Professional Communication:
THE CORPORATE INSIDER'S APPROACH

Daniel L. Plung
University of South Carolina

Tracy T. Montgomery
Idaho State University

THOMSON
™
SOUTH-WESTERN

Australia · Canada · Mexico · Singapore · Spain · United Kingdom · United States

SOUTH-WESTERN

THOMSON LEARNING

Professional Communication: The Corporate Insider's Approach, 1st Edition
Daniel Plung, Tracy Montgomery

Editor-in-Chief:
Jack W. Calhoun

Team Director:
Melissa S. Acuña

Acquisitions Editor:
Jennifer L. Codner

Developmental Editor:
Taney H. Wilkins

Marketing Manager:
Larry Qualls

Senior Production Editor:
Marci Combs

Manufacturing Coordinator:
Diane Lohman

Compositor:
Navta Associates, Inc.

Design Manager:
Rik Moore

Internal Design:
Brenda Grannan, Grannan Art & Design

Cover Design:
Brenda Grannan, Grannan Art & Design

Cover Image Source:
PhotoDisc, Inc.

Media Developmental Editor:
Josh Fendley

Media Production Editor:
Kelly Reid

For permission to use material from this text or product, contact us by
Tel (800) 730-2214
Fax (800) 730-2215
http://www.thomsonrights.com

ISBN: 0-324-27038-0

Library of Congress Control Number: 2002113838

BRIEF CONTENTS

A WORD ABOUT THIS TEXT AND ITS USE

This text departs from the strategies employed in most business and professional writing texts. The text is unique in that our strong academic credentials are amplified by extensive practical experience and a clear, firsthand corporate perspective of what's needed and how to provide it.

The text is also unique in its approach. Academic research has added greatly to our understanding of the discipline of professional communication; yet, the primary lens through which we view the discipline must remain the practical, real-world demands of business and technical environments. We need an experience-based balance of direction and perspective if we are to teach the Yankee rhetorical pragmatism of practical, professional communication.

Therefore, as in this Introduction, we have structured each chapter to reflect the direction and the perspective. The direction is provided to make clear how to achieve effective professional communication. The practical perspective looks critically at the popular models, concepts, and methods—advancing those that have merit and refuting those that may have limited application in the actual practice of professional communication. Although we do not call the segments out with specific headings or divisions, each chapter has three parts: 1) a practical perspective that examines the popular thinking on the topic, 2) the rationale and practical bases for the methods and concepts we advocate, and, 3) the specific instruction (the pedagogy) associated with the principles and tools provided.

This threefold structure, by natural extension, creates a certain tone and personality for this text. We have adopted a lecture-like format for our discussions. This format supports a mature treatment of the subject, while readily accommo-

---

FIGURE P.1

The Basic Framework of Professional Communication

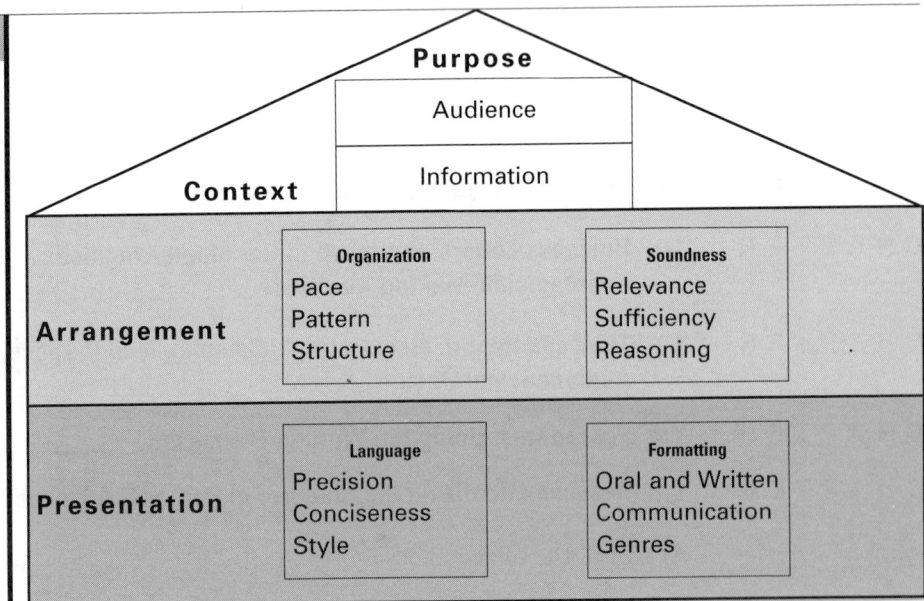

Purpose		
	Audience	
Context	Information	

Arrangement	**Organization** Pace Pattern Structure	**Soundness** Relevance Sufficiency Reasoning
Presentation	**Language** Precision Conciseness Style	**Formatting** Oral and Written Communication Genres

dating a comfortable, conversational tone. This tone is very important, for we see this work as the beginning of a dialogue. We want to invite students and instructors to appreciate the subject's depth—its science—while encouraging critical thinking, personal ownership of communications, and trust in their abilities rather than reliance on formula and prescription.

The format was also chosen to increase flexibility in how the materials are studied and taught. Approaches can be tailored to the comfort of both instructors and students. For example, groups of related chapters can be studied as units, or any chapter can be studied as a stand-alone topic. Similarly, the various media can be studied in any order. Within the individual chapters, similar flexibility exists. Discussions can center on any or all three parts of each chapter. The discussion of perspective can form the core of study and debate about popular lines of thought. The rationale can serve as a means of discovery, helping to derive a better understanding of the relationships and interactions among principles and methods. Or, the pedagogy can be isolated in the study of process and art. By using the various options, study can be tailored to fit any educational environment: undergraduate or graduate study; business school, technical school, or corporate training class. It can be also used in group discussion or for individual study. The exercises at the end of each chapter are provided to reinforce both principle and practice, accommodating group and individual activities.

In summary, our purpose in preparing this text is not to invoke a checklist approach but to encourage personal exploration of concepts and mastery of skills. Our purpose is not to teach mechanics or provide models but to promote an appreciation of the art and to provide a confidence of spirit that only comes with the knowledge that you are prepared for the communication challenges—now and in the future. Whether your interests lie with the Periodic Table of the Elements, organization charts, flowcharts, or spreadsheets, or whether your principal orientation is aligned with technical, professional, medical, scientific, or business communication, the values, tools, and principles that need to be mastered to communicate effectively remain the same.

As we are about to examine, communicating effectively in business is nothing less than demonstrating your facility with the discipline, the art, and the methods of professional communication.

ABOUT THE AUTHORS

DR. DANIEL L. PLUNG obtained his undergraduate degree from the City College of New York; his masters and doctoral degrees, in English, are from Idaho State University. Dr. Plung teaches professional and business communication in the Department of Business at the University of South Carolina and is on the Corporate Advisory Board of the Technical Communication Program at New Mexico Tech. Plung has more than 25 years experience in designing and managing publications and information functions. Having previously worked for Allied Chemical and Exxon, Dan currently is a senior manager for Westinghouse Savannah River Co. He is a recognized expert on procedure management whose work has earned a variety of national awards, including two Reinventing Government Awards. In addition to having authored dozens of articles on writing and communication, he co-edited two books for the Institute of Electrical and Electronics Engineers Press, was national secretary of the Professional Communication Society, and was the principal author of two national standards on procedures. He lives in Aiken, South Carolina with his wife and two sons.

TRACY MONTGOMERY is currently Associate Professor of English and Assistant Dean of the College of Arts and Sciences at Idaho State University. After completing her doctoral studies at Idaho State University, Montgomery worked as a technical writer, in-house writing teacher, and, subsequently, Publications and Procedures Manager at the Waste Isolation Pilot Plant, the nation's first geologic repository for low-level nuclear waste. After leaving the Waste Isolation Pilot Plant project, Montgomery integrated her practical experience into her academic career: Montgomery taught technical writing as an assistant professor at Washington State University. Thereafter, she returned to Idaho State University where her teaching assignments have included a variety of undergraduate and graduate communication courses. In addition to publishing in journals such as *The Technical Writing Teacher,* she is co-author of *Solving Problems in Technical and Professional Writing,* a textbook published by McGraw-Hill.

ACKNOWLEDGMENT

Foremost, the authors would like to thank Vickie for her encouragement, Bill and Nathan for teaching us about taking on the big challenges, and Dylan, who reminds us daily of the joy of writing.

We would also like to thank our academic colleagues at Idaho State University, the University of South Carolina, and New Mexico Tech. We want particularly to thank Dr. Niren Vyas and Gina Buckley of the School of Business at the University of South Carolina—Aiken. In addition, we would like to thank our professional colleagues, particularly Kevin Schmidt, Kathleen Powe, John Strack, and Laurie Hollick who, over the years, have contributed much to our understanding and appreciation of professional communication.

SUPPORT MATERIAL

A comprehensive set of support materials is available for *Professional Communication: The Corporate Insider's Approach* on an instructor's resource CD (ISBN: 0-324-27036-4.) These materials are designed to guide the instructor and to minimize class preparation time.

The instructor's resource CD includes:

✓ Instructor's manual

✓ Testing material for each chapter

✓ PowerPoint® for each chapter

To obtain a copy of the instructor's resource CD please contact Thomson Learning's Academic Resource Center at 1-800-423-0563.

PLACING PROFESSIONAL
COMMUNICATION IN PERSPECTIVE

As those of us who have made successful careers in business know, the ability to do well is inextricably intertwined with the ability to communicate effectively. Communicating effectively is a skill. It is a discipline and an art that can be learned, practiced, and purposely applied.

In business, performance translates into recognition and recognition into promotion. The opportunity to "perform" for most business professionals—whether mail clerks, middle management, or senior executives—comes in the form of the chance to communicate, to be recognized for the product of our labor and thinking. Few people in the business environment have titles that identify them as the "writers" or the "presentation staff," but everyone, especially if individuals are striving to get ahead, needs to know how to practice the discipline, art, and methods of effective communication.

In the course of the daily routine, the mail clerk communicates regularly, though informally, with every level of the organization. Middle managers are challenged to define and articulate new strategies and interpretations. Senior executives are measured by their abilities to look across large conference rooms and forge positive relationships with shareholders, Boards of Directors, and oversight agencies. Every individual in every level of the organization must communicate. Each is judged (whether it is formally considered in the annual job evaluation or not) on ability and performance as a communicator.

Misjudging communication by treating it merely as the memorization of corporate formats and templates, reducing process requirements to grammatical correctness, or misinterpreting the realities of the performance is a mistake that inevitably will be reflected in a poor communication performance. The performance we give and the grade we merit in business are based on our ability or inability to take an assignment, understand its implications, and create a reasoned and effective response. In business, communication is the opportunity to make the impressions that matter. What matters are the impressions we know how to make.

Despite these simple truths, most training aimed at improving the quality of communications in business is greatly lacking. As one survey published in *Training* reported, 54% of companies with 100 or more employees provided in-house training on communication.[1] Considering the investments in materials, instructors, and the time employees spend in the classroom instead of on the job, this training represents a major expenditure. The magnitude of this commitment and investment suggests a widening gap between corporate expectations and actual performance.

"For nearly 50 years, industrial and business leaders have described poor written communication skills as a continuing weakness . . . . Why this crucial skill has been and is still being so inadequately addressed is considered by some to be the single most egregious failure of the higher educational system." Beyond the severe penalty paid by corporations for poor communication capabilities, this lack of adequate preparation is also potentially detrimental to the students' careers: "The fact that the ability to write effectively assumes a much larger role as one advances in a technical career further compounds this problem. Almost every technical person can recall cases of ambitious and technically adept colleagues passed over for promotion because they could not write well enough to meet the demands of a higher position."[2]

A similar set of conclusions was reached in an article in the November 1999 issue of *The Chronicle of Higher Education,* a leading publication on university issues and developments. In an article entitled, "Technology Transforms Writing and the Teaching of Writing," the author noted that although computers induce people to write more (both in frequency and length), "they're absolutely not making them write better." In fact, the author suggests, quality and quantity appear to be in inverse proportion: the greater the volume, the poorer the quality. As one professor interviewed for the article remarked, student focus is on "electracy," fluency with the computer technology rather than on the syntax, the ideas, or the quality of the communication. "They strip mine what they read on the Internet." As a consequence, they produce merely "a collage of thoughts."[3]

Poor writing and unstructured presentations eventually cost and disadvantage everyone involved: the corporation, the practitioners, the customers, and the shareholders. These issues raise an important question: What can be done about the problem of poor communications in business? Clearly, recognizing that there is a problem is the first step; the next step, if we are to define a better path forward, is to understand what causes the problem.

WHAT'S WRONG WITH COMMUNICATION TRAINING?

As was noted above, the source of the problem does not lie with a lack of appreciation for the amount of communication that goes on in business or with its perceived value and benefit. Several dozen studies have dealt with these issues. As has been repeatedly pointed out, management spends nearly half of its time on communication tasks, with only slightly less time spent on such tasks by professionals and clerical personnel (Table I.1).[4]

Indicative of responses received when assessing the importance of communications in business, one survey of 254 top- and middle-level managers representing such diverse fields as the military, federal service, technology firms, and telecommunications concluded: "Ineffective writing can slow [individuals'] rise through

TABLE

I.1	PERCENTAGE OF TIME SPENT ON WRITING TASKS		
Percent of time	**Management (%)**	**Professional* (%)**	**Clerical* (%)**
20 or less	45	48	42
21–60	50	41	29
61–100	5	8	17

*Numbers may not equal 100% because not all respondents answered.

Source: Reprinted with permission of the Association for Business Communication

managerial ranks, and, perhaps, prevent their reaching top executive positions. Some even change career directions because of writing problems."[5] Stated quantitatively, the same survey of business professionals reflected in Table I.1 determined that 84% of managers and 82% of professionals indicated that "writing was either critically important or very important to their jobs." A proportion roughly equivalent to those who viewed writing as important also perceived a strong correlation between effective communication and promotional opportunities.

If we can, therefore, conclude that despite ample empirical data validating its costs and importance, problems persist with the quality of business communications, we can then infer that the problem lies with some combination of what is taught, how it is taught, and who is teaching it. We need to ascertain how effectively the instruction is addressing the discipline, the art, and the method of professional communication.

WHAT'S NEEDED: THE DISCIPLINE, THE ART, AND THE METHOD

Whether we specify "business communication," "technical communication," or some other subset of professional communication, as the name suggests, there are two distinct elements reflected in the discipline: the genus (communication) and the species (e.g., business, technical). The elements suggest that two distinct preparations are needed to teach the subject matter effectively. First, an instructor has to have excellent credentials in communication; second, the instructor must have knowledge, preferably firsthand, about precisely what happens in business and technical environments.

To assert the need for communication skills without regard for the differentiation demanded by the specifics of a business or technical application is to argue that any communication course, any set of communication materials, is equally acceptable to any other. If that were the case, we should never have had a problem, because poor communication performance should have been resolved by the universal requirement that all students complete a basic composition course in expository writing. Conversely, placing inappropriate emphasis on business or technical skills, thereby minimizing the communication orientation, would argue that necessary attributes of writing and speaking effectively are automatically assimilated as a consequence of completing a course of study in a business or technical discipline; no specific communication amplification is warranted. Representing the prevalent educational strategies in effect until the middle of the twentieth century, these two options clearly failed to resolve the dilemma.

Instead, these strategies were replaced with the current focus on specialization courses when industry, reinforced by empirical data, demanded more precise and targeted communication instruction to enhance the quality of writing and speaking. The result is a variety of communication courses: business communication, technical communication, professional writing, management communication, risk communication, and science writing. Knowing how we got to this stage will be helpful in formulating an understanding of how much further we need to go to resolve the continuing "egregious failure."

The first stage of the communication course evolution was announced by sprinkling communication personnel among the ranks of business and technical schools. Similar to the ventures to introduce etiquette among a student body more comfortable with laboratories than lawn parties, engineering schools, science schools, business schools, and medical schools introduced a limited planting of communication faculty among the technical staff. Team-taught courses were in vogue; however, an aloofness remained. Technical students encountering the communication faculty usually received two grades on assignments—one for content and one for communication. As if divisible elements of each project, the ability to state something well was segregated from the concept of having something worth telling.

At this stage in the evolution, the focus remained steadfastly on the application (business or technical) as the predominant feature. Definitions used to delineate one "type" of writing from another were essentially reflections of subject matter rather than attempts to differentiate among modes of expression or attempts to identify critical attributes and principles. Take, for instance, one popular textbook's explanation of the scope of business communication:

> Business communication refers to the process of transmitting business information from one person to another . . . . Business communication takes place whenever a sender relays business information to a receiver. The information, which deals with a business topic or activity, may be in various forms or media such as meetings, oral and written reports, letters, memorandums, and computer printouts.[6]

The second—and current—evolutionary phase occurred when industry and academia promoted professional communication as a unique discipline. At the university, this stage translated into specialized communication courses and new programs in professional, business, and technical communication. In the corporate world, newly populated organizations were chartered to provide word processing, graphic arts, writing, editing, and printing services. Though still rightly a subset of business, communication was first allowed and then encouraged in this era to hang out its own shingle. Communication as a field of study and as a career option was "open for business."

The generalist philosophy of the first phase gave way to a world of specialization and specialists. Territories were staked out among corporate departments and among university programs. At the university, the result was greater proliferation of courses. In the corporate world, the result was a mushrooming of style manuals and a hoarding of equipment exclusively devoted to publication production. Fueled by the initial encouragement received from business, academic programs and courses, just like their corporate organizational counterparts, continued to subdivide into finer and finer gradations.

Unfortunately, somewhere along the line, the parallels between business and academia were severed because of a number of factors: 1) Advances in computer hardware and software, coupled with decreased costs, democratized the world of desktop publishing. 2) Like their efficiency expert predecessors, the gurus of restructuring and reengineering instigated major budget and personnel reductions within support organizations. 3) Most significantly, businesses, regaining perspective on why they had originally signaled the need for specialized communication courses, reassigned accountability for effective communication from the dwindling support organizations to the owners and originators of the communications.

Despite these changes in business, academia has, for the most part, retained and continued to expand the great variety of communication options. The result has been a shading of the borders among program and course offerings. This creates two problems. First is the question of where one communication specialty ends and the next begins. For example, compared to the definition of business communication in which the activity was defined by subject matter, consider the following definition proposed in a textbook on technical writing:

"Technical writing is the practical writing that people do as part of their jobs. Whatever their position—from executive to middle manager, from specialized research scientist to secretary—people generate documents as an expected part of their duties . . . . memos, letters, reports, instructions, and proposals on many subjects in many situations."[7]

Here the earlier messages typified by the business communication definition we presented have been completely reversed. Everybody communicates, a variety of situations exist, and numerous subject matters are involved. As another technical writing textbook succinctly restates the point: "Technical writing, then, is defined not by its subject but by the author's purpose and the audience's needs."[8] While this definition is true, defining borders by audience and purpose makes differences among specializations even less distinguishable, as may be inferred by comparing the similarity in scope of coverage between business communication and technical communication courses. As an example, one survey of 14 textbooks (nine business communication and five technical communication) found that with the sole exception of "Technical Reports," the genres addressed in the 14 books were essentially identical.[9] (The Appendix provides a table detailing the scope of these textbooks.)

These similarities, coupled with industry's sudden redirection away from well-staffed and well-funded support organizations, gave rise to the second problem. With limited resources (with sufficient time and money for one or at most two courses), in which species of communication should the individual, the university, and the corporation make its investment? This particular question propelled a number of reassessments of university curricula. In one survey article that attempts to define how best to redesign professional writing courses to meet real-world writing challenges, the author concluded that the perplexing competition among communication specialties is an anachronism, both unresponsive to the needs of business professionals and counter to university realities: "the kinds of writing people do in their positions within organizations cannot be neatly defined as 'business' writing or 'technical' writing. Routine writing on the job is, in reality, a blend of both types, as they are now defined academically . . . . Attempts to separate students into specialized writing courses according to their majors is not justified."[10]

The conclusion reached by this author is that professional communication courses, to be effective, must "emphasize the common rhetorical principles that underlie the design and development of all writing."[11] Though the author of the definition of technical writing we quoted used a different vocabulary, he, too, was implicitly advocating a similar redesign of communication courses when he shifted attention away from subject matter to rhetorical considerations (audience and purpose).

THE DISCIPLINE OF PROFESSIONAL COMMUNICATION

These elements, which we see as the needed next evolution of professional communication, forge the basis of what we mean in this text when we refer to discipline: the fusing of rhetorical principle with practical, real-world communication applications and media.

> Discipline:
> the fusing of rhetorical principle with practical, real-world communication applications and media

The same author who indicted universities for their egregious failures in communication instruction identified three causal agents for the problem: "misrepresentation of student needs, inadequate training in the craft of writing, and a lack of relevance to the modern technical workplace." The first two problems refer to the issue of the scope of the course; the third concerns itself with the perspective imparted to the materials. These elements precisely correspond with the two components of discipline. The first two problems correspond to the need for a strong rhetorical orientation; the third problem is one of pragmatics.

Because the "discipline" is the heart of this text and represents perhaps its most unique dimension, we need to take a few moments to explore this item fully. In so doing, we will begin with discussion of the text's practical orientation and then address how that focus defines the rhetorical approach we have taken.

PRACTICAL COMMUNICATION. It is ironic that in all texts on communication, both professional and otherwise, there is always consideration of audience and purpose; yet, when it comes to professional communication texts, they miss the real audience and purpose entirely. The real audience is the corporate world that hires these individuals. The purpose is to fulfill our tacit promise that these individuals will be ably equipped to meet the demands of industry. As one article relating insights from business school deans detailed: "Business school faculties will no longer be able to force-feed irrelevant and outdated concepts to students . . . . The users of our services . . . are ultimately the firms who hire our students. We must increasingly think of our students not as the end users of our services but as products trained to meet the needs of the market. If our products prove defective, we will not be able to 'sell' them . . . ."[12] Failure to recognize the true target audience and purpose is the causal agent for a lack of real-world focus. This imprecise focus, in turn, translates into a "misrepresentation of student needs," not as the student might perceive them to be, but what the corporate world knows them to be.

In comparison to using the company as customer, the current pedagogical orientation is more myopic, measuring success exclusively as a function of immediate classroom rather than projected corporate performance. Typical of this misplaced attention, one study on improving performance of business writing begins "Student performance is the most important outcome of education." This internal focus leads to a popular but faulty premise: "Business writing students feel generally confident that with a little review of the principles of grammar, they will write effectively. A 'can-do' attitude is certainly preferred since it generally moves students to act. Because they feel they are good communicators and writers, they are more inclined to attend classes and to complete their homework assignments. Business writing students, thus, are generally confident they will do well in class."[13]

Confidence and doing well are unquestionably important, but they are not synonymous with strong corporate performance or effective communication. Perceiving oneself as a "good communicator or writer" is not responsive to the greater audience and purpose. Therefore, we might conclude, although the empirical studies have addressed the question of what types of documents professionals prepare, they have not, at least not correctly, answered the more important question of how do they prepare them well.

A second factor related to addressing the proper audience and purpose is the need to equip students with the necessary knowledge and tools to meet realistic challenges. Whether we rely on the feedback from students, from corporations, or from deans of many of America's finest business schools, the report is that not only are the essential skills missing, but the tools and knowledge critical to maintaining adaptability and flexibility are also apparently missing. Although we might be inclined to dismiss or discount a note in the *Journal of Education for Business* that "members of the corporate community . . . typically claim that they can safely ignore most business school research with impunity," it is much harder to ignore an assertion by the dean of one of America's foremost business schools that "As much as 80% of management research may be irrelevant."[14]

As Jerry Wind—a professor at the University of Pennsylvania's Wharton School of Business, founding director of the Wharton Think Tank, and head of the project to revamp the prestigious school's MBA curricula for the first time in almost 30 years—notes, "Business schools are kind of the last dinosaurs . . . . They teach a lot of theory, but there's not enough application." As Wind continues, "students need to know how to adapt and modify their approach over time, so that as new knowledge emerges they will be up to date and able to apply that knowledge . . . . With practice in problem solving, students will be able to avoid just following the latest trend published in one of the business magazines. Business schools should really be teaching critical thinking more than anything else."[15]

The issues are precisely the same when assessing preparations in professional communication. Effective instruction demands education that is meaningful, applicable, current, relevant, and adaptable. Just as Tom Peters challenged management instruction in his landmark book, *In Search of Excellence,* because "few management faculty have worked in management positions," so, too, business communication—to be taught or explained well—requires credible, extensive, and diverse firsthand business experience. In contrast, however, as accurately summarized in the journal *Education and Training:* "Few alternatives are currently offered to today's business communication instructor in terms of texts and other pedagogical choices. Probably the most serious problem in texts today, looking at those currently on the market, is that . . . the texts lack real-world 'savvy.' One tip-off is that texts present writing situations far too simplistically. Students are taught simply to identify a situation as one requiring a 'good news' response or 'persuasive' response and then are presented with standard organizational patterns for these various message 'types.' As anyone knows who has worked in a corporate setting, writing assignments within a business environment are not that simplistic."[16]

This need for practical, experienced senior corporate perspective was our primary motivation for developing this text. We write as true, tested, and experienced practitioners who have gained our expertise through careers spanning more than 25 years in corporate America—as publication professionals, as managers of publication functions, as middle-management, and as executive management. This text represents a unique authoritative dimension, derived from the perspective of experienced personnel who are representative of both the practitioners of the art and a real-world audience for each communication media addressed in this text.

In short, this is a text with credibility. This text provides the *real* scoop on what goes on, what is expected, and what tools you need to create effective communications. This toolbox begins with an understanding of the rhetorical underpinnings of effective communication.

THE RHETORICAL UNDERPINNINGS. Given the amount of time spent by business professionals on communication activities, not surprisingly, its importance is often posted alongside key personality attributes as an indicator of corporate success. As Henry Ford II once remarked in an interview when asked what features he thought primary in his most successful executives: "I'd like honesty, candor, good judgment, intelligence, imagination, and the ability to write clear, concise memos . . . ."[17]

"Clear," as Henry Ford II uses it, means more than reducing words to the fewest number of syllables or sentences to the fewest number of words. "Concise," likewise, is not necessarily a function simply of word count. The admonition to be clear and concise is shorthand for demonstrating several skills: a conscious, disciplined control of information; a purpose that is explicit, consistent, and acted upon; information, language, and logic that are appropriate and effective for the given audience; a presentation that is complementary to the message, compelling and appealing. Making all these agents click, yet maintaining their relative invisibility so that your audience speaks of your work in terms of "clarity" and "conciseness" is the end goal of effective communication. They are also the demonstration and consequence of effective use of rhetorical principles.

When "clear" is presented as a matter solely as of diction and "concise" solely a matter of length, we are embarking on a journey that substitutes form for substance and technique for insight. As the author who spoke of the "egregious failure" of communication preparation explains, "while format and technique make for important components of the overall . . . writing task, they assume predominance only after issues of logical thought, and organization, audience, topic, style, strategy, and relevance have been addressed."[18]

The prevalent and popular attention to format and technique stems from a rethinking of rhetoric that occurred in the latter part of the nineteenth century. This rethinking proposes that "the foundations of rhetoric rest upon grammar; for grammatical purity is a prerequisite of good writing." Although a "prerequisite" of good writing, "grammatical purity" is not synonymous with nor is it indicative of quality or effectiveness. As one practitioner warns, "before you order that supply of grammar workbooks, before you acquire that talking-head video," instructors should recognize that teaching grammar as a substitute for rhetoric does not address the core issues of our current gap in communication capability:

1. "Grammar does not teach anyone to write." Most important, it doesn't teach how to synthesize new sentences out of existing thoughts. The survey we quoted earlier that polled 254 managers noted that even those individuals who were generally proficient in grammar and punctuation still tended to produce "disorganized and ineffective writing."

2. Like the Inquisition, the pedagogy of traditional grammar is better attuned to punishing unwanted behaviors than it is to teaching the attributes of effective communication.

3. Concentrating on grammatical errors distracts from rather than highlights the most significant problem—writing that fails to communicate what the writer and the organization need to say.[19]

Attention must be on the quality and the effectiveness—on rhetoric rather than on models and mechanics. As one communication consultant effectively argues: "The many business and technical writing courses based on the school model— that is, the courses designed to tell people about the proper ways to write— share the same misdirection as the grammar-protection model. In promising to reveal the 'do's,' and 'don'ts,' they perpetuate the mistaken assumptions that correctness and uniformity to preordained models, rather than communication, is the goal of corporate writing."[20]

We are still left to answer the question of whether we need to propose different rhetorically based solutions for each of the various "types" of writing. As we previously noted, curricular distinctions are already limited, often differentiated only by subject matter. When we pursue the question of whether these writing distinctions represent differing sets of skills, that limited differentiation evaporates. In an article summarizing results from 10 different surveys of communication skills that professionals needed, the author concluded that "this conventional approach to course design [separate classes in business, technical, and scientific writing] is outmoded, that the rhetorical needs of writers in all types of jobs surveyed are basically the same."[21]

This core commonality among the writing types is made more evident if we take a moment to explore a brief history of the development of professional writing. If we forego the urge to argue that the description of the building of Noah's ark represents the origins of technical writing, almost every scholar will concur that Aristotle's *Rhetoric* is the foundation of the art and science of writing. Greatly simplifying the history and acknowledging that we are about to take the expressway rather than the scenic route, it is arguable that all professional writing, as well as composition as currently taught, found its way from Aristotle to New England and the rest of America by way of eighteenth-century Scotland. Hugh Blair, a Scottish cleric and rhetorician, and contemporaries of his (such as Adam Smith, the economist) made the strong argument for rhetoric as a cornerstone of an educated citizenry. Further, Blair, lecturing at the University of Edinburgh, expanded the study to include "belles lettres," which not only furthered practical affiliations of rhetoric, but also joined it with such "polite" arts as history and biography. In so doing, Blair and other founders of modern rhetoric instilled the idea that a well-organized presentation needs "interest," "unity," and "coherence" and can be employed both for persuasion and for increasing an audience's understanding of a subject.

Blair's lectures, published in 1783, soon made their way to America. By the early years of the nineteenth century, his *Lectures on Rhetoric and Belles Lettres* became the standard at several major American universities, including Yale, Harvard, and Dartmouth. In America, the practical application of oratory and persuasive writing was already well understood. Bolstered by the work of Benjamin Franklin and others who established the printing industry in America, and fueled by the debates, pamphlets, and broadsides published in the years leading up to the American Revolution, the early nineteenth-century American universities were receptive to this modern rhetoric, a reception aptly reflected in the sudden appearance of endowed chairs of rhetoric.

One of the first endowed chairs was the Boyleston Professorship of Rhetoric and Oratory established at Harvard in 1806. Signaling the marriage of rhetorical theory and American pragmatics, the first appointee to that position was John Quincy Adams, a senator who was later to become President of the United States. Practical values, rhetorical theory, and classical doctrine shared honors in Adams's lectures. With overtones of the Enlightenment and echoes of the language of the Declaration of Independence, Adams explained:

> The purpose of my lectures . . . has been in the first instance to make you familiarly acquainted with the principles, transmitted in the writings of the ancient rhetorical masters; and in the next to discriminate those parts of their precepts, which were inseparably connected with the social institutions and manners of the ages and nations, for which they wrote, from those, which, being founded upon the broad and permanent basis of human nature, are still applicable, and will ever retain their force.[22]

Adams's stamp on the Boyleston Professorship established a fitting precedent for a society whose triumphs, tribulations, and travails formed the subject of a half-century of great and celebrated debates.

As the nineteenth century prepared to enter its final quarter, two major related developments cast rhetoric into its current role. The first was the rise of the English Department. The second was the transformation of American liberal arts education. English Departments emerged in response to a decreasing interest in oratory and an increasing popularity in teaching the new field of English and American Literature. Endowed chairs in rhetoric found themselves pushed up against a buffet table of literature, linguistics, philology, elocution, speech, and composition. At the same time, replicating the German University model, universities added numerous courses of study to the curriculum. In addition, an elective system was introduced. With this "Young Yale" movement came a call for greater practical usefulness in university work. The response was dramatic.

At Harvard University, for instance, President Charles W. Eliot enlarged the curriculum with courses in areas such as political economy, physics, and international law; expanded the elective process so that by 1883 all students, from freshmen to seniors, could choose most of their studies; and elevated training in law, medicine, and engineering to a post-graduate level. With this recasting, the ancient classics, ethics, and rhetoric assumed a supporting role, conceding the dominant educational position to practical courses of study. As Eliot, himself a chemist by trade, remarked: "The chief merits of style" are valued most highly when assisting "those whose avocations require them to describe and discuss material resources, industrial processes, public works, mining enterprises, and the complicated problems of trade and finance."[23]

In support of Eliot's position, Adam Sherman Hill, a lawyer-turned journalist who occupied the Boyleston Professorship of Rhetoric and Oratory at the time, introduced his *Principles of Rhetoric*. Hill further displaced classical rhetoric, declaring "grammatical purity" as the requisite of good writing. In contrast to previous rhetorically based courses of study, Hill's *Principles of Rhetoric* examined "grammatical purity," "choice of words," "number of words," and "arrangement," followed by examination of description, narration, exposition, and argument.

Thus, with no overt champions of classical rhetoric or of its practical adaptation as handed down through modern rhetoric and Adams, the university soon experienced the advent of books dedicated to the study of practical writing. By 1916, we have what is considered by some to be the first important business writing textbook for college use, George Hotchkiss's *Business English*. Next to arrive were technical writing texts, made increasingly popular as America marched into the technological era of the mid-twentieth century. Science writing soon grew up and separated from its journalism roots. Second cousins, like medical writing and management communication, donned their caps and gowns and joined the academic procession shortly thereafter.

However, at the same time that the menu of writing courses was expanding, the competition resulted in assorted attempts to stake out unique territories. The result was a minimizing of the common attributes (the rhetorical foundation) and a maximizing of the differences. As one scholar attests: "The ancient subject of rhetoric, which at first showed signs of adapting itself to the changing times while preserving both its integrity and its vitality . . . lost both integrity and vitality by dispersing itself to academic thinness."[24]

Fortunately for us, now armed with three vital weapons—a knowledge of the history of professional communication, our perspective gained through extensive practical experience, and a realistic understanding of the true needs of both the student and the corporation—we have an opportunity to reverse this "thinness." We can shape a course of study that introduces rhetorical principles in the context of practical, real-world applications and media. We can revitalize and reinvigorate the Yankee rhetorical pragmatism (as we have named it) of John Quincy Adams to achieve the discipline of professional communications.

END NOTES

[1] K.W. Davis, "What Writing Training Can—and Can't—Do," *Training,* Vol. 32 (Aug. 1995), pp. 60–61.

[2] D.D. Bradney and M.E Courbat, "Technical Writing: Higher Education's Self-Inflicted Wound," *Tech Directions,* Vol. 57 (Jan. 1998), pp. 33–36.

[3] W. Leibowitz, "Technology Transforms Writing and the Teaching of Writing," *The Chronicle of Higher Education,* Nov. 26, 1999, p. A67–68.

[4] Table I.1 was adapted from: M.K. Kirtz and D.C. Reep, "A Survey of the Frequency, Types, and Importance of Writing Tasks in Four Career Areas," *The Bulletin,* Vol. 53, No. 4 (Dec. 1990), pp. 3–4.

[5] P.G. Aldrich, "Adult Writers: Some Reasons for Ineffective Writing on the Job," *College Composition and Communication,* Vol. 33, No. 3 (Oct. 1982), pp. 284–287.

[6] P.G. Campbell "Business Communication or Technical Writing?" *The Bulletin,* Vol. 54, No. 2 (June 1991), pp. 6–10.

[7] *Ibid.*

[8] *Ibid.*

[9] *Ibid.*

[10] E. Tebeaux, "Redesigning Professional Writing Courses to Meet the Communication Needs of Writers in Business and Industry," *College Composition and Communication,* Vol. 36, No. 4 (Dec. 1985), pp. 419–428.

[11] *Ibid.*

[12] A.R. Bailey, C.W. Chow, and K.M. Haddad, "Continuous Improvement in Business Education: Insights from the For-Profit Sector and Business School Deans," *Journal of Education for Business,* Vol. 74, No. 3 (Jan./Feb. 1999), pp. 165–180.

[13] D. Page, "Improving Undergraduate Student Involvement in Management Science and Business Writing Courses Using the Seven Principles in Action," *Education,* Vol. 119, No. 4 (Summer 1999), pp. 747–757.

[14] A.R. Bailey, C.W. Chow, and K.M. Haddad, "Continuous Improvement in Business Education."

[15] "Q&A: Professor Jerry Wind's Got a Radical Suggestion for Business Schools: Teach Students to Think," *Sales and Marketing Management,* Vol. 148, No. 3 (March 1996), pp. S12–S15.

[16] S.G. Thomas, "Preparing Business Students for Real-World Writing," *Education and Training,* Vol. 36, No. 6 (1994), pp. 11–15.

[17] Quoted in: P. Gasarch, "Rhetoric and Technical Writing: A Working Relationship," *The Bulletin,* Vol. 54, No. 2 (June 1991), pp. 3–5.

[18] D.D. Bradney and M.E. Courbat, "Technical Writing."

[19] D. M. Ricks, "Why Your Business Writing Courses Don't Work," *Training,* Vol. 31, No. 3 (March 1994), pp. 49–51.

[20] *Ibid.*

[21] Tebeaux, "Redesigning Professional Writing Courses to Meet the Communication Needs of Writers in Business and Industry."

[22] R. F. Reid, "The Boyleston Professorship of Rhetoric and Oratory, 1806–1904: A Case Study in Changing Concepts of Rhetoric and Pedagogy," *Quarterly Journal of Speech,* Vol. 45, No. 3 (Oct. 1959), pp. 239–257.

[23] Reid, "The Boyleston Professorship of Rhetoric and Oratory, 1806–1904."

[24] W.R. Parker, "Where Do English Departments Come From?" *College English,* Vol. 28, No. 5 (Feb. 1967), pp. 339–350.

CONTENTS

PART 1

THE DISCIPLINE AND ART OF PROFESSIONAL COMMUNICATION

CONTENTS

CONTENTS

CONTENTS

CONTENTS

THE DISCIPLINE AND ART OF PROFESSIONAL COMMUNICATION

CHAPTERS

Purpose
Deciphering the Creative Possibilities

Let's begin our journey at what should be the beginning of any communication task—defining the purpose and audience. We say at "what should be the beginning" because purpose and audience share the unique distinction of being the two topics that, while absolutely fundamental and critical to achieving success in professional communication, are often dismissed as if the answers were of little consequence or are automatically inferred by the communicator.

Purpose is generally cast as a minor step within an oversimplified framework that entails planning the job, drafting the document, revising the text, formatting the materials, and proofreading the text (Figure 1.1). Eager to press on with the issues of word selection and formatting principles, most discussions about purpose do little to explore the subject, advising only that purpose can be compressed into two simple actions: determining the objective and predicting the reaction. Audience, for its part in the communication process, is characterized as a matter of demographics—creating personality profiles of the prospective reader.

Both of these strategies grow out of the expository writing typical of composition courses; however, the assumptions do not hold true when it comes to business and professional communication. When dealing with the real world and the pragmatic demands it places on communication, we must be both equipped and adept at discovering overt and embedded

Life with a purpose

       ... or maybe life without a purpose

       ... or with a plethora of purpose

The real business of purpose

The discovery and creativity of purpose

The price of failure

A purposeful response to purpose

Communicating with purpose—the lessons

purposes. We must also be prepared to deal with the distinct communities of business audiences. Misperceiving purposes invariably results in documents that are ineffective; misreading audiences creates tensions that may be adverse to career goals. In Chapter 1, we will look at purpose from a business perspective to determine the real significance of and the strategies for responding to complex objectives. In Chapter 2, we will examine the concept of audience as it applies in the world of business.

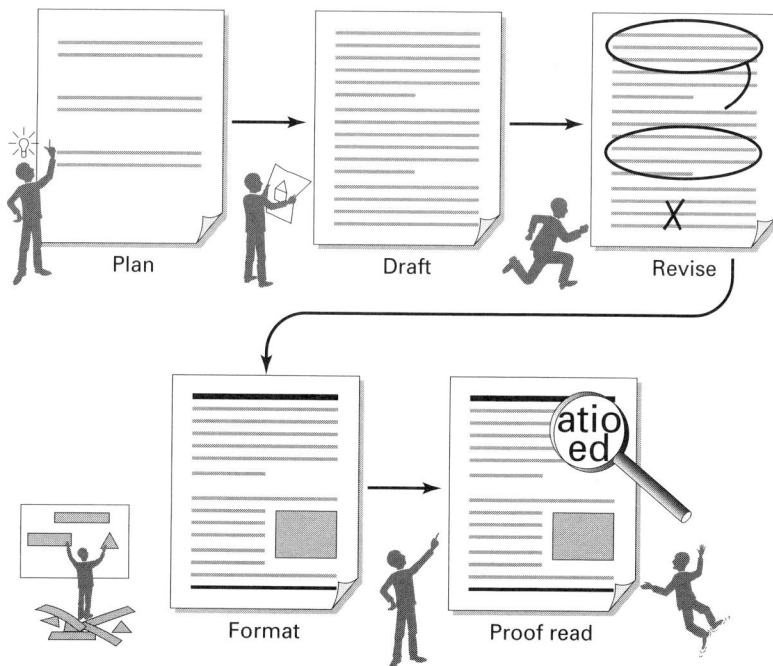

FIGURE 1.1

Typical Overview of the Writing Process

Plan

Draft

Revise

Format

Proof read

LIFE WITH A PURPOSE
LIFE WITHOUT A PURPOSE?

We might start off with the assumption that the purpose for any communication is an immediately evident item. As James Kinneavy notes in *A Theory of Discourse*, "Purpose . . . is all important. The aim of a discourse determines everything else in the process of discourse."[1] The first step, identifying purpose, should be quite easy and immediate.

Aristotle perceived of three primary purposes for communication: arguments presented in defense of individual freedom, discussions of the affairs of government, and eulogies. This simple structure did not, however, satisfy rhetoricians for long. Thereafter, an innumerable series of categorizations and taxonomies appeared. Sometimes the expansion of categories was modest, as illustrated when Kinneavy expanded the three purposes for communication proposed by Aristotle into four categories:

Discourse	Aim
Expressive	Displaying the reaction of the self
Referential	Expressing reality
Literary	Presenting the artifact
Persuasive	Requesting acceptance; attempting to elicit action, emotion, conviction

Not willing to settle for a simple expansion that converts three types of discourse to four, numerous studies attempted to define more precisely what people in business found to communicate about (Tables 1.1 and 1.2).[2] However, despite the appearance of precision, two problems remain with these categorization schemes: They are still too simplistic, and there is no means to translate (at least effectively) these categories into something helpful for the communication student. As an illustration, try to figure out what insight is gained, as reflected in Table 1.2, by knowing that 64% of the problems addressed constitute "everyday issues" or "something went wrong." Little further insight is gained by adding the clarification that, generally, when preparing memos or letters, our intent is "to inform" (Table 1.1).[3]

Responding to these generalizations, assignments tend to reduce statements of purpose to one dimension. However, statements such as "I want my proposal to persuade my supervisor to purchase new equipment" invariably prove insufficient for making communication decisions. "Failing to understand the multiple and competing purposes, may lead students to produce formulaic, ineffective communications."[4] Furthermore, cursory statements of this nature arbitrarily dismiss the embedded, overlapping, and competing purposes that tend to characterize business decisions.

Just beyond the one-dimensional model of purpose lies what is commonly called the heuristic approach, which relies on "unpacking" purposes by examining a series of characteristics: 1) the types of documents involved (e.g., sales letter), 2) the readers' knowledge of the topic, and 3) the critical interests of the organization and the writer.[5] The result of this inquiry is typically a checklist that distills and blends the essence of the inquiry with the types of purposes cited in Tables 1.1 and 1.2 (Figure 1.2). Inevitably, discovery of any specific purposes (the intended role of the inquiry) is blunted by the reintroduction of a predictable

1.1 TYPICAL REASONS FOR WRITING

Memos		Letters	
Reason given	Percent	Reason given	Percent
Inform of events	4	Communicate arrangements	5
Summarize approach	4	Request information	5
Summarize problems	4	Responses to issues	5
Report status	4	Summary of information	5
Describe materials sent	4	Clarify terms of agreement	10
Request action	7	Share information	10
Summarize a call	14	Document research	10
Describe a procedure	14	Inform	15
Inform of changes	20	Describe services or products	35
Share information	21		

Source: Reprinted with permission of the Association for Business Communication.

1.2 TYPICAL BUSINESS PROBLEMS ADDRESSED

Business Problem	Percent Indicating Problem
Client remiss	9
Bad news	9
Fee increase	9
Client unrealistic	9
Everyday issues	22
Something went wrong	42

Source: Reprinted with permission of the Association for Business Communication.

and finite range of purposes. Despite declarations about complexity, the conclusion is representative of a business world in which purposes are simple, limited, and relatively fixed. Yet, not all authors hold to this image of a highly predictable universe of purpose. There also exists a broad range of literature that suggests defining purpose is a problem so complex that it may be insolvable.

A Plethora of Purpose

While some authors struggle to reduce the types and purposes of writing to a number that will allow them to be dispatched with formulaic certainty, others see the subject of purpose as beyond capture.

> Purpose is problematic. Everyone agrees that it is an admirable thing: we encourage students to 'have' one and we are justly impatient with texts that don't. However, our traditional ways of talking about purpose—as that singular, stable entity one should possess—seem painfully limited. We may question if a simple 'authorial' purpose . . . even exists. We may conclude that the purposes behind any rhetorical or any human act are so multifold, so entangled and even contradictory that in the attempt to describe them, the notion of a willed, intentional act simply evaporates.[6]

Moving away from the 1960s model of how writing occurs (prewriting, writing, and rewriting), this new "entangled" sense of purpose grew out of the 1970s and 1980s, which placed great emphasis on attempting to decipher a more realistic representation of the cognitive processes that underlie communication. For simplicity sake, we might see the work as divided into two primary schools: speech-act theory and situational analysis. Trying to establish correlations between written and oral communication, speech-act advocates focused on the environment of the communication. Although oral communication had audience immediately present, written communication did not. Therefore, references were made to spoken communication as engaged and to written communication as detached. A few steps farther along the road and this detachment is transformed into a belief that there is an "autonomous production of text," that the writer creates his or her own context and purpose.[7] This creative allowance, in turn, gave credence to those who—unable or uninterested in pursuing writing's true purposes and context—proposed it as a rationale why they perceived writing to be so utterly unpredictable. As advocates for the proposed complexity theory argued, "Even though a teacher gives 20 students the same assignment, the writers themselves create the problem they solve. The reader is not the writer's only 'fiction.'"[8] (We'll return to the reader as fiction when we take up the subject of audience in Chapter 2.)

At the same time that these speech-theory personnel were arriving at the conclusion that the concept of assigned purpose in communication is a fiction, the situational analysts found themselves struggling to disentangle a "web of purposes" (see footnote 8 for reference). In contrast to the unfettered air of creating purpose, the web of purposes became so mentally challenging that it gave rise to a great "cognitive strain" (see footnote 8 for reference). All writers, the rhetoricians maintained, were inevitably stuck in this web because, as they went on to say, all "rhetoric is situational."[9] In fact, it was asserted that the situational element is an inescapable condition of communication.[10]

To help alleviate some of the strain, Linda Flower and John Hayes, who became the chief proponents of situational analysis, introduced use of protocols to assess the inescapable condition. Borrowed from psychologists who use the tools to analyze complex task performance, protocols involved having writers thinking aloud. Using surveys and interviews, writers explained why they responded in a particular way to writing assignments. As a consequence of these assessments, Hayes and Flower identified six components of the "rhetorical situation" (Figure 1.3). Of these, the first two components comprise the situation; the next four establish the writer's goals:

FIGURE 1.2

The Essence of
the Demographic
Approach

Explicit Purposes
Professional Communication

Primary Audience Purposes (what's the point)		What's expected
Support/encourage a decision	→	demonstrate validity
Provide status/update	→	add detail
Provide perspective (input)	→	provide insight
Apprise others—share information	→	provide new information
Change a decision	→	point out problems/alternatives
Move to action	→	create sense of urgency
Promote reconsideration	→	identify potential issues
Gain support	→	reinforce mutual benefits
Document to file	→	provide essential chronology

Primary Author Purposes (Personal)

☐ Make yourself look good

☐ Make yourself look smart

☐ Discredit someone else/someone else's idea/project

☐ Promote interpersonal/interorganizational relations

☐ Create sense of trust/credibility

1. Assignment—the task given to the writer
2. Audience—the intended readership
3. Reader—the effect intended on the audience
4. Persona—the "voice," or image the writer wants to send about himself or herself
5. Meaning—the "coherent network of ideas"
6. Text—the communication conventions associated with the assignment (e.g., beginning with an introduction)[11]

In subsequent explorations of purpose, Hayes and Flower amplified these elements, adding a series of factors that influence the dynamics of composing. These influences, called constraints, were generally of three kinds: 1) the demand for integrated knowledge—the retrieval and structuring of relevant information, 2) the linguistic conventions of written texts—the rules of grammar, syntax, and language; and 3) the rhetorical problem—adapting the knowledge and linguistic solutions to the problem at hand.[12] Despite the growing complexity of purpose, the bottom line of the research was clear: The ability to create effective communication is a direct function of how well we define the problems at hand and how well we respond to those problems (Figure 1.4).[13]

Although the constraint model represents a much more accurate depiction of purpose than that suggested by the idea that purpose is a fiction, the elements

FIGURE 1.3

Elements of
Purpose

Elements Contributed by the Rhetorical Situation	
Element	Example
1. *Assignment*	Develop a business plan for transitioning from mainframe applications to work on distributed servers
2. *Audience*	All corporate business and administrative departments and functions
Elements Stemming from the Writer's Interests	
3. *Reader*	I'll have to make clear that I understand the cost and schedule implications of the transition
4. *Persona or Self*	I'll need to make evident that this is not the first time I have administered a project of this nature
5. *Meaning*	I'll evaluate lessons learned from practical experience and benchmarking studies
6. *Text*	I'll include a transmittal letter that restates the principal conclusions in the Executive Summary

comprising the rhetorical situation are still not complete. Although Figure 1.3 appears to greatly expand the concept of purpose as explained by Aristotle and Kinneavy, we may not have progressed as far as we might first assume. Whereas we might see the picture much more clearly now, the rhetorical situation, as translated into writing direction, still leaves us with the basic admonitions to "pay attention to the assignment," and "know your audience." The true limits of how little distance we have advanced are suggested by Ronald Kellogg, who, in his book on the *Psychology of Writing,* provides a graphic depiction of theory advocated by the proponents of situational analysis. As this illustration suggests, purpose (now coupled with constraints in a unit called "Task Environment") is still potentially subject to being inappropriately dismissed as a topic warranting little further consideration (Figure 1.5).[14]

FIGURE 1.4

Recognizing
Purposes: A Key
Success Factor

	Situation	Other			
	Audience/ Assignment	Audience	Persona	Meaning	Text
Novice Writer	7*	0	0	3	7
Expert Writer	18	11	1	3	9

* Refers to number of references cited during interviews

Source: Copyright 1980 by the National Council of Teachers of English. Reprinted with permission.

FIGURE 1.5

A Depiction of
Situational Analysis

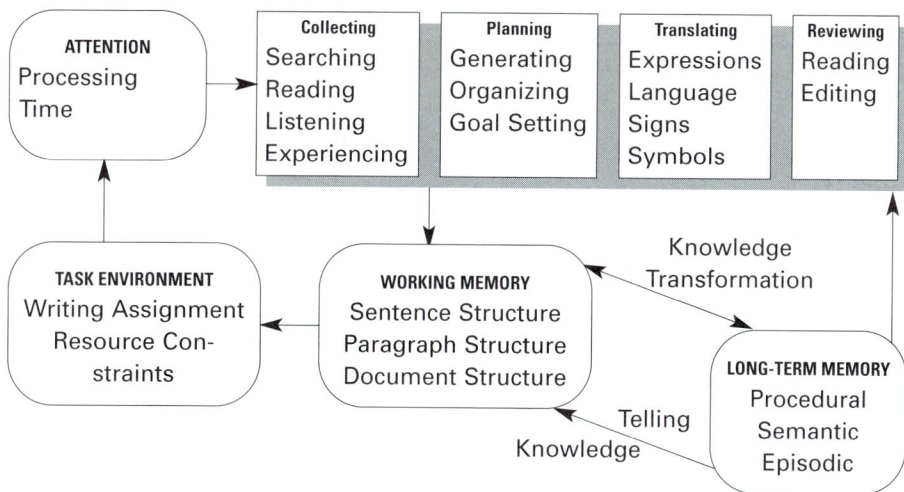

| ATTENTION Processing Time | Collecting
Searching
Reading
Listening
Experiencing | Planning
Generating
Organizing
Goal Setting | Translating
Expressions
Language
Signs
Symbols | Reviewing
Reading
Editing |

TASK ENVIRONMENT Writing Assignment Resource Constraints

WORKING MEMORY Sentence Structure Paragraph Structure Document Structure

Knowledge Transformation

LONG-TERM MEMORY Procedural Semantic Episodic

Telling Knowledge

Source: From the Psychology of Writing by Ronald T. Kellogg, copyright 1994 by Oxford University Press, Inc. Used by permission of Oxford University Press, Inc.

To counter these three positions (we proceed with no defined purpose; with a set of demographically defined purposes; or with an unlimited number of purposes), we might change our strategy. Rather than using the academic literature to gain perspective on business, let's look at business to get a perspective on the academic literature.

THE REAL BUSINESS OF PURPOSE

We might begin by suggesting that in the broadest terms, the purpose of business is to make money. A step down from this high-level perspective might reveal such contributing purposes as increasing sales, gaining political support, securing investments, etc. These same purposes might also be stated in the form of avoiding problems—avoiding reductions in sales, avoiding loss of political favor, or avoiding loss of investment money. Thus, for example, an Enron Corporation ostensibly sees its target as increased earnings for the corporation and its shareholders; it wants to encourage both investors and positive political support. On the other end of the business cycle, subsequent to the collapse of Enron Corporation, the Securities Exchange Commission and Congress see their mission as identifying causes so as to preclude a reoccurrence elsewhere in the economy. To generalize these statements and to establish a common vocabulary among all businesses, we might express these business activities in terms of risk and risk management (Figure 1.6).

As in professional communication, risk and risk management deal with assessing the issue (purpose) and postulating a response. As one expert on risk management notes: "The ability to sense and avoid harmful environmental conditions is necessary for the survival of all living organisms. Survival is also aided by an ability to codify and learn from past experience. Humans have an additional capability that allows them to alter their environment as well as respond to it. This capacity both creates and reduces risk."[15]

FIGURE 1.6

A Conceptual
Depiction of
Business Risk

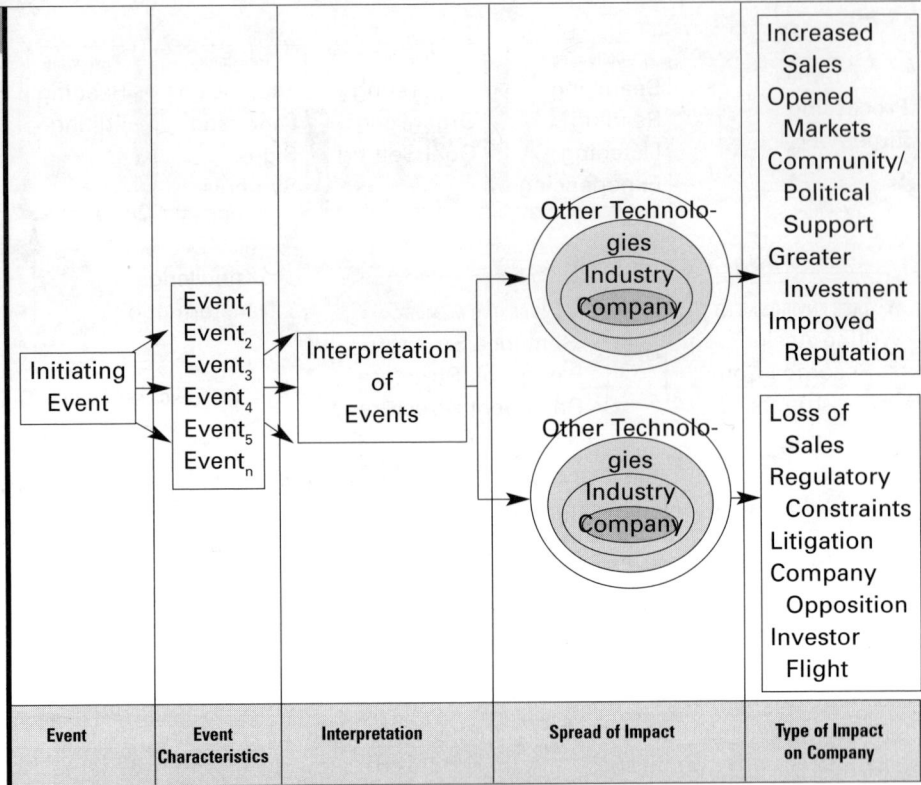

Event	Event Characteristics	Interpretation	Spread of Impact	Type of Impact on Company

Initiating Event → Event$_1$, Event$_2$, Event$_3$, Event$_4$, Event$_5$, Event$_n$ → **Interpretation of Events** →

Other Technologies / Industry / Company

Other Technologies / Industry / Company

Increased Sales, Opened Markets, Community/Political Support, Greater Investment, Improved Reputation

Loss of Sales, Regulatory Constraints, Litigation, Company Opposition, Investor Flight

For example, the goal of making money is directly affected by how well we understand and mitigate the risks. It might be seen as analogous to the relationship between gambling and probability. Gambling connotes a randomness, an equal chance to win as to lose; probability allows the odds to be better understood. The link is very strong; in fact, interest in doing better at gambling actually gave rise to our contemporary study of probability. In the seventeenth century, a gambler named Chevalier de M'ere would bet people that if he rolled a single die four times, he would get a six. Having achieved a reasonable degree of success with this bet, he changed the bet to say he would get a 12 (two sixes) if he rolled two dice a total of 24 times. Unfortunately, the second set of bets was proving less profitable.

He turned to a friend, Blaise Pascal, for an answer. The ensuing correspondence, which represents the founding of Probability Theory, pointed out that de M'ere's first set of bets had a 51.8% probability of winning versus 49.1% probability of winning the second set of bets. As for communication, we might refer to this knowledge as an "informing client," a condition that helps us better comprehend the risk, but doesn't necessarily lessen the risk. In business, knowing the risk may be insufficient. We may also want to pursue the means of lessening that risk. To understand a condition that influences rather than informs the decisions, let's continue our discussion of gambling.

When eight baseball teams formed the National Association in 1871, betting booths were a common feature at the ballparks.[16] Visited by fans and players alike, the betting booths often gave rise to rumors of fixed games. When the Louisville Grays threw the 1877 season, losing to the Boston Reds, attention focused on improving baseball's image as a national sport. Things seemed to be

1. **The assignment**	} **establish the goals**
2. **Influencing constituents**	
3. **Informing clients**	} **give shape to the goals**
4. **The writer's goals**	

FIGURE 1.7

The Elements of Purpose

improving until 1919 when Arnold Rothstein directed eight Chicago Black Sox players to throw the World Series. This influence resulted in a total ban on gambling for all ballplayers. The betting may have operated out of some "informed" knowledge of what was about to transpire. In comparison, the act of throwing the game or the series was a consequence of an influencing constituent.

Informing clients are those insights that allow keener appreciation of the event and its circumstance. Influencing constituents are those ideas, perspectives, and actions that can directly or indirectly change the risks and the outcomes. These informing clients and influencing constituents exist in all business contexts, not just in the world of professional gambling. They also exist as the underpinnings of all our communication activities.

We can use this clarification to help modify the work of Flower and Hayes to create a more complete portrayal of the communication task (or environment). In total, there are four types (or elements) of purposes at work in professional communications (Figure 1.7):

1. The assignment—the explicit task given to the communicator

2. The influencing constituents—those factors that immediately bear upon the primary purpose or introduce purposes that must be dealt with within the context of the assignment

3. Informing clients—those factors that further shape the nature of the primary and ancillary purposes

4. The writer's goals—the reader, persona, meaning, and text goals outlined by Flower and Hayes

THE DISCOVERY AND CREATIVITY OF PURPOSE

With this clearer sense of the nature of purpose in professional communication, we can now assess how to discover and respond to the elements of purpose. Here, too, the approach should be anything but formulaic. Let us offer an anecdote to introduce this area of discussion.

Several years ago, a moderately-sized research firm invited a communications professor to assess a number of documents that their scientists believed were essentially ready for publication in the open literature. As part of the review, the professor was asked by the Senior Vice President to meet with their senior scientists to discuss his observations. One scientist who felt the recommendations were infringing upon his artistic license attempted to dismiss the observations by inquiring if the principles of professional communication were not at odds with creativity.

As that individual was informed, and as reflected in this text, the answer is that creativity in communication derives directly from thinking about the options and alternatives and combining the vast, innumerable combinations of facts, their arrangement, and the strategy reflected in the reasoning. Creativity is also reflected in the selection of language and the stringing together of words to create a particular sound on paper. However, creativity starts, as in science, with the discovery process, the analysis, and the framing of the problem to be addressed.

To illustrate this point, let's begin with an article that appeared in the *Saturday Review* in 1968. As the article describes, a physics instructor gave his students a test, which included the following question: "Show how it is possible to determine the height of a tall building with the aid of a barometer."[17] The expected answer is one that any first-year physics student would know: The mercury in a barometer drops 1 inch for every 1000 feet of altitude; therefore, if you take a barometer reading at the base of the building and a second reading on the roof, you need only basic math to complete the calculation.

One student, however, offered a totally unanticipated solution: "Take the barometer to the top of the building, attach a long rope to it, lower the barometer to the street, and then bring it up, measuring the length of the rope. The length of the rope is the height of the building." No doubt, the method would work. The answer also met the requirement of having employed "the aid of a barometer." However, the physics professor pointed out, the rope method had not satisfied one of the embedded purposes—the implicit requirement to show competence in physics. The student was then given a second chance to answer the question. Undaunted, the student offered a new solution: "Take the barometer to the top of the building and lean over the edge of the roof. Drop the barometer, timing its fall with a stopwatch. Then, using the formula $S = \frac{1}{2} at^2$, calculate the length of the building." For this answer, the student received full credit. He had used the barometer and applied a principle of physics. This exercise in creative problem solving has, ever since, been a common fixture in physics classes.

The point of the anecdote is that understanding purpose allows for development of not only creative but also complete solutions to our communication assignments. The correlation between well-understood purpose and development of creative problem solving has always been a cornerstone of scientific thinking. (It also, as we shall discuss shortly, has application to the social sciences and to professional communication.) In this regard, Albert Einstein, unquestionably one of the greatest thinkers of the twentieth century, noted in *The Evolution of Physics:* "The formulation of a problem is often more essential than its solution, which may be merely a matter of mathematical or experimental skills. To raise new questions, new problems, to regard old problems from a new angle, requires creative imagination and marks real advance in science."[18]

FIGURE 1.8

The Basic Staircase Design

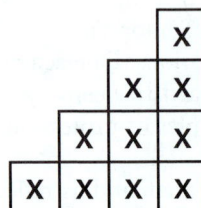

Before we turn to the relationship between creativity and problem solving in the more artistic disciplines, let's stop momentarily for a related anecdote from the development of mathematics. Let's say you are given a basic problem to solve. You are in charge of building a staircase along the wall in the hall. The staircase is going to be made up of square, carved panels, each the same size as the ends of the steps (Figure 1.8). The staircase is going to be 10 steps high. How many squares do you need to purchase at the store?[19]

One means of approaching the problem is to start adding: $1 + 2 = 3 + 3 = 6 + 4 = 10 + \ldots$. A more direct way might be to recognize that there is a recurring pattern at work—a pattern first discerned by a 6-year-old boy. What he noticed was that if he added the outside pairs of boxes, the sum of each of the succeeding pairs of outside numbers remained the same (in this case, 11). By adding the outside pair, therefore, and multiplying it by the number of pairs, he could quickly arrive at the answer. He would need 55 boxes (11×5 pairs) to complete the staircase (Figure 1.9).

This perception of the problem gave rise to an important theorem: $S = (n+1) \tfrac{n}{2}$. (In our example: $S = (10 + 1) \tfrac{10}{2} = 11 \times 5.0 = 55$.) More important than the theorem is what it may help prove to the aspiring professional communicator. It demonstrates, as Einstein concluded, that it is not skill in accomplishing the task (anyone can add the numbers from 1 to 10), but rather the perception (the visualization) of the problem that differentiates the quality (the creativity) of the solution.

We need not simply appeal to inferences to make this axiom more immediate to our current topic. In addition to scientific and mathematical associations, we can look to disciplines closer to home. For instance, we might consider the conclusion from a 10-year study that tracked artists during and after their studies at the Art Institute of Chicago. This study found direct parallels with Einstein's assertion that "problem finding may well be the origin of the creative vision."[20]

As this study, *The Creative Vision: A Longitudinal Study of Problem Finding in Art*, determined, artists, just like scientists, choose between two routes: a well-worn pathway of established technique, routines, and solutions or a less-trodden pathway where solutions and formulations have not yet been defined. Ultimately, the individual's success is not a factor of artistic ability, but rather a matter of whether the individual followed the presented or the discovered pathway. The former is the path of the copyist who arrives at a technically correct answer; the latter is the route of the artist who "discovers" an original, creative solution. While the copyist is judged on technique, the artist is appraised in terms of originality.[21] Envisioning the complete purpose and problem, we might deduce from this study, is the exclusive means of arriving at a complete and creative answer to any communication assignment.

Like the artist, the successful communicator is expected to provide a response that is not only accurate, but original. The less original, the less effective the response is perceived to be. Therefore, the first challenge the communicator

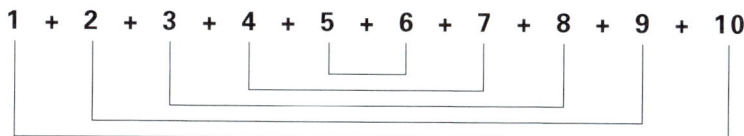

$$1 + 2 + 3 + 4 + 5 + 6 + 7 + 8 + 9 + 10$$

FIGURE 1.9

The Innovative Solution

must meet is whether the problem—in all of its dimensions—has been understood and effectively answered.

THE PRICE OF FAILURE

We have already seen what happens if we are not diligent in defining and discovering the full spectrum of purpose. We end up with simplistic representations of the assignment, with mechanically correct, creatively challenged solutions. However, that is only one dimension of the shortcoming that arises from treating purpose simplistically. The second issue is of more consequence to us as communicators: We may provide incomplete and inappropriate responses to the assignments we have been given. It is one thing to suggest an unimaginative solution to your boss; it is quite another to give your boss an inappropriate solution.

Because it should be relatively obvious that if we incorrectly formulate the problem (or purposes) that we will necessarily create an ineffective answer, we will not dwell on this matter any further. However, we do want to give a straightforward demonstration of how, if we are not diligent in discovering purposes, we can fool ourselves into believing we have the complete picture when, in fact, we don't. To do this, let's look at an experiment that was conducted with college students.[22] Instructions for the task are shown below. The chart referred to in the instructions is shown in Figure 1.10.

Responding to the task, the students indicated 36% of the problems were related to the starting system, 34% the ignition system, 7% mischief, and 23% to "other." This distribution appears reasonable, except for one thing. The most common reasons for a car not starting are not accounted for on the chart: the battery is dead, the car is out of gas, or something is "frozen" in the line. On closer examination, we would expect a much higher score to be cited in the category of "All Other Problems." (Figure 1.11 provides a more complete list of reasons the car won't start; Table 1.3 compares the students' scores when shown this complete version versus the shorter version shown initially.)

Instructions

Every day across the United States millions of drivers perform the act of getting into an automobile, inserting a key in the ignition switch, and attempting to start the engine. Sometimes the engine fails to start, and the trip is delayed. We'd like you to think about the various problems that might be serious enough to cause a car to fail to start so that the driver's trip is delayed for at least 1 minute.

The chart is intended to help you think about this problem. It shows three major deficiencies that cause a car's engine to fail to start. These major categories probably don't cover all possibilities, so we've included a fourth category, All Other Problems.

Please examine this diagram carefully and answer the following question: For every 100 times that a trip is delayed due to "starting failure," estimate, on the average, how many of those delays are caused by each of the four factors. Make your estimates on the blank lines next to the factors named below. Your estimates should sum to 100.

Source: Reprinted with permission of Cambridge University Press.

Not examining a problem thoroughly may lead us to the false assumption that we sufficiently understand the problem. We need to discover embedded purposes; we must make certain we know all the contributing factors. As these researchers pointed out, accepting the evident purposes without pursuing the complete picture and the embedded components is a strategy that can "lull people into complacency."[23] Yet, as communicators, we cannot accept, as these students did, a strategy of "out of sight, out of mind." We must be prepared to understand the complete set of purposes if we are to end up with a complete and creative solution.

Call it "complacency," "technician versus artist," "assigned versus discovered," or "mechanical versus creative," the conclusion is the same. If we simply accept the assignment as given and don't pursue both the complete implications (the influencing constituents and the informing clients) as well as the potential creative solutions, the risk is substantial—to the solution and to us as communicators.

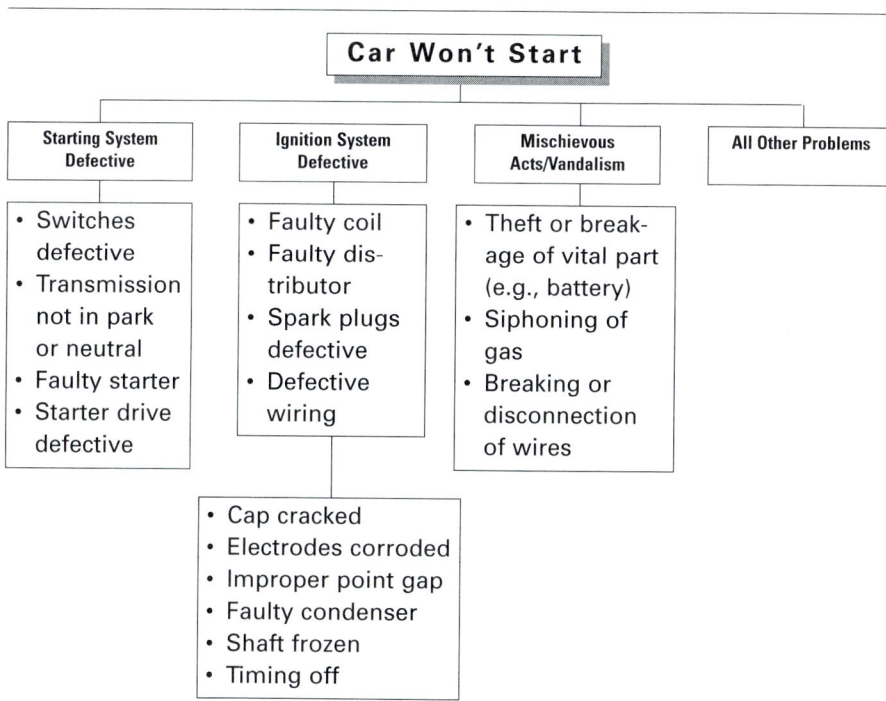

FIGURE 1.10

The Initial List of Potential Causes

Car Won't Start

| Starting System Defective | Ignition System Defective | Mischievous Acts/Vandalism | All Other Problems |

- Switches defective
- Transmission not in park or neutral
- Faulty starter
- Starter drive defective

- Faulty coil
- Faulty distributor
- Spark plugs defective
- Defective wiring

- Theft or breakage of vital part (e.g., battery)
- Siphoning of gas
- Breaking or disconnection of wires

- Cap cracked
- Electrodes corroded
- Improper point gap
- Faulty condenser
- Shaft frozen
- Timing off

Source: Reprinted with permission of Cambridge University Press.

TABLE 1.3 PERCENT OF FAILURE—A COMPARISON

Group	Battery	Starting	Fuel	Ignition	Engine	Mischief	Other
Partial Tree	—	35.7	—	34.3	—	7.3	22.7
Full Tree	26.4	19.5	19.3	14.4	7.6	5.1	7.8

Source: Reprinted with permission of Cambridge University Press.

FIGURE 1.11

The More
Complete List of
Possible Causes

Car Won't Start

Battery Charge Insufficient	Starting System Defective	Fuel System Defective	Ignition System Defective	Other Engine Problems	Mischievous Acts/Vandalism	All Other Problems
• Faulty ground connections • Terminal loose or corroded • Battery weak	• Switches defective • Transmission not in park or neutral • Faulty starter • Starter drive defective	• Insufficient fuel • Excess fuel (flooding) • Defective choke • Defective air filter	• Faulty coil • Faulty distributor • Spark plugs defective • Defective wiring	• Oil too thick • Piston frozen • Poor compression • Defective wiring	• Theft or breakage of vital part (e.g., battery) • Siphoning of gas • Breaking or disconnection of wires	
• Lights left on • Age • Cold weather • Defective generator • Cable broken • Alternator defective • Voltage regulator defective • Short circuit • Battery too small		• Out of gas • Clogged fuel line • Leaky fuel line • Dirt in tank/line • Fuel line frozen • Defective fuel pump • Defective/cracked carburetor • Leaky manifold	• Cap cracked • Electrodes corroded • Improper point gap • Faulty condenser • Shaft frozen • Timing off	• Wrong oil type • Broken ring • Leaking head gasket • Cracked cylinder head • Valves ruined • Piston or piston rings worn or broken		

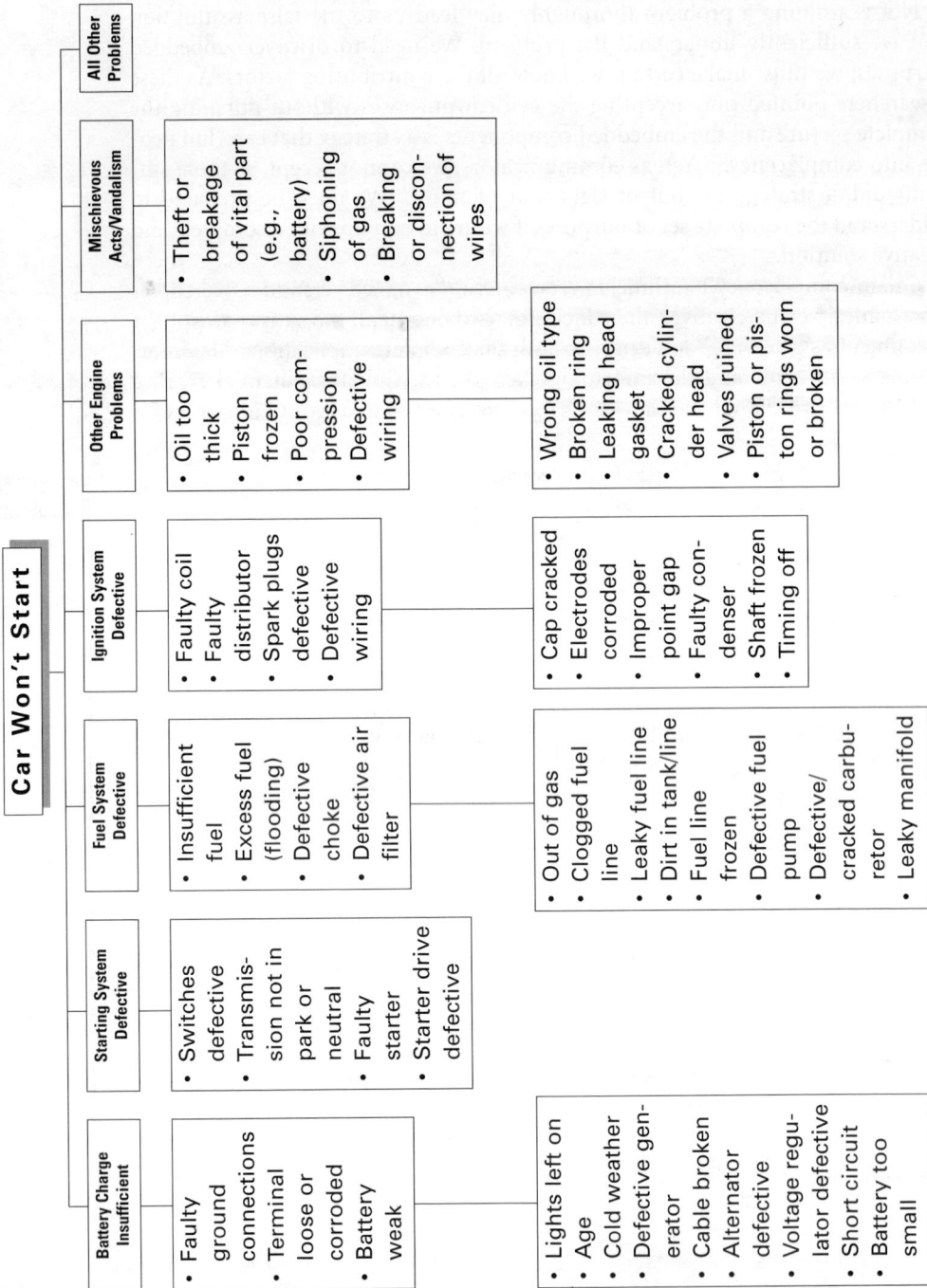

Source: Reprinted with permission of Cambridge University Press.

We recognize that this step from accepting the superficial sense of purpose to actively exploring the implications is a large stride; but we also know from experience that it is absolutely essential for anyone wanting to become a professional communicator. Choosing the easy way out will result in simple, incomplete solutions. Discovering and defining all the elements comprising the purpose—the assignment, the influencing constituents, the informing clients, and the writer's goals—contribute to arriving at and presenting effective responses. These responses completely answer the overt and embedded purposes as well as demonstrate your appreciation of the complexity of the business assignment. Putting together the elements we have been discussing, Figure 1.12 summarizes the questions you need to ask to ensure you have identified the full range of purposes in a business communication assignment.

A PURPOSEFUL RESPONSE TO PURPOSE

To put what we have been discussing in practice, let's try a simple exercise. In this exercise, you are Imma Buzz, regional supervisor at the R'N' Twee Electric Corporation, a firm that specializes in residential electrical work. Your primary activity is to make assignments to a crew of six electricians (four licensed, two apprentices). You are assisted in your work by your boss, S.C. Hock, who estimates the number of electricians for each job and the amount of time needed to do the job. In addition to dealing with your boss's expectations, you also need to follow a number of practices and protocols that have been agreed upon among the owners and the union (Figure 1.13). To add one more consideration, next week is the time your annual performance review is scheduled. This annual meeting with the boss often determines the size of your raise and the likelihood of promotion.

Table 1.4 lists the 16 jobs available to be worked today. Each job is accompanied by five pieces of information: 1) a basic description, 2) the time the job was

---

Explicit Purposes
1. What do you want to happen?
2. What impression do you want to make?

Embedded Purposes
3. What are the origins of the assignment?
4. To whom am I accountable?
5. What is the significance/importance of the activity?
6. How does this activity tie in with existing protocols/policies/corporate standards/corporate expectations?
7. Are there direct or indirect precedents?
8. What fundamental issues (underlying values) are involved or at stake?
9. Why is it important to take this action at this particular time?
10. Is there a particular incident or issue that set things in motion?
11. Are there issues/ideas/related activities my action will bring to mind?
12. Who in the corporation needs to see this (before and after I send it)? Who should not see it?

Discovering
Purposes

FIGURE 1.13

An Overview of
the R'N' Twee
Electric
Corporation

I. WHO YOU ARE:

You're Imma Buzz, Regional Supervisor of R'N' Twee Electric, a firm that specializes in residential electrical work. You've been with the company for nearly 15
years and believe you'll become Vice President when your boss, S.C. Hock, retires
in the next 2 to 3 years.

II. THE COMPANY:

A. Scheduling Jobs: At 6:00 A.M., S.C. Hock checks all the messages and all calls
received by the answering service. He then estimates the number of hours each
job will take and how many electricians are needed. (He is a great estimator and is
always right.) At 7:00 A.M., he dictates the information to the secretary who prepares a list of the day's jobs for you (including any jobs carried over from the previous day). You set priorities and assign the specific electricians. At 7:30, when the
electricians arrive, you hand out the day's schedule.

B. Union Contract: The company has a union contract with seven requirements:
1) Electricians cannot work more than 8 hours a day, but are paid for 8 hours even
if not scheduled for a full day's work. 2) A 1-hour lunch break must be provided
between 11 A.M. and 1 P.M. 3) Apprentices cannot work alone; they must work with
licensed electricians. (An apprentice and a licensed electrician meet the requirement for jobs requiring two electricians.) 4) Because of the hazards, electricians
not certified for high energy work must be accompanied by a licensed, certified
electrician. 5) After 12 months, you must recommend whether apprentices should
be licensed or terminated. If termination is recommended, the reasons must be
extensively documented and defended by you to a union review board. 6) As
supervisor, you are not allowed to do any electrical work yourself. You can, however, visit job sites for up to 4 hours a day. 7) An independent union audit will be
held annually (which is scheduled for next month). Violations can result in fines
that are to be negotiated between the union and your boss.

C. Your Boss: Once he calls in the day's jobs, your boss goes back to bed and
doesn't like to be disturbed. So you'll remember, he's posted key company guidelines in your office:
  1. Residential electrical safety is our mission.
  2. Customer satisfaction is critical. All calls received before noon of a working day
     should be completed before the end of the next working day.
  3. Promote a positive work environment. Personnel should be involved and effec-
     tively employed.

D. Your Crew: You have six electricians (four licensed and two apprentices):
Justin Time—A licensed electrician who tends to be a poor problem solver; not
              yet certified to work high energy jobs.
H. E. Fast—A licensed electrician who works quickly, but only because he tends to
              ignore people and shows little appreciation for public relations.
Bette Sharp—An apprentice 6 months into the program. Shows a great deal
              of promise; good problem solver. Wants to work with the best
              electricians.
H. Anginon—An apprentice 10 months into the program. Still struggling with
              basic technical problems. You haven't yet decided on a recommen-
              dation but are leaning toward termination.
Macon Anayme—A licensed electrician who has excellent leadership and technical
              skills. A natural to be the next regional supervisor if he doesn't
              leave because he prefers commercial work to residential.
Benton Tyred—A licensed electrician nearing retirement. A good problem solver
              who works slowly (especially as the day wears on).

1.4   R'N' TWEE ELECTRIC: ACTIVITY SCHEDULE—FRIDAY, JULY 14TH

	Job Description	Time Logged	People	Hrs	High Energy
1	The lights at the youth soccer league field are not working. Teams (and parents) for the regional games, which start tomorrow, began showing up in town last night.	4 P.M., Thurs	2	2	Yes
2	Several outlets in a private house are not working.	5 P.M., Wed	1	3	___
3	A woman said when she turned on the bedroom lights, there was a flash. She thinks the wall near the switch feels warm. She doesn't know if it's safe to stay in the house.	5 A.M., Friday	2	1	___
4	Power is out at a local school. The principal has cancelled morning classes, but has an important meeting scheduled in the afternoon.	6 P.M., Thurs	2	3	Yes
5	A building addition needs wiring. The homeowner's schedule is tight. He has scheduled the sheet rocking crew to begin Monday.	2 P.M., Thurs	2	3	___
6	The breaker box and basic wiring your boss volunteered to install for free at the local shelter for the homeless need work.	5 P.M., Thurs	1	3	___
7	A local contractor called. The wiring you put in the mall was not consistent with the drawings. The whole project may have to slip if you don't redo the work. He threatened never to contract work to your company again.	4 P.M., Thurs	2	3	Yes
8	A do-it-yourselfer tried to add a 240V line in his basement. He's fouled something up; power is out throughout the house. He's worried the summer heat will affect his three small children.	12 P.M., Thurs	1	3	Yes
9	A ceiling fan needs to be fixed. The fan is wobbling and the owner fears the light fixture is going to fall.	8 P.M., Wed	1	1	___
10	The outside lights are out at a rental property. The owner is scared that the house will be vandalized. He checked the breaker and the bulb and they appear to be fine.	6 A.M., Thurs	1	2	___
11	A local restaurant owner you know needs his kitchen rewired. Until it's done and the inspector signs off, the restaurant's closed. He says he'll cater the annual company party for half price if you get it done today.	5 A.M., Friday	2	2	___
12	The new stoplights need to be connected to the city power lines. The work has usually been done by city workers, but the City Council is testing the concept of subcontracting work to commercial firms like yours.	3 P.M., Thurs	2	3	Yes
13	The annual celebration of the city's founding is next week. The cabling to support all the outside electrical needs must be set up, along with two portable generators.	5 P.M., Wed	2	2	Yes
14	Two new outlets need to be added in a private home.	11 A.M., Thurs	1	1	___
15	The local retirement home has lost all central air-conditioning. The unit itself appears fine.	1 P.M., Thurs	2	3	Yes
16	A nonunion contractor you infrequently do work for says he needs help on a building that has been cited by city inspectors as being below code. If he doesn't get the wiring fixed, he could be looking at fines of up to $500 a day	7 P.M., Thurs	2	3	___

called in, 3) S.C. Hock's determination of the numbers of electricians needed, 4) a determination of how long the job will take, and 5) a notation of whether the job involves "high energy," indicating that the activity may be particularly hazardous and require someone with this special certification.

Each day at 7:00 A.M., you complete a work schedule (Figure 1.14) assigning the day's work to each of the electricians who begin work at 8:00 A.M. (A separate sheet tells the electricians the locations of the jobs. The electricians get that information directly from the secretary, so you need not concern yourself with that information.) Figure 1.15 is the schedule you completed for today. The numerical notations in the boxes indicate the job number to be worked by that electrician. Overall, you are pleased with the schedule you have prepared. You appear to have done well, leaving only one hour unaccounted for. Having now completed our initial work and having seen the electricians out the door, we are free to move on in our discussion of purpose.

Given our insights into purpose, we can now recognize that handling this assignment effectively demands more than merely filling out the schedule. We are now attuned to the fact that the scheduling responsibility has attached to it a number of informing clients and influencing constituents. One means of detailing all these factors is a Purpose Definition form (Figure 1.16). On this sheet, we can establish the relationship among the types of purposes. At the same time, we can make determinations about the relative significance of each purpose and identify each factor from our exercise that is essential to our decision making (Figure 1.17).

We should also be aware that this exercise, though complex, is actually simpler than the typical business communication assignment. Whereas in the exercise we clearly articulated all the major informing clients and influencing constituents for you, in most assignments you would have needed to ask the questions provided in Figure 1.12 to help you identify these elements of purpose.

Using our completed Purpose Definition form, let's return to the schedule we completed for our electricians. As Table 1.5 shows, we can now see that our schedule (Figure 1.15) has issues in almost every category. Although our solution is responsive to the union contract, it violates almost every one of our boss's expectations. Dismissing the boss's interests is not a very smart thing to do. Your performance evaluation next week may suffer if the boss believes that you perceive the electricians' lunch hour is more important than established corporate goals.

Another factor not previously apparent is that in our schedule we made no discernable effort to examine the relationships among purposes. One of the benefits of the Purpose Definition form is that it creates a clearer perspective of all the purposes involved, an essential ingredient of developing complete and creative solutions. As just one example, consider the implications had we made a decision to send H. Anginon by himself to Job 9.

At one level, such a decision would violate the union agreement allowing apprentices to work alone. Yet, there might be a compelling reason to take this action. There may be a hierarchy of purposes at play. In this particular instance, we might say that we were going to Job 9 with H. Anginon to monitor his work (instead of monitoring Benton Tyred at Job 8—an oversight action that is hard to justify). We could reasonably argue that we were taking this action to give the apprentice an opportunity to demonstrate that he had mastered elemental

FIGURE 1.14

Electricians' Schedule: R'N' Twee Electric Company

Electrician	8–9	9–10	10–11	11–12	12–1	1–2	2–3	3–4	4–5
					Time				
Justin Time									
H. E. Fast									
Bette Sharp									
H. Anginon									
Macon Anayme									
Benton Tyred									
Monitoring Imma Buzz									
Jobs Deferred:									

Sample showing Tyred working job numbers 1, 5, 9, and 11

Benton Tyred	1	1	5	5	Lunch	5	9	11	11

FIGURE 1.14

Sample Daily Work Schedule Form

FIGURE 1.15

Electricians' Schedule: R'N' Twee Electric Company

Electrician	8–9	9–10	10–11	11–12	12–1	1–2	2–3	3–4	4–5
					Time				
Justin Time	2	2	2	Lunch	5	5	5	11	11
H. E. Fast	7	7	7	3	Lunch	1	1	16	16
Bette Sharp	7	7	7	3	Lunch	12	12	12	15
H. Anginon	13	13	—	Lunch	5	5	5	11	11
Macon Anayme	13	13	10	10	Lunch	1	1	16	16
Benton Tyred	8	8	8	Lunch	14	12	12	12	15
Monitoring Imma Buzz	7	Office	8	Lunch	Office	12	Office	16	Office

Numbers of jobs carried over to July 15: 1 hr of job 16; 2 hrs of job 15; jobs 4, 6, 9

Completed Work Schedule

FIGURE 1.16

The Purpose
Definition Form

PURPOSE DEFINITION

Overall:

Specific Purposes

I. Informing Clients/ Author's Purposes		II. Influencing Constituents		III. Assignment Driven	
Priority	Essentiality	Priority	Essentiality	Priority	Essentiality
☐	☐	☐	☐	☐	☐
Priority	Essentiality	Priority	Essentiality	Priority	Essentiality
☐	☐	☐	☐	☐	☐
Priority	Essentiality	Priority	Essentiality	Priority	Essentiality
☐	☐	☐	☐	☐	☐
Priority	Essentiality	Priority	Essentiality	Priority	Essentiality
☐	☐	☐	☐	☐	☐
Summary		Summary		Summary	

electrical skills. If Anginon showed he could handle the work at Job 9, it would support keeping him on; if he was unable to handle this basic work at this point in his apprenticeship, it would have offered evidence that a termination decision was appropriate. Although we are aware of the conflicting purposes, we have acted upon the purpose with greater significance and immediacy.

Treating elements of purpose in isolation can potentially mask the overall picture and thus lessen the possibility of developing creative and far-reaching solutions. Sometimes, having defined and discovered the elements, you need to consider the interrelationships among them in order to determine opportunity for efficient and creative solutions. Like the staircase example, demonstrating that we can count may not earn a lot of points. In contrast, demonstrating that

FIGURE 1.17

Putting Purposes
Into Perspective

PURPOSE DEFINITION

Overall: Get the day's work scheduled so electricians can get to assignments; all electricians appropriately assigned.

Specific Purposes

I. Informing Clients/ Author's Purposes		II. Influencing Constituents		III. Assignment Driven	
Priority	Essentiality	Priority	Essentiality	Priority	Essentiality
8	✓	5	✓	2	✓
Union audit		**8-hour rule**		**Customer satisfaction**	
Priority	Essentiality	Priority	Essentiality	Priority	Essentiality
4	✓				
Determination of termination for H. Anginon		**Lunch requirement**		**24-hour rule on completing assignments**	
Priority	Essentiality	Priority	Essentiality	Priority	Essentiality
7	✓	3	✓		
Annual job performance review		**Apprentice 2-man rule**		**Residential vs. commercial work**	
Priority	Essentiality	Priority	Essentiality	Priority	Essentiality
		6	✓	1	✓
		Personality of personnel		**Urgency/safety of condition or job**	
Summary		Summary		Summary	
Need to complete evaluation of H. Anginon		Maintain contract items in light of upcoming audit		Assignments based more on urgency than 24-hr rule	

we can integrate the responses into a creative answer may be the ticket to recognition and reward. Equally important, if not more so, is that we have established the rationale for our actions. When the challenges come, as they frequently do in business, we will be able with confidence to articulate the reasons for the courses of actions we've chosen.

There is, in addition, one more point that becomes apparent when we fill out the Purpose Definition form. Sometimes not every purpose can be effectively integrated into a workable solution. When all the purposes can't be easily integrated into a workable solution, we need to start with an understanding of which elements represent the essential purposes, which have the highest priorities. Then we can work through the layers, making reasoned and defensible

1.5 AN ASSESSMENT OF THE SCHEDULE

Purpose	Priority	Potential Issues
Customer satisfaction	1	24-hour rule upheld; but several customers probably angered: jobs 4, 6, 16
Residential vs. commercial work	2	Some residential work deferred in opposition to commercial work
Urgency of job	3	Safety problems—job 15; future income—job 16; profit issues—one unworked hour H. Anginon paid for
Union regulation	4	—
Positive work environment	5	Issues with assignments to all six electricians
Evaluation of apprentices	6	No oversight of H. Anginon
Annual job review	7	Issues above probably will have an adverse effect on the review
Union audit	8	Problems with worker assignments and monitoring of apprentices may raise issue (though no fines will be incurred)

accommodations. Other strategies we can employ when competing purposes cannot be accommodated are to concentrate exclusively on a few elements that are most critical or to combine related purposes and treat them as a single unit.

As we noted, we can, at minimum, use the analysis as the basis for explaining our strategy in a way that shows we had a reasonable and purposeful approach to the problems at hand. Irrespective of which response structure we use and whether or not we have been able to work all the elements into our solution, by using the Purpose Definition approach, we will have accomplished the first obligation of a communicator—the purposeful response to purpose.

COMMUNICATING WITH PURPOSE—THE LESSONS

The important message in this chapter is that we need to begin our communication effort by identifying purposes in a disciplined manner. This process should begin with the overt, explicit purposes and then proceed through discovery of the embedded purposes. After the purposes are known, they can be used to prioritize, synthesize, integrate, and shape the response. (Figure 1.18 summarizes the process of using purpose.)

FIGURE 1.18

1. Begin by defining your explicit purposes (what you want to happen, what impression you want to make).
2. Dig out the embedded purposes:
    a) context: corporate demands
    b) situation: expected task outcomes
    c) audience: what the reader is anticipating
3. Record and prioritize the purposes, delineating which are essential, which are important, and which are peripheral.
4. Use your purpose to shape the line of attack.
5. Periodically, rereview the purposes and assess your effectiveness in responding to them.

Communicating
With Purpose:
The Process

Taken altogether, there are five critical lessons to learn about purpose in professional writing (Figure 1.19). Following these lessons will lead to successful conclusions; ignoring them will produce inappropriate, partial, or totally useless responses to communication assignments. Communication, done correctly, must consider purpose in every stage of writing: planning, writing, and reviewing. In the planning phase, you need to think about what you need and want to communicate. You need to work hard at surfacing all the purposes and not leaving yourself open to creating an incomplete and unsatisfactory response. In the development phase, you need to think whether you're effectively addressing the purposes and your audience. You need to pay attention to the strategies for dealing with multiple competing purposes. In the reviewing phase, you need to reassess whether you've actually achieved your goals and whether you have dealt effectively with the purposes. In the end, the question will be whether you are able to articulate your thinking and the soundness of your strategy or whether it has simply been a roll of the dice. It's your choice: to emulate Einstein or to shoot dice with de M'ere.

FIGURE 1.19

1. In business, assignments are not chosen; they are given.
2. Assignments may involve many people, but they are generally owned by only one.
3. Assignments don't occur within a vacuum. They are typically multidimensional with intertwined goals deriving from context, situation, audience, and personal expectations.
4. Sometimes not all purposes can be accommodated. You need to make defensible, deliberate choices and decisions.
5. You need to use a clear sense of purpose to evaluate your efforts before, during, and after writing.

Purpose: The
Message

☐ **Group**

1. Identify all the purposes you can think of for taking a course in professional communication. Prioritize these based on the following situations:

   a) You want to convince your boss to give you paid time off to take the class.

   b) You need to demonstrate improved communication skills in order to obtain a new assignment.

   c) You have three credits to fill on your schedule.

   d) You want to convince the instructor to allow you into a session that is already full.

2. Below is the organization chart for Minnesota Flamethrowers, Inc. The chart explains the basic responsibilities of the seven departments that report to the President. The head of Finance, your boss, just came up with a suggestion that she wants you to write up for her to deliver to her boss, the President, at the next staff meeting. (Staff meetings are attended by the heads of each of the seven departments, as well as by the President of the local Union of Flamethrowers and Fire-eaters.)

   Your boss's idea is to get rid of 50 (one-tenth) of the senior technicians (union members who assemble the flamethrowers) and replace them with people she expects human resources to hire at the local employment office. The savings, as she has figured, would be about $1,250,000 a year ($25,000 per technician). She knows there will probably be some objections, but with the company $1,000,000 in the hole, somebody has to do something fast!

   a) Using the Purpose Definition form (Figure 1.16), identify and prioritize the specific purposes your boss is going to have to address at the staff meeting in order to sell her proposal.

   b) So she can get some support in advance of the meeting, prepare a letter from your boss to one of the other department heads explaining why the proposal is in that group's best interests. (Use the elements identified on the Purpose Definition form to define the strategies you need.)

**Minnesota Flamethrowers, Inc.
President**

Finance	Human Resources	Operations	Quality Assurance
Auditing and ensuring cost-effective practices & operations	Hiring, benefits, EEO requirements, & overseeing union contracts	Assembling & testing flamethrowers; loading retardant in units	Ensuring all practices meet company & federal standards

Public Relations	Safety	Training
Promoting positive community relations & support	Ensuring worker safety; health; environmental compliance	Providing training and certification of workers

Individual

1. Complete a day's schedule for the electricians. Explain why you made the selection of jobs and how you assigned the work.

2. Your boss and the union rep just showed up at your office. They want to know your decision about H. Anginon. Let them know what you've decided and how you reached that decision.

END NOTES

[1] The quotation from Kinneavy is cited in Nancy Roundy Blyler, "Purpose and Composition Theory: Issues in the Research," in *Journal of Advanced Composition,* Vol. 9 (1989), pp. 97–111.

[2] Elizabeth M. Dorn, "Case Method Instruction in the Business Writing Classroom," *Business Communication Quarterly,* Vol. 62, No. 1 (March 1999), pp. 41–63.

[3] Nancy Roundy Blyler, "Teaching Purpose in a Business Communication Course," *The Bulletin,* Vol. 56, No. 3 (Sept. 1993), pp. 15–20.

[4] *Ibid.*

[5] *Ibid.*

[6] Linda Flower, "The Construction of Purpose in Writing and Reading," *College English,* Vol. 50, No. 5 (Sept. 1988), pp. 528–550.

[7] Deborah Brandt, "Toward an Understanding of Context Composition," *Written Communication,* Vol. 5, No. 2 (April 1986), pp. 139–157.

[8] Linda Flower and John R. Hayes, "The Cognition of Discovery: Defining a Rhetorical Problem," *College Composition and Communication,* Vol. 31, No. 1 (Feb. 1980), pp. 21–32.

[9] Lloyd F. Blitzer, "The Rhetorical Situation," *Philosophy and Rhetoric,* Vol. 1, No. 1 (Jan. 1968), pp. 1–14.

[10] Stanley Fish, *Is There a Text in This Class?* Cambridge: Harvard U. P., 1980.

[11] Flower and Hayes, "The Cognition of Discovery."

[12] Linda Flower and John R. Hayes, "The Dynamics of Composing: Making Plans and Juggling Constraints," in *Cognitive Processes in Writing,* ed. Lee Grien and Erwin Steinberg, Hillsdale, NJ: Lawrence Erlbaum Assoc. Publishers, 1980, pp. 31–50.

[13] Flower and Hayes, "The Cognition of Discovery."

[14] Figure adapted from Ronald T. Kellogg, *The Psychology of Writing,* New York: Oxford U. P., 1994, p. 26.

[15] Figure adapted from Paul Slovic, "Perception of Risk," *Science,* Vol. 236 (April 17, 1987), pp. 280–285.

[16] Much of the information on gambling was taken from J. M. Fenster, "Nation of Gamblers," *American Heritage,* Vol. 45, No. 5 (Sept. 1994), pp. 34–46.

[17] Alexander Calandra, "Angels on a Pin," *Saturday Review,* Dec. 21, 1968, p. 60.

[18] Cited in Jacob W. Getzels and Mihaly Csikszentmihalyi, *The Creative Vision: A Longitudinal Study of Problem Finding in Art,* New York: John Wiley and Sons, 1976, p. 4.

[19] Max Wertheimer, *Productive Thinking* (enlarged edition), Westport, CN: Greenwood Press, Publishers, 1959, pp. 108–112.

[20] Getzels and Csikszentmihalyi, *The Creative Vision,* pp. 250–251.

[21] *Ibid,* pp. 79–80.

[22] Paul Slovic, Baruch Fischhoff, and Sarah Lictenstein, "Fact Versus Fear: Understanding Perceived Risk," in *Judgment Under Uncertainty: Heurstics and Biases,* ed. Daniel Kahneman, Paul Slovic, Amos Tversky, London: Cambridge U.P., 1982.

[23] *Ibid.*

2

Audience
Bringing Business Communities Into Focus

Having gained a fuller appreciation of the complexity of purpose in professional communications, we now turn to the other keystone of effective communication—audience. The subject, like purpose, is deceptive. We can trace the need to pay attention to audience to each of the fathers of classical rhetoric. Yet, on this topic, we don't seem to have received more guidance than that which was made available several centuries ago.

> Aphorisms such as "consider your audience" and "adapt to your reader" have echoed off the walls of business communication classrooms for decades. Even Alta Guinn Saunders (*Effective Business English*, 1925), one of the field's premier early textbook writers, addressed the importance of reader analysis and adaptation.

> Despite this early concern about reader analysis, the business communication field's research in this area has slowed to a trickle . . . . Current business communication texts add little to the advice first offered by Saunders and her followers.[1]

What started off as a clearly defined and clearly understood concept has somehow gotten lost in a half-century of debate. Whereas purpose demands a sense of creativity to understand the environment and create the architecture, creativity seems to have been working overtime in trying to understand audience.

The issue of audience

The unknowable reader

- The novelist

- The film critic

- The anthropologist

The art of handling it

The truth about the fictional audience

Audiences are always real and concrete.

Each member of your audience has unique expectations.

The audiences for professional communications are eminently knowable.

Audience—the lessons

We need to put audience back into perspective if we are going to create effective communication. Purpose is all-important, but no more important than audience if we are going to know what needs to be said and how to say it well. Without a disciplined approach to purpose and audience, facts will never become information, and information will never become communication.

THE ISSUE OF AUDIENCE

Like purpose, audience is a commonly discussed, but little understood concept, particularly when applied to professional communication. Dating back to the works of Aristotle, Plato, and Cicero, communicators were directed to pay attention to audience. Yet, in the last half-century, we seem to have lost our way when it comes to audience. Recognizing this dilemma, Lisa Ede, writing in the 1970s, wrote:

> "CONSIDER YOUR AUDIENCE." Surely this is one of the most quoted and least understood of what might, for lack of a better term, be called composition commonplaces. Hardly a textbook exists that fails to give this advice; but few existing textbooks devote more than one or two pages to its elucidation.[2]

A number of writers have tried to answer the question of why the examination of audience is lacking. Reminiscent of our discussion of purpose, most researchers conclude the problem stems from a belief that audience is largely unknowable. This theory suggests that "a writer's acquisition of knowledge about the audience is more a mystery, more intuitive, and less easily describable and teachable than other steps in the writing process."[3]

Further, the unknowable is compounded by the ill-defined. Just as the audience itself has become increasingly nebulous, so the term "audience" has lost its precise meaning. A number of meanings can be inferred when we are invited to "consider our audience":

1. Anyone who happens to listen to or to read a given discourse: The audience applauded.

2. External readers or listeners defined by the rhetorical situation: The writer misjudged his audience.

3. An envisioned audience: What audience do you have in mind?

4. An audience implicitly defined by the communication: What does this paragraph suggest about the audience?[4]

The simple dictates of Aristotle, who advised his speakers to consider such audience characteristics as age and wealth (because these tend to make an individual more receptive to some arguments and less so to others) seemingly have been recast by a variety of approaches, theories, and pedagogical strategies that have variously emphasized the writer, the written product, and the audience. The writer model pushed hard for attention to self-expression. The product orientation model concentrated on mechanics and format. The audience model, the most popular pedagogical strategy for most of the twentieth century, maintained that in a communication, numerous interactions were taking place among all the elements (Figure 2.1).[5]

A number of schools and disciplines have helped complicate this simple picture of audience. Among these, a succession of psychological orientations has been heard. Perhaps foremost in its influence was the work of Young, Becker, and Pike. In their 1970 text, *Rhetoric: Discovery and Change,* they asserted that while classical tradition was founded on the assumption that man was fundamentally a rational animal, alternative interpretations might better explain how the human condition affects our communications. Among these alternatives cited were a Pavlovian interpretation that reduced man to a bundle of habits that can be changed and controlled, and a Freudian interpretation that argues we are intensely influenced by experiences suppressed in our unconscious mind. The classical, Pavlovian, and Freudian schools, as fundamentally different as they may seem, were—as Young, Becker, and Pike interpreted rhetoric—linked by a common, underlying goal: "the control of one human being by another."[6] The solution the authors offered to these "control" strategies was a reliance on the work of yet another psychotherapist, Carl Rogers.

FIGURE 2.1

Typical Audience-Response Model

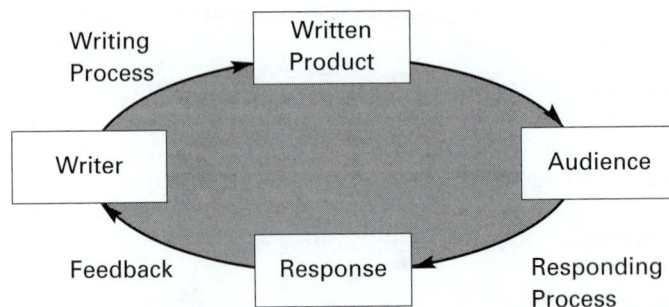

Writing Process — Written Product — Audience — Responding Process — Response — Feedback — Writer

Communication, as this interpretation argues, should focus on building bridges between writer and reader and should strive to establish an empathetic relationship with the reader, eliminating threats to the reader's beliefs and values. Not conceding the matter to "control" or "empathy," other social sciences proposed their own alternatives about how best to understand and deal with the audience. Sociolinguists, for instance, soon proposed that we concentrate on the audience's sociocultural background; in contrast, psycholinguists recommended that we make a more direct attack by anticipating the audience's processing needs.[7]

With a succession of opinions, by the 1980s, there was no longer anything approaching consensus as what was meant either by audience or by audience analysis. At the root of the problem was a running debate between two camps: those who believed "audience," as expressed by classical rhetoricians, applied to all forms of communication recipients (near and far, singular and plural); and those who insisted that "audience" was a concept that applies exclusively to a simple, immediate listener. Once the body of recipients grows in size or is reached through any form of indirect transmission (such as in written form), the notion of "audience," this second school argues, no longer applies. You might have "readers," but you no longer had an "audience."

The first component of the debate, "the one versus the many" (or an individual versus a collective audience), has echoes throughout rhetorical history (Table 2.1).[8] As interesting as this element of the discussion might be, it does not create the same degree of havoc for professional communication as does its close cousin—the debate between a present, immediate (enjoined) audience versus the distant (detached) audience. Little middle ground is offered between the attentive individual listener and "an ideal conception shadowed forth." The audience, we are led to believe, is either present or does not exist.

In what might initially be perceived as an attempt at synthesizing the two competing perspectives reflected in the debate, Chaim Perelman and L. Olbrechts-Tyteca took a new look at the relationship between speaker and audience. While they conceded a distant reader still could exist, they maintained his

TABLE

2.1 THE ONE AND THE MANY DEBATE

Rhetorician	"The One"	"The Many"
Plato	Judge	Crowd
Aristotle	Juror/Politician	Ceremonial Audience
Augustine	Upright Christian	Fallen Souls
Bacon	Scientist	Students
Hobbes	Monarch	Multitude
Locke	(False Abstraction)	Reasonable Man
Campbell	Men in General	Men in Particular

image was blurred by the distance. Specifically, in their highly influential text, *The New Rhetoric: A Treatise on Argumentation,* they concluded it is difficult, if not impossible, to know one's audience with anything approaching absolute certainty. Reminiscent of the advocates of the unknowable purpose, the image this creates is of a writer arbitrarily constructing both purpose and audience.

Their recommendation for addressing this dilemma was also a compromise of sorts. Communicators should address themselves to a "universal audience," a construction that would be unique to each writer and each culture. This universal audience would allow us to address an audience of ". . . common disposition, an aggregate formed from what the author knows of his men, in such a way to transcend the few oppositions he is aware of."[9]

THE UNKNOWABLE READER

As might be expected, rather than resolving the dilemma of audience, these authors only sparked further discussion. There now existed concepts of readers inside and outside of the text, readers who are real and readers who are not. There was focus on persuasion (control), opposed by focuses on sincerity, self-expression, and empathy. There were also universal as opposed to individual audiences. There were even questions of what was knowable and not knowable about our audience, and questions of whether the author actually had any intention at all of speaking to anyone.

Seemingly only befitting the debate, the psychologists, sociolinguists, and rhetoricians soon found themselves dealing with the voices of the poets on the issue of audience. Beyond just seeking reader empathy, the poets proposed that authors might simply engage themselves in conversation. This twist was introduced by T. S. Eliot in a lecture presented to the National Book League. In the opening comments of his lecture, "The Three Voices of Poetry," Eliot weaves together the capital elements of the audience debate, while introducing this entirely new dimension that as writers we may, in fact, be writing (or speaking) to ourselves:

> The first voice is the voice of the poet talking to himself or to nobody. The second is the voice of the poet addressing an audience, whether large or small. The third is the voice of the poet when he attempts to create a dramatic character speaking in verse; when he is saying, not what he would say in his own person, but only what he can say within the limits of one imaginary character addressing another imaginary character.[10]

None of the voices in the audience debate—the rhetorician's, the psychologist's, the linguist's, or the poet's—had effectively differentiated whether the audience debate was intended to be restricted to any particular mode of expression. The arguments could be applied equally to fiction writing as well as to the various forms of exposition. They could, in Eliot's words, pertain to both "dramatic and nondramatic verse."

Unchecked, over time, the audience debate spilled into all quarters of communication. The debate today remains enjoined among three schools of thought regarding the author's intentions toward and obligations to the audience. In partial acknowledgment of their respective heritages—but also to suggest the nature of their differing orientations—we refer to these three occupations of audience as the "novelist," "the film critic," and the "anthropologist."

THE NOVELIST

A few years before T. S. Eliot added his voice to the audience debate, composition theorists had introduced the idea of "mock readers," a limited acknowledgment that readers were out there, even if we weren't sure of their identities.[11] This limited acknowledgment, within the course of a few years, became more transparent; the barely known "mock" reader vanished. In the course of a single scholarly publication, the reader became a total "fiction." In his 1975 article, "The Writer's Audience Is Always a Fiction," Walter J. Ong challenged the classical concept of audience.[12] As Ong maintained, if the author does not have an audience—the "one," the "many" or, a "collectivity"—then an entirely different approach must be taken in constructing a sense of communication. While an orator has a true audience, a "collectivity," no such relationship or equivalent grouping exists when we discuss readers. Readership is, in fact, merely an abstraction:

> [I]t is really quite misleading to think of a writer as dealing with an "audience," even though certain considerations may at times oblige us to think this way. More properly, a writer addresses readers only, he does not quite "address" them either: he writes to or for them. The orator has before him an audience which is a true audience, a collectivity. "Audience" is a collective noun. There is no such collective noun for readers, nor, so far as I am able to puzzle out, can there be. "Readers" is a plural. Readers do not form a collectivity, acting here and now on one another and on the speaker as members of an audience do. "Readership" is not a collective noun. It is an abstraction in a way that "audience" is not.

> The contrast between hearing and reading (running the eye over signals that encode sound) can be caught if we imagine a speaker addressing an audience equipped with texts. At one point, the speaker asks the members of the audience all to read silently a paragraph out of text. The audience immediately fragments. It is no longer a unit. Each individual retires into his own microcosm. When the readers look up again, the speaker has to gather them into a collectivity once more. This is true even if he is the author of the text they are reading.[13]

The conclusion Ong reaches is that the fictionalizing of audiences is part of an age-old drama in which the writer and the reader willingly perform. For a communication to succeed, a fiction must be created by the writer and accepted by the reader. Not only must the writer "construct in his imagination . . . an audience cast in some sort of role," but the audience must also "fictionalize itself," must be willing to accept the role in which it has been cast by the writer. "A text is a kind of drama, with roles created for writer and reader, and the audience is invited to enact the role which the writer has created for the reader."[14]

This fictionalizing would not perhaps have had such an impact on professional communication if Ong had limited his assault to the writing of fiction. However, whereas others in the debate had allowed an overlap among the modes of communication to occur by default, Ong explicitly brings the issue of the audience as fiction to rest on the doorstep of every form of written communication—professional communication included: "The historian, the scholar or scientist, and the simple letter writer all fictionalize their audiences, casting them in a made-up role and calling on them to play the role assigned."[15]

The natural extension of this thinking is that we end up precisely back where Eliot suggested: "The process of imagining a reader . . . is not an attempt to approximate the knowledge and viewpoint of actual persons, but a process of projecting a self that the reader will try on and find agreeable."[16] We don't write, this thinking goes, for the audience or to the audience; we merely allow them to participate as they see fit. What this "novelist's" strategy leads to is a focus on questions that reflect the audience as projection: Who do I want my audience to be? What ideas or actions are to be encouraged? What distance between writer and reader should be maintained? What pieces of information do I want the reader to take for granted? What do I want to list in detail?

Fortunately, not everyone is willing to concede the audience as fiction. (Nor has professional communication yet been called upon to deal with "dramatism," the school of communication that asserts that life is not like a drama, but is a drama.) The novelists who promote the audience as fiction fail to acknowledge that readers' experiences, expectations, and beliefs play a central role in their reading of a text. The professional communicator, in particular, who does not consider the needs and interests of a real audience is creating a self-induced fiction.

While such a fiction may be sustainable through academic dialogue in the composition or literature class, it is totally inappropriate when dealing with professional communication. In this environment, the audience is not fictional; it is real, substantial, and knowable. Even more important, the business audience is often both the initiator and the recipient of the communication, inhabiting a much more commanding (and demanding) role than that conceded by the novelist. We already have learned the consequences of not answering the audience's expectations. A similar problem will arise for anyone who tries to dismiss the imposing reality of the audience itself.

THE FILM CRITIC

The novelists may have a unique perspective, but that doesn't mean that other equally speculative perspectives haven't divided the landscape of audience. For instance, living next door to the novelist is the film critic. The novelist is involved in inventing the audience, while the film critic uses a lens to filter an impression—a sense of the character of the audience. While the novelist creates the audience, the film critic construes it. Often this is an attempt to gain perspective on a diverse, heterogeneous audience. At other times, it approaches the kind of audience analysis more commonly associated with marketing products to the mass media.

Referred to variously in the literature as implied, invoked, projected, and simulated audiences, the readership, as viewed by the film critic, is a generally, though not solidly, known body of people. They exist—out there—but in a vague, undifferentiated manner. In one sense, they might be categorized consistent with the categories used in television marketing (Table 2.2).[17]

In media studies, the film critic's orientation to audience corresponds with the three models of audience as market: 1) audience as mass, 2) audience as outcome, and 3) audience as agent.[18] The audience as mass is the most common model of considering the media audience. In this model, whose roots lie in the Industrial Revolution, the audience is viewed as a commodity—a large collection of people scattered across time and space. The members of the collection act autonomously and have little, if any, immediate knowledge of one another. The audience as outcome, in contrast, considers the potential effects of the media on its audience. Most commonly, the audience as outcome—an outgrowth of the film research of the 1920s and 1930s—seeks to define how the power of media can produce a deleterious effect on an individual, and, by implication, on the overall society. Last, the audience as agent suggests a degree of free agency, with people actually

2.2 CATEGORIES OF AUDIENCE

Audience Concept	Prime Role Envisioned
Market	To sell via attention
Public	To serve a role
Fans of taste or culture	To feed an identity
Social group	To satisfy shared interest
Involved audience	To provide an enriched communication experience

selecting which media they will consume, using media to suit their own needs and interests. As an audience, they are, nonetheless, an aggregate rather than a series of individual, differentiated profiles.

To aid in the comparison with the mock and fictionalized audiences of the novelist, let's return to the world of professional communication and portray these marketing models along a continuum of audience interaction (Figure 2.2). At the far right of the spectrum are the commercial audiences among whom there is little chance for interaction. On the far left are the face-to-face encounters that even the novelists concede are among the few nonfictional interactions. Between these extremes lie the pedestrian audience (analogous to persons who happen to pass a soap box orator); the passive occasional audience (analogous to persons attending a lecture); and the active occasional audience (analogous to persons participating in a working session of a town council).[19]

In an attempt to "know" this "implied" audience, the film critics advocate a series of questions that consider four different dimensions of the writer-audience relationship: 1) the environment of the audience, 2) the subject as interpreted by the audience, 3) the relationship between the writer and the audience, and 4) the means for achieving the writer's goals (Table 2.3).[20]

These questions generally produce answers that hit wide of the mark. Speculation about the audience appears more important than knowing the audience. Empathy with the reader is more vital than a positive identification of the audience. The implied reader of the film critic is, thereby, only slightly more real, only slightly more attuned to the knowable audience of professional communication than is the novelist's fictions. This leaves us with one last interpretation of audience to review before we get down to business.

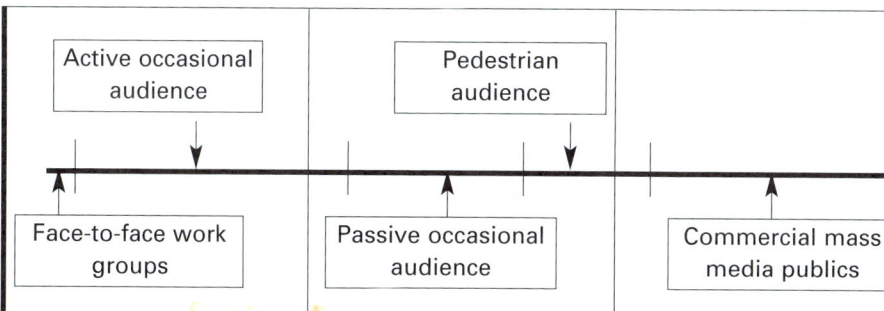

FIGURE 2.2

An Audience Continuum

2.3   A PROPOSED MODEL FOR AUDIENCE ANALYSIS

The environment of the audience	—What is the reader's physical, social, and economic status? —What is the reader's educational and cultural experience? —What are the reader's ethical concerns and hierarchies of values? —What are the reader's common myths and prejudices?
The subject as it might be interpreted by the audience	—How much does the reader know about what I want to say? —What is the opinion of the reader about my subject? —How strong is that opinion? —How willing is the reader to act upon that opinion? —Why does the reader react the way he or she does?
The relationship of the audience to the writer	—What is the reader's knowledge and attitude about me? —What are our shared experiences, attitudes, interests, myths, and prejudices? —What is my purpose(s)/aim(s) in addressing this audience? —Is this an appropriate audience for my subject? —What role do I wish to assign to the audience? —What role do I want to assume for the audience?
How best to achieve audience cooperation, persuasion, and identification	—What pattern/model/development is appropriate? —What tone? —What diction? —What level of syntactic sophistication (complexity of sentence structure)?

Source: Pfister and Petrick, "A Heuristic Model for Creating a Writer's Audience," *College Composition and Communication*. Copyright 1980 by the National Council of Teachers of English. Reprinted with permission.

THE ANTHROPOLOGIST

The novelist and the film critic presume the body of knowledge about audience is limited. The anthropologist, however, takes the opposite position. The anthropologist pursues an aggressive excavation of information, unearthing great volumes of (though often potentially irrelevant) information. Expanding on Aristotle's direction to consider such information as the audience's age and wealth, the anthropologist expands the original demographic approach from a search for individual characterization into a full-scale cultural analysis. In comparison with the novelist who invents the audience and the film critic who interprets it, the anthropologist enters on a protracted, multidirectional voyage of discovery. "You must keep in mind the concerns and values of the people you want to reach; you should have some knowledge of their educational and social backgrounds, how old they are, what kind of work they do, and whether they are, on the whole, liberal or conservative about religion, sex and politics . . . You will have to analyze your audience consciously, specify its traits, and decide what conclusions you can legitimately make about an audience with those traits."[21] The problem that soon arises, however, is that discovery devoid of context provides data but not insight.

Similar to the film critic's approach, this discovery process manifests itself in a series of questions that give definition to the types of information to be used, the style, and the language of the audience (Figure 2.3). Ironically, this self-induced complexity gives rise to a simplistic assessment of audience in which individual characteristics are deduced from the habits of the community to which the individual belongs. These communities represent groupings of individuals bound by a common interest or common sets of expectations or rules: "the community of engineers whose research area is fluid mechanics, alumni of the University of Michigan; Magnavox employees; the members of the Porter family; and the members of the Indiana Teachers of Writing."[22] Often these communities are replaced by "global" communities: Democrats and Republicans; "partisan, neutrals, and opponents"; and "novices and experts."[23]

Unfortunately, the more amorphous the group, the more global the community, the less likely that the distinct characteristics are retained—the more likely that audiences are implied or invoked, rather than known. Inevitably following this line of thought, audiences take up concurrent residency in both local and global communities, forcing a folding together of invented, interpreted, and discovered conceptions of audience.

To highlight this merger of audience perspectives, let's consider the graphical depiction used by the authors who were largely responsible for launching the debate about whether audiences were addressed or invoked. Their wheel depicting "concept of audience" shows the invoked and addressed audience roles in the form of "discourse communities." Because the communities identified on the

FIGURE 2.3

The Demographic Approach to Knowing Audience

Audience
Business Communication

Primary Audience Factors
(who's it for)

what's suggested

☐ What is their background? ──────► line of argument

☐ Educational level? ──────► language & analogies

☐ Technical/subject expertise? ──────► logic

☐ Potential relevant biases? ──────► level of detail

☐ Knowledge of the subject? ──────► focus, depth

☐ What do they want to know? ──────► organizing rationale

☐ What do they need to know? ──────► points to be made

☐ What is their purpose in reading? ──────► what are they inclined to

☐ What do I want to happen when ──────► link between
they're done?   audience & purpose

Secondary Considerations

☐ Are they open to my information?

☐ Are they open to me?

☐ Is the material competing with others?

☐ Are there particular issues to hit/avoid?

☐ What approach is best suited to them?

wheel are essentially the same for the invoked and addressed audiences, this clearly suggests a conclusion that the writer has gained little discrete knowledge of his audience from these competing models (Figure 2.4).[24]

As with several of the issues we examined when discussing purpose, the problem is evident: The novelist, the film critic, and (especially) the anthropologist are trying to assess rather than reflect the issues of audience as they occur in a business environment. From an external vantage point, certain attributes of audience may have been obscured.

Two critical problems arise from the acceptance of audience as fiction: we never appreciate the real challenge represented by artfully addressing business audiences, and we reinforce the erroneous notion of a limited set of business circumstances and purposes. The lack of appreciation for the sense of business audiences is reflected in the fact that two types of audience exercises are repeatedly stressed. In the first instance, students are assigned an audience and then are expected to adapt language and mechanics to the audience's presumed interests, character, and inclinations. In a similar assignment, but processed in reverse, students are given writing samples (most often advertisements) and asked to decode the traits of the audience (an exercise particularly common among the film critics and anthropologists). (The Appendix includes a sample of one of these oversimplified exercises.)

The second consequence of the fiction is that by conceding the faulty assumption that the audience is a somewhat blurry commodity, we reinforce the primary assumption we challenged in Chapter 1: There are only a fixed number of business circumstances requiring communication. If writing assignments are limited and highly predictable, attention to audience becomes less critical. The notions of limited purposes and minimally definable audience thereby reinforce and substantiate each other.

FIGURE 2.4

The Invoked and Addressed Communities

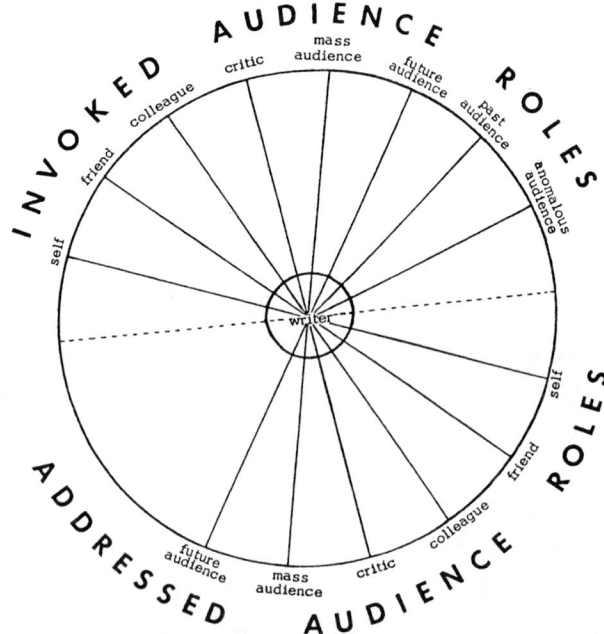

Source: Ede and Lunsford, "Audience Addressed/Audience Invoked: The Role of Audience in Composition Theory and Pedagogy," *College Composition and Communication.* Copyright 1984 by the National Council of Teachers of English. Reprinted with permission.

These two consequences are reflected in a conclusion from an article dealing with creating "a better understanding of reader analysis":

> The writer's responses . . . are almost always based on speculation. Business writers can use observation, analysis, and experience to gauge their reader's attitudes, beliefs, and needs. But their judgments can be no more than tentative and speculative because reader attitudes and motivations are dynamic and unpredictable, particularly when the reader is responding to a sensitive topic. These speculations force writers to make organizational, stylistic, and content choices that result in their creating in their messages a context—a kind of role, invention, or fiction they hope their readers will adopt or engage in. This context may require the reader to act as a straightforward businessperson, team player, unbiased analyst, understanding colleague, or to play other appropriate roles.[25]

However, neither the blurry audience nor the limited circumstances and purposes is true of professional communication. We deal daily with a complex universe of tightly integrated purposes. We will see presently that we also deal with real, immediately known and demanding audiences.

THE ART OF HANDLING IT

So, is the audience really a fiction? Must we invoke a general sense of the audience? Should we suggest how to proceed by gathering demographic and "societal" data about the audience? Just as the wheel of invoked/addressed audiences brought us full circle in defining audience characteristics, so the discussion of local and global communities brings us back to the concept of "the one" and "the many" as understood by Plato, Aristotle, Augustine, Bacon, Hobbes, Locke, and Campbell (Table 2.1).

Yet, the trip has not been for nothing. Cycling back to the traditional rhetorical views allows us to see the basics of the audience model (Figure 2.1) in better perspective. In fact, while negotiating the uneven terrain of the territories occupied by the novelists, the film critics, and the anthropologists, we may have inadvertently overlooked the cautions not to lose sight of Aristotle's fundamental rhetorical structure of speaker, subject, and audience:

> [T]he concept of audience has at last emerged from a period of complacency and stagnation—a long period during which the concept received only superficial treatment in most of our composition textbooks, as well as little theoretical elaboration and very little research . . . . Salutary as this renewed interest may prove for our field, we need to consider how unwise and unproductive it would be to swing from neglect of the audience to overemphasis, forgetting in our new enthusiasm the old lesson that writing involves a delicate balance among several elements of communication, of which the audience is but one. Aristotle reminds us that a speech (or any communication) is the "joint result of three things—the speaker, the subject, and the person addressed."[26]

To reinforce this relationship and to explore this "delicate balance," let's try an exercise that should place the orientations advocated by the novelist, the film critic, and the anthropologist into proper perspective.

You work for a company called Shoe n' Sole, Inc., a major producer of footwear. You are in charge of a new line of products known as SSAs (Super Shoes for Adults). One morning you arrive at the office and find a note in your inbox. The note was originally sent by someone named Joe in the Transportation Department to your immediate manager, the Vice President of Product Development. She, in turn, has forwarded the note to you. You have no idea who Joe is, but your boss has written across the bottom of the note a request for you to take care of the matter (Figure 2.5). You know precisely what that request means. Your boss expects the necessary actions to be completed before she gets back in the office.

What do you do? You try calling the Transportation Department, but find out Joe won't be in until the evening shift, 8 hours away. The note, given the imminent timing of the planned shipment of the new SSAs, has a sense of urgency. So, you sit down and start writing to the Vice Presidents. (Figure 2.6 provides a summary-level organization chart of the company.) Being a take-charge professional on the rise, you know from experience not to bring Vice Presidents a problem; they expect solutions. Accordingly, you dash off a quick response and send it to the Vice Presidents (Figure 2.7).

Having sent your secretary to hand deliver your notes to the Vice Presidents, you sit down to draft the note to Carol in the Design Department about how to amend the box inserts, the standard flier describing the shoes' superior craftsmanship and quality. You don't get far into this second project because your phone rings. In quick succession, you receive calls from each of the Vice Presidents.

Smile wants to know what the problem is and how it's going to change the marketing plan. He's got sales agreements for several thousand pairs of shoes and needs to know whether the sales need to be renegotiated. Also, the marketing program has never included any references to safety. How is there a safety issue with the shoe? Dough is livid. His warehouses are stuffed solid with pallets of shoes.

Dough can't hold the shoes beyond tomorrow because another production line is scheduled for receipt. He also can't spare his warehouse staff to unpack pallets and put in new inserts. Spy can't believe you've been sitting on a legal

---

FIGURE 2.5

The Delegated
Action

> **Shoe n' Sole, Inc.**
>
> To: V.P. Development
>
>   Reviewed the plan for the new line of Super Shoes for Adults. Looks like a real winner, but we could have issues with the laces. Someone could trip, fall, and SUE! I recognize this is the third line of shoes shipped this year and the flier's already crowded with specifications. I'm sure Carol in Design could fit in whatever's needed (wording/graphics) on the flier to keep us out of court without too bad a bump in the schedule. Sorry to hit you with this 2 days before we're ready to do final packaging, but with a stake in the company, I want to end up rich, not in court.
>
>   Obviously it's your action. Let Carol know what to add to the flier, and I suggest you fill the other VPs in on what we're adding, why, and the schedule impact.
>
>   Joe
>   Transportation
>
> *Please take care of this. I'll be back in the office the day after tomorrow.*
>   *Bigwig*

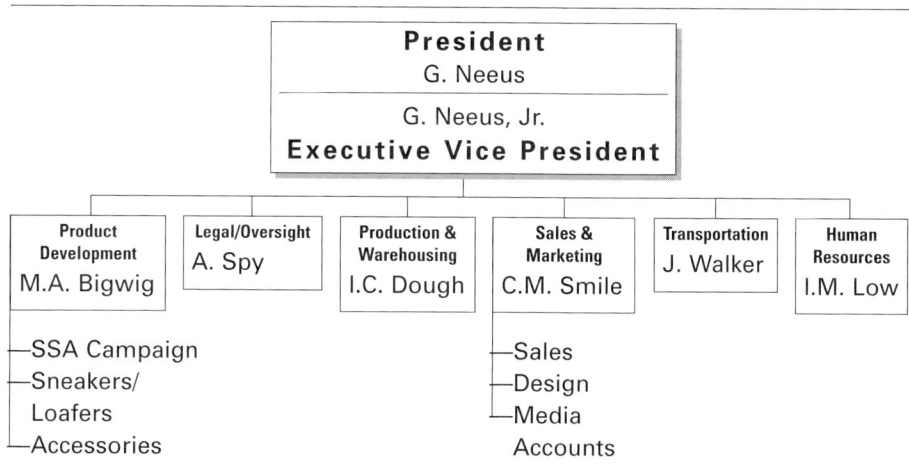

FIGURE 2.6

President
G. Neeus

G. Neeus, Jr.
Executive Vice President

Product Development	Legal/Oversight	Production & Warehousing	Sales & Marketing	Transportation	Human Resources
M.A. Bigwig	A. Spy	I.C. Dough	C.M. Smile	J. Walker	I.M. Low

—SSA Campaign
—Sneakers/
　Loafers
—Accessories

—Sales
—Design
—Media
　Accounts

problem and her office knows nothing about it. Who is to blame? What is the degree of exposure? Have we already received inquiries from any federal agencies or legal firms? Walker's already scheduled his drivers to begin trucking the SSAs beginning tomorrow morning. These union guys are going to be paid whether they drive or not; the trucks are going to cost whether they roll or not. Right behind the SSAs are two other lines of product that need to be transported. If your SSAs aren't out of the warehouse in 2 days, they'll have to sit for up to 3 weeks. Low calls wanting to know if she has to release some of the temporary workers she brought in to load the trucks. She also needs to know if she has to bring in a different crew entirely to help with the inserts.

You almost have a moment to yourself when G. Neeus, the President of the company, calls. This is your sixth call in 20 minutes. He wants a quick, detailed write-up in his office in the next 15 minutes. He wants all the details, the potential legal exposure, the potential lost revenue, the implications to current contracts, and an assessment of whether action needs to be taken to mitigate adverse impacts on the company's stock prices and bond ratings.

Where's the fiction? Is this really a matter of fictional audiences? It doesn't appear so since you have spoken to each of the six individuals. Do you need to invoke an image of the audiences? More likely, you are now trying to get the images of their distraught and angered faces out of your mind. Or was this a matter of deciphering the needs of a discourse community? These people certainly represent a community: the management of Shoe n' Sole, Inc. However, as their inquiries attest, each "member" of that society has a unique set of interests. These interests, if they weren't before, have been made painfully clear to you. This kind of misreading of audience may cost you dearly.

FIGURE 2.7

Vice Presidents
Shoe n' Sole, Inc.

A problem has been brought to my attention regarding an issue with our shoe that could lead to injuries and lawsuits. I've directed Carol to modify the package inserts to explain the proper procedure, negating our liability. My analysis suggests a delay of less than 4 working days.

J.M. Sharp

You can only imagine the additional anger you might have caused had you the time to have contacted Carol before the calls starting coming in. How would a harried counterpart of yours have reacted had she been told that she had to start redesigning the flier, had to accommodate a new design, and had to coordinate the printing of several thousand new inserts? If you thought the Vice Presidents were mad, just try dumping work on others who aren't organizationally accountable to you and you can signal the beginning of a major corporate feud.

Unfortunately for you, returning to the images of those Vice Presidents for a second, you don't have the answers to any of the questions asked by senior management. Having forgotten the need to assess the embedded issues, constraints, and purposes, you have manufactured controversy where none previously existed. Assuming somehow you survive long enough to contact Joe, the person who authored the original letter, maybe you can still demonstrate to management that you took prudent and proactive action. However, the last shock of your day, and most likely the last shock of your career at Shoe n' Sole, is yet to come. Joe is not a senior manager in Transportation; he is a mechanic who repairs trucks (Figure 2.8).

Not only did you not know the audience you were writing to, you didn't know the audience to which you were responding. A simple "thanks for your interest" note to Joe was all that was needed. Instead, you put your career at risk and gave

FIGURE 2.8

The Author of the Note to Your Boss

Source: Reprinted with permission of Sand River Photography

rise to the belief that the company's reputation, profit, and security may be at risk. Now, where's the fiction? You certainly created some corporate intrigue, but the drama had an entirely real cast—one you needed to read before you put pen to paper.

You should know, however, that it doesn't take a Joe or a contrived exercise to give rise to an opportunity to invite this type of response from your corporate colleagues. Let's give a real example. A manager sent out an e-mail to hundreds of personnel alerting them that for several days they should enter the production building by way of an alternate entrance. Her note, intended to avoid having people spend extra time outdoors should there be inclement weather, received anything but the notes of appreciation she was expecting. The culprit in this case is a single indiscriminant phrase.

As the author of the note indicated, the front lobby was going to be unavailable because it was "undergoing a face-lift." Almost immediately, she got a large number of responses—not from thankful customers, but from irate managers. For the most part, managers wanted to know how her group had money available to spend on frivolous activities when there were much more pressing corporate issues needing finances (Figure 2.9).

Her note had failed to make clear that the activity was not prompted by aesthetics, but by the need to respond to urgent safety and security issues. The response she got, however, was a good indication of her audience's concerns. She had implicitly invited the audience into her business by sending the initial note and now was faced with responding to the questions unintentionally raised by her message. As this one example illustrates, the business community is comprised of real, very distinct individuals, each of whom may have different corporately based interests, interpretations, and expectations. (We'll discuss more about the unintentional consequences of poorly directed e-mail in Chapter 10.)

FIGURE 2.9

When the Business Audience Responds

Initial e-mail

After years of trying to get a better looking lobby, we are finally going to receive our face-lift! Starting next week, on Wednesday according to the schedule, the construction crew will be roping off Customer Service and the front door to the building.

There is a price for this face-lift in terms of inconvenience to our customers and to ourselves in having the front door and nearby entrance into Illustrating closed off while the work is done.

During the renovation, we will need to use the side door. Signs will be posted for customers approaching the building that will lead them to that entrance and the temporary home of the Customer Service desk. Your assistance in directing customers to the new Customer Service desk will be appreciated.

Your patience during this period will certainly contribute to a smoother transition from the old look to the new!

Manager's Response

This really sends the wrong message. Sounds like we have extra money and are doing something that is not really necessary other than for aesthetic purposes! There are lots of places on-site that need a face-lift that we cannot afford to give. What are the structural and other issues behind doing the work? What is the distribution of this memo, i.e., how much criticism have we just invited?

THE TRUTH ABOUT THE FICTIONAL AUDIENCE

In the simplest terms, what we have learned is that there are a few key truths about audience in the world of business. Audiences are real and concrete. Each member of your audience has unique expectations. The audiences you will deal with are eminently knowable.

AUDIENCES ARE ALWAYS REAL AND CONCRETE

Although the Shoe n' Sole exercise may be contrived, it does make a number of key points. Foremost among these is a clear perspective on the multi-decade argument about an addressed audience versus an implied, invoked, or fictional audience. In professional communication, the audience is always real, irrespective of the logistical relationships they share with you. The audience is known—whether he, she, or they are with you in the room, are several hallways away, or are around the other side of the world. The issue was never really one of physical presence, but, rather, an issue of how diligent the writer is in defining the identity of the audience.

The limitation supposed by the novelist, the film critic, and the anthropologist alike was that the reader or audience resided somewhere between the unknowable and the presumed. One might presume such a consideration is valid in environments other than in business, but it has no validity when it comes to professional communication. Whether we consider the exercise about electricians we used in assessing purpose in Chapter 1, or the Shoe n' Sole exercise we just considered, there is a framework that can be applied to understand the business audience even in those circumstances where the particular people in your audience are not well-known to you. No matter where you are positioned within an organization, the audiences you deal with in a professional environment are generally comprised of 1) management—those to whom you report; 2) peers—those who have equivalent responsibility and authority to your own; 3) staff—the individuals who report to you, either directly or indirectly, and 4) customers—those individuals, either within or external to the company, who are dependent on your products and your organization.

Of course, this structure is directly affected by the size and complexity of the company. Larger companies may include several layers of management, including first-line supervision (those who directly oversee production activity), middle management (those who translate policy and vision into production activities), and senior management (those responsible for the policies and strategic directions of the company). (Figure 2.10 depicts a typical organizational structure.)

Unlike the unknown recipients of mass mailings, external audiences may also often be defined. This is true because most professionals who have responsibility for communicating with people or organizations outside of their company deal with a targeted audience. Targeted audiences are those organizations and customers who have a defined identity, generally as a consequence of having some form of relationship with the company. For example, the targeted audience may comprise previous customers, those who have responded to surveys, or organizations that have accessed your web site. In contrast, essentially only marketing and mass media personnel deal with an open audience, one that is only known in terms of limited information. The open audience is the only one of the eight communities where we often have to proceed based exclusively on demographic information. (Table 2.4 lists the eight audiences for professional communication.)

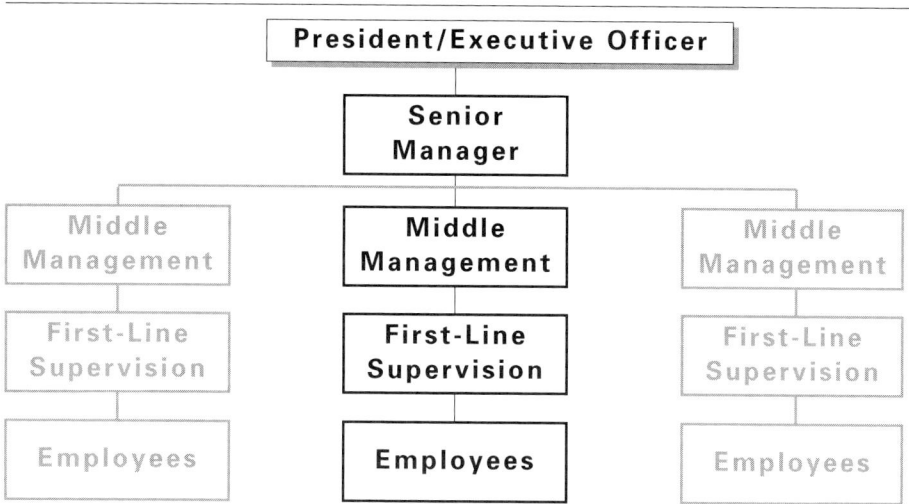

FIGURE 2.10

A Generic
Organization Chart

EACH MEMBER OF YOUR AUDIENCE HAS UNIQUE EXPECTATIONS

The eight communities represent the starting point, not the finish line. You should not make the mistake that you can simply deal with broad groupings of people in the same way that was suggested by the proponents of discourse communities. Some assignments, like the Shoe n' Sole assignment, although seemingly addressed to a common class of individual (the community of Senior Managers) might require several customized responses in order to respond to and accommodate the unique interests of the various recipients. Yet, at the same time, that doesn't mean that every communication assignment will demand dozens of tailored communications. In most cases, business communications don't entail messages to the whole corporate body. Whether the communication you prepare is intended to travel upwards to higher management, downwards to your staff, or laterally to colleagues, most communications entail travel to only one of the following four readers: to your immediate management, to your direct reports, to your direct peers, or to an external customer.

In an average week, as documented in various management studies, approximately half of a manager's communications are to direct reports. The other half is evenly split among communications with external audiences, counterparts,

TABLE 2.4 THE EIGHT PROFESSIONAL COMMUNITIES

Corporate	Local	External
Senior management	Your peers/counterparts	Defined (targeted) audiences
Middle management	Your staff	Undefined (random) audiences
First-line supervision		
All employees		

and superiors (Table 2.5).[27] Your responsibility is not to focus on the number of messages, but on the suitability of the messages. If one message is appropriate for many recipients, then just issue the one. If, in contrast, you don't want to invoke the kind of response illustrated in the Shoe n' Sole exercise, then you need to have more targeted, directed responses to the members of your audience.

THE AUDIENCES FOR PROFESSIONAL COMMUNICATIONS ARE EMINENTLY KNOWABLE

As we just discussed, the audience can first be understood as part of a hierarchical unit. This provides general attributes about the audience's tendencies and inclinations. Table 2.6 summarizes the characteristics of the six internal communities. Table 2.7 provides equivalent depiction of the two types of external communities.

You must not stop there with your assessment. Just as your communication will not exist within a vacuum, so the identities of the various audiences—individual and collective—can and should be known. Even assuming you are new to the organization and don't know the difference between Joe in Transportation and the Vice President of Production, the identities are far from hidden. In most organizations, you have ample opportunity to learn about the audience and their approach to conducting business.

To learn about individuals, you might make use of the corporate literature. Are there published organization charts? If so, these might define precisely where your intended audience is positioned, to whom the person reports, and who reports to him or her. What is the scope of the person's responsibility? Is it broad, narrow, or one-dimensional? This type of information is extremely valuable. As an example of how it might shape your response, consider that someone who administers a single program, one project, or one initiative may offer a fierce defense of that program. Any perceived threats or intrusions into such territory may be taken as a challenge and, therefore, demand more tact and reassurances—along with more detail—before the proposal might be accepted.

How about charters? Often large companies, agencies, and institutes will have published charters that articulate precisely what the group is responsible for and the reason for its existence. Similarly, you might look at job descriptions or job titles. Knowing an individual's title may offer broad insights, not only into that

TABLE 2.5   DIRECTION OF MANAGERIAL COMMUNICATION

Recipients	(%)
Subordinates	45.4
External others	23.6
Internal others	17.6
Superiors	14.6

Source: Reprinted by permission of Sage Publications Ltd. from Fred Luthans and Janet Larsen, "How Managers Really Communicate," *Human Relations,* Copyright © The Tavistock Institute, 1986.

2.6 THE SIX INTERNAL BUSINESS COMMUNITIES

Community	Primary Interests	Areas of Lesser Interest	Shared Attributes/Traits	Breadth/Depth of Knowledge
Senior Management	Corporate decisions Strategic issues Policy setting Profit/loss/risk	Operational details Local concerns	Accomplished Mature (politic) Good communicators Motivated Pressed for time Highly independent	Breadth: high Depth: low to moderate
Middle Management	Implementing policy Operational and adminis-trative matters Issues of interdepartmen-tal import	Any matters out-side their assigned scope of responsi-bility	Motivated Competitive Perceive themselves as liaison between execu-tive and all other man-agement levels	Breadth: moderate Depth: moderate to high
First-Line Supervision	Running operations Personnel actions and administration Deliverables/quotas/ schedules Performance metrics	Strategic matters (e.g., boardroom issues)	Commonly come up through the ranks (iden-tify with workers) Strong technical skills and expertise	Breadth: low Depth: high
Peers	Perspective equivalent in breadth to your own	Problems of other departments (unless they are affected)	Motivated Competitive Looking for opportunities to stand out	Breadth: same as yours Depth: same as yours
Staff	Technical areas assigned Priorities you set	Issues of other departments	Technical experts Share your perspective/ operational philosophy	Breadth: subset of yours Depth: high
Employees	Changes in personnel/pay practices Operational matters (e.g., procedure changes)	Matters that don't bear directly on their work	Representative of the scope of company activities/work Aligned most closely with immediate supervision	Breadth: limited to assigned activities Depth: generally are the "experts"

individual's responsibility, but it may also suggest how those individuals who set up the assignment see the position.

Beyond the inferences that may be drawn from documents that illuminate an individual's or group's corporate identity, you can also retrieve documents authored by that individual or organization. Letters, reports, and operational and strategic plans all can establish a picture of what a group is, how it sees itself, and what it contributes to the corporation. You might even evaluate the kinds of information posted on bulletin boards and office walls. A good deal can be learned by taking time to observe the images people find important to broadcast about themselves.

One other valuable means of gaining knowledge of your audience is to look at the procedures that they have developed to administer their activities. How detailed are the procedures? Do they suggest a tendency to delegate decisions to the lowest possible level, or do they restrict the decisions to management? Do they tend to dis-courage or encourage conformity? Creativity? Consistency? A little research can

2.7   **THE TWO EXTERNAL BUSINESS COMMUNITIES**

Community	Primary Interests	Areas of Lesser Interest	Shared Attributes/Traits	Breadth/Depth of Knowledge
Targeted (defined)	Customer information New opportunities Specific benefits/values	Internal politics Operational details	Diverse (unified only by a shared commodity interest) Limited potential for interaction (with the company or each other)	Breadth: limited to area of interest Depth: varied
Open (undefined)	Generally unknown Defined commonality is a function of the demographic analysis that identified the audience	Generally unknown Defined commonality is a function of the demographic analysis that identified the audience	Only known to the level of sophistication of the demographic analysis	Breadth: varied, but undefined Depth: varied, but undefined

offer substantive insight into your audience. (Figure 2.11 highlights some of the corporate resources you can use to determine audience characteristics.)

Although we don't recommend relying on the administrative controls, there is one more dimension of the corporate communication system that will be useful. The majority of professional communications are created within very exacting protocols. These protocols will establish, for example, who (or what management level) can authorize release of the various forms of communication. The new employee, even the degreed professional, for instance, is unlikely to be given authority for issuing letters to customers, the public, or oversight agencies without an intensive series of reviews and approvals. These reviews are demanded to ensure that the information, tone, and approach are appropriate for the audience, and to make certain that none of the embedded corporate purposes or philosophies is inadvertently violated. (Figure 2.12 is a flowchart showing a typical process for review and approval of professional communications.) However, these systems are designed to help catch an irregularity before it gets out. Reviewers will not take kindly if they suspect that you use the review process instead of doing your homework on purpose and audience analysis.

FIGURE 2.11

Developing a Sense of the Business Communities

I. Review information about the organization
   a. Organization charts
   b. Charters
   c. Titles/biographies

II. Review what the organization has published
   a. Letters
   b. Reports
   c. Strategic and operational plans
   d. Posters/awards/recognition activity

III. Review how the organization works
   a. Operating and administrative procedures
   b. Interdepartmental agreements

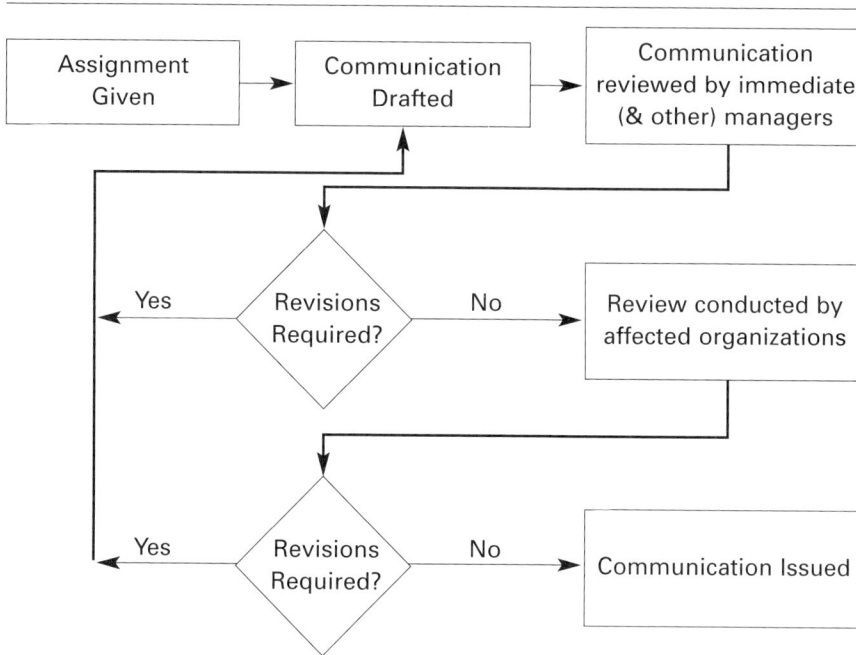

FIGURE 2.12

A Basic Review and Approval Process as Used in Business

AUDIENCE—THE LESSONS

Being successful in dealing with business audiences demands that you pay close attention to 10 guiding principles:

1. Audiences are real and immediate, even if they're not physically present.

2. Audiences for professional communication are comprised of eight communities.

3. Every community and the individuals in it have their own personalities and expectations.

4. You can learn about a particular community by assessing its literature (letters, reports, policies, organizational structure, charters, etc.).

5. Generally, even the external communities are known rather than unknown commodities.

6. Demographic analysis is usually only valuable for an undefined external community (never for an internal community).

7. The majority of communications travel one level: up, down or laterally (among peers).

8. A single subject may require multiple communications in order to accommodate different communities and individuals.

9. Most communications are internal, not external.

10. Corporate protocols will usually provide necessary, immediate feedback (such as through reviews) commensurate with significance and urgency of the communication. Use this system to validate your efforts, not to do your work for you.

☐ Group

1. You have been appointed Director of a new museum that is to be constructed in your town. Develop a plan that explains the following to the community and to the major contributors:

   a) The focus of the museum (e.g., modern art)

   b) The collections you intend to obtain for the museum

   c) The way in which the exhibits will be arranged to entice the audience (whomever you intend that to be)

   d) Any special features (e.g., recorded tours) you intend to help increase attendance and memberships

   e) Why your exhibits and special features should make the museum a success

2. You have just read an article in the local paper that details, despite the public's perception to the contrary, that not all bottled water is significantly better than tap water. In fact, in testing more than 1000 bottles of water from 103 brands, more than a third contained cancer-linked compounds and bacteria above acceptable drinking water standards.

   a) Choose one of the following purposes:

      1. to call for an immediate end to bottled water sales on your campus or in your company

      2. to call for an investigation of the brands sold at your campus or facility

      3. to support continued sales of bottled water

      4. a different purpose of your choice

   b) Prepare a letter to one of the following audiences:

      1. the President of the university or company

      2. the student council or Director of Safety

      3. the owner of the firm supplying bottled water to the campus or company

      4. the Dean of Facilities or Manager of Administration (who oversees vendor contracts)

   c) In a presentation, explain how your letter is targeted to the specific information needs and expectations of your selected audience.

☐ Individual

1. Using the organizational chart for Shoe n' Sole, prepare a letter (or letters) to explain to the Vice Presidents about a real problem: The stitching on the shoes is separating. Explain why you have taken the approach you've selected and explain how the letter is aligned with the specific needs of the various Vice Presidents.

2. Collect a series of procedures issued by three or four different departments in your university or company. Prepare an analysis that explains what insights the procedures provide about the organizations and how those insights might be used when communicating with those organizations.

[1] J. Suchan and R. Dulek, "Toward a Better Understanding of Reader Analysis," *Journal of Business Communication,* Vol. 25, No. 2 (Spring 1988), pp. 25–45.

[2] Lisa Ede, "On Audience and Composition," *College Composition and Communication,* Vol. 30, No. 3 (Oct. 1979), pp. 291–295.

[3] Fred Pfister and Joanne Petrick, "A Heuristic Model for Creating a Writer's Audience," *College Composition and Communication,* Vol. 31, No. 2 (May 1980), pp. 213–220.

[4] Douglas Park, "The Meanings of Audience," *College English,* Vol. 44, No. 3 (March 1982), pp. 247–257.

[5] Ruth Mitchell and Mary Taylor, "The Integrating Perspective: An Audience-Response Model for Writing," *College English,* Vol. 41, No. 3 (Nov. 1979), pp. 247–271.

[6] Richard Young, Alton Becker, and Kenneth Pike, *Rhetoric: Discovery and Change.* New York: Harcourt, Brace, & World, Inc., 1970, p. 7.

[7] Theresa Redd-Boyd and Wayne Slater, "The Effects of Audience Specification on Undergraduates' Attitudes, Strategies, and Writing," *Research in the Teaching of English,* Vol. 23, No. 1 (Feb. 1989), pp. 77–108.

[8] Adapted from: Thomas Willard and Stuart Brown, "The One and the Many: A Brief History of the Distinction," in *A Sense of Audience in Written Communication,* ed. Gesa Kirsch and Duane Roen, *Written Communication Annual,* Vol. 5, Newbury Park: Sage Publications, 1990, pp. 40–57.

[9] Chaim Perelman and L. Olbrechts-Tyteca, *The New Rhetoric: A Treatise on Argumentation.* Trans. John Wilkenson and Purcell Weaver. Notre Dame: University of Notre Dame Press, 1969, p. 33.

[10] T.S. Eliot, "The Three Voices of Poetry," in *On Poetry and Poets.* New York: Farrar, Strauss, and Cudahy, 1957.

[11] Walker Gibson, "Authors, Speakers, Readers and Mock Readers," *College English,* Vol. 11 (1949–1950), pp. 264–274.

[12] Walter J. Ong, "The Writer's Audience Is Always a Fiction," *Publication of the Modern Language Association (PMLA),* Vol. 90, No. 1 (Jan. 1975), pp. 9–21.

[13] *Ibid.*

[14] Kroll, "Writing for Readers: Three Perspectives on Audience," *College Composition and Communication,* Vol. 35, No. 2 (May 1984), pp. 172–185.

[15] Ong, "The Writer's Audience is Always a Fiction."

[16] Robert Roth, "The Evolving Audience: Alternatives to Audience Accommodations," *College Composition and Communication,* Vol. 38, No. 1 (Feb. 1987), pp. 47–55.

[17] Jay Blumler, "Recasting the Audience in the New Television Marketplace" in *The Audience and Its Landscape,* ed. James Hay, Lawrence Grossberg, and Ellen Wartella. Boulder, CO: Westview Press, 1996, p. 101.

[18] James Webster, "The Audience," *Journal of Broadcasting and Electronic Media,* Vol. 42, No. 2 (Spring 1998), pp. 190–208.

[19] Lisa Ede and Andrea Lunsford, "Audience Addressed/Audience Invoked: The Role of Audience in Composition Theory and Pedagogy," *College Composition and Communication,* Vol. 35, No. 2 (May 1984), pp. 155–171.

[20] Pfister and Petrick, "A Heuristic Model for Creating a Writer's Audience."

[21] Quoted in Kroll, "Writing for Readers: Three Perspectives on Audience."

[22] M. Jimmie Killingsworth, "Discourse Communities—Local and Global," *Rhetoric Review,* Vol. 11, No. 1 (Fall 1992), pp. 110–122.

[23] Theodore Clevinger, Jr., *Audience Analysis.* Indianapolis: The Bobbs-Merrill Co., 1966, p. 109.

[24] Ede and Lunsford, "Audience Addressed/Audience Invoked."

[25] Suchen and Dulek, "Toward a Better Understanding of Audience Analysis."

[26] Kroll, "Writing for Readers: Three Perspectives on Audience."

[27] Fred Luthans and Janet Larsen, "How Managers Really Communicate," *Human Relations,* Vol. 39, No. 2 (1986), pp. 161–178.

Facts

Attending to the Sociology of Business Information

Facts are everywhere. As people are fond of saying, we live in an information age. Even our leisure time is filled with facts. Sports announcers, for instance, whether discussing tennis, horse racing, or golf, regale us with innumerable facts and statistics. Since the axel was invented by Axel Paulsen in 1882 and the lutz by Alois Lutz in 1913, figure skating, as an example, has continued to increase in performance and statistical complexity. Technical merit and presentation are detailed with exacting reference to spins, revolutions, landings, and use of inside and outside skate edges. Although these facts and statistics of figure skating often remain muted until brought forward when controversy arises—as was the case with the pairs competition in the 2002 Olympic games— more commonly, the factual and statistical attributes of sports have matched, if not overtaken, the qualitative aspects of the commentary. Baseball, a prime example, has transformed a simple game of balls and strikes into a swarm of statistics: earned run averages; numbers of hits; runs batted in; strike outs with runners on first, or second, or third; the speed of each pitch thrown; the percentage of hits against each pitcher—whether starting, relief, or cleanup. Whether in the muted terms that accompany figure skating or like the bellowing chords accompanying baseball, facts and statistics impress themselves on every facet of our daily lives.

One dimension of the flood of information was evident in the waves of detail following the 2000 presidential election. As

All you need are the facts—a few questionable assumptions

- Whoever has the most facts wins
- Just give me the facts—any facts
- That's just your opinion
- My facts can beat your facts

The sociology of business information

The truth about facts—selection counts

The information we used to need, we still need

Facts—the lessons

the evening of the election wore on into weeks of political and legal squabbling, we experienced the media's intensive search for more data to add to the discussion. At first we were given details on how people had voted, then came information on the mechanics of voting equipment and on the cards people use to vote. Not only were we introduced to new items, such as the chad, but also a classification of chads: dimpled chads, hanging chads, and partial chads. By the time the election was officially decided, we had come to know dozens of Floridians along with their interests, political persuasions, and home-town dynamics.

If we back up one step, we see the same manifestation on a global scale. A quick visit to the Internet gives us access to hundreds of millions of web pages. Estimates suggest that about 80 million web pages existed in January 1997, 100 million by April of that same year, and more than 320 million approximately a year later.[1] With all experts in agreement that the Internet is nowhere near its capacity, the total number of web pages in the future may approach numbers beyond calculation.

Sorting among the hundreds of millions of web pages can be a challenge. The number of hits we get on an average search is staggering. Over 100 search engines and dozens of "meta-search" engines, which engage multiple independent search engines simultaneously, await our inquiries. The topics we can investigate are unlimited, as are the perspectives we can find on almost any subject. Almost any aspect of the universe we want to probe is within seconds of our reach.

In business, we have a similar (although not as voluminous) wealth of information. All kinds of statistics may be maintained: on performance of equipment as well as on performance of people; on sales and markets; on reliability and error rates. Bolstered by a growing number of corporate intranets, company information is now the source of great attention. Most notably, a growing industry has arisen in "knowledge management," the search for greater use of and access to information. As one set of knowledge management consultants maintains, a growing number of companies are in a race, "pursuing value-through-knowledge."[2] The values they are seeking, as depicted in Figure 3.1, range from interest in starting a new business to improving existing processes to transferring successful practices among various segments of the organization.

FIGURE 3.1

Application of
Knowledge
Management

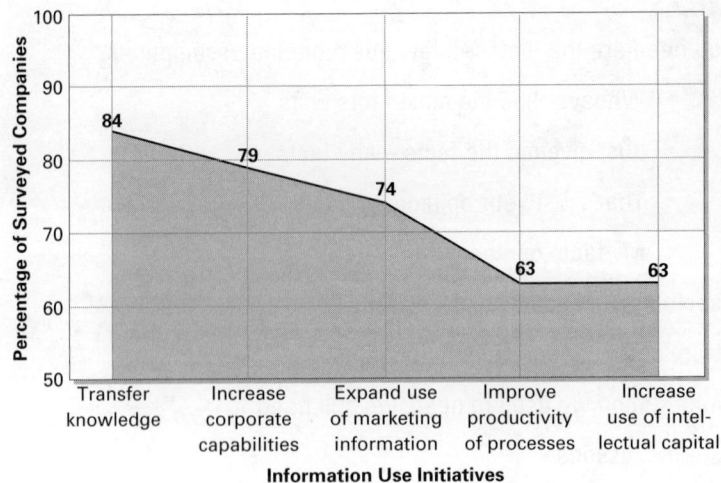

We should not, however, mistake the idea that this astounding growth in the volume of information available to us is synonymous with an equally acute improvement in our ability to make meaningful use—or even adequate selection—of information. Locating information is not necessarily synonymous with finding answers. Finding facts does not automatically define the means to use the facts to improve decision-making. In this chapter, we will look primarily at selecting facts. Chapters 4 and 5 will address the arrangement of information and application of information in the development of sound business reasoning.

ALL YOU NEED ARE THE FACTS— A FEW QUESTIONABLE ASSUMPTIONS

Let's begin our discussions by examining four questionable beliefs about the value of fact in the business context: 1) Whoever (or whatever argument) has the most facts wins. 2) The facts needed will be apparent. 3) Facts are the opposites of opinion. 4) Knowing the facts is sufficient. To look at these suppositions, let's take a short tour through three significant American events.

WHOEVER HAS THE MOST FACTS WINS

The date was March 18, 1836. The location was Washington, Texas. David Burnett, President of the Republic of Texas, was faced with a dilemma. Less than 2 weeks earlier, after 13 days of battle, a small mission, named for a Spanish cavalry unit that had occupied the mission in the early days of the nineteenth century, had been retaken by the Mexican army. Antonio Lopez de Santa Anna had succeeded in defeating the 189 men who had gathered at Pueblo del Alamolos (better known as the Alamo—Figure 3.2).[3] Among the dead were a number of men whose names we still recognize: William Travis, James Bowie, and Davy Crockett. On March 5, 1836, Colonel William Travis had drawn the famous line in the sand with his sword. All 189 men crossed over, signifying their intent to fight on. In the predawn hours of March 6, 1836, with bugles sounding the "Dequello," Mexican troops attacked the Alamo on all four sides; by 6 A.M., the Alamo had fallen. The heroes of the Alamo were all dead.

FIGURE 3.2

The Alamo

Source: Reprinted with permission of Sand River Photography

Despite the heavy casualties inflicted on the Mexican army, the men of the Alamo had been defeated. The dilemma that David Burnett now faced was how to maintain an army strong enough to drive the Mexicans off Texas soil. Rumors were spreading across Texas about the imminent threat to all of Eastern Texas. General Sam Houston's army was in need of replacements if it was to battle with the much larger Mexican forces. In addition, the government headed by Burnett had previously made plans to relocate to Harrisburgh, Texas—some distance farther removed from the fighting. Although not planned out of a desire to be free of any threat, would the move, nonetheless, be seen by his countrymen as a mark of imminent defeat for Texas? What could he do? There was no mass communication system by which to alert the citizenry. Newspapers were not widely read nor distributed with the frequency of their current incarnations. What he decided to do was issue a proclamation. Copies would be disbursed by messenger throughout Eastern Texas, delivered to local officials, and posted wherever people might congregate (Figure 3.3).

Burnett's goal was to make the facts clear. So, what facts does he report to his countrymen? Reading the Proclamation closely, we can account for only two "facts": General Houston has an army of 800 men, and the government is moving to Harrisburgh. Beyond those two statements, Burnett is appearing to put a "positive spin" on the events. He is attempting to show that the fall of the Alamo is not a "reverse," but the "surest guarantee of our ultimate success." How well can such a proclamation work? Inspired by the images of 800 men in pitched battle with more than 2000 Mexicans, the fallen Alamo, and a government on the move, would the homesteaders of Eastern Texas be inclined to stay and fight or would they pack their wagons and head for Oklahoma?

With so much opinion and so little fact on which to base our decision, we might—using our twenty-first century skepticism—feel extremely uncomfortable. Our conclusion might be that it's time to pack the wagon. We are distressed by not having answers to several critical questions: Exactly how many men does Santa Anna have? Where are they stationed? Which way are they moving? How many cannons does Houston have? The list might go on and on, soliciting the information we feel is needed to develop a complete picture of the possibilities and circumstances.

FIGURE 3.3

Proclamation to
the Citizens of
Texas

Executive Department of the Republic of Texas
Washington, Texas, 18th March 1836

To the people in Eastern Texas:

General Houston is at his post on the frontier with eight hundred men and reinforcements constantly arriving. Our army is in high spirits and full confidence. Yet in the midst of the security this state of things should inspire, the officers of Government are surprised and grieved to learn that a portion of the people of Eastern Texas under the influence of idle and groundless rumors are leaving their homes and by the circulation of false news may prevent others of their countrymen from repairing to the standard of their country where alone their homes and families are to be defended. Under these circumstances, I have thought proper to issue this my proclamation to the citizens of Texas, calling upon them to organize themselves under the laws of their country. I conjure you my countrymen to repair to the field forthwith and to deafen your ears against all rumors from whatever quarter they may come. The officers of your Government will take special care to obtain true information of the movements of the enemy and our own army, and keep their fellow citizens regularly informed on all matters, which may affect their safety. To the field then my countrymen, to the standard of liberty, and defend your rights in a manner worthy of your sires and yourselves.

PROCLAMATION

Citizens of Texas:

But recently called to discharge the executive duties of your government, it is with inexpressible regret that I observe the slightest indication of alarm among us. To provide for and protect our wives and children is a sacred duty, prompted by nature and sanctioned by every manly feeling. But in the manner of discharging that duty we may commit many and fatal errors. The best security of families is to be found in a gallant veering before the enemy. Our army is in the field and preparing to meet, and as it ever has done, to repel the enemy. General Houston calls for reinforcements, a small accession to his noble band will enable him to advance and speedily chastise the presumption of the invader. Rally, then, fellow citizens to the standard of freedom. Let not every idle rumor, circulated perhaps by the artifices of the enemy, paralyze your hands or divide your thoughts from one grand purpose, the "Independence of Texas." By an unbroken unanimity of voices, you have declared that Texas shall be "free, sovereign, and independent." Let us with equal unanimity resolve to sustain that declaration; to ratify it with our blood. Our fathers achieved their emancipation, and were abundantly rewarded for their toils. But they persevered through many reverses, surmounted many disasters, and gloriously triumphed. We have sustained no reverse. The fall of the Alamo is the surest guarantee of our ultimate success. The Spartan band that so nobly perished there, has inflicted on the enemy a terror and a loss that is equivalent to a defeat.

Rally, then, fellow citizens, to the standard of your country. While the army is between your families and the enemy, they are safe. Reinforce and sustain the army, and our wives and children are secure from pollution. The government will remove to Harrisburgh, but the removal is not the result of any apprehension that the enemy is near us. It was resolved upon as a measure conducive to the common good, before any such report was in circulation, and it has not been expedited by such report.

Again I conjure you, fellow citizens, listen not to every rumor that runs, trumpet-tongued, through the country. The government is perfecting arrangements, as rapidly as possible, to insure the transmission of official intelligence, on which they and you may rely with confidence. Let us acquit ourselves as men; gird up the loins of our minds, and by one united, prompt and energetic exertion, turn back this impotent invader; and, planting our standard on the banks of the Rio Grande, dictate to him the terms of mutual recognition.

David G. Burnett,
President of the Republic. Washington, March 18, 1836

Before we use our list of unanswered questions as a basis for faulting Burnett for his failures as a communicator, let's revisit some of the principles we learned about purpose and audience. First, let's consider purpose. Burnett has four primary purposes:

1. Create a sense of urgency—He needs as many able-bodied men as possible to join up with General Houston's army.

2. Convince people to ignore the rumors—He has to make certain that Texans believe they are safe, that they should stay on their lands, and they should hold strong to the ideals of a free republic.

3. Inspire and motivate—he needs to create a renewed zeal for the cause of freedom. Even for those who will not join up with Houston, Burnett needs assurances that they will stay and fight.

4. Convince people victory is at hand—Burnett needs people to see the Alamo as a victory, that Texas truly has "sustained no reverses." The goal of a free and sovereign Texas has to be envisioned as achievable and imminent. If citizens anticipate a protracted war with Mexico, they might be reluctant to follow the course Burnett is advocating.

Second, let's examine audience. Who are these people who have made their way to the Republic of Texas? Remember that the early part of the nineteenth century offered little in the way of developed roads and thoroughfares. Travel was slow and difficult. People traveling across the continent needed will and determination as much as luck and endurance. For families, travel meant covered wagons proceeding for weeks at a few miles per hour. What this tells us is that these settlers shared a deep-seated belief that they had earned their land through grit and determination.

To this attribute, we might add several other factors. These were staunchly independent people. Homesteading settlers were highly unlikely to care very much about the administration of government, whether that seat was in Washington, Texas, or Washington, DC. Their goal was to own a piece of land and to raise cattle, crops, and family. They also were "God-fearing" people who held steadfastly to the fundamental belief in right and wrong and to the ethical teachings of the Bible. Last, the nineteenth-century settlers and homesteaders generally might be understood as "common" folk, people who trusted common sense more than the pontificatings of any Philadelphia lawyer.

Reconsidering Burnett's purposes and audience, we might now reach a different conclusion about the appropriateness of the Proclamation. Rather than our initial thinking that the document suffered from a lack of information, we might acknowledge that Burnett's Proclamation gave the folks of Texas precisely the details and facts they needed to come to a decision—the decision Burnett was after:

- The Texan army has done well against the Mexicans.
- You've earned your land and the right to keep it.
- The brave men who died at the Alamo did no more than any man would do who believes in the sanctity of his freedoms.
- We have 800 men, but we need more.
- The government move has no bearing on the fight for freedom.

Though we may never know exactly how many men were actually influenced by the Proclamation, we still might draw some inferences from the following history. On April 21, 1836, only 46 days after the Proclamation was issued, General

Houston launched an attack at San Jacinto. With a battle cry of "Remember the Alamo," the army routed the Mexican army, and the Republic of Texas was born. Like the small army that gave Texas its freedom, the weight of evidence is not measured in number of facts presented, but in their strength—as judged by their success in meeting the rhetorical challenge.

To illustrate the point in a less-serious manner, we can quote from a satirical account of how Abraham Lincoln might have handled the Gettysburg Address were he more concerned with the volume of fact than the pertinence of message (and if he had an overhead projector to aid in adding "substance" to his address):

> A dense quiet came over the crowd as the President of the United States stepped to the speaker's table. He placed a transparency on the stage of the overhead projector, and onto the screen was projected a map of the original 13 colonies of the United States. "Eighty-seven years ago," he began, as the image of his finger was seen to trace the coastline from North Carolina to Delaware, "this was the new country that our forefathers brought to us: North Carolina, Virginia, Delaware, *et cetera*. The propositions on which they based their thinking are contained in this famous document." The screen went brightly blank for a moment as the 13 colonies disappeared. Then a page of beautiful calligraphy starting with the words "We hold these truths to be self-evident," splendidly illuminated, came into view. The President turned, looked in silence at the projected works and smiled, obviously moved by the impact of their message. "Now our nation," he continued, shuffling through the stack of transparencies on the table, "is divided by civil war"—another map appeared, appropriately rendered in blue and gray—"which not only tests the basic propositions"—back came the illuminated words of the Declaration of Independence—"on which the country is based, but also threatens its very existence." And with that, the President brought back the map transparency, took a wax pencil from his shirt pocket and proceeded to draw a saw-tooth black line, which rent the nation into two jagged-edged, broken, blue and gray parts. "We are here today . . ."[4]

The introduction of extraneous "factual" information to President Lincoln's speech is purely gratuitous and adds nothing to the speech's impact or clarity. In fact, the material is effective in detracting from both the message and the moment. As we shall see in Chapter 7, President Lincoln's speech achieves much more in a few words than might have been achieved were he to have presented dozens of transparencies and piles of facts. Let's now leave President Lincoln and turn to another potential issue associated with the use of facts.

JUST GIVE ME THE FACTS—ANY FACTS

Let's move forward about a century from President Lincoln's famous speech to the second half of the twentieth century. In response to Russia's successful launch of *Sputnik 1*, on October 4, 1957, President Eisenhower created the National Aeronautics and Space Administration (NASA) with the stated purpose of providing "for research into the problems of flight within and outside the Earth's atmosphere and for other purposes."[5] Aggressively pursuing these lofty goals, less than 4 months later, NASA launched its first Earth satellite, *Explorer 1*.

The enthusiasm for space exploration and the initial sense of urgency invoked by President Eisenhower was amplified when President Kennedy announced on

May 25, 1961, "I believe that this nation should commit itself to achieving the goal, before this decade is out, of landing a man on the Moon and returning him safely to Earth." With fervency, the agency pressed on, and NASA fulfilled the commitment, landing the *Apollo II* crew (Neil Armstrong and Buzz Aldrin) on the moon on July 29, 1969. By the close of the twentieth century, NASA had racked up more than 100 crewed space flights and six lunar landings, propelling a new strategic vision of achieving a permanent human presence in space.

As if announcing the successful passing from initial exploration to routine flight, in 1981, NASA made a transition from reliance and investment in one-time-use spacecraft to a reusable "Space Shuttle." With growing certainty in its technological capacity, NASA moved boldly forward on its quest. Along the way, only two catastrophic events marred the landscape. The first was the deaths of three astronauts who were killed when an *Apollo* capsule, still on the ground, caught fire. The second tragedy came two decades later on January 28, 1986.

There had been much hype surrounding Flight 51-L. Among the seven-member crew of the *Challenger* was a woman of growing celebrity, Christa McAuliffe, a schoolteacher who had been added to the crew in part to demonstrate the democratization of the space enterprise. In recognition of the routine nature of it all, an insurance company had given McAuliffe a million-dollar policy, and, to broadcast the success story, there was talk of a televised conversation between McAuliffe and President Reagan during his State of the Union address, scheduled for 10 hours after liftoff. However, the *Challenger* flight was not to last 10 hours. The *Challenger* blew up 73 seconds after its rockets were ignited.

At 11:38 A.M. EST, *Challenger* was launched. The morning was a chilly 36° F, 15 degrees cooler than any previous launch. Within the first second of liftoff, a puff of gray smoke spurted from one of the joints on the solid rocket booster. Within 2½ seconds, eight more puffs of smoke were seen. These puffs were blacker, indicative of a serious condition known as "blow by," meaning sooted grease was escaping past the O-rings that seal the various sections of the rocket to each other. At 45 seconds into the flight, there were three bright flashes, followed by emergence of a small flame 14 seconds later. Within seconds of the first flame, larger flames erupted from a leaking field joint (sections put together at Cape Kennedy rather than at the manufacturer) and engulfed the fuel tank, which subsequently ruptured and exploded. At 73.137 seconds into its flight, traveling at a speed of Mach 1.92 and at an altitude of 46,000 feet, *Challenger* was destroyed and all seven members of the crew were killed instantly. An intensive investigation was immediately launched.

Perhaps most significant, the investigation focused on a lengthy debate that had preceded the decision to launch *Challenger*. Following an extensive process of flight readiness reviews and checkouts on January 23, the *Challenger* flight (designated by NASA as Flight 51-L) was certified as ready to fly on January 27. At 12:36 P.M. of launch day, the mission was scrubbed because of high crosswinds at the launch site. In keeping with procedures, meetings were held to determine the feasibility of a launch the following morning. During these evening discussions, attention began to focus on performance of the O-rings. Since 1982, the O-rings had been designated a "Criticality 1" feature of the rocket design, signifying a failure point that—because there was no backup system—could result in a loss of life or the loss of the vehicle if the component failed (Figure 3.4). In a telephone conference among 30 engineers and managers, 16 from NASA and 14 from Thiokol, the main contractor, a debate began about whether to delay the launch.

FIGURE 3.4   ▸   Attention Focused on the Shuttle O-Rings

185 feet (56.4 meters)

Rubber O-rings, nearly 38 feet
(11.6 meters) in circumference;
1/4 inch (6.4 mm) thick.

The field joint
that leaked.

Upon ignition, smoke
leaked from this joint.
A flame burned through
59 seconds later.

Upper segment
of rocket casing

Primary O-ring

Secondary O-ring

Exterior wall
of rocket

Lower segment
of rocket casing

Inside of rocket
(filled with 500 tons of propellant)

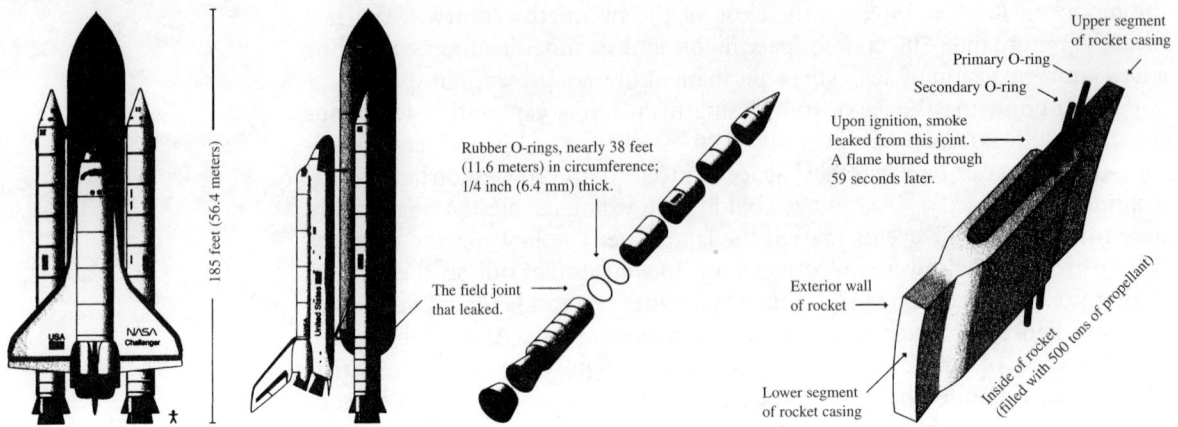

Source: Reprinted by permission, Edward R. Tufte, *Visual Explanations,* Graphics Press, Cheshire, CT, 1997.

In his testimony to the Presidential Commission investigating the accident, the Deputy Director of Science and Engineering at the Marshall Space Center characterized the exchange as "professional . . . not, in my view, uncharacteristic of discussions of flight readiness issues on previous occasions."[6] Specifically, the exchange centered around three points that Thiokol had developed in advance of the meeting: 1) The temperature for launching *Challenger* was at least 15° F colder than any previous flight. 2) The booster rockets had experienced the most O-ring damage during the coldest flight to date (Flight 51-L, launched at 53° F). 3) Using available data (both actual flights and test data), the launch should be delayed.

In a series of 13 charts, Thiokol explained its reluctance to proceed with launching the *Challenger*. As the principal spokesperson for the Thiokol Seal Task Force argued, the team had a "deep concern about launching at low temperature," particularly concerning the integrity of the primary and secondary O-ring seal—the contact to be maintained among parts during the first 2 minutes following ignition. The issue, as Thiokol portrayed it, was that "if erosion penetrates the primary O-ring seal, there is a higher probability of no secondary seal capability in the steady state condition."[7] O-ring failure would result in total and immediate destruction of the Shuttle. (The Appendix includes the two main charts used to explain the failure potential during the teleconference.) The last of the 13 charts, a handwritten list presented by the Thiokol Vice President for Engineering, stated Thiokol's principal recommendations, the first of which was that launches only proceed at temperatures at or above 53° F (Figure 3.5).[8]

While this representation of the technical debate would lead us to believe there was agreement that the launch should be delayed, several hours later, Thiokol sent the NASA Management at Cape Kennedy and the Marshall Space Flight Center its formal position: "MTI [Morton Thiokol Inc.] recommends STS-51-L launch proceed on 28 January 1986" (Figure 3.6).

What had happened in the intervening hours? A vehement position with consensus support among Thiokol's engineers and management had seemingly

FIGURE 3.5

Thiokol's
Concluding Slide

RECOMMENDATIONS :

° O-RING TEMP MUST BE ≥ 53 °F AT LAUNCH

  DEVELOPMENT MOTORS AT 47° TO 52°F WITH
  PUTTY PACKING HAD NO BLOW-BY
  SRM 15 (THE BEST SIMULATION) WORKED AT 53 °F

° PROJECT AMBIENT CONDITIONS (TEMP & WIND)
  TO DETERMINE LAUNCH TIME

evaporated. Instead of demanding a delay, Thiokol cleared the last hurdle to launch. The single step that might have saved the *Challenger* and its crew had been reversed!

The simple and unfortunate fact is that despite the volume of data presented, Thiokol did not offer a convincing argument. In interviews and testimony, there was consensus that Thiokol had offered a weak engineering argument. They had made a fateful mistake of letting the facts stand on their own. As one participant in the teleconference later stated: "I don't believe they did a real convincing job of presenting their data . . . . The Thiokol guys even had a chart in there that says temperature of the O-ring is not the only parameter controlling blow-by. In other words, they're not coming in with a real firm statement. They're saying there's other factors. They did have a lot of conflicting data in there. I can't emphasize that enough. Let me quote. On [one] chart of theirs . . . they had data that said they ran some sub-scale tests down at 30 degrees and they ran blow-by tests in a fixture at 30 degrees, and they saw no leakage. Now they're talking out of both sides of their mouth, see. They're saying, 'Hey, temperature doesn't have any effect . . . .'"[9]

FIGURE 3.6

Thiokol's
Recommendation
to Proceed
With the Launch

MTI ASSESSMENT OF TEMPERATURE CONCERN ON SRM-25 (51L) LAUNCH

0 CALCULATIONS SHOW THAT SRM-25 O-RINGS WILL BE 20° COLDER THAN SRM-15 O-RINGS

0 TEMPERATURE DATA NOT CONCLUSIVE ON PREDICTING PRIMARY O-RING BLOW-BY

0 ENGINEERING ASSESSMENT IS THAT:

    0 COLDER O-RINGS WILL HAVE INCREASED EFFECTIVE DUROMETER ("HARDER")

    0 "HARDER" O-RINGS WILL TAKE LONGER TO "SEAT"

        0 MORE GAS MAY PASS PRIMARY O-RING BEFORE THE PRIMARY SEAL SEATS
           (RELATIVE TO SRM-15)

            0 DEMONSTRATED SEALING THRESHOLD IS 3 TIMES GREATER THAN 0.038"
               EROSION EXPERIENCED ON SRM-15

    0 IF THE PRIMARY SEAL DOES NOT SEAT, THE SECONDARY SEAL WILL SEAT

        0 PRESSURE WILL GET TO SECONDARY SEAL BEFORE THE METAL PARTS ROTATE

            0 O-RING PRESSURE LEAK CHECK PLACES SECONDARY SEAL IN OUTBOARD
               POSITION WHICH MINIMIZES SEALING TIME

0 MTI RECOMMENDS STS-51L LAUNCH PROCEED ON 28 JANUARY 1986

    0 SRM-25 WILL NOT BE SIGNIFICANTLY DIFFERENT FROM SRM-15

JOE C. KILMINSTER, VICE PRESIDENT
SPACE BOOSTER PROGRAMS

MORTON THIOKOL. INC
Wasatch Division

In their testimony before the Commission, Thiokol's management also conceded that they had presented a less than convincing case for launch delay: "NASA concluded that the temperature data we had presented was inconclusive." As the Thiokol engineer who had argued most insistently for a launch delay conceded, "when we as engineers presented our data and were unable to quantify it, it left it somewhat open from the standpoint of we only had data down to 50 degrees."[10] Even the chart that had been used as the centerpiece of the Thiokol argument had argued against itself. Speaking about this chart, a Senior Vice President for Thiokol acknowledged that "we could conclude that this lower temperature doesn't affect the timing functions (O-ring sealing)."[11]

Faced with "inconclusive" data, the administration approved the launch. The problem, as the Presidential Commission was later to characterize it, was "a serious flaw in the decision making process leading up to the launch of Flight 51-L."[12] Stated in the context of a communication problem, the issue was that Thiokol presented essentially irrelevant facts that may have explained the context of their position, but failed to speak directly to (to quantify) the only real topic of consequence. Thiokol never provided facts that demonstrated or proved O-ring failure below 50° F. Although there were 13 charts of facts, the essential facts were missing—a conclusion shared by the Presidential Commission as well as by experts in both visual design and educational psychology.

As Edward Tufte, a leading authority on visual display of quantitative information, summarizes:

> There is a scandalous discrepancy between the intellectual tasks at hand and the images created to serve those tasks. As analytical graphics, the displays failed to reveal a risk that was in fact present. As presentation graphics, the displays failed to persuade government officials that a cold-weather launch might be dangerous. In designing those displays, the chart makers didn't quite know what they were doing, and they were doing a lot of it.[13]

An analysis provided by an expert on educational psychology offers a more scathing assessment of Thiokol's performance. He concludes that of the 13 charts, one was invalidated by its presenter and six contained no significant data about either O-ring temperature, O-ring blow-by, or O-ring damage. "Of the seven remaining charts containing data either on launch temperatures or O-ring anomaly, *six of them included data on either launch temperatures or O-ring anomaly but not both in relation to each other.*"[14]

Choosing and presenting facts as this illustration informs us is not simply a matter of what you know or what information is available to you; rather, the responsibility entails selecting facts purposely to meet the objectives. If 30 experienced, highly educated engineers and managers didn't get it right, there's plenty of opportunity for the rest of us to choose unwisely when it comes to information selection. This should also be a reminder that despite our supposed reverence for "objective" fact, we should remember that facts do not necessarily speak for themselves; nor will they close the gaps we unintentionally leave open.

THAT'S JUST YOUR OPINION

There's another facet of the *Challenger* story that is worth our attention here, but first let's establish some context for this point. Most Americans are familiar with opinion polls. Every major election and most consequential votes are preceded by polls that try to gauge (and sometimes sway) opinion. What do you think of this candidate? What about her views on the following subjects? Do you favor this initiative or that? Sometimes the polls are used to get a sense of where opinions lie. At other times, we hear about politicians who supposedly amend their stands based on measures of popularity. With all this reliance on opinions, we might suspect that opinions are highly valued in American political life. Yet, the literature would lead us to conclude just the opposite. In a half-century of debate, political scientists have argued two diametrically opposed theories: 1) "The democratic citizen is expected to be well informed about political affairs. He is supposed to know what the issues are, . . . what the relevant facts are, what alternatives are proposed, (and) what the likely consequences are."[15] 2) "The political ignorance of the American voter is one of the best documented features of contemporary politics . . . ." In the midst of these absolute positions, political scientists are forced, reluctantly, to admit that "the political significance of this political ignorance is far from clear."[16]

In assessing this "ignorance," political scientists have concluded there is something at work beyond explicit voter knowledge of the facts. This "something" is not merely a practical demonstration of jury theory that—as espoused by the Marquis de Condorcet in 1785—concluded that the probability of a prudent outcome of any vote or election was a direct function of group size. (Twelve jurors, for example, will probably arrive at a judicious court decision, whereas a smaller number of individuals might arrive at an "incorrect" decision.) Rather, the answer lies with a necessary recalibration of our ideas about the relationship between fact and opinion. To understand this point, let's back up a few centuries.

Facts, as originally understood from Aristotle through the latter part of the seventeenth century, were observable details. As Hobbes noted in *Leviathan* (1651), one of the most influential works of its time, human knowledge was of two types: the knowledge of facts and philosophical knowledge. As Hobbes explained, the knowledge of fact "is nothing else but Sense and Memory." It is a recording of what is observed or what one recalls to have observed.[17] So, too, today—though implicitly—we consider facts to be items of "correct" information, of truths that accurately reflect our world.

However, "some purported facts are more indisputably correct than others."[18] Is it a fact that smoking causes lung cancer? Is it a fact that increasing the minimum wage causes unemployment? These statements are offered as if they constitute fact, yet, they are surely not universally accepted. They are observations, but not in the sense spoken of by Hobbes. We can all look at the sky and agree it is blue. We may not all agree that changes in salary scales cause unemployment.

The determination of a statement's factual character and of its relevance may, in the end, represent as much subjective as objective responses. Voters may not be "totally" informed, but are informed of and attuned to information of particular consequence to them. As a result, people generally cast votes based on what political scientists call "low-information rationality." That is, people naturally assign information and statements the weight of fact based on how well it fits in with, supports, and reinforces the "facts" they already accept.

The cross over to our discussion of the *Challenger* accident and business in general is that business decisions, like voting, while based on fact, are not matters of absolute certainty. Were certainty always achievable, management would not require decision-making, only implementation. This relationship between knowledge (or opinion) and fact has not always been so difficult a concept to grasp. To quote from another seventeenth-century theorist, John Locke wrote in "An Essay Concerning Human Understanding": "Man would be at a great loss if he had nothing to direct him but what has the certainty of true knowledge . . .

he that will not stir till he infallibly knows the business he goes about will succeed, will have little else to do but to sit still and perish."[19] "Low-level rationality" may be a hallmark of both American politics and American business. They both put the information received into a meaningful context in order for it to make sense. They both establish where the line is drawn between fact and opinion, where one must act rather than "sit still and perish."

As such, we can better accept the determination that Thiokol's evidence was "inconclusive" as more a matter of fact than a matter of opinion. Information presented in a business context is subject to two tests: 1) Does the information have merit? Can the information be agreed-upon and accepted as fact? 2) Is the information sufficient to outweigh any competing information that is understood by the participants to be part of the accepted thinking or the established protocols already in place? That is, is new information sufficiently compelling to dispute and dethrone the body of already agreed-to facts? Both these tests contributed to Thiokol's information being characterized as "inconclusive." The fact that the O-rings would fail had not been established and, therefore, the information was not sufficiently compelling to reverse NASA's established decision-making processes.

First, Thiokol's argument failed the technical test. According to testimony by Thiokol's Vice President of Engineering, the teleconference focused mainly on the integrity and reliability of the technical conclusion. Although Thiokol had concluded that temperature would cause O-ring failure, other engineers involved in the conversation had differing opinions about what the bench tests had proven and had "presented a very strong and forthright rationale of what they thought was going on in that joint."[20] Because of the presentation of an alternative theory, the period between the initial presentation of the charts and the issuance of the recommendation to proceed with the launch was not a capitulation to public relations pressures but, rather, a period of vigorous examination of competing technical interpretations:

> We were concerned the temperature was going to be lower than the 50 or 53 that had flown the previous January . . . we were concerned with the unknown. And we presented that to Marshall, and the rationale was rejected. They said that they didn't accept that rationale, and they would like us to consider some other thoughts that they had had . . . . And he presented a very strong and forthright rationale of what they thought was going on in that joint and how they thought that the thing was happening, and they said, we'd like you to consider that when they had some thoughts that we had not considered . . . . So after the discussion with Mr. Mulloy, and he presented that, we said, well, let's ponder that a little bit, so we went offline to talk."[21]

The second part of the discussion dealt with the weight of the information in relation to the established process for determining flight readiness. Were the Thiokol "facts" consistent with the existing facts governing launch criteria? Approval to launch relies on a series of checks and balances involving multiple levels of certification of flight readiness. Among the checks was a list of Launch Commit Criteria, the best thinking on how to evaluate readiness to launch, as developed over many years of experience and research. If, as those involved were inclined to believe, these processes and protocols codified in the review cycles and the Launch Commit Criteria would catch issues warranting launch postponement, then the process should be followed, not revised at the last minute.

This deference to protocol is a basic principle of business and of most of the circumstances of our lives. Whether playing school-yard games or making business decisions, we expect that certain processes, procedures, and rules will be followed. Simply put, rules must be followed if matters are to proceed in a disciplined and reasoned fashion. You don't—in the school yard, in the research facility, or in the business office—change rules in the middle of the game unless the evidence and motivation for doing so is so overwhelming that there is little other choice.

The "inconclusiveness" of the Thiokol argument was a result of two analyses: the facts did not support the conclusion, and the facts were not sufficiently compelling to warrant rethinking the established decision-making process at NASA. As the manager for the Solid Rocket Booster program at the Marshall Space Flight Center was to explain regarding the discussion of the Thiokol recommendation: "There are currently no Launch Commit Criteria (LCC) for joint temperature. What you are proposing to do is to generate a new Launch Commit Criteria on the eve of launch, after we have successfully flown with the existing Launch Commit Criteria 24 previous times. With this LCC, i.e., do not launch with a temperature greater [sic] than 53 degrees, we may not be able to launch until next April. We need to consider this carefully before we jump to any conclusions. It is all in the context, again, with challenging your interpretation of the data, what does it mean and is it logical, is it truly logical that we really have a system that has to be 53 degrees to fly?"[22]

The decision to launch, therefore, was not a matter of scientists and administrators bowing to public relations pressures. Neither is it a story of a great ethical lapse. It is a lesson for all business communicators: 1) In business, facts represent both observable truths and the institutionalized opinions that have gained the authority of fact. 2) In business, fact is weighed on several scales, including merit and relevance. 3) In business, facts operate within an established context; facts are measured against norms, expectations, protocols, and institutionalized approaches to problem-solving. Every decision brings personal and business perspectives to bear, but the focus needs to be on what information is the most credible in terms of its sources, its substance, and its consistency with what is already known. Accordingly, instead of our general sense that every statement is either fact or opinion—a variation of Benjamin Disraeli's quip that the world operates on "lies, damned lies, and statistics"—we might more accurately depict the circumstances in business as more indicative of a kind of continuum (Figure 3.7). Your job as communicator is not to rest once you have selected, or even weighed, the facts, but to follow through and to ensure that the facts you present support business's needs to arrive at practical, time-dependent, judgment-based decisions.

MY FACTS CAN BEAT YOUR FACTS

There is still one more important lesson to learn about facts and factual information. To address this last element, let's leave the space program for a more routine mode of transportation—the automobile. Americans have always had a love affair with their vehicles. Not only do they represent a certain power and individualism, "at one level, they may represent the very ideals of democracy."[23] Maybe this is why we are both intolerant of anything that diminishes our driving pleasure and demanding that our safety be safeguarded—whether by industry standards or legislative mandate. One recent public debate that has tested our patience because it has disrupted this balance is the battle between Bridgestone/Firestone Tires and the Ford Motor Company.

FIGURE 3.7

The Spectrum of
Factual Legitimacy

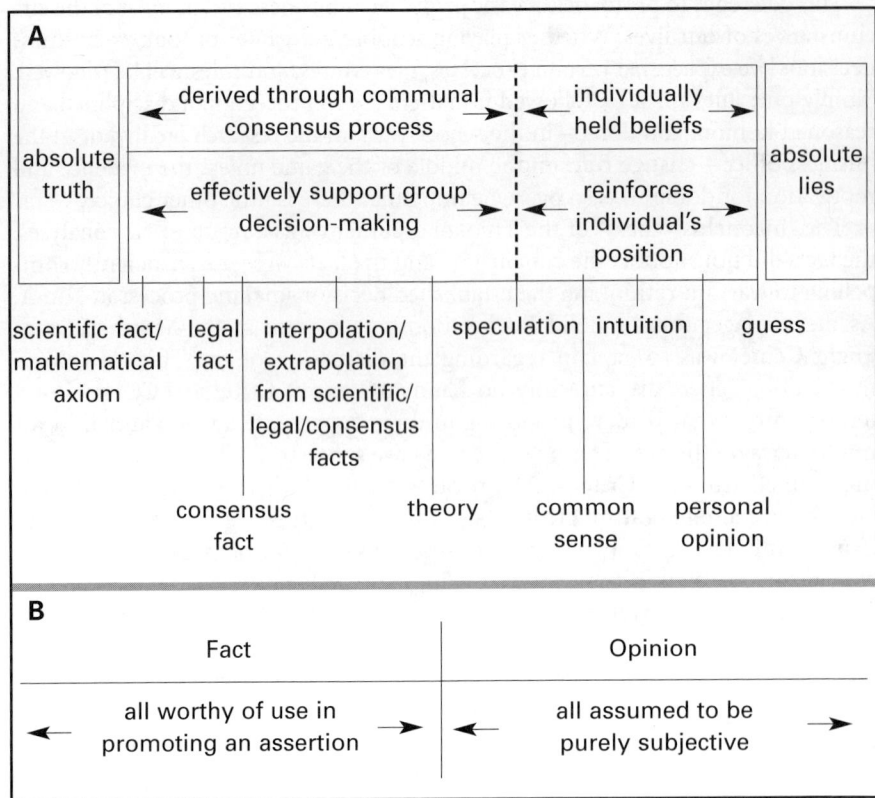

A

	derived through communal consensus process	individually held beliefs	
absolute truth	effectively support group decision-making	reinforces individual's position	absolute lies

scientific fact/ mathematical axiom	legal fact	interpolation/ extrapolation from scientific/ legal/consensus facts	speculation	intuition	guess

consensus fact   theory   common sense   personal opinion

B

Fact	Opinion
all worthy of use in promoting an assertion	all assumed to be purely subjective

In August 2000, the Firestone Company announced a plan to recall millions of all-terrain tires, an action taken in response to complaints received by the National Highway Traffic Safety Administration (NHTSA) that treads were separating from tires. As of May 2000, four fatalities were linked to the tires; by August, the numbers were up to 46 probable deaths. Among other vehicles, the Firestone tires in question had been included on most of the 3.6 million Explorers manufactured by Ford since 1990. The recall was going to be the biggest in the history of the tire industry. The previous record was also held by Firestone; in 1978, it recalled almost 14 million steel-radial tires, an action that nearly resulted in bankruptcy and contributed to the company being sold to Bridgestone in 1988.

The same month, as lawsuits mounted, Ford and Firestone began their public feud. While denying any ulterior motives, the Vice President of Communication at Ford cited issues with quality control at the Illinois plant where most of the suspect tires had been manufactured. As the Vice President stated, "We're not finger pointing, we're just telling what the statistics show."[24] The "statistics" included a failure rate for tires from the Illinois plant 10 times higher than at other Firestone plants, a bitter labor dispute that lasted from July 1994 to November 1996, and an NHTSA preliminary report that linked 20 of the 30 initial tire failures to the Illinois plant. By September, partially in response to Firestone's reluctance to expand the recall voluntarily, the House Commerce Committee began scheduling hearings. Ford, attempting to distance itself from the criticism, held a preemptive news conference in which it announced, "We are very disappointed with Firestone."[25]

Over the course of the next year, the public debate escalated. (Figure 3.8 is a time line showing some of the high points of the debate.) Firestone claimed the problem was with Ford's instructions that contributed to underinflated tires and with the design of the Explorer's steering system. Following a meeting with the Secretary of Transportation, the President of Firestone announced: "When tires fail . . . drivers should be able to pull over, not roll over."[26] Shortly thereafter, Firestone, citing that its relationship of "trust and mutual respect" had been "severely eroded," completely severed its 95-year partnership with Ford. (The Appendix contains the text of the letter severing the Ford-Firestone partnership.) For its part, Ford announced its intention to replace all 13 million Firestone tires on its sport-utility vehicles and pickup trucks—an initiative that would cost the company $3 billion.

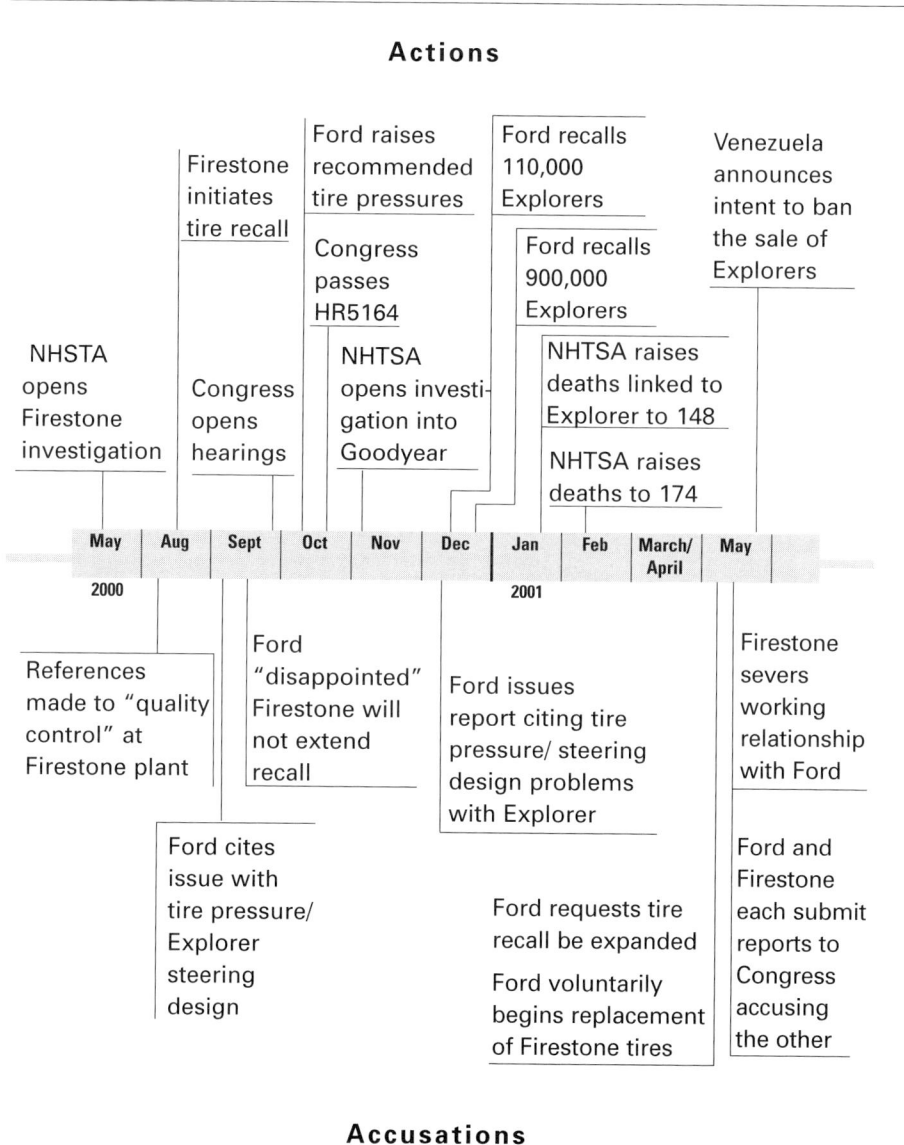

FIGURE 3.8

A Year of Feuding and Finger Pointing

Actions

Firestone initiates tire recall

Ford raises recommended tire pressures

Ford recalls 110,000 Explorers

Venezuela announces intent to ban the sale of Explorers

Congress passes HR5164

Ford recalls 900,000 Explorers

NHSTA opens Firestone investigation

Congress opens hearings

NHTSA opens investigation into Goodyear

NHTSA raises deaths linked to Explorer to 148

NHTSA raises deaths to 174

| May | Aug | Sept | Oct | Nov | Dec | Jan | Feb | March/April | May |

2000 — 2001

References made to "quality control" at Firestone plant

Ford "disappointed" Firestone will not extend recall

Ford issues report citing tire pressure/steering design problems with Explorer

Firestone severs working relationship with Ford

Ford cites issue with tire pressure/Explorer steering design

Ford requests tire recall be expanded

Ford voluntarily begins replacement of Firestone tires

Ford and Firestone each submit reports to Congress accusing the other

Accusations

CHAPTER 3   Facts: Attending to the Sociology of Business Information

By the summer of 2001, Ford and Firestone had been linked to approximately 200 deaths and hundreds of injuries. Neither Congress nor the National Transportation Safety Board (NTSB) had been able to define the cause or establish the blame. Public opinion polls conducted by *The Washington Post* at the time suggested that the public held Ford more accountable than Firestone (by a margin of 8:1).[27] By the early part of 2002, federal officials had linked more than 800 serious crashes, approximately 700 injuries, and 271 fatalities to accidents involving sudden tread separation on Firestone tires.

Opinions about which company is more culpable continue to swing back and forth. In November 2001, Bridgestone/Firestone paid approximately $40 million to settle a lawsuit brought by a collection of state attorneys general. As of Spring 2002, an equivalent investigation of Ford brought by these same attorneys general had yet to be settled. Beyond these state investigations, allegations continue as dozens of individual and class-action court cases weave their way through the judicial process.

Unlike the example with the Alamo where people needed only a few facts to help them reach a decision or the *Challenger* example where there were issues with factual consistency, relevance, and objectivity, here we have an example of facts without relative authority. All sources of information are overtly perceived as being of equal authority and equal currency. This equivalence, compounded by the sheer volume of information, creates an inability for the audience (Congress, the public, NTSB, and NHTSA) to establish exactly who is at fault. All parties appear equally (and appropriately?) subject to blame (or exoneration) based largely on their success in distilling the information into short television sound bites.

Despite the oversight of a congressional agency, several congressional hearings, testimony from dozens of experts, and an insatiable media, we are unable to evaluate the suitability of the facts and, therefore, unable to reach a conclusion. The failure to establish the relative value of the facts presented has ended in a stalemate to be fought out in the courts. The lesson we should take away from this is that facts must be given their voice. They must be assigned relative values and made meaningful in the intended context. Shoveling mounds of fact—even relevant facts—does little to aid the decision-making, and can have the opposite effect—forcing individuals to make poor decisions because the important information has been unintentionally buried amidst the less important (less relevant) information.

THE SOCIOLOGY OF BUSINESS INFORMATION

Having traveled down a century of history using a variety of modes of transportation, let's stop here to review what we've just learned. We have seen illustrations that we need to remain diligent when selecting and applying facts. We need to recognize the five common myths regarding facts:

1. The myth of absolute sufficiency—Facts are not weighed by numbers. Although people sometimes refer to documents passing a weight test, numbers of facts are not a suitable discriminator to assess whether you have made the necessary evidence available. (Remember the Alamo.)

2. The myth of preestablished relevancy—All facts are not equal. The Internet and site intranets may add to the volume of information available, but cannot help in defining which facts have immediate relevancy to the topic,

purpose, and audience. Just because facts fit the topic doesn't mean they are immediately relevant. Relevancy may be complete or partial. Facts, although of immediate importance, may establish context (the circumstance) of the topic, but may still fail to illuminate the precise issue or question under consideration. (Remember the *Challenger.*)

3. The myth of one-dimensional objectivity—Facts are not all equally accepted. A good percentage of facts (other than those that are simply descriptive of universally observable truth) are generally dependent on some degree of communal consensus. Businesses are not typically challenged to delineate fact from opinion in the sense of purely objective versus purely subjective statements; rather, the matter is to understand the subtext of consensus that promotes or challenges the credibility. (Remember Launch Commit Criteria.)

4. The myth of equal authority—Facts derive their relative statures from a number of contextual elements, including the source, currency, and forthrightness. Unlike formal debating in which there is a marshaling of armies of facts in support of multiple or alternative solutions, business demands that facts be delivered with clarity of context and the full weight of authority. (Remember the Explorer.)

5. The myth of certainty—As was illustrated in part by the *Challenger* accident, we must be careful not to confuse certainty with accuracy. When we are convinced we are right, we may become less objective in our assessment of the information. As an example of how this works, consider results from a series of experiments conducted using judges. Given details of a case, the judges' confidence in their determinations about the issues increased in direct proportion to how well they were "convinced of their . . . increasing understanding of the case." The tests demonstrated that certainty was not a measure of accuracy. Although intensely convinced of their conclusions about the case, the judges' "decisions became entirely out of proportion to the actual correctives of those decisions."[28] We must be objective about the facts, making careful assessments of the relative and absolute value of the facts we choose to present. (Remember the goal.)

Collectively, these five points, a sociology of business information, represent a framework in which to examine how the society of facts operates in a business culture. We need to always recognize that in business the three principles of reasoning are purpose, audience, and information. In so doing, we need to make certain we proceed through the planning steps in a disciplined and purposeful manner.

THE TRUTH ABOUT FACTS—
SELECTION COUNTS

We must be extremely diligent in selecting precisely the right information. At one level is our responsibility to ensure that there is a correct balance of context-setting information. Each business audience, given its orientation to and familiarity with a subject, generally needs a different percentage of the overall communication devoted to setting context. Our staff, generally fairly knowledgeable about the subjects of keen interest to us, needs considerably less context-setting information than does senior management. Senior management expects a clear articulation of context, the minimum sufficient to provide necessary perspective

FIGURE 3.9

The Relative
Percentages
of Contextual
Information

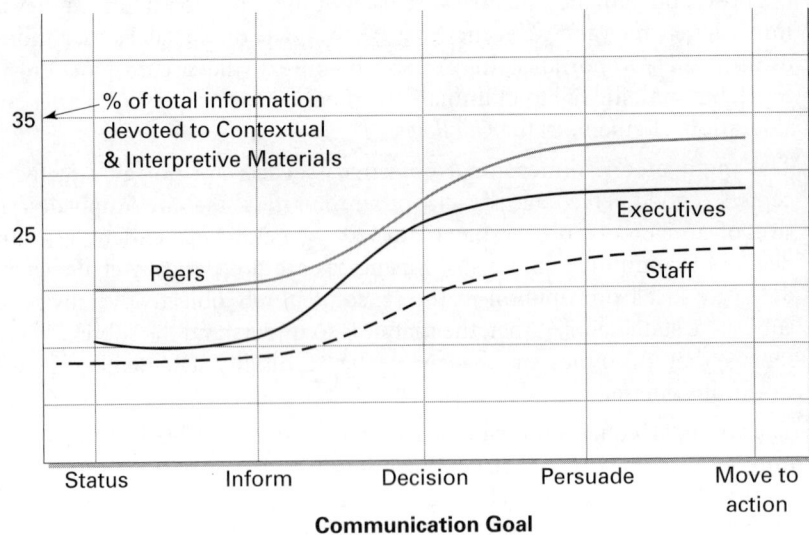

% of total information
devoted to Contextual
& Interpretive Materials

35

25

Peers

Executives

Staff

Status   Inform   Decision   Persuade   Move to
action

Communication Goal

on your critical recommendations and conclusions. Our peers, in contrast, may want substantial context to feel comfortable with accepting our proposed alignment of goals, issues, and commitments (Figure 3.9).

To accomplish these goals, facts should be selected based on their abilities to satisfy 10 criteria (Table 3.1). The facts must also be selected that relate to their

TABLE

3.1   SELECTING THE FACTS: THE 10 CRITERIA

1.	**Reasonableness**	Will the audience accept it?
2.	**Recency**	Does it represent current thinking on the subject?
3.	**Objectivity**	Does it appear to be free from inappropriate biases?
4.	**Authority**	Is the source recognized in the particular subject area?
5.	**Accuracy**	Is the fact a precise representation (e.g., direct quotation)?
6.	**Credibility**	Is the source reliable?
7.	**Consistency**	Is the fact in keeping with what is known and understood about the subject?
8.	**Clarity**	Will the audience readily understand the information?
9.	**Relevancy**	Is the information immediately applicable to the discussion at hand?
10.	**Particular Pertinence**	Are there considerations that make the fact particularly effective in supporting the assertion?

TABLE **3.2**

THE RELATIVE PERSUASIVE POWER OF FACTS

	Collectively Build Foundation	Provide Strength	Immediately Compelling
Reasonableness	√		
Objectivity	√		
Consistency	√		
Credibility		√	
Accuracy		√	
Recency		√	
Authority		√	
Clarity	√		
Relevance			√
Particular Pertinence		√	

application. Some types of information are best suited to building the foundation of the assertion. Other information is needed to create a case that is substantive, solid, and compelling (Table 3.2). To make the best use of our facts in creating a convincing argument, we might also benefit from an understanding of how the 10 criteria we have established are aligned with the mechanisms we naturally employ to develop, hold, and reinforce our personal belief structures. For example, as we saw with the Texas Proclamation, facts that have a particular pertinence—that resonate with our core values—are likely to create strong emotional reactions (Table 3.3).

THE INFORMATION WE USED TO NEED, WE STILL NEED

Having defined the selection criteria for our information, let's turn to the question of what kinds of information we need: the sources, the types, the levels, and the forms (Table 3.4). The Internet, amplified by corporate intranets, and knowledge management initiatives bring a universe of information into our offices. A simple CD-ROM or DVD now replaces a shelf of books. Yet, this access might easily mislead us from the important point that the information needs of business are not new. These information challenges have existed for decades. The ability to understand and answer that need is what separates someone who

Statement 1

Information needs arise from the problems, uncertainties, and ambiguities encountered in specific organizational situations and experiences. Such situations and experiences are the composite of a large number of factors that relate not just to subject matter, but also to contextual factors such as organization style, functional constraints, goal clarity and consensus, degree of risk, professional norms, amount of control, and so on. As a result, the determination of information needs must not stop at asking: "What do you want to know?" "What does your problem look like?" "What do you know already?" "What do you anticipate finding?" "How will this help you?" "How do you need to know it?"

Statement 2

We may feel confident that no one who has had extensive experience in management, or has made serious study of it, will question the value of research to the responsible executive of these days. Therefore our attention to that phase of this report should be primarily for completeness of the record and may be in the form of propositions.

1) Management involves problems relative to purposes, policies, programs, projects, plans and procedures; decisions are made by rational consideration of pertinent facts; the validity of a decision depends not only upon the soundness of the rational considerations, but also upon the completeness and accuracy of the facts.

2) The development of a complicated industrial organization has generated problems of management which are critical, perplexing and exacting in their demands for rational determination on the bases of facts which are numerous, and difficult of ascertainment and valuation.

3) The range of facts required by management in making its decisions is indicated by the following classifications: Facts relating to—

Materials: their fabrication and consumer uses.

Progress of the arts employed in industry.

Organization for and direction of transformative and distributive processes.

Human individual and group reactions to organization and direction procedures and relationships.

Consumer demand, and the general and particular markets.

Industrial tendencies pertinent to long run planning of policies and programs.

Environmental influences such as social customs, government regulation and international relations.

effectively uses information from someone who merely collects information. Being an information gatherer is not the same as being an information user. To make this point more evident, let's consider two statements.

Both statements concern similar areas of interest: the need to have information to solve problems, reduce uncertainties, promote the means for improving efficiencies, and better understand the dynamics of organization and technolo-

3.3   FACTS IN RELATION TO OUR BELIEF STRUCTURES

Belief Mechanism	Principal Orientation	Facts Most Readily Accepted	Related Selection Criteria
Lessons learned	Relationships established between items	Facts that have an established set of associations	Authority Relevancy
Critical thinking	Simple tests we apply automatically	Facts that are unbiased and acceptable	Objectivity and reasonableness
Needs we have to solve dilemmas	The information we seek	Facts that respond to the immediate needs	Credibility
The way we receive information	How information we receive is categorized	Facts that are accepted in the form transmitted	Accuracy Clarity
Emotional associations	The intensity of our response	Facts that promote an intense response	Particular pertinence
Memory	What we have stored	Facts that agree with our impressions	Consistency
Feedback	The responses we get	Facts that suggest the point matches current thinking	Recency

gies. To assist with our understanding, the authors of the two statements offer tabular representations of the types of information warranted (Tables 3.5 and 3.6, respectively).[29]

It is evident that the authors closely share an opinion of the types of information needed by business. What may be surprising, however, is that the first statement and its tabular representation (Table 3.5) is adapted from a recent text on information management. The second statement and its corresponding table (Table 3.6) are adapted from 1926 and 1931 writings of H.S. Person, Managing Director of the Taylor Society, an organization devoted to promoting the ideals of Scientific Management, a movement we will discuss further in later chapters.[30]

As the two cases from the farther ends of the twentieth century suggest, the information challenge has never been in finding the information or in knowing the questions that need to be answered, but in recognizing and isolating the information that effectively relates to the business purpose and audience. Our goal as professional communicators is to do the hard work of choosing just those pieces of information that, when assembled, explain the essence of the problem, prove the contention, or provoke action. Whether we talk about information in the context of operational problems, management philosophy, or specific versus general goals, we share the same basic needs for information—irrespective of what industries or sectors of the economy we represent. Stated simply, no matter what industry we represent, our success is a matter of how we choose and represent the facts of the case.

3.4   A HOST OF WAYS TO TALK ABOUT BUSINESS INFORMATION

Sources

Internal: from within the organization
External: from outside the organization
Primary: information from original sources
Secondary: information resulting from
processing other data

Time

Historical: information pertaining to past
operations or performance
Current: up-to-date information
Future: information pertaining to projections
or extrapolations

Types

Quantitative: numerical information
Qualitative: other than numerical
Formal: information developed using
established processes or procedures
Informal: information resulting from
less-defined means (e.g., conversation)

Frequency

Real time: information provided on an ongoing
basis
Periodic: information produced on a routine
basis
As-needed: information retrieved when
warranted

Levels

Strategic: information pertaining to
long-term goals or performance
Technical: information pertaining to
shorter-term management
Operational: information pertaining to
day-to-day operations

Use

Planning: information for developing insights
Control: information to monitor performance
or processes
Decision: information used to determine
actions or resolve problems

Form

Written: recorded language
Visual: video, photo
Aural: sound

Representations

Detailed: information based on large volume
of data
Aggregated: summarization of data
Sampled: information selected at some frequency from among the available information

FACTS—THE LESSONS

Where once people talked of fact versus opinion, or intuition versus reasoned decision-making, we can now understand that the foundations of purposely selecting facts derive from a common set of criteria. Being diligent in the application of those criteria is what separates success from failure, myth from reality, and fact from fiction in the business world. As communicators, we need to keep the 10 criteria in mind when choosing and presenting facts:

Reasonableness
Accuracy
Relevance

3.5 DIMENSIONS OF THE CONTEMPORARY INFORMATION CHALLENGE

Possible Information Orientations	Question To Be Answered
1. Design vs. Discovery	How much data is immediately available? Is that data sufficient or does it need amplification?
2. Well-structured vs. Ill-structured	How well defined are the pathways for collecting, defining, categorizing, and analyzing information?
3. Simple vs. Complex	How many facets are there to the problem and what degree of subdivision is needed to get at the critical elements?
4. Specific vs. Amorphous goals	What degree of the problem is understood based on accepted analytic practices and what percent is based on preferences and experiential conclusions?
5. Initial state understood vs. Initial state not understood	Are the underlying conditions and requirements documented and understood?
6. Assumptions agreed upon vs. Assumptions not agreed upon	Is there a general consensus about what constitutes the causal agents?
7. Assumptions explicit vs. Assumptions not explicit	Are all the assumptions defined, recognizable, and understood?
8. Familiar pattern vs. New pattern	Are the conclusions to be based on established precedents or will acceptance demand an appreciation of a new relationship among the facts and conclusions?
9. Magnitude of risk not great vs. Magnitude of risk great	Are the assumptions understood well enough that the implicit and explicit risks associated with the conclusions are reasonable and justified?
10. Susceptible to empirical analysis vs. Not susceptible to empirical analysis	Can the assumptions and conclusions be independently verified or must some elements be accepted based on subjective interpretations, extrapolations, forecasts?
11. Internal imposition vs. External imposition	To what degree are the assumptions and conclusions driven by internal business decisions and by the work or business environment?

Objectivity
Recency
Pertinence
Consistency
Authority
Credibility
Clarity

We also need to avoid becoming captive to a number of myths regarding the selection and use of facts (Table 3.7).

TABLE 3.6   THE FACTUAL NEEDS AT THE TURN OF THE TWENTIETH CENTURY

Collective Principles	1. Work Place	2. Shop	3. Personnel	4. Marketing	5. Finance	6. General Administration
Research	Engineering studies Economic studies Methods studies Time study Motion study Material behavior studies	Relationship between skills and facilities	Manual aptitude studies Job requirements Group/ organizations	Market analysis Quantitative Qualitative Consumer demand Distribution channels Studies of methods of selling/ sales and competition	Studies of market for capital Customer credits and collections Pricing Financial ratios	Industrial forecasting Managerial operating ratios
Standardization	Specifications of Materials Machines Products Methods Quality Quantity	Specifications regarding application of skills Production schedules	Hiring, promoting, and discharging Training and sharing of information Personnel and group relations	Sales schedules Quotas Channels of distribution Methods of selling Pricing Discounting Salaries and commissions	Standard costs Financial ratios	Policy Projects Plans Master schedules Master budgets Operating ratios
Control	Provision of materials and tools Product inspections Performance inspections	Analysis of orders Routing Scheduling and assigning of work Inspections	Direction of conduct	Functional separation of planning and execution	Inspection of financial activities, management	Inspection of conformity to budgets and schedules Attention to exceptional situations Prompt decision-

3.7 THE FIVE MYTHS OF BUSINESS FACTS

Myth	The Mistake
The myth of absolute sufficiency	It is not the number of facts that's important, but rather the applicability and substance of the facts you choose.
The myth of preestablished relevancy	All facts must be selected based on immediate applicability to the purpose, audience, and circumstance.
The myth of one-dimensional objectivity	Facts are judged within the specific context and through filters of the audience experience.
The myth of equal authority	Facts do not arrive with credibility and weight; the strength of the facts must be established and reinforced.
The myth of certainty	Facts must be judged to ensure they are not only relevant and substantive, but also accurate and true.

EXERCISES

☐ Group

1. Divide into three groups. Each group identifies 20 facts it feels will most effectively address the purpose and audience of one of the topics below. These facts are presented in terms of the 10 criteria (Table 3.1) and evaluated by the class.

Purpose	Audience
Results of lie detector tests should be allowed as evidence.	Panel of Criminal Court judges
The Electoral College system should be eliminated.	Regional conference of New England governors
More federal land should be opened to the mining and timber industries.	Annual meeting of environmental scientists

2. Discuss the following:

  a) how changing the audience for your assigned topic above to an audience of the general public affects the suitability and effectiveness of the facts that were selected.

  b) what types of facts you would have selected had the general public been your initial audience.

3. Select a major, unresolved public controversy (e.g., the link between cancer and tobacco use). Prepare a 15-minute presentation highlighting the issues involved, the types of information used by each of the participants in the controversy, the applicability to the 10 criteria (Table 3.1), and the demonstrations or repudiations of the five myths about facts, as listed in Table 3.7.

Individual

1. Select an editorial from a nationally recognized newspaper (e.g., *The New York Times*). Evaluate the author's use of fact.

2. Compare the use and reliance on fact in the editorial you used above with an editorial on the same (or similar) topic from a local newspaper.

END NOTES

[1] Zan D. Quible, "Guiding Students in Finding Information on the Web," *Business Communication Quarterly,* Vol. 62, No. 3 (Sept. 1999), p. 57.

[2] Adapted from Carla O'Dell and C. Jackson Grayson, Jr., *If Only We Knew What We Know Now.* New York: The Free Press, 1998.

[3] Photograph reprinted with permission of Sand River Photography.

[4] John Rigden, "The Lost Art of Oratory: Damn the Overhead Projector," *Physics Today,* March 1990, pp. 73, 75.

[5] Stephen J. Garber and Roger K. Launius, "A Brief History of the National Aeronautics and Space Administration," NASA Fact Sheet.

[6] Testimony of G. B. Hardy, *Report to the President by the Presidential Commission on the Space Shuttle Challenger Accident (PCSSCA),* June 6, 1986. Vol. 4, pp. 888–889.

[7] Testimony of R. Boisjoly, *PCSSCA,* Vol. 1, p. 88.

[8] Testimony of R. Boisjoly, *PCSSCA,* Vol. 1, p. 89.

[9] *PCSSCA.*

[10] Diane Vaughn, *The Challenger Launch Decision: Risky Technology, Culture, and Deviance at NASA.* Chicago: University of Chicago Press, 1996, p. 307.

[11] Testimony of A.J. McDonald, *PCSSCA,* Vol. 4, pp. 630–631.

[12] *PCSSCA.*

[13] Edward R. Tufte, *Visual Explanations: Images and Quantities, Evidence and Narrative.* Cheshire, CN: Graphics Press, 1997.

[14] Frederick F. Lighthall, "Launching the Space Shuttle *Challenger:* Disciplinary Deficiencies in the Analysis of Engineering Data," *IEEE Transactions on Engineering Management,* Vol. 38, No. 1 (Feb. 1991), pp. 63–74.

[15] Cited in J. H. Kulinski, P. J. Quirk, D. W. Schweider, and R. F. Rich, "'Just the Facts Ma'am': Political Facts and Public Opinion," *The Annals of the American Academy of Political and Social Science,* Vol. 560 (Nov. 1998), pp. 143–154.

[16] Larry M. Bartels, "Uninformed Votes: Information Effects in Presidential Elections," *American Journal of Political Science,* Vol. 40, No. 1 (Feb. 1996), pp. 194–230.

[17] Cited in Michael Ben-Chaim, "How Do Facts Speak for Themselves? The Doctrine and Practice of Classical Empiricism," *Journal of Technical Writing & Communication,* Vol. 26, No. 1 (1996), pp. 3–19.

[18] Kuklinski et al, "'Just the Facts, Ma'am.'"

[19] Cited in Ben-Chaim, "How Do Facts Speak for Themselves?"

[20] *PCSSCA.*

[21] Testimony of T. K. Lund, *PCSSCA,* Vol. 1, p. 94.

[22] Testimony of L. P. Mulloy, *PCSSCA,* Vol. 1, p. 96.

[23] Edward Tenner, *Why Things Bite Back: Technology and the Revenge of Unintended Consequences.* New York: Alfred A. Knopf, 1996.

[24] Frank Swoboda and James V. Grimaldi, "Ford Finds Tire Plant Had Many Failures," *The Washington Post,* Aug. 14, 2000, p. A1.

[25] Caroline Meyer and Frank Swoboda, "U.S. Issues Warning About More Tires," *The Washington Post*, Sept. 2, 2000, p. E1.

[26] Caroline Meyer and Cindy Skrzycki, "Firestone Wants Proof of Explorer Safety," *The Washington Post*, June 1, 2001, p. E1.

[27] *The Washington Post,* on-line http:\\www.washingtonpost.com

[28] Stuart O. Kamp, "Overconfidence in Case-Study Judgments," in David Kahneman, Paul Slovic, and Amos Tversky, *Judgment Under Uncertainty: Heuristics and Bases.* Cambridge: Cambridge University Press, 1982, pp. 287–293.

[29] Table 3.5 is adapted from: Chun Wei Choo, *Information Management for the Intelligent Organization*, 2nd ed. Medford, N.J.; Information Today, Inc: 1998. Table 3.6 is adapted from H. S. Person, "A Tabular Presentation of the Principles, Technique and Chronological Development of Scientific Management," in *Classics in Scientific Management: A Book of Readings.* Ed. D. DelMar and R.D. Collons. University, AL: University of Alabama Press, 1976, pp. 194–198.

[30] H. S. Person, "Management's Concern in Research," in *Classics in Scientific Management*, pp. 302–312.

4

Arrangement
Ordering and Visualizing
Business Information

Facts are everywhere. Our first step as communicators is to figure out which facts to choose. The next step is to ensure that these facts have perceived value. The way in which we cause facts to have value is in the choices we make about their presentation. Presentation involves a number of factors: 1) how we group (or organize) facts into packages, 2) how we present them, and 3) how clearly, efficiently, and accurately we portray the information.

Each of these three factors has to do with decisions about such things as the organizational strategies we use and the use of graphical versus text displays. The arrangement and presentation of information grows straightforwardly out of the material we have been discussing so far. Namely, its most immediate source is the types and quality of facts we select. Equally important, when done correctly, organizational strategies and presentation choices grow out of an appreciation of audience and purpose. Who will be accessing the information? What is the person's reason for reviewing the information? We need to be sure that information comes together in a disciplined fashion. We also have to pay greater attention to our graphic design responsibilities as professional communicators than to the graphic capabilities of the computer. Knowing the choices, their application, their basis, and their expectations offers us opportunity to be effective information designers.

LOOKING CLOSELY AT WHAT WE KNOW

In Chapter 3, we looked at the question of how to assemble the right types of facts to support our business assertions. Now let's move forward to discuss what we must do once the facts have all been collected. Let's begin roughly at the same point as we began in the last chapter.

Figure 4.1 shows the statistics cited on four football cards. These cards detail statistics for four well-known players, each from a different team, and each with a different assignment: quarterback, running back, wide receiver, and cornerback. Our quarterback card details such statistics as completion percentages for passes thrown and yards gained per catch. Our running back card gives us information on such statistics as yards per catch and yards per carry. The wide receiver among the group, not having an emphasis on running, adds statistics regarding yards per catch after the carry in addition to a column on yards per catch and percentage caught. Our one defensive player, the cornerback, offers three unique columns of numbers: tackles, sacks, and interceptions. In each of the four cases, the columns are neatly measured against categories of performance, how well the individual performed against teams in the same league, and

FIGURE 4.1

A Sampling of
Football Statistics

Quarterback
San Diego Chargers

Quarterback Rating	Yards/ Attempt	Completion %	
83.6	6.9	59.0	Vs. AFC West
78.0	6.7	57.0	AFC W. Avg
81.7	7.1	59.4	Vs. AFC
79.3	6.7	57.1	AFC Avg
80.4	7.1	59.0	Vs. NFL
79.3	6.8	58.2	NFL Avg

Running Back
Arizona Cardinals

Yards/ Carry	Yards/ Catch	Combined/ Game	
3.7	8.7	88.6	Vs. NFC East
4.2	8.1	73.4	NFC East Avg
4.0	7.9	89.0	Vs. NFC
4.0	7.9	65.6	NFL Avg
3.8	8.4	82.1	Vs. NFL
4.0	7.8	62.6	NFL Avg

Wide Receiver
Pittsburgh Steelers

Yards/ Catch	Yards After Catch	% Caught	
17.5	5.1	53.0	Vs. AFC Cent.
14.2	3.8	51.2	AFC Cent Avg
17.1	4.7	53.6	Vs. AFC
14.2	3.8	52.5	AFC Avg
15.4	4.4	56.3	Vs. NFL
14.0	4.0	54.8	NFL Avg

Cornerback
Dallas Cowboys

Tackles	Sacks	Interceptions	
3.0	0.0	0.0	Vs. NFC East
24.2	0.2	2.6	NFC East Avg
3.0	0.0	0.0	Vs. NFC
41.5	0.4	3.3	NFC Avg
3.0	0.0	0.0	Vs. NFL
53.5	0.5	3.3	NFL Avg

how well those compare with statistics for the National Football League (NFL) as a whole.

The most immediate question that probably strikes us is "So what?" We assume these statistics must be of some significance. Otherwise, why would anyone keep all these arcane numbers? The card company, you might argue, is simply filling space; however, they still have to get the numbers somewhere. Someone who studies the sport has found these statistics worthy of capture. Yet, our question still stands: What are these numbers supposed to tell us? If the quarterback has fairly consistent completion rates in the 50+% range, can we be assured that in the next game he plays, half his throws will be completed? And if, on average, he gains about 7 yards per carry, does that mean his next throw, if completed, will be for less than 10 yards? How about our running back? Will he carry the ball for less than 4 yards next time he gets it, or gain about 7 yards on each pass, yet never amass a total of more than 100 yards in any single game? How about our wide receiver? Can we expect when he's thrown to he'll gain 15 to 17 yards? Would it then stand to reason that if the quarterback throws to him 12 times, he'll score a touchdown (6 catches × 17 yards) no matter where the team takes possession of the ball? And, last, while our wide receiver is hurdling downfield, our cornerback may or may not provide a suitable defense, depending on which league the offensive players come from.

Are we prepared to accept that the dynamics of football have been neatly distilled into a simple statistical representation on the backs of football cards? We're certain the answer is no. Yet, before we spend any more time on the football field, let's take a look at a second set of statistics.

Let's assume you've decided that you need life insurance. You've found a company that doesn't require a physical. The company just requires answers to a few questions. The company has no former knowledge of you. You are not as well-known to them as our football players are now known to us. Yet, which set of information—the football statistics or the health survey—more readily allows its recipient to draw defensible conclusions? We will probably all say the health survey, but we might be uncertain why that is.

The first kind of information (the football statistics) is purely descriptive. It provides a summary of past history, but has little to do with establishing meaningful predictions. The insurance industry information, on the other hand, is purposely designed to allow decisions to be made—in this case, whether or not to issue a policy. The actuarial tables were established through extensive data collection and analysis. They allow the insurance industry to know, with a reasonably high level of confidence, which health factors increase the probability that the insurance industry will pay out the greatest share of the money taken in through premiums.

In statisticians' terms, these two categories are known as "descriptive statistics" and "inferential statistics." They either describe a situation of interest or they form the basis for reaching a conclusion about it. In business, both types of information are valuable, but we have to be extremely careful that we don't unintentionally use the former to try to achieve the latter. Trying to use the sports card statistics to predict what will happen in the next play or the next game is not supported by the available information. It has little to no predictive value.

In the news business, confusing the two can bring us back to the situation that occurred in Florida during the 2000 presidential elections. Having conducted exit polls (polls taken as voters leave the polling stations), television stations thought they had a sound basis for predicting who the winner of the election would be. First one then another station indicated Al Gore had won Florida, a state whose electoral votes were critical to the outcome of the election. As the evening wore on, the actual vote tallies seemed less aligned with the predictions. Several hours after their initial forecasts, television stations started indicating Florida was "too close to call." Thereafter, it was reported that George Bush had taken Florida and had won the election. No one, certainly not the media with all its descriptive data, was able to predict just how long it would be before the actual election results would be known.

Some of the implicit elements that need to be known regarding descriptive and inferential statistics might be illustrated using a puzzle attributed to Frederick Mosteller, a Harvard statistician. The puzzle involves three people: Mr. Z,

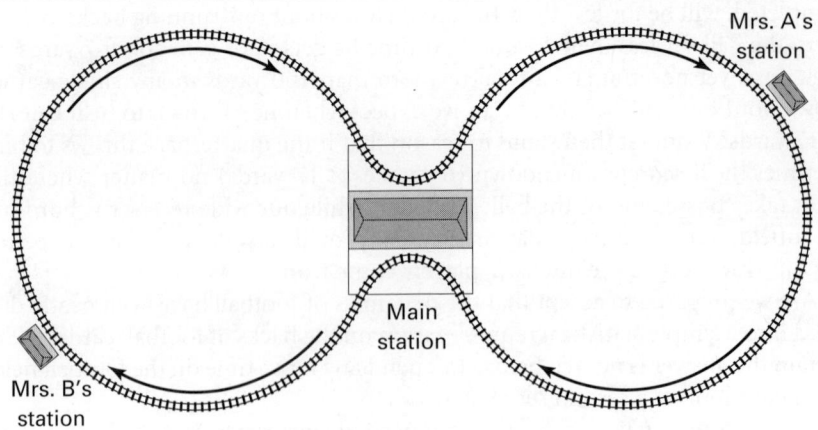

FIGURE 4.2

Visiting Friends

Mrs. A's station

Main station

Mrs. B's station

Source: Reprinted with permission of Gregory Kimble.

Mrs. A, and Mrs. B. Mr. Z, whose office is near the main railroad station, intends to visit his two friends (Mrs. A and Mrs. B) on an equal frequency. The two friends live on opposite sides of the city (Figure 4.2).[1] Rather than setting up a schedule, he leaves to chance who he will visit on a particular day: He goes to the train station and boards whichever train arrives first. He reasons that since it is equally likely to catch an eastbound train as it is a westbound train, he should see Mrs. A half the time and Mrs. B half the time. However, in his first 30 trips, he actually ends up visiting Mrs. A 21 times and Mrs. B only nine times. This distribution might have occurred purely by chance, or there may be other factors that created the imbalance.

For example, what if the two train segments are really not equal in length? What if one route has more stops than the other? What if there are differences in the quality of the tracks, causing the train to travel more slowly on one side of town than the other (Figure 4.3)?

Reinforcing what we discussed in Chapter 3, the typical conclusion is derived not from a single fact, but by collecting the facts that are immediately relevant to the problem. As a transition between the collection of facts and the development of a line of argument (which we will discuss in Chapter 5), we need to begin to put the information into packages of related data. To understand this better, let's begin with a situation that is common in business.

ORGANIZING TO MEET THE DEMANDS

You and a few friends have been working on a new idea that you think will be a great seller in the world of electronic commerce. You're at the point where you decide the product is ready for full-scale development. You've done research, prototyping, marketing studies, programming, and design work. You've held focus groups, done Beta testing, and completed all forms of financial forecasting and risk analysis. In short, you've sunk everything—all your talent, all your creativity, all your insights, and all your money—into the concept. In a world of dramatic market swings, you are betting that you're on the verge of becoming very rich entrepreneurs.

In essence, what you and your friends have developed is a computer disk that can be assigned a certain dollar value by a bank and then inserted into any computer and used to purchase materials and services on-line. Unlike credit cards,

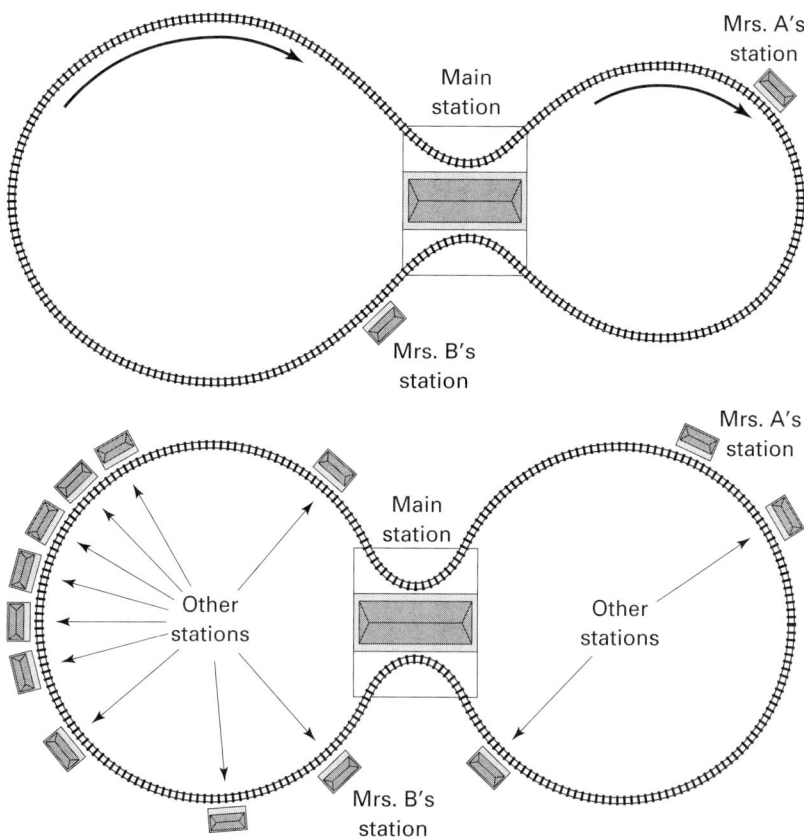

FIGURE 4.3

Some Rides Are
Longer Than
Others

Source: Reprinted with permission of Gregory Kimble.

your disk has a specific dollar amount and is totally separate from any of the user's financial information and records. If anyone steals the disk, the most the person could use it for is the preestablished dollar value. The person cannot use the information to tap into any other accounts, to steal personal records, to learn social security numbers, or to hijack identities. Your company, E-Disc, has invented a way to open up the world of on-line buying to even the most skeptical consumer. You believe that the value of the idea is enormous because it brings every bank and every company selling on-line a universe of new customers.

Tomorrow morning you have set up a meeting with some venture capitalists who are interested in finding places to invest their money. The only problem you foresee is that, as is a common phenomenon in business, yours is not the only firm they're visiting tomorrow. They have told you that they have no more than 45 minutes to meet with you. It may not be that they're going to be seeing other firms with comparable ideas, but they are seeing other firms in competition with you for the same pot of money.

Having benefited from Chapter 3, you have collected all the information into dozens of files, each with a number of subfiles and sub-subfiles (Table 4.1). Certainly, you're not going to sit at the meeting and rummage through your files. You know you can't show the thousands of pages of detail in only 45 minutes. You have a problem. You have all the data in the world, but you don't have all the time in the world to show the data. The ability to compress years of work into 45 minutes may mean the difference between success or failure of the company.

| 4.1 | **E-DISC FILES** |

Programming
- problems
- options

Market Analysis
- quantitative data
- qualitative data
- distribution

Liabilities
- financial
- legal

Competition
- on-line
- nonelectronic

Testing
- prototypes
- Beta testing
- focus groups

Costs
- development
- implementation
- maintenance

Schedule
- development
- implementation

Corporate Expertise
- biographies

Applications
- primary
- secondary

History
- how developed
- how it fits in
- previous related services

Expected Sales
- first 12 months
- first 3 years
- continuing

Necessary Partners
- computer security firms
- underwriters

Taking a cue from Chapter 3, you first go through the collection and pull out the relevant factual information. But that still leaves you with far more than can be presented in the allotted time.

In the initial steps of selecting individual facts, you employed a set of 10 criteria. Now you begin to package the information into usable bundles by asking a new series of questions determined by the purposes and audiences you need to address. In considering the audience's particular interests, the questions that seem most immediate are the following:

1. What is the idea?
   —what it entails
   —how it is like/unlike existing commodities
2. How does the idea work?
   —the sequence
   —steps involved
3. Where'd the idea come from?
4. How far along are you on the project?
5. What have been the costs to date?
6. How much money will it take to bring the product to market?
7. How much longer will it take to be ready to market?
8. What are the major markets?
9. Based on your projections, what is the earning potential?
10. What are the risks and liabilities?
11. What kind of a track record does your firm have?
12. What kind of financial arrangement are you expecting?
13. What's the return on investment?

ORGANIZING STRATEGIES

The questions you are asking correspond directly with organizing rationales that will support your need to present your information effectively (Table 4.2). Each

4.2 ORGANIZING RATIONALES

Questions to be answered	Organizing rationale
1. What the idea is	1. Definition/classification
2. How the plan works	2. Process analysis/description
3. How the plan was developed	3. Chronology
4. How it stacks up to the competition	4. Comparison/contrast
5. Costs/development to date	5. Status
6. Money/time needed to implement	6. Interpretation
7. Major markets/earning potential	7. Assessment
8. Risks and liabilities	8. Causality
9. Track record of the firm	9. Summary
10. Return on investment	10. Consequences

of these organizing rationales is briefly explained below. For those less-familiar forms that have several variations, examples are also provided. Following the individual descriptions, all 12 organizing rationales are summarized in Table 4.3.

DEFINITION—delineates exact dimensions of an item or topic. There are three common forms of definitions, 1) formal—quoting from a dictionary or some official standard to express how an item is understood by a major community; 2) experiential—establishing a definition from a frame of reference that derives from an actual circumstance, and 3) stipulated—a definition assigned to the item or topic at hand.

Definitional Types—An Illustration	
	Example: Three definitions of "acceptable risk"
Formal	A risk in which the benefits are perceived to be a factor of 3 greater than the perceived consequences.
Experiential	A risk like that of driving an automobile versus the risk of living next to an explosives factory.
Stipulated	For our purposes, we will consider acceptable risk to be any liability the company is willing to bear to be successful.

TYPE/CLASSIFICATION—establishes a commonality among known commodities. The two principal forms of classification are complete (in which all members of the population are included) and incomplete (in which a subset of the population is used).

Classification—An Illustration

Complete	In singles competition in figure skating, a competitor is expected to demonstrate a double axel, a double or triple jump, a jump combination, a flying spin, a layback or sideways leaning spin, a spin combination, and a spiral step.
Incomplete	In today's event, we are going to limit the focus to just the jump combination and the spiral step.

STATUS—provides a picture of an item in time. The three common forms of status are 1) over time—in which a historical context is established, 2) relative—in which the status is explained in relation to other events or activities, and 3) current—in which we provide the most recent perspective that can be reported.

Status—An Illustration

Over time	Since 1996, slow progress was achieved; thereafter, we completed the initial testing by 2000.
Relative	Our project has matured in direct correspondence with the increases of reliance on e-commerce.
Current	We are now 70% of the way toward full implementation.

SUMMARY—provides an overall picture or digest of the information. The degree of specificity varies greatly. At one end is the general summation—analogous to a lawyer's closing statement in which days of testimony are distilled into a few primary conclusions. At the other end of the spectrum is a detailed summary in which a large percentage of the main points and facts are reiterated.

DESCRIPTION—portrays the image of the item or topic. The primary forms are detailed and summary, differing in the specificity of the description.

CHRONOLOGY—provides a time-related depiction of the topic. In business, the two most common forms of organizing by chronology are sequential—detailing elements in a series (i.e., what came first, second, etc.) and historical (depicted over time). The time scale will vary depending on the topic.

PROCESS ANALYSIS—delineates the individual steps in the activity. The rationale relies on either a detailed depiction or summary depiction (which may or may not equate to the equivalent of "complete" and "incomplete" depictions). For example, we might tell you that to get to our office, go down I-80 to Exit 14 and then proceed 6 miles to Barnwell Avenue (summary). Conversely, we might explain that at Exit 14, make a right turn, cross through the intersection, and then go down eight lights, make a right when you come to the Industrial Park, and then proceed to the third building on your left (detailed).

COMPARISON/CONTRAST—defines the item or topic in relation to similar or differing items or topics. Often, the two strategies are integrated, introducing both similarities and differences to provide a complete image of the topic.

CAUSALITY—defines the contributing forces or elements that lead to an event. As we will discuss in Chapter 5, causality is often a much more complicated matter than may be readily apparent. However, we can summarize that causality is usually argued from one of two vantage points: primary, in which the overriding causal agent is identified, and sufficiency, in which the cumulative force of a number of causal agents are used to sustain a contention.

Causality—An Illustration	
Primary	The increase in cost of production results from increased inflation.
Sufficiency	Suppliers A, B, and C have each increased their prices by 3%. Because they are the main external costs for production, it seems that inflation is the cause of our problem.

INTERPRETATION—assigns meaning to a circumstance. In business, there are three common expressions of interpretation. Localized, personal, and corporate. Localized versions examine a particular event or circumstance. Personal bases the interpretation on some relationship between you and the event. Corporate attempts to put the interpretation into a larger, more global perspective.

Interpretation—An Illustration	
Localized	The Firestone tire problem will be most significant at the Illinois plant.
Personal	Our problem, however, is that our dealership has had a 40% drop in sales.
Corporate	The issue may be whether Firestone can return from the brink of a second near bankruptcy.

ASSESSMENT—provides a judgment of or sets a value on the issue or topic. Although many variations exist in the ways an evaluative conclusion might be stated, the two most common types are relative and absolute. Relative shows the value as compared to that of a similar item. Absolute does not rank a value, but sets a specific value.

Assessment—An Illustration	
Relative	We ranked all the senior foremen in the plant, and John is fourth on a list of 27.
Absolute	John's review showed an "excellent" in seven of 10 categories assessed.

CONSEQUENCES—projects implications: what may occur as a result of actions or inactions. In general, statements of consequence are presented in terms of two factors: time and certainty. The time factors are immediate (those that are imminent) and strategic (those that will occur at some point in the future). The certainty factors are potential (having varying degrees of probability [less than 100%] of occurrence) and certain (having a 100% probability of occurrence).

Consequence—An Illustration				
	Time		Certainty	
1.	Imminent	If we purchase the Roland Co., our stock prices will go up at least 20% this year.	3. Potential	If we purchase the company, we may also reduce risk of closing the Michigan plant.
2.	Strategic	Also, our market share should expand by at least 10 % over the next 5 years.	4. Certain	However, if we don't follow through, we know we have no choice but to close the Michigan plant.

TABLE

| 4.3 | **ORGANIZING RATIONALES FOR PROFESSIONAL COMMUNICATION** |

Strategy	Use	Options	Example
Definition	Delineates exact dimensions of item or topic	• formal • experiential • stipulated	Professional communication is a class that explains effective strategies for communicating in industry.
Type/ Classification	Establishes item's commonality with known commodities	• complete • incomplete	Professional communication is part of a group of courses derived from logic, rhetoric, and speech.
Status	Provides current picture/information	• over time • current • relative	Professional communication is often a core course in a business degree.
Summary	Provides overall abstract/distillation	• detailed • general	Professional communication developed over the past 100 years; its origin is rhetoric.
Description	Portrays image of the topic	• detailed • summary	Professional communication is comprised of several modules, including audience, purpose, and business formats.
Chronology	Provides logical/historical sequence	• sequential • historical	The first courses were offered in the nineteenth century. As business evolved, communication became more demanding.
Process Analysis	Delineates individual steps in the activity	• detailed • summary	Professional communication proceeds from development of purpose to audience analysis to selection of facts and strategies.
Comparison/ Contrast	Defines the item by relation to similar/differing items or topics	• similarities • differences • mixed	Professional communication is similar to composition in its reliance on rhetoric, but differs in its practical application.
Causality	Defines contributing elements/agencies	• primary • sufficiency	Professional communication's current status is a result of industry demanding that graduates bring more than technical skills.
Interpretation	Assigns meaning to circumstance	• localized • personal • corporate	Professional communication contributes to job opportunity precisely because it contributes to effective decision-making.
Assessment	Provides judgment/ assigns value	• absolute • relative	Used effectively, the principles taught in professional communication have been shown to contribute to job advancement.
Consequences	Projects implications	• immediate • strategic • potential • certain	Not having a background in how to communicate effectively may impede professional advancement.

So far we have defined the information we need and the organizational strategies to use with the respective pieces. Instead of having several filing cabinets worth of data, we might be faced with a stack of approximately 15–20 manila folders worth of information. A good start, but clearly the information has not been suitably compressed to allow us to make our pitch in only 45 minutes. What we do next is try to ascertain how to present the greatest volume of important information in the most concise form. Certainly a narrative account of each point presented as straight text won't do.

We recognize that rather than text, we need to rely on graphical and visual representations if we are going to succeed in compressing our data into a manageable form. Some ideas for this representation will easily come to mind: photos, drawings, graphs, tables. We may also already recognize that these solutions represent graphical equivalents of the organizing rationales we have been discussing. Each represents an option we might use to organize and present information in a manner more readily understood by our audience.

A HOST OF EVERYDAY STRATEGIES

Whether we recognize it or not, this preliminary recognition reflects both our familiarity with and acceptance of using graphics and visual displays to communicate large volumes of complex information. Although we may have paid little attention to them, these types of graphical equivalents greet us on a routine basis. When we travel, for instance, we rely on airline, train, or bus schedules. When we follow instructions for assembling a product, we are involved with process analysis. When we make determinations about why we didn't like a particular movie, we are making an assessment.

One place in which we have come to expect these graphical displays is in our local and national newspapers. All 12 organizational strategies typically find their ways into the articles we read. Graphical versions, both explicit and implicit, are also commonplace. Newspapers would be communication nightmares if they didn't effectively employ graphical representations to convey complex information. We would find it unacceptable if we woke to find the daily weather report displayed as lengthy discussions of temperatures and barometric pressure readings. We would be offended if we had to wade through lengthy text to determine the relative rankings of our favorite teams instead of having this information displayed in clear tables of descriptive statistics. We'd find ourselves confused when searching for that personal ad for a used car if the hundreds of ads, services, and garage sales randomly filled the newspaper's concluding pages instead of being grouped into related collections. We might not even know how to voice our dissatisfaction if the editors did not give a clear process for submitting comments.

PUTTING INFORMATION TO WORK

With this knowledge of organizational strategies and their graphical equivalents, let's return to our E-Disc interview. Where we had left off, the company had defined the topics to address and some of the means for conveying the information. The next step would be to consider the form each graphical solution might take (Table 4.4). Tying the process together, Table 4.5 denotes the relationship among the question we are answering, its graphical representation, and the organizational strategy represented.

Using the means we have been discussing to achieve graphical compression of information, your colleagues at E-Disc have come up with a series of 15 slides, including illustrations, pie charts, line charts, column graphs, flowcharts, area graphs, tables, and organization charts—a broad representation of graphical choices (Figures 4.4–4.18). The correspondence between the 10 points you want to make with the venture capitalists and the charts developed by your staff is shown in Table 4.6.

4.4 POTENTIAL STRATEGIES FOR GRAPHICAL/VISUAL REPRESENTATIONS

Information Being Presented	Potential Graphical Solution
1. What your idea is . . .	Photos/drawings/side-by-side images/cutaway views/exploded views
2. How the plan will work . . .	Flowcharts/schematics depicting process
3. How the plan was developed . . .	Time Line: Development history; causal agents leading to current status
4. How it compares to other ventures . . .	Table/Bar Graph: Your data compared to other comparable commodities
5. Costs/development to date . . .	Table: Activities completed; benefits; time frames Graph: Status completed
6. Money/time to implement the idea . . .	Graph/Pie Chart: Showing projections
7. Potential markets . . .	Graph/Table: Depicting market share
8. The risks involved . . .	Table/Graph: Comparative risks/benefits
9. Track record of the firm . . .	Table/Chart: Explanation of successes/credentials of the partners in E-Disc
10. Return on investment . . .	Chart: Comparison of earning anticipated over time

A PRELIMINARY ASSESSMENT OF GRAPHICAL PERFORMANCE

So, the story's complete! You can now make your pitch within the established time constraints. All we have to do is wait for tomorrow. Or, is the story complete? Your communication expert (Marketing V.P.) starts asking questions about what the graphs and tables mean. You answer that you'll be adding clarifications as you go. A similar argument was made by the NASA and Thiokol engineers at the congressional hearings. In fact, many of the slides presented at the hearings included a footnote that stated: "Information on this page was prepared to support an oral presentation and cannot be considered complete without the oral discussion."[2] This may be an attempt to sidestep your responsibilities as the designer of the graphical representation, but it's not a very sound approach.

Responding to this strategy, Edward Tufte noted: "Such defensive formalism should provoke rambunctious skepticism: they suggest a corporate distrust both of the chart maker and of any viewers of the chart."[3] Though you certainly will have opportunity to reinforce the charts and graphs, whether they are incorporated into a document or used as the substance of a presentation, there is an

TABLE 4.5 THE RELATIONSHIP BETWEEN GRAPHIC STRATEGY AND ORGANIZING RATIONALE

Action	Graphic Strategy	Organizing Rationale
What your idea is —scope —relation to known products	Photos/drawings/side-by-side images/cut-away views/exploded views	Description/Definition Classification
How the plan will work —Sequence/steps involved	Flowchart/Schematic: Steps, process, how your idea works	Process Analysis
How the plan was developed	Time Line: Development history; causal agents leading to current status	Chronology
How it compares to other ventures	Table/Bar Graph: Your data compared to other comparable commodities	Comparison/Contrast
Costs/development to date	Table/Graph: Activities completed; benefits; time frames	Status
Money/time to implement the idea	Graph/Pie Chart: Depicting relative progress versus remaining work	Interpretation
Potential markets	Graph/Table: Depicting market share	Assessment
The risks involved	Table/Graph: Comparative risks/benefits	Causality
Track record of the firm	Table: Detail on successes, magnitude of successes, credentials of E-Disc employees	Interpretation
Return on investment	Chart: Comparison of earnings anticipated over time	Consequences

TABLE 4.6 THE E-DISC OVERVIEW

The content/focus	Figure number
1. The idea	4.4
2. How the plan will work	4.5
3. How the plan was developed	4.6
4. How it compares to other ventures	4.7
5. Costs/development to date	4.8
6. Money/time needed to implement the idea	4.9–4.14
7. Potential markets	4.15
8. Risks involved	4.16
9. Track record of the firm	4.17
10. Return on investment	4.18

FIGURE 4.4

The E-Disc
Concept

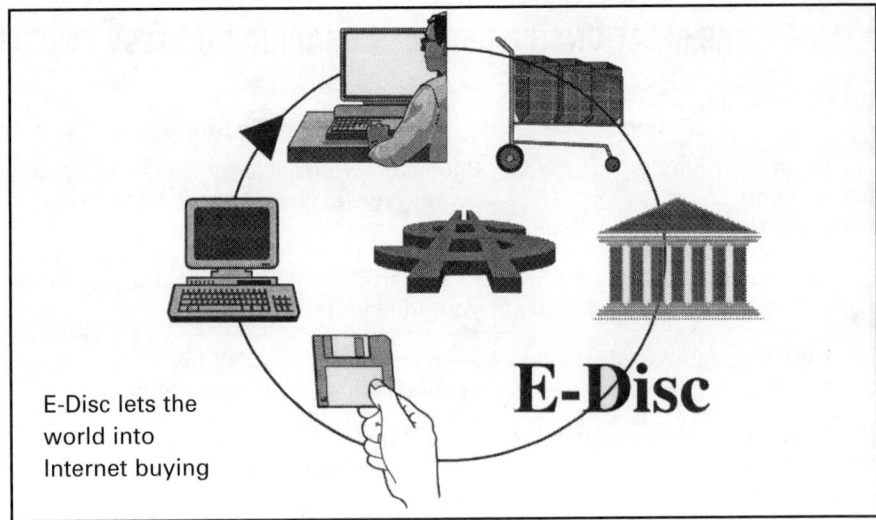

E-Disc lets the
world into
Internet buying

E-Disc

FIGURE 4.5

How the Plan
Works

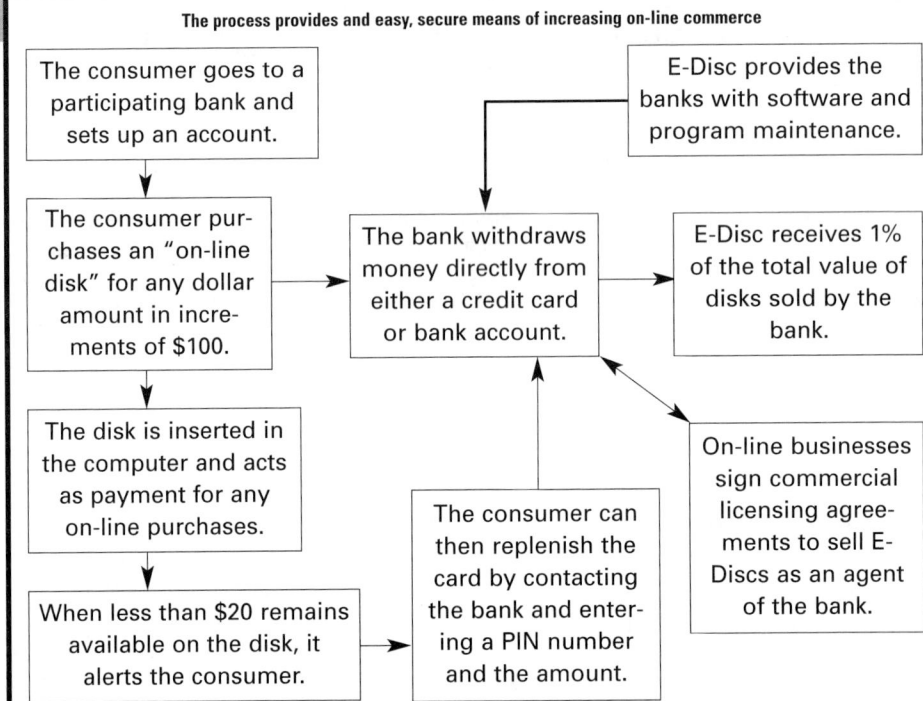

The process provides and easy, secure means of increasing on-line commerce

The consumer goes to a participating bank and sets up an account.

E-Disc provides the banks with software and program maintenance.

The consumer purchases an "on-line disk" for any dollar amount in increments of $100.

The bank withdraws money directly from either a credit card or bank account.

E-Disc receives 1% of the total value of disks sold by the bank.

The disk is inserted in the computer and acts as payment for any on-line purchases.

The consumer can then replenish the card by contacting the bank and entering a PIN number and the amount.

On-line businesses sign commercial licensing agreements to sell E-Discs as an agent of the bank.

When less than $20 remains available on the disk, it alerts the consumer.

FIGURE 4.6

The Chronology of
E-Disc

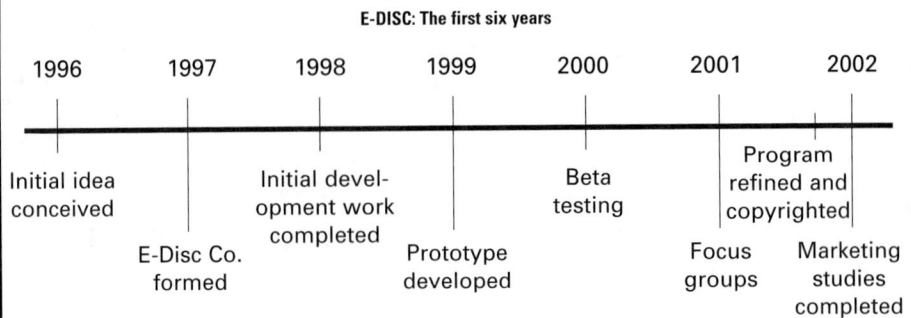

E-DISC: The first six years

1996	1997	1998	1999	2000	2001	2002

Initial idea conceived

E-Disc Co. formed

Initial development work completed

Prototype developed

Beta testing

Program refined and copyrighted

Focus groups

Marketing studies completed

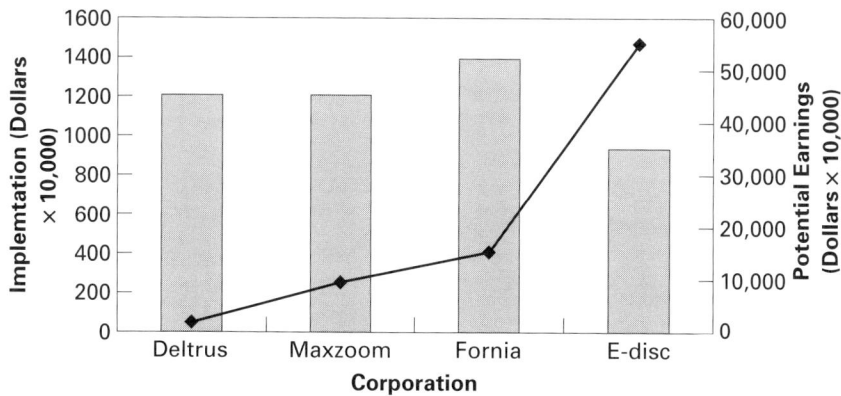

FIGURE 4.7

Comparative
Earnings Potential

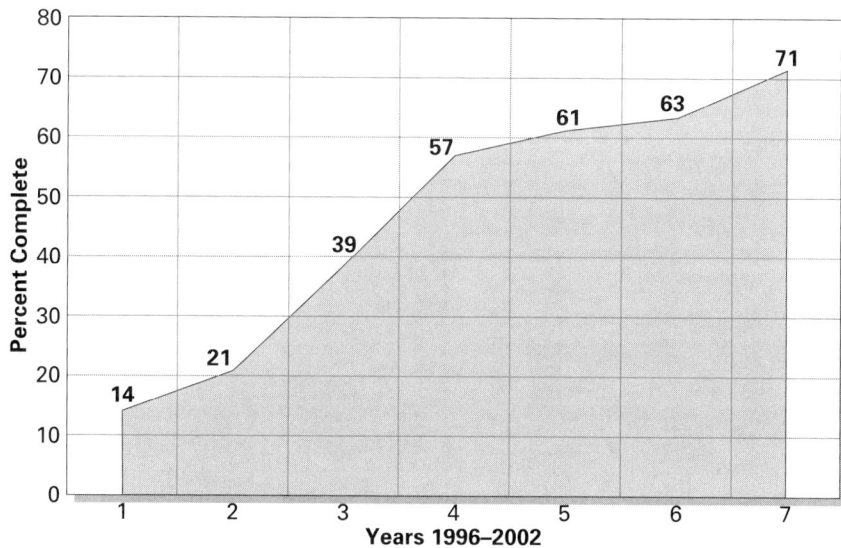

FIGURE 4.8

Development
Progress

FIGURE 4.9

Annual Expenses
by Category

	Travel	Salaries	Rent	Training	Supplies	Utilities	Phone	Misc	Subtotal
Jan	1200	8600	2200	800	130	210	140	110	13,390
Feb	1800	8600	2200	1100	120	300	190	240	14,550
March	3700	8600	2200	300	60	300	120	7900	23,180
April	2200	8600	2200	1700	90	240	350	140	15,520
May	1800	8600	2200	1400	140	260	210	640	15,250
June	4700	8600	2200	0	310	280	260	80	16,430
July	1200	8600	2200	2500	180	360	190	120	15,350
August	1500	8600	2200	0	120	410	170	1100	14,100
Sept	3900	8600	2200	0	530	340	140	370	16,080
Oct	2200	8600	2200	0	150	340	230	110	13,830
Nov	1800	8600	2200	3800	210	390	210	110	17,320
Dec	900	8600	2200	700	120	210	120	180	13,030
Avg.	$2241	$8600	$2200	$1025	$180	$303	$194	$925	15,669
Total	26,900	103,200	26,400	12,300	2160	3640	2330	11,100	188,030

FIGURE 4.10

Monthly Expenses

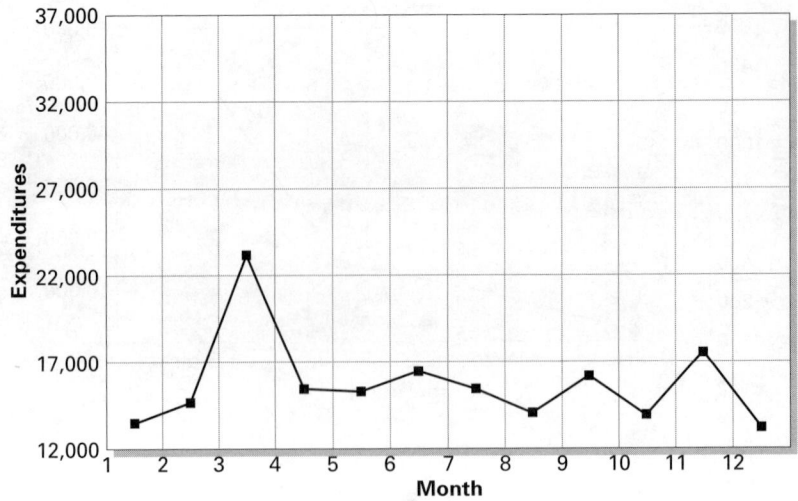

FIGURE 4.11

Comparative
Services Costs

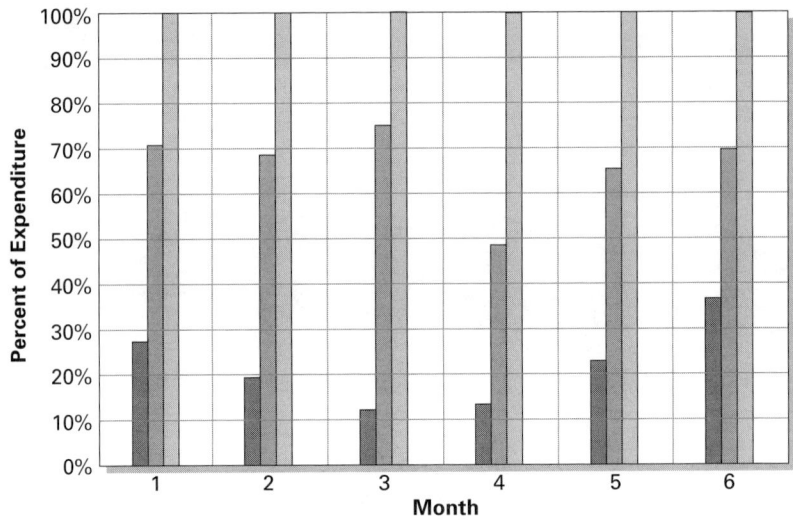

FIGURE 4.12

Services in
Perspective

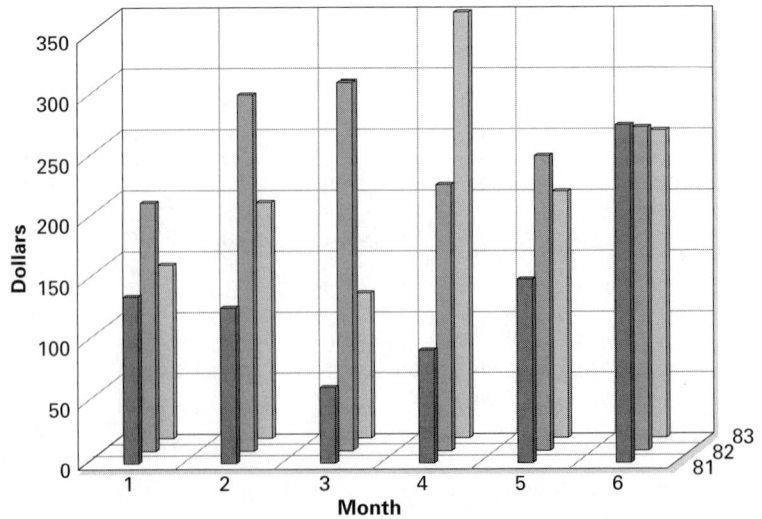

FIGURE 4.13

January Expenses

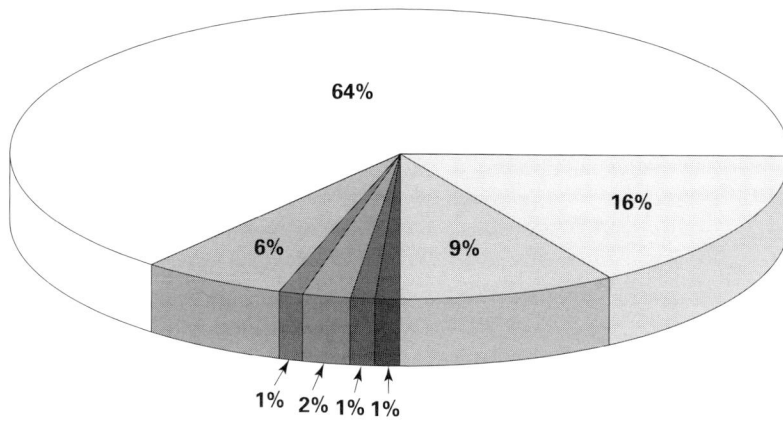

January Expenses

64%

16%

9%

6%

1% 2% 1% 1%

FIGURE 4.14

Phased Investment

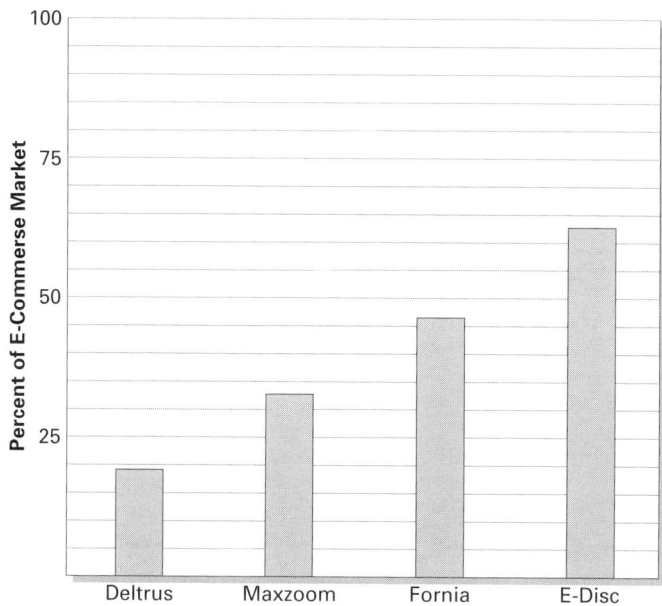

Phased Investment

Percent Complete

Cost in Thousands

Years 2001–2006

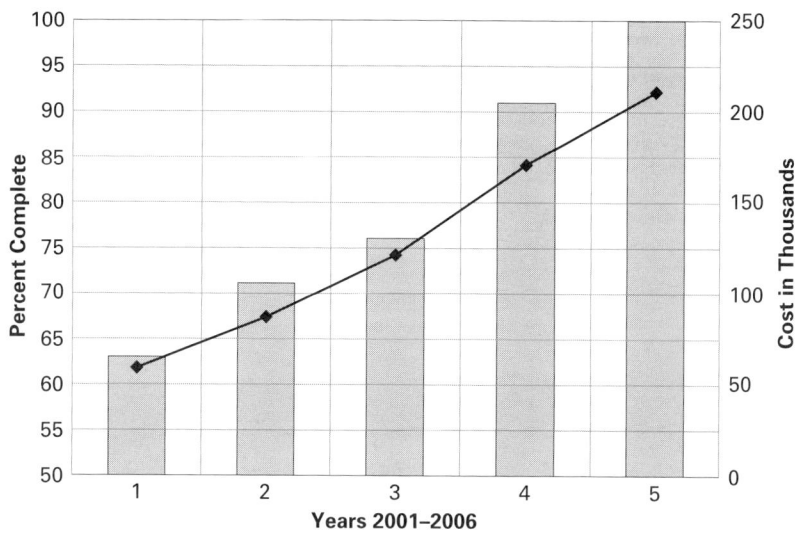

Percent of E-Commerse Market

Deltrus   Maxzoom   Fornia   E-Disc

FIGURE 4.16

The Relative Risks

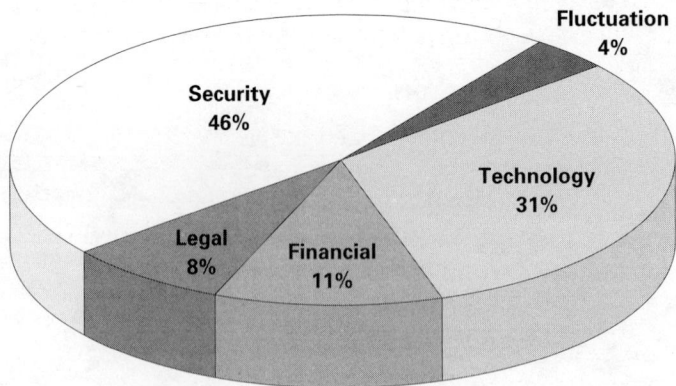

The Relative Risks pie chart

- Security 46%
- Technology 31%
- Financial 11%
- Legal 8%
- Fluctuation 4%

FIGURE 4.17

The Organization
of E-Disc

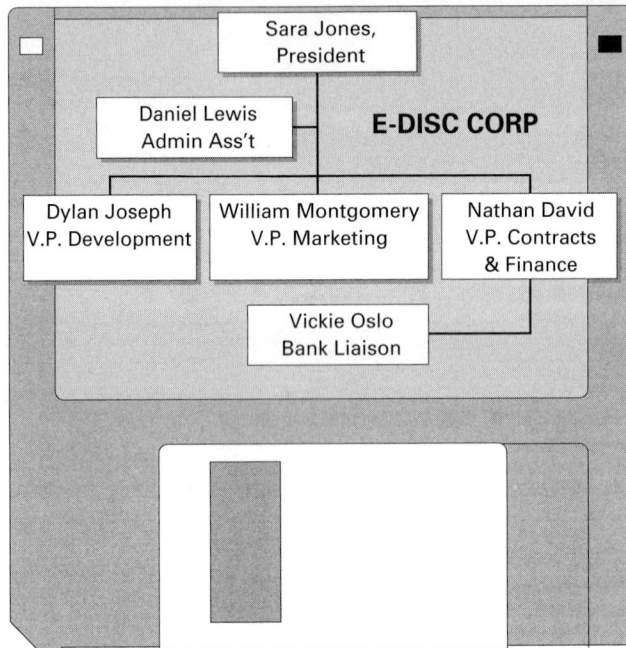

E-DISC CORP

Sara Jones, President

Daniel Lewis Admin Ass't

Dylan Joseph V.P. Development

William Montgomery V.P. Marketing

Nathan David V.P. Contracts & Finance

Vickie Oslo Bank Liaison

FIGURE 4.18

A Significant
Return on
Investment

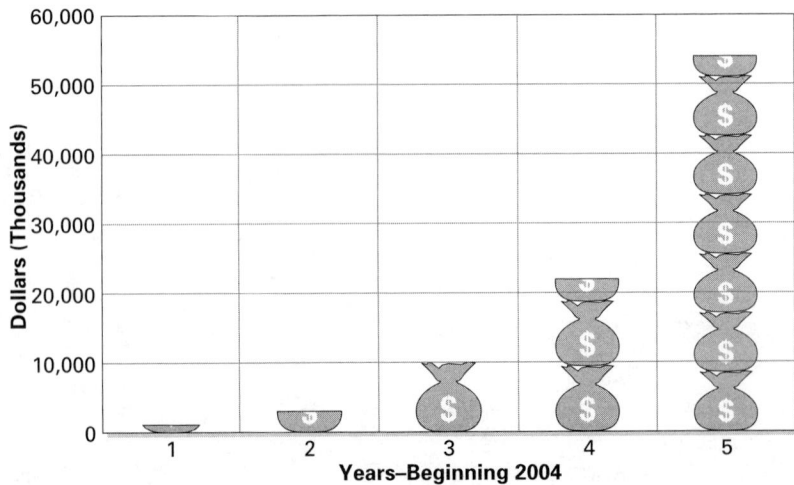

Dollars (Thousands) vs Years—Beginning 2004

Dollars (Thousands): 0, 10,000, 20,000, 30,000, 40,000, 50,000, 60,000

Years—Beginning 2004: 1, 2, 3, 4, 5

expectation that the graphs, figures, and tables will have the strength to do their jobs. We want our materials to represent a winning formula, not replicate the *Challenger* disaster.

Let's look at whether the E-Disc collection has done its job. We can do this most easily by restating the intent of each slide in the form of a question. For instance, since the first image was intended to explain the company's idea, our first question might be: Does the first slide (Figure 4.4) succeed in explaining the company concept? Each slide, in turn, can then be given a score based on its success. A score of "1" indicates the purpose has been attained, "2" indicates partial success, and "3" means the illustration misses the mark. If, as we presume, we have constructed our materials effectively, we should get straight 1's.

Far from the desired straight 1's, our assessment gives us a totally different impression of our performance: Of 15 slides, five do a good job of telling the story, five are partially successful, and five(an equal share) are completely off target (Table 4.7). Five of 15 (33%) is hardly an unacceptable grade. Before we use this analysis to begin our revision process, we need to recognize that there is still another scale that needs to be assessed. To understand this second score, we need to take a moment to understand the language and expectations of graphs and tables.

GRAPHICS: A BASIC OVERVIEW

Analogous to the concepts of descriptive and inferential statistics, graphs and tables can be designed to be either descriptive or inferential. Graphs and tables can have a number of purposes. In general, there are seven circumstances in which graphics may be particularly useful:

- To describe a complex or new idea
- To present abstract structures
- To convey spatial relationships
- To provide a meaningful context for unfamiliar information
- To assist readers in their attempts to solve problems
- To detail steps in a procedure
- To reinforce and help remember information provided in text

These seven circumstances correlate extremely well with those cited by the two leading experts on graphics and graphical display of complex information, Edward Tufte and Jacques Bertin. As one component of "graphical excellence," graphs, according to Tufte, must have "a reasonably clear purpose: description, exploration, tabulation, or decoration." Explicitly examining how graphics aid in communication, Bertin, in his book, *Semiology of Graphics,* maintains that graphical depiction of information serves to help the audience with three functions: 1) recording information, 2) communicating information, and 3) processing information.

The first role fulfilled by graphics is recording information. In performing their jobs, graphics create "a comprehensive inventory of information." The clear correspondences among the pieces of information eliminate any need for memorization. "The subway diagram which can be put into one's pocket, the highway map, the data table enable us to avoid the task of memorizing all the lines, all the correspondences, all the numbers. They are available in one document which assembles them and renders them conveniently accessible." At the next level are

4.7 ASSESSMENT OF E-DISC GRAPHICS—PURPOSE

E-Disc Slide	Figure #	Purpose	Ranking			Explanation of Ranking
			1	2	3	
1	4.4	Have I explained the concept?	✓			Materials appear to tell the story.
2	4.5	Have I explained how the idea works?	✓			Flow chart provides clear understanding.
3	4.6	Have I explained how the plan was developed?		✓		The time line shows the major components of the project, but does not at all address "how it was developed." What void is the project intended to fill?
4	4.7	Have I explained how E-Disc fares relative to other projects?		✓		The chart shows E-Disc is cheaper to develop and has a greater earning potential, but how have the others actually done? How are the others related?
5	4.8	Have I explained the cost/development to date?		✓		The percentage complete is explained, but there is no suggestion of costs to date.
6–11	4.9–4.14	Have I explained the money and time needed to implement the project?				
	4.9		✓			Details the specific anticipated expenditures
	4.10				✓	Adds no value, but it's pretty
	4.11				✓	Knowing the percentages of each of these three costs is absolutely meaningless.
	4.12				✓	And these tell us what?
	4.13				✓	Adds nothing of value beyond the detail provided in Figure 9.
	4.14		✓			Provides a worthwhile perspective over time
12 ket"	4.15	Have I explained the potential market?		✓		What does the "percent of e-commerce mar- mean? Can it be understood as a single entity? What market in particular?
13	4.16	Have I explained the risks involved?		✓		What is the likelihood that your venture capitalists will know how big the 100% risk is? Are all the risks important only in terms of dollars?
14	4.17	Have I explained the company's track record?			✓	Six names on an organizational chart do nothing to suggest past success, credibility, and credentials.
15	4.18	Have I explained the potential		✓		Certainly, the venture capitalists will see

graphics used to communicate information. With the help of our visual memory, these graphics create a memorizable image. Like sketches on a blackboard, these graphics are inscribed in our memory where they later can be recalled at the time of an exam, a conversation, a meeting about a research project, or the process of reaching a decision. Last, combining the attributes of the first two types of graphics, graphic representations can reduce large inventories of related information into a message that can be assimilated into memory. Like maps in an atlas, these collections allow us to see and discover the correlations and associations among the pieces, thus increasing comprehension, retention, and communication.[4]

These three levels of increasing sophistication (providing an inventory, communicating messages, assisting in discovery and resolution of problems) parallel the historical evolution of graphics as aids in professional communication. Originally graphs arose from observation, and, more specifically, from devices that mechanically recorded observation. As illustrated by the weather clock, invented in the latter part of the seventeenth century, and the Universal Wind Machine, invented in 1726, graphs were initially valued as representations of observable phenomena. The weather clock, which measured wind direction, rainfall, and temperature, recorded the data on a moving chart using a pen attached to a float on the surface of a thermostat. The Universal Wind Machine also used graphs to represent an inventory of observations. Writing about the invention—essentially an anemometer that recorded the strength and direction of the wind—a contemporary of the inventor noted: "That which is most singular about this anemometer is that one does not need to remain in its presence for observation and that one finds marked on the paper all the changes that have occurred either in the direction or the velocity of the wind, the time of these changes, and the duration of each wind."[5]

By the latter part of the eighteenth century and the early part of the nineteenth century, we see a movement toward graphs as vehicles for displaying messages and contributing to the purposeful analysis of experimental results. The two men most often associated with the transition, the "great inventors of modern graphical designs" were J. H. Lambert, a Swiss-German scientist and mathematician, and William Playfair, an English political scientist.[6] Advocating the use of graphical methods to assist with understanding observed events, Lambert wrote: "We have in general two variable quantities, x, y, which will be collated with one another by observation, so that we can determine for each value of x, which may be considered as an abscissa, the corresponding ordinate y. Were the experiments or observations completely accurate, these ordinates would give a number of points through which a straight or curved line should be drawn."[7]

Expanding significantly on the advances in the uses of graphical methods as a means of communication, Playfair published *The Commercial and Political Atlas*, credited with introducing most of the contemporary forms of charts and graphs. In the opening pages of his book, Playfair announces his intent to break with the past, to employ graphics to aid in the comprehension and appreciation of complex information:

> Information that is imperfectly acquired, is generally as imperfectly retained; and a man who has carefully investigated a printed table, finds, when done, that he has only a very faint and partial idea of what he has read; and that like a figure imprinted on sand, is soon totally erased and defaced. The amount of mercantile transactions in money, and of profit or loss, are capable of being as easily represented in drawing, as any part of

space, or as the face of a country; though, till now, it has not been attempted. Upon that principle these Charts were made; and, while they give a simple and distinct idea, they are as near perfect accuracy as is any way useful. On inspecting any one of these Charts attentively, a sufficiently distinct impression will be made, to remain unimpaired for a considerable time, and the idea which does remain will be simple and complete, at once including the duration and the amount.[8]

Over the two centuries since Playfair's work, there has been much research done on graphical display of information, including advances in information processing, perceptual sciences, statistics, human factors, design, and psychology. Together the insights gained have helped to define improved means of portraying information graphically. By the early days of the twentieth century, graphical displays were becoming a common part of business administration and decision-making, as is suggested by the 1909 recommendations made by Irénée Du Pont, Du Pont Corporation's Director of Development:

This is to suggest a wider use of plotting paper for indicating the results of sundry experiments. For instance, in the black powder investigation, if a plot be made showing the time of wheeling or the total number of revolutions as abscissae, and velocity as ordinates, the results are shown much clearer than by a simple tabulation. This method of quickly arriving at generalization has been found to be advantageous.[9]

With an enthusiasm and optimism equal to that voiced in Playfair's introduction, these twentieth century advances gave rise early to an overly optimistic belief that a single set of optimum graphical standards might be developed. As explained by the American Statistical Association in 1915: "If simple and convenient standards can be found and made generally known, there will be possible a universal use of graphic methods with a consequent gain to mankind because of the greater speed and accuracy with which complex information may be imparted and interpreted."[10] Nonetheless, further assessments of graphical displays demonstrated that, as with most communication activities, no absolutes exist.

THE EXPECTATIONS FOR GRAPHICS

Rather than relying on standards that provide for "universal use of graphical methods," your graphical representations must be customized, aided by guidelines that have evolved with the enhanced knowledge of how and why graphics help communicate. These guidelines, like many others we have discussed in the preceding chapters, do not relieve the obligations of the professional communicator. They merely assist the designer in maximizing the key attributes of effective graphics: efficiency, legibility, and accuracy.

EFFICIENCY

Graphics, like text, demand a certain precision, conciseness, and efficiency, a concept that Bertin expressed as a matter of "mental cost." "Efficiency is defined by the following proposition: If, in order to obtain a correct and complete answer to a given question, all other things being equal, one construction requires a shorter observation time than another construction, we can say it is more efficient for this question."[11] For our purposes, the three primary contributors to graphical efficiency are: 1) choosing the appropriate graphical format, 2) ensuring the shortest path to the primary information, and 3) eliminating extraneous decoration and distractions.

CHOOSING THE APPROPRIATE GRAPHICAL FORMAT. As a first step when examining the information you want to present, you need to determine whether the format should be text, table, or graphic. This decision is largely a function of three factors: 1) the amount of information, 2) the need to read versus the need to visualize the pieces of data, and 3) the relationship among the data. To assist us in this decision, we might employ the same guidance the journal *Human Factors* provides to potential authors. A simple flowchart allows clear definition of when to use text, when tables, and when graphs (Figure 4.19).[12]

This flowchart incorporates conclusions about the presentation of data from extensive research and numerous studies. Best known among these studies was a series conducted in 1927 that evaluated how accurately people could read and understand tables and charts. Washburne, the author of the study, compared various textual, tabular, and graphic presentations of data for three tasks: reading exact values (what he called "specific amounts"), comparing values ("static comparisons"), and identifying and comparing trends in the data ("dynamic comparisons"). His main conclusions were:

(a) bar graphs should be used for complex or slightly complex static comparisons;

(b) pictographs should be used for extremely simple static comparisons;

(c) line graphs should be used for dynamic comparisons; and

(d) tables should be used for portraying specific amounts.[13]

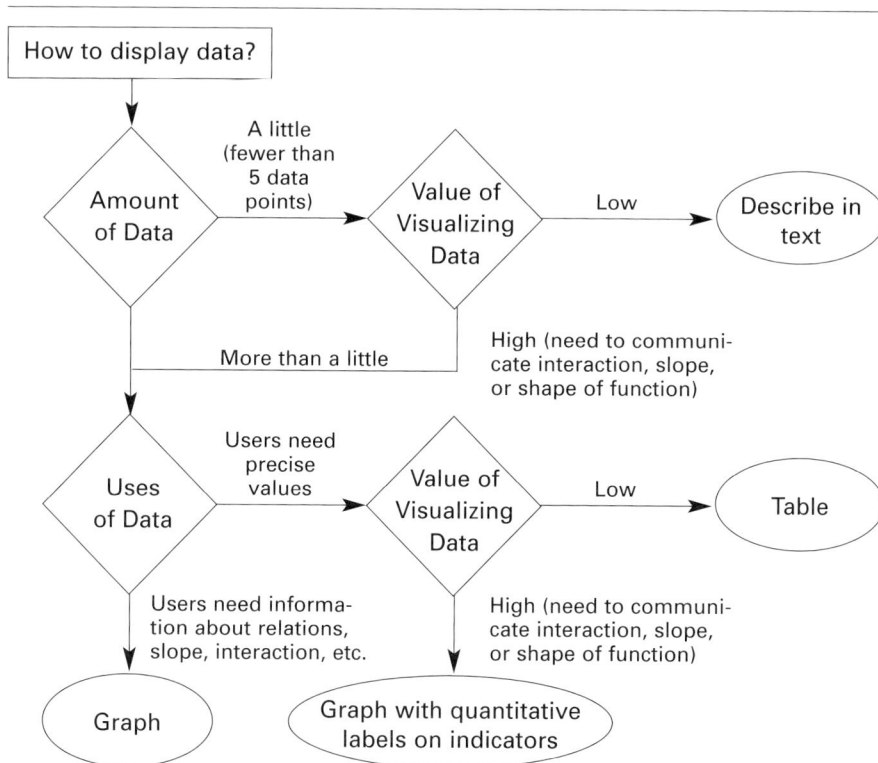

FIGURE 4.19

The Initial Decision Regarding Graphics

In the intervening years since Washburne's study, numerous studies have reconfirmed his conclusions; in addition, cognitive psychologists have provided what is believed to be the psychology underlying Washburne's observations. There is a "naturalness of bars for categorical information and lines for ordinal or interval data. Bars are like containers or fences, which enclose one set of entities and separate them from others. Lines are like paths or outstretched hands, which connect separate entities."[14] As the Human Factors and Ergonomics Society concludes, the collective research of three-quarters of a century supports a number of basic recommendations for selecting an appropriate form for presenting complex information:

- Use either a line graph or a bar graph if readers need to determine relative or absolute amounts.
- Use a line graph if readers need to determine the relationship between two functions (the *x*- and *y*-axes).
- Use a bar graph if readers need to determine the difference between functions.
- Use a pie chart or divided bar graph (stacked bar graph) if readers need to determine proportions but not absolute amounts.
- Use a scatter plot if readers need to determine the degree of correlation between two functions.
- Use a line graph if readers need to detect interactions between independent functions.[15]

ENSURING THE SHORTEST PATH TO THE IMPORTANT INFORMATION. Tables and charts can be as simple or complex as you choose to make them. Your goal, however, is to make certain your graphics are as useful as possible. Even the most accomplished communicators may become too focused on introducing a large number of information items and, thereby, lose track of the chart's usability and readability. For example, we might consider a chart published in *The Chronicle of Higher Education,* a publication read by many American university instructors (Figure 4.20).[16] The data have clearly overwhelmed the chart, making the graph difficult to read.

In comparison, let's return to the simple graphs produced in 1913 by the High Explosives Department at Du Pont (Figure 4.21).[17] Here the information is easy to read. Yet, this graph helps highlight an additional caution: Make certain any cross-hatchings in your graphs don't overpower the data.

To guard against such information overflow, the authors of *Graphing Statistics and Data: Creating Better Charts* offer some commonsensical approaches to simplifying graphical complexity:

- Too many bars? Choose a different type of chart.
- Jagged curves? Smooth them.
- Lots of curves? Draw several smaller charts. A line chart becomes difficult to read if it contains many intersecting curves. Drawing a suite of charts can clear up the picture.
- Lots of dots? Aggregate or draw several small charts in which you isolate critical portions of the larger graph.
- Complex comparisons? Place information needed to draw contrasts or comparisons as close together as possible; minimize the number of items between the images to be compared or contrasted.[18]

FIGURE 4.20 When Staying in the Lines Isn't Easy

	Stock Price 12/31/99	Stock Price 12/31/99
Apollo Group Inc.[1]	$20.06	$32.81
Agency Education Group Inc	4.44	5.75
Career Education Corp,[2]	38.38	50.75
Connthian Colleges Inc.[3]	23.88	40.25
DeVry Inc.	18.75	30.05
Education Management Corp.	14.00	32.63
ITT Education Services Inc.	15.44	27.10
Stayer Education Inc.	19.75	35.00
Sylvan Learning Systems Inc.	13.00	20.63
U. of Phoenix Online[4]	–	29.19
Whitman Education Group Inc.	2.75	3.00
Index		

[1]Stock split 3 for 2 on February 6.2001
[2]Stock split 2 for 1 on August 28, 2000
[3]Stock split 2 for 1 on December 18, 2000
[4]Closing price was $17.81 on first day
 of trading, September 28, 2000

Index: December 31, 1999 = 100

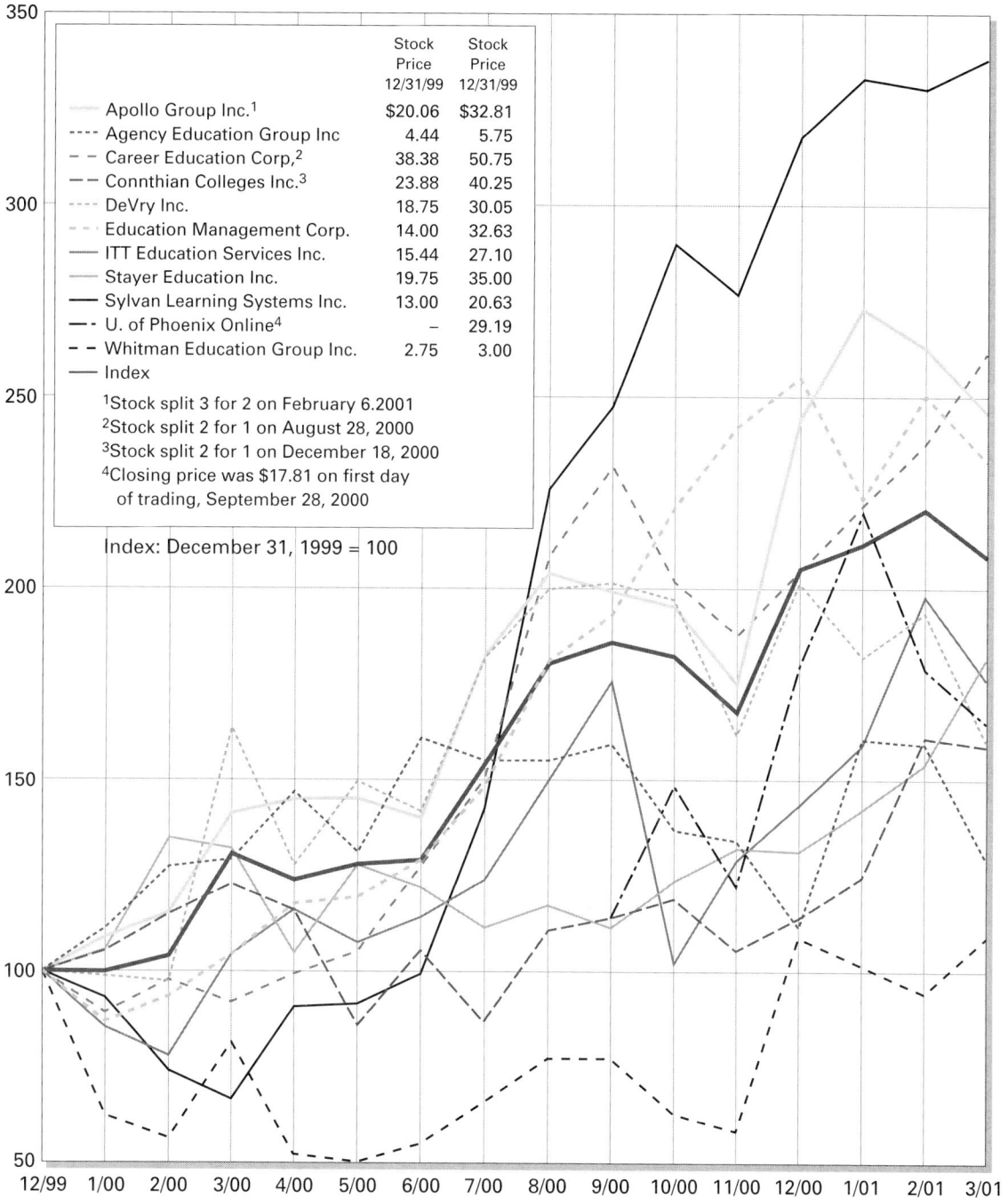

Source: Copyright 2001. The Chronicle of Higher Education. Reprinted with permission.

FIGURE 4.21

Easy Reading: The
Value of Simplicity

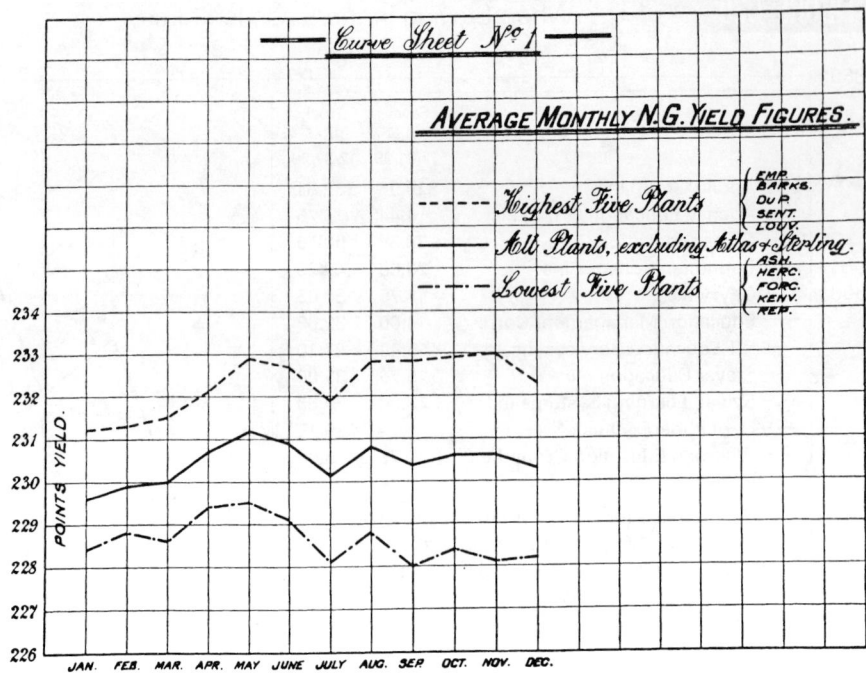

Source: Reprinted with permission of the Association for Business Communication.

ELIMINATING EXTRANEOUS DECORATION AND DISTRACTIONS. In his book, *The Visual Display of Quantitative Information,* Edward Tufte coined the term "chartjunk" to refer to any extraneous elements in a chart, whether they pertained to unnecessary borders, clever ways of changing the data into misleading images, or simply just "stuff" that adds no value. You, as designer, need to concern yourself with how to give the data grace and impact without diminishing the content by adding such unnecessary flourishes. As Tufte effectively summarized: "The best designs . . . are intriguing and curiosity-provoking, drawing the viewer into the wonder of the data, sometimes by narrative power, sometimes by immense detail, and sometimes by elegant presentation of simple but interesting data. But no information, no sense of discovery, no wonder, no substance is generated by chartjunk."[19]

LEGIBILITY

Sometimes the purpose of a graphic illustration can be clear and yet the reader has a hard time deciphering what is being presented. Graphical legibility is determined by the three D's: 1) density, 2) information definition, and 3) data clarity.

DENSITY. Density pertains to the use of available space. Did the designer cram in as many pieces of data as possible, or was the space used effectively and aesthetically? An example of an overly dense illustration is a railroad timetable (Figure 4.22). As Tufte points out when discussing this illustration,

> Space is poorly allocated; much of the paper is given over to categories at the top that labor incessantly to make only three binary distinctions (between New York/New Haven, leaving/arriving, and weekdays/week-

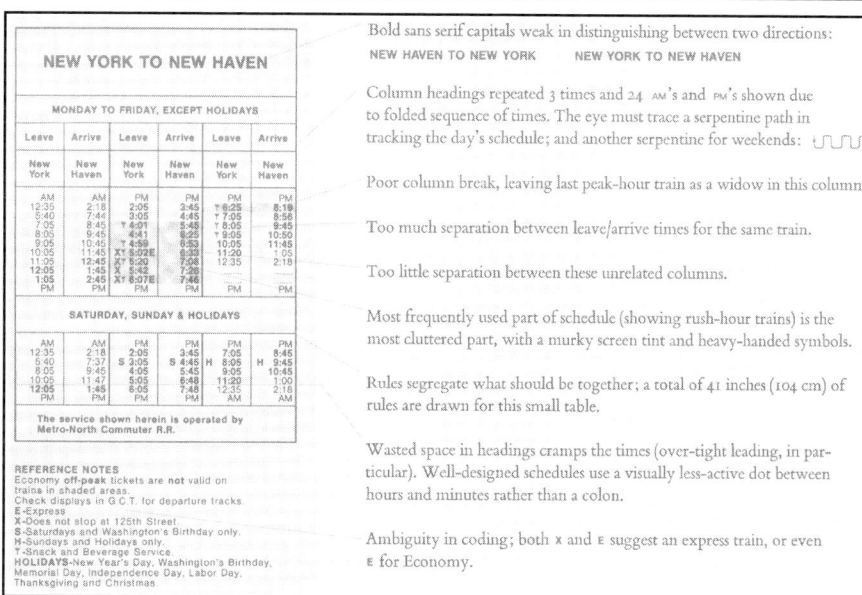

FIGURE 4.22

When Figures Waste Time (and Effort)

Source:: Reprinted with permission of Graphics Press LLC.

ends). All the little boxes create an elaborate but false appearance of systematic order . . . and so, in this timetable, left-over space beneath the introductory grids and rectangles reports on 80 different times of arrival and departure (410 characters). Only 21 percent of the timetable's area is devoted to display of times that trains run. Disorderly footnotes lurk in the basement, waiting to derail insufficiently vigilant travelers.[20]

INFORMATION DEFINITION. Density considers use of space. Information definition deals with the labeling of that space, primarily the labeling of axes and the legends (Figure 4.23). Careful consideration must be given to assigning meaningful terms for the legend (the information plotted on the graph) and for both the vertical and horizontal axes. You must also consider placement of the legend. As a number of studies have found, placing the label directly adjacent to the function or curve improves the speed with which a user can "read" the graph and "may even reduce the error rate where potentially confusing factor lines are dis-

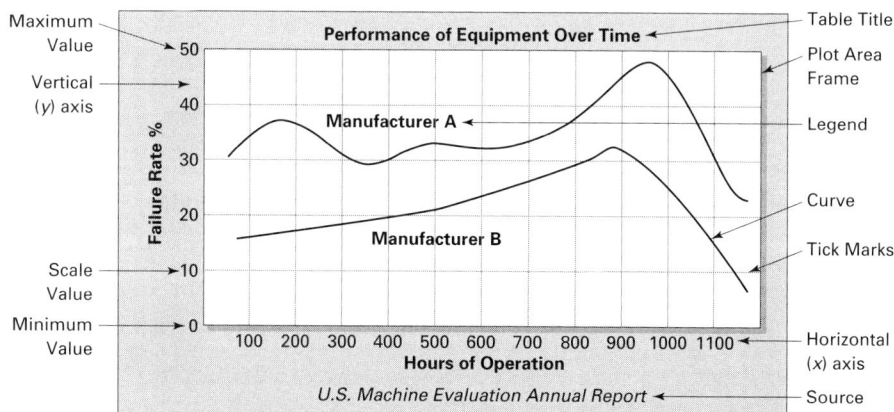

FIGURE 4.23

The Anatomy of a Graph

CHAPTER 4   Arrangement: Ordering and Visualizing Business Information

played."[21] (One reason for paying close attention to legend placement is that many computer programs that automatically convert tables and spreadsheets into graphs do not allow the curves to be labeled directly, instead creating a distantly positioned legend box.)

Last, you need to pay careful attention to scales. Not only should you identify minimum and maximum values, but you also need to consider the appropriate frequency of tick marks on both the *x*- and *y*-axes. Experts recommend that for absolute values you should use intervals that build on base 10, which we use in our counting systems (e.g., 1, 2, 3; 10, 20, 30; 100, 200, 300). For percentages, you should use intervals of 25 (e.g., 25, 50, 75, 100).[22]

DATA CLARITY. Data clarity is often a function of complexity. Yet, it is also often jeopardized when a designer becomes enamored with the drawing capabilities of the computer. Numerous drawing programs make it easy to create all types of perspectives, shadings, patterns, colors, and orientations. As designer, you need to think less about novelty and more about comprehensibility.

For example, if bar graphs are produced in a way that shows three columns of information receding from the reader, you must make certain that the information in the back row is not obscured by that in the first two columns. With colors and patterns, you must make certain the choices are clearly distinguishable from one another, and also that the difference will not be lost should the graphs be reproduced in black and white.

You must also pay attention to the more complicated issue of orientation because it may affect the accuracy of data interpretation. There are seven basic judgments readers make to extract quantitative information from graphs: 1) position along a common scale; 2) position along identical, but not aligned, scales; 3) length; 4) angle; 5) slope; 6) area of uniform objects; and 7) areas among nonuniform objects (Figure 4.24).

As research has shown, the orientation directly affects the accuracy of information extracted from charts. Judgments made after viewing charts whose data is portrayed using common or aligned scales (orientations 1 and 2) are most accurate, followed by those graphs that use length comparisons (orientation 3). Judgments reached using angles and slopes (orientations 4 and 5) are less reliable, and those based on area (orientations 6 and 7) tend to be the least reliable.[23] Specifically because spreadsheets can automatically be converted into dozens of graphical forms, you must make certain that all the factors affecting legibility—density, information definition, and data clarity—are carefully considered. You,

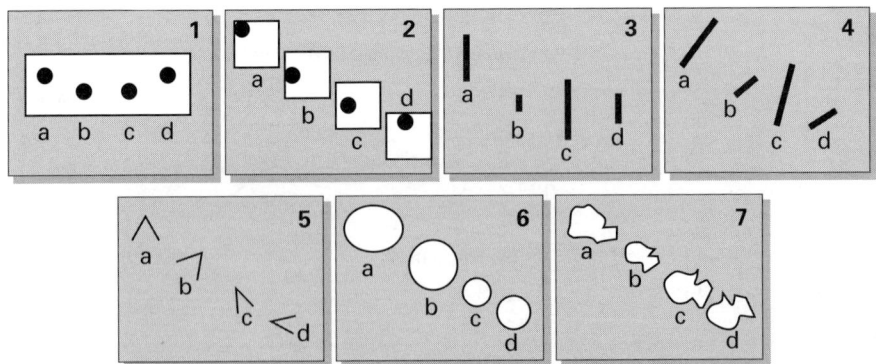

FIGURE 4.24

A Complication of Orientation

Source: Reprinted from *International Journal of Computer Studies,* Vol. 25, William J. Cleveland and Robert McGill, "An Experiment in Graphical Perception," pp. 491–500 (copyright 1986), by permission of Elsevier Science.

as designer, not the computer, are responsible for balancing aesthetics with usability.

ACCURACY

Although intending to create charts that accurately depict information, it is easy to unintentionally contribute to inaccuracy. Data and images conflict; incorrect inferences are drawn. In particular, three common errors contribute to inaccurate representations and readings of graphics: 1) suggestive sizing, 2) context-free data, and 3) maladjusted axes.

SUGGESTIVE SIZING. When values are portrayed as images, the relative sizes of the images must remain consistent with the data. Unintentioned as it may be, images that are disproportionate to the data prompt incorrect conclusions.[24] As a measure of the consistency between data and its portrayal, Tufte developed what he called, "the lie factor":

$$\text{Lie factor} = \frac{\text{size of effect shown in graphic}}{\text{size of effect in data}}$$

If the lie factor equals 1, then there is no distortion; values greater than 1.05 or less than 0.95 indicate a visual distortion. While sometimes the distortion results from ornate decorations or borders, most typically the distortion occurs when the graphic designer introduces clever graphical associations as a means of displaying information. Consider the following example. You want to depict the continuing decrease in the number of public payphones available in your city. Your research shows that in 1980 there were 7,500 machines. A decade later that number had dropped to 4,000. By the year 2000, the number had further decreased to 2,500. In the 20-year period you studied, a 66% decrease had occurred. Using an image of a payphone, you depict your research as shown in Figure 4.25. Unintentionally, you have created a graphic that may mislead your audience.

Based on the numbers they are intended to represent, the payphone on the left should occupy an area three times that occupied by the phone on the right. Instead, the phone occupies an area approximately 6 times as large. Using Tufte's formula, these differences in actual versus displayed values result in a lie factor of 2.08.

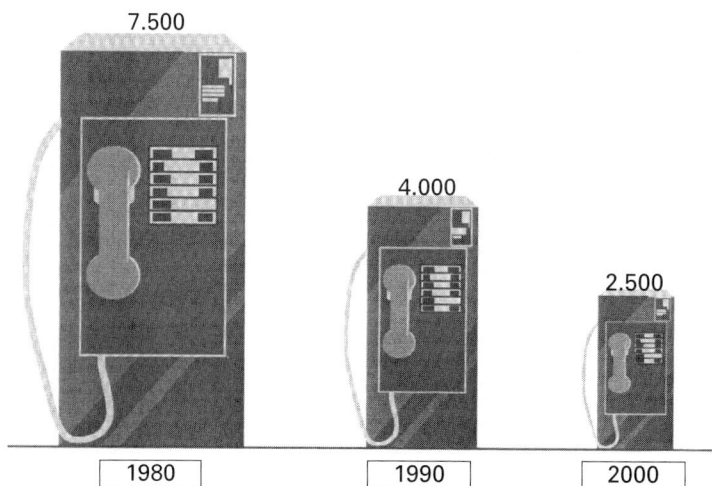

FIGURE 4.25

Demise of the Public Payphone

7.500

4.000

2.500

1980   1990   2000

$$\text{Lie factor} = \frac{\text{Difference in area occupied by payphones for 1980 vs. 2000}}{\text{Actual decrease in number of payphones}}$$

$$= \frac{6.25}{3.0} \qquad = \qquad \mathbf{2.08}$$

CONTEXT-FREE DATA. While suggestive sizing creates a competition between the data and the audience's perceptions, context-free data forces (or allows) the reader too much latitude when drawing conclusions that may or may not be consistent with the intended message. The direct equivalent of allowing facts to speak for themselves, this problem is one of leaving the reader to figure out what you intended, instead of making the context explicit. For instance, consider the following graph (Figure 4.26a). Simply announcing that the Dow Jones average did well in a particular month may be a fair interpretation. However, is the assertion that the market went up because of the announcement of a new cancer drug also valid? If the graph we present only shows one month's

FIGURE 4.26

A Questionable
Performance

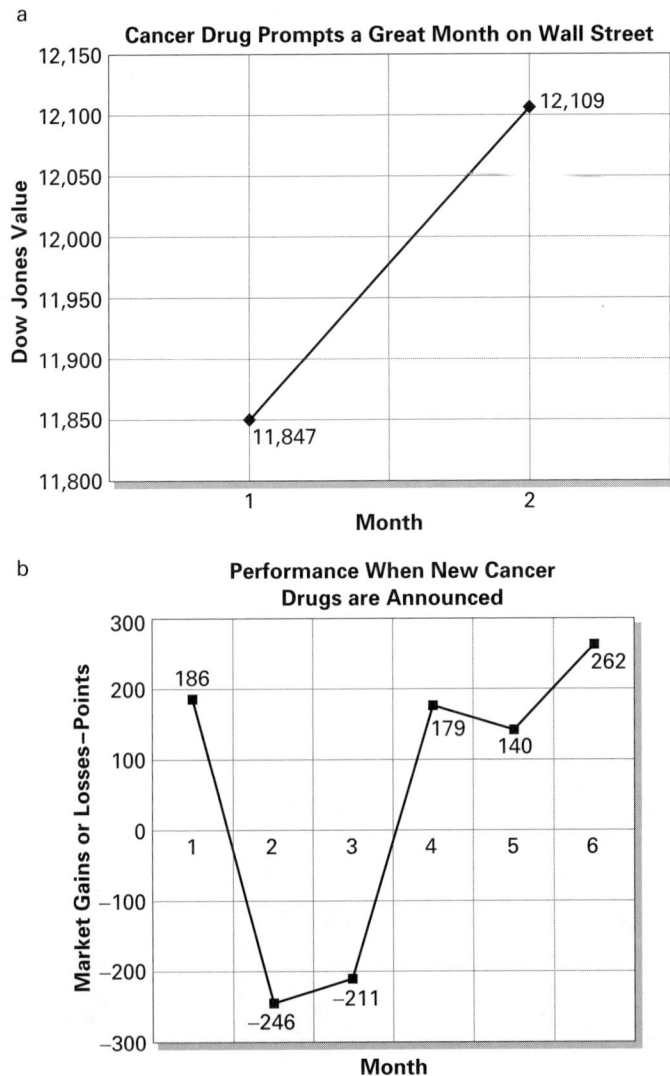

a

Cancer Drug Prompts a Great Month on Wall Street

12,109

11,847

Month

b

Performance When New Cancer Drugs are Announced

186

179

140

262

−211

−246

Month

performance, there may be little opportunity to gauge the appropriateness of this second assertion. However, quite a different story emerges if we are shown the market's performances for each of the last 6 months in which a cancer drug was announced (Figure 4.26b). The context, not previously available, may suggest the initial conclusion was questionable.

MALADJUSTED AXES. Another means of potentially affecting the graph's accuracy is by adjusting the scale on the vertical (*y*) axis. Shortening it may make large changes appear less dramatic; lengthening it, in contrast, can cause just the opposite effect. For example, Figures 4.27a and b depict the same data as shown in Figure 4.26a. Figure 4.27a, with a reduced scale, is suggestive of skyrocketing performance—a misrepresentation aided by the fact that the values themselves have been deleted on the line, and the highest value on the vertical axis is just less than the value of the line (12,109). In contrast, stretching the *y*-axis, as shown in Figure 4.27b, makes the performance appear insignificant, an impression also assisted by the removal of actual values. Your job as designer is to tell the story as accurately as possible: no inappropriate suggestive sizing, no context-free data, and no maladjusted axes.

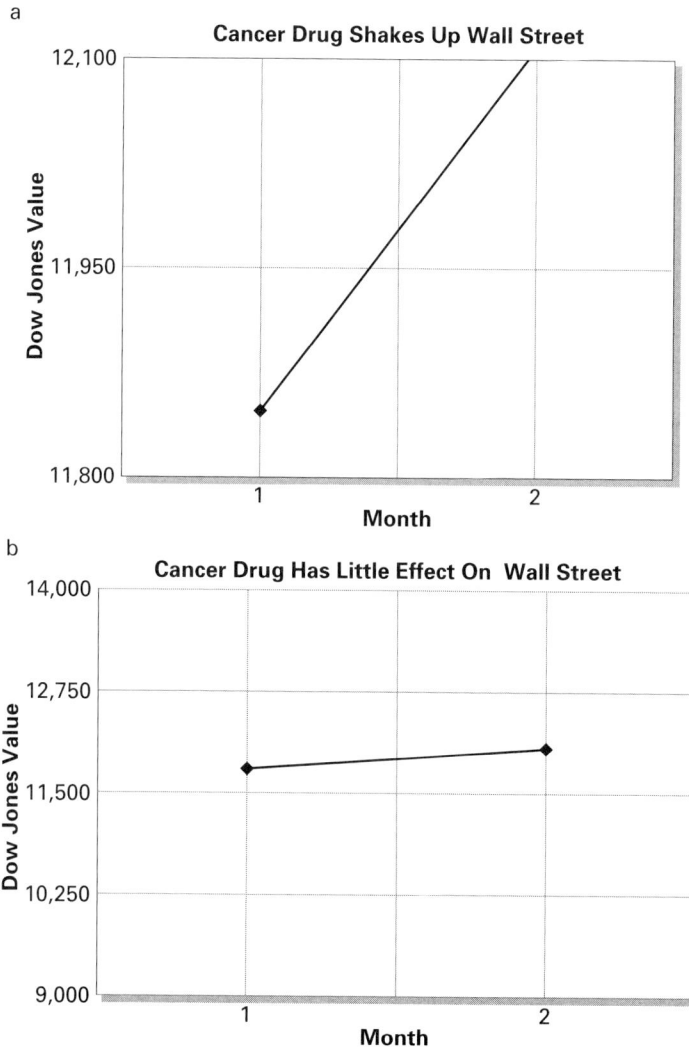

FIGURE 4.27

The Effect of Manipulating the *Y*-Axis

E-DISC GRAPHICAL PRESENTATION: AN ASSESSMENT

With our improved insights into the attributes of "graphical excellence," let's assess our 15 E-Disc slides, using the additional criteria we have just been discussing. When initially assessed, solely in terms of how well they fulfilled their designed purposes, five slides were deemed totally successful, five partially successful, and five totally unsuccessful. To this score let's now add a dimension based on overall effectiveness—or graphical excellence. Table 4.8 shows how well the E-Disc slides perform when evaluated using the criteria of efficiency, legibility, and accuracy.

As Table 4.8 indicates, only three of the 15 slides don't require attention (4.5, 4.6, and 4.9); the remaining 12 slides have areas that need attention. Of these, three of the slides have multiple issues (4.10, 4.14, and 4.18). If we now consider both sets of results (from Tables 4.7 and 4.8), we might be surprised to learn that of our 15 slides, only two (Figures 4.5 and 4.9) don't warrant some degree of rework. Although previously we limped away with a score of 33%, our real score is only a 14% acceptable rating. We've got a good deal of work to do to make tomorrow's meeting a success.

A WORD ABOUT OUTLINES

We'll return to discuss rework of the E-Disc package shortly when we get to the Exercises for this chapter. For now, let's discuss one last topic relative to organizing information—outlines. We have purposely left discussion of outlines until now because we didn't want to turn everyone off. Every student, somewhere during his or her education, has dealt with the instructor who adamantly maintained that every theme, every paper—irrespective of length or complexity—had to be preceded by an outline. It was as if we were all told that we were incapable of organizing or simply couldn't be trusted to organize information in our heads. Those instructions on outlining invariably proceeded from

Efficiency:
1. Using the appropriate graphical format
2. Emphasizing critical information
3. Minimizing extreme decoration and distractions

Legibility:
1. Using space effectively
2. Providing clear and accurate labeling of all information necessary to comprehend the graph
3. Making the data and data points clear

Accuracy:
1. Avoiding using images that are suggestive of impressions different from that supported by the actual data
2. Ensuring the context of the data is clear and appropriate
3. Establishing scales on the horizontal and vertical axes that are complementary to the information being presented

discussion of sentence versus topical outlines to a discussion of rules to follow, such as these:

- There should never be a single point; headings need to be developed by at least two subheads.
- Strict parallelism has to be maintained.
- A series of indentations must be employed to show coordination and subordination.
- Entries should be expressed as complete sentences (as statements, not questions).

In a world filled with short-term and long-term memory studies, it is almost a sign of weakness to suggest that outlines have value. Nevertheless, that is the

TABLE

4.8 ASSESSMENT OF E-DISC GRAPHICS—EFFICIENCY, LEGIBILITY, ACCURACY

E-Disc Slide	Figure #	Efficiency 1	2	3	Legibility 1	2	3	Accuracy 1	2	3	Explanation
4.4	1		✓		✓			✓			Clipboard background distracts from message.
4.5	2	✓			✓			✓			Clear, legible, accurate
4.6	3	✓			✓			✓			Clear, legible, accurate
4.7	4	✓				✓		✓			Issue with placement of legend; also, no values shown
4.8	5	✓			✓				✓		Using a scale to 75% suggests the company is further along than it actually is.
4.9	6	✓			✓			✓			Well designed, no extraneous information
4.10	7	✓				✓		✓			Scale is not good, legends and values missing
4.11	8	✓				✓			✓		Legend needs clarification and repositioning.
4.12	9	✓				✓		✓			Hard to read values, issues with legend, depths (orientation)
4.13	10	✓				✓		✓			Shading an issue; legend is of little value
4.14	11	✓				✓		✓			Legend a problem; scale appears to downplay E-Disc accomplishments to date
4.15	12	✓				✓			✓		No value shown
4.16	13	✓				✓		✓			Shading an issue; values missing
4.17	14		✓		✓			✓			The disk image looks good, but distracts from the main information.
4.18	15		✓			✓		✓			Chartjunk; also misleading. The scales used to depict the bags of money change from column to column, creating misleading impressions of profits.

position we wish to assert. Consider the E-Disc exercise. How many individuals would have had the capacity to organize an equivalent volume of information effectively without some assistance? That assistance, although we may not have recognized it, was provided by the outline we developed in advance of creating the 15 slides. Although the steps we followed did not obey the strict mechanics we have been taught about outlines, they did fulfill the intent. Our plan detailed a progression from selecting individual facts to combining related information to forming strategies to represent the grouped information. Last, we had opportunity to reevaluate and determine where we might make changes or improvements in the structure and the individual components.

Our process allowed our ideas to mature and crystallize. Our outlining process allowed us to visualize options and to analyze alternatives regarding scope, sequencing, depth of information, types of information, presentation strategies, organizational strategies, and conclusions. As such, our outlining process was exactly the type of dynamic, forward-thinking tool our teachers intended when they tried to convince us that outlines had value. You need some form of outline if you are going to use a large volume of information in support of an assignment.

The need for outlining is genuine, regardless of the form it takes. Without an outline, whether you use a sentence, phrase, or other outline form, there remains a strong possibility that information will get lost, or that you will get lost in the process of pulling the information together. With an outline, you can better ensure that each package of information (text or graphic) will be appropriately crafted and targeted:

1) to help contribute to achieving the purpose

2) to be an efficient expression of how that purpose can be achieved

3) to be a clear (legible) statement of ideas, assumptions, supporting data, and conclusions

4) to be an accurate and precise statement.

ORDERING AND VISUALIZING INFORMATION—THE LESSONS

Getting the story right is a function of putting the pieces together in a coherent package. It is the opportunity to make certain that the purpose is achieved and that the presentation is clear, efficient, and accurate. Whether we speak with text or graphics, there are expectations. Organizational strategies need to be aligned with the purposes. Similarly, when we employ graphics to communicate the information, send a message, or aid in the decision process, the choices of the types of graphics and their design must be understood as a series of deliberate choices. Having a plan for the arrangement and presentation of information makes the difference between an integrated package and a package of stuff. Organizing and visualizing information is a full-time job and one that must take place in every phase of developing your response to a communication assignment (Table 4.9).

4.9 ACHIEVING ORGANIZATION: THE MAKING OF A PLAN

Plan	Group related materials. Develop an outline that defines your key points and assertions. Establish a progression of thought that advances your point. Select and apply the appropriate organizing rationales for each segment.
Develop	Use your outline structure as a means of guiding and building your paper. Consider where graphical treatments might ease comprehension. Consider how your main assertions can form the headings, subtitles, and thesis sentences of your major segments.
Evaluate	Periodically check the arrangement, using the perspective of your audience. Assess whether you are maintaining a suitable balance among the segments. Reconsider where to apply narrative approaches and where to let graphics do the heavy lifting.

EXERCISES

☐ **Group**

1. Divide into three groups. The first two groups each rework the E-Disc graphics. The third team represents the venture capitalists.

   a) Each team has 45 minutes to present their revised package.

   b) The venture capitalists then have 15 minutes to explain to which revised package they will award the money. The evaluation criteria are:

      1) how well the package achieves its purpose (both the purpose as a whole and the purposes of the individual graphics)

      2) how well the package demonstrates the principles of efficiency, legibility, and accuracy.

2. Your group is responsible for designing a "Professional Communication" web page for your school or corporation. Using the format below, complete the directions for each of the web pages to be included:

Web-Page Development: Sample information for top page on "Letters"

Web Page Topic: Professional Communication

Development Page—Letters

Subheads	Organizing Rationale	Summary Sentence	Graphic
Components of the letter	Summary	The business letter has the following sections: heading, inside address, salutation, body, closing and signature.	Sample letter with call outs

---

a) the page title and the subheads that will appear on the page,

b) the organizing rationale for the information,

c) a summary statement that explains the relationship between the pages (and with the home page), and

d) the graphical displays that will be used to improve the effectiveness of the communications.

☐ Individual

1. You have just joined the staff of the local newspaper. You need to prepare a movie review for next week's edition. In the review, you are requested to demonstrate some of the strategies you have learned about organizing information.

Here is an e-mail that you received from your boss.

```
Movie Lover -

I need six paragraphs from you. You can cover either something new
or something out on video--your choice. I do need to fill space,
so     I     want     the     review     to     be     structured     as
follows:

Paragraph 1 - description (who's in it, basic details, etc.)
Paragraph 2 - summary (you know, plot)
Paragraph 3 - classification (what type of film is it?)
Paragraph 4 - comparison (how it stacks up against the other films)
Paragraph 5 - interpretation (what's the message?)
Paragraph 6 - assessment (so, is it worth my time and money?)

In the left margin next to each paragraph indicate the structure
(just to remind me in case I get sleepy). Make my readers happy!

                                                        City Editor
```

2. Using newspapers, journals, and magazines, identify narrative and graphical demonstrations of the various organizing rationales.

3. Select an article from a professional journal in your field of study. Assess how effectively the author incorporates and employs graphical representations.

[1] Gregory A. Kimble, *How to Use (and Misuse) Statistics.* Englewood Cliffs, NJ: Prentice Hall, 1978.

[2] *PCSSCA.*

[3] Edward R. Tufte, *Visual Explanations: Images, Quantities, Evidence & Narrative.* Cheshire, CN: Graphics Press, 1997.

[4] Jacques Bertin, *Semiology of Graphics: Diagrams, Networks, Maps.* Trans. William J. Berg. Madison, WI: University of Wisconsin Press, 1983.

[5] Laura Trilling, "Early Experimental Graphs," *British Journal for the History of Science,* Vol. 8, No. 30 (1975), pp. 192–213.

[6] Edward R. Tufte, *The Visual Display of Quantitative Information.* Cheshire, CN: Graphics Press.

[7] Quoted in Trilling, "Early Experimental Graphs."

[8] Quoted in Tufte, *The Visual Display of Quantitative Information.*

[9] Cited in Joanne Yates, "Graphs As Managerial Tool: A Case Study of Du Pont's Use of Graphs in the Early Twentieth Century," *The Journal of Business Communication,* Vol. 22, No. 1 (1985), pp. 5–33.

[10] Cited in T. H. Penniall, "Trends in Graphics," *Ergonomics,* Vol. 23, No. 9 (1980), pp. 921–933.

[11] Bertin, *Semiology of Graphics.*

[12] Douglas J. Gillan, Christopher D. Wickens, J. G. Hollands, and C. Melody Carswell, "Guidelines for Presenting Quantitative Data in HFES Publications," *Human Factors,* Vol. 40, No. 1 (March 1998), pp. 28–41.

[13] Joachim Meyer, "A New Look at an Old Study on Information Display: Washburne (1927) Reconsidered," *Human Factors,* Vol. 39, No. 3 (1997), pp. 333–340.

[14] Jeff Zacks and Barbara Tversky, "Bars and Lines: A Study of Graphic Communications," *Memory and Cognition,* Vol. 27, No. 6 (1997), pp. 1073–1079.

[15] Gillan et al., "Guidelines for Presenting Quantitative Data in HFES Publications."

[16] "The Chronicle Index of For-Profit Higher Education," *The Chronicle of Higher Education,* May 11, 2001, p. A–33.

[17] Yates, "Graphs As a Managerial Tool," p. 14.

[18] Anders Wallgren, Britt Wallgren, Rolf Persson, Ulf Jorner, and Jan-Aage Haaland, *Graphing Statistics and Data: Creating Better Charts.* Thousand Oaks, CA: Sage Publications, 1996.

[19] Tufte, *The Visual Display of Quantitative Information.*

[20] Edward R. Tufte, *Envisioning Information.* Cheshire, CN: Graphics Press, 1990.

[21] R. Milroy, E.C. Poulton, "Labeling Graphics for Improved Reading Speed," *Ergonomics,* Vol. 21, No. 1 (1978), pp. 55–61.

[22] Wallgren et al., *Graphing Statistics and Data.*

[23] William S. Cleveland and Robert McGill, "An Experiment in Graphical Perception," *International Journal of Man-Machine Studies,* Vol. 25 (1986), pp. 491–500.

[24] Tufte, *The Visual Display of Quantitative Information.*

5

Reasoning
Framing the Sound Business Argument

In the early part of the twentieth century when Chief Justice Oliver Wendell Holmes introduced the concept of the "market place of ideas" in his free-speech opinions, he solidified one of the major tenets of American life: We will never be able to suitably judge ideas if we silence voices. As such, free speech, a guiding principle of the Bill of Rights, has always been a hallmark of American life and American law. To some degree, a similar belief operates in the world of free enterprise.

Business relies on continuous decision-making, reinforced by the ability to deliver a sound argument. What must we do next to maintain market share? How do we improve the efficiency of business processes? Who among the staff should we promote? How might we better structure the organization? As we shall study in this chapter, business typically bases its decisions on four types of assertions, each with a unique expected formulation, and each dependent on a particular structuring of evidence. Promoting an effective line of reasoning that contributes to judicious decision-making is a demanding and challenging professional responsibility.

Part of the challenge is dealing with a well-ingrained notion that there must be some scientific method, some computer-driven strategy, or some descendent of formal logic that will allow business decisions to proceed with mathematical certainty. While the computer can perform complex calculations that aid in reaching a decision, it is not a substitute for reasoning. Similarly, the study of formal logic and logical fallacies does not respond to business needs or replicate the conditions for making business decisions. As we shall examine, the business of business is not a study of mathematical certainty nor one of purely logical constructions.

Business decisions rely on judgment as much as on fact, on reasoning as much as on logic. Several additional factors make business decisions unique: 1) Decisions are often made with less than complete information. 2) Business decisions react to circumstance, most typically reflected in a time-dependent environment: and 3) Business decision-making is focused on production of a practical, implementable outcome. Because of these considerations, business decisions are both more complex because of the environment in which they are made and simpler because the line of reasoning need only influence judgment, not withstand the mechanisms used to deconstruct formal truths.

Yet, we don't want to suggest a complete divorce among reasoning, logic, and mathematical proofs. The pathway to achieving effective business reasoning is via rhetoric, which, as we will also briefly examine, is a root of science, math, and logic. As such, we might propose that the answers about how to prepare a convincing business argument lie somewhere between the ancient rhetoricians and the modern businessperson.

Let's use two observations to bookend the discussion. At one end, we might consider the observation made by Heraclitis in 500 B.C. that no man can ever step in the same river twice, that we need to adapt our arguments to an ever-changing environment. As the other bookend, we might recall an observation attributed to one of America's premier business tycoons, Andrew Carnegie. Duly capturing the inherent dynamics of American business, Carnegie supposedly stated that "no one will be a millionaire until he's gone bankrupt at least three times." "Triangulating," as politicians tend to say, between the fifth century B.C. and the twentieth century A.D., observations might lead to two important conclusions: business reasoning is accomplished by careful design, not by computer design, and business reasoning is an art, not a science.

THE BUSINESS OF DECISIONS

In the years immediately preceding 2000, much of the industrialized world was debating the possibility that at precisely 12:01 A.M. on January 2000 all the power plants, banking systems, transportation infrastructure, and everything else from copiers to control rooms dependent on computer chips would cease to function. The anticipated consequences would be followed by global recession, food shortages, and social turmoil. According to the media and the professional literature, a "time bomb" was ticking, and a computer "meltdown" was imminent. Our world for decades to come was going to be embroiled in technologically digging out from the rubble. Even the federal government, anticipating an avalanche of lawsuits, hurried through a law intended to expedite the resolution of legal battles. The problem?

Decades earlier, computer programmers opted to represent years in the computer by a two-digit number: 1955 was 55, 1980 was 80. Year 2000 was going to become "00," a year potentially not decipherable by our computers. Consequently, the concept of a Y2K (Year 2000) bug was born.

No one who owned a computer was presumably immune to the ubiquitous infestation. In the three years leading up to 2000, estimates put the costs of reconfiguring computers to make them Y2K compliant at more than $500 billion. The United States price tag was placed at $100 billion; England spent $20 billion. Agencies such as the Internal Revenue Service spent $1 billion. When the critical moment arrived at midnight on January 1, 2000, and the time bomb essentially fizzled, the debate heated up.

As *Newsweek* was to look back 10 days into the year 2000, it stated that "we were left feeling like someone who worked through the night to board up the windows before a hurricane, evacuated and was delighted to discover an unharmed homestead upon return—a joy tempered by seeing that the house next door was equally pristine, when all the neighbor did was pop open a beer can and pull down the shades."[1] The initial January 2000 responses were harsh, with companies "threatening to sue the pants off their IT [Information Technology] suppliers. Computer experts . . . received death threats from disappointed fanatics. And university professors [began] . . . accusing software suppliers of making a fast buck by blowing the problem out of proportion."[2]

Even the computer journals were at odds with each other over whether the story was one of a crisis averted or a cataclysmic mistake in judgment. At one end of the spectrum, the argument was offered that the "non-event" was the result of preventive actions that had been taken. The preventive measures had averted calamity. These proponents were quick to point out that the millennium bug had indeed bitten. The safety systems in 10 nuclear power stations across the world had failed simultaneously, electrocardiograph machines in hospitals across the country had stopped working, and the United States' crucial defense intelligence satellites were out of action for hours. Summarizing this position, one computer journal noted: "In any other week any of these failures would have been big news. They seem trivial only because people, perhaps unsurprisingly given the hype, were expecting problems of apocalyptic proportion. The story could have been very different if organizations had not taken Y2K so seriously."[3] Other computer experts argued that Y2K was a monumental failure, demonstrating that our information-based society "couldn't cope economically with computer-based risks." We were, according to this interpretation, "whipped into a spending frenzy by doomsday consultants, self-serving vendors and blame dodging politicians" who cowered industry into "trying to attain a zero-risk status against unpredictable bugs."[4]

The question presented by these opposing camps was whether the world had been too hasty in committing hundreds of billions of dollars to the cause of eradicating the Y2K bug. Though conceding the government would have been criminally negligent not to have taken an aggressive approach, *Newsweek* noted "while it might not be so unusual for the federal government to devote billions of dollars toward fixing a problem that doesn't exist, real corporations operate on a reality principle that usually requires a reason to shell out huge sums."

The "reality principle" is the crux of business decision-making. Yet, that principle does not suggest all business decisions are well reasoned. To better identify and understand the principle, let's step down a notch. Instead of focusing on decisions of great import like a Y2K investment, let's consider a more mundane, everyday decision. Suppose you had a product locked in a decades-long rivalry with a competitor's product. Tens of millions are spent annually just in advertising, but then suddenly a consequential reversal occurs: your product, which had always had the predominant market share, begins to lose ground. Then the worst thing happens. You awaken one morning to learn you are no longer No.1; now you're No. 2. What should you do?

When faced with this problem, Coca-Cola frantically cast about for a means to unseat its rival, Pepsi-Cola. The response was to spend millions on a new formula and a new product line: New Coke. Coke had found an answer, but, unfortunately, to the wrong question. The real problem was image, not taste. Pepsi was winning the marketing war, not the taste test. As reported in *Fortune* magazine, the company "introduced New Coke after it outscored both Pepsi and the original Coke in taste tests. The unexamined assumption—that flavor mattered more than Coke's classic image—led to one of the biggest marketing debacles of all times."[5]

The Y2K and New Coke illustrations are intended to show that having ample information to use or money to spend is not necessarily any guarantee that business will make the best decisions. As Donald Carter, senior partner of Deloitte and Touche, further elaborated in the same *Fortune* magazine interview quoted above:

> You remember what a syllogism is—a logical construction with a major premise, a minor premise, and a deductive conclusion. Like this one:
>
> > All smart people are logical.
> > Businesspeople are smart.
> > Therefore, businesspeople are logical.
>
> Wrong. A syllogism is true only if both premises are. In this case, the major premise is untrue: Like writing or math, deductive logic is a learned skill. There is no reason to believe that all people possess it.

Although the appropriateness of Y2K decisions and the Coca-Cola decision might be debated, they point to the important consideration we suggested earlier, that business decisions represent unique challenges. Decisions may have to be reached before all the information is known. Decisions may involve varying degrees of uncertainty, and these decisions, by definition, entail risk. These are precisely the reasons why understanding how to shape and build an argument or assertion are so vitally important. Who wants to be the one to tell investors that you don't know why you invested millions in a war on a "bug," why you introduced a new product line that is now draining money from the company, or why you took some personnel action that has exposed the company to legal repercussions? In business, the strength of the argument and the confidence with which you are able to promote your ideas are critically and inextricably linked.

FIGURE 5.1

A Plan Without Reasoning

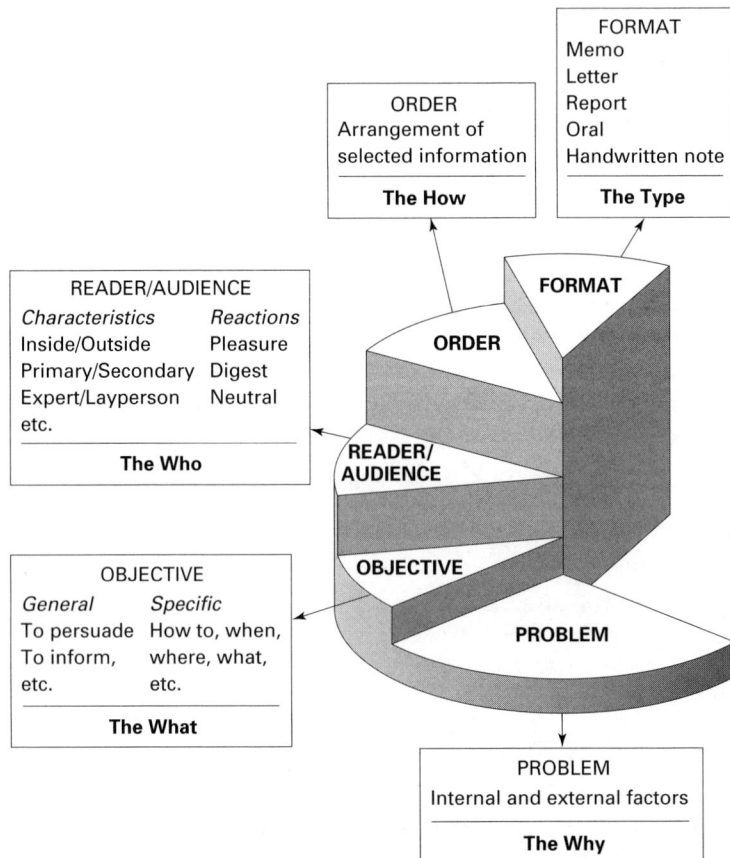

ORDER
Arrangement of selected information

The How

FORMAT
Memo
Letter
Report
Oral
Handwritten note

The Type

READER/AUDIENCE

Characteristics	Reactions
Inside/Outside	Pleasure
Primary/Secondary	Digest
Expert/Layperson	Neutral
etc.	

The Who

OBJECTIVE

General	Specific
To persuade	How to, when,
To inform,	where, what,
etc.	etc.

The What

PROBLEM
Internal and external factors

The Why

Source: Reprinted with permission of the Association for Business Communication

Getting a handle on creating effective business arguments begins with an understanding that, in the most general terms, business decisions fall into four categories:

1. Establishing objectives for your organization.
2. Directing the attainment of those objectives.
3. Monitoring the results.
4. Deciding whether and where course corrections are needed.

All levels of the organization participate in decisions relative to these four categories. Some organizations may have a corporate-wide responsibility; others may have decisions of more precise focus that, in turn, contribute to the broader corporate decisions. For example, a Research and Development Department is primarily concerned with future products. The Production Department focuses its attention on the efficient application of equipment, technology, and human resources. The Finance Department concentrates on cash flow, investments, and return on capital. Each of these departments may, in turn, have sections dealing with more specific elements of these decision areas. For instance, Finance may have units devoted to Accounts Payable, Travel, and Accounts Receivable. Responses to the critical issues, the health and success of the corporation, depend on how effectively the organizational units go about making decisions and how well the decisions are communicated to all organizations affected by or involved with the decisions and their implementation.

THE RHETORICAL FOUNDATION OF DECISION-MAKING

These decision-making capabilities derive directly from an understanding of how to communicate effectively. Thinking is central to the communication process, both in analyzing the information we have collected and in structuring a solid, sustainable, and convincing argument. This component is, nevertheless, often overlooked, as typified in an illustration depicting "critical-thinking skills" needed by professionals. In depicting the elements needed, no explicit reference is made to reasoning as a contributing skill (Figure 5.1).[6] The assumption, as reflected in this thinking, is that arrangement and formatting dictate reasoning. In actuality, the opposite is true. Reasoning defines the arrangement and for-matting of information.

To better understand how to construct a reasoned argument, let's begin by placing business reasoning in its correct rhetorical context. Remembering some of our earlier references to Aristotle, the correspondence should be clear. The simple goal of effective reasoning is the presentation of a convincing argument. In contrast, an argument that is not convincing is less likely to achieve its goal. For simplicity's sake, a continuum from convincing to unconvincing might be depicted as shown in Figure 5.2.

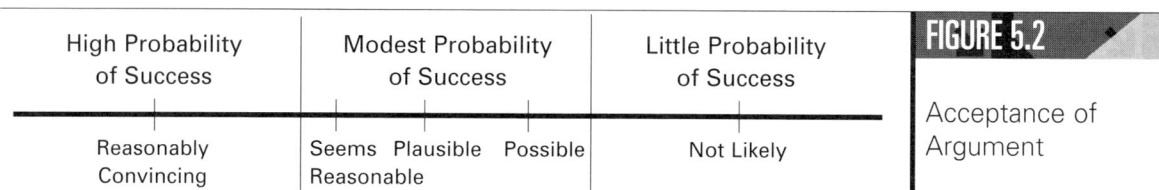

High Probability of Success	Modest Probability of Success	Little Probability of Success
Reasonably Convincing	Seems Plausible Possible Reasonable	Not Likely

FIGURE 5.2

Acceptance of Argument

The methods for constructing convincing arguments—whether business, legal, mathematical, or scientific—all share a common rhetorical ancestry. Aristotle identified three types of rhetoric: forensic, deliberative, and epideictic. The forensic, or legal, applied to defense of individual freedom, the deliberative to issues of domestic and foreign affairs of the government, and the epideictic to eulogizing a cause or an individual. Within a relatively short period of time, advancing the ability to think became a major force in western culture. As an initial step, the proliferation of rhetoric, and of forensic rhetoric in particular, contributed to the founding of democracy in Syracuse in the fifth century B.C. Forced to plead their own causes in court, the citizenry found an urgent need to gain proficiency in persuasive techniques. Once the practicality had been demonstrated, the intrinsic power of critical thinking soon caused rhetoric's application to spread far beyond exclusive focus on resolving arguments over property rights.

Rhetoric became the impetus behind the development of math and science. As was reasoned, if science is "the search for consensus of rational opinion among all competent researchers, [then] science . . . is an extension of rhetoric."[7] Proceeding from this assumption, Aristotle and Plato found the boundaries among rhetoric, science, and mathematics purely artificial. Crossing among the disciplines was a natural extension of thought. Bridging the relationship between science (natural and physical) and rhetoric, Aristotle assigned man the supreme link in the Great Chain of Being based on our superior power to reason.[8] Although often at odds with Aristotle over the significance of rhetoric, Plato took a somewhat parallel course in attempting to understand what he (like the Pythagoreans before him) believed was an ideal, mathematically organized universe. In a world where "God eternally geometrizes," Plato hoped a "few penetrating observations of the physical world would suggest basic truths that could then be developed through reason."[9]

Given the tension between intuitive association on the one hand and the search for a mathematical derivation of the universe on the other, reasoning and scientific certainty soon diverged, breaking into two distinct branches. The former—an outgrowth of Aristotle's work—retained a close tie to its rhetorical foundations. The other sought to enhance the platonic ideas through a search for absolute certainty and mathematical precision. We shall meet up with the former again when we arrive at our discussions of contemporary business decisions. For now, we will briefly follow the second branch, a pathway that indirectly illuminates critical dimensions of constructing an effective business argument.

THE SO-CALLED OBJECTIVITY OF DECISION-MAKING

THE FALLACY OF SCIENTIFIC DECISION-MAKING

In the evolution of science, several thousand years were dominated by Aristotle's influence. Rather than scientists observing, collecting, and interpreting data, knowledge of the natural world was to be taken upon the authority of Aristotle.[10] Beginning in the twelfth century, a change to this thinking began to occur. With Copernicus, Francis Bacon, and Isaac Newton at the forefront, scientists returned to relying on observing and analyzing natural phenomena. Discipline was added by means of validating theories and hypotheses, by experimentation, and by demonstrating the integrity of conclusions by having peers replicate experiments and methods. Together, this return to observation coupled with the experimental discipline introduced what became known as the Scientific Revolution.

This scientific rigor of the Scientific Revolution contributed to significant expansion of our fundamental knowledge of the universe. As an example of the transition from the Aristotelian model to the tenets introduced with the Scientific Revolution, let's consider the century-and-a-half collaborative and cumulative effort of completing the Periodic Table of the Elements. Displacing the prevailing theory that all matter was comprised of the Aristotelian elements, in 1783, Antoine-Laurent Lavoisier introduced the idea that water is a compound composed of hydrogen and oxygen. In so doing, he proposed that an element "be defined experimentally as any substance that can't be decomposed by chemical methods." Next came a suggestion about determining atomic weights. Building upon these theoretical foundations, by 1869, nearly 60 elements were known, allowing Dimitry Mendeleyev to construct a "periodic" table based on the similarities among elements. The table was subsequently filled in with the advent of several related discoveries and theories. Quantum mechanics explained the energy associated with the concentric circles in which electrons travel. Isotopes were identified, and synthetic elements were added. In summary, the development of today's Periodic Table reflected the disciplined compounding of theories, facts, and conclusions.[11] However, science—like business—does not always proceed so dispassionately. Frequently, the "reality principle" spoken of earlier is colored, tempered, or hampered by the introduction of a minimally predictable, less than disciplined "human factor." This factor can be effectively understood by using another illustration from the realm of science.

There is a lengthy history of scientific debates surrounding those scientists whose theories and ideas ran counter to the scientific current. Scientists such as Galileo and Kepler had to overcome a good deal of scrutiny and cynicism. Yet, as a prelude to the topic of the very human (semi-subjective) process of business reasoning, let's use a more modern scientific controversy to illustrate how the human factor influences reasoning, even as practiced in the absolute, objective, computer-reinforced world of contemporary science.

In 1950, Immanuel Velikovsky published a book entitled, *Worlds in Collision,* which hypothesized that the plagues brought upon Pharaoh in the book of Exodus as well as many of the miracles cited elsewhere in the Bible could be traced to near collisions between the earth and the nearby planets of Venus and Mars. (The Appendix includes a synopsis of the book as presented in a refutation by the scientist, Carl Sagan.) While on one hand Velikovsky was lauded as a scientific equivalent of Newton, Freud, Darwin, and Einstein, numerous other scientists disparaged his work. The volume and vigor of the debate was so substantial that in the heat of the moment, Macmillan, the book's original publisher, transferred its rights to Doubleday, sparking charges that the scientific community was practicing censorship.

Amidst the swirling controversy, numerous important voices of the twentieth century were heard trying to define the line at which "real science" becomes "pseudoscience," the point at which "true science" is corrupted by the idiosyncrasies and unscientific influences of the human factor. Notable among those on record, Albert Einstein, in an interview only 2 weeks before his death, offered a muted opinion of the book saying "It is not a bad book. No, it really isn't a bad book. The only trouble with it is, it is crazy." At the same time, asked if a scientist's contemporaries could differentiate a crackpot from a genius based exclusively on his lack of orthodoxy, Einstein was quick to note that "there is no objective test."[12]

While Einstein allowed the text was not "bad," the scientific community generally felt less tolerant of the work. One approach to refuting the "crazy" book was typified by Carl Sagan, who tried to show Velikovsky's hypotheses—such as the earth ceasing to rotate—were impossible. Reflective of the scientific and cultural magnitude of the controversy, Sagan began his refutation of Velikovsky's theory by quoting one of the famous exchanges between Clarence Darrow and William Jennings Bryan. In the Scopes Monkey Trial, a full quarter of a century prior to the publication of *Worlds in Collision,* Bryan and Darrow had also debated the feasibility of the earth standing still (Figure 5.3).

Where evolution once stood in opposition to creationism, Sagan brings quantum mechanics as the standard to bear against Velikovsky's hypotheses. Whereas Charles Darrow had to demonstrate issue with a fundamentalist interpretation of the Bible, Sagan offers calculations to refute the "scientific" interpretation of the same text. Based on Sagan's analysis, if the earth had stopped rotating for a single day, the average temperature would have gone up approximately 100°K, "enough to raise the temperature above the normal boiling point of water . . . it is doubtful," he goes on to conclude, "that the inhabitants would have failed to notice so dramatic a climactic change. The deceleration might be tolerable, if gradual enough, but not the heat."[13]

But dueling scientists and competing theories were not, in themselves, necessarily sufficient to resolve the debate. Other members of the scientific community—despite Einstein's urgings to the contrary—proposed a less-objective measure. Shifting from dueling theories to dueling theorists, some scientists proposed checklists to differentiate real science from pseudoscience, or, as referred to in an only slightly veiled allusion to Velikovsky, "to distinguish between 'crackpot work and good science.'" Using inventive (and subjective) weighting of a variety of traditional and novel measures to characterize the levels of scientific purity, this scale compared three points of reference: 1) a universally recognized scientist, 2) a discredited crackpot who advocates using dowsing rods to locate underground treasure, and 3) an advocate of extrasensory perception. Unlike the scientist who earned a score of 97 out of a possible 100 on this scale, the crackpot (Velikovsky) merited a score of only 28. (The Appendix shows the complete scoring in this comparison.) Drawing the dissatisfaction of the majority of the scientific community, the crackpot is assigned scores of 0 in such categories as public verifiability, controlled experimentation, authority, open-mindedness, and humility.[14]

FIGURE 5.3	
The Earth's Deceleration on Trial	Q. Now, Mr. Bryan, have you ever pondered what would have happened to the earth if it had stood still? A. No. The God I believe in could have taken care of that, Mr. Darrow. Q. Don't you know that it would have been converted into a molten mass of matter? A. You testify to that when you get on the stand. I will give you a chance. —*The Scopes Monkey Trial, 1925*

Belittled and embattled, Velikovsky neither retreated nor recanted his theories. Only time assigned Velikovsky to his proper place in the history of science: a rarely cited footnote. What science could not disprove and public opinion not discredit, simply faded, as Einstein predicted it would. Over time, it was not logic or scientific proof that succeeded; common sense and basic reasoning—the prerequisites of good business sense—prevailed.

A Sense of Logic

The human factor is also evident when we consider how our inexact senses may blunt the edges of objectivity. While few of us would want to maintain the absolute position of Plato, who was eager to dismiss almost everything known to the senses, most science tries to minimize the variability our senses introduce. We need not assess the legal debate about the acceptability of repressed memories or detail the fallibility of eyewitness testimony to gain a fair measure of our sensory vulnerability. Instead, we might illustrate the point more simply by using three nineteenth-century illusions (Figure 5.4).[15] The lines, in part a, an illusion devised around 1899, are the same length, though appear to us to be of different lengths. Looking at part b, an illusion devised around 1860, we would expect the oblique line on the right, if extended, to intersect the farthermost left vertical line well below where it is intersected by the oblique line coming in from the left. In fact, the two lines will meet at the upper end of the left-hand oblique line. Part c is an example of the "Herring Illusion," dating from about 1861. The straight horizontal lines give the illusion of curving in relation to the converging oblique lines.

While the illusions may suggest parlor tricks, they help represent a significant judgment factor that may potentially influence business decisions. Our expectations, often referred to as our "common sense," may predispose us to particular conclusions. Sometimes our intuition may be wrong. To illustrate this point, let's consider a second debate, one that traces its roots to Aristotle. If a ball is fired from a cannon and, at the same time and from the same height, a second ball is dropped, which ball will hit the ground first (Figure 5.5)?[16]

Most people assume, as Aristotle did, that the dropped ball will hit first because it is traveling a shorter total distance. However, the vertical distance is

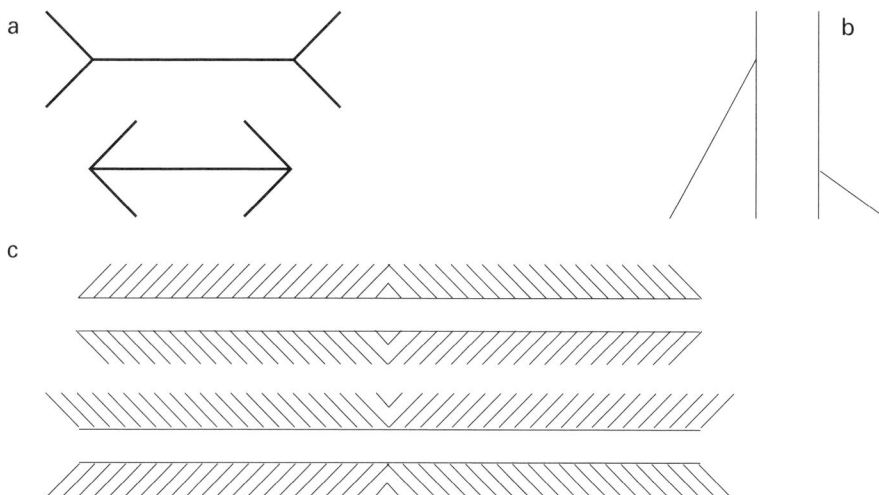

FIGURE 5.4

A Sense of Reality

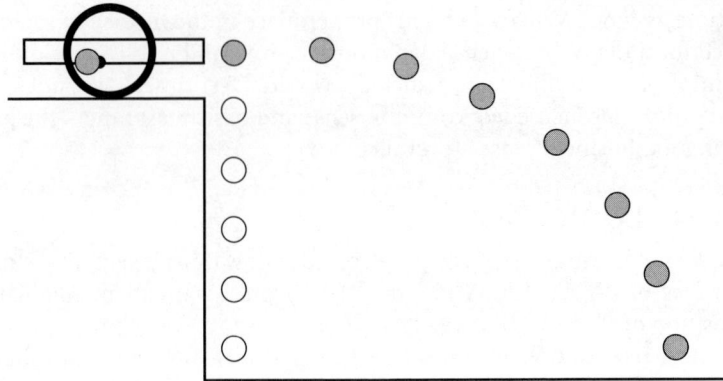

FIGURE 5.5

The Application of Intuitive Response

Source: From Uncommon Sense: The Heretical Nature of Science by Alan Cromer, copyright 1995 by Alan Cromer. Used by permission of Oxford University Press, Inc.

the same for the two balls. Assuming a perfectly level cannon, the correct answer—one that traces its roots to experiments conducted by Galileo in 1632—is that the two balls strike the ground at the same time. Despite differing trajectories, the propelled ball and its dropped counterpart remain equally captive to the laws of gravity and motion. What this second illustration reinforces is the simple principle that while our eyes were capable of misleading us when observing illusions, our brain may also mislead our eyes when we hold strong, intuitive beliefs about what should be "reality."

As the Velikovsky debate demonstrated, we have no litmus test to differentiate science from its less-scientific cousins, absolute certainty from theoretical probability, or business fact from business opinion. As a consequence, many scientific conflicts require some kind of arbitration. Often the arbitration comes in the form of lawsuits. As Alex de Tocqueville wrote in *Democracy in America* (1835), Americans have an unflagging trust that our courts can mediate all ostensibly intractable disputes. Today, a common feature of the judicial landscape is the battle of expert witnesses who give testimony on diametrically opposed, mutually exclusive interpretations of data. One expert might argue that available information irrefutably proves a client innocent; the opposing expert maintains that the very same information establishes guilt. In so arguing, the experts may rely on differing scientific bases or differing technologies to bolster their conclusions. They may also differ regarding the underlying assumptions, a critical factor, as we shall see shortly, that also affects the success of business arguments and reasoning.

While the scientific community continues to try to differentiate crackpot from scientist, the courts have the harder job of delineating "proven" (or accepted) theory from nonvalidated (or less popular) assertions. Despite decades of practice, the court appears equally daunted by the task. Starting with *Frye v. United States,* a case best known for establishing the inadmissibility of lie detector results, the courts have struggled with establishing the "legality" of science and scientific theory (Figure 5.6).[17]

Science, as it turns out—whether in the court of public opinion or in the court of law—does not readily allow for easy discriminators between popular science and proper science, between proper science and pseudoscience. Luckily,

FIGURE 5.6

General acceptance test (Frye v. United States (1923))

" . . . while courts will go a long way to admitting expert testimony deduced from a well-recognized scientific principle or discovery, the thing from which the deduction is made must be sufficiently established to have gained general acceptance in the particular field to which it belongs."

Federal Law of Evidence Section 702: Testimony of experts (1972, revised 1998)

"If scientific, technical, or other specialized knowledge will assist the trier of fact to understand the evidence or to determine a fact in issue, a witness qualified as an expert by knowledge, skill, experience, training, or education, may testify thereto in the form of an opinion or otherwise."

Formal acceptance test (Daubert v. Merril Dow Pharmaceuticals (1993))

[Guidelines to be used to assess testimony should include]

(1) "determining the 'falsifiability' of a theory: is it testable and has it been tested;

(2) the 'known or potential error rate' associated with applications of a theory;

(3) whether the findings have been subjected to peer review and publication; and

(4) the 'general acceptance' of the science being offered."

Testing the validity of scientific expert opinion (Revision to Sec. 702 FRE by the National Conference of Commissioners on Uniform State Laws)

(1) Is the theory applicable to the problem and sufficiently reliable to obtain the proposed result?

(2) Is the equipment or method used to apply the theory suitable for the intended purpose and reliable enough?

(3) Is the data proferred adequate and of sufficient quality to be reliable?

(4) Is the expert sufficiently qualified to understand the strength and limits of the theory, equipment and data to apply it to the present case in such a manner that his opinion is relevant and reliable?

(5) Can the expert validate his assumptions?

(6) Has the expert considered whether there are equally likely alternative explanations?

business is not so heavily challenged when it comes to weighing the validity and relevance of information. Business decisions actually tend to embrace rather than deny the imposition of the human factor when it comes to making decisions. However, before we examine the business of making business decisions, we need to discuss one other potential side road: the assertion that business decisions rely on (or need to rely on) the formalism of logic to determine the best course of action.

THE ILLOGIC OF LOGIC

While rhetoricians were charting a course for much of science, so their work on structure of arguments encouraged and inspired the mathematicians who were busily working on developing geometrical proofs. Raised in a culture that valued sound reasoning, the Greeks demanded convincing arguments in order to reach decisions. When people communicated or debated, convincing arguments were accomplished through the artful application of rhetorical principles. In mathematics, a sound argument relied on a refined system of formal logic.

Today, formal logic is understood as a systematic study of the techniques for formulating information in languages (including symbolic languages such as math) and for extracting information from linguistic formulations. With a bow to its origins, logic is concerned solely with the correctness and propriety of methods of reasoning, not with the processes of thought that people actually use. As a textbook on logic explains: "Logic is sometimes described as 'the study (or the science) of reasoning.' This is misleading. How people *actually* reason and what inferences they *actually* make are irrelevant to logic. Even if it were established that 99.9 per cent of all people think that 'Eggs are good for men' follows from 'Many people eat eggs often,' this inference would not thereby belong to the subject matter of logic, but rather to a social science such as psychology or sociology or anthropology."[18]

Accordingly, exhaustive discussion of the mechanics of logic (e.g., truth tables, Venn diagrams, and syllogisms) may be more tangential to than illuminating of business reasoning. Yet, although the distinction should make apparent why we are not stopping to study logical proofs in this text, we do need to spend a moment to explain further why we are not addressing two subsets of formal logic that commonly get intertwined with discussions of business reasoning: the confusion about inductive and deductive arguments, and the fallacy about fallacies.

THE INDUCTIVE/DEDUCTIVE DILEMMA. One commonly advocated strategy for establishing a well-reasoned argument is the use of inductive and deductive reasoning to define the line of thought. When proposed as an organizing rationale, the concepts of inductive and deductive reasoning are almost universally explained as a process of movement—proceeding from a particular case to a generalized conclusion (induction) or proceeding from application of a general principle to a particular case and conclusion (deductive). Based on these definitions, the following example represents deductive reasoning:

Books about professional communication need to discuss reasoning.

This book is about professional communication.

This book needs to discuss reasoning.

In actuality, the order of presentation (specific to general or general to specific) is irrelevant to establishing which type of argument is being invoked. Whether going from conclusion to premises or from premises to conclusion, the same set of premises and conclusions will always constitute the same form of argument. The real difference, as defined in formal logic, lies neither with motion nor issues of specific versus general conclusions. Rather, any argument in which the premises claim to prove ("entail" as logicians might say) is a deductive argument. All other arguments, those that imply probability rather than certainty, are considered inductive.

More importantly, the clarification offers little in the way of furthering our goals of learning to construct a well-reasoned business argument. Somewhat analogous to our discussions of descriptive and inferential statistics, we may use the terminology to describe a structure, but not to chart an effective path forward. Induction and deduction, whether explained correctly or not, are not pathways we can follow as a basis for constructing an effective and compelling business argument. Neither is it of immediate value to us in this context to expend significant effort learning the titles and attributes of dozens of logical fallacies.

THE FALLACY OF FALLACIES. Studying fallacies may give us a terminology to apply when assessing issues of insufficient evidence, linguistic ambiguities, and irrelevant conclusions in the type of expository writing done in composition class. These insights have limited applicability in professional communication. It's hard to imagine the business circumstance that parallels the kind of intentionally misleading arguments that propelled the development of studies devoted to identifying and eradicating logical fallacies. Even in the darkest recesses of corporate maneuverings, it is unlikely we will be able to trace parallels with the manipulative characteristics often used as justification for studying fallacies:

> You've taken a position on an issue, which you've thoroughly thought through. You have supporting data at your fingertips. You're a quick thinker and articulate. You unfold your argument in logical steps. Yet somehow you don't seem to be getting anywhere. The other guy keeps coming back with statements and questions that seem to be relevant, that seem to make sense. And yet somehow they're neither relevant, nor do they make sense. You become confused, frustrated, angry. What's wrong? The explanation may be simple—you're being conned . . . . What's happening is that your opponent is using what are commonly known as fallacies of logic.[19]

There are serious problems with the thinking evidenced in this excerpt. Some of the problems lie with the limited pedagogical value of studying fallacies: 1) Fallacy theory is inherently incomplete: "truth may have its norms, but error is infinite in its aberrations." 2) Fallacy theory is inherently negative; it highlights what to avoid rather than explain how to construct solid arguments. Furthermore, fallacies are not well defined or clearly distinguished from one another.[20]

Despite these limitations, studying fallacies might be beneficial were it not for the fact that there are three equally compelling issues that challenge the relevancy of studying fallacies in the assessment and development of business arguments. First, looking for fallacies mischaracterizes the nature of business decisions. Business decision-making is not a distant relative of "conning" opponents; business arguments generally do not proceed from a "win at any price" strategy. Second, focusing on a hunt for fallacies may totally misread the business context: dismissing the value of opinion, mischaracterizing shared beliefs as equivalent to unsupported conclusions, and mislabeling a corporately shared perspective as a demonstration of insufficient evidence. Only limited equivalents exist to the major and minor premises as identified in syllogistic reasoning.

In addition, if we look at another side of one of the issues we discussed in Chapter 3, we learn that fallacies are not discernable without due examination of the whole argument—both explicit and implicit. For example, if we state "Saturns are the best-made cars," is there a fallacy taking place? Is the statement an example of a "hasty generalization"? Or is it simply the statement of an accepted "truth" shared by the communities involved in the conversation? Even when business arguments are insufficiently supported, debate does not focus on deconstructing arguments or labeling fallacies; rather, such instances produce solicitations for more information and for enhanced collaboration among those who can add dimension and perspective to the business case.

Last, teaching fallacies fails to recognize the environment in which business decisions are made. What events preceded or initiated the matter at hand? How has the business performance affected the arguments? Do the social and political climates in which the company operates play a role? As we also noted in Chapter 3, the purpose, the audience, and the context all contribute to the evaluation of factual information. Isolating elements of an argument from its context is a difficult step and one whose analysis generally leads to clarifying problems associated with the underlying assumptions, not to matters of sufficiency or relevancy of evidence.

These problems associated with studying fallacies as a means of appreciating business reasoning might be made more concrete by examining the biggest business story of 2001 and 2002: the collapse of Enron Corporation. Formed in 1985 when Houston Natural Gas combined with a gas pipeline company, Enron's pioneering tactics in trading electricity and natural gas resulted in its rapid rise to the number seven position on the Fortune 500 list. While amazingly fast on the upswing, Enron's rise was dwarfed by its meteoric slide into bankruptcy.

Between the summer and early December of 2001, Enron completely fell apart: stock values plunged from $83 per share to a value of pennies; $60 billion of stockholder value vanished; $1 billion in employee savings disappeared; and approximately 15,000 people lost their jobs. The CFO who was honored by *CFO Magazine* in 1999 for "unique financial techniques," was summoned—along with current and previous CEOs of the corporation—to appear before a dozen or so congressional committees and subcommittees investigating the corporate collapse. By fall 2002, investigations and inquests began to be translated into criminal indictments of corporate officials. The impacts of the corporation's failure were widespread. Not only was Wall Street shaken, but the shadows stalked the halls of Congress. As noted in *The Washington Post* in early February of 2002, "Of the 248 members who sit on committees that plan to hold hearings on the scandal, an extraordinary 212 received money from Andersen [the firm's accounting and consulting firm] or Enron."[21]

Clearly Enron represents the pinnacle of corporate greed. While tens of thousands of investors and employees pondered their losses, the executive team had made millions based on elaborate investment schemes. The intrigue, as it continues to unfold in the congressional hearings, endless lawsuits, civil probes, and criminal probes, points to massive loopholes in our laws and regulations. More than two dozen bills have been drafted to address issues with how corporations calculate profit, account for assets, produce financial statements, disclose insider stock sales, administer pension funds, and account for donations to political candidates and campaigns.

At the same time, business schools and law schools perceived Enron as "the case study of a lifetime. Indeed, Enron is fast becoming as useful . . . as *Hamlet* is to the English Department."[22] Law schools used Enron as a case study in courses on conflict of interest and obligations of corporate directors. Business schools incorporated the Enron story into courses on leadership, auditing, executive compensation, and organizational culture.

Yet, nowhere among the inquiries, analyses, and case studies examining how insufficient information was made available to stockholders, auditors, government oversight agencies, and employees is there discussion about these shortcomings being a reflection of poorly crafted arguments or inadvertent introduction of logical fallacies. Ethical lapses, manipulation of standard practices, and deceit all contributed to masking the magnitude of the Enron problems. But even in this most extreme case, little insight would be gained by assessing logical frameworks or logical fallacies.

As villainous as we may perceive these individuals to be, the lessons being learned from Enron support the conclusion that even the most purposeful of business deceptions are reflections of tampering with the rules and regulations—maneuvering around the accepted criteria and assumptions that underlie conventional business practice. They are not matters of failed logic or logical fallacies. In an article published less than a week after Enron filed for bankruptcy, *Newsweek* summarized the truth of the calamity: "The Enron Affair reinforces two of the oldest lessons there are. To wit: When someone tells you he's changing the world for the better and getting rich at the same time, hold onto your wallet. And that when something sounds too good to be true, it probably isn't true."[23] We need to pay attention to what makes sense, not try to use the mechanics of logic to forecast the outcome.

Having established the proper perspective, and having clarified the relationship between logic and reasoning, we are ready to examine the true "science" of making business decisions and building effective business arguments.

THE SCIENCE OF BUSINESS

On our road to exploring how decisions are made in business, we need to make one last stop to appreciate how the scientific limb of rhetoric manifests itself in business. Paralleling the relationship between science and the human factor, business has undergone a succession of movements that have drawn it toward and then dragged it away from a reliance on mathematical and scientific modeling. The first major movement began approximately 150 years ago.

During the earlier parts of the nineteenth century, when factories began appearing on the landscape, approaches to management were generally informal. After the Civil War, the business landscape changed. Factories had to be equipped, a workforce comprising a large proportion of non-English-speaking workers had to be integrated into the operation, and the overall subject of management had yet to be defined. The answer about how to accomplish these ends caused what soon thereafter became known as Scientific Management. In addition to establishing the procedures needed to manage American enterprise, Scientific Management, as based on the concepts developed by Frederick Winslow Taylor, sought to impose mathematical rigor. Inventory control, linear and nonlinear programming, queuing theory, applied mathematics, statistics, and other quantitative techniques were applied to managerial problems. Henry Gantt developed bar graphs that tracked output against expectations. Frank and Jillian Galbraith pioneered industrial psychology and "time and motion" studies. The early Human Relations Movement introduced industrial psychology as a means to improve productivity and lessen the variability associated with worker performance.

Yet, in what may be one of the great ironies of the information age, the greater the breadth of information needed and available, the greater the resulting reliance on people to assess, synthesize, and define the "logic" of argument. In Chapter 3, we illustrated the correspondence between business information needs cited by representatives of Scientific Management and those of knowledge management. In a similar correlation, no matter what the circumstance or discipline of study, no matter what the level of technological sophistication applied, constructing a strong argument derives its strength—not from the rhetorical branch that went in search of scientific certainty—but from the branch that retained its lineage with the rhetorical heritage. Human reasoning, not formal logic, is the critical success factor. Even the newest kid on the block, Six Sigma, which explains process variability in terms of the number of standard deviations (or sigma) between actual performance and predicted values, grudgingly concedes an irreplaceable reliance on judgment and experience.

Constructing a "case" is a common feature and expectation of all disciplines (Figure 5.7). Whether they call their approaches scientific method, engineering analysis, or design process, professionals share a challenge to find answers to four primary categories of questions: 1) What exactly is the issue being examined? 2) What caused it to occur? 3) What is it worth? 4) What should be done about it?

THE SUBSTANCE OF BUSINESS ARGUMENT

With the preceding groundwork in place, we can better appreciate the four factors critical to correctly understanding the concept of business reasoning and argumentation:

1. Business argumentation is a direct descendent of classical rhetoric.

2. There are no scientific (or logic) models that will make business decisions for us.

3. Business decisions rely—to one degree or another—on judgment rather than certainty.

4. Business decisions are made in a time-dependent environment that may limit opportunity to search out or bring all facts to bear on the decision.

Does this emphasis on judgment—supported by scientific method, mathematical model, and logical validation—suggest we are any less equipped to handle the demanding decisions of business? Clearly, the Greek and Roman rhetoricians didn't think so. We are, with some basic assistance on how to structure a reasoned argument, quite capable of determining courses of action that are prudent, appropriate, and in the company's best interests. In fact, a

FIGURE 5.7	Scientific Method	Engineering Method	Design Process	Business Process	Standard Process	Six Sigma
Problem Solving Processes	Develop hypothesis	Conduct preliminary analysis	Analysis	Think	Define the problem	Define the problem
	Define experiment	Refine issues	Synthesis	Plan	Analyze the problem	Measure
	Conduct experiment	Conduct design activities (e.g., conceptual, functional)	Evaluation	Do	Establish goals and objectives	Analyze
	Analyze results		Decision	Check		Improve
	Compare results with hypothesis	Select option(s)	Optimization	Revise	Select best solution	Control
	Refine hypothesis	Conduct final design activities	Revision		Implement	
	Redo experiments	Initiate project				
		Monitor vs. plan				

"reasonable" answer may, at times, be better than that arrived at through scientific method, mathematical model, or logical validation.

In the 1950s, the following question supposedly appeared on the written portion of the driver's license test in New York. A fire engine, a police car, an ambulance, and a mail truck are each approaching an intersection. They are coming from four different directions and each arrives at precisely the same time (Figure 5.8). At each of the four corners is a stop sign. The ambulance, fire engine, and police car have their sirens blaring and their lights flashing. Who has the right of way?

Logic would suggest we try to deduce some means by which to rank the relative urgency of the activities associated with ambulances, police cars, and fire engines. Is a building on fire? Are people in dire medical straits? Is a major crime in progress? Is one of these conditions more urgent or more dependent on the arrival of rescue personnel than the other two? Scientific or mathematical methodologies might suggest we gather statistics or establish some procedure by which to assign point values. After a while, the problem may seem reminiscent of trying to select an appropriate course when faced with competing scientific theories or when responding to the competing testimony of dueling expert witnesses. On the surface, the vehicle problem seems impervious to logic or formulaic analysis. Further, because of the context in which the problem is being addressed, no additional information is available, nor can any be solicited. So, what's the answer?

The correct answer, at least according to this test, is "mail truck." Why? Among the four vehicles—remembering this is supposed to be the 1950s—the mail truck was the only federal vehicle. Extending the general principle that federal agencies have jurisdiction and precedence over local and state agencies led the authors of the question to the following conclusion:

Federal activities take precedence over state and local activities.

The mail truck is part of a federal activity.

Therefore, the mail truck should take precedence.

Yet, for our purposes, even more important than the "right" answer is your reaction to the answer. We would expect that you find the answer totally unacceptable. Although the explanation for answering "mail truck" may be valid and logical (i.e., it conforms to acknowledged rules), it is neither sensible nor "reasonable." Whether your final answer was police car, ambulance, or fire truck, those answers seem more rational to us than does mail truck.

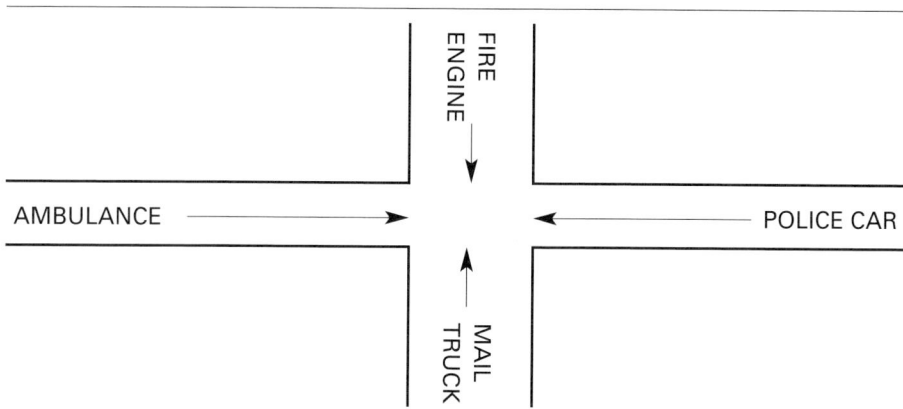

FIGURE 5.8

Reasoning and Logic: A Practical Illustration

Your dissatisfaction with the mail truck answer attests to your natural capacity to make decisions, even when the decisions may appear contrary to the dictates of formal logic. The means by which you reached a decision demonstrate all the elements necessary to make sound business decisions: 1) You presumably had sufficient information to make a determination. 2) You had a rationale for your decision—doing the right thing "naturally" meant granting precedence to one of the emergency vehicles, not the mail truck. 3) You believed you understood all terms and criteria (even though, ultimately, you may have been proven wrong). 4) The format and sequence of information presentation appeared clear. Given these factors, you proceeded to make a decision and take action. You didn't rely on any system or mathematical model to reinforce your conclusion, you exercised judgment, and you reacted in keeping with the hypothetical urgency of the decision. As a consequence, when you selected one of the emergency vehicles as your answer, you made a valid—even though a technically illogical—decision. The assumptions you used made the critical difference between a defensible answer and a logical answer, the difference between a "reasoned" answer and a guess. Welcome to the world of building business arguments.

CONSTRUCTING THE BUSINESS ARGUMENT

In stark contrast to the complexities of applying scientific methods, logic, and the predicting of absolute certainty, constructing effective business arguments is relatively simple. In fact, it can be represented by an intersection of the four evidence factors cited above with the four major categories of business decisions (Table 5.1):

- Propositions—Arguments explaining precisely what something is and how it should be treated.

- Analyses—Arguments explaining what caused an event or what the effect was. Analysis is the equivalent of inquiring how we arrived at our present condition.

TABLE

5.1 THE ESSENCE OF EFFECTIVE BUSINESS ARGUMENTATION

Evidence factors	Application			
	Propositions	Analysis	Assessment	Proposal
Clarity of trends	✓	✓	✓	✓
Sufficiency of information	✓	✓	✓	✓
Applicability	✓	✓	✓	✓
Order of presentation	✓	✓	✓	✓

- Assessment—Arguments explaining whether the action or process will result in a positive or negative outcome. What is the value?
- Proposal—Arguments asserting what needs to be done.

PROPOSITIONS

Propositions occur routinely in business. For example, suppose your company is about to reorganize—nothing major, just some realignments. For years, your company has had both a fire brigade that responds to fires and a separate fire engineering function that designs fire water-systems and determines the placement of sprinklers and other fire-suppression systems. In the past, these two groups have reported to different departments. The fire brigade reports to the Security Department, and fire engineering reports to the Safety Division. The question has arisen whether any economies might result from assigning both functions to a single department and which department should it be. Figure 5.9 suggests the basic pattern for developing and presenting this form of business reasoning.

To show how the model would be applied, let's assume you intend to argue that both functions should report to the Safety Division. Your objective, then, is to offer definitions and examples that support the premise that the most important factor shared by the two groups is their contribution to safety (Figure 5.10).

ANALYSES

Business is continually engaged in trying to fix what's gone wrong and emulate what's going right. An example that may yield either of these two conditions is the routine analysis of variances. It is a common practice that on a periodic basis managers look at current performance (often referred to as "actuals") versus anticipated performance (often referred to as "projections"). These actuals may be how much money has been spent to date on a project, the number of cars that have come off the assembly line, or the number of tires that have failed to meet quality standards. In each instance, the goal is to identify and explain any discrepancies between actuals and earlier projections. What caused us to spend less or more money than planned? Why are we 10% behind in automobile production? Why are tires failing at a rate of 3% instead of at a rate of 1% as expected? Each function in the company is challenged to demonstrate that it can explain the irregularities, correct any deviations, and produce the desired level of

| What specifically is the proposition? |
| Are there any terms or assumptions that need to be defined? |
| What is the essence of your argument? |
| What examples offer compelling evidence? |
| What is the most obvious point to be refuted? |

Success factor:
1) The definitions must be clear, unambiguous, and applicable.
2) The terms should offer suggestion of the commonality of the elements.
3) The examples must be immediately applicable.

FIGURE 5.9

Proposition

FIGURE 5.10

A Sample
Proposition

Proposition: Both fire response and fire engineering should report to the Safety Division.

Supported by Terms

Fire Response has a primary mission of ensuring the safety of personnel during emergency conditions. The contribution that fire response makes to security is limited to supporting personnel accountability during evacuations.

Fire Engineering has a primary role of ensuring that proper safety specifications are reflected in the design and operation of facilities. Personnel are experts in National Fire Safety Codes.

Essence of Argument *It's been proven that improved safety and reduced costs result from aligning safety-related functions.*

Example

In Company Y, merging these groups has resulted in numerous benefits, such as faster response times because personnel are more knowledgeable of critical fire engineering systems and also less costly fire protection designs accomplished by integrating both the practical and engineering expertise in the design process.

Refutation

In maintenance, while some initial issues were incorporated (a simple refutation), we made a similar reorganization of the operating and engineering functions responsible for the plant's safety systems. There have been considerable reductions in the administrative costs, greater coordination on complex assignments, and fewer failures of safety systems than last year.

---

performance. Yet, as seemingly straightforward as this may appear, arguing about cause can be tricky. As was shown earlier in the Coca-Cola example, it is easy to incorrectly assume cause, relying too readily on proximity or associations without validating that they are the true causal agents.

Surely, the most famous of the demonstrations of the complexity of searching for an elusive causal agent in business is reflected in the Hawthorne Experiments, a series of studies that fundamentally transformed our thinking about workers and productivity. In the 1920s, the Western Electric Company plant in Hawthorne, Illinois, was a hallmark of enlightened management. However, despite the generosity of the pension and benefit plans, production wasn't meeting expectations. Soliciting the help of Harvard University, the company began a series of experiments aimed at improving productivity. In the initial test, experimenters identified that changes in lighting brought about positive changes in productivity. Luckily, before enormous sums were spent on redoing the lighting system in the factories, the experimenters tested other variables.

Quizzically, every variable tested—pay scales, rest breaks, work schedules—elicited similarly positive results (Table 5.2). The underlying cause that was finally deduced was that the workers were responding not to the specific change as much as they were reacting positively to attention from management. In a seeming refutation of some principles of Scientific Management, the experiments caused the whole concept of management to change from an essentially exclusive focus on charts and numbers to a greater interest in workers and

5.2 | **HAWTHORNE EXPERIMENTS (WESTERN ELECTRIC COMPANY, HAWTHORNE, ILLINOIS)**

Test Condition	Effect on Productivity
1. More light	↑
2. Less light	↑
3. Workers operate in dark (by sense of touch)	↑
4. Hourly work changed to piecework	↑
5. Workers given two 10-minute rest breaks	↑
6. Breaks lengthened, coffee provided	↑
7. Workers allowed to leave 1/2 hour early	↑
8. Workers let off 1 hour early	↑
9. Workers put back on original schedule	↑
10. Working hours reduced from 48 to 40	↑
11. All original conditions reinstated	↑

worker satisfaction. Once again the human factor had introduced itself into the hunt for objective certainty.

Of all the disciplines that have routinely struggled with differentiating true causes from mere associations, of all disciplines that have had to acknowledge the human factor, none has pursued the matter with more diligence than the field of epidemiology, the study of disease in a population. This is not surprising given the consequences of incorrectly identifying the causes of major heath risks. Of particular value to us as communicators is that the epidemiological circumstances, in many ways, parallel the business environment: potentially complex sets of inputs, high variability, significant potential consequences of mistakes, and a sense of urgency. Therefore, before offering our business model, it might be worthwhile to summarize the criteria that epidemiologists have developed to delineate causal agents from associations.

In 1965, Sir Austin Bradford Hill, a professor emeritus of medical statistics and then President of the Occupational Medicine section of the Royal Society of Medicine, defined what have remained the nine aspects used by epidemiologists to establish causation. Only one of those nine, "Biological Gradient," has no apparent corollary in business. The remaining eight are as follows:

1. Strength—Is the association substantial?
2. Consistency—Has the relationship been repeatedly observed by different persons in different places, circumstances, and times?
3. Specificity—Is the association limited to a specific set of effects?
4. Temporality—Have we established precisely "which is the cart and which the horse"?

5. Plausibility—Are we certain we're dealing with the cause? To quote Sherlock Holmes, "When you have eliminated the impossible, whatever remains, however improbable, must be the truth."

6. Coherence—Does the data agree with or seriously conflict with generally known facts?

7. Experiment—Can experimental evidence be introduced?

8. Analogy—Are there immediately applicable comparisons and analogies that can be drawn?[24]

Using these means for delineating cause from association, we can now suggest a model for constructing an argument based on analysis (Figure 5.11).

As an illustration of this form of argument, let's return to the matter of variance explanations. Suppose you are in charge of a $10 million, multiyear project. Initially, you projected that you would spend $4 million of the project money in the first fiscal year. You now need to explain a fiscal variance: Why, only 4 months into the year, have you already spent $2 million of the $4 million (Figure 5.12)?

FIGURE 5.11	What specifically is cause/effect?
	Are there any terms or assumptions that need to be defined?
Analysis	What is the essence of the argument?
	What causes are proposed?
	How do you show that the causes were at work?
	What causes need to be refuted?
	Success factor: Defining acceptable and sufficient causes at work at the time

FIGURE 5.12	**Primary Cause:** The reason for the variance is that major procurements are ahead of schedule.
A Sample Analysis	**Terms Needing Definition:** Major procurements: purchases of greater than $250,000
	Essence of the Argument: The budget was built upon an expectation that major procurements would be equally spaced throughout the year.
	The primary causes: • The plan was to procure major equipment earlier than forecast to allow the overall schedule to be accelerated. • Management wanted to try to get the next major project milestone completed by the fall. • The political climate suggested that the money for next year may be tight; so the early allocation funds may avoid layoffs next year.
	How you demonstrate the causes were in effect: A review of the project correspondence over the past 3 months will confirm each of the causes (assuming these would not already be known to the review committee).
	Causes to be rejected: None

ASSESSMENTS

Business is dependent on ensuring that activities and investments add value. Evaluations focus equally on what "value added" accrues from work and from people. Such evaluative discussions tend to introduce multiple perspectives. While one organization may feel itself critical to an operation, others may consider the same organization as peripheral, or even unnecessary. The tension in such discussions is generally high because telling someone that their work, their solutions, or their performance is below expectations is not a conversation geared toward quiet consensus. As might be apparent, the critical feature in assessment is the choice of criteria—and in making those criteria explicit (Figure 5.13).

ASSESSING PEOPLE. A fundamental responsibility of business is to provide direction and feedback to people on how well they are performing. This type of assessment reveals why appropriate criteria selection is so important. When someone is undergoing a performance review, the clarity of the terms used and the clear articulation of the criteria are the determinants of success or failure.

For example, in a typical performance review, the employee may be expecting a glowing report. He has a good number of nice compliments from customers and coworkers, hasn't made any great mistakes, and attendance has been commendable. Thirty minutes into the performance review, the employee is confused, angry, and ready to quit. Or, now convinced that the performance issues lie with his manager, that employee may be getting ready to contact the union steward, file a grievance, or take the matter up to the next level of management. What went wrong?

The short answer is that the criteria used by the person being reviewed may have been different from those used by the reviewer. The difference, in and of itself, may cause some friction, but the real rub is that each of the participants entered and left the room without having established the common vocabulary (the criteria) by which evaluations are being made. The primary fault is with the reviewer. The employee should have known, well in advance of any formal review sessions, precisely what constituted good performance. If not, the reviewer may have to explain herself not only to the disgruntled employee, but, potentially, to upper management, Human Resources, and others.

Using the model cited in Figure 5.13, the answer is straightforward: establish what precisely is being reviewed: performance, development, opportunity for advancement, or all of the above. Then articulate and explain the criteria being used, preferably well in advance of the face-to-face meeting. (We will examine the specific expectations of face-to-face meetings in Chapter 8.) As an example,

• What is the assessment?
• Are there terms or assumptions requiring clarification/definition?
• What criteria are being used to support the assertion?
• Why are these criteria the primary, appropriate ones?
• What is the specific performance against the criteria?
• What criteria/examples need to be reflected?
Success factors: defining defensible criteria and providing sufficient examples of performance relative to those criteria

FIGURE 5.13

Assessment

FIGURE 5.14

Assessment
Criteria

	DISCIPLINE	ACHIEVEMENT	POTENTIAL
PROFICIENCY	Knowledge, Skills: How much an individual knows with respect to the area of expertise	Productivity: How much an individual accomplishes in doing work	Innovation: How much improvement an individual is likely to make in the area of proficiency
FUNCTIONALITY	Pertinence: How relevant an individual's expertise is to the organization's primary work	Closure: How successful an individual is in completing work	Adaptability: How readily an individual responds to changes in work requirements
CREDIBILITY	Customer perception: How customers regard the individual as a service provider	Program contribution: How successful an individual is in completing work	Independence: How customers and others regard an individual's reliability in working without ongoing direction/oversight

Figure 5.14 details nine criteria that might be used in a performance review. Figure 5.15 shows how these factors might be weighted and tailored to the assessment of employees with different levels of experience and responsibility.

ASSESSING WORK. Consistent with the intense contemporary focus on value, companies periodically reassess whether each element of the business represents a worthwhile investment. For instance, a photographer may have to decide if it is worth her while to continue developing pictures or if she should limit her work exclusively to taking pictures. A company that provides research on air pollution might assess whether it should release the person who has been providing photography services and, instead, establish a service contract with a local business to provide a photographer on an as-needed basis.

At the same time, a manufacturing plant might consider whether the consulting firms it hires on an as-needed basis are costing too much or whether they should hire a full-time air pollution engineer. Each of these businesses is involved in essentially the same exercise—determining whether a certain activity (often referred to as a "scope of work") adds value commensurate with its cost. In the case of the photographer, cost may be equipment investment; for the air pollution firm, it is utilization of personnel and resources; and for the manufacturing firm, it is actual outlay of cash.

The probability of each individual or organization reaching the decision appropriate to its circumstance remains the same as reflected in the performance assessment we just discussed, namely, that success will be determined by how well each defines appropriate criteria. To balance our performance review example, let's look at three brief examples that suggest the need for carefully crafted criteria selection when assessing a scope of work.

The first example illustrates how criteria need to be reconciled against one another. The next two examples illustrate how two different circumstances affect the criteria for a common scope of work. Businesses, especially those operating in a highly regulated environment, are required by law to keep records documenting performance (e.g., records that prove benefits programs were compliant with federal law or chemical emissions were below regulatory limits). In addition, much information is retained to allow companies to analyze and

FIGURE 5.15

Tailoring the Criteria

Junior Professionals	DISCIPLINE		ACHIEVEMENT		POTENTIAL	
PROFICIENCY	Knowledge, Skills	Hi (9) Med (4) Low (0)	Produc-tivity	Exceeds (9) Meets (4) <Satisfactory (0)	Innovation	Hi (9) Med (4) Low (0)
FUNCTIONALITY	Perti-nence	Leadership (3) Applicable (2) Inapplicable (1)	Closure	Exceeds (3) Meets (2) <Satisfactory (1)	Adapt-ability	Flexible (3) Compliant (2) Inflexible (1)
CREDIBILITY	Customer perception	Authority (3) Org Rep (2) Not (1)	Program contri-bution	High-initiative (3) Follows thru (2) Lacks (1)	Indepen-dence	Leader (3) Responsive (2) Destructive (1)

Senior Professionals	DISCIPLINE		ACHIEVEMENT		POTENTIAL	
PROFICIENCY	Knowledge, Skills	Hi (3) Med (2) Low (1)	Produc-tivity	Exceeds (3) Meets (2) <Satisfactory (1)	Innovation	Hi (3) Med (2) Low (1)
FUNCTIONALITY	Perti-nence	Leadership (9) Applicable (4) Inapplicable (0)	Closure	Exceeds (9) Meets (4) <Satisfactory (0)	Adapt-ability	Flexible (9) Compliant (4) Inflexible (0)
CREDIBILITY	Customer perception	Authority (3) Org Rep (2) Not (1)	Program contri-bution	High-initiative (3) Follows thru (2) Lacks (1)	Indepen-dence	Leader (3) Responsive (2) Destructive (1)

Managers	DISCIPLINE		ACHIEVEMENT		POTENTIAL	
PROFICIENCY	Knowledge, Skills	Hi (3) Med (2) Low (1)	Produc-tivity	Exceeds (3) Meets (2) <Satisfactory (1)	Innovation	Hi (3) Med (2) Low (1)
FUNCTIONALITY	Perti-nence	Leadership (3) Applicable (2) Inapplicable (1)	Closure	Exceeds (3) Meets (2) <Satisfactory (1)	Adapt-ability	Flexible (3) Compliant (2) Inflexible (1)
CREDIBILITY	Customer perception	Authority (9) Org Rep (4) Not (0)	Program contri-bution	High-initiative (9) Follows thru (4) Lacks (0)	Indepen-dence	Leader (9) Responsive (4) Destructive (0)

predict performance trends. To some degree, there are even regulations about the processing, storage, retrievability, and destruction of records. However, there is no requirement that a company manage its own records versus subcontracting for that service.

At one large industrial firm, the Controller determined that it would be cheaper to subcontract than maintain records. However, management inquired whether there were other factors to consider before proceeding with the subcontract. In this particular instance, extensive analyses revealed that although subcontracting would result in cost savings, more important criteria existed: 1) Business sensitivity—the records collection contained business-sensitive information that could not be guaranteed appropriate safeguarding in an off-plant warehouse. 2) Legal liability—regulatory inquiries demanded timely availability of the records; any delays in retrieving records could contribute to substantial fines and penalties. 3) Lost knowledge—expertise associated with development of the records collection would be lost, adversely affecting the company's ability

FIGURE 5.16

Balancing the
Elements of the
Work Environment

LIBRARY UNIVERSE

Interpersonal
Decisions

Strategic
Decisions

BUSINESS UNIVERSE

to respond to audits and external reviews. Weighing the additional criteria, management concluded it was better not to subcontract the records function.

As our second example, let's examine decisions associated with funding a corporate library. In an article entitled "Strategic Decision Making in a Time of Information Overload," the authors explain that maintaining the research library's funding is contingent on "matching and weighing the traditional library choices with an understanding and appreciation for the business framework in which it operates."[25] Accordingly, gauging the library's performance demanded attention not only to the library's information function (i.e., making resources available to patrons), but also to the library's business functions (i.e., making prudent, defensible use of the library's budget) (Figure 5.16). Responding to the dual sets of criteria, the authors developed a basic decision logic that clearly details the criteria used to ensure that purchases are in the best interests of both the business and information responsibilities of the library (Table 5.3).

In contrast to the library discussed above, which was responding to the need to prove itself a worthy corporate citizen, let's examine a second library facing a very different set of challenges. The Carnegie Library of Pittsburgh is one of the 100 largest libraries in the nation. Recognizing its responsibility to the community, this library is restructuring its criteria for assessing performance, moving away from a focus on administering expenditures, and instead "trying to shake off the dust to play a bigger part in local residents' lives." As an example, challenging the traditional criteria associated with safeguarding the collection, the library's director is asking "Why, if a book hasn't been taken out for two or three years by anyone, is there a rush to get it back in three weeks? What is the point of fines if they just turn people off?" He is also challenging the traditional criteria that a library must be a quiet, sedate, staid environment; he "envisions such shocking changes as coffee-slurping readers . . . opening whole stacks of books to circulation that have long been guarded carefully inside the thick walls and even shifting some collections to the nearby university libraries where they'd get more use."[26] The comparison between the efforts undertaken by the two libraries makes evident that criteria are not driven by the scope of work but by the immediate circumstance, by the explicit purposes and goals.

When constructing a business case or argument, in positioning your organization to make effective decisions, you need to make certain that the criteria selected and their relative weightings appropriately reinforce the desired outcome. Each case and each circumstance must be carefully analyzed and the appropriate criteria selected.

5.3 THE CRITERIA FOR BUYING LIBRARY RESOURCES

Access	Quality	Perspective	Media	Format
Single source	Recommended	Collective resource	Easy to use	Directly usable
Shared/licensed	Reliable	Sum is greater	Accessible	Needs equipment
number of users	Well	than collective	Upgradable	(reader, printer,
Reference material	researched	parts	Supported	etc.)
Circulating materials	Ephemeral	Offers multiple	Equipment	Special skills
Number of copies	Reference	entry points	needs	required
Single location	Unique	Valuable for a vari-	available	Reproducible
Use in-house only	Irreplaceable	ety of users and	Special care in	Transportable
Unlimited access on	Archive	occasions	use or storage	Easy to see and
intranet	Temporary	Value improves	Dependable	read
Familiar, no training	Familiar	with use	Convertible	Legible
needed	Regular	Continues to	(paper to	Design supports
Use in location	updates	build/grow	electronic)	content
where and when		Index supported	Lasting value	
needed		Searchable	and quality	
Password access		Keyword access	Command	
only by request		Index/gateway to	language	
		other resources	searches	

What precisely is the problem?
   Why did the problem occur?
   What is the significance of the problem?
What should be done to resolve the problem?
What are the consequences of following or not following the recommendations?
What is the specific action needed?

Success factors: Establishing a strong link among the problem, the urgency to act, and the clear impression that the proposed action will resolve the problem

FIGURE 5.17

Proposal

PROPOSALS

The last of the four major decision-making frameworks is the proposal—inviting the audience to take action. Because almost all business communication seeks to support an assertion, most forms of business communication—whether letters, reports, or presentations—seek to promote action. Because the line of reasoning employed in the proposal will be further developed in subsequent chapters, for now we shall simply lay out the basic proposal model (Figure 5.17).

CHECKING THE LINE OF REASONING

There are two primary means of checking the soundness of your line of reasoning once the argument has been put together: responding to a series of questions about the sufficiency and suitability of the evidence, and visualizing the argument.

ASSESSING THE SUFFICIENCY AND SUITABILITY OF THE EVIDENCE

Building upon the lessons in Chapter 3, the final step is to ensure that our evidence substantiates our assertions and correctly defines the course of action. To accomplish these goals, we can ask ourselves the following questions before we try our argument out on our peers or our boss.

1. Is there enough evidence? Will our audience perceive that we have offered enough evidence to convince them about the validity of our assertions?

2. Is the evidence clear? Will our audience understand the evidence as intended?

3. Is the evidence generally consistent with already known evidence? Will our audience see our evidence as in line with what they already accept as reasonable?

4. Is the evidence verifiable and reliable? Will our audience feel confident about the sources, accuracy, and currency of our evidence?

Now is the time to review the guidance we have discussed on defining purpose and audience, and to reassess our selection and presentation of facts, allowing us to see both the explicit statements and the implicit assumptions. Now is also the appropriate time to assess if there are any weaknesses in the argument that need to be addressed.

VISUALIZING THE ARGUMENT

Stephen Toulmin, a British philosopher, developed an effective means of deconstructing and visualizing arguments. As he explains, rational arguments involve a basic framework in which we establish grounds for the argument, establish the bases for the argument, and then offer a conclusion. Along the way, the bases are informed by specific validating statements, clarifications, and limitations. To use Toulmin's terminology, argument is composed of the following elements:

1. Claims—the position or conclusion you are asking the audience to reach

2. Grounds—the foundation on which you make your claims

3. Warrants—the means by which you establish that the grounds lead inevitably to your claims (e.g., laws, statutes, engineering formulas)

4. Backing—the supporting information and unstated assumptions that need to be articulated to ensure that the audience is comfortable with the warrants you have cited.

5. Modal qualifiers—terms (e.g., commonly, often, infrequently) that establish the degree of certainty or probability

6. Possible rebuttals—the factors, conditions, and/or assumptions that must be in effect for the assertion to be true. (For example, you might argue that the company will only make money if the average inflation rate remains below 4.5%.)[27]

Using these six terms (designated respectively as *C, G, W, B, M,* and *R*), Toulmin offers a model to visualize an argument or line of reasoning (Figure 5.18).

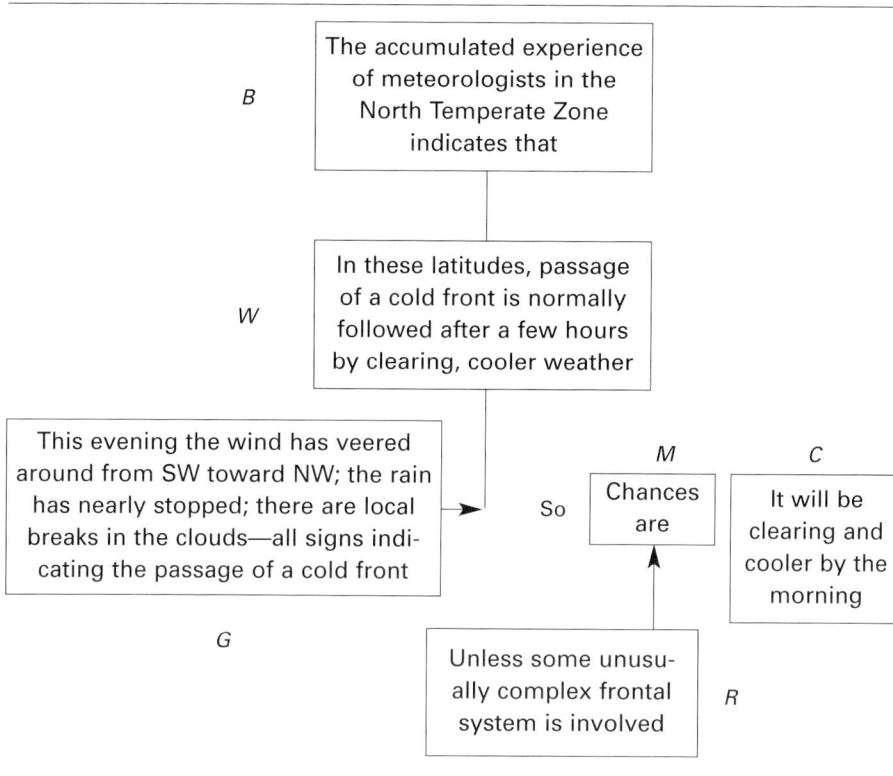

FIGURE 5.18

Toulmin's Structure for Visualizing Argument

B The accumulated experience of meteorologists in the North Temperate Zone indicates that

W In these latitudes, passage of a cold front is normally followed after a few hours by clearing, cooler weather

G This evening the wind has veered around from SW toward NW; the rain has nearly stopped; there are local breaks in the clouds—all signs indicating the passage of a cold front

So **M** Chances are

C It will be clearing and cooler by the morning

R Unless some unusually complex frontal system is involved

Source: Toulmin/Rieke/Janek, AN INTRODUCTION TO REASONING, 2/E (c) 1984, p. 124. Reprinted by permission of Pearson Education, Inc. Upper Saddle River, New Jersey.

Combining this visualization technique with the questions on information sufficiency and with your understanding of the basic tenets of business reasoning will provide a substantive means to assess the strength and validity of your argument.

A WORD ABOUT REFUTATION

Although the goal in business reasoning is generally a collaborative effort to secure the best possible outcomes for the company, this does not necessarily mean that all decisions are reached without exchange and challenges. When called upon to refute a colleague's position, you can employ a structure or line of argument similar to those used when constructing your own argument:

1. State precisely what element of the position you intend to address. Where possible, employ the same terminology as used in the position as originally presented.

2. State concisely what the issues are and what objections you intend to raise.

3. Introduce the evidence or reasoning that supports your contentions. Also, explain where you rely on different assumptions.

4. Explain precisely how the new evidence demonstrates that your position is a more appropriate course of action than that proposed by your colleague.

5.4 | **A REVIEW OF BASIC EXPECTATIONS FOR REASONING**

Type of Assertion	Audience Expectations
Asserting what something is (or the type it is aligned with) *"Information is power."*	Definitions of all terms are acceptable. Examples are convincing and verifiable.
Asserting a cause/effect relationship *"Inflations leads to unemployment."*	Causes are acceptable, credible, defined, and sufficient to lead to the event or conclusion.
Asserting a value (relative or absolute) *"Product X is not a good investment."*	Evaluative criteria are enumerated, valid, sufficient, and acceptable.
Need to take action *"We need to sell our stock today."*	Significance and urgency of problem are established. Recommendations are in line with magnitude and immediacy of the issue.

REASONING—THE LESSONS

Building an effective line of reasoning to support a business decision demands a sound appreciation of how decisions are reached. We cannot rely on scientific methodology or formal logic, except as these may provide sources of evidence that contribute to the proof. In each case—whether making a proposition, an evaluation, an analysis, or a proposal—we have the responsibility to make certain that the dimensions of the discussion are clearly established; the audience's expectations about appropriate and adequate information are satisfied; the assumptions and criteria are clearly articulated and consistently applied; and the actions or conclusions are derived directly from the arguments advanced. Table 5.4 summarizes the key expectations associated with the four types of business assertions.

EXERCISES

☐ Group

1. Using the newspaper article shown on the following page, develop a proposal that your university or company support and fund development of a degree in astrology.

2. Identify an initiative underway at your university or company. Analyze how the argument for the initiative is structured; also, identify what you see as opportunities to strengthen or refute the line of reasoning.

Stars bode well for school of astrology

By GIOVANNA DELL'ORTO
ASSOCIATED PRESS

SCOTTSDALE, Ariz. — The stars were favorably aligned this month for the Astrological Institute, says founder Joyce Jensen, whose students learn to write horoscopes and give advice about the future.

The modest school in suburban Phoenix won accreditation from a federally recognized body in what's thought to be a first for a school of astrology. Now the institute can seek approval from the U.S. Department of Education for its students to get federal grants and loans.

From her observation of the celestial array, Jensen said she sees that "this was a very good time" for her school. But Jensen — a 60-year-old Scorpio — also said she has been seeking accreditation for years, and wouldn't have stopped no matter what the stars indicated.

Her institute, where courses include a "master class on the asteroid goddesses" and "how to write an astrological column," offers one program: a diploma in astrology and psychology.

The institute received accreditation from the Accrediting Commission of Career Schools and Colleges of Technology after demonstrating that its teachers are qualified and that its graduates can be placed in jobs, said Elise Scanlon, head of the Arlington, Va.-based commission. Scanlon and other officials in her field knew of no other accredited astrology schools.

Judith Eaton, head of the Council for Higher Education Accreditation in Washington, said the accreditation does not validate astrology, but only recognizes that the school fulfills what it promises its students.

Tuition is $5,300, with classes offered in the day and evening. Full-time students can earn a diploma in 12 months. But a majority of the 32 students now enrolled come at night, after working day jobs. For a diploma, they must pass three courses each in astrology and psychology, plus at least four electives.

Source: Reprinted with permission of The Associated Press.

☐ Individual

1. Using the newspaper article, prepare an outline for one of these three business cases:

   a) Proposition—An explanation answering why the astrology program should be part of the communication program

   b) Analysis—An explanation explaining why astrology needs to be considered central to a comprehensive communication program

   c) Evaluation—An argument about the value the astrology program will add to the communication program

2. Present your line of reasoning to the class for discussion and review.

END NOTES

1 Stephen Levy, "The Bug That Didn't Bite: Billions of Dollars Later, Y2K Bug Is on the Run," *Newsweek,* Jan. 10, 2000, p. 41.

2 Bill Goodwin, "Y2K Bug Was a Costly Non-Event," *Computer Weekly*, Jan. 13, 2000, p. 14.

3 Ibid.

4 "The Y2K Ransom," *Computerworld,* Jan. 10, 2000, p. 47.

5 Quoted in Thomas A. Stewart, "Being Smart Doesn't Mean You Can Think," *Fortune,* July 30, 1990, Vol. 122, No.3, pp. 247–248.

6 John J. Stallard, Sandra F. Pierce, and E. Ray Smith, "A Strategy for Teaching Critical-Thinking Skills in Business Communication," *The Bulletin,* Vol. 55, No. 3, Sept. 1992, pp. 20–22.

7 Alan Cromer, *Uncommon Sense: The Heretical Nature of Science.* New York: Oxford University Press, 1993.

8 Philip K. Wilson, "Origins of Science," *National Forum,* Vol. 76, No. 1 (Winter 1996), pp. 39–43.

9 Morris Kline, *Mathematics and the Search for Knowledge.* New York: Oxford University Press, 1985.

10 Wilson, "Origins of Science."

11 Alan Cromer, *Uncommon Sense: The Heretical Nature of Science.*

12 I. Bernard Cohen, "An Interview with Einstein," *Scientific American,* July 1955, pp. 69–73.

13 Carl Sagan, "An Analysis of *Worlds in Collision,*" in *Scientists Confront Velikovsky,* ed. Donald Goldsmith. Ithaca: Cornell University Press, 1977.

14 Fred J. Gruenberger, "A Measure for Crackpots," *Science,* 145 (Sept. 25, 1964), pp. 1413–1415.

15 The illustrations and their descriptions are adapted from Kline, *Mathematics and the Search for Knowledge.*

16 Figure from Cromer, *Uncommon Sense: The Heretical Nature of Science.*

17 Summarized from Carl Meyer, "Distinguishing Good Science, Bad Science, and Junk Science," in *Expert Witnessing: Explaining and Understanding Science,* ed. Carl Meyer, New York: CRC Press, 1999.

18 Nicholas Rescher, *Introduction to Logic.* New York: St. Martin's Press, 1964.

19 Irving David Shapiro, "Fallacies of Logic: Argumentation Cons." *ETC: A Review of General Semantics,* Vol. 53, No. 3, (Fall 1996), p. 251–265.

20 Richard Fulkerson, "Technical Logic, Comp-Logic, and the Teaching of Writing," in *College Composition and Communication,* Vol. 39, No. 4, (Dec. 1988), pp. 436–452.

21 Quoted in George F. Will, "Soft Money, Odd Thinking," *Newsweek,* Feb. 11, 2002, p. 64.

22 Daniel McGinn, "The Ripple Effect," *Newsweek,* Feb. 18, 2002, pp. 29, 30, 32.

23 Allan Sloan, "Lights Out for a Giant," *Newsweek,* Dec. 10, 2001, pp. 50–51.

24 Austin Bradford Hill, "The Environment and Disease: Association or Causation?" in *Evolution of Epidemiological Ideas: Annotated Readings on Concepts and Methods,* ed. Sander Greenland. Chestnut Hill, MA: Epidemiological Resources, Inc. 1987. Also see: Linda S. Erdech, "Using Epidemiology to Explain Disease Causations to Judges and Juries," in Carl Meyer, *Expert Witnessing.*

25 Kathleen B. Powe and Daniel L. Plung, "Strategic Decision Making in a Time of Information Overload," *Information Outlook,* Vol. 5, No. 11 (Nov. 2001), pp. 22–30.

26 Theresa F. Lindeman, "Would You Like a Latte With That Best Seller? Carnegie Library Is Trying to Shake Off the Dust to Play a Bigger Part in Local Residents' Lives," *Pittsburgh Post Gazette,* Feb. 18, 2001, Business Section, pp. 1–3.

27 Stephen Toulmin, Richard Rieke, and Allen Janik, *An Introduction to Reasoning.* New York: Macmillan Publishing Co., 1979.

6

Language and Readability
Thinking Out Into Language

Having established the communication foundations of purpose, audience, information, organization, and argument, we eventually get around to putting our thoughts down as we intend to present them, whether in written or spoken form. At this moment, there is a grand transition, what Cardinal Newman termed "a thinking out into language."

This "thinking out" does not seek to discriminate one type of writing from another or define the environment in which to apply it. Yet there has developed a certain misperception that the concept of style is for the poetic, for the fanciful, perhaps even for the academic, but not for the business environment. Can this really be?

The business world is awash with words. The digesting of reports and the assimilation of presented materials is the heart of business. Can we then think that in business, the goals are tedium, dullness, and lack of style? The businessperson, often reading long into the night, is no more prepared to withstand the sleep-inducing potion of a dull manuscript or presentation than any other reader. To be successful as communicators, we need to create an identity through language. We must grasp precisely the right words, and we must string the words into an effective message—a message that makes its point with grace and style.

THE BUSINESS OF STYLE

In the business world, we often have missed the mark by reducing the meaning of style to something synonymous with mechanics. Style guides, such as the *MLA (Modern Language Association) Style Sheet*, the *Handbook for Authors of Papers in the Journals of the American Chemical Society, The Chicago Manual of Style*, the *Associated Press Stylebook*, or the American Psychological Association (APA) *Publications Manual* are valuable in establishing consistency among publication guidelines such as format, spelling, and citations. However, these guides represent "house style," not the individual style announced in "thinking out into language."

In business, house style reaches far into the workplace. At a national level, there are broad-reaching style guides, such as the United States Government Printing Office *Style Manual*, whose authority derives from federal law (Figure 6.1).[1] At a more immediate level, there are corporate-specific manuals developed to ensure communications within a corporation share a common format and adhere to a common interpretation of mechanical requirements (e.g., punctuation, abbreviations, capitalization, spelling, and technical expressions). Certainly, it can be agreed that operating the United States Government or specific corporations demands a great degree of consistency among agencies, courts, embassies, and offices. However, consistency is not necessarily indicative of style.

Perhaps we can make the distinction between "house" (or "press") style and the style alluded to by Cardinal Newman a bit clearer if we add a few voices to that of Cardinal Newman. Alongside "style is the thinking out into language," we might add four other well-known expressions about style:

- A man's style is his mind's voice. (Emerson)
- Style is the dress of thoughts. (Lord Chesterfield)
- Style is the sound . . . words make on paper. (E. B. White)
- Style, in its finest sense, is the last acquirement of the educated mind; it is also the most useful. (Alfred North Whitehead)

FIGURE 6.1

A Congressionally
Mandated Style

> **EXTRACT FROM THE PUBLIC PRINTING LAW**
> (TITLE 44, U.S.C)
> SECTION 1105. THE PUBLIC PRINTER SHALL DETERMINE THE FORM AND STYLE IN WHICH THE PRINTING OR BINDING ORDERED BY A DEPARTMENT IS EXECUTED, AND THE MATERIAL AND THE SIZE OF TYPE USED, HAVING PROPER REGARD TO ECONOMY, WORKMANSHIP, AND THE PURPOSES FOR WHICH THE WORK IS NEEDED.

These quotations point out five important attributes of style: 1) Style is synonymous with who we are. 2) Style reflects the clarity of our thoughts. 3) Style provides the precision of our ideas. 4) Style gives voice to both meaning and sound. 5) Style represents a skill that can be acquired.

While the poets and philosophers have a valuable perspective on style, social and natural scientists, communities closer to our immediate interests, have added appreciably to the insights concerning the nature of and need for style. The first of these insights is that style is what gives strength to our communications. While George Orwell, author of *Animal Farm* and *1984,* clarified that language was an "instrument" for expressing thought in his influential essay, "Politics and the English Language," others have taken this point much further. Asserting "the study of language is a way of studying thinking," V.V. Nalimov, a noted Russian mathematician, offers this modest conclusion to his book *In the Labyrinth of Language: A Mathematician's Journey:* "For some reason or other, words with rhythm have acquired a peculiar power. They may intoxicate the listener. Those who are masters of such words possess in the human world an unlimited attractiveness for others. Words have acquired power over people. By means of words great changes in . . . society have been made."[2]

As powerful as the message is coming from the world of mathematics, by far the most poignant elaboration on style comes not from a poet, a politician, or a mathematician. Having experienced the consequences of war and having sired the atom bomb, the greatest weapon known to man, J. Robert Oppenheimer, writing in *The American Scientist* only 4 years after the end of WW II, offered the following insights:

> The problem of doing justice to the implicit, the imponderable, and the unknown is, of course, not unique to politics. It is always with us in science, it is with us in the most trivial of personal affairs, and it is one of the great problems of writing and of all forms of art. The means by which it is solved is sometimes called style. It is style which complements affirmation with limitation and with humility; it is style which makes it possible to act effectively, but not absolutely; it is style, which in the domain of foreign policy, enables us to find harmony between the pursuit of ends essential to us, and the regard for the views, the sensibilities, the aspirations of those to whom the problem may appear in another light; it is style which is the deference that action pays to uncertainty; it is above all style through which power defers to reason.[3]

The last insight we need to take with us as we journey into this world of style is that style is not only an "integral part of us," but is a dynamic capability that improves not through attention to rules, but with our improved mastery of individual expression. As H.L. Mencken, an American essayist and scholar on American English, argued: "Style is always the outward and visible symbol of a man, and it cannot be anything else." In so stating, Mencken also celebrated the individualism of style: "For the essence of a sound style is that it cannot be reduced to rules—that it is a living and breathing thing, with something of the demoniacal in it—that it fits its proprietor tightly and yet ever so loosely, as his skin fits him . . . . If he has fed it well, it is mellow. If he has gastritis, it is bitter."[4]

Putting these insights of the poets, political theorists, mathematicians, and scientists into perspective, we can see a number of factors that contribute to style: diction, sentence structure, sentence variety, imagery, rhythm, coherence, emphasis, and arrangement. As such, this basic understanding of style serves as a backdrop for understanding the role of style in professional communication. In business, we have a major challenge—to offer arguments that are concrete, precise, effective and appealing. We must be able to create the sounds that give voice to our thoughts in exactly the way we intended. We must be able to marshal ideas in a manner that represents the argument well. We must be prepared to offer the power of language and style that allows action to pay deference to uncertainty and power to defer to reason.

THE ESSENTIALS OF STYLE

Let's begin our discussion of style by considering a sample from a publication familiar to most adult Americans—the instructions for filing taxes. If we put aside the 44,000 pages of tax code and focus exclusively on the tax instructions, we should have no difficulty defining the audience and purpose. The audience is all Americans who have established themselves as wage earners. The purpose is to help us to determine what we owe in taxes to the government. Accordingly, we might expect that the information and its organization correspond with our need to complete the forms, make the calculations, and conclude our transaction either by asking for money back or submitting a check. Additionally, of most interest to us in the context of this chapter, the language should be clear, precise, and comprehensible (readable).

To isolate these stylistic components, let's compare the guidance that the Internal Revenue Service (IRS) provides regarding one simple but critical decision: deciding whether to itemize deductions or to take a standard deduction. Figures 6.2 and 6.3 show the explanations provided to assist with completing returns for the years 1980 and 2000. In 1980, instructions were presented as very dense text. Over the years, narrative was shortened and tables added, so that by 2000 a much more readable text is accompanied by a simplified chart. This progression reflects the advancing emphasis on clarity, as well as on recognition of the value of style.

Not unlike a number of government agencies, in the 1970s and 1980s, the IRS recognized that its inability to communicate with the public contributed to a significant loss of credibility. This lack of clarity also contributed to thousands of incorrectly completed returns. Consequently, the IRS introduced a series of courses on "Effective Revenue Writing." Taught by Calvin Linton, a professor of English and Dean of Columbia College at George Washington University, these courses forced thousands of government employees to consider how they might "take a dull subject and make it seem interesting, an obscure subject and make it seem clear, an unpleasant subject and make it appear palatable."[5] Accomplishing these improvements meant attacking what Linton called the five "common diseases" of government writing:

a. when you retired, or

b. on January 1, 1976, or January 1, 1977, if you retired before the later date on disability or under circumstances which entitled you to retire on disability.

Use **Form 2440**, Disability Income Exclusion, to figure the amount of any exclusion. Enter the exclusion from Form 2440 on this line.

Note: *Be sure to include the full amount of your disability pension on Form 1040, line 8.*

Line 30

Total Adjustments

Add lines 23 through 29. Enter the total on this line.

Line 31

Adjusted Gross Income

Subtract line 30 from line 22. If line 31 is less than $10,000, you may be eligible to claim the Earned Income Credit. Please see the instructions for line 57 on page 13.

If line 31 is less than zero (0), you may have a net operating loss that you can carry to another tax year. If you carry the loss back to earlier years, see **Form 1045.** For more information, please get **Publication 535,** Business Expenses and Operating Losses.

Tax Computation

Line 32

Enter the amount from line 31.

Line 33

You will fall into one of the three classes below:
- You MUST itemize deductions, or
- You choose to itemize, or
- You do not itemize.
  The three classes are described below.

You MUST Itemize Deductions

You must itemize deductions if:

A. You can be claimed as a dependent on your parents' return and had interest, dividends, or other unearned income of $1,000 or more. Generally, this means that you must complete Schedule A and Schedule TC, Part II.

There are two exceptions to this rule:
   1. You don't have to itemize or complete Schedule A, or Part II of Schedule TC, if you have earned income* of $2,300 or more if single ($1,700 or more if married filing a separate return). Enter zero (0) on line 33 and go to line 34.
   2. You don't have to itemize and use Schedule A if you know that your earned income* is more than your itemized deductions. In this case go directly to Schedule TC, Part II, after completing line 32 of Form 1040.

Note: *If your unearned income is less than $1,000, you don't have to use Schedule A or Schedule TC—enter zero (0) on line 33 and go on to line 34.*

In any case, be sure to check the box on line 33.

B. You are married, filing a separate return, and your spouse itemizes. (There

is an exception to this rule: You don't have to itemize if your spouse is described in item **A** above and enters earned income* instead of itemized deductions when completing Part II of Schedule TC.)

C. You file Form 4563 and exclude income from sources in U.S. possessions. (Please see **Form 4563,** and **Publication 570,** Tax Guide for U.S. Citizens Employed in U.S. Possessions, for more details.)

D. You had dual status as a nonresident alien for part of 1980, and during the rest of the year you were either a resident alien or a U.S. citizen. However, you do not have to itemize if you file a joint return with your spouse who was a U.S. citizen or resident at the end of 1980 and you and your spouse agree to be taxed on your combined worldwide income.

Generally, you must complete Schedule A (Itemized Deductions) if item A, B, C, or D, above applies to you. After you've completed Schedule A:
a. If Schedule A, line 40, is more than line 39, do not fill in Form 1040, line 33. Go to Schedule TC instead and complete Part II to figure the amount to enter on Form 1040, line 34.
b. If Schedule A, line 39, is more than line 40, enter the amount from Schedule A, line 41, on Form 1040, line 33.

You Choose to Itemize

You may choose to itemize your deductions if you are:
- Married and filing a joint return, or a Qualifying widow(er) with dependent child, and your itemized deductions are more than $3,400.
- Married and filing a separate return, and your itemized deductions are more than $1,700.
- Single, or a Head of household, and your itemized deductions are more than $2,300.

If you do itemize, complete Schedule A and enter the amount from Schedule A, line 41, on Form 1040, line 33.

Caution: *Certain taxpayers must itemize even though their itemized deductions are less than the amount shown here for their filing status. See "You MUST Itemize Deductions" above.*

You Do Not Itemize

If your itemized deductions are less than the amount shown above for your filing status (or you choose not to itemize), enter zero on line 33 unless you MUST itemize as described above.

__Earned income__ is income you receive for personal services you have performed. It includes wages, salaries, tips and professional fees.

Generally, your earned income is the total of the amount(s) you reported on Form 1040, lines 8, 13, and 19.

Earned income does not include pay for your services that included a distribution of earnings and profits other than reasonable compensation for your work for a corporation.

If you were engaged in a trade or business in which both your services and capital were important income-producing factors, your earned income will be based on a reasonable allowance for the services you performed. However, the earned income may not be more than 30 percent of your share of the net profits from the business.

FIGURE 6.2

When Making a Decision Isn't Easy

1. Weak Writing—concealing the subject or the verb of a sentence; weakly constructing the relationship among the parts of the sentence; and ignoring the logical relationships among pieces

2. Obscurity—constructing sentences that either say nothing or say something other than what the author intended.

3. Confusion—authoring letters and reports that have no clear sense of meaning or relevance.

4. Incorrectness—producing mechanically flawed communications

5. Unattractiveness—proceeding without style, without "any sense of the power of personality in expository writing"[6]

Using these "diseases" to assess the IRS samples, we can now understand what causes our increasingly positive response to instructions as they evolve from

---

FIGURE 6.3

The IRS Enters the Twenty-First Century

Line 35b

If your spouse itemizes deductions on a separate return or if you were a dual-status alien, check the box on line 35b. But if you were a dual-status alien and you file a joint return with your spouse who was a U.S. citizen or resident at the end of 2000 and you and your spouse agree to be taxed on your combined worldwide income, **do not** check the box.

Line 36

Itemized Deductions or Standard Deduction

In most cases, your Federal income tax will be less if you take the **larger** of:

● Your itemized deductions or
● Your standard deduction.

⚠ **CAUTION** If you checked the box on **line 35b**, your standard deduction is zero.

Itemized Deductions

To figure your itemized deductions, fill in **Schedule A.**

(Continued on page 32)

Standard Deduction Chart for People Age 65 or Older or Blind—Line 36

If someone can claim you (or your spouse if married filing jointly) as a dependent, use the worksheet below instead.

Enter the number from the box on line 35a of Form 1040 . . . . ▶ [ ]

⚠ **CAUTION** Do not use the number of exemptions from line 6d.

IF your filing status is . . .	AND the number in the box above is . . .	THEN your standard deduction is . . .
Single	1	$5,500
	2	6,600
Married filing jointly or Qualifying widow(er)	1	$8,200
	2	9,050
	3	9,900
	4	10,750
Married filing separately	1	$4,525
	2	5,375
	3	6,225
	4	7,075
Head of household	1	$7,550
	2	8,650

Standard Deduction Worksheet for Dependents—Line 36   *Keep for Your Records*

Use this worksheet **only** if someone can claim you (or your spouse if married filing jointly) as a dependent.

1. Add $250 to your **earned income***. Enter the total . . . . 1. _____
2. Minimum standard deduction . . . . 2. __700.00__
3. Enter the **larger** of line 1 or line 2 . . . . 3. _____
4. Enter the amount shown below for your filing status.
   ● Single—$4,400
   ● Married filing separately—$3,675
   ● Married filing jointly or qualifying widow(er)—$7,350
   ● Head of household—$6,450
   } . . . . 4. _____
5. **Standard deduction.**
   a. Enter the **smaller** of line 3 or line 4. If under 65 and not blind, **stop here** and enter this amount on Form 1040, line 36. **Otherwise,** go to line 5b . . . . 5a. _____
   b. If 65 or older or blind, multiply the number on Form 1040, line 35a, by: $1,100 if single or head of household; $850 if married filing jointly or separately, or qualifying widow(er) . . . . 5b. _____
   c. Add lines 5a and 5b. Enter the total here and on Form 1040, line 36 . . . . 5c. _____

***Earned income** includes wages, salaries, tips, professional fees, and other compensation received for personal services you performed. It also includes any amount received as a scholarship that you must include in your income. Generally, your earned income is the total of the amount(s) you reported on Form 1040, lines 7, 12, and 18, minus the amount, if any, on line 27.*

1980 to 2000. In 1980, we were faced with a seemingly impenetrable mountain of detail. Information was clumped together, drifting in and out of focus. Decisions were embedded in the text. Interpretations were positioned within the text and buried in the footnotes following the text. Paragraph upon paragraph pulls us along, but away from the information we seek. With the exception of mechanical incorrectness, all the remaining horsemen of "common writing disease" are here: weak writing, obscurity, confusion, and unattractiveness.

By the time we reach the 2000 instructions, the deep brush we had been wading through is gone. White space on the page gives us opportunity to isolate each independent element of the instructions. Even the intimidating footnote regarding Earned Income seems less daunting — both in the length of the explanation and in its physical presentation. When deciphering the IRS's instructions, we now have an easily approachable, much more understandable, more precise and significantly more attractive communication.

The evolution reflected in just these two samples when combined with the attributes of style reflected in our earlier analysis yields a framework for addressing and developing style, for "thinking out into language." To understand and develop a writing style that will let us communicate effectively in business, we need to know the method, the discipline, and the art of style. Specifically, we need to appreciate the four critical elements of style (Table 6.1). In this chapter, we will deal with the method of style (language and readability). In Chapter 7, we will examine the discipline and art (the rhetoric of grammar and stylistic tactics).

LANGUAGE: THE BEGINNINGS OF STYLE

The fundamental elements of establishing style are 1) selecting and using words appropriately, 2) avoiding jargon, and 3) controlling readability. These elements, which supply the backbone of effective style, warrant close attention.

USE AND SELECTION OF WORDS

Word choice and use can prove critical to the effectiveness of a communication. In some instances, word choice can even become a matter of life and death, as was demonstrated in May 1996. A simple confusion of terms contributed to the May 11, 1996, crash of ValuJet Flight 592 in the Florida Everglades. Before loading excess oxygen cylinders (used to feed passenger oxygen masks in the event of cabin decompression) into the hold of the airplane, mechanics were supposed to follow a basic procedural requirement: "If generator has not been expended, install shipping cap on firing pin." If any residual gas remained in the cylinder, extra precautions were needed to ensure against an accidental release or worse.

TABLE

6.1	THE ELEMENTS OF BUSINESS STYLE	
Method	Language	
	Readability	
Discipline	The rhetoric of grammar	
Art	Stylistic tactics	

However, instead of verifying the contents of the cylinder, the mechanics checked the dates the canisters had been placed into service. As these mechanics were later to explain during investigations, they were "replacing generators because they had expired." Unfortunately, for the 110 people who died that day, "expired" is not synonymous with "expended," and shelf life is not an indicator that the contents have become inactive. When the cylinders heated up in the hull of the plane, fire erupted, and ValuJet 592 went down.[7] Everyone on board was killed, ValuJet was forced to shut down all operations for more than 3 months, mountains of civil suits were processed, and criminal prosecutions were sustained against the airline's maintenance contractor in Miami.

Like the *Challenger* accident, the consequences of poor communications were tragic. Although few of us will ever make errors in correctness, diction, precision, or word choice that will produce equivalent consequences, the lesson is there for all of us to heed. We need to pay careful attention to connotation and precision of language.

CONNOTATION AND DENOTATION. Connotation and denotation are terms familiar to us from our studies in basic diction. Denotation addresses a word's literal meanings. Connotation deals with a word's associations and implications. In business, as in all enterprises, language can convey much more than literal meaning. To understand the roles played by these elements, let's look at some phrases that are heard by thousands of workers every year: the expressions associated with "firing" or "terminating" an employee.

In a book on business slang, *Big Talk 1, American Business Slang and Jargon*, David Burke provides numerous alternative phrases businesses might use to communicate the process of "downsizing" (Table 6.2).[8] By no means exhaustive, Burke's list could be expanded to include such novel additional terms as "restructuring" and "redistribution." What we say often has two meanings (if not more), and we need to make certain the connotation and the denotation fit our purposes and audience.

PRECISION. Accompanying the issue of connotation and denotation is one of precision. Is the selected phrase a solid and specific articulation of the thought we intended to convey? Precision represents a broad set of considerations and gets quickly to the heart of many problems evidenced in business communication. More specifically, imprecision is the root cause of many of the "diseases" cited earlier: obscurity, weak writing, confusion, and incorrectness. To keep our discussion of imprecision to a length appropriate for our purposes here, we will restrict ourselves to three categories of imprecision: 1) the seemingly precise, 2) soft diction, and 3) business jargon.

Seemingly precise communication often masquerades as its exact counterpart. For example, Figure 6.4 shows the distribution of common terms used to communicate the idea of "error" in analytical chemistry publications.[9] Though the terms all imply the general idea of "error," there are very distinct differences among the choices. These differences, though not apparent immediately until the variations are listed side by side, represent the short distance between the precise and the seemingly precise. Like the choices used to express the concept of "error," the problem is that the precision is only skin-deep, a communication that barely misses its target. The seemingly precise has the appearance of precision without actually delivering it.

As an example of this near-miss approach, suppose you are a volunteer for the local police department. Your primary duty involves preparing descriptions of felons being sought in open cases. You receive a report about two men seen fleeing the scene of a shooting. You type up the report, using the details provided by the

6.2 THE LANGUAGE OF LAYOFFS

Term	Denotation	Business Use
Axe someone	To kill someone with an axe	I hear the boss is planning to axe three people from this department.
Boot someone (to get the boot)	To kick someone with a boot	The boss said he didn't need me anymore, so he gave me the boot.
Cut back	To reduce one's cost	I just heard the company is going to be making cutbacks soon.
Downsize	To reduce costs	Our company is going to have to downsize if it is to remain profitable.
Dump someone	To dispose of someone	Unfortunately, Jim was the first in sales to get dumped.
Show someone the gate (door)	To point out the exit	He wasn't pulling his load, so the boss showed him the gate.
Give someone the ol' heave-ho	A nautical command to sailors to pull hard on a line	I can hardly believe it. The boss just gave me the ol' heave-ho.
Kick someone out	To remove someone by giving them a kick	Just 'cause he talked back, John kicked him out.
Lay off	To dismiss someone	There's going to be a layoff starting tomorrow.
Let someone go	To release a person	I just saw them let Jane go.
Ride someone out of town on a rail	Forcibly evict someone from town	When Mark hit his supervisor, he was ridden out of town on a rail.
Throw someone out on their ear	To eject someone forcibly	The boss was so angry, he threw Dan out on his ear.
Trim the fat	To cut the fat off a piece of meat	The only way to make this office more productive is to trim the fat.
Walking papers (pink slip)	To be handed a termination notice	The entire department was handed its walking papers.

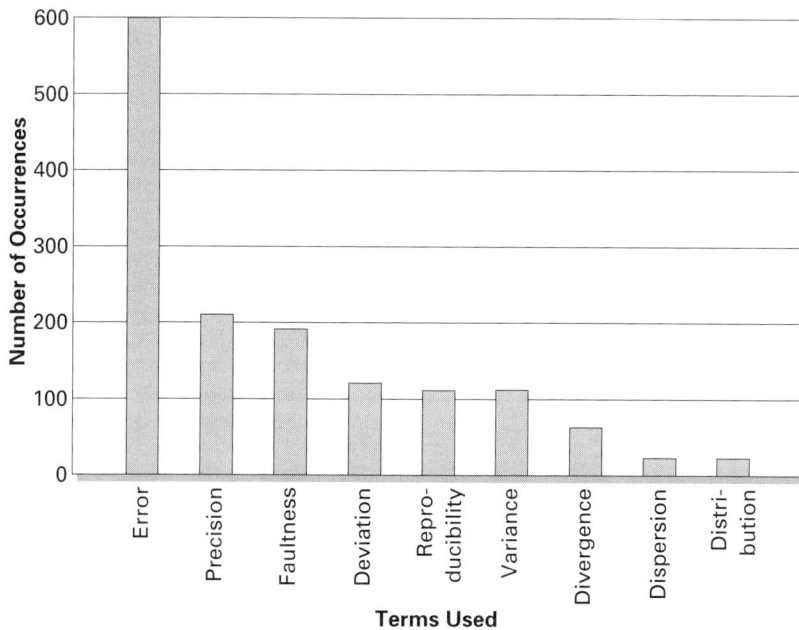

FIGURE 6.4

A Matter of Error

CHAPTER 6   Language and Readability: Thinking Out Into Language

sole eyewitness: "two men, one tall and stocky, one short and thin." You hand your description to the sergeant who seems perturbed. The next morning the sergeant appears at your desk and hands you a chart (Figure 6.5). He tells you to fill in the blanks and leaves.

Your original language was, at best, seemingly precise, especially compared to assigning specific heights and weights. The crossover from imprecision to precision in this example demands a translation system, a basic equation that assigns a value to the descriptive terminology, creating a bridge between the seemingly precise and the actually precise (Figure 6.6). The difference may be of little consequence to you, sitting comfortably at the police station, but it makes all the difference in the world to the officer on the beat—your audience.

Although generally done unintentionally, sometimes the seemingly precise is produced with conscious intent to avoid accurate communication. Sometimes, when stretched beyond credibility, purposeful imprecision can become almost comical. As an example, there is a joke about the Cold War that goes as follows:

During an important meeting between Western and Eastern powers, the Soviet and American leaders challenged each other to a foot race. The U.S. leader won, and the American press reported: "The president defeated the chairman of the U.S.S.R. in a two-man foot race yesterday."

FIGURE 6.5

Reporting the Information

	First Subject		Second Subject	
Height	_____ Feet	_____ Inches	_____ Feet	_____ Inches
Weight	_____ Pounds		_____ Pounds	

FIGURE 6.6

Converting the Imprecise to the More Precise

Average Values		Official Adjustments			
		Height		**Weight**	
5'6"	155	Short = 5'6" to 5'8"		Emaciated: Subtract 40 lb	
5'7"	160			Thin: Subtract 20 lb	
5'8"	165				
5'9"	170	Average = 5'9" to 6'0"		Slender: Subtract 10 lb	
5'10"	175			Medium Use Average Value	
5'11"	180				
6'0"	185	Tall = 6'1" to 6'3"		Stocky Add 15 lb	
6'1"	190			Heavy Add 25 lb	
6'2"	195				
6'3"	200	Very Tall = 6'4"+		Fat/Obese Add 55 lb+	

	First Subject		Second Subject	
Height	**6** Feet	**1** Inches	**5** Feet	**7** Inches
Weight	**205** Pounds		**135** Pounds	

Now the Soviet leader's defeat posed a problem for the Soviet press, which was bound to present things in a positive light or as a victory for Communism. The undaunted Soviets reported: "The chairman of our republic competed in an international foot race yesterday in Moscow. Our leader brought honor to the Soviet Union by finishing second. The president of the United States, however, finished next to last." [10]

We often encounter similarly misleading (seemingly precise) tactics used in business. Here there is no purposeful goal of lying, but a basic lack of precision in the language (Table 6.3). Concrete terms offer us ideas that are solid and specific; less concrete terms allow the same thoughts to slip into vagueness, abstraction, and obscurity. We need to look for clear statements of what happened, who did what, the consequences, and the recommendations.

While it would be easy to fill dozens of pages with examples of business's use of and reliance on the imprecise, a select group of "Memos from Hell" cited in *Fortune* magazine (amplified by a few choice words from among a half dozen industries) should give a clear suggestion of the type of statement we need to watch out for (Figures 6.7 and 6.8). [11]

The solution to eliminating the seemingly precise is to assess concreteness from the perspective of the audience. If the terms used are nebulous to you in the imagined role of audience, that lack of precision will be magnified in the real audience's mind.

The second subset of imprecision is soft diction, manipulating or adding new meanings to words. This elasticity, as Mencken called it, may be a natural characteristic of the English language, but it should not be taken as an open invitation

TABLE 6.3 BUSINESS IMPRECISION

Seemingly precise phrase/sentence	The sentence without euphemism
For your convenience, have your transaction ready.	To improve efficiency of our service, please have your transaction ready.
For your convenience, all transactions enacted after 3 P.M. will be recorded the next day.	If you bring your transaction in after 3 P.M., we will not process it until tomorrow.
For your convenience, please check your packages at the Courtesy Desk.	To control shoplifting, please check your packages.

—Top management helicoptered this vision.
—Added value is the keystone to exponentially accelerating profit curves.
—We need to dimensionalize this management initiative.
—We utilized a concert of cross-functional expertise.
—Don't impact employee incentivization programs.
—Your job, for the time being, has been designated as "retained."
—The plane had an unanticipated vertical impact with the ground.

FIGURE 6.7

Memos of Imprecision

FIGURE 6.8

A Bit of Business
Imprecision

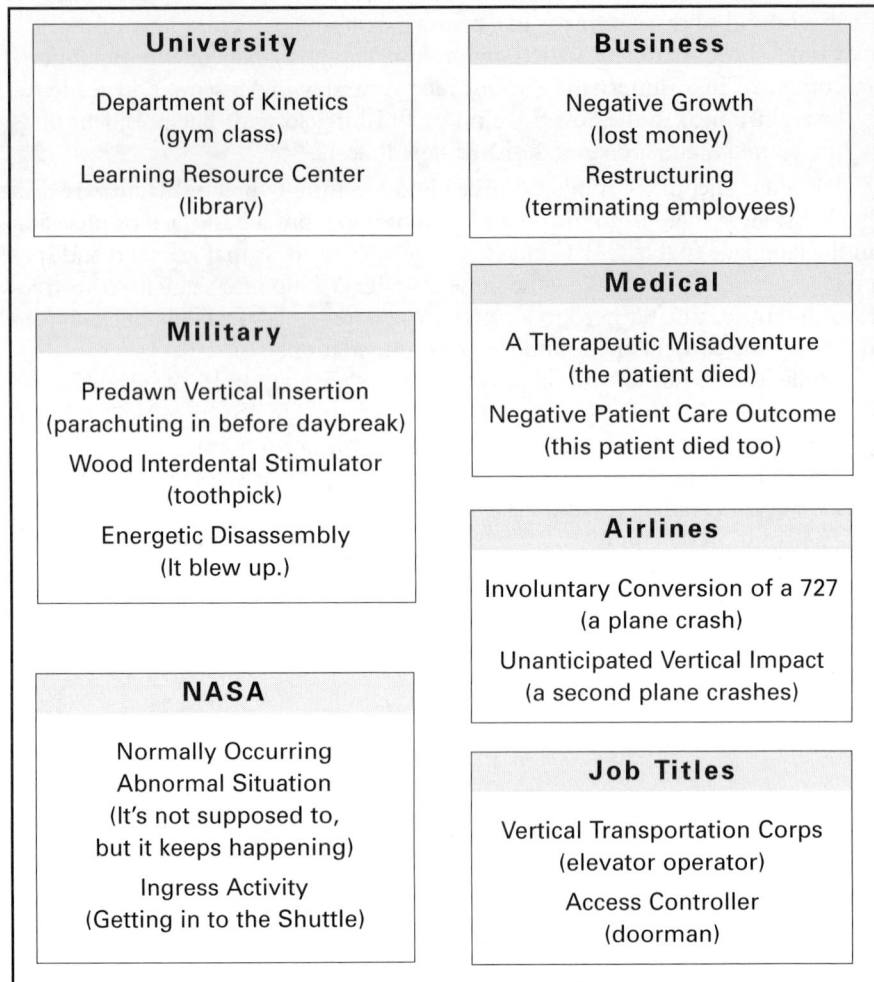

University	Business
University Department of Kinetics (gym class) Learning Resource Center (library)	**Business** Negative Growth (lost money) Restructuring (terminating employees)

University

Department of Kinetics
(gym class)

Learning Resource Center
(library)

Business

Negative Growth
(lost money)

Restructuring
(terminating employees)

Medical

A Therapeutic Misadventure
(the patient died)

Negative Patient Care Outcome
(this patient died too)

Military

Predawn Vertical Insertion
(parachuting in before daybreak)

Wood Interdental Stimulator
(toothpick)

Energetic Disassembly
(It blew up.)

Airlines

Involuntary Conversion of a 727
(a plane crash)

Unanticipated Vertical Impact
(a second plane crashes)

NASA

Normally Occurring
Abnormal Situation
(It's not supposed to,
but it keeps happening)

Ingress Activity
(Getting in to the Shuttle)

Job Titles

Vertical Transportation Corps
(elevator operator)

Access Controller
(doorman)

to dismiss the precision of language. While we may want to temper the counsel of the author of the book of Ecclesiastes, who advised, "Let thy words be few," we shouldn't assume there are too few words or meanings to make our points.

This invitation to create may have reached its pinnacle with the explosion of terms needed to explain the evolution of computer technology, but the instinct is part of a much older tradition. Ambrose Bierce, an early twentieth-century American social critic, echoed this invitation in his book *The Devil's Dictionary*, in which he classified the dictionary as "a malevolent literary device for cramping the growth of a language and making it hard and inelastic."[12] For language to remain precise, there must be a common point of reference to understand the terms we use. Also, there must be a commitment to consistency and a conscientious avoidance of soft diction.

THE GENERICS OF JARGON

A third problem of precision is an undue reliance on jargon, the peculiar, idiosyncratic language or a particular discipline, profession, or community. How does all this jargon get created? There are at least three primary ways to become a prisoner to jargon: 1) invent new words, 2) blunt the edges of the words we have, and 3) simply choose the wrong word for the job.

COINING NEW WORDS. New words and phrases (e.g., e-commerce, service provider, Internet provider, and on-line resource) are all attempts to name the new and dynamic. In many instances, introduction of new words is a valuable means of creating a common understanding. We must be careful, however, not to create just because we can. For example, were we to examine a list of all the words created in the period between the invention of the computer and the current use of the Internet, we could fill a separate book.

Sometimes we create new words in a more indirect manner. To avoid writing two or three words, we add prefixes and suffixes to words, changing the sounds, the nature, and the meaning of the words. Even professional writers, when not guarding against these habits, can slip into these awkward constructions, as was illustrated when *Newsweek* contributed "gunocracy" to our vocabulary.[13] Documenting our insatiable capacity for creating words using prefixes and suffixes, a book entitled *Ologies and -Isms* lists more than 1200 nouns ending in *ism* or *ist*, and approximately 250 more ending with the suffix *phobia* (Figure 6.9).[14]

When not in the word-creation business, we may often be found attempting to summarize difficult ideas by using simple descriptors. As one science reporter described it, this effort at simplification is our attempt to "coax the zap-factor from the unwilling boffin,"[15] a contrivance to satisfy the media's time constraints, the public's lack of attention, and the scientist's eagerness to capture the public's imagination. Put simply, the "zap factor" is the commercialization of language: "in vitro fertilization" becomes "test-tube baby"; "acid precipitation" becomes "acid rain"; major environmental analyses are reduced to the "greenhouse effect"; and the universe is created with a "big bang." The complicated concept becomes the simple image; the precise explanation gives way to the imprecise expression; and the concreteness of language succumbs to the inexactness of jargon and soft diction.

Amoxophobia	Fear of riding in vehicles
Cathisophobia	Fear of sitting down
Deipnophobia	Fear of dining or dinner conversation
Dromophobia	Fear of crossing streets
Ergasiophobia	Fear of work
Erythrophobia	Fear of the color red
Graphyrophobia	Fear of crossing a bridge
Graphophobia	Dislike of writing
Hylephobia	Intense dislike of wood
Ombrophobia	Fear of rain
Pedophobia	Fear of dolls
Phonophobia	Fear of noise
Politicophobia	Fear of politicians
Siderodromophobia	Fear of railroads or being on trains
Telephonophobia	Fear of using the phone
Teratophobia	Fear of monsters or giving birth to a monster
Theatrophobia	Fear of theatres
Tridecaphobia or Triskaidekaphobia	Fear of the number 13
Xerophobia	Fear of dryness or dry places (e.g., deserts)

FIGURE 6.9

A Phobic Response

BLUNTING THE EDGES. Often we don't want to work hard enough to create new words, so we blunt the edges of the ones we have. We force words from out of the precise context in which they have been established into an open circulation whereby the public and the other disciplines can use them in a less precise, more casual manner. Then through a kind of cultural osmosis achieved by continued repetition, the slightly distorted meaning takes precedence over its exact forerunner. Referred to as "Popularized Technicalities," in H. W. Fowler's cornerstone work, *A Dictionary of Modern English Usage*, these words and expressions have been "drained . . . of their very souls" by common misusage (Table 6.4).[16]

This phenomenon is also evident throughout business, where we accept without questioning an array of phrases swiped from other disciplines: Holy Grail, circuit breakers, deadwood, deep-six, parachute, meltdown, headhunter, knee-jerk reaction, turnkey, road maps, turkey, point person, kicker, honcho, feeding frenzy. The consequences of our acceptance are twofold: 1) the popularized technicalities we employ every day are less and less precise as their application continues to widen; and 2) many words that once had precise meanings within the world of business have likewise been hijacked into becoming popularized technicalities (Figure 6.10).[17]

CHOOSING THE WRONG WORD. Ever since the first American-edited dictionary was published by Noah Webster in 1806, we have continued to bend, blunt, and bolster the language. Numerous dictionaries, such as *Fowler's Modern English Usage*, have arisen as arbiters of correctness, attempting to referee etymology and usage. Business certainly needs such guidance. Many managers remain uncertain whether to use *among* or *between, bring* or *take, affect* or *effect*. Others blithely go about using *principle* as an adjective, or *adverse* as a verb. The list of these common errors has remained essentially the same over time (see the Appendix for a list of these examples).[18] The challenge we have is to whittle away at these errors in diction, misused word by misused word.

TABLE

6.4 | A SAMPLING OF POPULARIZED TECHNICALITIES

Original Source	Popularized Terms
Philosophy	Optimism, pessimism
Religion	Devil's advocate
Logic	Dilemma, beg the question
Chess	Checkmate, gambit, stalemate
Science	Acid test
Seamanship	Dead reckoning, underway
Psychology	Ego, psyche, phobia

FIGURE 6.10

The Evolution
of a Popularized
Technicality

Clearinghouse: An institution in London established by the bankers for the adjustment of their mutual claims for checks and bills, by exchanging them and settling their balances.

1832:	In London this is avoided by making all checks paid into bankers pass through what is technically called the "clearinghouse."
1848:	The clearinghouse to which every city banker sends each afternoon all the checks on other bankers which he has received during the day.
1881:	France acting as a clearinghouse between England and India.
1883:	The Charity Organization Society is a central exchange or clearinghouse for all the single relief organizations.
1903:	What is wanted is first a human clearinghouse, or, in other words, compulsory examination of all immigrants.
1943:	The new Council has, among other things, become a clearing-house for regional research.
1961:	The Committee of Vice Chancellors . . . is now proposing to set up a central clearinghouse which will handle all applications . . . .
1995:	The association will also serve as a clearinghouse of information on the subject of security.

THE SPECIFICS OF BUSINESS JARGON

The term jargon is generally applied in one of three principal ways: (1) the specialized vocabulary of a science, art, class, trade, or profession; (2) the hybrid speech of different languages; (3) the use of long words, circumlocution, and a general awkwardness of expression. Of these three definitions, in business the last is of most concern to us in learning to create clear and effective communications. We are, to put the discussion into its American vernacular, interested in elimination of "gobbledygook."

When Maury Maverick, the chairman of the Smaller War Planes Corp., coined the term *gobbledygook* in *Time* magazine in 1944, he created what was to become the best-known onomatopoeia of the post-war era.[19] In an article he authored for *The New York Times Magazine* about a month later, Maverick elaborated on the word he had created to describe the inexactness of government writing: "I do not know [how I got the word]. It must have come in a vision. Perhaps I was thinking of the old bearded turkey gobbler back in Texas, who was always gobbledygobbling and strutting with ridiculous pomposity. At the end of his gobble there was a sort of gook."[20] Melding jargon and imprecision into a single term, "gobbledygook," as Maverick went on to explain is "talk or writing which is long, pompous, vague, involved. . . . It is also talk or writing which is merely long, even though the words are very simple, with repetition over and over again, all of which could have been said in a few words." All-in-all, not a bad image of confused, befuddled, unintelligible language—a turkey gobbling away on a ranch in Texas! Gobbledygook, as he also stated, was "wasted words," a point he illustrated with the writing sample shown below in Figure 6.11. (Figure 6.12 is the cartoon that accompanied the article.)

The original

Whereas, national defense requirements have created a shortage of corundum (as hereafter defined) for the combined needs of defense and private account, and the supply of corundum now is and will be insufficient for defense and essential civilian requirements, unless the supply of corundum is conserved and its use in certain products manufactured for civilian use is curtailed; and it is necessary in the public interest and to promote the defense of the United States, to conserve the supply and direct the distribution and use thereof. Now, therefore, it is hereby ordered that . . .

The rewrite

It could have been written: National defense requirements have created a shortage of corundum. This order is necessary to conserve the supply for war and essential civilian uses, and . . .

Source: Copyright Abner Dean. Used by permission of the Trustees of Dartmouth College.

Before we return to our folks at the IRS (as Maverick's work certainly invites us), we do want to make certain that it's clear that business professionals and government employees are not alone in their ability to generate gobbledygook. For instance, each year since 1995, the scholarly journal *Philosophy and Literature* has sponsored a "Bad Writing Contest" to celebrate the "most stylistically lamentable passages" found in scholarly books and articles. A winning entry—a 94-word sentence—that was chided because it "bullies the reader" should be sufficient to demonstrate that gobbledygook is alive and well on America's college campuses.

The move from a structuralist account in which capital is understood to structure social relations in relatively homologous ways to a view of hegemony in which power relations are subject to repetition, convergence, and rearticulation brought the question of temporality into the thinking of structure, and marked a shift from a form of Althusserian theory that takes structural totalities as theoretical objects to one in which the insights into the contingent possibility of structure inaugurate a renewed conception of hegemony as bound up with the contingent sites and strategies of the rearticulation of power.[21]

Going the academicians one better, lawyers have been accused (and accused themselves) not only of generating, but thriving on an impenetrable form of gobbledygook sometimes referred to as "occupational protectionism." As reported in an article in *Forbes,* "despite what they've been told in law school writing programs, a lot of young lawyers thrill to the idea that they are now members of an exclusive club whose members communicate in a language incomprehensible to the uninitiated." This interpretation suggests a theme of "information is power," a purposeful attempt to keep outsiders from penetrating a veil of secrecy.

> Lawyers write obscure and impenetrable prose for the same reason the medieval Church didn't want the Bible printed in the vernacular. They want to control and limit access to vital information. They don't want a sales manager to look at a statute and decide for himself that his rebate program is legal; or a plant operations manager to read an EPA [Environmental Protection Agency] regulation and figure out how to get his effluent discharges within the legal limit. The legal profession wants them to call lawyers to do these things for them.[22]

Although we might disagree about the motives, few of us would disagree with the assertion that legalese is particularly difficult to understand. Whereas the academicians managed a sentence of almost 100 words to win an award for bad writing, we might have to work especially hard to determine a suitable award for the ability of lawyers to string incomprehensible ideas together. What award might we give, for instance, for the following single sentence that runs 515 words (Figure 6.13)?[23]

With this understanding of the universality—or at least universal potential—for jargon, we can return to our friends in government, recognizing that they are examples of, but not alone in manufacturing, bad writing. Although opportunities for improvement abound, we also have reason for optimism. As the federal tax instructions at the beginning of the chapter illustrated, our government is making concerted efforts to improve the quality and comprehensibility of its communications.

ADDRESSING THE ISSUES OF JARGON

In 1998, the President and Vice President of the United States weighed in on the urgency of making the language of government more accessible. On June 1, 1998, President Clinton issued a memorandum on "plain language in government writing": "The federal government's writing must be in plain language. By using plain language, we send a clear message about what the government is doing, what it requires, and what services it offers."[24] (The Appendix shows a copy of the Presidential Order issued by President Clinton.)

FIGURE 6.13

A Legal Sentence

In the event that the Purchaser defaults in the payment of any installment of purchase price, taxes, insurance, interest, or the annual charge described elsewhere herein, or shall default in the performance of any other obligations set forth in this Contract, the Seller may: at his option: (a) Declare immediately due and payable the entire unpaid balance of purchase price, with accrued interest, taxes, and annual charge, and demand full payment thereof, and enforce conveyance of the land by termination of the contract or according to the terms hereof, in which case the Purchaser shall also be liable to the Seller for reasonable attorney's fees for services rendered by any attorney on behalf of the Seller, or (b) sell said land and premises or any part thereof at public auction, in such manner, at such time and place, upon such terms and conditions, and upon such public notice as the Seller may deem best for the interest of all concerned, consisting of advertisement in a newspaper of general circulation in the county or city in which the security property is located at least once a week for three (3) successive weeks or for such period as applicable law may require and, in case of default of any purchaser, to resell with such postponement of sale or resale and upon such public notice thereof as the Seller may determine, and upon compliance by the Purchaser with the terms of sale, and upon judicial approval as may be required by law, convey said land and premises in fee simple to and at the cost of the Purchaser, who shall not be liable to see to the application of the purchase money; and from the proceeds of the sale: First to pay all proper costs and charges, including but not limited to court costs, advertising expenses, auctioneer's allowance, the expenses, if any required to correct any irregularity in the title, premium for Seller's bond, auditor's fee, attorney's fee, and all other expenses of sale occurred in and about the protection and execution of this contract, and all moneys advanced for taxes, assessments, insurance, and with interest thereon as provided herein, and all taxes due upon said land and premises at time of sale, and to retain as compensation a commission of five percent (5%) on the amount of said sale or sales; SECOND, to pay the whole amount then remaining unpaid of the principal of said contract, and interest thereon to date of payment, whether the same shall be due or not, it being understood and agreed that upon such sale before maturity of the contract the balance thereof shall be immediately due and payable; THIRD, to pay liens of record against the security property according to their priority of lien and to the extent that funds remaining in the hands of the Seller are available; and LAST, to pay the remainder of said proceeds, if any, to the vendor, his heirs, personals representatives, successors or assigns upon the delivery and surrender to the vendee of possession of the land and premises, less costs and excess of obtaining possession.

Later that month, Vice President Gore presented the first "Plain Language Award" to the Occupational Safety and Health Administration (OSHA), stating that "as we in the federal government put our communications into plain language, we will not only be cutting words and phrases, we will be reexamining the original purpose of our rules and regulations." Further promoting the "plain language initiative," Vice President Gore created the "No Gobbledygook Award" as part of a government-wide "Plain Language Network" (Figure 6.14). In recognition of simpler regulations, easier-to-use forms, and more comprehensible guidance, beginning in June 1998, Vice President Gore gave out 27 "No Gobbledygook Awards," the last on December 22, 2000, shortly before the Clinton Administration left the White House. (Figures 6.15 is a sample of the quality of the improved government writing.)

When President Bush took office, the initiative continued, with the Plain Action Network becoming the Plain English Network (PEN). Using the original web site and the existing network of agency representatives, volunteers continue to promote the relatively new tradition of improving "communications from the federal government to the public." Given several years of support by the White House, the initiative has continued to spread well beyond the federal framework. At the state government level, for example, in January 2002, California's Office of Innovation in Government initiated a "Clarity Award" for agencies that simplify state government documents.

FIGURE 6.15

A Sample of Rewritten Regulations

Hazardous Waste Rule Making

Previous
Exemption got listed hazardous waste containing low concentrations of hazardous constituents and managed in landfills and monofills.
  (a) Any hazardous waste listed under this subpart, any mixture of such a listed waste with a solid waste, or any waste derived from the treatment, storage or disposal of such a listed waste is exempt from regulation as a hazardous waste under parts 262–266 and 270 of this chapter if it meets the requirements in 263.37(b) and (d) (including the requirement that all hazardous constituents present in the waste be at or below the levels listed in appendix XI to this part and that the waste be disposed in a landfill or monofill, but not a land application unit). To maintain the exemption, the waste must satisfy the conditions of 261.37(e). Any such waste which also meets the requirements of 261.37(f) is also exempt from the requirement of part 268 of this chapter.

Plain English Version
What waste is eligible for exemption?
(a) Three types of waste are eligible for exemption from the requirements in parts 262–266 and 270 of this chapter.
  (1) Any hazardous waste listed in this subpart
  (2) Any mixture of such a listed waste with a solid waste
  (3) Any waste derived from treating, storing, or disposing of a listed waste
(b) To be exempt, the waste must meet the requirements in 261.37(b) and (d)
(c) To remain exempt, the waste must meet the requirements in 261.37 (e)
(d) If the waste also meets the requirements of 261.37(f), it also is exempt from the requirements of part 268 of this chapter.

Announcing the award, the Director of the Office noted: "The Pythagorean Theorem contains 24 words, while the Ten Commandments consists of 179 words and the Gettysburg Address is all of 286 words long. By contrast, California regulations on catching trout and salmon consume 18,897 words." (Figure 6.16 is the January 2002 winner of the "Clarity Award" in the category of public information.)

Even the American Bar Association has caught the fever, adopting a resolution to promote clearer communications (Figure 6.17).

As the government's experience instructs us, making the right choices about language is the first step to creating style. This demands that we pay attention to a number of principles:

- Use simple, accurate words (focus on convincing readers, not impressing them).
- Use words precisely (connotation, denotation, accepted definitions).
- Be concise and concrete.
- Avoid the urge to create words using suffixes and prefixes (e.g., *-ize, -ism, -wise, -phobia*).
- Avoid fostering occupational protectionism.
- Avoid creating popularized technicalities.
- Avoid redundancy of expression (e.g., "the color red," "the sport of baseball").
- Avoid stacking nouns when a direct name can be used (e.g., "a training session participation audit matrix" instead of "a basic audit").
- Use acronyms, initialisms, and abbreviations only when they are readily recognizable by the audience and are accepted as part of the community's vocabulary.
- Recheck any sentence of more than 20 words to be sure that it remains clear and doesn't mix numerous thoughts under one set of punctuation.

FIGURE 6.17

The Lawyers
Join In

AMERICAN BAR ASSOCIATION
SECTION OF ADMINISTRATIVE LAW AND REGULATORY PRACTICE
SECTION OF STATE AND LOCAL GOVERNMENT LAW
SECTION OF ENVIRONMENT, ENERGY AND RESOURCES
COALITION FOR JUSTICE
RECOMMENDATION—1999

RESOLVED, That the American Bar Association urges agencies to use plain language in writing regulations, as a means of promoting the understanding of legal obligations, using such techniques as:

- Organizing them for the convenience of their readers;
- Using direct and easily understood language;
- Writing in short sentences, in the active voice; and
- Using helpful stylistic devices, such as question-and-answer formats, vertical lists, spacing that facilitates clarity, and tables.

To avoid problems in the use of plain language techniques, agencies should:

- Take into account possible judicial interpretations as well as user understanding;
- Clearly state the obligations and rights of persons affected, as well as those of the agency; and
- Identify and explain all intended changes when revising regulations.

FIGURE 6.16

Winner of the
2002 California
"Clarity Award"

California Department of Forestry and Fire Protection

Homeowners Checklist

How To Make Your Home Fire Safe

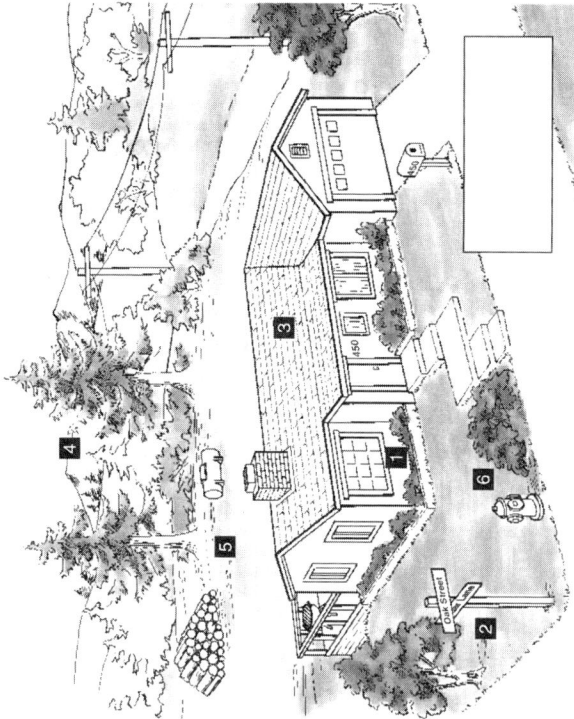

www.fire.ca.gov

OUTSIDE

1 Design/Construction

— Consider installing residential sprinklers
— Build your home away from ridge tops, canyons and areas between high points on a ridge
— Build your home at least 30-100 feet from your property line
— Use fire resistant materials
— Enclose the underside of eaves, balconies and above ground decks with fire resistant materials
— Try to limit the size and number of windows in your home that face large areas of vegetation
— Install only dual-paned or triple-paned windows
— Make sure that electric service lines, fuse boxes and circuit breaker panels are installed and maintained as prescribed by code
— Contract qualified individuals to perform electrical maintenance and repairs

2 Access

— Identify at least two exit routes from your neighbourhood
— Construct roads that allow two way traffic
— Design road width, grade and curves to allow access for large emergency vehicles
— Construct driveways to allow large emergency equipment to reach your house
— Design bridges to carry heavy emergency vehicles, including bulldozers carried on large trucks
— Post clear road signs to show traffic restrictions such as dead end roads, and weight and height limitations
— Make sure dead end roads, and long driveways have turn around areas wide enough for emergency vehicles
— Construct turnouts along one-way roads
— Clear flammable vegetation at least 10 feet from roads and five feet from driveways
— Cut back overhanging tree branches above roads
— Construct fire barriers such as greenbelts
— Make sure that your street is named or numbered, and a sign is visibly posted at each street intersection
— Make sure that your street name and house number are not duplicated elsewhere in the county
— Post your house address at the beginning of your driveway, or on your house if it is easily visible from the road

3 Roof

— Remove branches within 10 feet of your chimney and dead branches overhanging your roof
— Remove dead leaves and needles from your roof and gutters

— Install a fire resistant roof. Contact your local fire department for current roofing requirements
— Cover your chimney outlet and stovepipe with a nonflammable screen of ½ inch or smaller mesh

4 Landscape

— Create a "defensible space" by removing all flammable vegetation at least 30 feet from all structures
— Never prune near power lines. Call your local utility company first
— Landscape with fire resistant plants
— On slopes or in high fire hazard areas remove flammable vegetation out to 100 feet or more
— Space native trees and shrubs at least 10 feet apart
— For trees taller than 18 feet, remove lower branches within six feet of the ground
— Maintain all plants by regularly watering, and by removing dead branches, leaves and needles
— Before planting trees, close to any power line contact your local utility company to confirm the maximum tree height allowable for that location

5 Yard

— Stack woodpiles at least 30 feet from all structures and remove vegetation within 10 feet of woodpiles
— Locate LPG tanks (butane and propane) at least 30 feet from any structure and maintain 10 feet of clearance
— Remove all stacks of construction materials, pine needles, leaves and other debris from your yard
— Contact your local fire department to see if open burning is allowed in your area, if so, obtain a burning permit
— Where barn barrels are allowed, clear flammable materials at least 10 feet around the barrel, cover the open top with a non flammable screen with mesh no larger than ¼ inch

6 Emergency Water Supply

— Maintain an emergency water supply that meets fire department standards through one of the following:
  ▪ a community water/hydrant system
  ▪ a cooperative emergency storage tank with neighbors
  ▪ a minimum storage supply of 2,500 gallons on your property
— Clearly mark all emergency water sources
— Create easy firefighter access to your closest emergency water source
— If your water comes from a well, consider an emergency generator to operate the pump during a power failure

FIRE YOUR POWER

December 2001

CHAPTER 6   Language and Readability: Thinking Out Into Language

Keeping these principles in the forefront of our writing efforts will help begin the march toward a promising style. The next step is gaining a greater appreciation of what needs to be done to ensure we maintain an appropriate readability of our material.

READABILITY

THE CONTEXT AND BACKGROUND

The final principle listed above is something we have only alluded to—sentence length. We certainly don't want to emulate the sentence that won the Bad Writing Award or the lawyer's amazing 515-word sentence. Where we can maintain clarity and precision while reducing sentence length, we should do so. We should also vigorously pursue opportunities to reduce syntactical weight: reducing sentences to phrases, replacing clauses with a single adverb or adjective, and combining related thoughts into single sentences.

Yet, at the same time, we don't want to be too fast in following one of the most vocal and popular trends: the discrediting of sentences more than a few words long. Calvin Linton, as an example, is most vehement when dealing with the subject of sentence length: "The longer the expression, often the tinier the meaning. About economy, then, I think we can come as close to justifiable dogmatism as we can about any feature of writing."

For Linton, the dogmatism translates into the prescription that sentences should not be more than 12 words long. For others, the prescription translates into calculations that claim to establish a text's precise readability. Often partnered with the attack on gobbledygook, readability formulas, like other rules and templates, have limited application in professional communication—a fact that begins to become evident when we look at their origins and assumptions.

Instead of in business offices or university studies, readability, as a focus of study, grew up in elementary schools. Teachers, challenged by the annual exercise of selecting textbooks, wanted some method—other than subject matter—to differentiate the appropriate grade level for each text. As a starting point for developing such a tool, E. L. Thorndike in 1921 published *The Teachers' Wordbook,* a ranking of some 20,000 words based on how common they were. By 1928, this listing of the most common words had been integrated into a multiple regression formula for predicting textbook grade levels. Grade index, as this formula predicted, was determined by four factors:

1. The number of different words per thousand words of text

2. The number of uncommon words (those not in *The Teachers' Wordbook*)

3. The number of simple sentences contained in a selection of 75 successive sentences

4. The number of prepositions per thousand words [25]

While uncritical application of these readability guidelines was discouraged by the developers, the temptation was too great. Soon the initial formula for assessing children's literature was joined by formulas for assessing material written for parents, personal health notices, and popular journals.[26] In only a slight variation from their *Wordbook* origins, each successive new formula considered a combination of four elements:

1. Vocabulary Load—numbers of common and uncommon terms

2. Sentence Structure—sentence length, average number of words per sentence, and average number of simple sentences

3. Idea Density—the numbers of nouns, verbs, and prepositional phrases; the fewer of these elements, the less "dense" the text was presumed to be

4. Human Interest—the number of personal pronouns, the preferred means of engaging audiences

This new specialty of readability labored in the annals of psychology, reading, and elementary education journals until the years leading up to World War II. Overnight, readability was propelled off the pages of the academy digests and into the public vocabulary. With the onset of World War II and immediately after the war, a national interest arose in reaching larger audiences. More people had to fill out tax forms. More people had to be convinced to buy war bonds. More people had to cooperate in various war activities.

Commercial media, at the same time, were eyeing how to increase their markets. Though radio, television, and movies were growing in popularity, reading remained the most popular single pastime among Americans. Competition for the minds and wallets of America was growing ever steeper. The result was application of a common-denominator logic: Great literature was good, but good literature—readily digestible information—was better. Accordingly, numerous strategies were invoked to gain the public's attention.

In 1935, Pocket Books, Inc. launched the first publishing firm exclusively dedicated to publishing paperbacks. Ten years later, in April, 1945, within days of the death of President Roosevelt, Pocket Books rushed into print *FDR: A Memorial*, the first book written specifically to be published as a paperback. As with the invention of moveable type, suddenly access to information was everywhere. While paperbacks were competing with clothbound books, newspapers experienced an even greater challenge. Newspapers were often competing against each other for the same market. This competition was intensified as other media began to make serious inroads into what had always been the newspapers' territory. Radio already had a strong following by the late 40s. Movie theaters were not far behind, as became evident when, on February 18, 1948, 20th Century Fox Movie Tone News began its first daily newsreel telecast. Television, the newest upstart, was gaining in popularity.

Every publisher—book, journal, and newspaper—was looking for the key to make publications clear, entertaining, and more marketable. Rummaging about for a solution, publishers soon focused on the research done on assessing elementary school and adult literacy texts. The intuitive judgment of editors and the basic rule-of-thumb guidance given to journalists gave way to the predictability of the readability calculations. No longer concerned that these predictors had never been intended for assessing general literature, editors became more and more engrossed. While at first the attempts to improve readability using the research had an academic flavor, the tempo and the temperature were turned up when *The Wall Street Journal*, in a full-page advertisement, boasted to the world that it had "the most readable front page in the country."

The claim was founded on an analysis done by Robert Gunning who, doing business as "Readable News Reports," had been helping about 30 U.S. daily newspapers to "stop talking over their readers' heads." As he reported, "most editorial writers seem to confuse dignity with pomposity. Their marathon sentences, foggy words and abstractions put their pieces completely out of reach of all but the upper 5 to 10% of their readers."[27] His attack on "foggy words" and "marathon sentences" soon became what has been known ever since as the "Fog

Index," a tool that turned many inventors of readability systems into some of business's earliest consultants. In the frenzy for simplification and the urgency of publishers to defend their markets, nuance was lost, and the uncritical application of readability formulas became the norm.

Alongside the shorthand references to gobbledygook and Fog Indexes, readability advocates pursued shortcuts to increase the marketability of their assessment tools. At the same time, shortcuts were sought to the four initial readability considerations: language, stylistic expression, content expression, and interest. Focus turned first to typography as an indicator of legibility, then from legibility to reading speed. Content became a subset of human interest. Style of expression became syllable counting. Shortly, only a few readability contenders remained: 1) the Flesch Reading Ease Score—an attempt to link stylistic expression and human interest; 2) the Dale-Chall formula—a vocabulary-load approach descended from *The Teachers' Wordbook*; and 3) Gunning's Fog Index—a structural formula based on sentence length.

For our purposes, we can dismiss the Dale-Chall formula. Based on the 3000 most commonly recognized words by students in Grade 4, the formula has no applicability to business communication. In contrast, both the Fog Index and the Flesch Reading Ease Score, which were subsequently turned into book-length treatises by their authors, established footholds that still are evident today. In a recent article in *Public Relations Quarterly*, for example, the author suggested: "To check the readability of text [you] . . . will find it useful to rely on the Rudolf Flesch Reading Ease Formula and the Gunning-Mueller Fog Index. [These] are . . . invaluable in evaluating copy readability."[28]

So, are these devices "invaluable" or without value? Although knowing the formula's origins should suggest the answer, their lingering staying power demands that we take a moment to examine how these readability systems fare in a real business context. To make this evaluation, we will use two different writing samples, the first of which comes from an article in the *Journal of Small Business Management* (Figure 6.18).[29] The article's authors present a straightforward

---

FIGURE 6.18

Mission Statements in Small and Medium-Sized Businesses

Small and medium-sized enterprises (SMEs) are often characterized by strong entrepreneurial leadership. However, as a small business grows and develops there is an increasing need for the introduction of formal structures, systems, procedures, and controls. As part of this process, many entrepreneurs introduce strategic planning systems. An essential component of planning systems in large organizations is an organizational mission statement. This article uses Irish SMEs to replicate Pearce and David's landmark study of mission statements in large organizations. The results of this research question the validity of the widely referenced Pearce and David study. Research findings suggest that mission statements per se are not correlated positively with SME performance.

All growth businesses experience difficulties during organizational transitions. The transition from a small entrepreneurial organization to a "mature" business organization is characterized by a number of important internal and external changes. The small business often finds that success attracts the attention of others; new small start-ups and/or large competitors may enter the market. Increases in growth may necessitate expansion into overseas markets. Internal changes include the introduction of professional management to manage the increasingly complex organization; the introduction of outside equity to finance growth; and introduction of organizational systems and procedures.

---

discussion about the use and development of mission statements. Reading the abstract (italicized paragraph) and the first full paragraph of the article, we encounter few words that are either difficult or indicative of any occupational protectionism. Accordingly, we should expect this sample to fare well when evaluated by the readability systems.

Let's begin with the older system, Flesch's Reading Ease Score. In the front of his book, *The Art of Readable Writing,* he offered a chart that simply required drawing a straight line from the farthest left-hand column (highlighting the average number of words per sentence) to the farthest right-hand column (average number of syllables per 100 words) (Figure 6.19).[30] In so doing, the line intersects the center column, establishing the passage's Reading Ease Score. A score of 100, by this scale, is perfectly easy to read; a score of 0 is seemingly beyond comprehension.

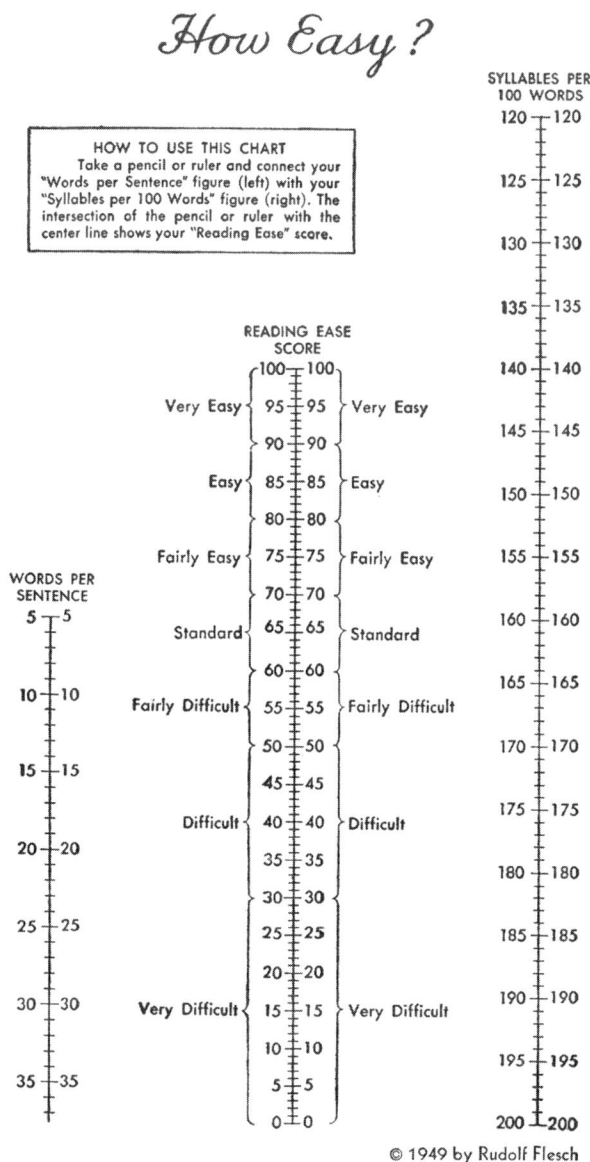

How Easy?

FIGURE 6.19

When Reading Gets Too Easy

HOW TO USE THIS CHART
Take a pencil or ruler and connect your "Words per Sentence" figure (left) with your "Syllables per 100 Words" figure (right). The intersection of the pencil or ruler with the center line shows your "Reading Ease" score.

© 1949 by Rudolf Flesch

Source: "How Easy?" from THE ART OF READABLE WRITING by RUDOLF FLESCH. Copyright 1949, © 1974 by Rudolf Flesch. Reprinted by permission of HarperCollins Publishers Inc.

For use when the book wasn't handy, Flesch provided the underlying formula. To apply the formula, you sample a passage of approximately 100 words, then count both the number of words per sentence and the total number of syllables. These values are then converted to a "difficulty" scale by means of Flesch's equation (Figure 6.20).

Using the abstract and the initial paragraph from the article, we find both passages earn ratings as "very difficult" (Figure 6.21). Are these samples really so difficult? Are they beyond the typical writing we encounter daily in business? Perhaps the writing samples will fare better when tested using Gunning's Fog Index.

In a masterful stroke of simplicity, Gunning's formula uses factors like those in the Flesch Reading Ease Score but requires less mathematical skill to apply. A Fog Index of 17 supposedly requires the reading capability of a college graduate, 13 the reading ability of a high-school graduate, and 6 the reading ability equivalent to that necessary to read a comic book. Returning to our samples from the article on mission statements, we can now also calculate their Fox Indexes (Figure 6.22).

FIGURE 6.20

Deciphering the Reading Ease Score

Reading Ease Score = 206.835 − [(1.015 × Average sentence length) + (0.846 × Number of Syllables)]

0–15	= very difficult
20–40	= difficult
45–55	= fairly difficult
60–65	= standard
70–75	= fairly easy
80–85	= easy
90–100	= very easy

FIGURE 6.21

The Difficulty of Business Writing

Difficulty of the Abstract =

206.835 − [(1.015 × 15.3) + (0.846 × 206)] = 206.835 − [15.530 + 174.276] = 17.03 = "Very Difficult"

Difficulty of the Sample in the Article Body

206.835 − [(1.015 × 29) + (0.846 × 205)] = 206.835 − [29.435 + 173.43] = 3.97 = "Very, Very Difficult"

FIGURE 6.22

Business Writing Gets Foggy

Fog Index = 0.4 × [Average sentence length + Number of words with three or more syllables]
(Gunning does not count capitalized words or verb forms made three syllables by the addition of (-*ed* or -*es*).)

Fog Index of Abstract = 0.4 × [14.4 + 26] = 16.16
Fog Index of Text = 0.4 × [26.25 + 23] = 19.3

As calculated, these results are no better. Relying on word count and syllable count, the Fog Indexes for our passages still suggest that the authors are writing at a level comprehensible only to graduate students and university professors, not average readers or business professionals. The suggestion is that sentences like "small and medium-sized enterprises are often characterized by strong entrepreneurial leadership" must be much more difficult than we would naturally surmise. Although we hardly suspect any business student or practitioner would find these samples particularly difficult, let's give the tests one more chance. Perhaps, since this first sample appeared in a scholarly publication, it really is more difficult than we admit.

Let's take as a point of comparison a sample from a business publication aimed at the widest of audiences, the annual report (which we will study at length in Chapter 13). Surely, we can assume that the annual report is written to reach and be comprehensible by the broadest possible array of readers. After all, this is the document that helps convince the public that their investments in the company are secure, prudent, and potentially profitable. Recognizing the significance of the document, companies typically assign a small army of people in communications, public relations, design, marketing, and accounting to ensure the document is attractive and the narrative portions are easy to understand.

Applying the Reading Ease Score and the Fog Index to the annual report of the UCB Group, one of the largest pharmaceutical and chemical companies in Belgium, we get an equally perplexing answer.[31] The annual report fares much worse than the academic publication, supposedly demanding the capabilities of a post-doctoral student to comprehend. (Figure 6.23 is the calculation for the sample page, Figure 6.24.)

How did we go so wrong? The article on mission statements from the college professors was 68% easier to read than the annual report? The entire team of executives, writers, and designers has jeopardized an international conglomerate that includes the oldest chemical factory in Belgium? Not at all!

These formulas don't work because the criteria they apply and the assumptions they use are inappropriate. While claiming to foster more readable communications, these formulas take indiscriminant aim at all long words. As Flesch explained about his formula:

> The significance of the Formula A [Reading Ease Score] will be more easily understood when it is realized that the measurement of word length is indirectly a measurement of word complexity . . . word complexity in turn is indirectly a measurement of abstraction . . . . Similarly, the measurement of sentence length is indirectly a measurement of sentence complexity . . . . Sentence complexity, in turn, may again be considered as a measure of abstraction. Formula A, therefore, is essentially a test of the level of abstraction."[32]

The quality of professional communications is dependent on more important factors than word count or numbers of syllables. The ease of readability and comprehension is predicated on rhetorical considerations, not superficial calculations. In professional communication, the arguments for readability formulas don't hold up. We need to use precise words regardless of their length. Length may not add up to complexity; complexity isn't necessarily a function of abstraction. Similarly, sentence length needs to be determined by how we can most clearly communicate ideas, not based on counting words or syllables.

FIGURE 6.23

The Annual Report
Bombs Out

Reading Ease Score = $206.835 - [(1.015 \times 39) + (0.846 \times 212] =$
$$206.835 - [39.585 + 179.352] = -12.101$$

"Mega-mega difficult!" (Literally, off the scale)

Fog Index = $0.4 (39 + 32) = 28.4$ (Ph.D.+?)

FIGURE 6.24

A Sample Page

the existing synergies between them. For the majority of the factories or subsidiaries, which are in Benelux, France, Germany or the USA, the satisfactory profits of the preceding year have been confirmed or improved.

At Ghent, the "packaging" activity has been re-organised on the site, resulting in necessary refurbishing and significant investments, including a new nine-colour gravure press and a new three-layer co-extruder

On the other hand, at La Cellophane Española SA (Burgos), the conversion activities have been transferred at the end of the year to a separate company, called UCB Packaging España SA, which will enable the structures to be better adapted to the different "film" and "packaging" activities.

The Research & Development teams have essentially devoted their efforts, both in Belgium and in Germany, to the development of multi-layer co-extruded films of high added value. These new films have been particularly developed as a substitute for PVC and for laminates based on aluminium, enabling the manufacture of packaging having excellent barrier properties, whilst at the same time making them lighter and more ecologically suitable for the food packaging market.

The efforts devoted to restructuring the activities of the Sector, and the planned undertaking of investments in certain ranges with higher added value, whilst disinvesting in others, enable us confidently to forecast, unless there are unforeseen economic circumstances, a significant improvement in the results for 1992.

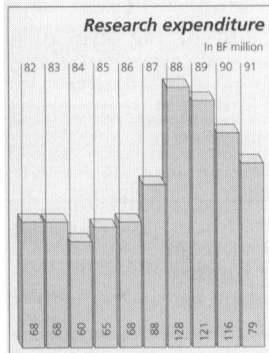

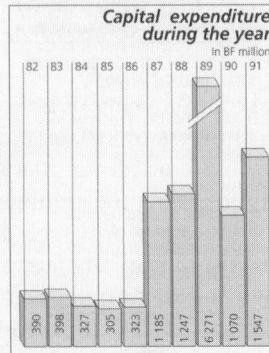

UCB Packaging Ltd at St Helens (Great Britain), has developed a specific pack for a new range of snacks. This laminated film combines the qualities of long shelf-life with protection against UV light and with easy opening.

Research expenditure
In BF million

82	83	84	85	86	87	88	89	90	91
68	68	60	65	68	88	128	121	116	79

Capital expenditure during the year
In BF million

82	83	84	85	86	87	88	89	90	91
390	398	327	305	323	1 185	1 247	6 271	1 070	1 547

Source: Reprinted with permission of UCB-Group.

READABILITY IN BUSINESS COMMUNICATION

So what ensures readability in business communication? As shown in Table 6.5, readability in business communication is synonymous with the two foundations of style: language precision (which we have been addressing) and effective content presentation.

In Chapter 4, we examined organizational patterns, showing how blocks of information can be effectively assembled. In content presentation, we expand that discussion to include the design used to assist with comprehending our material. Content presentation is, as Table 6.5 shows, an attack on idea density achieved through control of design and pace.

DESIGN. We have already seen illustration of some design techniques. The evolution of the IRS instructions and the page from the UCB Annual Report rely on design as a strategy for promoting comprehension. The UCB design invites the reader into the material. A partial column of text is complemented by an eye-catching montage of examples of packaging materials manufactured by UCB. The illustration summarizes and amplifies, in graphical form, the information provided in the narrative. Further, even before we have had opportunity to read the legends on the accompanying graphs, we have clear impressions of positive trends and business successes. Content is presented in an engaging manner. We are not overwhelmed, but led through the detail in a manner that consistently reinforces the conclusion that the company is doing well and our investments are safe. The sample clearly has overcome Linton's final disease, "unattractiveness," not just by dressing up ideas, but by giving them voice.

PACE. A close relative of design, pace represents the speed at which information is imparted, the speed with which the reader is allowed to gather in information. Although we might assume pace is synonymous with design, not all well-designed communications provide for an appropriate pace; nor does an appropriate pace ensure the effectiveness of design. To understand the relationship, let's examine a common document type—the instruction manual that accompanies products requiring assembly. Figure 6.25 is a sample page from the assembly instructions for a computer cabinet. The illustrations and design are nice enough; nevertheless, the purchaser may find the instructions difficult to follow.[33]

First, there is a misreading of the audience. We can deduce a number of audience attributes: 1) They have average mechanical and carpentry skills; otherwise they would have no reason to rely on the instructions. 2) They represent a spectrum of clients, essentially anyone who might own a computer. 3) They probably expect that the time invested in assembling the piece of furniture will represent a reasonable trade-off against the savings from buying the kit versus buying preassembled furniture.

TABLE 6.5 | READABILITY OF BUSINESS COMMUNICATIONS

Readability/ Formulaic Considerations	Vocabulary (abstractness)	Idea Density (comprehension)
Business Equivalents	Precise Language	Content Presentation

FIGURE 6.25

When the Going
Is Too Fast

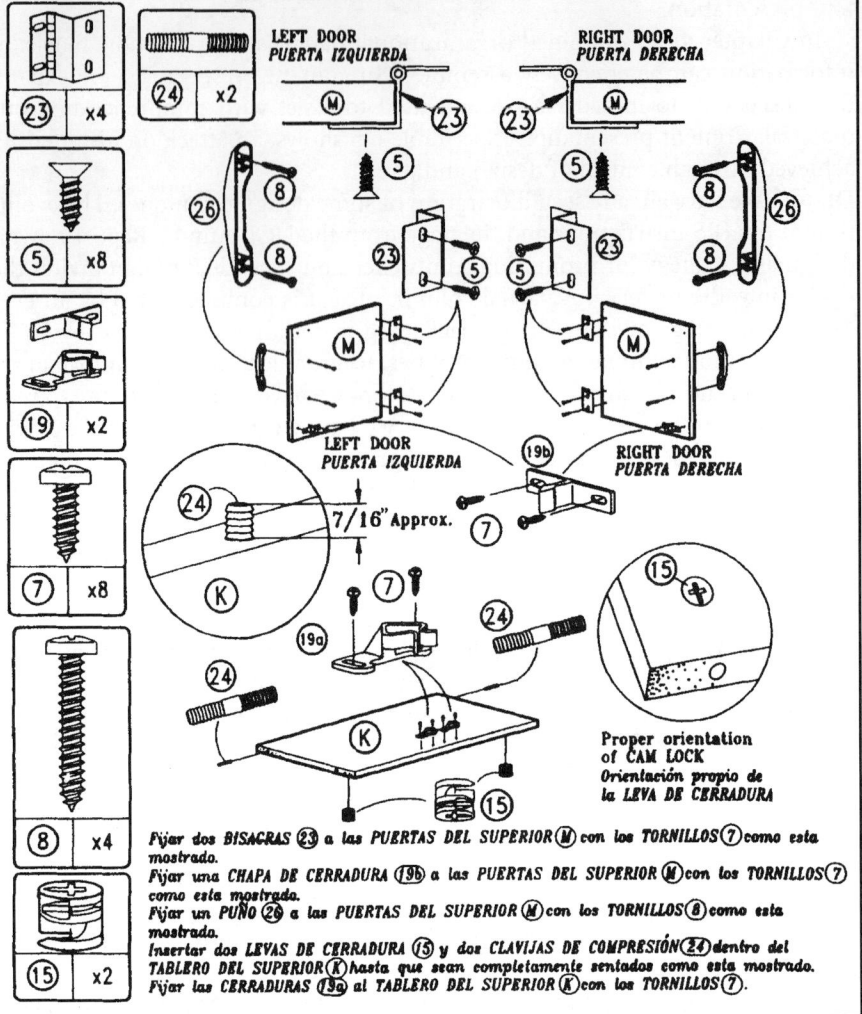

5

Fasten two HINGES ㉓ to HUTCH DOORS ⓂwithSCREWS ⑤ as shown.
Fasten STRIKE ⑲ⓑ to HUTCH DOORS Ⓜ with SCREWS ⑦ as shown.
Fasten a HANDLE ㉖ to HUTCH DOORS Ⓜ with SCREWS ⑧ as shown.
Insert two CAM LOCKS ⑮ and two COMPRESSION DOWELS ㉔ into HUTCH SHELF Ⓚ
until they are fully seated as shown.
Fasten CATCHES ⑲ⓐ to HUTCH SHELF Ⓚ with SCREWS ⑦.

LEFT DOOR
PUERTA IZQUIERDA

RIGHT DOOR
PUERTA DERECHA

7/16" Approx.

LEFT DOOR
PUERTA IZQUIERDA

RIGHT DOOR
PUERTA DERECHA

Proper orientation
of CAM LOCK
*Orientación propio de
la LEVA DE CERRADURA*

Fijar dos *BISACRAS* ㉓ a las *PUERTAS DEL SUPERIOR* Ⓜ con los *TORNILLOS* ⑦ como esta
mostrado.
Fijar una *CHAPA DE CERRADURA* ⑲ⓑ a las *PUERTAS DEL SUPERIOR* Ⓜ con los *TORNILLOS* ⑦
como esta mostrado.
Fijar un *PUÑO* ㉖ a las *PUERTAS DEL SUPERIOR* Ⓜ con los *TORNILLOS* ⑧ como esta
mostrado.
Insertar dos *LEVAS DE CERRADURA* ⑮ y dos *CLAVIJAS DE COMPRESIÓN* ㉔ dentro del
TABLERO DEL SUPERIOR Ⓚ hasta que sean completamente sentados como esta mostrado.
Fijar las *CERRADURAS* ⑲ⓐ al *TABLERO DEL SUPERIOR* Ⓚ con los *TORNILLOS* ⑦.

Source: Reprinted with permission of Dorel Industries, Inc.

Given this audience, the pace of the information presented is too fast. Users are forced to do too much work to make use of the information effectively and efficiently. Step 5 is not really a single step, but a series of tasks. To accomplish each task, we need to isolate the appropriate instructions, locate the right components, sort out the hardware, and assess the relationship among elements from the orientations provided. (The difficulties recall many of the tests we discussed regarding graphical performance in Chapter 4.) Getting any of these interpretations wrong means more work, more time invested, and more dissatisfaction. Maybe, contrary to Linton and others, economy may not always be the best policy.

In contrast (as shown in Figure 6.26), any of a number of actions might have been taken to reduce the rate of transmitting the information to make the pace

FIGURE 6.26

Allowing the
Information to
Build

5.

(5) x8	(7) x8	(8) x4	(13) x2	(15) x2	(23) x4	(24) x2

Hardware better aligned

1).Fasten two HINGES (23)
Fijar dos BISAGRAS (23)

(23) x4

to HUTCH DOORS (M) with SCREWS (5)
a las PUERTAS DEL SUPERIOR (M) con los TORNILLOS (5)

(5) x8

as shown.
como esta mostrado.

CHES (99) to HUTCH SHELF (K) with SCREWS (7).

**Single step;
English and Spanish
side by side**

LEFT DOOR
PUERTA IZQUIERDA

RIGHT DOOR
PUERTA DERECHA

(23)   (23)

(5)   (5)

**4. Insert two CAM LOCKS (15) and two COMPRESSION
DOWELS (24) into HUTCH SHELF (K) until they are
fully seated as shown.**

(15) x2

(24) x2

(24)

$7/16''$ Approx.

**Drawing expanded,
enlarged; all elements of
a single task put together**

(K)

(24)

(24)

(K)

(15)

(15)

**Proper orientation
of CAM LOCK**

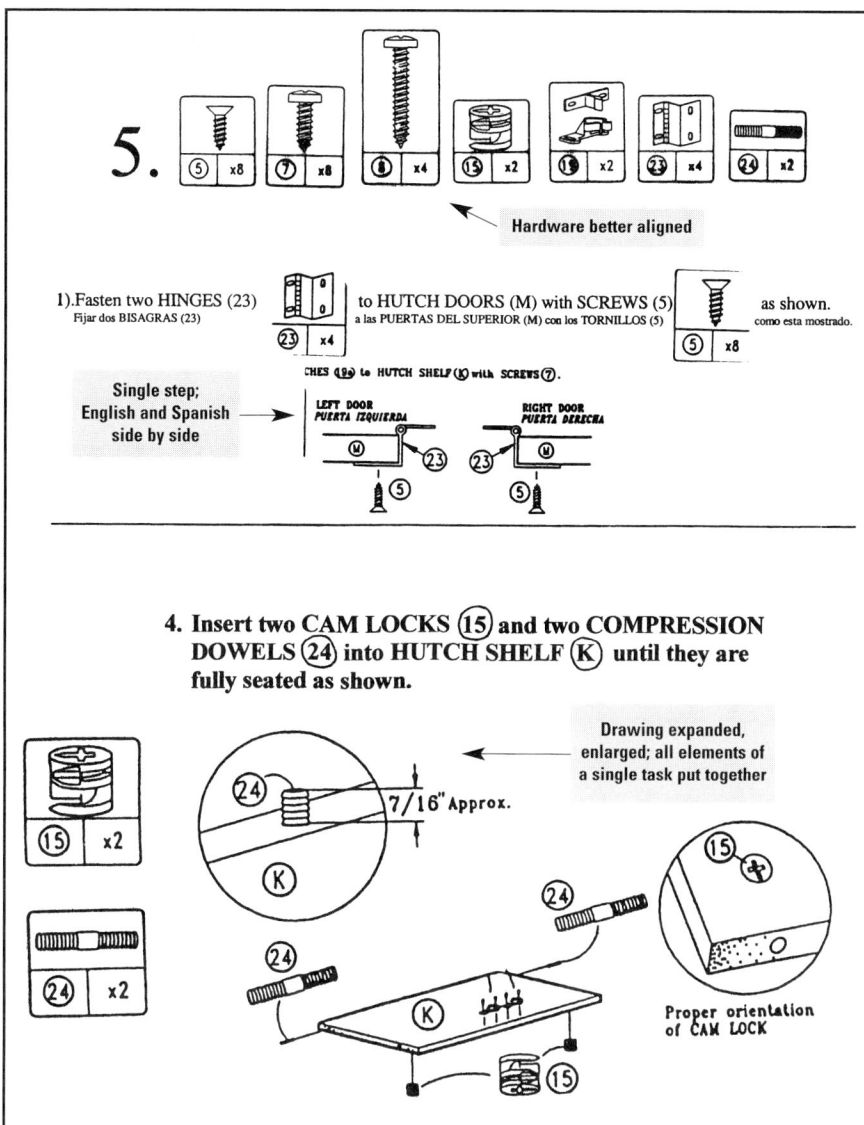

more appropriate for the activity, for the audience, and for the material:

- Steps and substeps might be numbered.
- Space might be added between tasks.
- Parts might be color-coded.
- Capital and lowercase letters might be varied.
- The Spanish text might be repositioned next to the English text.
- Hardware might be better aligned with the tasks.
- White space might be added to isolate information, components, or tasks.
- Parts might be shown in tables.
- Individual components might be better delineated.
- Images might be enlarged.

The lesson we just learned is that pace is most immediately linked to two factors: the complexity of the information and the audience's familiarity with the material. Not paying attention to these factors can result in a pace that is either too fast or too slow. A pace that is too fast may lose readers because they don't know how to interpret the information being presented. A pace that is too slow (Figure 6.27) may lose readers because they get tired of waiting for the substance and move on to another topic. Figure 6.28 depicts the basic factors pertaining to pace.

Expanding the list of possibilities, Robert Rathbone, a professor in the Department of Humanities at the Massachusetts Institute of Technology, offered 14 ways to achieve the right alignment of pace and presentation:

- Change from a statement to a question.
- Vary the length of sentences and paragraphs.
- Emphasize important material by placing it in a prominent position.
- De-emphasize secondary material by relegating it to a secondary position.
- Show parallel thoughts by placing them in parallel constructions.
- Relieve difficult text by introducing visual aids.
- Use analogy.
- Shift from straight line of prose to columnar listing.
- Break up large units of text by inserting headings and subheadings.
- Change the size of typeface.
- Use white space to relieve the eye and/or isolate text.
- Modulate "voice" by underlining, italicizing, or using parentheses.
- Repeat, and repeat, and repeat.
- Regulate choice of words.[34]

FIGURE 6.27

When We Move Along Too Slowly

Dear _____:

Our auditable subsidiary accounting records reveal that the subject containers have been issued to addressee activity and are on this date in this possession.

It is respectfully requested and essential that we be advised the status and actual location of the foregoing listed containers no later than fifteen (15) calendar days from the date of this letter.

If you have other returnable containers in your possession, not listed on the attachment, please add same to attachment enabling us to update our records.

If you have empty containers in your possession, please cause them to be returned. This will enable us to stop demurrage [a charge for detaining something], use charges or obtain deposit credit, as the case might be. Please transmit your timely response directly to the undersigned.

Pursuant to policy we are looking to the respective managers, or related counterparts where other than . . . corporation is involved, to whom a specified custodian responds, for timely and personal cooperation in the assurance that our input to the controller is satisfactory in all respects.

FIGURE 6.28

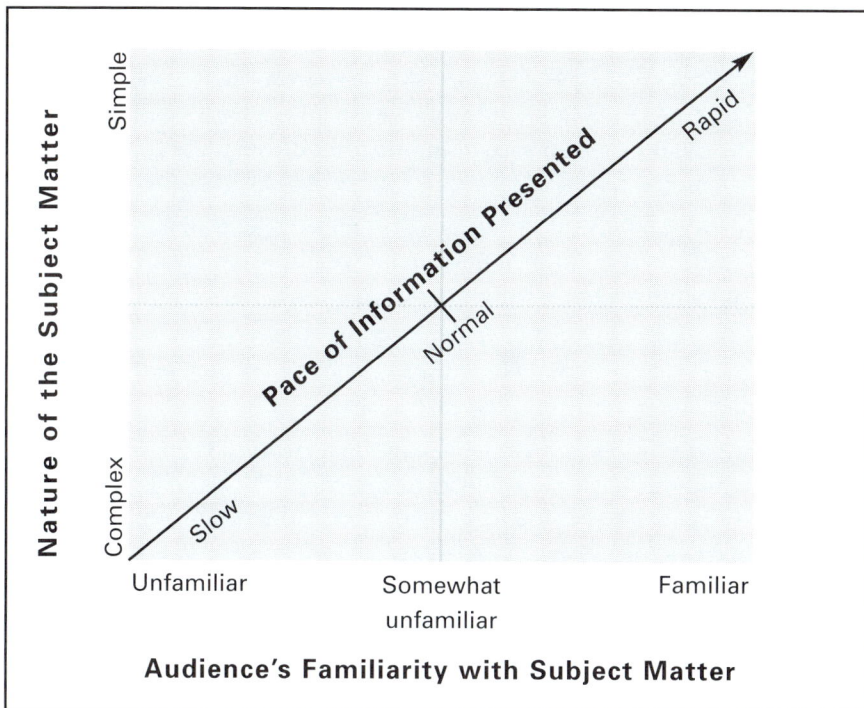

Nature of the Subject Matter (Simple → Complex)

Pace of Information Presented — Rapid / Normal / Slow

Audience's Familiarity with Subject Matter (Unfamiliar / Somewhat unfamiliar / Familiar)

LANGUAGE AND READABILITY—
THE LESSONS

Selecting and assembling information is only part of the writer's responsibilities. Effective communication demands purposeful decisions about how information is imparted: careful selection of language, the diction, pace, and information design. We must make a conscientious effort to ensure language is precise—that it has been inoculated against the diseases of weakness, obscurity, confusion, and incorrectness. We must also make purposeful decisions regarding pace and design of information in order to eradicate the disease of unattractiveness. We must, to return to Cardinal Newman, concentrate on how we can artfully and purposely "think out into language."

☐ Group

1. Select a page from a recent article in a business journal or periodical. Rewrite the page using a) an increased pace of information delivery and b) a decreased pace of information delivery.

2. Choose any of the forms that people use in filing taxes. Conduct an analysis of the form's readability, and then develop a revised form. Explain to the class the issues you identified and how you resolved or improved them.

3. On April 9, 2002, *The Wall Street Journal* introduced a new design for the newspaper, overhauling not only the "most readable front page in the country," but "refreshing" the paper "from first page to last."

   a) Review copies of the paper from before and after April 9, 2002 and discuss how pace and design contributed to the paper's goals of letting "time-pressed readers . . . get the news they need in the most convenient form possible."

   b) Review a local newspaper and explain what types of adjustments you would propose to improve the paper's pace and readability.

☐ Individual

1. Select two pages from a document published by the government. Identify any violations of Linton's writing "diseases."

2. Determine the Reading Ease Formula and the Fog Index for a page from a business text. Explain whether the indications are fair and why.

3. Choose an article from a journal in your field of study. Explain why the diction, pace, presentation, and readability are appropriate or inappropriate.

END NOTES

[1] *United States Government Printing Office Manual of Style.* Government Printing Office: Washington, DC, 1984.

[2] V.V. Nalimov, *In the Labyrinths of Language: A Mathematician's Journey.* Philadelphia: ISI Press, 1974.

[3] J. R. Oppenheimer, "The Open Mind," *The American Scientist,* Vol. 5, No. 1 (Jan. 1949), pp. 3–5.

[4] H.L. Mencken, "On Style," in *A Mencken Chrestomathy.* New York: Alfred A. Knopf, 1974.

[5] C. D. Linton, *Effective Revenue Writing: 2,* Government Printing Office: Washington, DC (Training No. 129–Rev. 7), 1962.

[6] *Ibid.*

[7] William Langeweische, "The Lessons of ValuJet 592," *Atlantic Monthly,* March 1998, pp. 81–98.

[8] D. Burke, *Big Talk 1: American Business Slang and Jargon.* Los Angeles: Optima Books, 1993.

[9] Nalimov, *In the Labyrinths of Language.*

[10] Paula LaRorque, "Deliver the truth, not just empty words," *The Quill,* Vol. 86, No. 7 (Sept. 1998), p. 63.

[11] "Memos from Hell," *Fortune,* Vol. 135, No. 2 (Feb. 3, 1997), p. 210.

[12] A. Bierce, *The Devil's Dictionary.* Thomas V. Cromwell Publishers, New York: 1911.

[13] R.J. Lifton, "The Psyche of a 'Gunocracy.'" *Newsweek,* Aug. 23, 1999, p. 49.

[14] L. Urdang, H.G. Zettler, and C. Hoequest, *-Ologies & -Isms: A Thematic Dictionary,* 2nd ed. Detroit: Gale Research Company, 1981.

[15] B.A. Billingsley, "Scientists Have A Word For It." *New Scientist,* Vol. 133, No. 1811 (March 7, 1992), pp. 53–54.

[16] H.W. Fowler, *A Dictionary of Modern English Usage,* 2nd ed. New York: Oxford University Press, 1965.

[17] J.A. Simpson and E.S.C. Weiner, *Oxford English Dictionary,* 2nd ed. New York: Oxford U.P.: 1989.

[18] P. Williams, J.D. Scriven, S. Wayne, "A Ranking of the Top 75 Misused Similar Words That Business Communication Students Confuse Most Often," *The Bulletin,* Vol. 34, No. 4 (Dec. 1991), pp. 19–25.

[19] "People," *Time,* April 10, 1944, p. 57.

[20] M. Maverick, "The Case Against Gobbledygook," *The New York Times Magazine,* May 21, 1944, pp. 11, 35–36.

[21] John Leo, "Tower of Pomobabble," *U.S. News & World Report,* Mar. 15, 1999, p. 16.

[22] D. Seligman, "The Gobbledygook Profession," *Forbes,* September 7, 1998, pp. 174–175.

[23] Cited by the Plain English Campaign, England's equivalent of the Plain Language Network, url: http://www.plainenglish.co.uk/ouch.html.

[24] *Federal Register,* Vol. 63, No. 111 (June 10, 1998), pp. 31,885–31,886.

[25] I. Lorge, "Readability Formulae—An Evaluation," *Elementary English,* Vol. 26, No. 2, (Feb. 1949), pp. 86–94.

[26] *Ibid.*

[27] D.L. Plung, "Add Style to Your Writing," *Hydrocarbon Processing,* Vol. 62, No. 5 (May 1983), pp. 123+.

[28] F. Grazian, "Frequently Asked Questions (FAQ) about Readability," *Public Relations Quarterly,* Vol. 41, No. 3 (Fall 1996), pp. 19–20.

[29] O'Gorman and R. Doran, "Mission Statements in Small and Medium-Sized Businesses." *Journal of Small Business Management,* Vol. 37, No. 1 (Oct. 1999), pp. 59–66.

[30] R. Flesch, *The Art of Readable Writing.* New York: Harper & Brothers, Publishers, 1949.

[31] *1991 Annual Report,* UCB Group.

[32] D. Plung, "Evaluate Your Technical Writing," *Hydrocarbon Processing,* July 1981, pp. 195+.

[33] "Computer Hutch Instructions," Model 41152, Dorel Corporation, Wright City, MO.

[34] R. Rathbone, *Communicating Technical Information,* Boston: Addison-Wesley, Publishing, 1985.

7

The Rhetoric of Grammar and Style
Orchestrating the Sounds
Words Make on Paper

In Chapter 6, we concluded by defining readability as a function of precise language (diction) and content presentation (design and pace). However, as we noted at the beginning of that chapter, readability is not synonymous with, but rather a subset of, style. Word selection, word use, and readability constitute the foundation, the method on which to build style. The other elements of style, as the formulators of readability formulas determined, are human interest and sentence structure. Expanding on the thoughts of the readability experts, we can conclude that the equation of style looks something like this:

$$\text{Style} = \text{Readability} + \text{Appeal}$$

We might be inclined to gloss over the idea of "appeal" and simply accept as a given that business communications are by definition of interest to business professionals; therefore, no additional attention to style would be warranted. However, that dismissal is inappropriate. Are we really going to assume that as long as the subject matter is business oriented, we are finished with our work on style when we have ensured appropriate word selection and idea density? Are we to assume that all business writing that shares a common vocabulary and similar information density is equal? Two authors examining the same subject and using the same language and format can create two significantly different business communications—perhaps turning an intriguing question into a truly boring

The rhetoric of grammar

- Expanding opportunities with sentences

- Creating appropriate emphasis

- Establishing strong relationships among ideas

The rhetoric of style

- The lessons of Lincoln

- A brief look at Kennedy

- A brief look at Martin Luther King, Jr.

- Style and business

A note on achieving style

Style—the lessons

presentation or transforming a routine assessment into an "appealing" set of conclusions. The difference between these extremes is a consequence of employing or ignoring the discipline and art of style.

Rudolf Flesch, like others advocating that readability could be quantified, equated "human interest" with use of personal pronouns, producing a scale that complemented the Reading Ease Score (Figure 7.1).[1] This scale, like its companion (Figure 6.19), has minimal applicability to business, where communications tend to be impersonal and more objective than writing in popular magazines and newspapers targeted by Flesch and his colleagues. Yet, impersonal does not imply lifeless.

As Table 7.1 suggests, the business equivalent of human interest is accomplished by attention to the rhetoric of grammar and style. These factors breathe life into the stylistic foundations established when we present ideas with precision, clarity, and comprehensibility. With this added dimension and increased sophistication of style, we advance from the sounds that words make on paper to the music of language.

THE RHETORIC OF GRAMMAR

We have chosen to call this discussion the rhetoric of grammar because we are going to focus on that important intersection where grammar (the rules of language) meets rhetoric (the means of the effective use of speech). In attempting to define a "mature style," Francis Christensen, author of *Notes Toward a New Rhetoric*, noted: "Grammar and rhetoric are complementary . . . . Grammar maps out the possible; rhetoric narrows down the possible to the desirable or effective."[2] Achieving "desirable" and "effective" communication demands that we approach grammar as something more than etiquette. We must approach grammar as a complement to style, as a means of promoting rhythm and effect.

FIGURE 7.1

Rudolf Flesch's
Human Interest
Scale

How Interesting?

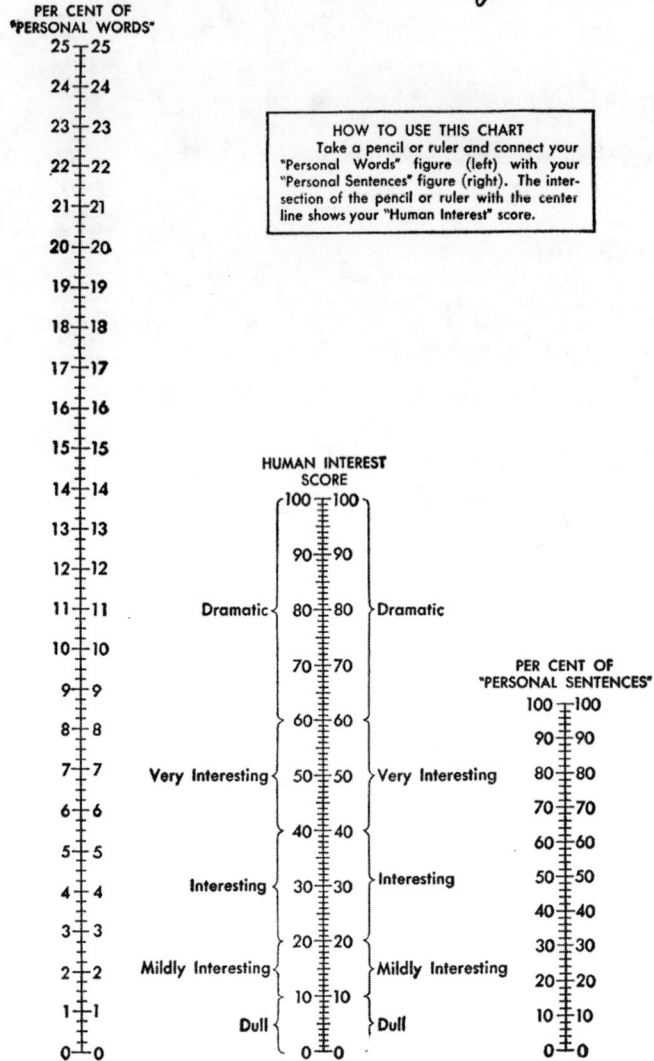

PER CENT OF
"PERSONAL WORDS"

25 — 25
24 — 24
23 — 23
22 — 22
21 — 21
20 — 20
19 — 19
18 — 18
17 — 17
16 — 16
15 — 15
14 — 14
13 — 13
12 — 12
11 — 11
10 — 10
9 — 9
8 — 8
7 — 7
6 — 6
5 — 5
4 — 4
3 — 3
2 — 2
1 — 1
0 — 0

HOW TO USE THIS CHART
Take a pencil or ruler and connect your "Personal Words" figure (left) with your "Personal Sentences" figure (right). The intersection of the pencil or ruler with the center line shows your "Human Interest" score.

HUMAN INTEREST
SCORE

100 — 100
90 — 90
Dramatic 80 — 80 Dramatic
70 — 70
60 — 60
Very Interesting 50 — 50 Very Interesting
40 — 40
Interesting 30 — 30 Interesting
20 — 20
Mildly Interesting 10 — 10 Mildly Interesting
Dull 0 — 0 Dull

PER CENT OF
"PERSONAL SENTENCES"

100 — 100
90 — 90
80 — 80
70 — 70
60 — 60
50 — 50
40 — 40
30 — 30
20 — 20
10 — 10
0 — 0

Source: "How Interesting?" from THE ART OF READABLE WRITING by RUDOLF FLESCH. Copyright 1949, © 1974 by Rudolf Flesch. Reprinted by permission of HarperCollins Publishers Inc.

TABLE 7.1 **A DEFINITION OF STYLE REVISITED**

Style = Readability + Appeal

Readability Scholars	Word Choice and Use	Idea Density	Human Interest and Sentence Length
Business World	Precise Language (diction)	Content Presentation (e.g., pace)	The rhetoric of grammar and stylistic tactics

This view is not an attempt to abandon the standard approach to teaching grammar, but, rather, a revival of tradition. As cited in *Linguistics and English Grammar*, "Grammar is one of those rare subjects where improvement might sometimes be made by turning the clock back." We need to recover the science of language, the appreciation that grammar is not a "mere collection of rules, but a system into which the rules fit in a significant and revealing way." In fact, to gain the ability to use grammar effectively as a tool to enhance the effectiveness of our communications, we must rescue grammar from the common model where it "has been a Cinderella consigned to scouring the grimiest pots in the composition classroom."[3] To achieve style, we must reassess not the rules, but the intellectual value of grammar.

Counting syllables, identifying commonly recognizable terms, and pruning sentence length are unreliable means of improving the comprehensibility and effectiveness of our communications. Words may be selected that are short, but also imprecise. Familiar words can be comforting but uncommunicative. Sequences of independent clauses can be punctuated deliberately or haphazardly, providing arbitrarily defined lengths of segregated words. Something more is needed to achieve style. Rather than maturity of style springing from numbers of words, maturity grows from the mastery of using sentences—the building blocks of thought—to interweave multiple ideas, to maneuver gracefully among the challenges of putting phrases and clauses together into an artful construct.

The idea that individual sentences may capture multiple ideas is, at a grammatical level, a restatement of the fact that sentences come in a number of forms: simple, compound, complex, compound-complex. In a grammarian's world, such reminiscences would lead us back to the days of diagramming sentences. We could invest a great amount of time relearning the mechanisms, beginning with the 26 diagrammed patterns first described in the 1850s, proceeding to the Reed and Kellogg diagrams popular during the 1950s, and advancing to such contemporary diagramming techniques as immediate constituent constructions. These adventures (somewhat analogous to our discussions of logic versus reasoning) would yield only greater appreciation of the syntactical dimensions of language, not provide critical insights into the issues of immediate interest to us. To clarify this point, let's return to another elementary school image: the crossing sign (Figure 7.2).

FIGURE 7.2

The Crossing Sign

Even if we don't have a driver's license, we are quick to understand the sign's intended message: Drive slowly. There may be children crossing. (Were we to add voice for the sign's color and shape, the message is understood as not just a statement, but a warning: Caution! Drive slowly because there may be children crossing.) Were we to attempt a literal reading of the sign, we might be somewhat anxious and confused: "children slow crossing"? We might wonder why the children opted to cross "slowly," or whether the crossing was for "slow" children only (and whether slow was describing a physical or a mental limitation). And, having now located where these "slow" children are crossing, we might want to apprise ourselves about where their counterparts, the fast children, might be crossing. However, the reason we have little difficulty understanding the intended meaning is that the information's presentation (spacing, type sizes, relative positioning of words), the language used, and the idea structure (or pace) all are complementary, resulting in an effective communication.

In addition to the lessons we studied in the last chapter about diction and readability, this simple illustration suggests at least two additional factors important to the study of constructing effective business communications: 1) Audiences are well prepared to deal with complex sentences that impart multiple ideas, just as long as the presentation strategy is appropriate. 2) The signals we choose to send regarding the relationships among ideas (which ideas are being emphasized, subordinated, clarified, or amplified) are critical to ensuring the audience interprets our message correctly. Let's focus our discussion of the rhetoric of grammar on accomplishing three goals: 1) expanding opportunities with sentences, 2) creating appropriate emphasis, and 3) establishing strong relationships among ideas.

EXPANDING OPPORTUNITIES WITH SENTENCES

When we discussed pace, we highlighted several approaches for improving comprehension by adjusting sentence structures and presentation. Those techniques were just a few of the available options. In addition to modifying sentence type and length, as communicators we have considerable freedom in choosing the way in which we begin sentences. The selection of sentence openers has the immediate consequence of inviting the audience in or turning the audience off. To illustrate the point, let's examine a short paragraph about a fictitious corporation called Brice Company (Figure 7.3).

FIGURE 7.3

The Tale of Brice Company

Brice Company has opportunity to expand its local and national product lines. Brice Company can either add variations to its existing line of products or can seek a merger with another compatible enterprise. The company would, given our current portfolio, be better-suited to a merger than an expansion. Brice Company management has identified at least two primary candidates for merger or corporate consolidation. We believe aligning with Rolsting will build a stronger production capability. Brice Company might also join with Cavlico Inc., which would bring a more complete domination in our primary markets. We would gain several patents crucial to expanding successfully into Asian markets. Brice Comp[any would, at the same time, strengthen our research and development team, a concern cited in several external analyses of our strategic viability. Brice is, potentially, in a position to launch simultaneous takeover bids on both these candidates. Brice management feels that selecting one would minimize market upheaval, reduce vulnerability to a hostile takeover of our company, and quiet growing union concerns.

The paragraph does not suffer from language issues (lack of familiarity, lack of precision or concreteness). It does not suffer from sentences that are too lengthy (only three sentences are more than 20 words long). The paragraph does not suffer from sentence variety. It contains simple sentences and complex sentences. Nonetheless, it is uninviting and repetitious. The reason for this response is that all the sentence openers are essentially the same. Every one of the 10 sentences begins with the subject. Even when we alternate among *Brice Company, we, the company,* and *management,* we are still employing essentially the same subject opening. We are "hearing" the grating sounds made when style is absent from our writing. Recalling the concept that "style is the sounds words make on paper," we need to listen for our sounds, a lesson that begins with the opening words of each sentence.

English provides numerous choices when it comes to selecting sentence openers. Though not exhaustive, Table 7.2 lists 10 possible choices, along with a brief explanation of the grammatical terms, and an example as it might appear in our

TABLE

7.2 A BEVY OF SENTENCE OPENERS

Opener	Explanation	Example
Adverb	Modifies a verb, an adjective, or another adverb	Very clearly, we now have opportunity to . . .
Adverb phrase or clause	A phrase or a clause that functions as an adverb	Although Brice has limited capital on hand, pursuing Cavlico now . . .
Adjective clause	A clause functioning as an adjective	Being positioned as we are on the verge of entering the Asian market, Brice . . .
Gerund phrase	A phrase employing a verb that, presented in its *-ing* ending, is functioning as a noun	Borrowing from our strategic reserves, we can . . .
Infinitive phrase	A phrase employing a verb that, presented in its "to be" form, is functioning as a noun	To build up a presence in Asia, we need to . . .
Absolute word/ phrase	A parenthetical word or phrase that qualifies the clause or sentence	True, Brice has available resources to pursue both mergers, but . . .
Interjection	A short exclamation	How meaningful, if Brice suddenly overcame . . .
Noun clause	A subordinate clause used as a noun	Whichever corporate merger we pursue, Brice will have . . .
Prepositional phrase	A phrase introduced by a preposition	By this time next month, the executive board can announce . . .
Appositive phrase	A phrase equivalent to a noun, which is placed near that noun to help identify it or to add an explanation	The leader in the aviation industry, Brice Company announced today . . .

discussion of Brice Company. Variety, however, must always be introduced as a complement to the message, not at the sake of the message. We must balance "attractiveness" and "desirability" with effectiveness, economy with readability. Forgetting the former, we end up with our original paragraph on Brice Company; forgetting the latter may lose clarity, comprehensibility, and precision. The appropriate answer lies at the intersection of grammar and rhetoric.

One proposed solution on how to reach this intersection, analogous to the solutions postulated by our readability scholars, was to reduce writing to a set of quantitative measures. The supposition is that there is an ideal distribution of sentence openers, a performance that can be measured by a "sentence opener scale." Merging the work of the readability scholars, the authors of this scale assessed both the type of opener used and the lengths of sentences. A "mature style," the authors proposed, needed 1) at least 8 to 10 different grammatical constructions in sentence openings, and 2) to limit subject-first openers to no more than one-fourth or one-fifth of the sentences.[4] (Figure 7.4 is a before and after sample provided by the system's authors; each dash denotes three words.)

Unfortunately for the system's authors, some researchers actually tested the proposed ratios, using the writing of professionals like H.L. Mencken. The research showed subject openers were used 75% of the time, the exact opposite of the percentages expected by the "sentence opener scale." Of the remaining 25% of the sentences using a nonsubject opener, 90% used some form of adverbial expression: clauses, prepositional phrases, adverbs, or nouns used in an adverbial function.[5] (Collectively, these represent about one-third of the options cited in Table 7.2.)

Had the formula's authors been thinking about message instead of numbers, they would have deduced a more appropriate set of proportions. The subject opener is always going to be primary structure because, as Dr. Christensen points out: "The natural function for an opener is to prepare the mind of the reader for the statement to follow."[6] This insight also makes evident why the adverb is the second most common opener: Adverbs set the stage for the main idea, providing a directional signal (time, cause, condition) for our mental traffic.

To rely on a formula that proposes constructions—even though grammatically correct—without appreciation of or consideration for the context, the subject, the audience, or the message is at best presumptuous, and, at worst, dangerous. Defaulting to these prescriptions will set you racing down a highway with no signposts. Knowing where to turn and how to avoid a rhetorical accident become matters of sheer guesswork. Rather, the beginnings of style, like the beginnings of your sentences, demand attention to purpose, audience, and message. A smooth start relies on an ear for the sounds being made by the words and attention to what is both desirable and effective.

CREATING APPROPRIATE EMPHASIS

As we have been discussing, opportunities abound to enliven sentence openers. But, as we were quick to point out, what grammar allows, rhetoric endows. The same relationship between grammar and rhetoric exists when we examine means of creating emphasis within and among sentences.

At the sentence level, the two most enduring debates concern the positioning of information and the use of active versus passive voice. The first of these debates, which arises from a narrow interpretation of a psychological principle, needs only a brief discussion here. Psychologists have identified that we are most likely to remember best the information that is presented first and the informa-

Before	Opener Type	Sentence Length
It was difficult to sit calmly in one of Professor Harris's chemistry classes.	1. Subject	— — — —
He was constantly on the move.	2. Subject	— —
He would breeze into class like a whirlwind, dressed always in blue pants and an old white linen coat.	3. Subject	— —
He lectured in nervous tension, his blue eyes dancing, his fingers twitching.	4. Subject	— — — — — —
He became irritable rather often.	5. Subject	— — — —
He was a good teacher, but we all felt the strains of his personality.	6. Subject	— — — — —
I can see his fingers crunching his notes to this day.	7. Subject	— — — —

After	Opener Type	Sentence Length
To sit calmly in one of Professor Harris's chemistry classes was difficult.	1. Infinitive	— — —
Tall and energetic, he was constantly on the move.	2. Adjective	— —
Like a whirlwind, he would breeze into class, dressed always in blue pants and an old white linen coat.	3. Prep. phrase	— — — —
His blue eyes dancing, his fingers twitching, he lectured in nervous tension.	4. Absolute phrase	— — —
Rather often, he became irritable.	5. Adverb	— —
Although he was a good teacher, we all felt the strains of his personality.	6. Adverb clause	— — — — —
To this day, I can see his fingers crunching his notes.	7. Prep. Phrase	— — —

FIGURE 7.4

Closing the Book on the "Sentence Opener Scale"

tion presented last. We are less inclined to remember information sandwiched in the middle. Known respectively as the Rule of Recency and the Rule of Primacy, these considerations are important when numerous pieces of information are being presented, not when fashioning individual sentences. (We will study these principles at some length in Chapter 9.) To illustrate this point, let's consider a single example that has been employed to try to promote the argument that these rules apply at the sentence level (Figure 7.5).[7]

The assertion by those who argue that these principles have application at the sentence level is that supposedly the first sentence would gain John the gratitude of the company. The second sentence would gain him a termination notice. Although the ultimate consequence of making these statements may, indeed, lead to congratulations or termination, that result is not a function of the positioning of the three adjectives. The emphasis on "slow" in the second sentence is not a function of what we recall best, but is achieved by the particular structuring of the series of adjectives (a stylistic device we will examine momentarily). The point is that clarity and conciseness are at play at this level, not issues of our innate limitations for processing information.

By far the more enduring and most impassioned war at the sentence level is waged over the matter of using active or passive voice. The simple matter of assigning a direct object to a verb (active voice) versus converting that direct object into the subject (passive voice) is often held up as a discriminator between a well-written and a poorly written sentence, between a competent writer and a novice (Table 7.3). Split an infinitive or two, create an awkward sentence, confuse *affect* and *effect*, and there is little attention paid. Yet, throughout the literature—from the earliest works on business communication such as Hotchkiss's *American Business English* to the government's current campaign for plain language—we are implored to avoid passive voice.

Yet, contrary to this thinking, we would suggest that this absolute dismissal of passive voice is inappropriate. Like slavishly manipulating introductory phrases to score well on the "Sentence Opener Scale," purposely introducing proper pronouns to score well on the "Human Interest Scale," or searching the thesaurus to identify a mountain of monosyllabic words to get the best Fog Index, avoiding passive voice at all costs is placing mechanics above message. Avoiding passive voice—or defaulting unthinkingly to active voice—is not always in your best interests.

Active voice is assuredly preferable when one intends to emphasize the subject or doer of the action. Whether being praised or fired, John (Figure 7.5) is the point of emphasis; his behaviors and habits are secondary. Yet, surely, there must be appropriate use of passive voice as well. Understanding that passive voice, a construction that is grammatically 100% correct, has valid purpose brings us to one of the crossroads between grammar and rhetoric—the intersection of popular thinking and rhetoric.

TABLE 7.3 THE VARIOUS FACES OF ACTIVE AND PASSIVE VOICE

Active Voice	Passive Voice
We voted on the recommendation.	The recommendation was voted on by us.
Congress will enact the law.	The law will be enacted by Congress.
The Board has decided to execute the merger.	The merger has been decided on by the Board.
Production is retooling the line.	The line is being retooled by Production.
The Architecture/Engineering firm was constructing the new store.	The new store was being constructed by the Architecture/ Engineering firm.

FIGURE 7.5

A Position of
Consequence

(1) John is slow, painstaking, and meticulous.
(2) John is meticulous, painstaking, and slow.

If there's a community in business that knows when action needs to be focused on the subject and when attention should be focused on what was done, it's lawyers. Your client is on the stand, your job is to tell the jury her side of the story—carefully distinguishing among moments when:

- you want to assert that the individual's identity is irrelevant,
- you want the jury's attention to be riveted on your client,
- you want their attention to be on what happened,
- you want their attention to be on how it happened,
- you want your client to be seen as a unique individual,
- you want her to be seen as part of a larger class or community, and
- you want their attention to be on an individual other than on your client.

Success, stated very simply, is a matter of whether you know when to use active voice and when to use passive voice (Table 7.4).[8]

TABLE 7.4 PUTTING THE PASSIVE VOICE TO WORK

Situation	Example of Passive Voice	Example of Active Voice
When the actor's identity is irrelevant: you want to omit it	The statute was enacted in 1968.	Congress enacted the statute in 1968.
When the action's recipient is the focus: you want to keep the attention on the subject	Smith, because he knows the workings of the department, has lasted for more than a year. Nevertheless, he will probably be asked to resign.	Smith, because he knows the workings of the department, has lasted for more than a year. The President, nevertheless, probably will ask him to resign.
When placement of the actor at the end of the sentence adds to the dramatic effect	The tapes were hidden by the President of the United States	The President of the United States hid the tapes.
When avoiding overuse of the pronoun "one" to express a generalization of an entire class	Here are seven situations where the passive voice is preferred.	Here are seven situations where one prefers the active voice
When the identity of the actor is unknown	The files were mysteriously destroyed.	Someone mysteriously destroyed the files.
When you want to conceal the actor's identity	I regret to inform you that your file has been misplaced.	I regret to inform you that I lost your file.
When you want to avoid unnecessarily clumsy antecedents and pronoun constructions	An application must be filed with the personnel office. A complete educational background should be included.	An applicant must file his/her application with the personnel office. He/she should include his/her complete educational background.

Knowing how to construct the proper opening for the sentence and how to handle the intricacies of the sentence's internal organs, we are now ready to look at the options relative to the sentence's concluding notes. When examining the sentence's concluding elements, what we are considering is the means to successfully hammer together a proper paragraph, the residence sentences co-occupy in their attempt to coalesce into strong, functional, indivisible blocks of related information.

ESTABLISHING STRONG RELATIONSHIPS AMONG IDEAS

Four primary ingredients foster and signal the relationships among ideas, whether working within an individual sentence, among sentences in a paragraph, or between paragraphs. These four ingredients are 1) punctuation, 2) transitions, 3) opening and concluding sentences, and 4) managing the relationships among ideas.

PUNCTUATION. Punctuation, like other elements of grammar, needs to be recognized not as a means merely to enforce correctness, but as a valuable contributor to the clarity, conciseness, and comprehensibility of business communications. We are only partially correct when we suggest that there is only one way to punctuate any pattern of words. As one text, *American Punctuation,* correctly informs us, "Skillful writers have learned that they must make alert choices between periods and semicolons, semicolons and commas, commas and dashes, and dashes and parentheses, according to meaning and intended emphasis."[9]

To illustrate this principle, let's begin with the simplest form of expressing a complete thought, the simple sentence (a single independent clause). To build on this basic structure, we can provide amplification in three locations: 1) in front of the clause, 2) after the clause, or 3) within the clause (between the subject and predicate). These three options, in turn, are supported by three essential punctuation patterns (Figure 7.6). Expanding this basic set of relationships, we quickly come to see how the entire spectrum of punctuation options can be employed to enhance the thoughts we are trying to express (Table 7.5).[10]

From this foundation, we can examine how the options (which are applicable to all sentence structures, not just a simple sentence) can help us from a rhetorical standpoint. We can also explore further how punctuation aids in articulating precise relationships among ideas.

FIGURE 7.6

Building Up
Sentences

1. Amplification before the clause:
Structure: *Amplification + punctuation + independent clause*
Example: Being the newest company, Brice has the power to initiate the merger.

2. Amplification after the clause:
Structure: *Independent clause + punctuation + amplification*
Example: Brice has the power to initiate the merger, being the newest company.

3. Amplification positioned within the clause:
Structure: *Subject + punctuation + amplification + predicate*
Example: Brice, being the newest company, has the power to initiate the merger.

7.5 BASIC INTERNAL PUNCTUATION PATTERNS

Pattern	Punctuation Options	Example
1. Amplification + punctuation + independent clause	Comma Colon Dash	• Being the first in electronics, Brice can benefit . . . • We will win the bid: Brice is by far the strongest contender. • First in electronics—Brice is guaranteed to lead the industry.
2. Independent clause + punctuation + amplification	All punctuation options are possible for this pattern	Brice is the unparalleled leader in electronics, having just engineered a new deal with the Department of Defense.
3. Subject + punctuation + amplification + predicate	Commas (paired) Dashes (paired) Parentheses (paired)	• Brice, being first in electronics, is sure to win the new contract. • Brice—long positioned as the industry standard—is poised to win. • Brice (maker of Centurian Systems) is guaranteed a lucrative contract.

To help illuminate the role that punctuation plays in articulating precise relationships among ideas, let's return momentarily to our elementary school crossing sign. Let's suppose that we want to post a sign on which the two ideas—drive slowly and children crossing—are written out as we would expect to see them on a written page. At the same time, we have also decided to position the thought about "driving slowly" first in order to assign it the primary emphasis.

Figure 7.7 suggests six different punctuation options. (It is probably possible to construct versions using a question mark or parentheses, but such options would, more than likely, not communicate the same message.) Each of the six selections is grammatically correct, and each meets our criteria for beginning with "slowly." Yet, they are not precisely equivalent statements.

The differentiating factor is the rhetorical dimension of punctuation. Each set of sentences reflects a slightly different relationship between the two ideas—different degrees of separation and different degrees of idea independence or dependence. Selections 1 and 6 present the ideas as two thoughts completely separate from each other. There is a total stop between thought one (slow) and thought two (children crossing). Although the two versions are similar, Selection 1 makes its assertion more emphatically.

---

1. Slow. Children crossing.
2. Drive slowly; children are crossing.
3. Drive slowly: children crossing.
4. Drive slowly—children crossing.
5. Slow, children crossing.
6. Slow! Children crossing.

FIGURE 7.7

Punctuation Options

Selection 2, the semicolon, imposes a break, but does not demand complete separation; we read the two thoughts as independent elements of a single unit. Selection 3, the colon, uses the first idea to build anticipation of the second: we are carried forward with minimal hesitation as we move from one thought to the next. Use of the dash, Selection 4, inserts a break equivalent in time to that imposed by the colon, but substitutes emphasis for anticipation—stressing the second half of the message. Last, the comma (Selection 5) insists on minimal independence between the two parts of the sentence. We are led, in a single step, to reconcile the close relationship between slowing down and remaining alert for children. (Table 7.6 summarizes these separation differences.)

Complementary to the intent of using punctuation to establish purposeful relationships among thoughts, punctuation can also be used to establish emphasis (a slightly different nuance than the matter of separation). To this end, Table 7.7 illustrates how punctuation can be used effectively to help clarify and communicate ideas.

TRANSITIONS. Building bridges among ideas is not exclusively a function of what happens within the body of the sentence. It is largely a function of establishing relationships between sentences—the jurisdiction of transitions. Transitions announce and strengthen temporal relationships (relative positions in time) and spatial relations (relative distances, both actual and metaphorical). Transitions, much like sentence openers and punctuation, have elements of both correctness and intention, creating opportunities for purposeful selection and use. Transitions can be introduced as adverbs, pronouns linking ideas forward and back, phrases, sentences, even entire paragraphs. The purpose of transitions is to make an explicit announcement: Here is how Idea A relates to Idea B. Without transitions, audiences are left to infer the relationships between ideas, something they may or may not do correctly. As we have seen in previous chapters, it's best not to leave the audience to surmise meanings because they may construe materials in a way you didn't intend.

TABLE 7.6 THE RHETORIC OF PUNCTUATION

Mark	Position	Degree of Separation
Exclamation Point (!)	Final	Full—emphatic
Question Mark (?)	Final	Full—anticipatory
Period (.)	Final	Full—momentary
Colon (:)	Internal	Medium—anticipatory
Semicolon (;)	Internal	Medium—momentary
Parentheses (())	Internal	Medium—explanatory
Dash (—)	Internal	Medium—emphatic
Comma (,)	Internal	Minimum

TABLE 7.7 USING PUNCTUATION TO MAKE YOUR CASE

Emphasis	Example
Two separate and equal thoughts	1. Jones wrote the proposal. He was aiming to land the account.
Two equal parts of one thought	2. Aiming to land the account, Jones wrote the proposal.
Emphasis assigned to second thought	3. Jones wrote the proposal. He was aiming to land the account!
Creating emphasis through anticipation	4. Jones—aiming to land the account—wrote the proposal.
Using the second thought to expand the meaning of the first thought	5. Jones wrote the proposal. (He was aiming to land the proposal.)
Creating disbelief about the first thought	6. Jones wrote the proposal. He was aiming to land the account?
Creating close alignment between first and second thoughts	7. Jones wrote the proposal; he was aiming to land the account.
Restating the first thought	8. Jones wrote the proposal; he was aiming to land the account.

"He shot the gun several times. It hit its mark." There is no clear, intuitive way to be certain how to read these two sentences. Is the second sentence simply restating a fact that should be obvious from the first statement, or is something else going on? Try inserting any of the following words before the word *it*, and suddenly you have a variety of specific, but different, meanings: *finally, occasionally, no doubt, furthermore, doubtless, even though.* Table 7.8 lists a sampling of potential transitions and their associated purposes.

OPENING AND CONCLUDING SENTENCES. As we begin to expand the groupings of information—proceeding from a simple sentence, to a sentence with openers, amplification, and transitions—we are naturally progressing into the realm of the paragraph. Effective paragraphs must satisfy three primary obligations: 1) They need to have something to say; they must represent a collection of related ideas that convey a single "chunk" of information. 2) They need to have a tight internal unity. 3) They need to create a transition to the next paragraph. The same lessons we have learned about sentences—about controlling the openings, structure, internal cohesion, punctuation, and transitions—hold true for paragraphs as well.

Literary and expository paragraphs do differ, however, when it comes to the roles they assign to introductory and concluding sentences. While a simple announcement of direction is generally sufficient for opening sentences, in business communication, the introductory sentence has two purposes: to create the path (the transition) to the paragraph and to put the substance of the paragraph into context.

| 7.8 | **USING TRANSITIONS EFFECTIVELY** |

Transitional Words/Phrases	Purpose
1. and or, nor, also, moreover, furthermore, indeed, in fact	adding an idea
2. for instance, for example, similarly, likewise	adding and illustrating a point
3. therefore, thus, so, finally, in other words, in short	adding up consequences; summarizing elements so as to make a major point
4. frequently, occasionally, in general, usually, especially	adding a qualifying point or illustration
5. of course, no doubt, certainly, granted, doubtless	conceding a point to the opposition, recognizing a point that may lie outside the major theme
6. but, however, yet, on the contrary, surely	reversing the thought, usually bringing the focus back to your central theme
7. still, nevertheless	returning to your arguments after making a concession to your audience
8. although, though, whereas	attaching a concession to your point
9. because, since, for	connecting a reason to an assertion
10. if, provided, unless, when	qualifying and restricting a major point
11. as if, as, as though, even though	suggesting a tentative or hypothetical condition that strengthens your point
12. this, that, these, it, they, them, many, few, several, he, she, who	tying things together by referring to a specific antecedent, pointing back to the preceding idea(s) while carrying the reference ahead

This is accomplished by summarizing information, giving direction on how information should be understood or interpreted, and establishing the paragraph's contribution—its additive value to the preceding and subsequent information. As such, the opening sentence is somewhat like a handshake, both extending a welcome and demonstrating that there are no hidden weapons. The opening sentence reaches out and gains trust while providing insight into what's coming.

Creating well-rounded opening statements is accomplished by stopping to place the entire substance of the paragraph into context. To do this, we can use a variety of methods: 1) putting the paragraph's intended message in the form of a question, 2) stating the central idea of the paragraph as a problem, or 3) creating a single statement that combines the general theme of the paragraph and its principal conclusion or assertion. To illustrate these approaches, let's return to our original write-up about Brice Company.

Using the three methods of devising an appropriate introductory sentence, we can produce three types of opening sentences for our paragraph:

1. What opportunity will best serve Brice's strategic market?

   (opening with a question)

2. We need to strengthen our market position.

   (presentation of a problem statement)

3. Brice Company can gain strategic advances in market share through a merger with Cavlico Corporation.

   (general statement—"opportunity arises from mergers"—combined

   with a specific one—"A merger with Cavlico is Brice's best opportunity")

All three examples satisfy the first obligation of an opening sentence—announcing the subject. Selecting the best of the three, therefore, may depend on which one does the best job of meeting the second obligation—establishing the scope of the paragraph. To let us gauge this second dimension more readily, let's isolate each of the 10 thoughts that comprise the paragraph:

1. Brice has opportunity to expand.
2. The options are expand or merge.
3. Merger is preferable.
4. Two candidates exist.
5. Merger with Rolsting strengthens production.
6. Merger with Cavlico aligns market strategies.
7. The Asian market would benefit from patents.
8. Research and development would be expanded.
9. Brice could take on both Rolsting and Cavlico.
10. The recommendation is to merge with Cavlico.

Isolating the ideas makes it evident that there are three principal points being made in the paragraph: 1) Brice needs to merge with another company. 2) The primary goal should be to strengthen market share. 3) Cavlico is the best merger candidate. Using our insight into the content and scope of the paragraph, we can assess the relative effectiveness of our three paragraph openers (Table 7.9).

To appreciate the importance of meeting both these obligations, try to keep in mind two uncomfortable experiences every professional has had. The first

TABLE

7.9 THE RELATIVE EFFECTIVENESS OF THREE PARAGRAPH OPENERS

Opener	Content	Scope		
		Merger	Market	Cavlico
What opportunity will best serve Brice's strategic market?	√		√	
We need to strengthen our market position.	√		√	
Brice Company can gain strategic advances in market share through a merger with Cavlico Corporation.	√	√	√	√

image is of a speaker who is scheduled to address a topic of keen interest to you. She introduces the topic and explains that she is going to address subtopics 1, 2, and 3. After speaking about items 1 and 2, she sits down, leaving you unsatisfied and your expectation unfulfilled. The second image is of the speaker who announces his intention to speak about items 1, 2, and 3, but some time later is interminably rambling on about items 7, 8, and 9. This second speaker has violated a similar implicit agreement between communicator and audience. Failure to correctly speak about the paragraph's scope in your opening sentence is the equivalent of breaking these pacts with your audience, signaling an intention and then not following through with your announcement.

MANAGING THE RELATIONSHIPS AMONG IDEAS. Meeting the two obligations that frame the role and scope of the paragraph is also the surest means of assessing the adequacy and appropriateness of paragraph length. Paragraphs are not made easy or difficult as a consequence of the number of words or sentences they contain. They become difficult if too broad a scope is assigned, if they give the impression of being poorly confined or ill-focused. Rather than counting words, use your introductory sentence as a means to control pace—establishing clearly defined and purposely segregated units of thought that can be readily understood and managed by your reader.

As research has demonstrated, readers base their expectations for the paragraph on the signals you provide: clear shifts in topics, sentence openers, and transitions. One study showed that even when the paragraph indentations were removed, 75% of the time people could identify where the paragraph separations should go based on the availability of "paragraph cues."[11] In another study, researchers confirmed that when the signals were provided, the length of the paragraph did not have a significant effect on the ease of comprehension.[12]

What was also learned in this research was that we can, if we're not diligent, introduce other types of errors that impede the comprehension of our paragraphs. As the researchers reported, the four most common errors that diminish comprehension lie at "the intersection of grammar, meaning, and style."[13] Listed in order of the frequency in which these errors were observed to occur, the four most common problems in managing the relationship among multiple ideas and clauses are:

1. embedding—mismanaging the relationship among ideas, often hiding the main thought in a less than obvious position in the sentence;

2. syntax shift—failing to fulfill grammatical expectations announced within the sentence;

3. parallel structure—failing to retain the same grammatical structure for all elements in a series;

4. direct/indirect speech—mishandling incorporation of quotations, paraphrases, summaries, or other source material (Table 7.10).

We now have three of the four components of developing a mature style: diction, readability, and the rhetoric of grammar. We now can command language, idea density, and—as Francis Christensen termed it—"the rhetorical theory of the sentence." We have added to our abilities an appreciation that sentences should "not be managed arbitrarily for the secondary concerns such as variety. They [should] be treated functionally and the variety . . . allowed to grow from the materials and the effort to communicate them to the reader."[14] Only one additional set of tools needs to be added to make our style kit complete.

TABLE 7.10 — MEANS OF DIMINISHING COMPREHENSION

Error	Example Sentence	The Issue
Embedding	It is my opinion that one of the primary reasons for which the new media lends itself for such exaggerations in their coverage of health risks is entertainment.	The point is not clear: Is the issue the media, exaggerations, or entertainment?
Syntax Shifting	The data represents 85% of the automobiles are moving or obeying the laws of driving an auto.	The culprits, drivers, are never brought into the sentence.
Parallel Structure	Family life is eroding because of gender liberation, divorce, teenage sex, and, lastly, because people's morals just aren't what they used to be.	Is it not clear whether morals are an issue or not.
Direct/Indirect	Single-parent households, 24%, which include mother only, 21.6% and father only 3.1%, "so sadly to say that with the divorce rate on the rise . . ." some fathers are choosing to leave their families so that they can find employment in other places.	The statistics and quotations are fragmented and incomplete.

THE RHETORIC OF STYLE

We now know that style is not simply a function of word count, sentence count, arbitrary sentence variety, or any basic calculation of proper pronouns. Yet, we still may not have the complete means by which to create precisely the sounds we want to make on paper. To take this last step, we need to examine the specific stylistic attributes we want to emulate, a process that begins by asking how specifically do we give words a "sound," how do we create a unique stylistic identity? Another means of approaching this question is to ask what it is that stylistically separates one writer or speaker from another. What is it, for instance, that transforms a Kennedy administration into Camelot, and a Nixon administration into—as Nixon's Vice President, Spiro Agnew, referred to the administration's critics—"nattering nabobs of negativity."

At the more immediate level of communication, we might ask why, among the thousands of speeches throughout American history, three speeches stand out: Abraham Lincoln's Gettysburg Address, John F. Kennedy's Inaugural Address, and Martin Luther King, Jr.'s "I Have a Dream" speech. We don't often find the words of Everett Emerson, the main speaker at Gettysburg, being memorized in high schools. More than 40 Presidents have given Inaugural Addresses, but few are remembered, or quoted. Martin Luther King, Jr., was not the only civil rights leader who spoke that crisp autumn day in front of the Lincoln Memorial. We know the three speeches have little in common with one another, differing in subject, length, circumstance, and setting. Despite these facts, these speeches are routinely referenced in history and rhetoric texts. Taking a lesson from nineteenth-century educational theory, we need to ascertain what gives these speeches endurance, what it is about them that we can emulate.

The Lessons of Lincoln

Abraham Lincoln's Gettysburg Address represents one of the most impressive uses of short words, short sentences, and short paragraphs (Figure 7.8). Of the 264 words Lincoln spoke that morning, 245 have only one or two syllables; of the approximately two dozen remaining words, none is more than four syllables. Furthermore, in a mastery of economy that surpasses even the greatest zealotry of the readability scholars, Lincoln uses words of few letters. More than half the words in the Gettysburg Address have four or fewer letters. (Figure 7.9 graphs the absolute simplicity and economy of language comprising this speech.)

FIGURE 7.8

The Gettysburg Address

Four score and seven years ago our fathers brought forth on this continent, a new nation, conceived in Liberty, and dedicated to the proposition that all men are created equal.

Now we are engaged in a great civil war, testing whether that nation, or any nation so conceived and so dedicated, can long endure. We are met on a great battle-field of that war. We have come to dedicate a portion of that field, as a final resting place for those who here gave their lives that that nation might live. It is altogether fitting and proper that we should do this.

But, in a larger sense, we cannot dedicate—we cannot consecrate—we cannot hallow—this ground. The brave men, living and dead, who struggled here, have consecrated it, far above our poor power to add or detract. The world will little note, nor long remember what we say here, but it can never forget what they did here. It is for us the living, rather, to be dedicated here to the unfinished work which they who fought here have thus far so nobly advanced. It is rather for us to be here dedicated to the great task remaining before us—that from these honored dead we take increased devotion to that cause for which they gave the last full measure of devotion—that we here highly resolve that these dead should not have died in vain—that this nation, under God, shall have a new birth of freedom—and that government of the people, by the people, for the people shall not perish from the earth.

FIGURE 7.9

The Simplicity of Lincoln

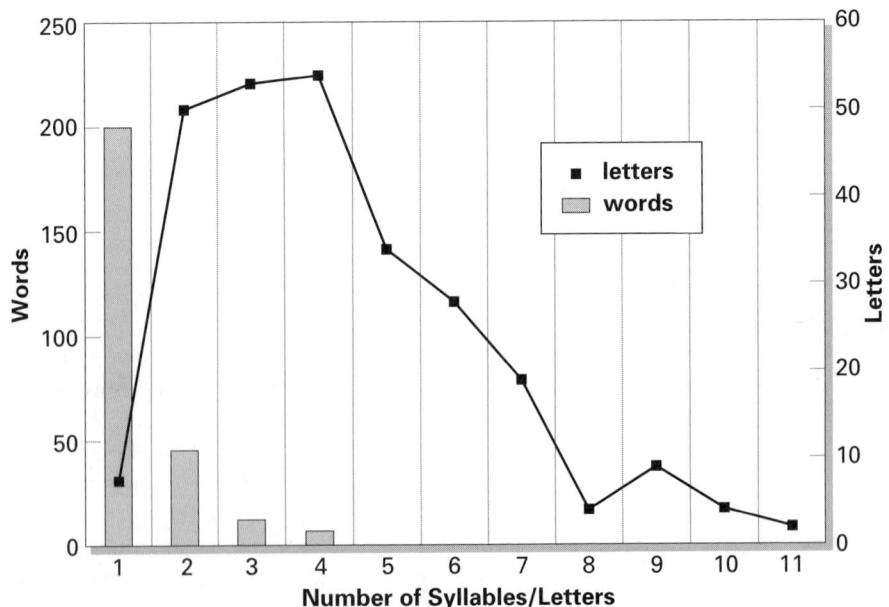

Lincoln far surpasses all standards for brevity, simplicity, and economy. His presentation was so brief that there are no photographs commemorating Lincoln's speech. He stood up, delivered his remarks, and sat back down before cameras could be positioned. But, as we have been arguing, short words are not an answer. A good reading on the Fog Index does not attest to style. In fact, despite Lincoln's achievement in using short words, the readability of the Gettysburg Address—when gauged simply as a function of simplicity—can, computers show us, be improved. (Figure 7.10 is a side-by-side comparison of Lincoln's document with an "enhanced" version generated by an automated writing program.[15])

Comparing the two versions provides the first suggestion of what truly is at the heart of Lincoln's style. The computer's elimination of certain critical phrases from the original text gives the revised version a hollow ring, as if the very identity of Lincoln has been drained from the text. The rhythm, the emotion, the strength, the force are all gone. The words do not sing; they barely hum.

Gone is the lyricism of the opening lines: "Four score and seven years ago." Gone is the cadence of the closing line: "government of the people, by the people,

Eighty seven years ago, our grandfathers created a free nation here. They based it on the idea that everybody is created equal. We are now fighting a civil war to see if this nation or any similar nation can survive. On this battlefield we are dedicating a cemetery to those who died for their country. It is only right. But in another sense, the task is impossible, because brave men, living and dead, dedicated the place better than we can. Hardly anyone will notice or remember what we say here, but nobody can forget what those men did. We should continue the work they began and make sure they did not die in vain. With God's help, we will have freedom again, so that the people's government will endure.	Four score and seven years ago our fathers brought forth on this continent, a new nation, conceived in Liberty, and dedicated to the proposition that all men are created equal. Now we are engaged in a great civil war, testing whether that nation, or any nation so conceived and so dedicated, can long endure. We are met on a great battle-field of that war. We have come to dedicate a portion of that field, as a final resting place for those who here gave their lives that that nation might live. It is altogether fitting and proper that we should do this. But, in a larger sense, we cannot dedicate—we cannot consecrate—we cannot hallow—this ground. The brave men, living and dead, who struggled here, have consecrated it, far above our poor power to add or detract. The world will little note, nor long remember what we say here, but it can never forget what they did here. It is for us the living, rather, to be dedicated here to the unfinished work which they who fought here have thus far so nobly advanced. It is rather for us to be here dedicated to the great task remaining before us—that from these honored dead we take increased devotion to that cause for which they gave the last full measure of devotion—that we here highly resolve that these dead should not have died in vain—that this nation, under God, shall have a new birth of freedom—and that government of the people, by the people, for the people shall not perish from the earth.	**FIGURE 7.10** The Computer and the President

for the people shall not perish from the earth." The body no longer stirs with the powerful juxtapositions of thought: "The world will little note, nor long remember . . . " The rhythm of language is no longer evident: "we cannot dedicate—we cannot consecrate—we cannot hallow—this ground." And the images have disappeared: "a new nation conceived in liberty." Although the computer-generated version is grammatically correct, it represents grammar without rhetoric, rule without identity, voice without sound. These attributes are added to our work when we employ stylistic devices, the purposeful stringing together of words to create emphasis, rhythm, and image.

The enduring life of the Gettysburg Address is not a function of who said the words, the occasion, or the simplicity of language. The success lies in how Lincoln used stylistic devices to weave a story of the birth, life, death, and rebirth of a nation—all in the span of only 264 words. (Table 7.11 lists the 14 stylistic devices used in the Gettysburg Address; Figure 7.11 shows their application within Lincoln's speech.)

Lincoln's masterful use of style leads to two questions: Which devices have relevance to the study of professional communication? How can we gain mastery over them? In answer to the first question, many stylistic devices exist. Efforts to catalog these devices have their origins with classical rhetoricians such as Cicero and Quintillian. Teachers of rhetoric, such as Isocrates, used the study of stylistic devices as the foundation of learning. In Elizabethan times, style enjoyed a prominent cultural role. In parallel with the evolving vocabulary for defining musical style, Elizabethans, such as Henry Peacham, were aggressive catalogers, recording hundreds of stylistic devices in works such as *The Garden of Eloquence* (1577). Yet, like word count, our interest is not with numbers.

FIGURE 7.11

The Devices in the Gettysburg Address

Four score and seven years ago our fathers brought forth — allusion / assonance
a new nation, conceived in Liberty, and dedicated to the — metaphor
proposition that all men are created equal.
Now we are engaged in a great civil war, testing whether — epistrophe
that nation, or any nation so conceived and so dedicated,
can long endure. We are met on a great battle-field of that
war. We have come to dedicate a portion of that field, as — anaphora
a final resting place for those who gave their lives that the
nation might live. It is altogether fitting and proper that we
should do this.
But in a larger sense, we cannot dedicate—we cannot — tricolon
consecrate—we cannot hallow—this ground. The brave — antithesis
men, living and dead, who struggled here, have consecrated
it, far above our poor power to add or detract. The world — personification
will little note, nor long remember what we say here, but — parallelism
it can never forget what they did here. It is for us the living, — expletive
rather, to be dedicated here to the unfinished work which — epistrophe / allusion
they who fought here have thus so far so nobly advanced.
It is rather for us to be here dedicated to the great task
remaining before us—that from these honored dead we
take increased devotion to that cause for which they gave — alliteration
the last full measure of devotion—that we here highly
resolve that these dead shall not have died in vain— — tricolon, anaphora / metaphor
that this nation, under God, shall have a new birth of
freedom—and that government of the people, by the — climax, asyndeton, epistrophe
people, for the people, shall not perish from the earth.
— litote

206

7.11 THE STYLISTIC DEVICES EMPLOYED BY LINCOLN

Device Name	Explanation	Example
1. Alliteration	Recurrence of initial consonant sounds	The serpent slithered and cowered the cautious creature.
2. Allusion	Indirect reference to a famous historical or literary person or event	Plan ahead. You know, it wasn't raining when Noah began work on the ark.
3. Anaphora	Repetition of the same word(s) at the beginning of successive phrases, clauses, or sentences	Not time, not money, not laws, naught but practice will lead to success.
4. Antithesis	Juxtaposing ideas to highlight the stark contrasting between them	"To err is human, to forgive divine." Alexander Pope
5. Assonance	Repetition of similar vowel sounds in successive or proximate words	"A city on a hill cannot be hid."
6. Asyndeton	Omitting conjunctions between a series of words, phrases, or clauses	He was a lawyer, businessman, orator, CEO, inventor.
7. Climax	Arranging words, phrases, or clauses in a series of increasing weight, importance, or emphasis	That ball is going, going, going, gone!
8. Epistrophe	The repetition of the same word(s) at the end of successive phrases, clauses, or sentences	Without time, running out of time, generally short on time, make time. Buy Brice stock.
9. Expletive	A single word or short phrase interjected between ideas to draw attention to each of the two thoughts	"All truth is not, indeed, of equal importance; but if little violations are allowed, every violation will in time be thought little." Samuel Johnson
10. Litote	An understatement in which the expected term is replaced by an unusual equivalent	Heat waves are not rare in the south during the summer.
11. Metaphor	An implied comparison in which the comparative terms *like* and *as* have been omitted	The lightning-fast strike totally caught all competitors off guard.
12. Parallelism	Arranging words, phrases or clauses in a series; each segment using the same syntactical construction	I helped her to her car, threw the door open, waved for her to enter, waited for her, and then closed it after her.
13. Personification	Providing an inanimate object with human or animal characteristics	The table began to creak and protest as the CEO pounded each point home.
14. Tricolon	A form of parallelism in which three syntactically equivalent phrases, clauses, or sentences are presented	He did no work, offered no solutions, and left without complaint.

Our job here is not to postulate a comprehensive list of devices, but to isolate those patterns that are particularly pertinent to professional communication. To do so, let's return to the business of politics, refocusing our attention from the best-known American speech of the nineteenth century to the two best known speeches of the twentieth century: John F. Kennedy's Inaugural Address, and Martin Luther King, Jr.'s "I Have a Dream" speech. Identifying the intersection among the stylistic devices used in the works of Lincoln, Kennedy, and King should serve as a practical approach to defining the elements of style of interest in professional communications.

A Brief Look at Kennedy

On January 20, 1961, John F. Kennedy delivered his Inaugural Address. Like the Gettysburg Address, the speech is still frequently quoted, in particular the line that invited Americans to volunteer in the service of their country: "Ask not what your country can do for you, but what you can do for your country."

Kennedy's stylistic success was a matter of conscious choices in selecting and applying language. Theodore Sorensen, who served as a key White House advisor to and speechwriter for Kennedy, articulates the Kennedy administration's emphasis on attention to the sounds that words make on paper—and to the ear:

> The test of a text was not how it appeared to the eye, but how it sounded to the ear. His best paragraphs, when read aloud, often had a cadence not unlike blank verse—indeed at times key words would rhyme. He was fond of alliterative sentences, not solely for reasons of rhetoric but to reinforce the audience's recollection of his reasoning . . . .
>
> Words were regarded as tools of precision, to be chosen and applied with a craftsman's care to whatever the situation required. He liked to be exact . . . . he disliked verbosity and pomposity in his own remarks as much as he disliked them in others. He wanted both his message and his language to be plain and unpretentious, but never patronizing. He wanted his major policy statements to be positive, specific, and definite . . . . At the same time, his emphasis on a course of reason—rejecting the extremes of either side—helped produce the parallel construction and use of contrasts with which he later became identified.[16]

The elements of Kennedy's style are neatly laid out: 1) short words, 2) short phrases and sentences, 3) a commitment to precision, conciseness, and clarity, 4) a conscious application of emphasis, 5) attention to sound: rhyme, cadence, alliterative sentences, parallelism constructions, and 6) the juxtaposition of opposites to emphasize contrasts. Not surprising, given Kennedy's emphasis on certain sounds, all 14 devices employed in the Gettysburg Address are found in the Inaugural Address, along with five additional devices of potential use to business communicators. (Table 7.12 lists the five new devices; Figure 7.12 gives examples from the Inaugural Address of the 19 stylistic devices.)

A Brief Look at Martin Luther King, Jr.

Two points, it is said, define a straight line, but for our purposes, we may want to introduce a third data point to ensure we have a representative pattern. We saw a strong correspondence between the stylistic devices employed by Lincoln and Kennedy; if King's speech, believed by some to be the most famous American speech of the twentieth century, shares points in common with these other

7.12 **ADDITIONAL STYLISTIC DEVICES EMPLOYED BY KENNEDY**

Device Name	Explanation	Example
1. Anadiplosis	Repeating the concluding word, phrase, or clause at the beginning of the next syntactical element	"In the beginning was the word, and the word was with God, and the word was God." John 1:1
2. Antimetabole	Repeating—but reversing—the words of a phrase or clause in two successive clauses or sentences	All work and no play is no better than all play and no work.
3. Metonymy	A form of metaphor in which an item closely associated with the object or idea is used in its place	a) The White House said today (The White House replaces President.) b) The mercury is rising.
4. Polysyndeton	The opposite of asyndeton, inserting conjunctions between every member of a series of words, phrases, or clauses	He talked, and he studied, and he met, and he reviewed, and he analyzed, and he contemplated, and, finally he took action.
5. Rhetorical Question	Phrasing an idea as a question whose answer, being evident, is already known to the audience and speaker (Generally, the question requires merely a yes or no response.)	Are you going to stand there and tell me that Brice never intended a hostile merger with Cavlico?

FIGURE 7.12

Kennedy's Use of Stylistic Devices

Alliteration—"dark powers of destruction"

Allusion—"irony tyranny" (communism)

Anadiplosis—"has always been committed, and to which we are committed."

Anaphora—"let both sides . . . let both sides"

Antimetabole—"Ask not what your country can do for you; ask what you can do for your country."

Antithesis—"wishes us well or ill"

Assonance—"jungle of suspicion."

Asyndeton—"pay any price, bear any burden, meet any hardship, support any friend"

Climax—"born in this century. . . unwilling to witness"

Epistrophe—"the power to destroy nations under . . . control of all nations."

Expletive—"it is for us the living, rather, . . ."

Litote—"shall not perish"

Metaphor—"chains of poverty"

Metonymy—"huts and villages"

Parallelism—"united . . . divided"

Personification—"the world will little note . . ."

Polysyndeton—"where the strong are just and the weak secure, and the peace preserved . . .

Rhetorical Question—"Can we forge . . . unwilling to witness . . . you join me . . . ?"

Tricolon—"both sides overburdened, both rightly alarmed, yet both racing . . ."

speeches, we should be able to assert with confidence that we have identified a credible subset of stylistic devices applicable to professional communication.

Delivered only 8 months after Kennedy's Inaugural Address, King's speech utilizes many of the same devices we have just identified in the Gettysburg Address and the Inaugural Address.

Standing in the "symbolic shadows" of the Lincoln Memorial, King presented America with an obligation to fulfill the promise of democracy decreed in the Declaration of Independence and sealed in the Emancipation Proclamation. As his presentation unfolds, King moves the framework from past, to present, to future—imploring America to respond to the "fierce urgency of now" so as to avoid the "rude awakenings" that will accompany the "whirlwinds of revolt" (Figure 7.13).[17]

Throughout his oration, King makes frequent and powerful use of metaphor. The image of America's debt is carried through a succession of references to banks, vaults, cashing checks, and insufficient funds. Justice and freedom are cast in the form of daybreak, light, and streams, contrasted with the "islands of despair," the darkness, and the extended night of oppression and slavery. Even the journey to freedom is expressed in the form of an extended metaphor (Figure 7.14). Along this journey, King uses numerous allusions to suggest the forces and events that shaped—and were shaping—the American landscape (Table 7.13).

FIGURE 7.13

The Unfinished Business of Freedom

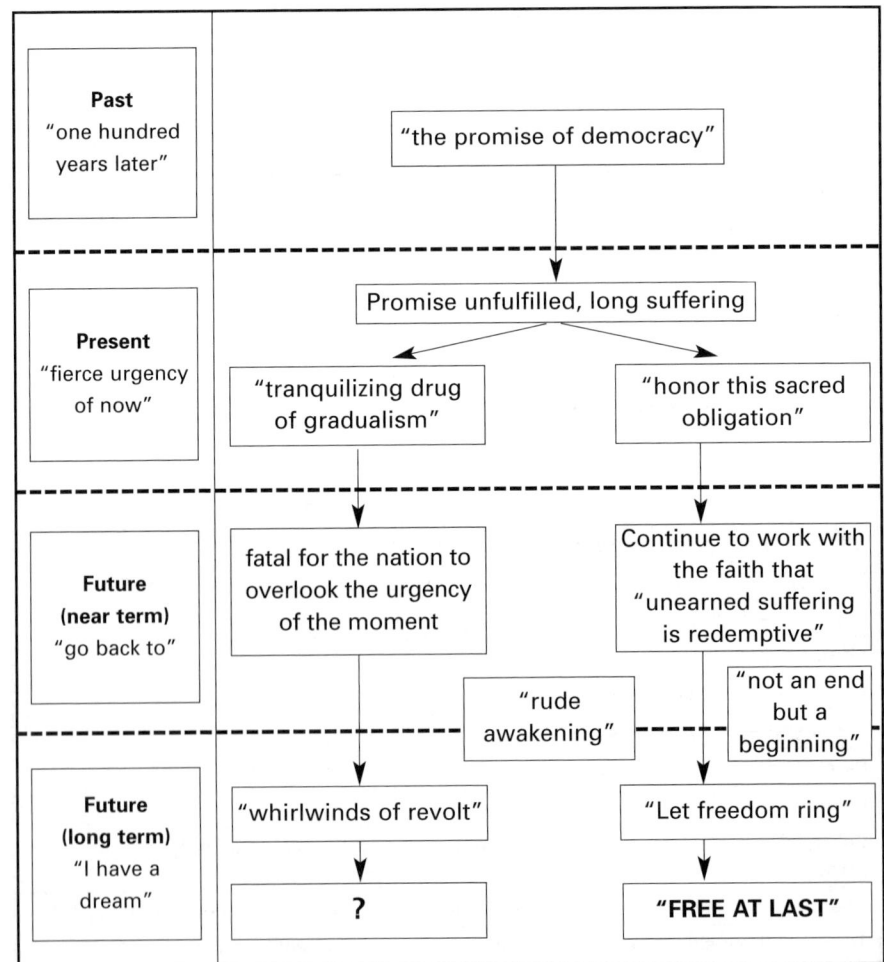

Past "one hundred years later"	"the promise of democracy"
Present "fierce urgency of now"	Promise unfulfilled, long suffering → "tranquilizing drug of gradualism" / "honor this sacred obligation"
Future (near term) "go back to"	fatal for the nation to overlook the urgency of the moment / Continue to work with the faith that "unearned suffering is redemptive"
	"rude awakening" / "not an end but a beginning"
Future (long term) "I have a dream"	"whirlwinds of revolt" → ? / "Let freedom ring" → "FREE AT LAST"

FIGURE 7.14

	Time	Distance	Spiritual
Past	"five score years ago"	"lives on a lonely island of poverty" "we have come to this hallowed spot"	"covenant with Abraham"
Present	"one hundred years later" "fierce urgency of now"	"you have come here out of your trials and tribulations" "go back"	life in bondage deliverance
Future	"I have a dream"	"Let freedom ring from every state and every city"	redemption

The Mighty
Journey

TABLE

7.13 KING'S ALLUSIONS

Quotation	Allusion
five score years ago	The Gettysburg Address
symbolic shadow	Abraham Lincoln
seared in the flames	Cross burnings
we will not be satisfied until justice rolls down like waters and righteousness like a mighty stream	Amos 5:24
soul force	Peaceful resistance (Mahatma Ghandi)
marvelous new militancy	Black Panther movement
We hold these truths to be self evident	Declaration of Independence
every valley shall be exalted . . . the crooked places will be made straight	Isaiah 40: 4–5
My country 'tis of thee	The patriotic anthem often referred to as America's national song.
Stone Mountain, Georgia	Ku Klux Klan
Lookout Mountain, Tennessee	Civil War

In the course of his delivery, King makes use of all but a few of the devices we identified in the works of Lincoln and Kennedy. He also adds five new devices to our list (Table 7.14). (Figure 7.15 illustrates the spectrum of stylistic devices used by King.) This high degree of commonalty among the devices used in these three speeches is not accidental. The writers of the speeches shared common goals: to make their positions and assertions not only clear but forceful, their messages not only informative but inspiring, and their opportunity not only memorable but enduring. (Figure 7.16 provides a graphical representation of the commonalty of style devices shared by Lincoln, Kennedy, and King.)

TABLE

7.14 ADDITIONAL STYLISTIC DEVICES EMPLOYED BY KING

Device Name	Explanation	Example
1. Epanalepsis	Repeating the same word(s) or phrase at the beginning and end of a clause or sentence	Our eyes saw it, but we couldn't believe our eyes.
2. Onomatopeia	Using words whose sounds are suggestive of the meaning	We will soon hear the plop, plop, plop of money dripping into our coffers.
3. Oxymoron	The juxtaposition of seemingly contradictory and mutually exclusive words or phrases	A wealth of poverty is what we face in this country.
4. Simile	A comparison of ideas or objects in which the word *like* or *as* is used.	Merging with Cavlico will be like launching a Titan rocket.
5. Symploce	The combined use of anaphora and epistrophe	Sales of new products at Brice will increase, sales of old products will increase, sales of all products will increase.

FIGURE 7.15

King's Use of Stylistic Devices

> **Alliteration**—"citizens of color are concerned"
> **Allusion**—"not an end but a beginning" (an allusion to Kennedy's Inaugural Address)
> **Anadiplosis**—"come to cash a check, a check . . ."
> **Anaphora**—"one hundred years later. . . one hundred years later"
> **Antithesis**—"joyous daybreak to end the long night of captivity"
> **Assonance**—"jungle of suspicion."
> **Asyndeton**—"every valley . . . every hill . . . every mountain . . ."
> **Climax**—"free at last, free at last, thank God Almighty, we are free at last."
> **Epanalepsis**—"It is a dream deeply rooted in the American dream"
> **Epistrophe**—"a person . . . cannot vote . . . has nothing for which to vote."
> **Expletive**—"I say to you, my friends, . . ."
> **Litote**—"I am not unmindful that"
> **Metaphor**—"vaults of opportunity"
> **Metonymy**—"interposition and nullification"
> **Onomatopeia**—"lips dripping," "jangling discords"
> **Oxymoron**—"creative suffering"
> **Polysyndeton**—"to work together, to pray together, to struggle together, to go . . ."
> **Simile**—"justice rolls down like waters . . ."
> **Symploce**—"we cannot . . . vote . . . we . . . cannot . . . vote"
> **Tricolon**—"black men and white men, Jews and Gentiles, Protestants and Catholics"

FIGURE 7.16

	Stylistic Device	Gettysburg Address	Inaugural Address	I Have A Dream Speech
Image Setting	Allusion	√	√	√
	Eponym			
	Metaphor	√	√	√
	Metonymy		√	√
	Personification	√		
	Simile			√
Rhythm	Alliteration	√	√	√
	Assonance	√	√	√
	Asyndeton	√	√	√
	Climax	√	√	√
	Parallelism	√	√	√
	Polysyndeton		√	
	Tricolon	√	√	√
Emphasis	Anadiplosis		√	√
	Anaphora	√	√	√
	Antimetabole		√	
	Antithesis	√	√	√
	Epanalepsis			√
	Epistrophe	√	√	√
	Expletive	√		√
	Litote	√		√
	Onomatopeia			√
	Oxymoron			√
	Rhetorical Question		√	
	Symploce			√

A Shared Reliance on Stylistic Devices

STYLE AND BUSINESS

We still must make the leap from the works of King, Kennedy, and Lincoln to the world of business. Do the same devices work equally well when discussing matters other than the politics of business? Do we have to achieve the oratorical excellence of Lincoln to use these devices to give voice to our thoughts? If, as we have been asserting, these devices represent a commonly employed subset applicable to professional communication, we should be able to find them being used in the everyday communications of professionals.

To test our assertion, let's look briefly at one more speech. To step forward in time and to bring the subject matter more up-to-date, let's consider the keynote address made at E-Day 2000, an event sponsored by the Boston University School of Management. The speech, "E-Business Is Still Business," was delivered in January 2000 by Michael Bronner, the founder and chairman emeritus of Digitas Corporation.

Table 7.15 lists the devices used by Bronner in his remarks. Compared to Lincoln who used 14 of our devices, Kennedy who used 19, and King who used 20, Bronner uses 18 in his 15-minute presentation. Interestingly, the number of devices used by our twentieth-century entrepreneur corresponds to the precise average of devices used by Kennedy, King, and Lincoln. The inevitable conclusion is that it is not circumstances, subject matter, or station that makes a difference in whether we develop a style of communication. The difference is the commitment we make to creating a positive sound on paper.

7.15 STYLISTIC DEVICES IN THE E-DAY 2000 SPEECH

Alliteration—"I believe it has the **p**ower and **p**otential to more deeply affect **p**eople's lives."

Allusion—"I'm not talking about the exciting . . . things millions of people have been enabled to do as a result of the Internet: buy books and CDs easily, buy and sell stocks at lower commissions, buy airline tickets cheaply" (allusion to Amazon.com, E-Trade.com, Priceline.com).

Anadiplosis—"We have done this because of an **obsession**—an **obsession** with serving customers . . ."

Anaphora—"surround yourselves with great **people**—**people** you work for . . . **people** who work for you . . . **people** who work with you"

Antithesis—"My colleagues and I have done this together by focusing not on the **future** but on the **past**."

Assonance—"What we have learned over the past two decades is that the emergence of the Internet and the proliferation of technologies has caused traditional boundaries to be blurred."

Asyndeton—"I believe it has the kind of power and potential . . . to bring communities of people together . . . bring nations together, to promote understanding and tolerance; to foster safety and security . . . to enable more scientific research . . . to entertain in ways as yet undreamed of; to truly educate people . . . share and distribute resources . . . to bridge the gap between the franchised and the disenfranchised; to support a global Information Technology (IT) or e-infrastucture."

Epanalepsis—"Talking about the **potential** of the Internet this way may sound 'Utopian,' but I believe it has that kind of **potential**."

Epistrophe—"Put simply, hire **talented people**, work for **talented people**, and work with **talented people**."

Metonymy—"Consequently they move from one service provider to another at the speed of a click."

Metaphor—"We're living in a new economy and some of these guys are still in the Middle Ages bleeding patients."

Onomatopeia—"The operative word for all this is 'disintermediation.'"

Oxymoron—"I want to talk about the hype surrounding the Internet phenomenon. This hype is grossly . . . understated."

Parallelism—"We are known as a leader who has recognized paradigm shifts ahead of others—a leader in promotions . . . in direct marketing . . . in customer management and direct sales . . . integrated marketing across the enterprise."

Personification—"The fear I experience keeps me honest, and makes me work harder. Fear only exists in the shadows, because I keep it in its place."

Rhetorical Question—"I was twenty years old then. Do you think I was scared when I presented to American Express? Do you think I was afraid that I might fail?"

Symploce—"an **obsession** with understanding and serving their **needs** . . . an **obsession** with being leaders . . . in the use of new technologies that enable customers to meet their **needs**."

Tricolon—"Put simply, the combination of deregulation . . . the impact of new Internet technologies . . . and the emergence of a global economy is radically transforming the business and social landscape."

Having brought the devices firmly into the contemporary business world, we want to go one step further. You don't need to search out politicians or CEOs to find demonstrations of the devices. The devices are employed in the advertisements and commercials we read and listen to on a daily basis. The same reason we vividly recollect the key phrases and principal themes of the works of Lincoln, King, and Kennedy is why we are so readily inclined to recall advertising jingles and product slogans. Advertisers make their livings being sensitive to the kinds of sounds and images that will stay with us as consumers. Is it any surprise, therefore, that we can find the stylistic devices we have been examining at play when we read magazines or watch television (Figure 7.17)?

The opportunities, as these varied examples suggest, are available for each of us to gain a voice, an identity, and a style. The opportunity exists to bring an identity into focus, to present information with imagery, rhythm, and emphasis. The opportunity is there for each of us to strive for the style that Kennedy demanded: short, precise communications that provide for clarity and comprehension without pomposity or verbosity. Most importantly, the opportunities are available to everyone—from entry level professional to CEO—to continue to strive for and improve our abilities at "thinking out into language," to add music to "the sounds words make on paper."

FIGURE 7.17

A Sampling of Devices in General Use

Alliteration—"Being diabetic doesn't mean being disabled." *Liberty Mutual*	
Anadiplosis—"The heat activates the gel. The gel releases the shine. The shine attracts the eye." *Thermasilk*	
Anaphora—"TWA's Ambassador Class to Europe: More room to sit. More room to work. More room to relax. *TWA*	
Antimetabole—"You can take Salem out of the country, but you can't take the country out of Salem." *Salem*	
Antithesis—"Life insurance isn't for the people who die. It's for the people who live." *Life Insurance*	
Asyndeton—"We would never change the most trusted, proven, gentle, pediatrician-recommended medicine you can give." *Tylenol*	
Epistrophe—"Traffic-free. Crowd-free. Now—$20 free. *Toytime.com*	
Metaphor—"Your twenties were just training wheels." *Kraft cottage cheese*	
Metonymy—"Perfect for couch potatoes." *Ritz Crackers*	
Oxymoron—"Look at the world—under a microscope." *Scientific American*	
Parallelism—"Fast talk gets you in a corner. Straight talk gets you out." *Inter First Bank*	
Personification—"Making filing come alive." *Pendaflex*	
Rhetorical Question—"Want to chop, dice, and cut prep time?" *Campbell's Soup*	
Simile—"Coke is like family. You can never have enough." *Coke*	
Tricolon—"Affordable mobile technology. Excellent support. In-depth training." *Gateway Computers*	

A NOTE ON ACHIEVING STYLE

Your primary attention as communicator must always remain on what you want to say, who you want to say it to, and what you expect of that audience as a consequence. When we take the next step in gaining mastery of our communications, we can consider the diction, precision, and appropriateness of language, the pace at which we impart information, the comfort of the presentation, the rhetoric of grammar, and the rhetoric of style. Each instance must be tempered by an appreciation of how selections and choices aid comprehension and clarity—not how they can be made impressive and imposing.

The only path to achieving these ends is, like the punch line to the old Henny Youngman joke: How do I get to Carnegie Hall?—practice, practice, practice. Lincoln, Kennedy, and King were most likely strangers to terms such as polysyndeton, symploce, and antimetabole, but not to the purposeful intent of creating rhythm, image, and emphasis. They understood that achieving style demanded application and observation—the two critical dimensions of practice.

The first dimension, application, occurs in two broad stages. The first stage requires taking conscious advantage of what we have been examining. This can be done by stopping and making conscious choices about language and phrasing: Should the contrast you are proposing be made more dramatic and compelling by using antithesis? Should the comparison be enhanced by metaphor or simile? Should a series be set up in the form of a tricolon, or should the series be made more compelling by using climax? Should the elements of the series be isolated from one another by use of polysyndeton or less pronounced through use of asyndeton? Should antimetabole be used to create a clearly memorable catch phrase? These are the types of questions that, when asked with regularity, contribute slowly but surely to style.

The second stage occurs when you find yourself more automatically, more intuitively, making stylistic choices because the sounds have a particularly pleasant sound or cadence. With each use, the devices become more of a natural extension of your identity, a more spontaneous reflection of your style.

Complementing practice is observation. In the seventeenth, eighteenth, and nineteenth centuries, writing and speaking were learned (both in terms of correctness and style) through a process of imitation. Not only did students listen and read, they copied page after page of well-written discourse into their notebooks, assimilating stylistic elements as a consequence of the effort. Style, like vocabulary, was understood to be a study best mastered through a combination of observation and imitation.

Assigning names to the devices is only a small step toward developing style; it is no more than the vocabulary that makes the elements of style more visible and distinguishable. The major step involves observation and imitation. Even Kennedy studied the Gettysburg Address in preparation for writing his Inaugural Address. As Theodore Sorensen, who worked alongside Kennedy in the White House, points out, Kennedy worked hard at attaining style, often honing phrases and sentences until they had the sharp, crisp ring with which he was identified (Figure 7.18).

The value of imitation and observation has been proven many times. People who read a great deal generally have better vocabularies than those who try memorization techniques. People who practice and listen for the elements of style are more likely to incorporate the devices into their own writing and speaking. We retain ideas—and words—in context, much as we use context to help us

FIGURE 7.18

First Draft	Next-to-Last Draft	Final Draft
We celebrate today not a victory of party but the sacrament of democracy	We celebrate today not a victory of party but a convention of freedom	We observe today not a victory of party but a celebration of freedom
Each of us, whether we hold offices or not, shares the responsibility for guiding this most difficult of all societies along the path of self-discipline and self-government.	In your hands, my fellow citizens more than in mine, will be determined the success or failure of our course.	In your hands, my fellow citizens, more than mine, will rest final success or failure of our course.
And if the fruits of cooperation prove sweeter than the dregs of suspicion, let both sides join ultimately in creating a true world order—neither a Pax Americana, nor a Pax Russiana, nor even a balance of power—but a community of power.	And if a beachhead of cooperation can be made in the jungles of suspicion, let both sides join some day in creating, not a new balance of power, but a new world of law . . .	And if a beachhead of cooperation can push back the jungle of suspicion, let both sides join in creating a new endeavor, not a new balance of power, but a new world of law . . .

Kennedy's Reworking of Language

understand the meanings and connotations of words. Therefore, building a style, like building vocabulary, benefits from observation (reading), complemented by use (application in writing or speech). The gains you achieve will be directly proportional to the investment you make.

STYLE—THE LESSONS

Business communications do not have to be lifeless. They should be clear, precise, concise, and immediately comprehensible—a function that derives from diction, pace, information presentation, the rhetoric of grammar, and the prudent employment of stylistic devices. When we find ourselves dizzied by a dense text or bored to distraction when attending a presentation, we are experiencing the presenter's lack of style. The penalty is that important information and great ideas go unheeded, unappreciated, and unapplied.

In business, we will be called upon to handle a range of subjects—some mundane, some unfamiliar, some safe, and some accompanied by great risk. What we do with those opportunities is up to us, the tools we use, the choices we make. We can choose to apply the needed discipline and art, or we can let the words fall as they may. Each word, each phrase, each clause, each sentence, each paragraph, each page, and each slide is a chance to succeed—or to fail—at our obligations to make the salient information clear and comprehensible. It is also an opportunity to succeed or fail at gaining the kind of positive recognition that should accompany a job well done.

We should never lose sight that what we learn today about communication must be consistent with the common sense that has been the keystone of all good communication theory. Scholars, consultants, and dilettantes may dress up the attributes of communication in various clothes. They may coin new terms to restate the principles handed down from the Greeks. They may introduce new technologies to aid in the capture, manipulation, indexation, and transmission of information. However, at its core, the fundamentals of sound writing—business or otherwise—haven't changed and will not change.

At the core of your responsibilities as a communicator are seven fundamental obligations:

1. Make certain you have an appreciation of the full scope and dimensions of the purpose of your assignment.

2. Know and respect the audience and the communities you are addressing.

3. Assemble facts that relate precisely and effectively to the subject at hand.

4. Arrange your information in a manner that will assist the audience with understanding your assertions and conclusions.

5. Build your material into a clear and cogent business argument.

6. Use language that makes your points clearly, precisely, and forcefully; use a pace that allows the points to be gathered in and processed.

7. Employ the rhetoric of grammar and the rhetoric of style to make your argument both compelling and appealing.

On our journey so far, we have been focusing on explaining how to achieve each of these goals. We have established in these first seven chapters the discipline and art of professional communication. Now, with this base, we are ready to engage in examining how these tools and principles are applied to the various products and genres of professional communication.

EXERCISES

☐ Group

Divide into teams.

1. Select several business letters. Examine and report on the use of language, grammar, and style.

2. Identify as many of the 23 stylistic devices as you can, using national and local advertisements. Discuss the appropriateness and effectiveness of each example.

3. Select an Inaugural Address (other than Kennedy's). Prepare an essay in which you discuss the President's message and how his style (or lack of style) contributes to the clarity and effectiveness of that message.

☐ Individual

1. Rewrite the paragraph about Brice Company, making use of a variety of sentence openers, punctuation, transitions, and stylistic devices. Explain how your choices improve the quality of the paragraph.

2. Select any speech published in the journal *Vital Speeches of the Day*. Identify the stylistic devices that are used and how they contribute to the message.

[1] Rudolph Flesch, *The Art of Readable Writing.* New York: Harper & Brothers, Publishers, 1949.

[2] F. Christensen, " The Problem of Defining a Mature Style," *English Journal,* Vol. 57 (1968), pp. 572–579.

[3] H. A. Gleason, Jr., *Linguistics and English Grammar.* New York: Holt, Rinehart and Winston, Inc., 1965.

[4] D. M. Wolfe, "Variety in Sentence Structure: A Device," *College English,* Vol. 11, No. 7 (April 1950), pp. 394–397.

[5] *Ibid.*

[6] F. Christensen. "Notes Toward a New Rhetoric—I. Sentence Openers," *College English,* Vol. 25, No. 1 (Oct. 1963), pp. 7–11.

[7] D. Bush, "Sensitivity to Emphasis." *Technical Communication,* Vol. 39, No. 3 (Aug. 1992), pp. 442–443.

[8] C. E, Good. "When the Passive Voice Is Preferred," *Trial,* Vol. 32, No. 7 (July 1996), pp. 98–100.

[9] Cited in J. Dawkins.. "Teaching Punctuation as a Rhetorical Tool," *College Composition and Communication,* Vol. 46, No. 4 (Dec. 1995), pp. 533–548.

[10] Tables 7.5 and 7.6 are adapted from Dawkins, "Teaching Punctuation as a Rhetorical Tool."

[11] Cited in M. Markel , M. Vaccaro, and T. Hewett. "Effects of Paragraph Length on Attitudes Toward Technical Writing," *Technical Communication,* Vol. 39, No. 3 (Aug. 1992), pp. 454–456.

[12] *Ibid.*

[13] E. Barton, E. Halter, N. McGee, and L. McNeilly, "The Awkward Problem of Awkward Sentences." *Written Communications,* Vol. 15 (Jan. 1998), p. 69 (1).

[14] Christensen, "Notes Toward a New Rhetoric."

[15] D. Plung, "Evaluate Your Technical Writing," *Hydrocarbon Processing* (July 1981), p. 195+

[16] Theodore Sorensen, *With Kennedy.* New York: Harper & Row, 1965.

[17] The idea for this chart was derived from: M. Solomon, "Covenanted Rights: The Metaphoric Matrix of 'I Have a Dream,'" in *Martin Luther King, Jr., and the Sermonic Power of Public Discourse,* ed. C. Calloway-Thomas and J.L. Lucaites, Tuscaloosa: The University of Alabama Press, 1993, pp. 66–84.

THE METHODS OF PROFESSIONAL COMMUNICATION

One-on-One and Group Meetings
Making the Human Moment Purposeful

Speaking is natural to us. We grow up using speech as the primary means of communication. In business, we keep this tradition—also relying extensively on oral communication. We talk in one-on-one sessions with peers and managers, we talk in meetings in which people have assembled to deal with a specific topic of common interest, and we make formal presentations.

Employers generally expect that employees are prepared to interact orally with the various components of the business community. Yet, that doesn't mean that our natural ability to speak should be interpreted as a natural ability to speak or communicate well. There are expectations for each of the communication settings—individual interaction, meetings, and formal presentations. To do each one well demands both an appreciation of the rhetorical principles we have been examining in Part 1 of this text and an understanding of each situation's unique expectations.

In this chapter, we will look briefly at the role of oral communication in business, with particular attention to one-on-one discussions and interactions in meetings—the two primary forms of oral communication in business. In Chapter 9, we will examine the development and delivery of formal presentations.

TALKING, TALKING, TALKING

In a 1998 article in *Harvard Business Review,* Jay Conger, a professor of organizational behavior at the University of

California's Marshall School of Business, argued that managers need to hone their oral communication and skills of persuasion if they are to become and remain successful in the contemporary business environment. In a workplace where "ideas and people flow more freely than ever around the organizations," the "fine art of persuasion," is a necessity, not a nicety. Demonstrating our ability with oral communication is, as Conger announces, a predicate of success: "If there was ever a time for businesspeople to learn the fine art of persuasion, it is now." One reason, succinctly stated, is that "work today gets done in an environment where people don't just ask What should I do? But Why should I do it?"[1] Another reason is that oral communication is the cornerstone of a variety of interactions. As one survey of more than 100 companies determined, 80% of personnel were involved with job interviews, 75% with seminar discussions, 76% with oral reports, 78% with oral instructions to subordinates, and 75% with interaction with clients.[2] The challenge of oral competency is not, however, restricted to management.

At the same time that managers need to be practicing their oral competency to stay ahead in business, entry-level professionals need to be ready to demonstrate their oral competencies as well if they expect to get a foot in the door. As one survey of more than 350 managers in a wide range of businesses (retail, wholesale, manufacturing, service, public administration, transportation, finance, insurance, and banking) reported, oral communication is cited as the most important competency affecting hiring decisions (Table 8.1).[3]

Given the diverse nature of business responsibilities, business professionals tend to rank the importance of direct, personal interactions very highly, even more so than business faculty, who tend to give priority to presentations and presentation techniques (Table 8.2).[4]

The variety of exchanges is one reason for the rankings assigned by business professionals. The rankings are made more apparent when we consider the frequency

8.1 RELATIVE RANKING OF COMPETENCIES IN HIRING DECISIONS

Competency/Characteristic	Ranked #1	Ranked in Top 5	Weighted Score
Delegation	1	29	413
Basic computer	4	34	525
Creativity	3	39	632
Academic performance	17	62	750
Work experience	27	88	1046
Personal appearance	10	93	1063
Time management	8	100	1178
Written communication	7	110	1211
Teamwork	19	111	1407
Human relations	37	159	1608
Leadership	49	150	1634
Decision-making	21	78	1755
Problem-solving	36	200	2011
Self-motivation	52	193	2016
Oral communication	65	231	2237

Source: Reprinted with permission of the Association for Business Communication.

8.2 RANKED ORDER OF ORAL/INTERPERSONAL COMPETENCIES

Competency	Rankings Assigned	
	Business Professionals	Business Faculty
Listens effectively	1	2
Uses telephone effectively	2	16
Maintains eye contact	3	4
Asks appropriate questions	4	13
Uses voice effectively for emphasis (speed, pitch)	5	5
Uses appropriate tone of voice (formal or conversational)	6	8
Establishes rapport with audience	7	6
Organizes presentations effectively	8	1
Conducts/participates effectively in interviews	9	11
Uses appropriate techniques in making oral presentations	10	3
Is poised; controls nervousness	11	7
Uses proper interviewing techniques	12	15
Uses appropriate body actions in interpersonal oral communication	13	14
Objectively presents information in oral reports	14	9
Analyzes the audience before, during, and after an oral report	15	10
Uses audiovisual aids effectively	16	12

Source: Reprinted with permission of the Association for Business Communication.

that various oral communication skills are employed (Table 8.3).[5] As this table points out, the three most commonly employed skills are: 1) listening skills, 2) conversational skills, and 3) following instructions. Rounding out the picture of oral communication in the workplace, Table 8.4 indicates rankings assigned to other related competencies that contribute to the effectiveness of oral communication.[6]

From these tables, we can infer that there are three primary areas of activity when it comes to oral communication in business: 1) direct, one-on-one interactions, 2) meetings, and 3) formal presentations. Recognizing these conclusions, the authors of the survey comparing the relative rankings of various oral communication competencies suggest that in professional communications courses, formal classroom presentations need to share the stage with conflict resolution and meeting skills. To be successful practitioners of the fine art of persuasion, we need to learn how to negotiate both one-on-one and group meetings.[7]

LET'S FACE IT!—MEETING ONE-ON-ONE

Although our "networked" society may give rise to the impression that communication is conducted primarily by e-mail, the majority of communication in business is still conducted the old-fashioned way: one-on-one and face-to-face. Depending on which study is quoted, 60% to 80% of business communication is done face-to-face (Figure 8.1).[8] Further, the numbers remain relatively static whether discussing communication going up or down the organizational hierarchy (Table 8.5). [9]

TABLE 8.3 **ORAL COMMUNICATION SKILLS IN BUSINESS**

Skill	Importance*	Frequency of Use*
Following instructions	4.66	4.52
Listening skills	4.60	4.74
Conversational skills	4.47	4.53
Giving feedback	4.00	3.86
Communicating with the public	3.98	3.91
Meeting skills	3.74	3.52
Presentation skills	3.66	3.48
Handling customer complaints	3.52	3.48
Conflict resolution skills	3.48	3.43
Negotiation skills	3.33	3.18
Taking customer orders	3.09	2.93
Teaching/instructing skills	2.67	2.72
Interviewing skills	2.55	2.21

*Responses ranged from a minimum of 1 to a maximum of 5

Source: Reprinted with permission of the Association for Business Communication.

| TABLE | 8.4 |

RANKED ORDER OF RELATED COMPETENCIES

Competency	Rankings Assigned	
	Business Professionals	Business Faculty
Applies ethics, morals, and values to determine socially responsible actions	1	2
Understands personal values and shows sensitivity to the values of others	2	5
Uses principles of time management effectively	3	4
Assesses own needs and behaviors; locates outside sources to improve skills	4	3
Collects, classifies, and analyzes information about business situations; uses creative thinking in formulating solutions	5	1
Exhibits leadership by influencing and persuading	6	9
Plans, conducts, and follows up meetings effectively	7	8
Knows the importance of feedback	8	6
Uses appropriate data-analysis tools to solve problems	9	7
Applies knowledge of intercultural differences in communication situations	10	10
Applies knowledge of demographic diversity	11	11

Source: Reprinted with permission of the Association for Business Communication.

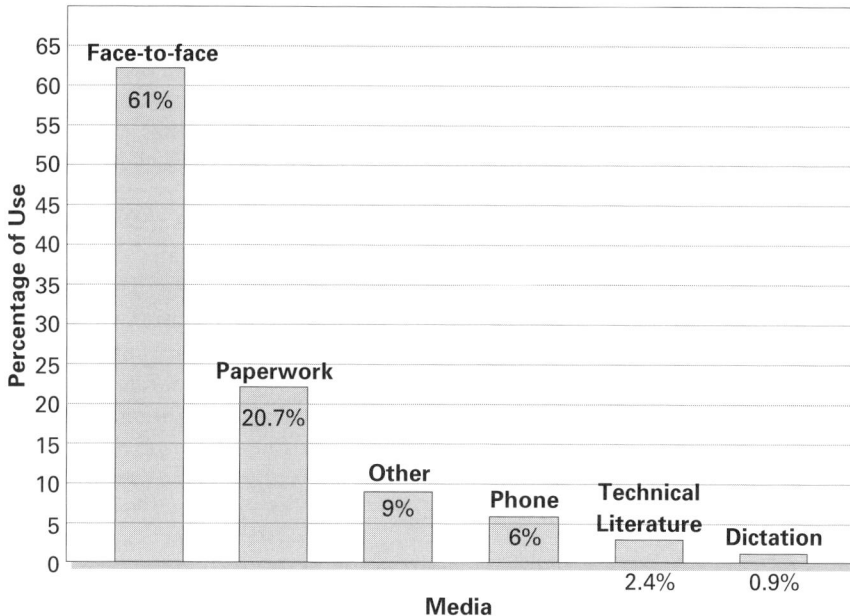

FIGURE 8.1

Types of Communication Media Used in a Normal Working Day

Source: Reprinted with permission of the Association for Business Communication

8.5	**FACE-TO-FACE MANAGERIAL COMMUNICATIONS**	
	Subordinates	**Superiors**
From	81.1%	76.9%
To	83.4%	82.4%

WHAT'S EVERYONE TALKING ABOUT?

Several approaches have been taken to categorize exactly what constitutes the subject of all this one-on-one discussion in business. At the foundation are two types of information being exchanged: technical information about how the work is to be done and social information about the organization, personnel, and working group. Years of discussion in the professional literature have refined these two categories, highlighting seven types of information typically shared in one-on-one business discussions:

1. Technical information—how to execute required tasks
2. Referent information—what is required and expected of the employee
3. Social information—the interrelationships among employees
4. Appraisal information—evaluation of the employee's performance and behavior
5. Normative information—explanation of the organization's culture
6. Organizational information—details of the firm's structure, procedures, and policies
7. Political information—explanation of the distribution of power within the organization.[10]

Table 8.6 provides details of some of the elements that comprise each of these seven categories of information.[11]

The relative volumes of information shared in each category are a function of experience with the organization. As newcomers, for instance, we need to actively pursue all categories of information. In contrast, if we reach the ranks of senior management, we may be involved in imparting all seven categories of information to subordinate communities in the office; yet, we will most likely only receive information in one or two categories (e.g., updates of technical information or annual evaluations of our performance).

To appreciate these categories, Figure 8.2 suggests the relative volumes of information newcomers receive as a consequence of active inquiry and as a result of passive receipt—information received through various corporate programs, explicit instructions received from supervisors, and informal interactions with coworkers. Adding to the explanation of the types of one-on-one exchanges that support these types of information, Figure 8.3 shows how new employees tend to rank the relative usefulness of the seven types of information received.[12]

As we might readily infer from these three figures, face-to-face and one-on-one interactions go on continuously within the business environment—between coworkers and between managers and subordinates. The health of the business, the alignment of objectives, the minimization of uncertainties and job anxieties, and the effective assimilation of new employees all are contingent on maintaining open lines of communication and active interaction.

8.6 **DIRECT INFORMATION SHARING**

Category	Examples of Information Topics
Technical Information	1. How to perform specific aspects of the job 2. How to perform one's job efficiently and effectively 3. How to balance the demands of the job 4. Definitions and technical terms related to the job 5. Where to obtain needed supplies and information
Referent Information	1. Performance standards associated with the position 2. How much authority the position entails 3. The responsibilities associated with the position 4. Reward criteria associated with the position 5. The goals and objectives of the job 6. What is expected of the individual in the position
Social Information	1. How to get along with people in the organization 2. The behaviors and personalities of coworkers 3. How to deal with politics at work 4. Who to trust and who not to trust 5. How well one is fitting in 6. The appropriateness of one's social behavior 7. How well one is getting along with coworkers
Appraisal Information	1. Feedback on the adequacy of one's job skills and abilities 2. Feedback on how well one is performing the job 3. Feedback identifying problems in one's performance 4. Feedback on how others are evaluating one's work 5. Feedback on one's potential for advancement
Normative Information	1. The history of the organization 2. The company's philosophy and goals 3. Promotion criteria in the organization 4. The organization's customs and rituals 5. Appropriate ways to behave and interact 6. What it takes to succeed in the organization 7. The behaviors and attitudes the company expects
Organizational Information	1. Organizational policies and procedures 2. The structure of the organization 3. The financial position/performance of the organization 4. Services or products provided by the organization 5. Where individuals and departments are located 6. Benefits provided by the organization
Political Information	1. Who makes the important decisions in the organization 2. Who controls critical resources in the organization 3. Who has authority over whom in the organization 4. Who's who in the organization

Source: E.W. Morrison, "Information Usefulness and Acquisition During Organizations Encounter," *Management Communication Quarterly,* Vol. 9, No. 2 (Nov. 1995), pp. 131–155, copyright 1995 by Sage Publications Inc.

FIGURE 8.2

Active and
Passive Receipt of
Information From
Direct Interaction

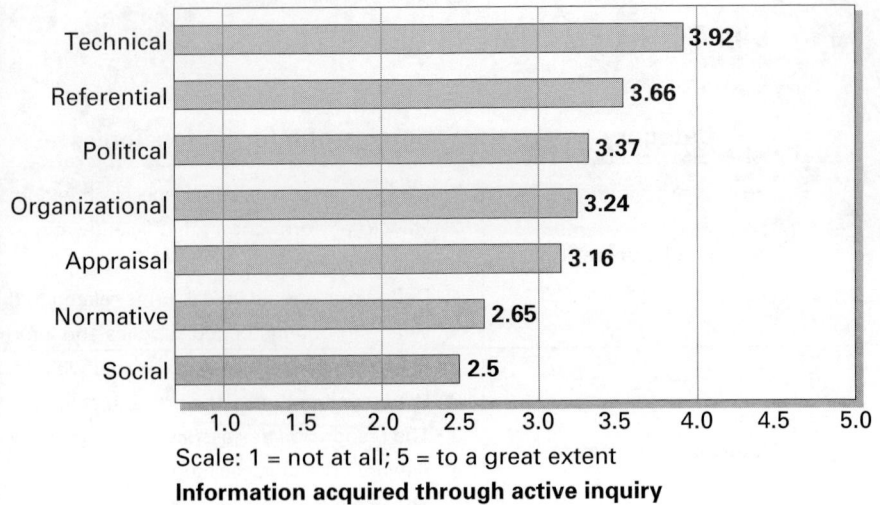

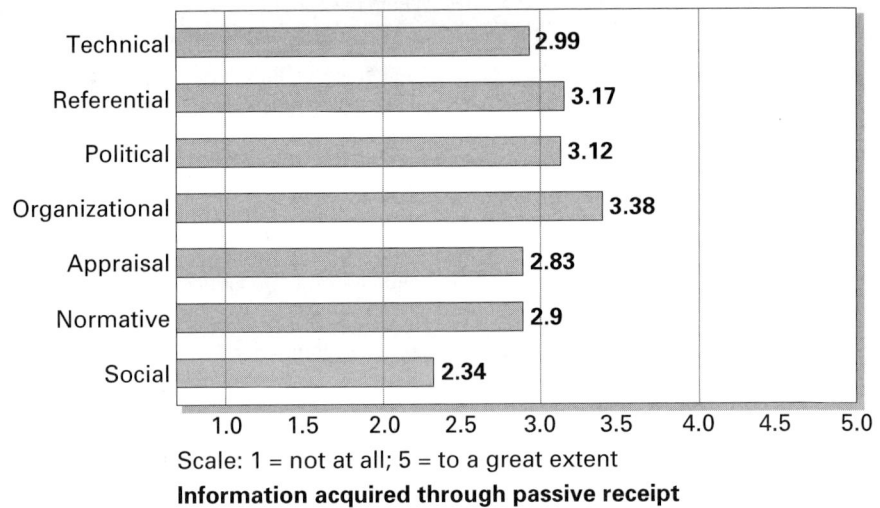

Category	Value
Technical	3.92
Referential	3.66
Political	3.37
Organizational	3.24
Appraisal	3.16
Normative	2.65
Social	2.5

Scale: 1 = not at all; 5 = to a great extent

Information acquired through active inquiry

Category	Value
Technical	2.99
Referential	3.17
Political	3.12
Organizational	3.38
Appraisal	2.83
Normative	2.9
Social	2.34

Scale: 1 = not at all; 5 = to a great extent

Information acquired through passive receipt

Source: E.W. Morrison, "Information Usefulness and Acquisition During Organizations Encounter," *Management Communication Quarterly,* Vol. 9, No. 2, (Nov. 1995), pp. 131–155, copyright 1995 by Sage Publications Inc.

We can also deduce much about the nature of office relationships. For example, although technical information is most readily provided (whether solicited or not), appraisal information is less immediately forthcoming. Technical information is generally neutral; appraisal information can be both subjective and highly charged. Typically, those categories of information where the greatest difference exists among the volunteered information, solicited information, and information usefulness are indicative of interactions that are more formal, more constrained. Conversely, categories of information where there is a close correspondence among volunteered information, solicited information, and information usefulness generally represent those interactions that are more casual, less restrained, and more likely to occur without formal arrangement.

Furthermore, these sets of inferences lead to some valuable insights into one-on-one business interactions: employees may have to work hard at getting the comprehensive information they need to feel comfortable in doing their jobs.

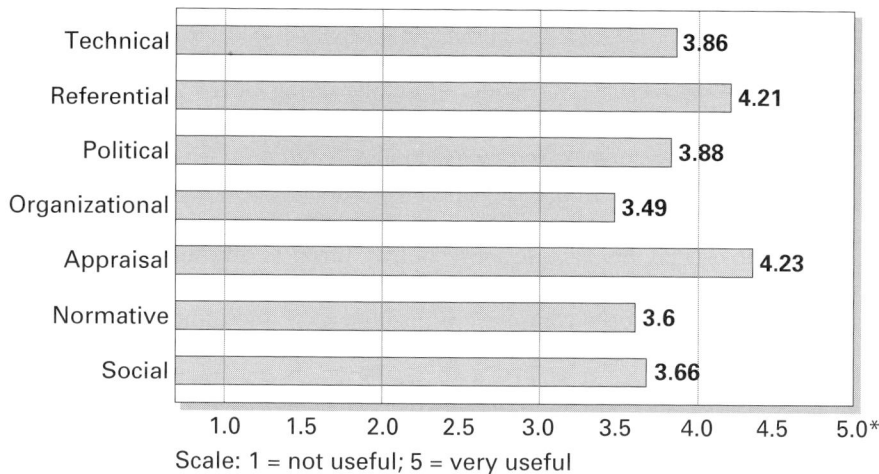

FIGURE 8.3

Perceived Usefulness of Information Gained Through Interaction

Figure 8.3 bar chart:
- Technical: 3.86
- Referential: 4.21
- Political: 3.88
- Organizational: 3.49
- Appraisal: 4.23
- Normative: 3.6
- Social: 3.66

Scale: 1 = not useful; 5 = very useful

Source: E.W. Morrison, "Information Usefulness and Acquisition During Organizations Encounter," *Management Communication Quarterly*, Vol. 9, No. 2, (Nov. 1995), pp. 131–155, copyright 1995 by Sage Publications Inc.

On the other side of the coin, there may be some reluctance—among coworkers and managers—to share openly some types of information. This tension may not be exclusively limited to sharing difficult information such as appraisal information. Reluctance to share information occurs generally because providing information takes time and energy, often with little return for the person giving the information, and because individuals are often reluctant to convey unpleasant messages or get involved in what they anticipate will be uncomfortable interactions. (We will discuss the issue of delivering bad news at length when we discuss "politeness theory" in Chapter 12.) Yet, beyond the simple discomfort that may impede immediate communication of information, there are other reasons that interfere with effective one-on-one interactions—most significantly the inappropriate reliance on technology when interaction is needed.

THE DISAPPEARING HUMAN MOMENT

In a December 2001 article in the *Chronicle of Higher Education,* a professor of computer science stated that the wiring of his campus had almost eliminated interaction with students outside the classroom. What had begun as a "great vision" to put everyone in touch with everyone else on campus and "through the Internet, everyone else in the world" had not only changed how personnel taught and did research. The "subtler consequences" included a change in the "campus culture."[13]

The same consequences, as reflected in the scenario below, may become evident in a "networked" office where "on-line" communication is used to replace—and avoid— "in-person" contact.

At an electronics company, a talented brand manager is increasingly alienated. The problem started when his division head didn't return a phone call for several days. She said she never got the message. Then the brand manager noticed that he hadn't been invited to an important meeting with a new advertising agency. What's wrong with my performance? he wonders. The man wants to raise the question with the division manager, but the opportunity never seems to arise. All their communication is by memo, e-mail, or voice mail, which they exchange often. But they almost never meet. For one thing their offices are 50 miles apart, and for another, both of them are frequently on the road. During the rare moments when they do see each other in person—on the run in a corridor or in the parking lot at corporate headquarters—it is usually inappropriate or impossible to discuss complex matters. And so the issues between them smolder.[14]

The antidote for this "smoldering" problem is a face-to-face, one-on-one conversation. Writing in the *Harvard Business Review*, Dr. Howard Hallowell, a psychiatrist who offered the example above, noted: "Business communication can fail if lack of face-to-face interaction leads to misunderstandings. Voice mail, e-mail, and memos can help speed communication, but lack of the 'human moment' can lead to complications." Speaking specifically of the brand manager and his division head, Hallowell counseled: The brand manager is driving himself "crazy for no reason . . . . [He needs to] experience what I call the human moment—an authentic psychological encounter that can happen only when two people share the same physical space." Highlighting the significance of such interactions, Hallowell goes on to explain: "I have given the human moment a name because I believe that it has started to disappear from modern life—and I sense that we may all be about to discover the destructive power of its absence."[15]

The corollary to the problem of having individuals unwilling to meet because of a discomfort they feel about sharing evaluative information or bad news or the inappropriate reliance on mediated communication is the problem of not recognizing that sometimes meetings are essential. Information is information, but not all forms of communication delivery are equal. Sometimes information can simply be transmitted (in written or electronic form); at other times, the communication demands a personal, human component. You need to promote one-on-one interactions when one of two conditions exist: A transmitted message will not convey the richness of the communication, or a transmitted message will not convey the complete picture.

THE RICHNESS OF INTERACTION. The first condition necessitating one-on-one interaction occurs when the relationship between the individuals is a critical component of success. As we pointed out, the technical dimension of a job is only one of seven categories of business information. Our overall success requires that we gain both technical knowledge and a sense of community—with coworkers, managers, and subordinates. No one wants to feel isolated, cut off from the "inside" information, the inside scoop on what's going on. We are, by nature, social creatures; even the most automated of offices or factories cannot diminish or compensate for the natural propensity we have toward personal communication and community.

The "subtle consequences" that changed the culture at the networked university were the losses associated with diminished interactions—among students, between students and faculty, and even among faculty members. Students lose the richness of a traditional college career; interaction is replaced by e-mail, "a painless and guilt-free means of communication." While it may be "painless" and "guilt-free," it is without the embodiment of community. Faculty, for their part, "may never know the true joy of teaching." The lack of interaction seriously diminishes the health of the environment and the success of the organization.

The conclusion this author reaches holds a valuable lesson for the business world: Although we may "have the power and resources of a world that moves at blinding speed," we can easily and inadvertently lose the critical sense of community, the soul and identity of the organization.[16] The lesson we all must learn in business is that regardless on which side of the desk we sit, we need to make certain that we seek and employ one-on-one meetings to reinforce not only the human moment, but also the momentum and richness of the relationship. Only if we have this dimension will we maintain the sense of community that is vital to communication—not only the communication of interaction, but also the other forms of communication that are indirectly strengthened through the growth of a healthy work environment.

THE COMPLETENESS OF MESSAGE. While the psychological dimension of one-on-one interactions is important, these encounters are vital to carrying on the physical work of the corporation. Specifically, a second set of conditions warrants personal interactions. These conditions include two primary circumstances: The individual's presence is the essential ingredient, and important verbal and non-verbal cues must be made evident.

To illustrate the first condition, let's give an example of a situation we encountered a few years back. An executive was assigned responsibility for a large operation that had several managers and almost 100 workers on shifts other than Monday to Friday, 8 A.M. to 5 P.M. When given the assignment, the manager was informed that there had been a lengthy history of employee complaints and grievances, performance was less than optimum, and serious dissatisfaction had been voiced by customers. In response, among the first actions the manager took was to establish a series of meetings.

Some meetings were held around 6 P.M. to coincide with shift changes, when the largest group of workers was available; other meetings were held later in the evening (some as late as 1 A.M.). Some meetings were held with small groups; others were held with individual employees in their work locations. Most meetings were informal, and the topics ranged freely from policy to office politics to pay practices. The goals of these get-togethers were twofold: to allow personnel the opportunity to make their issues, interests, and grievances heard, and to establish a personal rapport with the employees. While many of the initial meetings were tense and the exchange of information somewhat one-sided, the temperament changed as the relationships matured.

What was heard repeatedly at the onset was that most of these employees didn't think the company was interested in shift personnel. They assumed that management had little interest in—as they characterized themselves—second-class corporate citizens. In fact, as the manager was also told repeatedly, most of the employees could not remember ever meeting with (or even seeing) a member of senior management.

These interactions, as the managers and the employees came to see them, were establishing that human component of the environment. Over time, all involved were able to solidify common goals and objectives and to arrive at balances between individual interests and corporate commitments. Performance improved, the number of complaints and grievances decreased, and customer satisfaction went up. The human dimension, missing previously, was satisfied not by what information was being presented, but by the fact that the information was being presented face-to-face, and often one-on-one. The ingredients to this type of success, as Hallowell notes, are simple: "The human moment has two requisites: people's physical presence and their emotional and intellectual attention. That's it." Making communication work means that the one-on-one interaction needs to occur, no matter who initiates the interaction.

The significance can be understood from a variety of perspectives. As the seven categories of information demonstrate, first there are basic educational exchanges that help reinforce the corporate culture—the themes, mores, standards, and expectations of the organization. Second, there is the perspective of the information recipient, who is trying to gain insight into how effectively and efficiently to negotiate the work demands and the work environment. Third, amplifying the perception reflected in the analysis of the "human element," we can view the interactions from a more fundamental level, from what some organizational psychologists call Needs Theory. Using this perspective, we can interpret the interactions as fulfilling subconscious goal-oriented motives of the employees and the managers: 1) a duty motive—the need to make certain that workers have the essential understanding of their roles and work environment; 2) inclusion—the need to share and maintain a satisfactory work relationship; 3) affection—the need to achieve closeness and community; and/or 4) control—the need to maintain the careful balance among responsibility, accountability, and authority.

FACE TIME

However we choose to view or interpret the one-one-one communication activities within business, there are some undeniable truths: The interactions are continuous, important, and necessary. Having this appreciation, we can readily establish a set of three primary expectations if these interactions are to be successful and mutually beneficial. Participants in these face-to-face exchanges have to 1) face up to the moment, 2) be engaged, and 3) avoid hiding out.

FACING UP TO THE MOMENT. As has been made evident, we need to use one-on-one time to share information and exchange opinions and evaluative information. If you have valuable information, consider whether it needs the intimacy of a one-on-one interaction (e.g., providing feedback to someone on job performance). If the information is neutral, then you may want to transmit it electronically or in written form (e.g., a memo). However, if the human presence is needed, make certain to give the information face-to-face.

One way to decide if a personal interaction is warranted is to consider the implications of delivering the information without any accompanying visual or verbal cues. If any of the five following conditions exist, visual and verbal cues are needed—meaning it's time to meet face-to-face:

1. The information or situation has a unique sensitivity that is inappropriate for an indirect form of communication; you need to address the person, his or her sensitivities, and the circumstance in a personal, interactive manner.

2. The information or situation demands attention and responsiveness; you need to have proof that the other person is paying attention.

3. The information or situation demands that there is a clear interpretation of the attitudes and intentions; you need to have opportunity to establish the right emphases and intensity, to use tone and volume of voice for impact.

4. The information needs to be amplified by visual cues; you want an opportunity to use body language and gestures to reinforce the seriousness or intensity of the communication.

5. The information demands an immediate visual feedback; you want to be able to gauge visually whether the recipient of the information has the right interpretation, that the recipient's response communicates that he or she understands, believes, disbelieves, is surprised by, is pleased by, or displeased by the information.

BEING ENGAGED. If you decide there is need to interact directly, act accordingly. As Hallowell pointed out, the two conditions for success in one-on-one encounters are physical presence complemented by conscious attention. Almost as bad as avoiding necessary interactions is holding one-on-one exchanges in which the two participants have only physical proximity, where one party is in the room in body, but not in spirit. Think about meetings you have had where the person sitting across the table has appeared disinterested, inattentive, or seemingly unaware of your presence. Then do the opposite:

1. Don't keep glancing at your watch as if waiting for a chance to end the meeting or as if broadcasting that you'd rather be doing something else. Chances are, even if you're trying to do this glancing act surreptitiously, the other person is probably aware of your distraction and signaled disinterest.

2. Put beepers on vibrate; turn cell phones off. If the meeting is important enough to hold, it should be important enough to hold your attention for the allotted period of time. Even if the other person is polite enough to offer to let you answer a page or call, the message will already have been sent that you're only halfheartedly engaged.

3. Avoid potential interruptions. Before the meeting, transfer your phone calls to someone else or ask the secretary to take messages. Inform the secretary that you are not to be interrupted. Phone calls and drop-in visitors have the same disruptive power as activated beepers and cell phones.

4. Maintain eye contact. Although a meeting is not intended to be a staring contest, neither should it appear that you are drawn to papers on the desk, images on the computer screen, or your stack of unreturned message slips. Maintaining eye contact is one of the most potent discriminators of interest; don't let your eyes send a message that you don't want transmitted.

5. Keep the focus. Keep the subject appropriately focused and keep the interaction going only as long as there's substantive exchange underway. The focus should be business-related and businesslike. When the business matter has been completed, the exchange should be drawn to a close. Knowing when to make an exit is every bit as important as knowing when to make an entrance. You don't want to dawdle about as if you have nothing else important to do. You've taken care of business; now go take care of business.

6. Be prepared to cover the essential topics. Most important in getting comfortable with sharing information is the recognition that being forthright is not the same as being mean-spirited or dispassionate. If you are uncomfortable with the information you have to share, rehearse your approach and strategy in advance of the meeting. Think about what you need to say, why you need to say it, and what the other person is expected to do with the information. Putting the complete context together will assist in making the session less confrontational and less of an immediate challenge to you or the information recipient.

7. Make notes of critical items warranting follow-up. You shouldn't spend your time documenting the conversation (an action likely to be interpreted as a threatening gesture), but you do want to record items that warrant a follow-up. Generally, it's best to make these notes toward the end of the discussion and to review what you've written down with the other party to secure not only agreement, but the recognition that the meeting has generated appropriate results.

8. Conclude the meeting by summarizing results and with a thank you. Meetings should not simply fade into nothingness. Assuming a substantive need precipitated the meeting, conclude the discussion by summarizing what's been decided and thanking the person for agreeing to meet. A closing that is both definite and polite (even when the subject may have created some tension) provides the necessary foundation for a sustained working relationship, allowing appropriate opportunity for continued communication.

AVOIDING HIDING OUT. The opportunity to meet face-to-face, as we have learned, is important to both the health of the company and the emotional well-being of the employee. If you have something that needs to be said, say it. Dodging the subject or relegating it to an inappropriate genre such as e-mail is not a satisfactory alternative. If the information is important—even if it's something the other person may not want to hear—the best service you can do for that person is to share the information.

Not being forthright, in addition to lessening the other individual's ability to act based on comprehensive knowledge, may also adversely affect your credibility. As Conger explains in the article quoted earlier, to become successful in communicating, "the first hurdle persuaders must overcome is their own credibility." As he goes on to explain: "In the workplace, credibility grows out of two sources: expertise and relationships." The first of these sources you supposedly already possess because you have information that needs to be shared. Therefore, attention should be focused more immediately on the second source—relationships. The relationships that you need to foster will be affected by the reputation you develop.

Reputation grows out of a consistent behavior. "People with high credibility have demonstrated—again, usually over time—that they can be trusted to listen and to work in the best interests of others. They have also consistently shown strong emotional character and integrity; that is, they are not known for mood extremes or inconsistent performance. Indeed, people who are known to be honest, steady, and reliable have an edge when going into any persuasion situation. Because their relationships are robust, they are more apt to be given the benefit of the doubt."[17]

Not hiding out should be seen as your intent to be "honest, steady, and reliable," to build a reputation for integrity. Viewed from this perspective, it becomes clear that beyond just helping people to do their work better, your willingness and forthrightness in sharing information—all types of information—best serves both the sender and the recipient.

ABOUT FACE

Business, as we have seen, relies heavily on face-to-face interactions to ensure that employees are effectively assimilated, that there is an alignment of goals and commitments, and that work is accomplished efficiently and effectively. Having a sense of how well you are contributing to these objectives is, as should be evident, extremely important to your performance and that of the company. To gain insight into overall communication effectiveness in one-on-one interactions, researchers analyzed the communication style and characteristics of a large population of management personnel.

These analyses resulted in a basic model delineating the characteristic behaviors exhibited when it comes to face-to-face interactions (Figure 8.4). In this model, there are two continuums: one extending from "Mechanistic Isolate" to

FIGURE 8.4

A Continuum of
Face-to-Face
Interaction

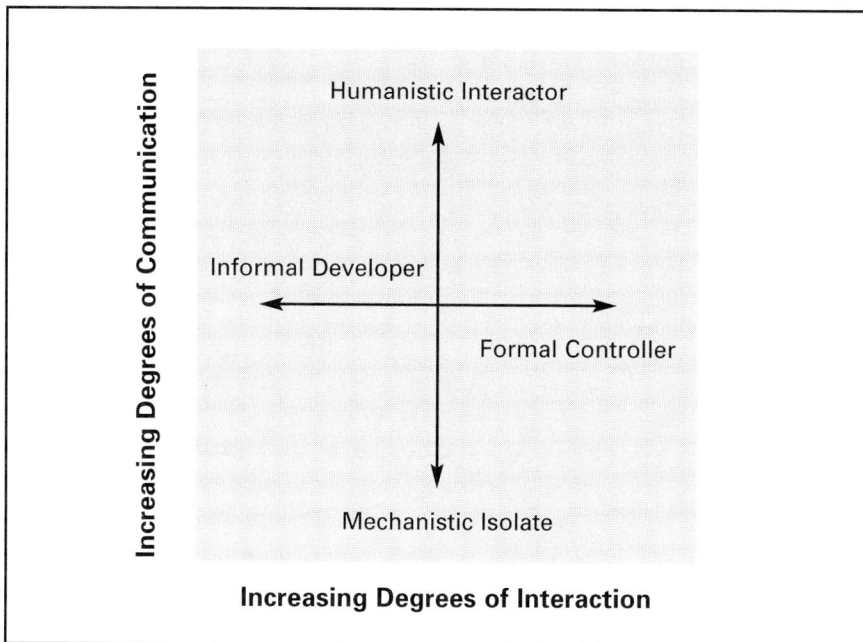

Source: Reprinted by permission of Sage Publications, Ltd. from F. Luthans and J. Larsen, "How Managers Really Communicate," *Human Relations,* Copyright © The Tavistock Institute, 1986.

"Humanistic Interactor" and the other from "Informal Developer" to "Formal Controller." The first line reflects the degree of open, active communication; the second line reflects the nature of the interaction.[18] Although developed through analysis of managers, the model can be used as a basic self-assessment tool for all interactions. To expand its application for nonmanagement personnel, simply make a few substitutions in the vocabulary to reflect the user's orientation (such as replacing the word *subordinate* with *coworker*).

When examining the model, as the designation suggests, Mechanistic Isolates represent those who tend to communicate very little, in any direction. Face-to-face communication is generally brief and infrequent. They tend to pay limited attention to employee assimilation, development, and performance.

These Mechanistic Isolates also tend to find themselves more regularly engaged in conflict resolution because of their lack of communication. At the other end of this spectrum are the Humanistic Interactors. These individuals, as the terminology suggests, are more personally engaged with their staff. They tend to communicate frequently with subordinates and superiors, exhibit more interest in developing employees, and tend to promote more harmonious environments—and thus engage in less conflict management.

On the horizontal line of the continuum, Formal Controllers represent those who engage in structured face-to-face interactions such as scheduled appointments and periodic reviews. They tend to initiate and control the flow of the communication and are more engaged with their superiors than with their subordinates. As might be expected, Formal Controllers evaluate and monitor the performance of subordinates more by inspecting work and examining performance data than by means of open communication channels. As a consequence of their limited interaction, they tend to be more frequently engaged in managing conflict.

Informal Developers are much better attuned to open communication, unrestricted exchange, and more frequent and less structured one-on-one interactions. They typically are seen as the coaches and mentors who assist employees with their assimilation and development "by communicating spontaneously (or informally) with subordinates and superiors."[19]

Where you lie on the two lines is a function of choices you make—choices about facing up to the moment, being engaged, and not hiding out. You can fulfill your responsibilities and gain credibility, or you can dodge them and find yourself continually engaged in managing employee issues and conflict. Your goal should be purposeful exchanges, characterized by forthright discussions, a mature relationship, and a conscious appreciation of how the types and quality of interactions affect you, the information recipient, and the company.

THE MEETING: KNOWING WHERE YOU STAND

As with one-on-one meetings, it might be reasonable to assume that the computer's presence in business has reduced the need and frequency of getting groups of people together to discuss issues and resolve problems (Figure 8.5).[20] Yet, once again, the computer, while a major productivity enhancer, takes a back seat to the natural inclination for people to get together. Depending on which studies are quoted on this topic, estimates are that there may be as many as 20 million business meetings held every day in the United States.[21]

Ironically, the computer, along with changes in technology and business strategies, may actually be contributing to an increase in business meetings. Technology has made it easier for people to meet, even when separated by long distance. Not only do we have meetings where people share a common conference room, but we also have videoconferencing (first demonstrated by AT&T in 1964 at the New York World's Fair), and desktop and wireless videoconferencing. Recently introduced business strategies have complemented the technology by adding reasons to meet. As reported in a *Newsweek* article in October 2000, "Experts lack ironclad data on the number of hours spent in conference rooms, but they point to several reasons meetings appear to be mushrooming—and becoming more of a bother. As computers have automated away routine paper-pushing jobs, more workers are doing project-oriented work, which requires updates and elaboration. Other trends, such as outsourcing work to suppliers and the rise in joint ventures and mergers, lead to more external meetings, too."[22]

FIGURE 8.5

The Meeting as Communication Genre

> **Meeting:**
> A social form that organizes interaction in distinctive ways. Most specifically a meeting is a gathering of three or more people who agree to assemble for a purpose ostensibly related to the functioning of an organization or group (e.g., to exchange ideas or opinions, to make a decision, to formulate recommendations). A meeting is characterized by multi-party talk that is episodic in nature and participants develop or use specific conventions for regulating this talk. The meeting form frames the behavior that occurs within it concerning the 'business' of the group or organization.

Just how consuming business meetings have become is evident in related estimates of how much time business personnel spend in conference rooms. The lower scale of the estimates suggests business personnel spend from 1½ days per week to 2 months a year in meetings.[23] At the upper regions, the estimates can range as high as a full 20 weeks per year spent in meetings.[24] While the amount of time may not appear overly significant, the problem arises when these same surveys tend to reflect the participants' impressions that the meetings are "more of a bother" and frequently unproductive. In one survey, meeting participants claimed that approximately a third of meetings were a total waste of time; much of the remainder of the meeting time was variously characterized as "boring," "poorly organized," "unstructured," "purposeless," "chaotic," and "too long."[25] These attitudes are complemented by a clear sense that nothing of consequence tends to happen in these exchanges, no actions are taken, and no decisions reached. (Figure 8.6 offers two often-quoted impressions of meetings.)

Answering this critical challenge to the efficiency of American business is, as the literature would lead us to believe, a fairly simple and straightforward task. Stated simply, the answer is, as one article concludes, "for companies and managers . . . to make meetings more productive for the organization and those who attend them."[26] If that's all it takes, then this communication genre should have been fixed long ago. Unfortunately, the accompanying recommendation about how this productivity enhancement is to be accomplished is often lacking in substance, interested more in the mechanics of meetings than in making meetings more meaningful.

ENTER THE MEETING ENGINEER

Much guidance exists regarding how to "make meetings more productive." However, discussions usually focus on the mechanics of meetings; they do not aid the communication process—the primary reason for initiating the meeting. The directions tend to highlight the administration of the meeting, such as setting an agenda, assigning roles to play (e.g., timekeeper, recorder), and facilitating discussion. Largely, this line of recommendation tends to concentrate most intently on the role played by the chair of the meeting, especially in handling difficult circumstances and behaviors (Table 8.7).[27] These facilitation recommendations, though helpful in maintaining direction and decorum, have limited effect on the quality of the communication. Nevertheless, running a well-orchestrated meeting offers more in the way of substance than does much of the remaining guidance.

For instance, one author has advocated a "science of chair administration," a belief that "where chairs are uncomfortable or unscientifically arranged, minds and persons tend to wander from the meeting."[28] Under this fine art of chairmanship (the seat, not the individual), sometimes called proxemics, we are invited not only to consider the type of chair (e.g., reclining or the amount of padding in the seat), but also the proximal relationship among the seats. Like lessons learned from

FIGURE 8.6

"Meetings are places where minutes are taken and hours wasted."

"Hate working alone? Make decisions? Hold a meeting! See people. Draw flowcharts. Impress your colleagues. All on company time. Meetings: the practical alternative to work."

The Negative Perception of Meetings

8.7	BASIC GUIDANCE FOR CHAIRING A BUSINESS MEETING	

Objective	Problem Needing to be Addressed	Techniques to Employ
Unite the group	Aggression	Allow individuals to let off steam Use opening statements to temper interaction Do not take sides Bring others into the discussion Stick to the facts
Focus the group	Digression	Stay alert Question Check understanding Paraphrase/summarize
Mobilize the group	Squashing	Protect the weak/shy Check around the group Record suggestions Build on ideas

King Arthur's Court, people must—as this line of study tells us—face each other to "symbolize equality and the importance of every person's contribution." As we have already examined in this chapter, there is value in having people face each other, but there is little value in expending much energy on furniture. Unless you are hosting an international summit, little likelihood exists that every meeting is going to be uniquely staged, or new props, such as cushy chairs, added. Yet, here again, in comparison to other recommendations in the literature, even chair administration appears meaningful.

A step well beyond the rational call for active facilitation or even a dalliance with the "science of chair administration" is a proposed concern for the "ecology of meetings." Not sufficiently convinced that a controlled discussion will contribute toward or lead to success, this theory about an "ecology of meetings," first proposed in 1995, advises a deeper concern for "the interplay of personalities, ideas, and environment."[29] The road to success—or at least physical comfort—is one of "synomorphy: the importance of a good fit between the physical, psychological, and social aspects of a setting." Suddenly, we are asked to turn our attention away from the substance of the meeting to the meeting environment. And not only the environment, but the climate as well, to "research that demonstrates cold temperatures reduce reaction times; how crowding can lead to withdrawal in competitive environments; how most people associate bright lighting with optimism and increased activity; the importance of having a secure room where comments cannot be overheard and of providing movable furniture to facilitate face-to-face seating."

Once past the manipulation of temperatures, spatial allowances, and lighting, this study turns to more basic creature comforts, to "hospitality"—providing for the "physical and psychological needs of participants." The scene suddenly metamorphoses from business meeting to church social: "Grace notes, such as a warm greeting, ice breakers, introducing new members, providing food and beverage, celebrating participants' special achievements, and treating everyone with respect, are key determinants in whether meeting participants want to enhance, end, or otherwise alter their relationship with others in the group."[30]

An extended roster of roles must be assigned to support this extensive ecology of meeting interests. Where previously the meeting rosters were limited to such needs as timekeepers and recorders, these more traditional roles appear secondary to the new disciplines such as "meeting engineer": "Given the many variables that affect meeting outcomes, managers are wise to share the burden of leadership with other participants—people whose jobs are to make sure environmental, hospitality, productivity, and enthusiasm objectives are planned for and strategies for their implementation carried out. These roles can include a meeting engineer to make room and technology arrangements; a host to greet new members, provide food and beverages, and prepare a list of successes to celebrate; a scribe to regulate the recording of information; and a timekeeper to make sure equitable amounts of time are devoted to each agenda item."[31]

. . . AND EXIT THE REAL PURPOSE

There are two very important, though subtle, messages in the above description of meeting assignments. Time management is mistakenly placed in competition with productivity, and the definition of purpose is relegated to a secondary position. Here the real purpose somehow becomes displaced. Where the initiating condition was a matter of corporate or organizational significance, the attention is shifted to the satisfaction and physical comfort of the attendees. Let's look briefly at these two deviations from purpose.

Almost without variation, advice on holding meetings begins with the idea of setting an agenda. The agenda is seen as a driver for the meeting, the taskmaster that sets the tone and tempo. Sometimes the agenda has time limitations assigned for each element; other times an equal time allotment is assumed for every item. As such, this step may become the first barrier to achieving organizational purpose. Although meetings may have a time constraint (because of room or technology availability, or the urgency of the matter), that constraint should not be used as an arbitrary means of hindering discussion. The agenda, like every facet of meeting facilitation, has to be carefully crafted, reflecting a keen appreciation of the depth and complexity of the exchange needed to achieve the goals set for the meeting.

The meeting is not a race in which you post a stopwatch and then sprint to the finish line. The only meaningful indication of a well-facilitated meeting (whether controlled by an agenda, a facilitator, Roberts Rules of Order, or any other group-defined mechanism) is that the intended outcome has been achieved as a consequence of complete and thorough analysis. The trick to achieving this goal is accommodating the constraints, not adding to them or becoming artificially constrained by them. Sometimes meetings demand active—even heated—exchanges. Some subjects may require deeper, lengthier analyses than others do. Some items may have more intense sensitivities associated with their resolution than others do. Each of the conditions must be understood and accommodated, an activity that may demand considerably more insight and attention than achieved by posting an agenda at the beginning of discussion.

Irrespective of the conventions, administrative controls, and physical and psychological trappings, the only successful outcome of a business meeting is a position, solution, recommendation, or plan that is responsive to the meeting's initiating condition. "Whether the business meeting is called to gather the various disciplines needed to formulate a safe and immediate response to an unanticipated process problem or to ascertain the clerical perspective on a proposed change to an administrative policy, the goal [of the meeting] is the same. The goal is to tap into the relevant knowledge; promote exchange and evaluation; and, finally, to arrive at the best and most appropriate response to the initiating condition."[32]

Instead of advocating a structure evaluated exclusively against the meeting's performance in achieving its obligations to the corporation or organization, the literature on meeting mechanics promotes comfort over conclusions and proxemics instead of attention to purpose. "[W]here direction on improved product is needed, instead the guidance in the literature—including the popular texts on business and professional communication—devolves into a trite recipe on meeting administration and logistic: set an agenda, set a time limit, be inclusive, be facilitative, keep meetings short, assign roles (e.g., scribe), restate comments to ensure comprehension, publish minutes, and close the loop on open items. Complementing these vagaries are directions on proxemics, the psychology of seating arrangements that purports to improve corporate physical and mental health through better positioning—and arrangement—of chairs ... Unless comfort equates to productivity, we are left to make a rather large intellectual leap if we want to argue that these practices promote better decision making."[33] A facilitator who keeps attendees from a healthy exchange, an agenda that artificially limits discussion, or a meeting engineer who creates merely an atmosphere of optimism is promoting the equivalent of a magician's misdirection.

We need to make certain that we don't allow or contribute to a misdirection that allows the communication responsibility of the meeting to be hijacked. Logistical features and physical comforts are important, but are not the goals of the meeting. What we want is a balance. We want a meeting where administrative, logistical, and other features are tailored to promote one exclusive aim—resolution of the problem that necessitated the meeting.

We do not want to make business meetings into church socials. Neither do we want to emulate the practices of Admiral Hyman Rickover, the father of the nuclear navy. Admiral Rickover, as a demonstration of control and to assess character, was notorious for purposely staging uncomfortable meetings—going so far as to provide chairs with legs of different lengths so that the chairs were unsteady and wobbly.

To achieve and maintain the proper balance, we must focus primarily on purpose, recognizing that sometimes a meeting may require an extremely rigid structure; in others, a free-flowing debate may be more appropriate. Some meetings might best he held in a secluded conference room; others may be more appropriately conducted at a conference center, a manager's office, in a restaurant, or outdoors. The determining factor is how to achieve the purpose, secondarily the amenities—not vice versa.

A MEETING OF THE MINDS

Having gained a better appreciation of what's needed, we can better define how to get where we need to go. Concerned foremost with the time and energy that meetings consume, most proposed fixes have concentrated on numerical measures—how to reduce either the number or the length of meetings. Solutions range from the implementation of "Meeting-less Fridays" to banning meetings one day a week to more sophisticated exercises in time management. However, the orientation needed to improve communications has to be rhetorical, not mechanical. More precisely, the resolution needs to begin with a refocusing of attention on purpose and audience—most particularly on three primary demands:

1. Meetings must be purposeful.
2. The performance of the meeting participants must be aligned with the end goal.
3. The meeting must always maintain a precise focus on the assigned purpose.

PURPOSEFUL MEETINGS. You need to choose your genre wisely. Don't send an e-mail to do the work of a personal exchange, don't write a letter to do the business of a procedure, and don't use the meeting as a means to accomplish what is best left to a single individual. In the words of one author, "sorting out true motivations for meetings may require some serious soul-searching."[34]

First, "participative" management does not mean that everyone has to gather together to consider every new idea, action, or suggestion. Meetings should not be held simply to rubber-stamp a decision; nor should they become "a roll call where attendance is the measure of success."[35] Furthermore, meetings should not be called just to demonstrate that you have the power to make everyone show up. "Joy and money love company. But they're not enough of a reason to bring people together in a business meeting."[36]

These inappropriate reasons account for many unnecessary meetings, but not nearly as many as occur to camouflage the initiator's unwillingness to accept individual responsibility or accountability for a planned action or decision. "More and more these days, managers are calling meetings not to find ideas and solve problems, but simply to cover themselves. A manager who should be making decisions on his own is not. Instead he calls 10 or 12 colleagues and subordinates together, secures a consensus and announces the decision. If the decision turns out to be poor, he can always say: 'Don't blame me. That was what the participants in our August 23 meeting wanted. It was their idea, not mine.'"[37]

Attendees are quite efficient in deciphering whether they have been invited to a meeting for valid reasons. Those who realize that their presence is important will make the greatest contributions; others who feel the meeting—or their attendance at the meeting— is unnecessary will quickly disengage, no matter what the setting or the seating. If the meeting didn't have to happen, or if certain attendees didn't need to be there, their attention will go elsewhere (Figure 8.7).[38] The loss resulting from this unnecessary gathering is, however, much more costly than the momentary disinterest of a few employees.

FIGURE 8.7

Knowing When You Shouldn't Be in a Meeting

Here are some tell-tale signs that your time could be used more effectively elsewhere rather than in a meeting:
—dismantling your pen and losing that little spring;
—being more interested in finding that spring than listening to what is going on;
—writing shopping lists/love letters/your obituary;
—making impressive mini-sculptures out of paper clips;
—being annoyed with yourself for forgetting to bring a newspaper/lunch/bed;
—making paper airplanes;
—doodling;
—looking out of the window on a sunny summer's day and wishing you were the person sitting on the mower.

Unnecessary meetings, whether called in the name of power, distributed accountability, or misconstrued interpretations of collaboration, dilute the quality and meaning of necessary, substantive meetings. Not only are these unnecessary assemblies great time wasters, but big money wastes as well. One estimate suggests company meetings may cost up to $15,000 an hour.[39] Consider, for instance, the cost implications illustrated in Figure 8.8.[40]

As summarized in *Management Review*, there are only three good reasons for a business meeting:

1. To create a forum. A forum is an opportunity to share perspectives, for people with different values, ideas, and experiences to learn from each other. Forums may range from loosely assembled town meetings to tightly structured gatherings.

2. To make decisions. A decision-making meeting is intended to analyze alternatives and decide the best course of action. The subject of this type of a meeting may range from strategy or policy formulation to policy solving.

3. To build a team. A team-building meeting has to do with developing group capabilities, promoting a sense of togetherness and a commitment to collective performance.

These three types of meetings form a natural line of development: A forum identifies issues and options that provide the grist for a decision-making meeting; aided by team building, a subsequent group can then implement the selected solution.[41]

MEETING PERFORMANCE. Although we hear repeatedly about assigned roles in meetings, equally, if not more important, are the unassigned roles: each individual

---

FIGURE 8.8

When Meetings Just Don't Make Sense

I learned not long ago of a meeting at a small plastics manufacturing firm. Present were a division manager, six department heads and the heads of three sections. The topic: Should a replacement be hired for a recently injured secretary, or should a typist be secured from a temporaries service and kept on a week-to-week basis?

It took 50 minutes to reach a consensus on that question. Actually, the decision should have been made privately by the division manager or by the manager of the one office involved.

What was decided is not important. The effect of such meetings on the company is. Because of the length of the discussion about the secretarial replacement, time ran out before a second topic could be considered. A decision on it was not reached until another meeting weeks later. The topic: Should a new fluorescent lighting system for the plant be installed? Involved were not just one office but four departments—not to mention a $28,000 investment.

It should not be that way. First of all, meetings are expensive. When 12 people, each paid $15 to $25 per hour, meet for two to three hours, the cost for one session may easily exceed $500. Such a price is justified when it is necessary to bring representatives from engineering, production, finance and marketing together to solve a legitimate problem. But when the session is held to get a consensus on whether coffee breaks should be taken at 10 A.M. and not at 10:30, or whether the copying machine should be moved 50 feet, blowing $500 worth of time on a meeting is unconscionable.

is in attendance because he or she has something meaningful and important to add to the forum. The first obligation of every attendee, therefore, is the need to make your presence and voice heard. As Bernard Baruch once said, "The ability to express an idea [in a meeting] is well nigh as important as the idea itself."[42] To fulfill your obligation to the organization and the group, you need to practice a few important behaviors.

- Present your thoughts with conviction.
- Be prepared to hear the multiple voices represented in the room.
- Present your ideas directly and with confidence.
- Present your ideas as specifically as possible. The more general your explanation, the less clear and precise the audience's interpretation.
- Propose your ideas succinctly.
- Listen to objections and challenges rather than planning your rebuttal.
- Don't withdraw your proposal for the sake of harmony. Support your ideas and proposals until convinced there is a more appropriate, more compelling alternative.
- If you don't have something to say, don't say it. You are not expected or obligated to comment on every issue.
- "Don't harpoon an idea because it's a poor swimmer. Listen to and support ideas that make sense."
- Settle for measured success when a compromise position is in the best interests of the company.
- Participate even if your ideas get shot down. You're in the meeting to participate, not pout.[43]

As a representative of the company as well as your immediate organization, you also need to do more than just offer your opinions and advice. You need to assist in ensuring that you and others in the meeting are not detracting or distracting from the work at hand. These distractions come in four forms:

1. Whisperers—people who chatter and hold side conversations
2. Loudmouths—people who try to overpower the meeting by bullying other participants and drowning out their voices
3. Interrupters—people who continuously try to "put everyone else right," who cannot accept the fact that they don't have all the answers
4. Broken records—people who return to the same point over and over again as if no one was bright enough to have understood the point the first half dozen times it was proposed[44]

If the meeting is purposeful, the matter of making the meeting successful is contingent on participants who take their responsibilities seriously and professionally. That responsibility, as we have mentioned, is to achieve the right goals. **PRECISION OF PURPOSE.** Although we have already discussed some of the detours meetings may take when attention shifts from the corporate purpose to the individual's comforts, there are other detours that are more common and more damaging. These detours occur when the participants can not (or choose not to) differentiate the corporate goals from those of the individual interests of the organizations the attendees represent. Let's illustrate.

The members of a City Council are called into session by the mayor to respond to a beneficial opportunity of a federal grant having been awarded to the city. A response must be returned promptly to the federal government explaining how the grant is to be applied. As you might expect, each of the departments represented at the meeting (Fire Department, Health Department, Police Department, Chamber of Commerce) has its own ideas. The Fire Department, as example, is interested in adding new firefighters, fire trucks, and a fire station. The Chamber of Commerce thinks that expanding the airport will not only increase tourism but also attract new industry. Given the comfortable setting for City Council deliberations, we can assume that the meeting environment, ecology, synomorphy, and proxemics are all excellent. That being the case, the meeting begins with all the collegiality of a family reunion—pleasantries are exchanged, several light-hearted references to ongoing activities are made. Then the meeting gets down to business.

The federal grant is far less than needed to satisfy all the interests at the table. Moreover, there are direct conflicts between certain projects; for instance, the proposed airport expansion would directly interfere with the optimum placement of the new fire station. Round after round of give-and-take is followed by a series of negotiations—some overt, some not. As the evening wears on, each department head becomes more resolute, more determined that the projects his or her department has proposed are of greatest merit. The more entrenched each department head becomes, the less accommodating each becomes of other projects. Finally, exhausted by the exercise and hoping to reach a reasonable compromise, the mayor offers a resolution that each department will receive a share of the money proportional to the current department budgets. After some continued grumbling, the attendees agree, the paperwork is completed, and the response faxed to the federal agency in Washington. Their work done, the members of the City Council withdraw to celebrate their success.

The next morning, however, all the City Council members awaken to a surprise. The local paper offers a most embarrassing banner headline:

**CITY COUNCIL SQUANDERS FEDERAL MONEY: BICKERING LEADS TO
LOSS OF GOLDEN OPPORTUNITY!**

What went wrong? The simple answer is that the participants derailed the meeting by substituting a new purpose. Instead of looking at what would be best for the city (the intended audience and purpose), the attendees decided to focus on what was best for them individually.

The two purposes are not necessarily synonymous. Had the City Council established the real purpose first, they might have defined the criteria to use: Do we want to improve the welfare of our citizens? Do we want to increase the tax revenues? Do we need to concentrate on improving safety? These criteria would have assisted and guided the ensuing discussion. Projects could have been objectively assessed in light of the established criteria. Without the purpose, without a fully defined rationale for evaluating proposals, the attendees, perhaps unintentionally, each go their own way and arrive at vastly different conclusions.

That is not to say that the attendees are not to promote their cases vigorously. It does mean that they must acknowledge a greater obligation to the overriding purpose of the meeting. Remember, you're there to participate, not to pout. You're also there to participate, not to posture.

To restate another guideline, a measured success is better than a hollow victory or an outright failure. The outcome of the City Council exercise, as the newspaper headline announced, was not only detrimental to the city, which lost a prime opportunity, but also potentially detrimental to each member of the

City Council who now may face the wrath of angry voters. It is one thing to be a disruptive influence, someone who exhibits bad behavior in a meeting. It is something significantly more serious to be seen as someone unable to grasp the bigger picture, to be a team player. Pulling together toward a commonly understood goal benefits the company and the participants alike. Pulling against one another leads you into protracted circles—exhausting the energies, goodwill, and enthusiasm of your peers and management.

MEETING OBLIGATIONS—THE LESSONS

Meetings are a valuable and frequent form of business communication that rely on careful application of the rhetorical principles we have been examining. The audience is the individual, group, organization, or agency that has commissioned you with a charter to assist in finding an answer or setting a direction. Your purpose is that charter—the initiating condition. The secondary purposes are to ensure that the organization you represent is comfortable with and prepared to support you and the team in the decision reached. The information—its arrangement, reasoning, and language—needs to be limited to precisely that collection that will allow the team members to make prudent and appropriate decisions.

Whether you are leading or participating in a business meeting, you need to remain keenly focused on eight factors:

1. Hold meetings only for which there is a valid, verifiable purpose.

2. Establish the precise purpose before anything else takes place in the meeting.

3. Invite only those people essential to developing a complete and appropriate perspective of the issue or topic.

4. Tailor administrative controls (e.g., the facilitation, agenda) to the team, purpose, and circumstance.

5. Make your voice heard and your opinions known, but not to the exclusion of listening to and supporting contrary positions that make good sense.

6. Be prepared to represent yourself and your organization—both in the discussions and in following through with the implementation of the decision.

7. Monitor your performance to make certain that you are contributing to and not detracting from the group's mission.

8. Most importantly, make certain that you and your colleagues maintain focus on the true purpose. Avoid detours or misdirections that—although more immediately satisfying or more likely to ease tensions or mollify participants—are, nevertheless, not as completely responsive to your audience and purpose.

In summary, meetings—whether one-on-one or group—are dependent on your abilities as a communicator. You have the opportunity to make the meeting count, to assist in advancing the ends of your organization and your company. You can, if you practice the fine art of persuasion, ensure that the human moment does not inappropriately disappear from the business landscape. Only when you fulfill your responsibilities to the company and to your coworkers can you make certain that the human moment remains important, substantive, and purposeful.

☐ Group

1. Form teams of threes. Take a few minutes to review each of the four scenarios below. Then, in sessions of 10–15 minutes, take turns being the recipient of the news, the one transmitting the news, and an observer. After each session, discuss as a team what features of the interaction went well, which might be improved, and which created the greatest difficulty for the participants.

   a) A session informing an employee that he will not be getting a much sought after promotion

   b) A session in which an employee is told she is being transferred

   c) A session in which an employee is asked to take responsibility for training a new recruit to help take over some of her job responsibilities

   d) A session in which you must respond to an angry customer

2. As a class, discuss the four scenarios and the observations made during the role-playing.

3. Divide into groups. Then, as a class, watch the 1957 version of the film *12 Angry Men*. Each group (as assigned by the instructor) monitors and assesses the meeting performance of one or more of the 12 jurors in the film. After you have viewed the film, meet as groups and prepare an analysis of how your character(s) contributed to or detracted from the jury's purpose. Present these analyses for discussion with the rest of the class.

☐ Individual

1. Attend an open meeting in your community (e.g., Board of Education, City Council). Prepare a report explaining what major purposes were established, what other purposes came into play, what administrative controls were used, how appropriate they were, and an overall assessment of the meeting.

2. Prepare an essay explaining how you would approach one of the scenarios listed in Group Exercise 1.

END NOTES

[1] Jay A. Conger, "The Necessary Art of Persuasion," *Harvard Business Review,* May–June 1998, pp. 84–95.

[2] Quoted in Fred Luthans and Janet Larsen, "How Managers Really Communicate," *Human Relations,* Vol. 39, No. 2 (1986), pp. 161–178.

[3] Jeanne Maes, Teresa Weldy, and Marjorie Icenogle, "A Managerial Perspective: Oral Communication Competency is the Most Important for Students in the Workplace," *Journal of Business Communication,* Vol. 34, No. 1 (Jan. 1997), pp. 67–80.

[4] Karen Warner, "Business Communication Competencies Needed by Employees as Perceived by Business Faculty and Business Professionals," *Business Communication Quarterly,* Vol. 58, No. 4 (Dec. 1995), pp. 51–56.

[5] Jeanne Maes, Teresa Weldy, and Marjorie Icenogle, "A Managerial Perspective: Oral Communication Competency Is the Most Important for Students in the Workplace."

[6] Karen Warner, "Business Communication Competencies Needed by Employees as Perceived by Business Faculty and Business Professionals."

[7] *Ibid.*

[8] S.V. Volard and M.R. Davies, "Communication Patterns of Managers," *Journal of Business Communication,* Vol. 19, No. 1 (Winter 1982), pp. 41–53.

[9] Adapted from: Fred Luthans and Janet Larsen, "How Managers Really Communicate."

[10] Elizabeth Wolfe Morrison, "Information Usefulness and Acquisition During Organization Encounter," *Management Communication Quarterly*, Vol. 9, No. 2 (Nov. 1995), pp. 131–155.

[11] *Ibid.*

[12] *Ibid.*

[13] Frank W. Connolly, "My Students Don't Know What They're Missing," *The Chronicle of Higher Education*, Dec. 21, 2001, p. B-5.

[14] Edward M. Hallowell, "The Human Moment at Work," *Harvard Business Review*, Vol. 77, No. 1 (Jan.–Feb. 1999), pp. 58–66.

[15] *Ibid.*

[16] Connolly, "My Students Don't Know What They're Missing."

[17] Conger, "The Necessary Art of Persuasion."

[18] Fred Luthans and Janet Larsen, "How Managers Really Communicate."

[19] *Ibid.*

[20] Quoted in: Paul Hart, Lynne Svenning, and John Ruchinskas, "From Face-to-Face Meeting to Video Conferencing," *Management Communication Quarterly*, Vol. 8, No. 4 (May 1995), pp. 395–423.

[21] Bill Lawren, "Seating for Success," *Psychology Today*, Vol. 23, No. 9 (Sept. 1989), pp. 16–18.

[22] Daniel McGinn, "Mired in Meetings," *Newsweek*, Oct. 16, 2000, p. 52.

[23] Robert W. Keidel, "Only Three Reasons to Meet," *Management Review*, Vol. 80, No. 5 (May 1991), p. 5.

[24] Paul Sandwith, "Better Meetings for Better Communication," *Training and Development*, Vol. 46, No. 1 (Jan. 1992), pp. 29–31.

[25] *Ibid.*

[26] *Ibid.*

[27] Keith Reynolds, "Sorry I'm Late, I've Been to a Meeting," *Management Accounting* (British ed.) Vol. 78, No. 2 (Feb. 2000), pp. 66–67.

[28] Lawren, "Seating for Success."

[29] Thomas Clark, "Teaching Students to Enhance the Ecology of Small Group Meetings," *Business Communication Quarterly*, Vol. 61, No. 4 (Dec. 1998), pp. 40–52.

[30] *Ibid.*

[31] *Ibid.*

[32] D. L. Plung, "The Bald General Dancing in Our Basement: The Rhetoric of Business Information," unpublished article.

[33] *Ibid.*

[34] Quoted in Dianne Booher, "Holding Your Own in Meetings, But Working as a Team," *Training and Development*, Vol. 48, No. 8 (Aug. 1994), pp. 54–63.

[35] *Ibid.*

[36] *Ibid.*

[37] Norman B. Sigland, "The Use of Meetings," *Nation's Business*, Vol. 75 (Feb. 1987), p. 28.

[38] Reynolds, "Sorry I'm Late, I've Been to a Meeting."

[39] McGinn, "Mired in Meetings."

[40] Sigland, "The Use of Meetings,"

[41] Keidel, "Only Three Reasons to Meet."

[42] Quoted in: Booher, "Holding Your Own in Meetings, But Working as a Team."

[43] Booher, "Holding Your Own in Meetings, But Working as a Team."

[44] Winston Fletcher, "How to Keep Cool in the Hot Seat," *Management Today*, Nov. 1999, p. 40.

9

Formal Presentations
Being Understood, Accepted, and Remembered

Having now addressed one-on-one discussions and participation in meetings, we turn to the third most common component of oral communication in business—making presentations. Making an effective presentation demands more than a facility with presentation software or hardware. It demands more than consideration of what clothes you wear or how you use your hands. Whether making your presentation with transparencies, 35-mm slides, computer-projected visuals, or with no slides at all, presentations are a challenging communication task, the success of which lies with your ability to offer a message that is understood, accepted, and remembered.

TALK UP

Presentations come in a variety of purposes, lengths, and forms. As one extensive survey of scientific, technical, and managerial presentations identified, more than two-thirds of professionals indicated that they "frequently" or "very frequently" gave presentations (Table 9.1). Of these presentations, approximately 50% were given to colleagues; at 41%, managers were the next most common audience (Table 9.2). Further explaining the nature of these presentations, professionals noted that the majority of presentations were intended to share information, instruct, or persuade (Table 9.3).[1]

Talk up

Look who's talking

- The body language authorities
- The computer jockeys
- The speechwriters

A business perspective

Being understood, accepted, and remembered

- The rhetoric and aesthetics of slide design
- A bit of reasoning

A word or two about delivery

- Giving slides no more than their due
- Handling the question-and-answer period

The slide-less presentation

Presentations—the lessons

TABLE 9.1 FREQUENCY OF BUSINESS PRESENTATIONS

Frequency	% Responses
Very frequently	25.5
Frequently	42.5
Seldom	30.2
Never	01.9

Source: H.J. Scheiber and Peter J. Hager, "Oral Communication in Business and Industry: Results of a Survey on Scientific, Technical, and Managerial Presentations," *Journal of Technical Writing and Communication,* Vol. 24 (2)—Pages 161–180 (1994). Copyright Baywood Publishing Co., Inc.

TABLE 9.2 AUDIENCES FOR BUSINESS PRESENTATIONS

Audience	% Responses
Internal Colleagues	23.5
External Colleagues	11.1
Mixed Colleagues	15.6
Technical Managers	17.9
General Managers	11.3
Senior Managers	12.4
International	05.5
Other	02.6

Source: H.J. Scheiber and Peter J. Hager, "Oral Communication in Business and Industry: Results of a Survey on Scientific, Technical, and Managerial Presentations," *Journal of Technical Writing and Communication,* Vol. 24 (2)—Pages 161–180 (1994). Copyright Baywood Publishing Co., Inc.

TABLE 9.3 BUSINESS PRESENTATION OBJECTIVE

Objective	% Responses
To inform	14.8
To share data	28.9
To instruct	24.1
To persuade	18.0
To clarify	12.5
Other	01.6

Source: H.J. Scheiber and Peter J. Hager, "Oral Communication in Business and Industry: Results of a Survey on Scientific, Technical, and Managerial Presentations," *Journal of Technical Writing and Communication,* Vol. 24 (2)—Pages 161–180 (1994). Copyright Baywood Publishing Co., Inc.

Despite this wide diversity of activity, we often tend to think of only two aspects of business presentations: content and delivery. As expressed in *Communication World*, "On one side, you have speechwriters focusing almost exclusively on content. And on the other side, you have voice experts, body language authorities, dress for success advisors and media consultants focusing almost exclusively on delivery."[2] Sometimes a third side is added to the discussions: the computer jockeys, who focus on improving our facility with presentation hardware and software. Yet, we might well wonder how our rhetorical principles get factored into these discussions. The problem is, as we shall examine, that these camps tend to exchange mechanics for substance, image for structure.

LOOK WHO'S TALKING

Dressing for success or dressing the presentation up with a lot of fancy images and animation are not necessarily the substance of success. To appreciate the real measures of success, let's look briefly at these three predominant schools of thought: 1) the body language authorities, 2) the computer jockeys, and 3) the speechwriters.

THE BODY LANGUAGE AUTHORITIES

Body language strategists are the contemporary equivalents of the dress-for-success advocates. The problem with their message is that it demonstrates less than a keen appreciation of audience. As Table 9.2 made evident, the vast majority of presentations are made to colleagues. Although some circumstances may dictate formal attire, in most situations, you are expected to dress consistent with the expectations of the audience. If everyone in the company, from the President down, wears T-shirts and jeans, you would look out of place if you show up in a business suit. The more telling element of the body language message is that the advice favors appearance over substance, visual reference to the speaker over formal assertions of the speech.

The message unduly emphasizes delivery. Whether using the types of assessment forms typically employed in classrooms (Figure 9.1), or self-assessment forms advocated by the "pros" (Figure 9.2), the body language school is a powerful lobby that delivers a disproportionate emphasis on how you look, where you look, and what you do to engage the audience.[3] Although it is important to look good on stage, we have yet to see a single employee evaluation that cites such factors as "handles microphone well," "avoids nervous gestures," or "wears professional, coordinated attire." Making business presentations is not the same as a speech at Toastmasters (a popular society that emphasizes public speaking and communication skills). Neither is it an invitation to put on a Hollywood-quality production.

THE COMPUTER JOCKEYS

If you can't look good yourself, maybe—this second school might lead us to believe—the key is making your slides look impressive.* Today it is relatively commonplace to see digital projectors run by laptop computers using presenta-

---

* Throughout this chapter, the terms *slide, viewgraph, visual,* and *transparency* are used interchangeably.

Oral Report Evaluation Form

Team _____   Evaluator _____
       Please print   Name or Student Number

Rating Key: **4** = Very good; **3** = Acceptable; **2** = Needs improvement; **1** = Needs much improvement

Insert ✓ in one square opposite each numbered item. Add comments, especially for 4 and 1 ratings.

Content & Organization	4	3	2	1	Delivery (continued)	4	3	2	1
1 Introductory Remarks ▪ Aroused audience attention ▪ Prepared audience for report ▪ Introduced team members ▪ Used an agenda/partition statement		*Comments*			**6 Nonverbal Messages** ▪ Organized entry and exit ▪ Posture, freedom from swaying ▪ Smooth transition of speakers ▪ Natural movements and gestures ▪ Professional, coordinated attire		*Comments*		
2 Body (space for outlining on back) ▪ Soundly organized ▪ Clear transitions between points ▪ Each main point developed effectively ▪ Appropriate detail enabled audience to understand research results		*Comments*			**7 Presentation Aids (Slides)** ▪ Clear, readable, correct text ▪ Appropriate, graphics ▪ Slides advanced at proper times ▪ Speakers referred to some slides ▪ Appropriate number of slides		*Comments*		
Delivery					**Content & Organization (continued)**				
3 Style ▪ Poised, confident, enthusiastic ▪ Continuity (among speakers) ▪ Planned, prepared, rehearsed ▪ Audience awareness, rapport ▪ Eye contact; if read, speaker glanced frequently at audience ▪ Formal tone		*Comments*			**8 Conclusion** ▪ Moved to closure without hesitation ▪ Included a *final summary* that aided memory ▪ Placed report into larger perspective/organization's future		*Comments*		
4 Voice (all presenters) ▪ Enunciation, clarity ▪ Projection ▪ Variety in pace, pitch, volume		*Comments*			**9 Questions and Answers** ▪ Offered to answer questions ▪ Evidently planted questions in audience ▪ Repeated each question aloud ▪ Answered directly and briefly ▪ Gave thoughtful answer (no sarcasm) ▪ Made eye contact with questioner		*Comments*		
5 Language ▪ Word choice appropriate for audience ▪ Clear expression of ideas (research problem, procedure, outcomes) ▪ Correct grammar, proper idiom		*Comments*			**More Comments** _____ _____ _____	**Scoring** Total: _____ of 36 Grade points: ___ Letter grade: ___			

FIGURE 9.1

A Typical Classroom Presentation Evaluation Form

- Chose a title that tied audience interest to the topic
- Used an attention-getting opening
- Presented the body of the speech in an organized, logical sequence
- Used a conversational tone
- Demonstrated an appropriate degree of formality
- Used personal pronouns
- Avoided jargon
- Explained technical terms
- Handled notes unobtrusively
- Handled the microphone professionally
- Avoided nervous gestures or posture
- Made eye contact with individuals in the audience
- Avoided staring at one section or person in the audience
- Used gestures that supported, rather than detracted from, words
- Used pertinent, inoffensive humor
- Spoke loudly enough
- Varied the speaking pace
- Avoided speaking too fast or too slowly, and used emphasis appropriately
- Paused for audience reaction
- Avoided pause filers (er, uh, ok)
- Varied voice pitch
- Spoke clearly
- Pronounced words and acronyms correctly
- Dressed appropriately
- Met time requirements, within 5 minutes
- Presented a memorable conclusion

FIGURE 9.2

Evaluation Criteria Recommended by the "Pros"

FIGURE 9.3

The PowerPoint
Rangers

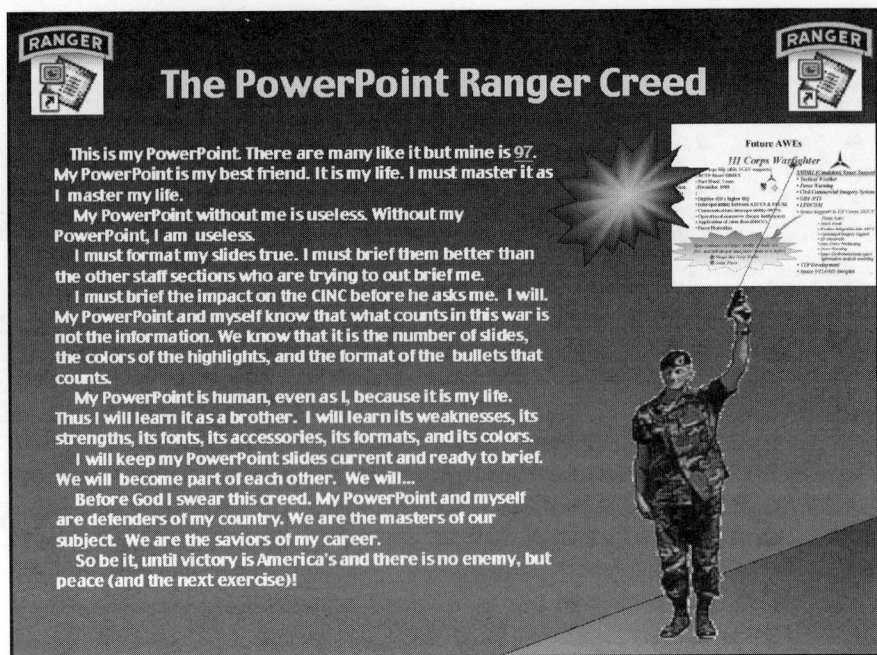

The PowerPoint Ranger Creed

This is my PowerPoint. There are many like it but mine is 97. My PowerPoint is my best friend. It is my life. I must master it as I master my life.

My PowerPoint without me is useless. Without my PowerPoint, I am useless.

I must format my slides true. I must brief them better than the other staff sections who are trying to out brief me.

I must brief the impact on the CINC before he asks me. I will. My PowerPoint and myself know that what counts in this war is not the information. We know that it is the number of slides, the colors of the highlights, and the format of the bullets that counts.

My PowerPoint is human, even as I, because it is my life. Thus I will learn it as a brother. I will learn its weaknesses, its strengths, its fonts, its accessories, its formats, and its colors.

I will keep my PowerPoint slides current and ready to brief. We will become part of each other. We will...

Before God I swear this creed. My PowerPoint and myself are defenders of my country. We are the masters of our subject. We are the saviors of my career.

So be it, until victory is America's and there is no enemy, but peace (and the next exercise)!

tion software that allows all types of animations, multimedia formats, automated advances, and impressive image manipulation. However, before you get too excited about delving into these practices, you might remember an easily overlooked notion in Table 8.1 of Chapter 8: Although oral communication, in general, was ranked No. 1 in hiring decisions, computer competency was ranked No. 14 in a 15-horse race! The business world, as the ranking implies, does not equate ability to communicate effectively with an ability to create dazzling animations that dance across the screen. Performance is gauged on what you communicate, not the technology and software tools you have mastered.

In fact, in some cases, contrary to this camp's affinity for technique and technology, there is a growing backlash against use of slides that do every type of trick except make the message clear. As highlighted on the first page of the April 26, 2000 edition of *The Wall Street Journal,* the Pentagon declared "war on electronic slide shows that make briefings a pain". In particular, as the article points out, the Chairman of the Joint Chiefs of Staff has initiated battle with "Power-Point Rangers," "a derogatory term for desk-bound bureaucrats more adept at making slides than tossing grenades" (Figure 9.3).[4]

Further, for those who believe that the technology is a recent development that negates the need to acknowledge the rhetorical underpinnings of business presentations, let's acknowledge just how deep the roots of our current technology run. The digital, multimedia projector we use today was preceded by the 35-mm slide projector. The 35-mm slide projector was preceded by the overhead (transparency) projector, which still remains the most commonly used piece of projection equipment for business presentations. Moreover, the overhead projector was predated by the stereopticon—a nineteenth-century optical projection instrument that used "magic lanterns" to cast a magnified image on a screen. This device was sophisticated enough to allow dissolving views or combinations of images to be projected. By the early part of the twentieth century,

Illustrated Talks Given by Phonograph Outfit
Popular Mechanics, July 1915

For giving illustrated phonographic lectures, a Colorado professor has devised a stereopticon attachment for a talking machine that operates automatically and may be timed for any record. The pictures to be shown on the screen during a talk are mounted in a disk frame which revolves before a lens of the projector, bringing each slide into a place at the proper instant. The shifting is accomplished by means of a series of "dogs" arranged on the back of the picture rack. A shaft connecting the disk and obtaining its power from the phonograph actuates the turning mechanism and makes the various slides appear in sequence and at whatever time intervals are requisite, so that as different topics are reached in the lecture, the desired pictures are projected on the screen without necessitating the attention of an operator. The device has been used by the inventor for schoolroom purposes.

this early precursor of today's multi-media capability even provided for automatic advances between images (Figure 9.4).[5]

The point is that the technology—though indeed helpful—is not the source of success, but simply another tool in your arsenal. Though clearly more vehement about the matter than most busy business managers and executives, Richard Danzig, then Secretary of the Navy, maintained in *The Wall Street Journal* article that an overly sophisticated, multimedia presentation is "only necessary for two reasons: If field changes are changing rapidly or if the audience is 'functionally illiterate.'" The message you are sending the audience with an overly elaborate multimedia barrage may be something completely different from the message you intended. The audience may feel you are more involved in your image than you are attuned to their interests or needs. If this becomes the case, you might as well use your 15 minutes of boardroom fame to say goodbye; you probably will not be invited back anytime soon.

What's true for the Navy audience is true of the business audience: the audience does not want to have its time wasted on frills and fanfare. Furthermore, you don't want your colleagues and managers leaving the room thinking that you have both insulted them and picked their pockets by wasting time they're paying for. They want message instead of show; they want elaboration instead of elaborateness; and they want meaning instead of mesmerizing displays.

THE SPEECHWRITERS

Our third group of presentation experts advocates that we concentrate on content—a good idea, except that what passes for content may not necessarily be a synonym for substance. This miscue is made evident if we review and explain the 10 tips cited in *Communication World* as a means to "connect content and delivery" (Table 9.4).

By most scorecards, these tips (the author's intent aside) appear to concentrate (by a ratio of 9:1) on delivery as opposed to content. Even Tip 3—the tip most evidently linked to substance—offers little to guide us toward enhanced substance. This disconnect between content and substance becomes even more pronounced when we look at eight tips provided by a second content-oriented advocate:

TABLE

9.4

DECIPHERING THE SPEECHWRITER'S TIPS

The Tip	The Author's Explanation
Make it [the presentation] shorter	The author means reduce the length.
Make it sharper	The author advises "clever" statistics and "shocking" contrasts.
Use greater variety in your research	The author says expand the resource base.
Start strong	The author wants openings with "guts" and "spunk."
Use stylistic devices	Key, according to the author, is repetition: "if you have a particularly good phrase or clever line, repeat it. Again. And again."
Include rhetorical questions	The author wants an engaged audience.
Avoid using audiovisual aids as a crutch	The author wants you to step out from behind the podium.
Use a light touch of humor	It's not so much for the audience; rather, the author thinks humor relaxes the speaker.
Respect wordsmithing	The author wants you to expand your circle of friends by getting "friendly with a speechwriter."
End strong	Once done, the author warns you to pack it in and get off the stage.

1. Plan your presentation.
2. Develop your notes.
3. Make training aids.
4. Rehearse the presentation.
5. Arrive early.
6. Cultivate a positive attitude.
7. Plan for questions.
8. Finish on time.

Here again we get a single tip (e.g., develop your notes) linked to substance. Yet, closer examination of the tip makes apparent that it is an aid to delivery, not a means of ensuring substance. The tip, as the author explains, means that we should create a series of key phases and words to serve as memory joggers during the presentation. These aids should be prepared in large type so they can be read easily, be stored in three-ring binders, be cross-referenced to the associated slides, and numbered in the event that they spill out of the binders.[6]

Surely there needs to be something more to effective presentations than physically protecting materials. We know the answers don't lie with the body language authorities who have us looking good, even if out of place. The answers don't lie with the computer jockeys, whose unrelenting attachment to the tools has the slides looking good, even if the message is buried in the fanfare. We know the answers don't lie with the speechwriters, who, although interested in merging content and delivery, create impressions of completeness by making reference to content while actually concentrating on delivery and performance.

A BUSINESS PERSPECTIVE

Dressing up—whether it's the speaker or the slides; using technology and software (paraphrasing Ben Franklin) to confuse motion with action; or substituting "clever" statistics and "shocking" contrasts for substance and structure may all add up to greater showmanship. Yet, they may not add up to a better showing (and, more than likely, not to a better showing on your own behalf). The answer, to the contrary, lies with recognizing the educational aspect of presentations, the need for a tightly woven persuasive strategy. Recognizing this important principle, one author jokingly argued, "a presentation is an opportunity to give other people a present that none of them wants." This article goes on to explain this cryptic comment:

> Question: What's the present and why don't they want it?
>
> Answer: The present is information, but unfortunately, this is the Information Age, so everyone is already swimming in information. Nobody is out there thinking: "Gee, I've only been bombarded by several thousand advertisements, memos, letters, and messages today—I can't wait for the next piece of information. Who knows, maybe this will be the one that makes my brain explode."[7]

The challenge, alluded to above, is therefore to transform your opportunity to speak to your colleagues, clients, or managers into a real present that the audience realizes it not only wants but also needs. The single most important feature in accomplishing this goal is recognizing that business presentations represent acts of persuasion. The presentation is not about how you look, how glitzy the slides might be, or the volumes of research you assembled on your way to the podium. The presentation is a communication the success of which relies on you having a clear business purpose and a clear strategy for achieving that purpose.

Highlighting this rhetorical nature of business presentations—the need for a persuasive strategy—a Director of Marketing, Planning, and Development explains what really must be understood about standing center stage at the podium.

> Much is at stake in making presentations. One rarely has a second chance to sell a product, service, or idea; persuade a board of directors to enter a new venture; convince colleagues that one's idea is best; or even ask the boss for a raise. Presentations have to be right the first time, and that takes more than just having a good idea. Persuasion requires clear goals and a sound strategy. Many people believe that the most crucial stage of an effective presentation is the delivery. In fact, the most important element is the goal setting that precedes it. Eliminate this step in haste, and the presentation is left to chance.[8]

Stating this concept of goal-oriented communication in a more generic fashion, we might trace a clear pathway that leads to successful business presentations. To be effective, business presentations must accomplish three things:

1. The presentation has to be understood
2. The presentation has to be accepted
3. The presentation must be remembered if it is to be acted upon.

BEING UNDERSTOOD, ACCEPTED, AND REMEMBERED

Making a presentation understood demands close attention to the rhetoric and aesthetics of slide design. Having a presentation accepted is a function of establishing a clear, recognizable, and transparent reasoning that allows delineation of a well-supported assertion. Last, for a presentation to be remembered, we must pay attention to a few principles about how people process information.

THE RHETORIC AND AESTHETICS OF SLIDE DESIGN

Effective business presentations rely on a variety of factors beyond the substance and structure of the presentation: audience factors, environmental factors, and perceptions of the speaker. Interestingly, one of the variables that affects all of these factors is the use of visuals. Twenty years ago, a study at the University of Pennsylvania showed that people are more likely to say yes and act upon recommendations when you use visuals. "You will be perceived as more professional, persuasive, credible, interesting, and better prepared. The probability of the audience reaching consensus is 79 percent vs. 58 percent without visuals. The evidence points overwhelmingly to the conclusion that a picture is worth a thousand words. Visuals make information easier to understand, promote interest, improve retention, and allow one to clarify or reinforce points."[9]

More recent studies have reached similar conclusions. Visuals enhance the persuasiveness of the material as well as the audience's perception of the presenter. These enhanced perceptions, in turn, contribute to improved attention, comprehension, agreement, and retention (Figure 9.5).[10] Tables 9.5 and 9.6 detail the results from studies that evaluated the impacts that visuals have on the presentation and on the audience's perception of the presenter.[11]

As these tables suggest, audiences respond not only to the use of visuals, but also to various characteristics of the visuals, such as the use of animation. Many

---

FIGURE 9.5

Perceived Impact of Visuals

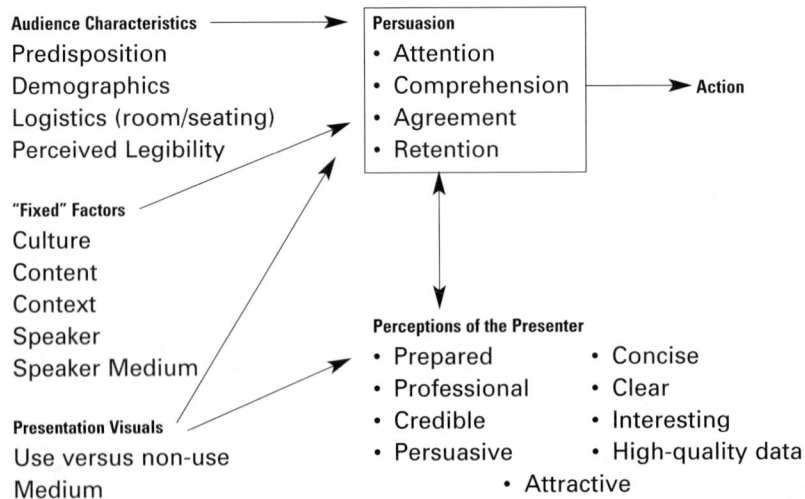

Audience Characteristics
Predisposition
Demographics
Logistics (room/seating)
Perceived Legibility

"Fixed" Factors
Culture
Content
Context
Speaker
Speaker Medium

Presentation Visuals
Use versus non-use
Medium

Persuasion
• Attention
• Comprehension
• Agreement
• Retention

→ **Action**

Perceptions of the Presenter
• Prepared   • Concise
• Professional   • Clear
• Credible   • Interesting
• Persuasive   • High-quality data
          • Attractive

Source: Reprinted from *Information and Management*, Vol. 33, J. Morrison and D. Vogel, "The Impacts of Presentation Visuals on Presentations," pages 125–138. Copyright 1998, with permission from Elsevier Science.

of the characteristics of effective presentation visuals are the same as the features we discussed about graphics in Chapter 4: efficiency, legibility, and accuracy of graphical depictions. In addition to these factors, there are several considerations particularly vital to making presentation visuals work for you instead of against you.

Just as the navy felt its presentations were being overwhelmed by gratuitous use of animation and other dynamic features of presentation software, so, too, a

TABLE

9.5 **THE EFFECT PRESENTATION VISUALS HAVE ON PERSUASION**

Persuasive Element	No Visuals Used	Visuals Used	Black and White	Color
Attention*	3.46	3.72	3.54	3.69
Agreement*	3.51	3.71	3.65	3.74
Comprehension**	10.89	11.80	11.58	11.98
Retention**	9.07	10.07	9.82	10.53

* 1 = very low; 5 = very high   ** Maximum number correct = 14

Source: Reprinted from *Information and Management,* Vol. 33, J. Morrison and D. Vogel, "The Impacts of Presentation Visuals on Presentations," pages 125–138. Copyright 1998, with permission from Elsevier Science.

TABLE

9.6 **THE EFFECT OF PRESENTATION VISUALS ON PERCEPTIONS OF THE PRESENTER**

Evaluation Category	No Visuals Used	Plain Visuals Used (no animation)	Animated Visuals Used
Prepared	5.58	5.08	5.76
Concise	5.00	4.75	5.06
Professional	4.17	4.58	5.06
Clear	5.33	5.33	5.71
Persuasive	3.08	3.67	3.71
Credible	3.50	4.25	4.12
Interesting	2.58	3.08	3.29
Attractive	3.67	3.75	3.88

1 = very low perception;   7 = very high perception

Source: Reprinted from *Information and Management,* Vol. 33, J. Morrison and D. Vogel, "The Impacts of Presentation Visuals on Presentations," pages 125–138. Copyright 1998, with permission from Elsevier Science.

presentation can become lost in a sea of colors, a parade of fonts, and a host of garish backgrounds and slide designs. To avoid putting visual display into competition with your message, conscious choices must be made about color, type, layout, and animation.

COLOR. Not too long ago, use of color slides often invoked anxious discussions about the costs of the presentations. The common availability of presentation software and color printers has essentially eliminated the cost of color production as an issue. However, color used badly may still be worse than using no color at all. Color, whether used for the text, the background, or the graphic material incorporated into the slides, should be used only for the following reasons:

- to emphasize key points
- to establish groupings among items
- to provide continuity

- to highlight important information
- to create a certain mood
- to increase reading speed and comprehension.[12]

Excellent advice on using color for backgrounds and text to achieve these ends was provided by Marie Flatley in an article that appeared in *Business Communication Quarterly*:

Careful attention to background, text, and color principles for graphics plays a vital role in the contribution a visual makes to a presentation. Background color is the single most important element. A presenter should choose a background with the ease of the audience's readability in mind. Room lighting is a major factor in selecting background intensity. The general consensus among graphic designers is that the darker the room, the darker the background . . . . Text color is important for readability too. Basically, it should contrast with the background color, and the greatest contrast should be between the title and the background color. A presenter will also want to limit the number of colors used since too many can confuse the reader and clutter the message. However, to get more color while keeping the color choice simple, a presenter could vary the tints and shades of colors. To highlight a point, a presenter might use the high contrast color for the point and the subdued or dimmed color for the other points.[13]

TYPE. As one author remarked, "Type defines a publication's personality."[14] The same is true in constructing presentations. In particular, two type factors demand your attention: font and size.

FONT. A font refers to a set of letters, numbers, punctuation, and symbols that share a common appearance and design (e.g., Helvetica, Times Roman, Palatino). For each font, you also generally have a variety of options such as bold or italics. Although there is some literature that argues for one font over another, the choice is pretty much a matter of personal preference. However, a firm choice has to be made—and made consistently. For instance, you might choose one font to use for all titles, a second for use with the body of the slide. Sometimes a limited number of fonts can be mingled with positive effect; too many fonts and the effect is lost. The fonts you choose are an extension of your message, promoting a sense of harmony, of a comfortable relationship among the pieces of information. To this end, you need to think how you want the visual message and harmony reinforced before making your selection of font.

The next decision is whether to use a serif or sans serif type. Serif refers to the small finishing strokes (or feet) at the bottom of the character. Although in publications serif type is often recommended, most presentations work better with a sans serif type (Figure 9.6). Last, you need to think about case—the use of capital, lowercase, or mixed-case letters.

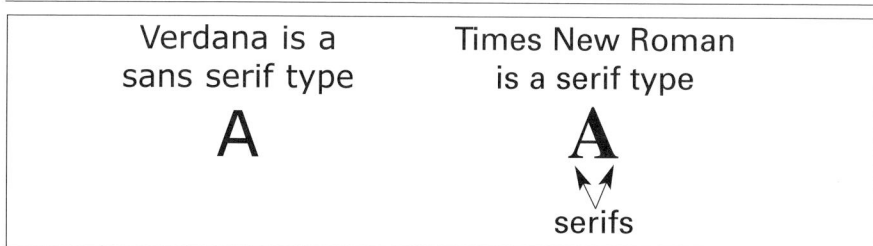

FIGURE 9.6

Sans Serif and
Serif Types

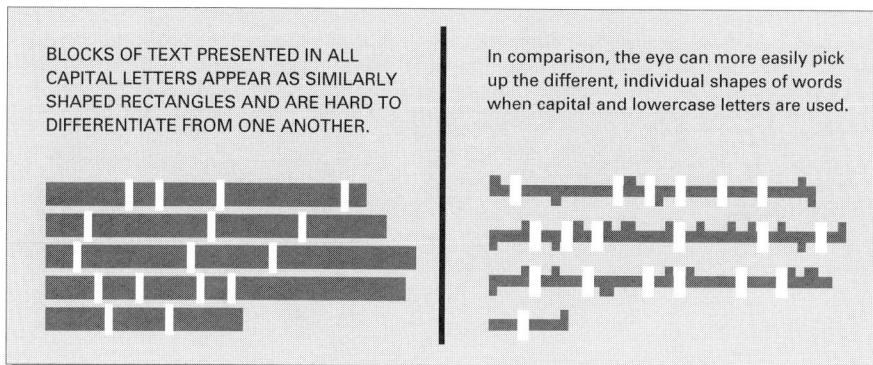

FIGURE 9.7

A Case of Images

As Figure 9.7 illustrates, when words are presented using mixed case, each word takes on a distinguishing shape. This visual image aids in the word's recognition, and, by extension, the comprehension of your material. Mixed case, it has also been shown, aids in reading speed. (Blocks of text written in upper- and lowercase can be read approximately 12% faster than text written using all capital letters.)[15] Therefore, you should restrict your use of all capital letters for creating emphasis. Titles should be written either with an initial uppercase letter (as in a sentence) or with an initial capital letter for each main word (often referred to as "title case"). The body of the text, in contrast, should use an initial uppercase at the beginning of the statement or bullet, with the remainder of the words—with the exception of proper nouns—written in lowercase letters.

SIZE. Misuse of fonts and case may cause some difficulty with the transmission of your information; misuse of the size of type, in contrast, may make the transmission impossible. Type size is measured in points (approximately 72 points equal 1 inch), a system devised back in the days when a separate block of lead was cast for each character and then the characters were set one-by-one into a printing tray (Figure 9.8). The x-height of a font is the minimum vertical space occupied by lowercase letters. Point size, originally measured by the height of the lead casting, is now measured from the height of letters extending above the x-height (known as ascenders) to the bottom of letters extending below the x-height (known as descenders). Just as we can calculate what constitutes a size easy for a report reader to follow, so, too, we can calculate—using what is referred to as a visual angle—the size of type needed when projecting text (Figure 9.9).[16] However, unless the location for your presentation represents an extremely unique set of physical demands, we recommend you simply use some standard guidelines:

Titles—use 20–27 point sans serif type.
Body—use 16–20 point sans serif type.

FIGURE 9.8

Measuring Type

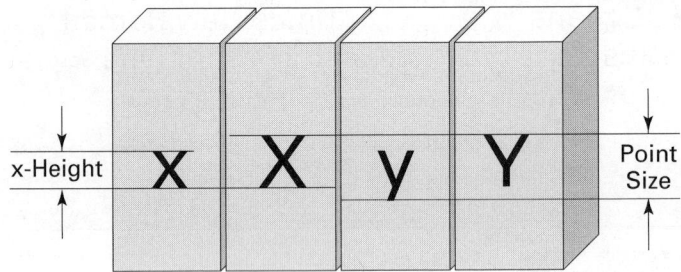

x-Height | Point Size

FIGURE 9.9

Measuring Type
Size for Projection

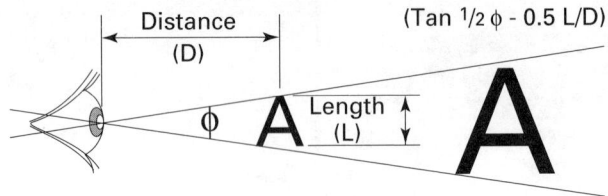

Distance (D)

$(\text{Tan } 1/2 \, \phi - 0.5 \, L/D)$

ϕ A Length (L) A

For text to legible to 90% of the audience
Letter Size$_{90}$ = 0.003D
For text to be legible to 100% of the audience
Letter Size$_{100}$ = 0.007D

Source: Reprinted with permission of Batelle Press.

FIGURE 9.10

Some Suggested
Formatting
Guidelines

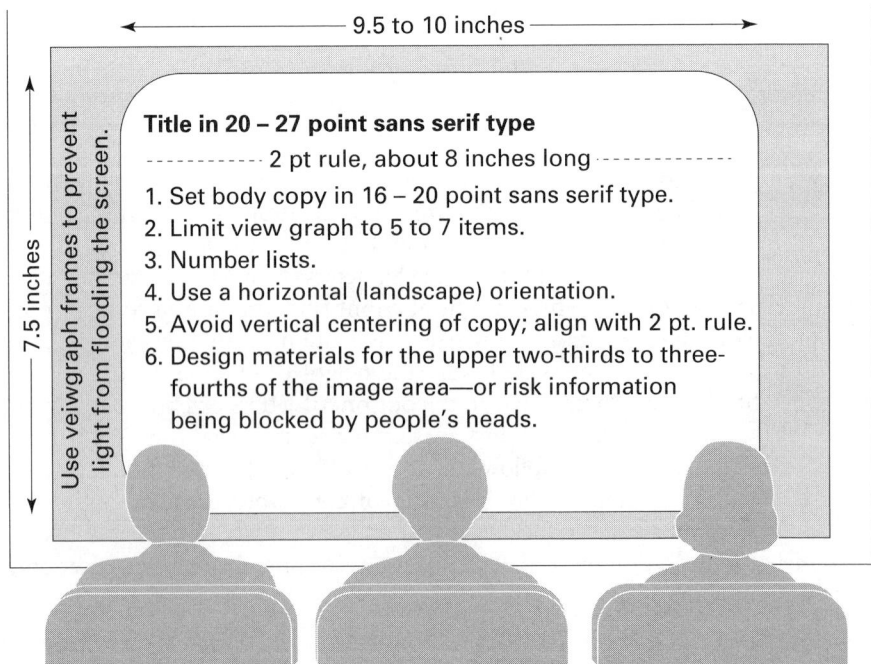

9.5 to 10 inches

7.5 inches

Use veiwgraph frames to prevent light from flooding the screen.

Title in 20 – 27 point sans serif type
----------- 2 pt rule, about 8 inches long -------------
1. Set body copy in 16 – 20 point sans serif type.
2. Limit view graph to 5 to 7 items.
3. Number lists.
4. Use a horizontal (landscape) orientation.
5. Avoid vertical centering of copy; align with 2 pt. rule.
6. Design materials for the upper two-thirds to three-fourths of the image area—or risk information being blocked by people's heads.

LAYOUT. As a few moments spent with any presentation software will convince you, you need to decide how items should be laid out on the slide. As shown in Figure 9.10, you should use the following guidelines:

- Set slides up in landscape rather than portrait mode.
- Don't extend your text or images to the very edge of the slide frame.
- Number lists (bullets) to assist you when making reference to information.
- Design materials for the upper two-thirds of the slide to minimize images that may be blocked by front rows of the audience.[17]

ANIMATION. Last, let's return to one of the options that has created much debate—animation. As the navy's experience should teach us, animation needs to be approached cautiously. As Table 9.5 detailed, when compared to non-animated slides, animation increased the audience's positive impression of the presenter in every category except "credibility." You can readily jeopardize your credibility by giving the impression that your main focus is on show, not substance. Animation for animation's sake is not good; you only have to sit through one presentation where every bullet makes a trumpeted appearance from stage left to know the truth of this axiom. Use animation sparingly and only when it substantively reinforces the clarity or substance of your message, as might be the case when you need to emphasize information on complex visuals to increase audience comprehension.[18]

As with each choice relative to the rhetoric and aesthetics of slide design, you need to be thinking of the slide template as a harmonizing, organizing, and integrating platform. You want a consistency that causes the audience to recognize a relationship among the elements. The choices of color, type, layout, and animation all must be part of an integrated persuasive strategy. Only when you have established this necessary canvas can you begin to artfully paint the argument itself.

A BIT OF REASONING

Presentations are expected to support assertions. Therefore, at the heart of any presentation must be a structure reflective of our discussions in Chapter 5 (also see Figure 9.11). Whether offering a proposition, demonstrating a causal relationship, assessing the relative value of alternative solutions to a problem, or soliciting a specific action from your audience, the presentation must proceed through a reasoned set of steps. In presentations, this structure is accomplished by developing a package consisting of four components:

Business Purpose	Basic Logic Template	FIGURE 9.11
1. Offer a proposition	• I intend to demonstrate . . .	
2. Show cause	• I will accomplish this by explaining (demonstrating) the following points . . .	The Basic Line of Thought
3. Evaluate an option	• Which will be supported by the following facts . . .	
4. Solicit action or support	• Which, given the following constraints and conditions . . .	
	• Along the way, I will show why/how this position is preferable to the alternatives.	
	• And, having made this argument, I will expect the following response/action . . .	

1. The title slide—an announcement of who you are (not only your name, but some suggestion of your relevant credentials, e.g., your title), the subject, the audience, and the place and date

2. An agenda slide—a slide that announces the principal subtopics of the presentation

3. The main-point slides—the individual pieces that support the assertion being made

4. A conclusion slide—the assertion, supported by a restatement of the main arguments (Figure 9.12).

THE SEQUENCE OF DEVELOPMENT. The most important step when beginning to develop these segments is to begin with the end in mind; therefore, rather than starting with the title, agenda, or main-point slides, you begin with the concluding slide. The reason for beginning with the concluding slide as a starting point is twofold: First, articulating the conclusion statement establishes a firm grip on precisely what is to be accomplished. Establishing the specific end point lessens the possibility of meandering or ending up somewhere other than might be intended (as was demonstrated in the City Council exercise in Chapter 8).

Second, setting the conclusion slide first establishes the boundaries for the presentation, both in prescribing the principal lines of argument needed to secure your purpose and in helping to isolate the types, volume, and relationship among the detailed information needed to support your assertion. Each of the bullets on the concluding slide will direct you to the subtopics that need to be developed in separate slides within the body of your talk. These main-body slides are thereby outlined in a preliminary form on the concluding slide. The concluding slide captures the principal assertions (what you intend to prove or substantiate), then links each of the major premises (the bullets on the concluding slide) to that assertion. When you begin to flesh out the presentation, each bullet on the slide, in turn, can then form the outline for the detailed evidence needed to support the individual premises (Figure 9.13).

Once the conclusion slide is complete, you have the necessary basis for proceeding logically through the remainder of the presentation. With the

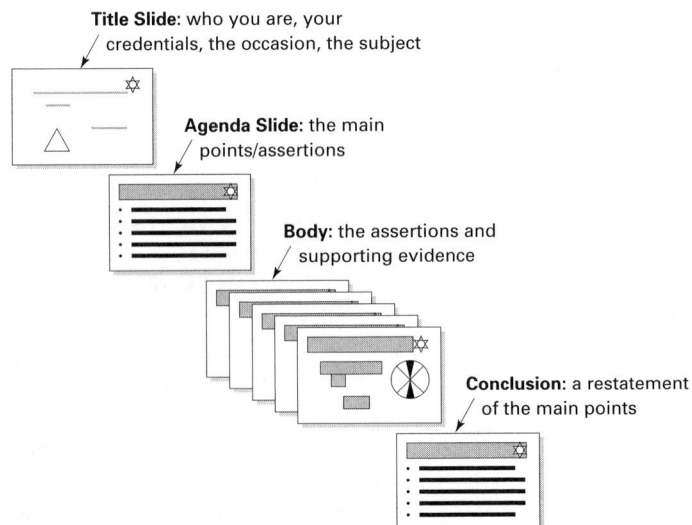

FIGURE 9.12

The General Presentation Framework

Title Slide: who you are, your credentials, the occasion, the subject

Agenda Slide: the main points/assertions

Body: the assertions and supporting evidence

Conclusion: a restatement of the main points

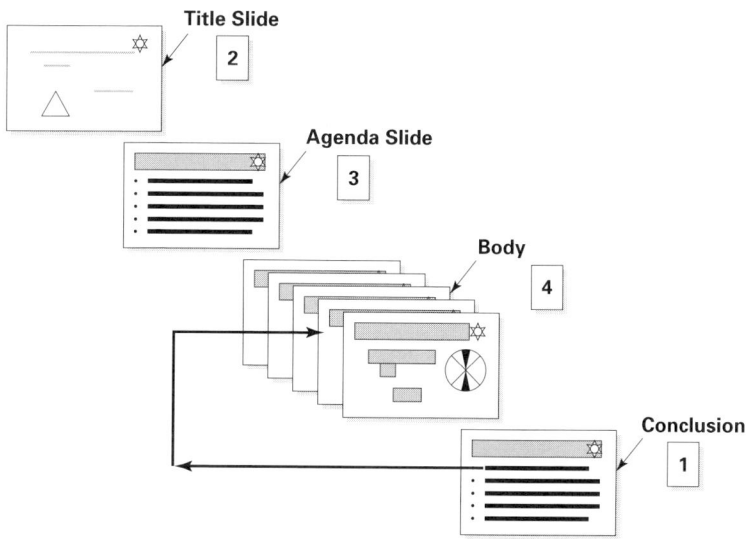

FIGURE 9.13

Begin by Defining What You Want the Audience to Remember

conclusion slide as a road map, you can develop the other components. The main-title slide is developed as a variation of the assertion cited on the concluding slide. The agenda slide profiles and forecasts much of the substance of the concluding slide; the main-point slides are the necessary amplification of the bullets on the concluding slide.

These individual main-body slides are developed, armed with a basic strategy (Figure 9.14):

The message of each slide = thesis + proof + a little assistance from credibility

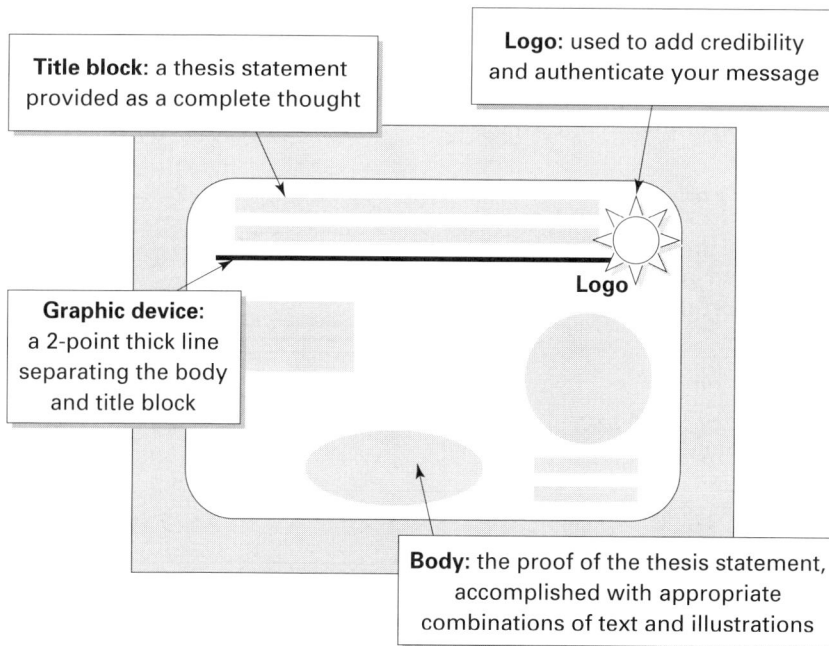

FIGURE 9.14

Message = Thesis + Proof (Implicitly Supported by Credibility)

Title block: a thesis statement provided as a complete thought

Logo: used to add credibility and authenticate your message

Logo

Graphic device: a 2-point thick line separating the body and title block

Body: the proof of the thesis statement, accomplished with appropriate combinations of text and illustrations

FIGURE 9.15

The Viewgraph
Title Should Be
a Complete
Thought

**Thesis should be stated
as a complete thought:**

• A declarative sentence
• Primary and secondary
  elements separated
  by a colon
• A rhetorical question

To achieve this formula, each slide is constructed of four elements:

1. A title block that sets the thesis in the form of a complete thought (Figure 9.15)

2. A graphical device separating the title from the remainder of the slide

3. A body that provides the critical information (text and/or illustrations) that proves the thesis (Figure 9.16)

4. An authenticating icon (e.g., a logo or an organizational label) that, like a signature, establishes your credibility and authenticates the slide.

CHECKING THE FLOW. When the title slide, concluding slide, and all the main-body slides have been completed, you have two things left to do to validate the overall clarity of the reasoning: align the agenda and concluding slides, and verify the correct flow of the argument. The first of these actions requires that you look at the agenda and concluding slides side by side. You want to make certain that the road announced by the agenda slide is still consistent with the road you have taken to the conclusion. Sometimes when developing the details, you may find that you have taken some detours along the way or may have lingered more deliberately over one point versus another. At the same time, you want to make certain that the agenda and concluding slides, though linked, are not absolute mirror images of each other. One is an announcement that provides a

FIGURE 9.16

The Body Proves
the Thesis
Statement

**Text and graphics are
combined in the body
to support the case:**

• Line art
• Photographs
• Tables/Graphs
• Quotations
• Clip art
• Anything else that
  illustrates, amplifies,
  or elucidates the
  thesis statement

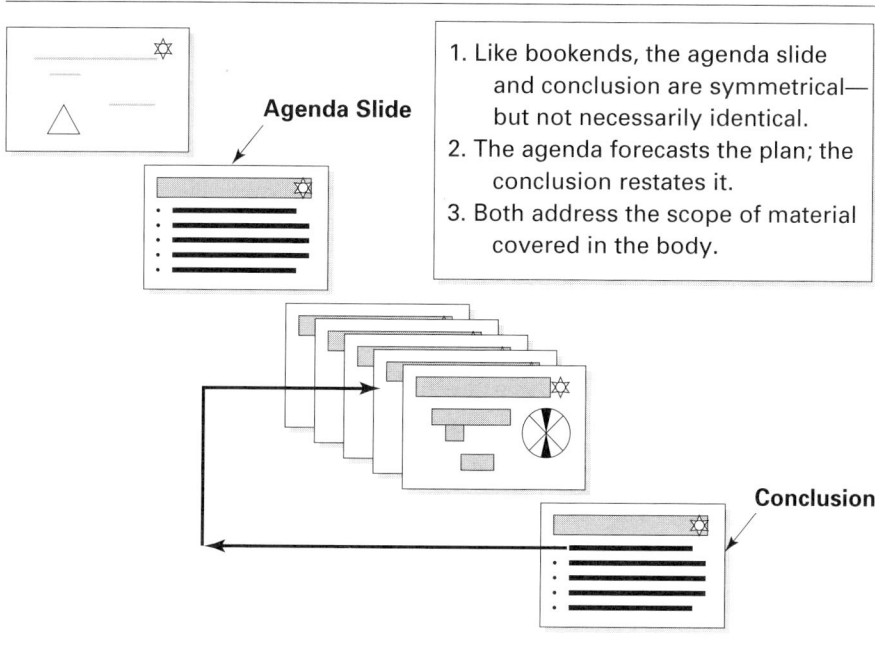

FIGURE 9.17

Agenda Slide

1. Like bookends, the agenda slide and conclusion are symmetrical—but not necessarily identical.
2. The agenda forecasts the plan; the conclusion restates it.
3. Both address the scope of material covered in the body.

Conclusion

The Agenda and Conclusion Slides Set the Scene and Close the Sale

basic starting point and prepares the audience for the trip. The other is a more complete restatement of your argument, meant to encapsulate the thinking that you maintain substantiates your conclusion (Figure 9.17).

The second action to be taken in validating the flow of the argument is called storyboarding. Not much different from the techniques used in laying out the scenes in a movie, storyboarding provides a single glimpse of the whole picture. By laying the pages side by side on a table or by taping them to a wall, you can examine how well the pieces fit together. This step is extremely important because the development stage often has you focusing intently on each individual slide; less attention is generally paid to the relationship among the slides.

Once you have positioned the slides so that you can see all of them, then you can begin to think about how you're actually going to talk about each slide. Which slide most easily supports the transition to the next thought? Are there slides that need to be regrouped to make the story more meaningful, more fluid, or more effective? Are there slides that need to be added or deleted? You may also want to think about the titles on each slide; sometimes by changing a few words or adding ellipsis points (. . .), you can better announce the relationship among thoughts to your audience. Take your time; try different arrangements. Walk through the presentation. Envision yourself standing at the podium. This is the stage where you are not only rehearsing your delivery, but also rehearsing the slides' role in making your argument as effective as possible (Figure 9.18).

A NOTE ON REMEMBERING. Figure 9.19 is a list of 21 sets of letters. Shown the list for about a minute, an average individual will tend to recall between five and seven of the letter sets. Commonly, the remembered sets will be among those at the tops or the bottoms of the three columns; far fewer sets are recalled from among the center rows. Both these phenomena (the number of sets remembered and their relative positioning) are important to us when developing presentations.

FIGURE 9.18 • Use Storyboarding to Gain Perspective and Fix the Flow

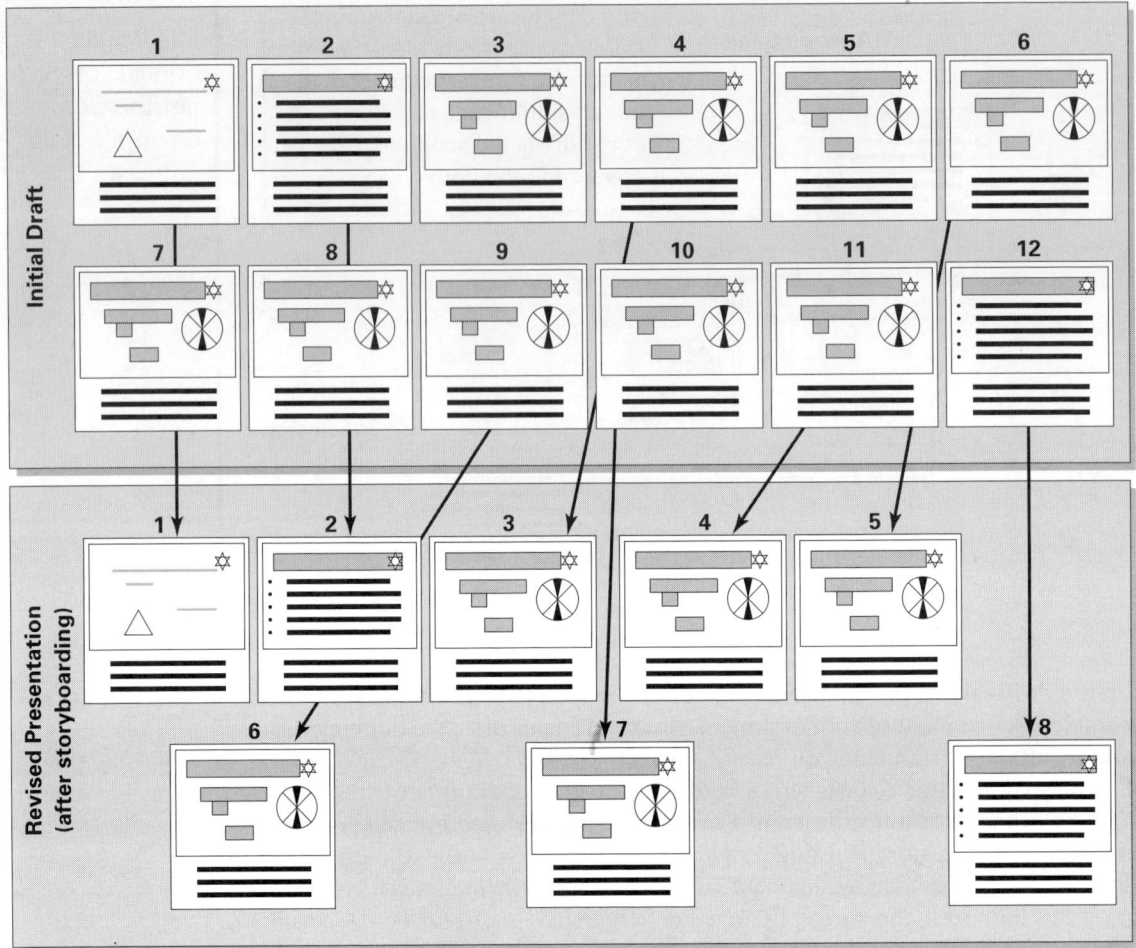

FIGURE 9.19 • A Bit of Nonsense

NWX	HWP	YFK
DPC	MKG	PCX
LGM	WYY	QLA
VPQ	NBH	PGR
FKB	LSW	TMC
RTV	VCP	PQX
JZI	ZJW	RKF

Remembering items at the top and bottom of the list demonstrates the rules of primacy and recency: people tend to remember best what they see first (primacy) and what they see last (recency). Numerous studies have shown that irrespective of the length, complexity, or timing of materials presented, the probability of recall increases among those items that appear first or last, as opposed to recollection of those in the middle.[19] Therefore, as the first principle contributing to having your material remembered, you need to place the most significant information correctly—both within the presentation as a whole, and within the individual slides.

The second phenomenon—the number of letter sets remembered—is also part of the psychology of human information processing. Dating back to the mid-1950s, researchers identified that immediate (short-term) memory has a limited retention capacity, a fact first summarized in an article entitled, "The Magical Number Seven, Plus or Minus Two: Some Limits on Our Capacity for Processing Information." In that article, George Miller placed our inherent limitations for short-term recollection somewhere between an ennobled characteristic of the human condition and a grand coincidence:

> And finally, what about the magical number seven? What about the seven wonders of the world, the seven seas, the seven deadly sins, the seven daughters of Atlas and Pleiades, the seven ages of man, the seven levels of hell, the seven primary colors, the seven notes of the musical scale, and the seven days of the week? What about the seven-point rating scale, the seven categories of absolute judgment, the seven objects in the span of attention, and the seven digits in the span of immediate memory? . . . Perhaps there is something deep and profound behind all these sevens, just calling out for us to discover it. But I suspect that it is only a pernicious, Pythagorean coincidence.[20]

Design or coincidence, the research, supported many times in recent years, shows our "span of attention," our "span of immediate memory," lies in the range of five to seven items. Therefore, to maximize the probability that points will be seen, heard, differentiated from one another, understood, and remembered, you should limit the number of pieces of information on any single slide to between five and seven items. You should also strive to build your line of argument around no more than five to seven principal points.

This limitation also has implications for the presentation as a whole. What if, as is often the case, the particular theses require more than seven bits of information to support them? What if the overall line of argument contains more than seven pieces of information needed to establish proof of the assertion? The answers to these questions lie in the technique generally known as "chunking"—the aggregating of ideas into larger blocks of thought or information.

As a simple demonstration of the principle, assume you wanted to have your audience remember a number that had 18 digits. (For simplicity's sake, we'll only use zeros and ones.)

$$\boxed{1\ 0\ 1\ 0\ 0\ 0\ 1\ 0\ 0\ 1\ 1\ 1\ 0\ 0\ 1\ 1\ 1\ 0}$$

Shown the series of numbers above, some people will try to process the information as 18 discrete pieces of information. Others will begin to group numbers into larger packets of two- three-, or four-digit numbers. What the audience in this latter case is doing is chunking, creating more readily recalled blocks of information. However, you don't need to entrust the responsibility for chunking to your audience. Being the one in control of the presentation, you have the option of doing this chunking for the audience. Instead of the series above, you could, for example, as shown in Figure 9.20, present the information in chunks. In so doing, you can increase the probability of your success—that information is remembered—by aggregating information so that the total number of individual packets of information remains in the targeted range of five to seven items.

FIGURE 9.20

Original 18 Numerals

| 1 | 0 | 1 | 0 | 0 | 0 | 1 | 0 | 0 | 1 | 1 | 1 | 0 | 0 | 1 | 1 | 1 | 0 |

9 Groupings of 2

| 10 | 10 | 00 | 10 | 01 | 11 | 00 | 11 | 10 |

6 Groupings of 3

| 101 | 000 | 100 | 111 | 001 | 110 |

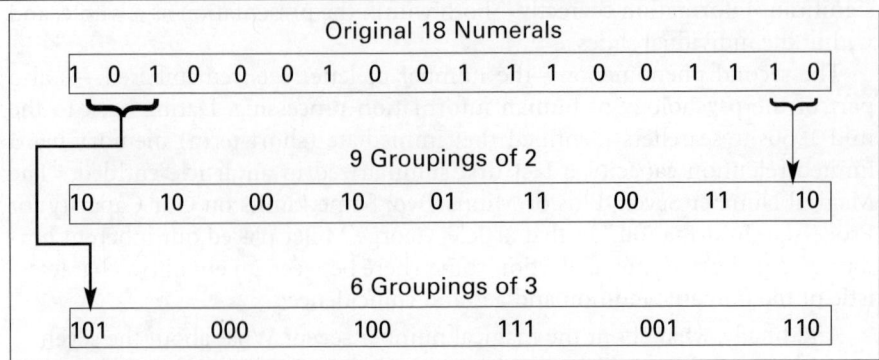

Chunking, whether digits, words, phrases, or other types of information, allows great flexibility in controlling the probability that your audience will retain the salient elements of your message. As defined in the early work of Miller, chunking allows a means of increasing both the volume of information transmitted and the probability of audience retention, despite our natural five-to-seven item limitation: "In order to speak more precisely, therefore, we must recognize the importance of grouping or organizing the input sequence into units or chunks. Since the memory span is a fixed number of chunks, we can increase the number of bits of information that it contains simply by building larger and larger chunks, each chunk containing more information than before."[21]

Understanding these two phenomena (limitations and placement) also helps explain another dimension of the presentation structure. As we have already learned, audiences respond more effectively to visually reinforced presentations. At one level, we can say that this occurs because the media reinforce the points we are trying to communicate. At the same time, we can say, from the audience's perspective, that the message is reinforced because we increase the number of sensory registers—using the audience's eyes as well as their ears—to translate the message into short- and long-term memory.

Once information is in short-term memory, as shown in Figure 9.21, various control mechanisms help determine what gets moved into long-term memory.[22] Taking advantage of these insights, for instance, the agenda slide, reinforced by the concluding slide, is providing repetition, a form of rehearsing performed for the

FIGURE 9.21

Environmental Input → Sensory Registers [Visual, Auditory, ⋮, Haptic] → Short-term (working) memory [Control Processes: —rehearsal, —coding, —decisions, —retrieval strategies] ⇄ Long-term (permanent) memory

Control Processes → Response Output

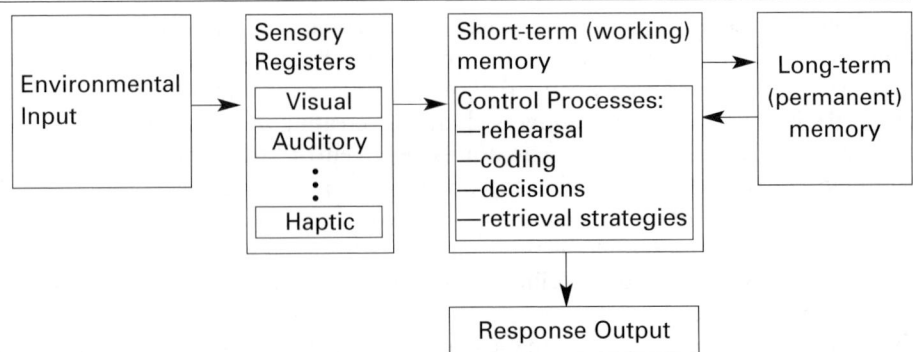

Source: Reprinted with permission of Allen Beechel.

audience. We therefore improve the probability that information will be transferred from short- to long-term memory. The more successful the transfer—the greater the number of transfers—the more successful you will have been.

Last, before we leave this topic of human information processing, let's consider how insights in this field can help resolve an age-old question: How many slides constitute the right number of slides? In an article in the journal *American Statistician*, a group of authors evaluated a series of "presentation myths." The No. 1 myth they cited was that "presentations require a magical number of visual aids." In attempting to debunk this myth, the authors explained: "Who has not been asked the question before a presentation, 'How many slides do you have?' That question is as relevant as the student who asks how many questions will be on the final exam. This is because some visual aids require 5 seconds of explanation and some 5 minutes! Of course, we have all seen the 5-minute slide that is presented in 5 seconds. A personal favorite is a transparency full of mathematical detail that the presenter clearly does not have time to cover, yet feels compelled to flash by the audience, perhaps as vindication that he or she did, in fact, prove a result."[23]

Without doubt, slides will differ greatly in how long they need to be on-screen, but one thing about all slides remains constant. The text of your slide—or your discussion of it—needs to accommodate a corollary to the five-to-seven item limitation. That is, there is a minimum amount of time that it takes for a piece of information to make the move from short- to long-term memory. "The psychological reality of the chunk has been well demonstrated, and the chunk capacity of short-term memory has been shown in the range of five to seven. Fixation of information in long-term memory has been shown to take about 5 to 10 seconds per chunk."[24]

The slide that shoots by too quickly may be shortchanging you and the audience, lessening your effectiveness by not allowing sufficient time for the information to register completely. Conversely, the slide that lingers too long on-screen may have outlived its usefulness and purpose long before it actually disappears from view. If you follow the five-to-seven rule about the number of items presented per slide, you may want to amplify the value of the lesson by practicing your delivery time. If there are five to seven pieces of information, and each takes 5 to 10 seconds to sink in, then you should practice spending

Understood	✔ effective use of visuals ✔ complementary text and graphics ✔ effective slide design	**FIGURE 9.22** Being Understood, Accepted, and Remembered
Accepted	✔ clear reasoning ✔ convincing logic ✔ compelling style	
Remembered	✔ persuasive argument ✔ positive perceptions of speaker ✔ application of basic tenets of human information processing —primacy and recency —5–7 limitation —reinforcement	

approximately a minute per slide. Coupling these two values will provide the highest probability that you are giving the audience an appropriate dose of information along with sufficient time to let the information go to work.

So, when is a presentation effective? A presentation, as shown in Figure 9.22, is effective when it is understood, accepted, and remembered.

A WORD OR TWO ABOUT DELIVERY

Just as a tightly structured approach resolved the long-standing problem of how many slides are enough, so, too, the approach will aid with delivery. Visual cues—the complete thesis statement on each slide and the consistent placement of critical information—indirectly assists with such factors as eye contact and minimizing the effects of nervousness. Instead of having to read entire slides to determine what you wanted to say and where you are in the presentation, you can, at a glance, use the cues to add to your comfort on stage and to trigger the response you need to speak meaningfully about each slide. There are, however, a few additional delivery-specific matters that need your attention: giving the slides no more than their due and effectively handling the question-and-answer period that generally follows any business presentation.

GIVING SLIDES NO MORE THAN THEIR DUE

The slides you have prepared carry the tune, but they're not the featured soloist—you are. Make certain you give the talk to the audience, not read the talk to them. Not surprisingly, the second presentation myth cited in the *American Statistician* article was the suggestion that the "audience can't read," an important reminder that you are not on the podium to read your slides verbatim to the audience. As the authors' explanation points out, "the slide's job is to focus the audience on the point—your job is to explain the point."

You need to maintain a healthy balance between the slide's contribution and your contribution as speaker. If you really believe the slide is there to do all the talking for you, you might as well turn on the projector and then sit down. It will be less insulting to the audience than reading the text to them. Conversely, if the slide has been designed with nothing to contribute, turn off the projector and start talking.

HANDLING THE QUESTION-AND-ANSWER PERIOD

Perhaps the most deflating experience is getting through your presentation only to do poorly in the question-and-answer period. With the exception of being set upon by someone whose only intention is to punish you, there's no reason why you should ever have the experience of seeing your presentation spin out of control during the endgame. Just as you have control when you are preparing and making your presentation, there's no reason to assume you cannot prepare for and maintain control in the question-and-answer period. The difference between success and failure in this session is—as is the case with all communication strategies—purely a matter of preparation.

The same information you used to prepare the presentation is the foundation for preparing for the question session: What are the audience's interests? What are their political sensitivities? What are the environmental challenges? What is the technical orientation of the audience? What differing organizational perspectives are reflected in the audience? Much like preparing for a job interview, sit down and think through the possible questions the audience is likely to have because of their organizational perspectives, technical backgrounds, and, most importantly, because of issues your presentation is likely to raise. Ask yourself what your opinion might be if you were an attendee at the meeting instead of the presenter. Last, be honest with yourself: What are the inherent weaknesses in your presentation? Every presentation has elements that are stronger or more likely to be immediately acceptable to the audience than are other parts. Focus on what questions you think need attention. Once you've done this analysis and soul-searching, then build your stock of answers and strategies.

To orchestrate this response development, you might, as one communication consultant recommends, sort the questions you have identified into three lists: the known, the knowable, and the notable.

1. The known list contains the questions to which you know the answers. Depending on how well you know the particulars, you may want to write out the answers and practice them out loud.

2. The knowable list contains possible questions to which you don't know the answers. Do the research, find out the answers, and practice them until you're comfortable.

3. The notable list contains the questions that demand a strategy. These are the broad questions that do not have simple answers or, which, when answered imprudently, may jeopardize the success of the presentation—if not more.[25]

While a known question might ask the specific sales figures for your department, and a knowable question might ask how the department fared against an agency elsewhere in the corporation, a notable question might ask you to clarify why you are promoting a particular action when previously your department had advocated the opposite path. These questions may challenge your authority or credibility by examining your sources. They may prod at the underlying assumptions by assessing your compatibility with corporate philosophy and history. They may question implicit political implications by examining contrary positions assumed by other departments. They may even test your strength of conviction by asking for levels of clarification and assurance of success. As demanding as these notable questions might be, you should be able to see these questions coming as readily as you can the known and the knowable questions. The additional obligation you have in regard to these challenges is to preplan a response strategy, validate the strategy against the continuity of the presentation, assess the most concise means of expressing the strategy, and then rehearse.

Using the practiced answers and strategies will allow you to negotiate the question-and-answer period. Almost always, the careful anticipation of questions gives the speaker a broader range of responses than demanded in the question period. The only other consideration is making sure that your preparations are made to work. Accomplishing this goal requires that you follow a few commonsense guidelines when responding to questions.

• Answer questions; don't give a speech.

• Listen closely to each question; don't start answering until the questioner is through.

• Pause to think before you answer; don't let your mouth get in gear before you have engaged your brain.

- Ask for clarification if you're not sure what was meant by the question; don't say what you think is important instead of answering the specific question that has been asked.

- Be honest; if you don't know an answer, say so. You may offer to get back to the questioner with an answer, but don't invent facts. Making up answers will invariably trip you up sooner or later—bringing the entire presentation into question.

- Answer as directly and concisely as possible; don't use the floor to start your presentation over again or to restate all your information. Offer only what's needed to respond to the question.

- When you've handled the final question, yield the floor and sit down; don't diminish your performance by offering a stuttering conclusion—adding extraneous information, valueless asides, or dozens of offers to answer additional questions at a later date. If people want to follow up later, they know where to find you.

THE SLIDE-LESS PRESENTATION

Some presentations offer different challenges than those we've already discussed. While we have essentially absolute control of the floor while flashing slides for the audience, not all presentations will demand or allow for the inclusion of visuals. Sometimes, because of time constraints or audience preferences, individuals are asked to make business presentations without props. These moments offer challenges that demand application of some different, but related strategies.

Preparation for this type of presentation begins with the same development stages as used for all presentations: articulating the precise purpose, defining the major points that need to be made, and determining the necessary evidence that needs to be offered to support the theses and assertion. However, the delivery stage shifts from an emphasis on the rhetoric and aesthetics of slide design to the design of a rhetoric of recollection.

Without the slides and the thesis statements projected on-screen as a reminder, you have to develop an internalized equivalent of these cues. This internalization is not intended to be a matter of memorizing a formal script, but it does mean that you may have to challenge yourself to remember.

At first, this shift to reliance on memory may be intimidating. No longer a mark of value or virtue, memory has lost much of its cultural standing—a conclusion well stated some years back in the *American Scholar* by Clara Park:

> We ask ourselves, and our children to remember nothing these days—not the multiplication tables, for we have calculators; not the presidents or the periodic table or the great dates of history; not 1066, not 1453, not 1517, not 1789, not even perhaps, 1914 and 1917 and 1939. We may make an exception for things we really care about—baseball statistics, for instance. The educated man, however, need not burden his memory. He has learned how to look things up .... We have come a long way ... from Saint Thomas Aquinas and Albert Magnus, for whom the cultivation of memory was a part of Prudence and one of the four cardinal virtues; from the elaborate Renaissance methods of memory training; even from the illiterate Vermont countryman of a hundred years ago who took the orders of isolated farm wives on back country roads and brought back from town unerringly

the three spools of thread, the packet of embroidery needles, the pound of tea. Memory now is the marker of outmoded and sterile education. What is important, after all? Not, surely, meaningless cultural facts, still less the great stories of the past or the great, weighted sentences and phrases . . . . We license ourselves to forget. Who needs memory?[26]

Yet, if we return to the rhetorical roots of business communication, we are greeted by a strong and lengthy linkage between memory and presentation. Memory, what Cicero referred to as the "firm perception" in *De Inventione* some 2000 years ago, was one of the five canons of rhetoric. Memory, as the Greeks believed, was the province of the goddess Mnemosyne, whose adulterous interlude with Zeus gave birth to the nine muses. As such, memory was the agent believed by the Greeks to underlie much of the creative impulse. It was memory that allowed such amazing feats as Homer's ability to recite more than 12,000 lines of *The Odyssey* by heart. Moreover, it was memory that served as a predicate for both wisdom and reasoning. Memory, as Aristotle argued, made a "man readier [more ready] in reasoning."[27]

Today, despite being aided by laptops, intranets, Internets, and PDAs (Personal Data Assistants), sometimes we are left to stand on our own devices. At these moments, we may again want to emulate the great rhetoricians, maybe not so much in devising mnemonics ("memory systems" as the Greeks called them), but in understanding the principles underlying these devices.

With clear correspondence to what we have already been learning about how to enhance the audience's recollection of the information we present, we know today, because of research in information processing, that any device intended to improve efficient memorization needs to follow four basic rules:

1. Information has to be in the form of small basic units, with no more than four or five individual items in any section.

2. The sections must have an internal organization, allowing the various parts to be fit together in a logical, self-ordering structure.

3. There must be an external relationship between the information to be learned and materials that have already been learned, so that they fit neatly together.

4. Any mental activity performed on the material (e.g., forming associations) increases the depth of processing, thereby automatically helping to form the relevant connections that improve retrievability.[28]

Therefore, what needs to be done when preparing for the slide-less presentation is to begin with our chunking technique—establishing the five to seven critical points or pieces of information. For each of these chunks, assign an association (e.g., an image or a keyword) that will aid with its recall. These recall aids should be assigned in the same sequence you intend to use when presenting the chunks. Next, remembering the control processes we discussed earlier, you need to do some rehearsing. Repeat the recall aids a number of times until they begin to jump readily to mind as if being cued like lines in a play. What you will have instilled in your memory is the equivalent of the conclusion slide. In fact, one mental image that works very well is to envision the images equivalent to the agenda, main body, and concluding slides.

Armed with the techniques of the ancient rhetoricians and with the insights of contemporary information-processing scientists, you are now prepared to meet the challenges of both the slide-less presentation and the slide-supported presentation.

PRESENTATIONS—THE LESSONS

Presentations are the opportunity to share information and persuade audiences of the value and reasonableness of your assertions. To accomplish these goals, you need to call upon all the rhetorical principles we studied in Part 1 of this text: audience, purpose, facts, arrangement, reasoning, and style. In some ways, your presentation is like that of an expert witness appearing before a jury. Your studies have given you critical information that, to be helpful, needs to be understood, accepted, and remembered by the jury.

Taking this analogy one step further, we might conclude this discussion by citing some of the advice given to lawyers when preparing expert witnesses on how to present scientific information in court testimony. The correspondences between the advice for expert witnesses and the details developed in this chapter should be quite evident.

You, like the expert witness, can create a presentation that wins over the jury by presenting a case that is understood, accepted, and remembered:

1. Clearly identify the issues that must be resolved. The expert "must highlight the issues . . . so the jury has a framework for understanding the . . . evidence."

2. Provide key evidence both early and late in the case. Expert testimony is "more influential when . . . presented early . . . . Toward the end of the trial, expert witnesses should summarize the evidence so that the jury has a reminder of the important points."

3. Provide internal summaries. "Before moving out to a new topic, concept, or idea, pause to repeat what went before."

4. Use demonstrative exhibits. "The . . . expert . . . should spend time developing exhibits that are comprehensible and persuasive . . . ."

5. Illustrate only one concept at a time. "Most people can acquire new information if it is presented in small palatable pieces."

6. Stick with the basics. "Give the jury the basic building blocks of information before moving on to the next level of complexity."

7. Enumerate. "Let the jury know how many points you will be making under each topic and subtopic."

8. Develop a theme. "Develop a theme for the case . . . that you can be committed to . . . . and that you can refer to frequently throughout your testimony."

9. Give a reason for providing the information and establish your credentials. "The juror's perception of an expert's credibility is closely related to their perception of why he is in the courtroom."

10. Provide a step-by-step road map of the expert analysis. "Describe precisely the scientific assumptions upon which the expert opinion is based. Connect the assumptions to the facts of the case and show the jurors how the facts support the opinion."

11. Use vivid language. "Remember the number of visual learners that are probably in the courtroom."

12. Thoroughly explore contrary opinions. "Part of the teaching function is to explore contrary opinions. The expert must explain why the scientific

evidence does not support the contrary opinion of the other party's expert. She should anticipate questions, acknowledge the disagreement between the parties and explain why her opinion is more sensible than the other expert's opinion."

As if summarizing the message of this chapter, the guidance on expert witnessing offers this summation: "The total presentation should be designed to make the jury feel comfortable with the conclusion they are being asked to reach."[29] You have the responsibility to offer a presentation that is understood, accepted, and remembered.

EXERCISES

☐ Group

1. Form teams of threes. Select a Fortune 500 Company and develop a 15-minute presentation to convince the other teams that your company represents the best place to make a $100,000 investment. (The period of the investment will be three years.) After each group has made its presentation, the class votes on which company receives the investment.

2. Using the feedback received from the presentation, prepare a revised presentation suggesting why your company remains the best company for the investment.

☐ Individual

1. Attend a presentation (other than a classroom lecture). Prepare an assessment of how effective the presentation was in terms of:

   a) slide design

   b) use of slides

   c) pace of information

   d) overall success in being understood, accepted, and remembered.

2. Prepare the conclusion slide for a presentation addressing the subject of "Creating Effective Presentations." Then write a one-to-two-page explanation for the following:

   a) why you selected the particular bullets to frame your presentation.

   b) how you would use graphic displays and your insights into human information processing to cover this topic in a 10-minute presentation.

END NOTES

[1] Tables 9.1, 9.2, and 9.3 are adapted from: H.J. Scheiber and Peter J. Hager, "Oral Communication in Business and Industry: Results of a Survey on Scientific, Technical, and Managerial Presentations," *Journal of Technical Writing and Communication*, Vol. 24, No. 2 (1994), pp. 161–180.

[2] Joan Detz, "Delivery Plus Content Equals Successful Presentation," *Communication World*, Vol. 15, No. 5 (April–May 1998), pp. 34–36.

[3] Donna J. Abernathy, "Presentation Tips from the Pros," *Training and Development*, Vol. 53, No. 10 (Oct. 1999), pp. 19–24.

[4] Greg Jaffe, "What's Your Point, Lieutenant? Just Cut to the Pie Charts," *The Wall Street Journal*, April 26, 2000, p. A-1.

[5] Mary Seelhorst, "Think It's New? Think Again!" *Popular Mechanics*, Vol. 178, No. 4 (April 2001), p. 148.

[6] Thomas K. Kollins, "Tips for Speakers," *Association Management*, Vol. 48 (August 1996), pp. 175–176.

[7] Paul Hellman, "So, You're Giving a Presentation!" *Management Review*, Vol. 79, No. 10 (Oct. 1990), p. 61.

[8] Frank K. Sonnenberg, "Presentations That Persuade," *The Journal of Business Strategy (Sept–Oct. 1988)*.

[9] *Ibid.*

[10] Figure 9.6 is adapted from: Joline Morrison and Doug Vogel, "The Impacts of Presentation Visuals on Persuasion," *Information and Management*, Vol. 33 (1998), pp. 125–135.

[11] Tables 9.5 and 9.6 are adapted from: Joline Morrison and Doug Vogel, "The Impacts of Presentation Visuals on Persuasion."

[12] Scott L. Jones, "A Guide to Using Color Effectively in Business Communication," *Business Communication Quarterly*, Vol. 60, No. 2 (June 1997), pp. 76–88.

[13] Marie E. Flatley, "Using Color in Presentations," *Business Communication Quarterly*, Vol. 59, No. 1 (March 1996), p. 90 (3).

[14] Valerie J. Vance, "Typography 101," *Business Communication Quarterly*, Vol. 59, No. 4 (Dec. 1996), pp. 132–134.

[15] Figures 9.7 and 9.8 are adapted from: Douglas Wieringa, Christopher Moore, and Valerie Barnes, *Procedure Writing: Principles and Practices.* Columbus, OH: Battelle Press, 2nd ed 1998, pp. 84, 85.

[16] Figures 9.9 and 9.10 are adapted from Douglas Wieringa, Christopher Moore, and Valerie Barnes, *Procedure Writing: Principles and Practices*, pp. 81, 82.

[17] We are greatly indebted to John Strack of Westinghouse Savannah River Company for design of Figures 9.10–9.18.

[18] Joline Morrison and Doug Vogel, "The Impacts of Presentation Visuals on Persuasion."

[19] Figure 9.22 is adapted from figures in Richard C. Atkinson and Richard C. Shiffrin, "The Control of Short-term Memory," *Scientific American*, Vol. 225 (1971), pp. 82–90.

[20] G.A. Miller, "The Magical Number Seven, Plus or Minus Two: Some Limits on Our Capacity for Processing Information," *Psychological Review*, Vol. 63 (1956), pp. 81–97.

[21] *Ibid.*

[22] Richard C. Atkinson and Richard C. Shiffrin, "The Control of Short-term Memory."

[23] Richard Becker and Sallie Keller-McNulty, "Presentation Myths," *The American Statistician*, Vol. 60, No. 2 (May 1996), p. 112 (4).

[24] Herbert A. Simon, "How Big Is a Chunk?" *Science*, Vol. 183 (Feb. 8, 1974), pp. 482–488.

[25] Diane DiResta, "Grace Under Pressure: Managing the Q & A," *Training and Development*, Vol. 50 (May 1996), pp. 21–22.

[26] Clara Claiborne Park, "The Mother of the Muses: In Praise of Memory," *American Scholar*, Vol. 50 (Winter 1980/81), pp. 55–71.

[27] Cited in Daniel L. Plung, "The Bald General Dancing in Our Basement: The Rhetoric of Business Information," unpublished article.

[28] Donald A. Norman, *Memory and Attention: An Introduction to Human Information Processing.* New York: John Wiley & Sons, Inc., 1976.

[29] Carl Meyer, ed., *Expert Witnessing: Explaining and Understanding Science.* New York: CRC Press, 1999, pp. 139–142.

10

E-mail
Securing the Great Link in Daily Business

Until the latter part of the nineteenth century, much of America's business was conducted orally; little written direction or documentation was needed or desired. Written communication existed primarily in the form of business letters used to correspond with clients and suppliers. In 1877, M. L. Sperry, treasurer for the Scoville Manufacturing Company, a manufacturer of brass and brass products, offered the following rationale for operating without reliance on excessive paper or written direction:

> We have never had any shop rules printed. There is a general understanding that ten hours constitute a day's work and that the hands are expected to do a day's work if they get paid a day's pay. Each department is under the direction of a foreman, in whom we trust and who sees that the hands are industrious and attend their business. If they do not do it, he sends them off and gets others . . . . We do not think printed rules amount to anything unless there is somebody around constantly to enforce them and if such a person is around, printed forms can be dispensed with.[1]

As localized businesses grew into industries, and particularly with the advent of Scientific Management, the tides changed. Attention began to focus on documentation—for communication with customers, directions to workers, and tracking and trending of business performance. This change

The uses and benefits of e-mail

- Greater speed and flexibility
- Denser connectivity
- Flatter hierarchies/broader participation
- More teamwork
- Greater boundary permeability

A history of the great links

- The infancy of on-line style
- A lesson in adaptation

E-mail: the issues

- The empty auditorium
- The half-empty cup
- The overflowing bank
- The full-court press

Doing e-mail right—the lessons

also corresponded with the growth of literacy in America: Functional literacy was the "direct result of the growth of bureaucracy and the need to understand the increasing number of documents which that bureaucracy produced."[2] Continuing with Scoville Company as our example, the company increased its staffing from 400 in 1876 to 4000 in 1914. Accompanying the growth in size came a growth in the use and volume of communication. In 1879, Scoville used a single bound volume (known as a press book) to maintain its correspondence with each of its branch sites. By 1880, it needed five press books, and by the year 1900, that number had doubled to 10.

The growth in paperwork began to change the whole approach to office administration. Even the simple office desk was transformed to accommodate the growing need to manage paper. While earlier offices might have made due with simple, unadorned desks, the office of the late nineteenth century was given over either to "pigeonholes," storage systems that provided neat, segregated compartments for various forms and incoming correspondence, or to "secretarial" desks, imposing pieces of patented furniture that—as their advertisements claimed—incorporated "everything that ingenuity can suggest or devise to facilitate desk labor."[3]

By 1913, E.A. Cope, an expert on filing systems, noted that with the change from an oral to a written tradition, the entire communication structure in business was evolving. Paperwork was quickly becoming the foundation on which the industrial world was being built:

A large business in the modern sense means an enormously increased specialization, a division into departments, a sub-division of work. It means also an enormous multiplication of the quantity of business papers, and a multiplication of the kinds and varieties of business papers. Special records not needed in the comparatively small businesses of the past are necessary to enable the details of the great businesses of the present to be traced, to enable the work of departments to be supervised and kept under effective control, and thus to prevent the doings of the huge modern concern from getting out of hand.[4]

Today, we take all this for granted. Written communication is as much a part of everyday interaction in business as is oral communication. Yet, like business itself, the evolution in written communication is far from over. The early transitions to a reliance on written communication started first with the business letter, a product that descended directly from the practice of classical rhetoric. Scientific Management introduced the memo, a corresponding means for conducting and coordinating internal activities. To these two enduring forms of written communication, the latter part of the twentieth century introduced e-mail, both a form and a capability that has challenged not only the role of the memo and the letter, but also the use of the office telephone, one-on-one meetings, and business meetings as well.

We need, however, to make certain we do not let the novelty or dynamics of the tools do our talking—or our writing. We need to take the time to be sure that our delivery mechanisms fit the purpose, audience, and circumstance of our communications. To begin to understand the benefits, limitations, and applications of the various written communication forms, in this chapter, we examine the unique demands, expectations, and potential pitfalls of e-mail. In the following chapters, we will deal with memos and letters. Let's begin our discussion of e-mail with an examination of its benefits and historical context.

THE USES AND THE BENEFITS OF E-MAIL

Although there have been innumerable explanations of the value of e-mail, one of the best summations was provided in the journal *American Archivist*: "The union of abilities to create, access, interact with, store, display and disseminate information by means of linked individual workstations provides the basis for professional changes in the way organizations work."[5] Enabled by e-mail, these changes, the author explains, can be summarized in the form of five trends: 1) greater speed and flexibility, 2) denser connectivity, 3) flatter hierarchies/broader participation, 4) greater teamwork, and 5) greater boundary permeability.

GREATER SPEED AND FLEXIBILITY

There is no shortage of impressive-sounding illustrations of the speed of on-line communications. The entire works of Shakespeare, or the Bible, or the *Encyclopaedia Britannica* can be transmitted in seconds. Equally impressive is the speed of interaction. The time between sending an initial message and the expected response continues to shrink. In the days of using paper as the primary communication form, replies were expected on the order of days (for internally distributed memos) to weeks (for externally distributed letters). With e-mail, often we have not had time to turn away from the computer before a response is received. As an example, one study of some 75,000 e-mail messages conducted at Rand Corporation, one of America's leading think tanks, showed that approximately 40% (31,000) of the messages were replies. Of these replies, more than 10% were received within 15 minutes of sending of the original message; approximately 30% of the replies were received within an hour (Table10.1).[6]

10.1 RESPONSE TIMES FOR E-MAIL REPLIES

Hours From Receipt	E-Mail Replies
0.25	4183
0.5	6844
1.0	9853
1.5	12,066
2.0	13,608
4.0	17,205
8.0	19,897
12.0	20,957

Source: Reprinted from *American Archivist* by permission of the Society of American Archivists

DENSER CONNECTIVITY

The number of people with access to e-mail is growing so rapidly that quoting any number is likely to be instantaneously wrong. However, some facts about e-mail usage are clearly indicative of its ubiquitous application. The American Messaging Association reports that as of late 2001, more than 100 million people used e-mail within a 24-hour period. Fifty-seven percent of American business executives replied to messages using e-mail. Forrester Research adds another dimension to the equation, advising there were 3 billion commercial messages in 1997 versus 250 billion anticipated in 2002.[7] The number of people interacting using e-mail is no longer limited to the small, intimate circle of computer-savvy technicians or to the immediate coworkers within a given company, industry, or locale. As Table 10.2 illustrates, even with communications largely within the same corporation, equivalent communications would have occurred only half as frequently, and among less than half the number of people had it not been for e-mail.[8] Adding to this insight, Table 10.3 makes clear that almost 40% of the communication exchanges would not have taken place at all had an e-mail network not existed. [9]

FLATTER HIERARCHIES/BROADER PARTICIPATION

As the *American Archivist* article notes: "New electronic media can help overcome not only barriers of space and time but also constraints on group involvement typically imposed by status." E-mail tends to have positive effects on participation and cohesion. This participation is implicit in the numbers represented in Tables 10.2 and 10.3. The cohesion is best understood as a consequence of the next benefit—teamwork.

10.2	CHARACTERISTICS OF E-MAIL COMMUNICATION PARTNERS	
	Characteristic	Percentages
How well is recipient known to sender	Well	23
	Somewhat	30
	Not at all	47
Physical distance between sender and recipient	In same location/building	43
	In same city	25
	Further away	32
Organizational relationship between sender and recipient	Work in same department/organization	58
	Work in same company	31
	No corporate relationship	11

10.3	PROBABILITY THAT COMMUNICATION WOULD NOT OCCUR WITHOUT E-MAIL
Messages characteristics	**Probability that message would not have been sent (%)**
Total sample	40
People who do not know one another	18
People who only communicate electronically	28
People who are spatially distant	28
People who are organizationally distant	27

MORE TEAMWORK

Speaking of teamwork, the authors of the *American Archivist* article summarized: "The tendency to rely more on teams to get work accomplished is closely related to the trend of flatter hierarchies and broader participation." With the steady increase in project- and process-oriented assignments, hierarchical units are regularly complemented by teams that cross functional and departmental lines. At the same time, these teams are reconfigurable over time, responding to changing and developing needs of the organization. With this dynamic situation, individual employees may belong to more than one team—directly contributing to flatter hierarchies, broader participation, and more teamwork. This teamwork, in turn, also creates a broadened permeability.

GREATER BOUNDARY PERMEABILITY

As the preceding discussion suggests, electronic communication "makes boundaries more permeable." Explaining this point, the authors note: "Work teams can cross internal unit boundaries even when the units are in geographically disparate divisions of an organization."[10]

Approaching the changes promoted by e-mail from a slightly different vantage point, another study concludes that there are five categories of "new communications," interactions that electronic mail makes significantly less costly for industry:

1. New communications between people who do not know one another
2. New communications between people who do not communicate other than by electronic mail
3. New communications between people who are spatially distant
4. New communications between people who are organizationally distant
5. New communications sent and received through distribution lists[11]

A HISTORY OF THE GREAT LINKS

Undeniably, e-mail has had profound effects on the dynamics of business. These changes, in turn, have inspired discussion of new behaviors, new etiquette, and new protocols. Yet, the new medium has numerous challenges and potential pitfalls not announced in these analyses. Rather, there are a variety of issues associated with the business use of e-mail: issues of style, legal issues, application issues, and utilization issues that must be considered by users. To put them all in perspective, let's take a moment first to understand how e-mail fits within the overall evolution of business communication.

As we shall see, the benefits attributed to e-mail are not new as important business values. Although the digital age has offered us a new means to accomplish these business goals, interest in speed, connectivity, participation, teaming, and interaction regarding business communication is not something that sprang into existence with e-mail. Only the means of achieving those aims has changed. The effort to introduce these capabilities is more correctly a story that parallels the evolution of commercial enterprise than it is a modern-day phenomenon.

The earliest "and very possibly, the most fundamental" innovation in American communication was the system designed to deliver mail. Confined to the eastern seaboard until around 1790, mail service was intended to provide a reliable means of making time-sensitive information about commerce and public affairs available to business. By 1828, the service "had become ubiquitous throughout much of the vast trans-Appalachian hinterland." Well in advance of the telegraph, the United States experienced its first communications revolution. The magnitude of the impact on daily life and business was effectively captured by Francis Lieber, a political theorist, who, in 1832, declared that the postal system deserved to be ranked alongside the printing press and the mariner's compass as "one of the most effective elements of civilization."[12]

Shortly thereafter, in 1837, Alex de Tocqueville reinforced this conclusion, referring to the American postal system as a "great link between minds," one that penetrated the "heart of this wilderness." During this same time frame, the postal system had been designated a government agency by President Jackson and consisted of twice as many post offices as in Great Britain and five times as many as existed in France. It was, as political theorist Benjamin Rush had explained some years before, the "true non-electric wire of government," the only means of "conveying light and heat to every individual in the federal commonwealth."[13]

Within a relatively short period of time, the postal system was to be joined by the first communications system to be based on electricity—the electric telegraph. As early as the 1770s, people conceived of the concept that electricity flowing through wires could be used to convey information. As described in the journal *American Heritage:* "The first system actually built, in Geneva in 1774, used one wire for each letter of the alphabet. The current would charge a pith ball with static electricity, which in turn would attract a bell, ringing it. This alphabetical carillon actually worked, after a fashion, but it was hardly a practical system."[14]

While the electrical challenges were being worked out in the electric telegraph, Claude Chappe created his own variation, the optical telegraph. Put into use by Napoleon, who used the device to coordinate military campaigns, Chappe's invention was a kind of land-based semaphore, consisting of a chain of towers located an average of 10 miles apart. Human relays, known as "mutes," manipulated a pair of shutters; the positions of the shutters told the message. Placing the optical telegraph in some rather peculiar company, one author suggests "along with the guillotine, it [the optical telegraph] deserved to be remembered as one of the principal technological innovations spawned by the French Revolution."[15] The obvious drawbacks of the system (for example, its reliance on clear, sunny days, and the probability of error associated with the successive copying and repeating of the message) limited its fame and endurance. Yet, Chappe's invention offered one enduring footnote on the history of communication: it was Chappe who coined the term *telegraph* (which means "writing at a distance").

While the optical telegraph had limited practical application, the electrical telegraph merely had to overcome a series of technical problems on its way to becoming the backbone of nineteenth-century communications. So, when Joseph Henry, a professor at the College of New Jersey (now Princeton), helped his friend Samuel Morse to resolve these electrical issues (such as the use of electrical relays to maintain the strength of the electrical signal), the electrical telegraph was officially born. By the time Alexander Graham Bell's "electrical toy," the telephone, was invented in 1876, the United States was crisscrossed by 214,000 miles of telegraph wire delivering 31,703,181 telegrams through 8500 telegraph offices.[16] Specialized telegraphs, such as the fire-alarm telegraph that signaled the location of fires, printing telegraphs, and telegraphs that served the special interests of investment houses and brokerage firms, were an accepted part of the American business landscape. (Interestingly, Bell discovered the telephone while working on a harmonic or musical telegraph intended to permit 30 or 40 messages to be sent simultaneously over the same wire.)[17]

The transition from a culture that relied either on word of mouth or formal letters to one that employed a mediated communication system brought about changes and challenges not altogether different from those faced by contemporary business's transition from a paper-based existence to its current heavy reliance on e-mail. In the broadest sense, these changes fell into two categories: style and application. Before we turn to the contemporary e-mail equivalents, we will look at these changes because they help explain our current challenges.

THE INFANCY OF ON-LINE STYLE

Initially, the plan for the telegraph was that it would use a cumbersome dictionary to translate words and phrases into a numeric format. These numeric notations would then be transmitted over the wires. Later, under the coaxing of his assistant, Alfred Vail, Morse changed to the dot and dash system for which he is known. One immediate consequence of the letter-by-letter transmission was that the longer the message, the lengthier the transmission process, and the more costly the communication. Accordingly, the inherent limitations of the system led inevitably to a spare, immediate style of writing. The spare style, which began as a strained accommodation to the telegraph, was soon codified when the press began extensive use of the telegraph as a principal means of getting stories back to their publishers.

Prior to the use of the telegraph, news stories could take weeks or months to arrive—especially for international stories. With the arrival of the telegraph, newspapers ran stories the next day. However, two factors drove journalistic style away from an ornate, narrative style to a more bare-bones approach. The first was simply cost. Forced to pay by the word, writers and editors began to demand attention to a concise—rather than an embellished—mode of discourse. Second, with the growth of wire services, journalists (particularly freelancing writers) strove to make stories marketable to papers throughout the country. Rather than responding to the unique, idiosyncratic voices of individual editors and newspapers, writers wanted to expand the potential marketability of every story they wrote. Selling a story once was good; selling it a dozen times was a way to make real money. This migration to a concise style gained literary currency when former *Toronto Star* correspondent Ernest Hemingway turned to fiction. In a land of accents, the telegraph represented a mediated norm, a common language among professional writers.[18]

Although the argument is questionable, some critics assert that telegram writing actually reached the level of an art form. "Telegram writing requires more discipline than writing haiku. Haiku writes most everything in seventeen syllables. The telegram, as an art form, demands that the writer use only fifteen words, Western Union's basic telegram rate."[19] Continuing this argument, the author concludes that "Morse's deep desire for simplicity of language was a reaction against the flowery New England transcendentalists who dominated the literary Establishment . . . . Morse loved the brief, the clear, the bold, a style epitomized in his code"[20] (Figure 10.1).

Whether having constructed the notation system with a certain stylistic prejudice in mind or not, Morse and his invention had proven that a communication delivery system could force people to adapt their writing styles. Important to our understanding of the allure of e-mail, for the first time, an on-line system had demonstrated how style might become tailored to and held captive by the means of communication.

A LESSON IN ADAPTATION

Samuel Morse had envisioned his invention as an additional mode for accomplishing the same principal objective for which the postal system had been established:

FIGURE 10.1

The Terse and Often Witty Language of the Telegram

An exchange between the playwright, George Bernard Shaw, and the Prime Minister of England, Winston Churchill:

Shaw: Have reserved two tickets for my first night. Come and bring a friend, if you have one.

Churchill: Impossible to come to first night. Will come to second night, if you have one.

"to wit: The rapid and regular transmission of intelligence."[21] However, much of this grand projection was overwhelmed by what one historian referred to as "a mad era of methodless enthusiasm."[22] Anyone who wanted to could start a telegraph company, and anyone with the money could be part of the newly wired nation. As a direct consequence of this "methodless enthusiasm," letter writing diminished in direct proportion to the increase in telegram traffic.

Clearly, the millions of telegrams sent each year were not focused on the enlightenment of the populace or even with what might ordinarily be conceded as a "regular transmission of intelligence." In fact, every manner of subject was in the air. While numerous new enthusiasts championed the expanding democratization being accomplished by the telegram as it intruded itself on all manner of business and common life, some Americans remained skeptical about the invention's implications. Speaking for the wireless minority, Henry David Thoreau said, "We are in great haste to construct a magnetic telegraph from Maine to Texas, but Maine and Texas, it may be, have nothing important to communicate."[23]

The great volume of telegrams, as Thoreau might have argued, added credibility to the earlier assertions made in the Federalist Papers (No. 10) by James Madison: that poor rather than voluminous communications might be a greater guarantee of political stability. As Madison had envisioned it, the movement from selected information access to a seemingly unbridled access to limitless volumes of information had its own unique perils. At the same time, the telegraph was providing a "great link" among the populace, promoting a "methodless enthusiasm" among the entrepreneurs, and contributing to a disquieting of a peaceful society. The telegraph was inspiring the "electric" opening into the portals of the world's information and—as claimed by the communication theorist, Marshall McLuhan—ushering in an "age of anxiety."[24] A balance was needed between an ability to disseminate information and a reasoned and disciplined rationale for that dissemination.

It is interesting, and not completely coincidental, that with the end of the telegraph's history (approximately 1970), e-mail's history begins. While the telegraph introduced the world to an electronic form of communication, e-mail furthered the destiny, providing the speed, flexibility, and connectivity only aspired to by the advocates of the electric telegraph. (Figure 10.2 lists select highlights in the history of e-mail.)

Yet, while e-mail bettered the telegraph's abilities, it also amplified the potential issues—especially as they apply within a business context. Where it was argued the telegram required more "discipline" in writing, e-mail has promoted greater informality; where the telegraph allowed some increased connectivity, e-mail has created an avalanche of interactions. E-mail has also muddied the waters between the "transfer of intelligence" and the "discipline of decision-making."

Last, where the telegram had profound effects on conducting business, e-mail has unveiled a host of unanticipated (and sometime unintentional) liabilities for users and their employers. These issues of style and adaptation, along with the lessons learned by American business through its use of the telegraph, help illuminate some of the current issues faced when using e-mail. In their contemporary form, these issues might be understood as representing four conditions:

1. The empty auditorium
2. The half-empty cup
3. The overflowing bank
4. The full court press.

FIGURE 10.2

Great Moments in
E-mail History

	First e-mail sent: from UCLA to Stanford. Computer immediately crashes. (1969)
1970s	Ray Tomlinson, working on Arapanet (Advanced Research Projects Agency Network) creates first messaging software. Tells colleagues "Don't tell anyone. This isn't what we're supposed to be working on." (1971)
	Tomlinson's first message sent. Content forgotten. Tomlinson later explains that he didn't think his invention was particularly momentous. (1971)
	Tomlinson selects @ for addresses "I got there first, so I got to choose the punctuation I wanted." (1972)
	First international e-mail sent. Arapanet user notifies colleagues he will be delayed owing to the delivery of a new baby. (1973)
	Queen Elizabeth II becomes the first head of state to send e-mail. (1976)
	Jimmy Carter and Walter Mondale use e-mail on a daily basis to coordinate itineraries during their presidential campaign. (1976)
	Kevin MacKensie invents emoticons. Unintentionally also sparks first case of flaming with suggestion that " -)" be used to indicate "tongue in cheek." (1979)
1980s	Colby College in Maine becomes one of the first universities to assign e-mail accounts to every student. (1983)
	Recovered e-mails, supposedly deleted by Oliver North, serve as powerful evidence in proving his guilt in the Iran-Contra hearings. (1986)
	Attempting to clarify corporate and e-mail user rights, Congress passes the Electronic Communications Privacy Act. (1986)
	Supreme Court acknowledges that Fourth Amendment rights extend to use of e-mail. (1987)
1990s	Radio gives e-mail a boost; National Public Radio reads its first e-mails from listeners. (1993)
	Advertising green-card services, Arizona law firm, Canter & Siegel, introduces the world not only to on-line legal aid—but also to spamming. (1994)
	Advertising their displeasure, Cleveland Browns fans inundate the media, politicians, and the NFL with 2 million e-mail messages protesting the team's relocation to Baltimore. (1996)
	Confronted with his recovered e-mail during the course of Microsoft antitrust trial, Bill Gates disavows recollection of his e-mail inquiry: "Do we have a plan . . . to undermine Sun?" (1998)
	TV gives e-mail a boost: Featured on Ally McBeal, the "dancing baby" becomes the most forwarded e-mail feature. (1998)
	100+ million estimated users in any 24-hour period. (2001)
	Annual number of e-mail messages estimated in excess of 250 billion. (2002)

E-MAIL: THE ISSUES

We have all heard the horror stories about the employee who inadvertently sends an e-mail message about some intimately personal subject to a distribution of hundreds, or of the college president who unintentionally makes his personal business the substance of every faculty conversation on campus (Figure 10.3).

FIGURE 10.3

Whoops!

IT WAS EARLY MORNING when Warrick L. Carter, the president of Columbia College Chicago, sent a mortgage lender an e-mail message detailing his financial problems and divorce settlement. Rife with grammatical and spelling errors, the message also revealed that he had been laid off from his previous job—something students and professors didn't know.

What Mr. Carter didn't know was that when he clicked the "send" button on January 11, he fired off the message to all 1,100 faculty members at the college—and every staffer as well.

Mr. Carter thought the message would reach only a loan officer at a Georgia bank, so he candidly discussed glitches in his credit report. "The entries during late 1998 and early 1999 were the result on my being laid off from the Disney Company," Mr. Carter wrote.

Students and professors, however, had been told that Mr. Carter stepped down as Disney's director of entertainment arts to assume the college presidency, in 2000. "He misrepresented himself to the faculty and the college community," said Amber Holst, editor of the student newspaper, *The Columbia Chronicle*.

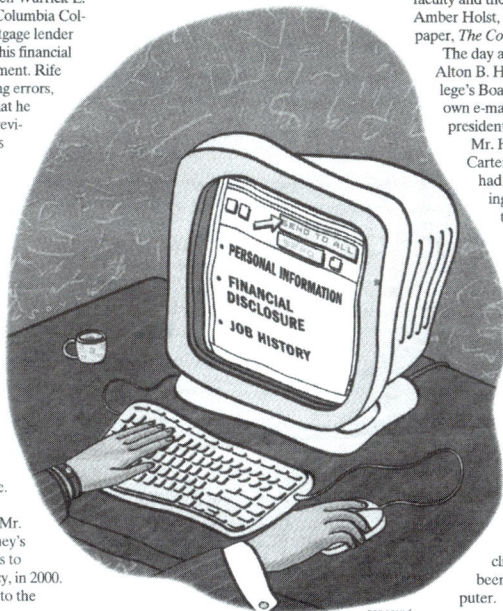

The day after Mr. Carter's blunder, Alton B. Harris, chairman of the college's Board of Trustees, sent out his own e-mail message to defend the president.

Mr. Harris explained that Mr. Carter's job changes at Disney had been prompted by the closing of one unit, and stressed that the president had "openly and candidly" discussed the situation with Mr. Harris before being hired.

One professor, reached in her office during the college's term break, expressed anger at the attention the gaffe had drawn and said it was irrelevant.

Mr. Carter agreed, insisting that the blunder was a "non-issue" at Columbia College. "We've moved on."

As has the send-to-all icon that he mistakenly clicked, said Mr. Carter: It's been removed from his computer.   —JENNIFER JACOBSON

BOB SOULÉ

Source: Copyright 2001, *The Chronicle of Higher Education.* Reprinted with permission.

Certainly, the technology of e-mail can, if we don't pay attention, cast us into an embarrassing light. However, in the larger scheme of business communication, the technology is not what should concern us most. We should be paying attention to the e-mail problems we make for ourselves.

THE EMPTY AUDITORIUM

Although the brevity and conciseness of telegrams may have fostered a spartan style of writing, e-mail sparks the opposite response. The isolation of computer-mediated writing often brings out writing traits that are not well suited for the professional business environment. In an apt image for the phenomenon, a member of a computer conference offered the following reflection about her on-line e-mail experience: "I feel that I am essentially standing up in front of an empty auditorium."[25]

Expanding on the concept that e-mail is more monologue than dialogue, more self-reflective than audience-oriented, one author explains that on-line we "often find neither discussions nor conversations, but, a set of asocial monologues." As he goes on to point out, although people are linked by a network, each is "writing energetically, all writing simultaneously, and no one reading and responding very much—not listening as much as they would in a face-to-face, spoken encounter." The result is what he calls "divergent monologue, rather than convergent conversation." The consequence of this "asocial" communication is that "we have created a context that isolates the individual participant, masking the essentially social nature of human discourse."[26]

Our previous discussion about audience in Chapter 2 warned us of the inappropriateness and the possible consequences of acting as if business communication is a monologue—of acting as if we are "in front of an empty auditorium."

When this mistake is made while using e-mail, we see evidence of three types of problems: flaming, self-absorption, and inappropriate familiarity.

FLAMING. Flaming is the e-mail equivalent of rude and offensive behavior. E-mail is especially susceptible to flaming because we seem readily inclined to forget the real people to whom we are writing when actively engaged by our computer. As numerous studies have shown, without the cues associated with physical interaction among people, writers become less concerned with what others will think, which presumably leads to uninhibited behavior.

Individuals reported experiencing rude behavior an average of four times a month in their face-to-face encounters. Flaming occurred an average of 33 times a month in the e-mail they received.[27] The types of e-mail behaviors people reported included:

- Remarks containing swear words, insults, and personal name calling
- Ranting and raving
- Impolite and improper statements: flirting, exclamations, expressions of personal feelings toward others
- Direct attacks, either on individuals or work groups, including disparaging comments about the organization or company.[28] (Figure 10.4 is an illustration of flaming.).[29]

Although swearing, profanity, and disloyalty may not be common elements of business e-mail, 33 instances a month certainly constitutes more than a petty annoyance. Further, flaming might also be understood to be something more than messages with explicit cursing. Sometimes it may be understood as an out-of-character message that seemingly conveys an inappropriate level of antagonism or animosity.

Physical interactions between individuals in business establish an implicit norm of behavior. For example, lengthy experience with a particular manager may establish an opinion that the individual is polite and personable. The expectation is readily transferred to interaction via e-mail. E-mail communications, like face-to-face interactions, are assumed to proceed within the established character of the relationship. When, instead of a cordial response, we receive a terse, chiding e-mail from the manager described above, it may invoke an intense emotional response, akin to having received a flaming e-mail.

FIGURE 10.4	
A Flaming E-Mail	Date: 26 Apr 19:35 EDT (Tuesday) From: Subject: That which is TRULY MONSTROUS To: [Product] Interest.pa It's great to worry about fine points, but I think we should concentrate on getting rid of those aspects of [product] which are TRULY MONSTROUS to the native user (such as yours truly). I had to ask about three people to figure out how to get the @#$%*ing insertion point beyond a graphics frame, the answer, it appears, is some incredibly arcane nonsense about show structure, select after anchor, and repaginate. WHY CAN'T I JUST POINT THE BLOODY MOUSE BELOW A GRAPHICS FRAME AND GET AN INSERTION POINT?

Source: Reprinted by permission, L. Sproull and S. Kiesler, "Reducing social context cues: Electronic mail in organizational communication," *Management Science,* vol. 32, no. 11 (Nov. 1986). Copyright (c) 1986, the Institute for Operations Research and the Management Sciences (INFORMS), 901 Elkridge Landing Road, Suite 400, Linthicum, Maryland 21090-2909 USA

Consider how the following e-mail might be perceived: "Read your report. I expected more detail. You need to get a quality report back to me no later than tomorrow P.M." Were there an already tense relationship between sender and recipient, such a note might be seen as totally in keeping with what is expected. If, in contrast, the relationship is friendly and cordial, the same message might be quite intimidating.

The tone and abrupt style might be perceived as every bit as flaming as if profanity had been used. In fact, it may be perceived as more deeply concerning. There is no other apparent interpretation than that the boss is deeply dissatisfied with you and your work. The change in temperament may also be inferred as a change in your relationship. Unfortunately, the message may be completely innocuous, more a manifestation of the style invited by the medium. You may not be able to deduce what the correct interpretation is unless you trace a pattern of the style and tone represented in the particular individual's e-mails. Have you been flamed? Maybe, maybe not.

SELF-ABSORPTION AND UNDUE FAMILIARITY. Two other issues derive from the absence of social context. As shown in Figure 10.5, not having geographic cues (a position

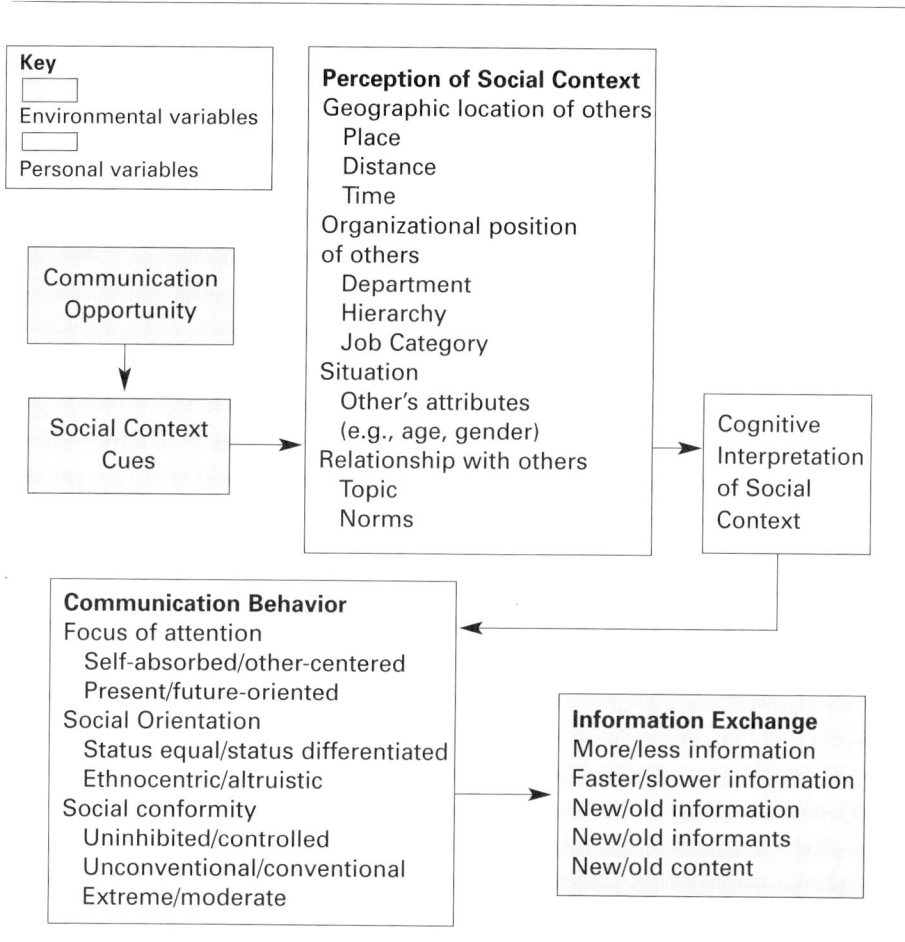

FIGURE 10.5

The Social Context of Communication

Source: Reprinted by permission, L. Sproull and S. Kiesler, "Reducing social context cues: Electronic mail in organizational communication," *Management Science*, vol. 32, no. 11 (Nov. 1986). Copyright (c) 1986, the Institute for Operations Research and the Management Sciences (INFORMS), 901 Elkridge Landing Road, Suite 400, Linthicum, Maryland 21090-2909 USA

in time and space), organizational cues (a position within the company or hierarchy), or situated cues (elements that describe the particular communication activity) may give rise to a variety of communication behaviors in conflict with the norms of business communication.[30] The first of these problems is a tendency by e-mail users to make themselves part of the discussion, turning the focus from a business case to a personal testimony or personal story. Like a television reporter who trains the camera on herself during an interview she is conducting, the misdirection both distracts from the real substance and detracts from the clarity of the message.

Often this misdirection of attention is reflected in a chatty style suggestive of talking out loud or talking to oneself. As example, consider Figure 10.6 in which an individual replies to a general message that had been distributed regarding the health effects of video display terminals. How many of us, as this woman did, would be eager to volunteer personal information to an audience of more than 3000 people?[31] In concert with the tendency to speak about ourselves is an inclination to speak to all recipients in an equally casual manner. While it can be

---

FIGURE 10.6

An Example of Self-Absorption

Date:	28 April 2:38 pm EDT (Thursday)
From:	
Subject	Re: VDTs—A NEW SOCIAL DISEASE
In-reply-to	Men's message of 17 April
	6:53 pm EDT (Wednesday)
To:	ALLNYC ALLCHI ALLPGH
Cc:	ALLSEW ALLPHL ALLNEW
Reply-to:	WOMEN.LA WOMEN.PGH

As a user of glasses only for reading (you know, the old age bit, where you could see 500 miles away, but can't read 2 inches in front of you, and your arms aren't made of elastic, therefore won't stretch far enough): I recently decided to purchase bifocals (thinking they would be better than my reading glasses) and I definitely say they are only good for reading material that you could position at the level you want. I am not of the same opinion as you in that it can be a problem only if you make it a problem. Even if you sit back and look through the top part of the lens, I find then that I'm better off without my glasses. You have to remember there are different degrees of distances farsighted people can see. My bifocals are not only entirely useless for the screen AND keyboard, but in trying to position my neck, face, head, shoulders, in order to work at the keyboard properly, I have worsened some very severe problems in my neck.

I found that my very first reading glasses (with the smallest prescription possible) were the best for working with the screen. The reason I say "were" is because I broke the frame the other day.

I sure hope someone comes up with a solution to all this. Until all this started coming over the electronic mail, I was silently suffering to myself, thinking I was the only one in such a dilemma.

Source: Reprinted by permission, L. Sproull and S. Kiesler, "Reducing social context cues: Electronic mail in organizational communication," *Management Science,* vol. 32, no. 11 (Nov. 1986). Copyright (c) 1986, the Institute for Operations Research and the Management Sciences (INFORMS), 901 Elkridge Landing Road, Suite 400, Linthicum, Maryland 21090-2909 USA

argued that such uninhibited communication is a positive democratizing agent within the world of business—the broader permeability we spoke of earlier—there is, nonetheless, some measure of distance and deference that is often warranted. For example, consider an e-mail's salutation. A boss familiar to you may find it appropriate to be addressed by her first name in an e-mail, just as she would expect were she engaged in a face-to-face conversation with you. Conversely, if we had not been previously introduced to the Senior Vice President, it might be inappropriate to begin our e-mail with an overly casual "Hi, Bob," or "Hey, Mary." Or consider the impression conveyed by the e-mail that was transmitted by a student to his professional communication instructor (Figure 10.7).

E-mail style has been the subject of considerable attention in the literature. Generally, the warnings show the need to maintain a more deliberate, more polite tone. Although you are employing a computer-mediated approach to communication, you need to focus on a human audience. Typical of the proposed etiquette, or "netiquette" as it is sometimes called, are the 10 "Core Rules of Netiquette" published by Virginia Shea, a leading authority on on-line style (Figure 10.8).[32]

Lapses into the overly familiar style are often reflective of a lack of attention. The computer, along with the perceived informality of e-mail, can promote a certain inattention to grammar and format. More importantly, this lack of respect for the basic conventions of writing may also be seen as an implicit disrespect for

---

Date: January 22, 11:40 EDT (Thursday)
From:
Subject   Prof Communication 345

Dear professor:

My name is Don and I'm the student who had to leave earl on last Thursday night. I understand from some of the students in clas that we have an assignment that is due o Thursday and you took up the other assignment that were due. I had with me my assignment and I was wonder if it was possible could you seen me the work as an attachment.

Thanks in advance.

Don

FIGURE 10.7

Making the Wrong Impression

Rule 1.   Remember the human—never forget that the person reading your mail or posting is, indeed, a person, with feelings that can be hurt.
Rule 2.   Adhere to the same standards of behavior on-line that you follow in real life.
Rule 3.   Know where you are in cyberspace.
Rule 4.   Respect other people's time and bandwidth.
Rule 5.   Make yourself look good on-line.
Rule 6.   Share expert knowledge.
Rule 7.   Help keep flame wars under control.
Rule 8.   Respect other people's privacy.
Rule 9.   Don't abuse your power.
Rule 10. Be forgiving of other people's mistakes.

FIGURE 10.8

Core Rules of Netiquette

the audience. This conclusion is reinforced by the fact that the majority of the 10 most common mistakes people make in business e-mail are not a function of the writer's inabilities. Therefore, the errors may be assumed as a measure of the writer's implicit disrespect for the audience:

- Unclear subject line
- Poor greeting (or none at all)
- Unfamiliar abbreviations
- Unnecessary copies (CCs)
- Sloppy grammar, spelling, and punctuation
- All caps in the message
- No closing or sign-off
- Rambling, unformatted message
- Unfriendly tone
- No clear request for action.[33]

Two further illustrations of the degrees of unrivaled familiarity are reflected in the use of emoticons, the face-like symbols used to convey the emotional interpretation of what has been said, and the use of abbreviated slang. Would you be equally inclined to stamp "happy faces" on an internal memo to your boss? Or would you interject a stage direction like "laugh out loud" in the middle of a hallway conversation with your corporate vice president? As we discussed earlier, we must be careful not to mistake jargon (in this case, inappropriate use of abbreviations and emoticons) for clear writing (Table 10.4).

TABLE

10.4 IMAGES OF E-MAIL FAMILIARITY

Abbreviations	Emoticons
BTW = by the way	(= -) = sender is happy
FAQ = frequently asked questions	(:-< = sender is unhappy
FYI = for your information	(:~ = message is tongue in cheek
IMHO = in my honest opinion	(B-) = sender wears glasses
JTYLTK = just thought you'd like to know	(:-D = sender laughing
LOL = laugh out loud	(;-) = sender winking
PLS = please	(:-@ = sender screaming
RFC = request for comment	(>:-> = a devilish remark
RTM = read the manual	(>:-<) = sender very mad
TTYL = talk to you later	(%-) = sender confused
YR = your	

Neither should we forget about the overall image of ourselves we transmit along with our e-mail. Writing in *The New York Times,* Naomi Baron, author of *How Written English Evolved and Where It's Heading,* offered valuable insights into how informality of "e-style" reveals much about who we are and "whether we care about people's responses." Speaking of the "easy disregard for written standards," Baron notes: "Constantly we reveal who we are (or wish to be) through our speech and writing. This is how we create our 'public face.' . . . E-mail encourages communication where conventions and public face seem to matter little."[34] In business, we can't risk allowing flaming, inappropriately informal advances, and inattention to style and business convention to tarnish our public face—the images we wish to portray of ourselves as serious, focused, and respectful professionals. To this end, we might do well to keep in mind the conclusions reached in one of the earliest analyses of the need for a formal etiquette when using e-mail.

Barely a decade after e-mail's inception, the Rand Corporation recognized the seriousness of maintaining certain rules of behavior when communicating via e-mail (Figure 10.9). Sandwiched between their reports on the *R&D Process and Technological Innovations in the Chinese Industrial System* and the report on *Contingency Plans for War in Western Europe:1920–1940,* the Rand Corporation issued a report entitled *Toward an Ethics and Etiquette for Electronic Mail.* This report, prepared for the National Science Foundation, cited rules "found useful for electronic mail." The conclusion reached in 1985 is every bit as pertinent today.

Electronic mail is in its infancy, as is our understanding of it. We have collected some guidelines that seem to point in proper directions, and have

FIGURE 10.9

The Rand "Rules of Behavior"

In sending messages
- Create single-subject messages whenever possible.
- Assume that any message you send is permanent.
- Have in mind a model of your intended audience.
- Keep the list of recipients and Cc:s to a minimum.
- Separate opinion from non-opinion, and clearly label each.
- If you must express emotion in a message, clearly label it.
- Other content labels are useful.
- Think about the level of formality you put in a message.
- Identify yourself and your affiliations clearly.
- Do not insult or criticize third parties without giving them a chance to respond.

In receiving and responding to messages
- If you receive a message intended for another person, don't just ignore it.
- Avoid responding while emotional.
- If a message generates emotions, look again.
- Assume the honesty and competence of the sender.
- Try to separate opinion from non-opinion while reading a message, so you can respond appropriately.
- Consider whom you should respond to.
- Consider alternative media.
- Avoid irrelevancies.

In acting as a coordinator/leader of an interest group
- Perform relevant groupings.
- Use uniform packaging, especially in the "Subject:" line.
- Exercise reasonable editorship.
- Timeliness is important.

personally used them in our own use of the medium. Many of them appear to be common sense in a new guise, but they are included because we've seen them violated too often to ignore. Electronic mail and messaging systems have novel characteristics that will lead toward their becoming a key, even dominant, communication medium in the coming decades. Understanding the unique attributes of this medium, and their effect on users, will help us all to avoid unwanted side-effects while obtaining the benefits from this new and important means of communication.[35]

THE HALF-EMPTY CUP

As one executive quoted in *The New York Times* said, e-mail is "a phenomenal way to communicate trivia."[36] Paralleling the informality of style, writers often act as if e-mail sanctions issuing communications that are neither complete nor responsive to business interests. As one author notes, "Writer's block has never been a problem on the net . . . . Possessed of the mistaken but reassuring notion that paperless communication is not really communication at all, e-mail users shed the self-conscious character of their other lives in writing. People who would normally labor over multiple versions of any document instead fire off quick, serviceable first drafts . . . ."[37] Like the restraint needed to maintain a businesslike style, writers also need restraint to avoid substituting these "quick, serviceable first drafts" for final products; to avoid turning corporate computer resources into the twenty-first century equivalent of gossiping at the water cooler; and to avoid using the send button to prematurely distribute an incomplete communication.

The many variants of this activity represent the "half-empty cup": 1) using e-mail to involve colleagues in your business obligations, 2) intermingling work and nonwork in your e-mail, and 3) manufacturing an open-ended e-mail discussion.

The first of these three forms of premature dissemination involves the distribution of incomplete work. As we discussed in Chapter 1, your obligation as communicator is to identify, define, and respond to the multiple tasks associated with the assignment you have been given. Transmitting an ill-thought response, a draft that clearly is lacking, or a poorly constructed e-mail to your boss (or even indirectly to those who may have some influence on your circumstances) is not a prudent business action. A common variation of this issue is the "look-at-me" syndrome, which is made worse by e-mail.

Eager to show how smart you are, you send an e-mail in which you implicitly solicit feedback, suggestions, and reviews from colleagues. However, possibly because of time constraints, but more likely because you really didn't want the input to begin with, you discard any advice or recommendations you receive. Like the boy who cried wolf, you can only do this trick so many times before people catch on and, suspecting your real motives, they simply ignore your requests for assistance.

For example, Figure 10.10 shows a series of e-mails. The first e-mail, which arrived the day before the Fourth of July weekend, asks for assistance in reviewing a technical paper. The second e-mail, essentially saying that the first should be ignored, arrived just after the weekend, but not before the colleague had begun the review. Whether the speed of e-mail allowed premature delivery of the product or the sender was simply fishing for accolades for her work is not the most important issue here. Since either reason for sending the e-mail is inappropriate, the only sure thing is that the next time this individual requests support from her colleague, the support will be a bit slower in coming and considerably less enthusiastic.

FIGURE 10.10

The "Look-at-Me"
E-Mail

E-Mail received Thursday, July 3
Attached is the paper and comments we received from the vice-chair of the session. She was not familiar with last year's paper. She and I subsequently had a phone conversation to discuss the relationship between last year and this year. She seemed to finally conclude that maybe what we need was some more context. I made some changes in the introduction and the conclusion to provide additional context to link this paper with last year's paper. Please provide a comprehensive review to determine if you think we have sufficiently addressed the reviewer's comments and if the design features are sufficiently clear. Have a great Fourth of July. (See attached file)

E-Mail received Tuesday, July 8
Hope you had a good Fourth of July. We got caught with the schedule demon so here's a copy of the paper we submitted.

Talk with you later.

Thanks.

A second category of inappropriate colleague involvement refers to use of e-mail for nonwork purposes. The informalities and inexpensive nature of e-mail make it easy to shade the boundaries between personal and business activities, and equally easy for users to rationalize its nonwork usage. However, the rationalizations generally are inconsistent with business's perspective. The company pays for the computer and for your time. The company expects both—the equipment and the employees—to do the work of the company, not their own work. This disparity in perception is one of the principal reasons why a growing proportion of companies have both e-mail policies and monitoring software: to dissuade employees from nonwork use of e-mail (a related subject that we will take up shortly).

Studies regularly report that e-mail traffic is 30, 40, even 50% nonwork. (Tables 10.5 and 10.6 show results from two different studies of corporate e-mail usage.)[38] The fact that the e-mail system is the contributing factor in this license to steal time is evident in that studies also show the nonwork usage of e-mail is 6 to 7 times more frequent than nonwork usage of the telephone. Employees averaged using the phone 6 times a week for nonwork communications. This same group reported using e-mail for nonwork purposes 38 times per week.[39] In the second study, though recognizably of a very small sampling, the authors concluded approximately 50% of the e-mail messages were nonwork (with approximately another 10% representing messages of mixed work and nonwork content).[40]

TABLE 10.5 NONWORK E-MAIL TRAFFIC: AN OVERVIEW

Topic of message	Partner Unknown		Known	
	Old Info	New info	Old info	New info
Work	65	177	340	170
Nonwork	18	339	54	85

Source: Reprinted by permission, L. Sproull and S. Kiesler, "Reducing social context cues: Electronic mail in organizational communication," *Management Science,* vol. 32, no. 11 (Nov. 1986). Copyright (c) 1986, the Institute for Operations Research and the Management Sciences (INFORMS), 901 Elkridge Landing Road, Suite 400, Linthicum, Maryland 21090-2909 USA

10.6 CONTENTS OF CORPORATE E-MAIL MESSAGES

Subject	Work Related	Mix of Work and Nonwork	Nonwork
Work activities	27	2	–
Personal	–	3	6
Political	–	1	10
Outside activities	–	1	16
Jokes and other humorous materials	–	–	10
Total	27	7	42

The loss to your company in time and productivity may seem insignificant when you consider the losses associated with a single employee. However, the numbers add up quickly. You need to be mindful of what you're communicating and why. Using your company's e-mail for purposes other than work is bad etiquette and can, depending on your company's policies, be bad for your career as well.

Last is the matter of initiating or contributing to an open-ended discussion. E-mail, while a very effective vehicle for communicating information, is not nearly as strong a vehicle for decision-making. This limited applicability may be a consequence of a number of factors: the nature of electronic interaction, the lack of social context, or its displacement of roles and hierarchical relationships. Whatever the cause, instigating a lengthy set of replies and responses may not be the most efficient means of resolving a complex decision—as opposed to a meeting or face-to-face exchange.

In one study evaluating the types of media used for various tasks, business professionals indicated a strong preference for using the phone when it came to making decisions, communicating personal messages, expressing opinions, and answering questions. In contrast, less than 20% of the respondents had a preference for using e-mail for these same tasks. The lowest score recorded (12%) was in response to the advisability of using e-mail to help make decisions. E-mail was seen as the preferred method of communication when simply transmitting information: 58% found the medium useful for delivering documents; 69% (the strongest showing) favored e-mail to circulate memos.[41] (The Appendix contains the detailed results of this survey.) Interactions and decision-making are best suited to a medium where there is active exchange. Although not necessarily an "asocial monologue," in these business applications e-mail is more attuned to transmittal than to interaction or dialogue.

As business has learned, you need to make certain that you use e-mail where it is best suited and not try to make it the exclusive communication vehicle you employ. You need to tailor the means to the purposes, to make purposeful choices about how you communicate (Table 10.7).[42] Although e-mail can be used for almost any communication task, it is not an appropriate substitute for other genres when circumstances warrant interaction and decision-making.

10.7	**PREFERRED COMMUNICATION MEDIUM**

Task or kind of information		Medium of Communication*			
		Face-to-face	E-Mail	Phone	Paper
Salary news	Raise	9.4	0.3	0.2	0.1
	No raise	8.6	0.9	0.3	0.2
Recommendation	Enthusiastic	5.3	2.2	1.7	0.9
	Halfhearted	4.4	2.8	1.9	0.9
Evaluate Colleague	Compliment	5.8	3.0	1.0	0.2
	Criticize	7.1	2.1	0.7	0.1
Solve Problem	To Secretary	6.0	2.8	1.0	0.05
	To Boss	6.0	3.3	0.7	0.03
Negotiate	To Secretary	7.5	1.5	0.7	0.25
	To Boss	7.3	2.3	0.3	0.06

*Mean preference on a 10-point scale

Source: Reprinted by permission, L. Sproull and S. Kiesler, "Reducing social context cues: Electronic mail in organizational communication," *Management Science,* vol. 32, no. 11 (Nov. 1986). Copyright (c) 1986, the Institute for Operations Research and the Management Sciences (INFORMS), 901 Elkridge Landing Road, Suite 400, Linthicum, Maryland 21090-2909 USA

THE OVERFLOWING BANK

On the flip side of the ability to create and send e-mail without due personal introspection or project completion is the consequence of overwhelming the recipients' abilities to process or respond to the material. The first matter is one of sheer volume. Analogous to our discussions in Chapter 3 in which we examined the implications of attempting to measure a communication's success by the number of facts, e-mail has an equal capacity to create a competition between weight and volume. Companies that rely on e-mail need to rely on the discretion of writers to target their communications rather than to employ a shotgun approach that distributes every e-mail to everyone in the company. In an early survey of Sun Microsystems, for instance, the 13,000 employees of the company sent an average of 1.5 million messages a day. (Every employee, on average, was sending more than 100 messages a day.) Equally significant in terms of productivity is the ability of the e-mail recipients to deal with the contents of the hundreds of daily messages. For example, we might try to imagine the time demanded of the company chairman who, according to this study, received an average of 200 messages a day.[43]

At one level of concern is the associated cost. This cost is sizable even if we consider only the composing time and not the time spent by the recipients. To suggest the magnitude of the cost, let's make some assumptions about the employees at

Sun MicroSystems. If we assume that each e-mail has 10 recipients, then each employee of Sun Microsystems is composing at least 10 e-mails a day. If we assume that each message takes 15 minutes to compose and, true to averages cited in the studies, that approximately 40% of the messages are nonwork-related, then the company cost is equivalent to having almost 2000 employees (15% of the workforce) being paid to do work of no value to the company (Figure 10.11).

Beyond issues of cost, receiving the massive volume of e-mail decreases the probability that messages will get more than cursory attention. In fact, the careless distribution of e-mail has demanded novel strategies to survive what one author calls the "e-mail tsunamis."[44] As one means of attempting to stem the tide, one university dean added the following appeal to his e-mail: "Do not reply to this e-mail. Please do not say yes, do not say no. Just come if you can."[45] Other types of survival strategies are more dramatic.

Many senior personnel, executives, and public figures equate an unguarded e-mail address with a published phone number; it is a solicitation for hundreds of unwanted messages. John Sculley, ex-chairman of Apple Computers, tells his friends to fax him important messages, not to send e-mail. Bill Gates, the Chairman of Microsoft, learned this lesson the hard way. When a Microsoft employee was fired for using company e-mail to launch a campaign against Ukrainian Communists, Gates was overwhelmed with e-mail messages. Similarly, when *The New Yorker* published Gates's e-mail address as part of a profile, he immediately received more than 5000 messages. In response, Gates employed what is known in cyber slang as a "bozo filter," which redirects his e-mail to an archive where it can be retrieved if the recipient decides to look for it.[46]

Your obligation, before you make that mouse click that sends your e-mail to an entire department, institution, or corporation, is to think about the reasons you want each of those recipients to hear from you. As we noted in the discussion of the "half-empty cup," perhaps the worst reason is that you want to involve everyone in your business. Here is an example of the consequences of indiscriminate distribution.

A bright and rising manager was given the assignment to develop a new policy. The group that would be directly affected by the initiative was relatively small. To many, that would be seen as a plus, the more likely that you can create something worthwhile and get it through the necessary reviews and approvals. This manager, however, saw things differently. From his vantage point, the limited audience corresponded with low visibility. He wanted more notice, more acknowledgement for his efforts and creativity. The solution as he saw it was

---

FIGURE 10.11

E-Mail's Cost in Productivity: An Example

> **Time spent composing e-mails = 2.88 hours per day per employee**
> (1.5 million e-mail messages ÷ 10 recipients × .25 hours) ÷ 13,000 employees) = 2.88 hours per day (36% of an employee's 8-hour day!)
>
> **Time spent composing nonwork e-mails = 1.15 hours per day per employee**
> 2.88 hours/day × 40% nonwork = 1.15 hours/day
>
> **Total hours wasted per day = 14,950**
> 1.15 hours/day wasted × 13,000 employees = 14, 950 total hours
>
> **Personnel equivalent = 1868 totally nonproductive employees**
> 14,950 hours ÷ 8 hours (the average workday) = 1868 people

easy. Instead of limiting the distribution of his proposed solution to the involved few, he would add the senior management of the company as CCs. The consequence was the opposite of what he intended. Numerous contradictory comments were provided to him, the senior management expanded the circulation to members of their own staffs, and the simple resolution evolved into a major debate (something we have already learned is not the best to conduct via e-mail). The manager turned a short-term assignment into a lengthy commitment of his time and energy. The policy, once held captive to the e-mail debate, was never issued, a fact that was most visibly reflected in the manager's subsequent performance review.

Beyond the implicit invitations for everyone to join in the discussion, the question of distribution also involves being conscious of the business environment. Adding people to the distribution of an e-mail message is generally done for one of three reasons: 1) Something in the letter has direct significance to the individuals or the operations they represent. 2) The recipient is being solicited to help persuade (strong arm) someone else (most likely someone you were unable to persuade yourself). 3) You want to go on record simply to avoid any accountability should there be a problem later. The first reason is prudent. The next two are highly questionable.

As some of the testimony in Figure 10.12 makes evident, expanding the distribution may be a less than honorable—or professional—action.[47] As one article notes, undue attempts to use an indiscrete distribution "increases the likelihood of embarrassment" and, at the same time, may be viewed by those involved "as unjustifiably dirty."[48] Not only may you be perceived as negative, deceptive,

FIGURE 10.12
When Distribution Goes Bad

1. The typical tactic [for getting someone to do something] is to carbon copy the message to management. Like, "Please do this," and it's carbon copied to both your managers. Now you've got the force of the manager looking over your shoulders. I don't do it, because I consider it extremely rude. I would never do that to someone.

2. I ask someone to do something that needs to be done and they don't do it. So I keep a copy of what it is I've asked them to do. A week later it's still not done, it's been a long enough time, I send them a message saying, "Have you had a chance to do this yet?" and I tack on electronically the first message I sent them that has the first date, and if necessary I carbon their boss, so that their boss is seeing these messages. You'd be surprised how efficient that can be!

3. I'll send [my boss] a message saying "This has been done." Basically, it's to have it on record that the problem's been reported and solved. So, if someone comes back later and says, "You didn't do this," I can say, "Ha! It's here." "You keep it on record."

4. I dislike blind CCs. It's negative, deceptive. To think it's only the two or three of you discussing something, and in the meantime, there are two or three [others] in on it.

5. I think a lot of persuasion is intended when people forward copies of other people's messages to the extent, "See, I really should be ticked off about something like that. Look at what I just got." [That] kind of thing. It's that kind of persuasion technique that's usually used.

6. If you make people mad due to an e-mail message you have sent them, they can easily forward that message to someone of higher status. "You don't know that you've screwed up."

manipulating, and unprofessional, but, having instigated a round of e-mail warfare, you may be opening one of those Pandora's boxes that doesn't close easily. Because you want to assume the high road whenever possible, you should assess your motives before expanding your distribution list. Once lost, integrity and reputation are infinitely harder to retrieve than an ill-distributed e-mail.

THE FULL-COURT PRESS

Just from our discussion of the percentages of nonwork e-mail messages, it should be evident that companies, while acknowledging the many benefits, also see e-mail as a liability. In one 1999 survey of e-mail managers, 31% stated they were routinely using monitoring software; an additional 21% had plans to install monitoring software.[49] Another study in 2000 indicated 27% of major U.S. firms check employee e-mail, up from 15% in 1997. The financial services industry leads in electronic monitoring (68%), followed by business and professional services (51%), and retailers and wholesalers (47%).[50] While the percentage of companies conducting monitoring is steadily increasing, fewer companies reported that they were telling employees about their monitoring activities (91% in 1998, 84% in 1999).[51] Although the nonwork usage of e-mail represents a significant corporate expense, industry has not made this staggering investment in monitoring software merely to improve productivity.

The problem, as corporations see it, is much more than productivity. The informality in style, the chattiness, the willingness to engage in extensive "dialogue," and the self-absorption all have potential for contributing to more significant risks: defamation and harassment, disclosure of trade secrets and proprietary information, and copyright infringement. Before we examine these liabilities, it will be beneficial to place e-mail monitoring in its proper legal context.

MONITORING. Most people have at least a passing familiarity with the Fourth Amendment, which provides a guarantee of protection from unreasonable searches and seizures. All through the crime dramas on television, we see overly zealous detectives being chided by judges for infringing on the suspect's Fourth Amendment rights: for performing illegal searches and seizures of evidence. To a limited degree, this same privacy protection extends to use of e-mail. Specifically, in the case of *O'Conner* v. *Ortega* (1987), the Supreme Court recognized that a person's Fourth Amendment rights extended to e-mail: 1) if the employee has a reasonable expectation of privacy, and 2) when the "intrusion" is seen as disproportionate to the employer's needs.

In this regard, privacy rights assigned to e-mail use follow the same dictates originally associated with wiretapping as established in the 1928 *Olmsted* v. *United States* decision, and subsequently reinforced 40 years later in *Katz* v. *United States*. In those cases, the court established two important predicates: 1) "The Fourth Amendment protects people, not places." 2) A warrant is required to authorize eavesdropping or tapping into electronic communications.[52]

At the same time the Court was reaffirming privacy rights, it also acknowledged: "Individuals do not own the records maintained by someone else (e.g., a bank), and therefore the records are beyond an individual's 'zone of privacy.'" While at work, employers may monitor the telephone calls of employees, even if they are private.[53] Furthermore, in cases relating to *O'Conner* v. *Ortega*, corporations were given substantive rights to protect themselves against inappropriate use of their electronic resources.

The Court's decisions in support of both individual privacy and corporate protections gave rise to the Electronic Communications Privacy Act (ECPA).

Passed by Congress in 1986, ECPA amends the Omnibus Crime Control and Safe Streets Act, commonly referred to as the Federal Wiretapping Statute. The ECPA expands the spectrum of electronic communications to include "any transfer of signs, signals, writing, images, sounds, data, or intelligence of any nature transmitted in whole or in part by a wire, radio, electromagnetic, photo electronic or photo optical system that effects interstate or foreign commerce . . ." In addition, while reaffirming the prohibitions against unwarranted interceptions, use, or disclosure of protected electronic communications, the ECPA establishes clear guidelines on conditions that do allow employers to access their employees' e-mail.

Specifically, business can monitor communications when two condition are met: 1) An employer can access electronic communications that are readily accessible to the public (for example, messages posted on bulletin boards). 2) An employer can access an employee's e-mail where one of the parties to the communication has given prior consent. As has been established through Court rulings, consent is established when employees have been informed of monitoring practices, and a clear policy has been developed regarding the company's intent to monitor e-mail. Further, under what is known as the "service provider exception," companies that provide the e-mail system to their employees, by definition, own the rights to the e-mail generated using the system.

Where companies have established policies consistent with ECPA guidelines, essentially all e-mail "invasion of privacy suits" have been dismissed. (The Appendix contains a typical set of legal requirements that must be met for a company to have an e-mail policy consistent with ECPA.) Essentially, for an employee to prove a case of e-mail invasion of privacy, the employee must sustain an argument known as "intrusion upon seclusion," meaning that the employer's actions were so egregious as to offend an average individual.

This ownership extends to the archived collection and beyond. As established by the ECPA, if the company has established an e-mail policy and if employees have been informed of the policy, the company has the full right to monitor the activities of employees—both in the course of their daily business activities and accessing the archived collections of e-mail messages.[54] Not only does the employer's ownership include active components of the e-mail system, but it also extends to deleted messages.

The technical ability to retrieve deleted messages along with its legal significance first became highly visible during the Iran-Contra scandal, a controversy that embroiled the presidencies of Ronald Reagan and George Bush. Although America had no official involvement in an ongoing war between Iran and Iraq, a covert operation run by the National Security Council (NSC) was selling weapons to Iran in exchange for its assistance in negotiating release of American hostages being held in Lebanon by Pro-Iranian terrorists. In addition, profits from the arms sales were being illegally funneled by the NSC to rebels in Nicaragua (known as Contras) who were attempting to overthrow the Marxist government. When the activities were discovered in 1986, a lengthy congressional hearing followed.

Among the centerpieces of the evidence introduced at the Tower Commission hearings against John Poindexter, President Reagan's National Security Advisor, and Lt. Col. Oliver North, one of Poindexter's aides, were tapes used to back up the White House e-mail system. These tapes included more than 5000 e-mail messages that Poindexter and North believed they had electronically deleted from the system. In testimony before the Senate, North said, "We all sincerely believed that when we sent a PROFS [the White House e-mail system] message to another party and punched the button 'delete' that it was gone forever. Wow, were we wrong."[55] (The Appendix has the text of one of North's retrieved e-mails used in the Tower Commission hearings.)

The ability of an archived e-mail to take center stage in formal testimony has been revisited and revalidated numerous times since the Tower Commission hearing. The basic conclusion is that technology, complemented by allowances stipulated in the ECPA, gives companies control, access to, and ownership of your e-mails. Acquainted with the corporation's legal right to monitor what you're doing on e-mail, we can now turn back to a discussion of precisely what the corporation is seeking to protect itself from and against.

THE LEGAL IMPLICATIONS. Recognizing that the company has a vested interest and full legal right in monitoring your e-mail, what specifically are the high-potential problems the corporation is guarding against? We mentioned several in passing, but before we come to those, one more element needs to be brought into prospective. No one expects that a high percentage of e-mail users are going to be intentionally involved in promoting a hostile working environment, disparaging colleagues, or creating financial or legal liabilities for their companies. Yet, the odds of transgressions happening increase significantly with use of e-mail. In part, it derives from the casual behaviors we see manifest in the informal style, the increased flaming, and the increased departure from an absolute focus on matters of business. It is only a short ethical distance from the minor indiscretions of a self-absorbed conversation to a wholesale, although unintentional, lapse in professional ethics.

The ethical lapse occurs when we are not mindful of our moral compasses. (If the equivalent lapse was intentional, we would be speaking of criminal violations rather than ethical misjudgments.) Each of us must carefully guard against what may be viewed as unguarded suggestions of harassment. Although most Americans go their entire career without sensing or being on the receiving end of some form of harassment or discrimination, that doesn't mean it isn't more common than we may want to believe. Furthermore, it also does not mean that many businesspeople may not inadvertently contribute to harassment.

The underside of business is more often a matter of nuance than explicit statement—more a matter of implicit collusion than overt participation. The very reasons we value e-mail are the means of unwittingly entrapping us. The greater connectivity creates opportunity to disseminate that which should be silenced. The informal style encourages use of a less tolerant language and vocabulary that can sting at the core of a person's being. The greater boundary permeability may lead us to bend the accepted rules of basic decorum and politeness. Our baser communication instincts—as suggested in our willingness to use the system for nonwork applications or to focus attention on a colleague's unwillingness to give in to our demands—are readily amplified by e-mail. E-mail contributes to a shortening of the distance between ethical and unethical business behavior.

The unfortunate validation of these truths is that the number of cases focusing on the inappropriate use of e-mail as a vehicle for harassment, discrimination, and development of a hostile work environment continues to grow. In 1993, fewer than 35 such cases were filed; within 4 years that number had gone up more than 350% (125 cases) and has continued to rise with e-mail's popularity and the increasing sophistication of retrieval technology. In 2001, the American Management Association issued a report on workplace monitoring and surveillance. Of the several hundred companies surveyed, 10% reported having received a subpoena for employee e-mail; 15% indicated they had been involved in some form of legal action concerning employee use of e-mail or the Internet.[56]

A Closer Look at Discrimination and Harassment. A survey prepared by the FBI in 1996 and conducted by the Computer Security Institute found that 31% of 563 responding businesses "had incurred financial loss from employee misuse of the Internet, including e-mail, for sexual harassment."[57] While e-mail is less involved in the kinds of quid pro quo harassment cases in which sexual demands are tied to employment-related actions, it plays a significant role in cases where claimants have been subjected to a "hostile environment," as established in 1986, any workplace that the employee finds unpleasant or in which it is difficult for the employee to do his or her job. A short summary of a select number of high-profile cases (one for racial discrimination and three for sexual harassment) should be sufficient to suggest e-mail's potential role in both creating and providing evidence of harassment and discrimination in the workplace (Figure 10.13).[58]

Release of Confidential Information. While e-mail has increased the number of harassment and discrimination court cases, it has also made it increasingly difficult to protect the information assets of a company. As one law journal notes, because "the use of e-mail is so widespread, employers . . . need to protect trade secrets and proprietary information that could intentionally be improperly

---

FIGURE 10.13

E-Mail's Role in Discrimination and Harassment Lawsuits

In *Young* v. *State Farm Mutual Automobile Insurance Co.*, the court held that several e-mail messages discouraging the plaintiff from seeking a promotion after she filed a charge of discrimination with the EEOC supported the plaintiff's retaliation claims.

Four female employees received a settlement of $2.2 million, plus legal fees and court costs, from Chevron Corp. for sexual harassment at the Chevron Information Technology Division. While Chevron denied the charges, the women claimed among other things, to have been subjected to offensive e-mail messages. One message titled "Why Beer Is Better Than Women" listed 25 reasons, including: "beer doesn't demand equality" and "a frigid beer is a good beer." The e-mail, considered along with other evidence, contributed to a ruling that a sexually hostile environment existed.

In *Strauss* v. *Microsoft Corp.*, Redmond, Wash., a female employee alleged Microsoft had failed to promote her because of her gender. Included in the evidence were e-mail messages from her supervisor. One e-mail message labeled "Alice in Unix Land," mixed computer language with sexual innuendo. Other messages included graphic and offensive sexual allusions. The court concluded the e-mail messages could lead a reasonable jury to conclude that " . . . [Microsoft] failed to promote [Strauss] as a result of gender discrimination."

In *Petersen* v. *Minneapolis Community Development Agency,* a male employee alleged that inappropriate e-mail messages were sent to him by a female administrative assistant who worked for his boss. The administrative assistant, though repeatedly requested to stop, sent a series of e-mails in which she pursued a relationship. The e-mails, considered with other evidence, were viewed by the court as sufficient to support the sexual harassment case.

disseminated through e-mail both inside a company to those without a need to know the information or outside of a company."[59] This issue of inadvertent dissemination of critical information has several dimensions.

At one level may be information that is actually classified, information that by government standards represents a potential risk to national security if inappropriately released. Classified information is part of the basic knowledge infrastructure of dozens of government agencies and thousands of contractors and subcontractors that support them. In addition to the obvious ramifications to national security, inadvertent release of classified information can result in dire business consequences, including fines, loss of contracts, and extensive "cleansing" of computer equipment and networks.

E-mail has made it increasingly easier to inadvertently disseminate or release classified information. This violation can occur by expressing too many details on a sensitive subject, or attaching an inappropriate drawing, specification, calculation, or procedure. (Again we hear echoes of the informality, the boundary permeability, and the increased connectivity in the background.) Though an extreme example, a government agency received what appeared to be a reasonable e-mail request for information. A wholesaler who had purchased equipment in a government auction needed to know more about the design and operation of the equipment. In response, the agency sent an e-mail with several lengthy attachments. Subsequently, the wholesaler submitted paperwork to allow him to resell the equipment to a foreign country. In the course of reviewing that application, a second government agency determined the information previously provided detailed a highly sensitive, classified nuclear technology. An inquiry later revealed that the informality of the e-mail request had lulled the agency into paying less rigorous attention to standard protocols regarding release of government information.

At a level much more common in business, an equivalent concern exists regarding the security of confidential information that constitutes vital trade secrets that represent the company's competitive edge. Information of this nature that is inadvertently released may jeopardize markets and even end the employer's exclusive rights to the information. For example, the Uniform Trade Secrets Act requires that for a company to be awarded compensation for a misappropriated trade secret, it must demonstrate it made "efforts that are reasonable under the circumstances to maintain its secrecy." The effort must be substantive, sustained, and aggressive. Saying that the information was casually e-mailed to an inappropriate recipient may not provide the legal basis for suitable legal resolution. Similarly, ideas that a company may be considering for patent may be barred from patents if publicly released in advance of filing a patent application because an idea that can be shown to exist in the public cannot be patented. If someone on staff has sent e-mails to colleagues outside the company discussing the idea or invention, the patent office may rule those e-mails are sufficient reason to preclude proceeding with a patent application or invention disclosure.

A third concern for business is inappropriate use of copyrighted materials—both those owned by the company and those owned by other corporations. The more adept people become with their computer skills, the more imaginative they become with their e-mails. Instead of summarizing a journal article to a colleague, they now may attach the entire issue in which the article appeared. Instead of using the company logo in its registered or copyrighted form, they may manipulate the image to "cleverly" reinforce some point they are making.

Instead of a simple text message, they may introduce a multimedia display, complete with lengthy musical clips from CDs, video from DVDs, and photos downloaded from the Internet. As a favor to a colleague, the employee may also attach to the e-mail the latest version of a new software.

Each of these situations represents a possible copyright violation. For example, transmitting the copyrighted journal articles, photos, video, and musical clips may constitute violations of "fair use" clauses that allow limited reuse of material. The transfer of software may be a violation of the "software piracy" laws intended to discourage the public from unlawful copying and redistribution of copyrighted software. The manipulation of the corporate logo may void the legal prohibitions that keep other companies from stealing your corporate identity (the kind of issue often suggested by highly publicized lawsuits in which a major corporation seeks damages from a company whose logo is too similar to or highly suggestive of the logo owned by the corporation). In each case, the company is left holding the bag. As long as you are understood to be acting as an agent of the company, a status essentially conferred to you by your use of the corporate e-mail system, the company foots the bill: paying for copyright infringement, software privacy, or the loss of its very image and identity.

These reasons, collectively, are why companies are so zealous in monitoring employee use of e-mail. They are concerned that, without their knowledge and certainly contrary to the interests or goals of the company, employees are creating liabilities for the company by using e-mail to:

1) Foster an environment that accepts a loss of productivity

2) Contribute to a hostile environment

3) Jeopardize vital information and trade secrets

4) Violate intellectual property laws.

In each of the categories, you have the control. Your conscious, deliberate, professional use of e-mail will make sure that you and your company derive e-mail's benefits, not pay the penalty for a system that is making communication decisions for you.

DOING E-MAIL RIGHT—THE LESSONS

ECPA establishes the basis for employer monitoring of e-mail. It has also engendered the use of e-mail policies to warn employees against the inappropriate uses of e-mail. Yet, for our purposes, the message is not that you concern yourself with getting caught. You should concern yourself with using e-mail professionally. You need to make certain that you do not confuse the allure of informality with allowance for unprofessional behavior. The style, the format, the completeness, the appropriateness, the distribution, and the substance are all matters for you to treat seriously. A single typo may not be as offensive as a disparaging remark about a counterpart, but it may be just as detrimental to your image—the public face you are trying to portray to your colleagues and customers.

Looking back on the revolution he unleashed a quarter century earlier, Ray Tomlinson, the inventor of e-mail, stated somewhat wistfully, "I miss the anarchy." The anarchy, the lack of convention that may have been acceptable in the early days of the invention, is no longer an acceptable trait—at least not in business. If you work for yourself and want to use your computer resources to undermine your credibility, then no one has the right to tell you otherwise.

However, if you are being paid by someone to do a job, then their resources, their image, and their goals have to become your values as well.

A little harmless misuse of e-mail is every bit as unethical as going to the supply cabinet and taking home a few dozen computer discs, or making personal copies of corporate software, or stealing clients. Yet, in comparison, misguided use of e-mail may have the most significant consequences for you and the company. Unlike Tomlinson's first message, which went uncaptured and unremembered, your e-mails may be around for as long or longer than you are. Equally important, they will remain part of a referenceable and retrievable universe of corporate information. Summarizing the lessons we have been learning about electronic communication, Figure 10.14 is a checklist to use when preparing business e-mail. Table 10.8 summarizes the use and applicability of e-mail.

FIGURE 10.14

An E-Mail Checklist

I. E-Mail You Create

Style (the empty auditorium)
1. Is the language appropriate?
2. Have I avoided any suggestions of flaming?
3. Is the tone correct?
4. Do I focus on the topic and not me?
5. Have I used the appropriate format?
6. Have I been as concise as possible?

Completeness (the half-empty cup)
1. Is the message ready/suitable for comment/distribution?
2. Is the focus exclusively work-related?
3. Does the information warrant sending?

Distribution (the overflowing bank)
1. Who is the principal recipient?
2. Do others need the information?
3. Have I limited the CCs to the essential distribution?
4. Are there any CCs that should be reconsidered?

Appropriateness (the full-court press)
1. Is there any confidential/sensitive information?
2. Is there any use of copyrighted information/trademarks? If so, is it going only to those with a "need to know"?
3. Is there any information/language/context that may be perceived as offensive/inappropriate?

Overall
1. Does the message need to be sent?
2. Am I sending it for the right reasons?
3. Am I sending it to the right people?
4. Am I sending the right image of myself?

II. E-Mails You Receive
1. Does the e-mail need/warrant a request/forwarding?
2. Who needs to be on that response/forwarding?
3. Are there ethical issues raised by the e-mail to which I need to respond?

10.8 E-MAIL—AN OVERVIEW

Primary uses	Communicate information Transmit information Ephemeral information
Style	Casual, informal, conversational (e-chat) Limited internal cues and signposts (e.g., headings, salutations)
Distribution potential	Virtually unlimited
Permanence	Generally not officially retained in corporate archives, but still retrievable if needed
Associated accountability	Distributed involvement creates a shared accountability for information content
Response expected	Tends to invoke a "daisy chain" of responses, even if none is solicited
Subject breadth	Generally focused on highly specific topic (e.g., a particular meeting)
Company involvement (review/approval)	No review generally precedes issuance
Authorship	Can be generated and issued by anyone with a company e-mail account (generally all employees)
Associated risks	The empty auditorium (inappropriate informality) The half-empty cup (distribution of inappropriate/unfinished work) The overflowing bank (excessive involvement of colleagues and staff) The full-court press (legal issues and corporate liabilities)

EXERCISES

☐ Group

1. The company you work for is concerned that inappropriate e-mail may create a liability for the corporation. As a team, draft a policy detailing how you expect e-mail to be used. Defend your positions and explain how the policies will not interrupt the necessary open communication among coworkers.

2. As a team, see how many issues you can identify in the e-mails drafted by your classmates (from Individual Exercise 2 below).

☐ Individual

1. Review the e-mails in your in-box. Using the e-mail checklist, explain any issues you see with the e-mails and suggest how you would resolve them.

2. Draft an e-mail in which you introduce as many problems as possible (using the e-mail checklist).

3. As a member of an international research team that is under great pressure to complete an assignment, you have just received a copy of the company's new e-mail policy (from Group Exercise 1 above). Draft a response to the new e-mail policy expressing any concerns you might have.

END NOTES

[1] Quoted in Joanne Yates, "From Press Book and Pigeonhole to Vertical Filing: Revolution in Storage and Access System for Correspondence," *The Journal of Business Communication,* Vol. 19, No. 3 (Summer 1982), pp. 5–26.

[2] Malcolm Richardson, "Business Writing and the Spread of Literacy in Late Medieval England," in *Studies in the History of Business Writing,* ed. George W. Douglas and Herbert W. Hilderbrandt. Urbana., IL: The Association of Business Communication, 1985.

[3] Quoted in Joanne Yates, *Control Through Communication: Rise of Systems in American Management.* Baltimore: The Johns Hopkins University Press, 1989, p. 31.

[4] Yates, "From Press Book and Pigeonhole to Vertical Filing."

[5] Tara K. Bikson, "Organizational Trends and Electronic Media: Work in Progress," *American Archivist,* Vol. 57 (Winter 1994), pp. 44–68.

[6] *Ibid.*

[7] Quoted on Graphic Decisions Website (*http://www.graphic-decisions.com*)

[8] Table 10.2 adapted from Martha S. Feldman, "Electronic Mail and Weak Ties in Organizations," *Office Technology and People,* Vol. 13, (1987) pp. 83–101.

[9] Table 10.3 is also adapted from Feldman, "Electronic Mail and Weak Ties in Organizations."

[11] Bikson, "Organizational Trends and Electronic Media."

[11] Feldman. "Electronic Mail and Weak Ties in Organizations."

[12] Richard R. John, "The Politics of Innovation," *Daedalus,* Vol. 127, No. 4 (Fall 1998), pp.187–214.

[13] *Ibid.*

[14] John Steele Gordon, "Technology of the Future," *American Heritage,* Vol. 44, No. 6 (Oct. 1993), pp. 14–15.

[15] Richard John, "The Politics of Innovation."

[16] Sidney H. Aronson, "Bell's Electrical Toy: What's the Use? The Sociology of Early Telephone Usage," in *The Social Impact of the Telephone,* ed. Ithiel de Sola Pool. Cambridge, MA: The MIT Press, 1977.

[17] *Ibid.*

[18] Rosa Harris-Alder, "Creation of the E-nation," *Canadian Geographic,* Vol. 115, No. 6 (Nov.–Dec. 1995), pp. 40–57.

[19] Marvin Kitman, "Introduction" to *Barbed Wires: A Collection of Famous Funny Telegrams,* ed. Joyce Denebrink. New York: Simon & Schuster, 1965.

[20] *Ibid.*

[21] Richard John, "The Politics of Innovation."

[22] Rosa Harris-Alder, "Creation of the E-nation."

[23] *Ibid.*

[24] *Ibid.*

[25] Charles Moran, "We Write, But Do We Read?" *Computers and Composition,* Vol. 8, No. 3, pp. 51–61.

[26] *Ibid.*

[27] Lee Sproull and Sava Kiesler, "Reducing Social Context Cues: Electronic Mail in Organizational Communication," *Management Science,* Vol. 32, No. 11 (Nov. 1986), pp. 1492–1512.

[28] Prashant Bordia, "Face-to-Face Versus Computer-Mediated Communication: A Synthesis of the Experimental Literature," *The Journal of Business Communication,* Vol. 34, No.1 (Jan. 1997), pp. 99–120.

[29] Sproull and Kiesler, "Reducing Social Context Cues."

[30] *Ibid.*

[31] *Ibid.*

[32] Virginia Shea, The Core Rules of Netiquette (Summary), (*http://www.albion.com/netiquette/book*)

[33] "E-mail Blunders," *Training and Development,* Vol. 54, No. 3 (March 2000), p. 19.

[34] Naomi S. Baron, "Put on a Public Face," *The New York Times,* OP-ED, April 11, 2001, p. A27.

[35] Norman Z. Shapiro and Robert H. Anderson, *Toward an Ethics and Etiquette for Electronic Mail,* July 1985. Rand Corporation Report (R-3283-NSF/RC)

[36] G. Pascal Zachary, "It's a Mail Thing: Electronic Messaging Gets a Rating-Ex," *The New York Times,* June 22, 1994, p. 1.

[37] Anne Eisenberg, "E-mail and the New Epistolary Age," *Scientific American,* April 1994, p. 128.

[38] Sproull and Kiesler, "Reducing Social Context Cues."

[39] Dominique Deckmyn, "More Managers Monitor E-mail; Computer World Survey: Fearing Lawsuits, Loss of Secrets, Employers Scan More Messages." *Computer World,* Oct. 18, 1999, p. 1.

[40] Feldman, "Electronic Mail and Weak Ties in Organizations."

[41] Christopher B. Sullivan, "Preferences for Electronic Mail in Organizational Communication," *The Journal of Business Communication,* Vol. 32, No. 1 (Jan. 1995), pp. 49–64.

[42] Sproull and Kiesler, "Reducing Social Context Cues."

[43] G. Pascal Zachary, "It's a Mail Thing."

[44] Rob Nixon, "Please Don't E-mail Me About This Article," *The Chronicle of Higher Education,* Sept. 29, 2000, p. B 20.

[45] *Ibid.*

[46] G. Pascal Zachary, "It's A Mail Thing."

[47] Steven R. Phillips and Eric M. Eisenberg, "Strategic Uses of Electronic Mail in Organizations," *The Public,* Vol. 3, No. 4 (1996), pp. 67–81.

[48] *Ibid.*

[49] Deckmyn, "More Managers Maintain E-mail."

[50] Fox, "The Boss Knows," *Communications of the ACM,* Vol. 43, No. 2 (Feb. 2000), p. 10.

[51] *Ibid.*

[52] Among articles used to develop this section are:

Douglas M. Towns and Jeana Gerard, "Superhighway or Superheadache? E-Mail and Internet in the Workplace," *Employee Relations Law Journal,* Vol. 24, No. 3 (Winter 1998), pp. 5–29.

Donald H. Selfman and Craig W. Trepanier, "Evolution of the Paperless Office: Legal Issues Arising Out of Technology in the Workplace," *Employee Relations Law Journal,* Vol. 21, No. 3, (Winter 1995/1996), pp. 5–36.

Jon H. Samoriski, John L. Huffman, and Denise M. Trauth, "Electronic Mail, Privacy, and the Electronic Communications Privacy Act of 1986: Technology in Search of Law," *Journal of Broadcasting and Electronic Media,* Vol. 40 (1996), pp. 60–76.

Janice C. Sypior and Burke T. Ward, "The Darkside of Employee E-mail," *Communications of the ACM,* Vol. 42, No. 7 (July 1999), p. 88+.

[53] Samoriski, Huffman, and Trauth, "Electronic Mail, Privacy, and the Electronic Communications Act of 1986."

[54] Selfman and Trepanier, "Evolution of the Paperless Office."

[55] "Iran-Contra: White House E-mail," The CNN Perspectives Series On-Line.

[56] Dana Hawkins, "Lawsuits spur rise in employee monitoring," *U.S. News and World Report,* Aug. 13, 2001, p. 53.

[57] Janice C. Sypior and Burke T. Ward, "The Ethical and Legal Quandary of E-mail Privacy," *Communications of the ACM,* Vol. 38, No. 12 (Dec. 1995), pp. 48–54.

[58] Cases cited in Selfman and Trepanier, "Evolution of the Paperless Office," and in Sypior and Ward, "The Darkside of Employee E-mail."

[59] Selfman and Trepanier, "Evolution of the Paperless Office."

11

Memos

Relaying the Voice of Management

In Chapter 10, we discussed the use of e-mail. Now we will turn to the two other forms of daily written business communication: memos and letters. These two forms exist side by side in almost every business environment. Each has its own history, applications, and expectations (Table 11.1). Each, as Joanne Yates and Wanda Orlikowski of the MIT Sloan School of Management have explained, reflects a separate "genre of organizational communication."

As these two authors explain, "a genre of organization communication . . . is a typified communicative action invoked in response to a recurrent situation. The recurrent situation or socially defined need includes the history and nature of established practices, social relations, and communication media within organizations . . . . The resulting genre is characterized by similar substance and form. *Substance* refers to the social motives, themes, and topics being expressed in the communication (e.g., the positive or negative recommendation and the supporting characteristics of the recommendee; the proposing of the project including its rationale and design). *Form* refers to the observable physical and linguistic features of the communication (e.g., inside address and salutation of a letter; standard sections of a proposal)."[1]

In particular, business letters and memos, over time, developed distinct forms as a consequence of their differing substances. Our ability to use these forms correctly relies on our clear understanding of this history, the unique applications (substance), and specific expectations (form) of business letters and memos. In this chapter, we will look briefly at the memo. To

Memos: an introduction

Where memos come from

A marriage of form of function

Losing sight of form and function

When good marriages go bad

- Incompatibility

- Not acting one's age

- Generally misbehaving

- Staying out late

A couple reunited

From corporate policy to memo: a short walk

Memos—the lessons

11.1 EMERGENCE AND INSTITUTIONALIZATION OF BUSINESS LETTERS AND MEMOS

Form of the Genre

Business Letter Form:
Content, placement, and style increasingly standardized

Memo Form:
Addition of subject lines, compression of salutation and address; use of subheads; less formal style

E-mail Form:
Informal style; few formatting conventions

Substance of the Genre

Business letters used as routine means to conduct external business affairs	Business letter use increases with expanded breadth and volume of American industry	Memos emerge as a genre to assist in conducting internal affairs; business letter use continues to increase	Memo format and style become more streamlined and standardized; use of memo and business letter increases proportionately with expanding demands of business	Business letters and memos remain critical for conducting business, but large volume of less formal communications handled by e-mail
Prior to 1800	**1800–1870**	**1870–1920**	**1920–1970**	**1970–Present**

Communication prominence

some degree, the use of e-mail has largely overshadowed the use of the memo, but the memo still maintains its vital role in the business world. In Chapter 12, we will examine the business letter, a genre that also continues to have a vital role in conducting America's business.

MEMOS: AN INTRODUCTION

Memos are clearly the least discussed form of business communication in the professional literature and current textbooks. When the memo is written about, it generally is in disparaging terms. For example, journalist Roy Rowan writes in *The Intuitive Manager* that "Ross Perot claims he operated a memo-less company. Like Napoleon, who reportedly tossed out all written reports from his generals, figuring he'd already heard the important news, Perot prefers to conduct all of his business by personal contact." Enveloping all written communication in a single unworthy package, Perot, the reference goes on to state, dismisses the memo because "Written reports stifle creativity."[2]

Further disparaging memos as the instrument of bureaucracy, Thomas Peters, in *The Washington Monthly*, argues for a change in managerial behaviors: "Here's how managers could encourage nonbureaucratic behavior . . . . Refuse to send memos; use the phone or personal contact instead. After getting a memo from the boss, managers should pop into his or her office with an answer, not retire to an office for three days to write a treatise in response. Send back without comment all 'information copies' of memos."[3]

Perot and Peters share a certain imprecision of vocabulary; they both implicitly declare memos synonymous with any written communication. They also share an opinion that memos have little real value, and certainly no discrete purpose in business. As Table 11.1 suggests, and as we will take up shortly, both these assumptions are incorrect.

A reason for memos receiving scant treatment is a belief that memos, if not supposedly already accounted for within the general discussion of business letters, must have been superceded by e-mail. As we discussed in Chapter 10, e-mail certainly has become the most ubiquitous form of communication, but it does not replace the memo. Memos can share some of the common pitfalls with e-mail, but they do not share a common substance. To put the memo's role in proper perspective, let's begin by expounding on the history summarized in Table 11.1. By doing so, we might resolve a peculiar irony: "In spite of those who disparage its use and in spite of its relatively recent appearance and the scanty attention it receives in textbooks on written modes of management communication, the memo is, according to many surveys . . . the most frequently used type of written communication in business."[4] Another article published in *Business Communication Quarterly* echoes this point: "Given the complexity of teaching students to write memos, it is surprising that the matter is so infrequently discussed in educational journals. The ERIC [Educational Resources Information Center] contains only two articles that relate specifically to teaching students to write memos."[5]

WHERE MEMOS COME FROM

Most commonly known in years past as "interoffice correspondence" or "departmental letters," the memo, or memorandum, grew out of a very specific business need. As explained by Yates and Orlikowski, until the mid-nineteenth century, internal correspondence was a secondary means of communication, generally employed when face-to-face discussion was not possible, as when people were out of the office on sales calls. As corporations expanded in the latter part of the nineteenth century, more levels of management were added, individual functions were compartmentalized, and greater control and consistency were required. As a consequence, in the 50 years from approximately 1870 to 1920, corporations began to stress "the importance of documenting operational processes and outcomes and of establishing flows of written communication for internal coordination and control. Written documents were preferred to oral exchanges in many cases because documents could be stored for later consultation and analysis. They created a form of organizational memory."

Further, as these two authors point out, "even though the telephone, widely adopted by businesses shortly after its introduction in 1876, facilitated oral communication within and between the growing factories and plants of this period, it did not satisfy management's demand for documentation. To respond to this demand, managers increasingly turned to internal correspondence."[6]

In her book, *Control Through Communication: The Rise of System in American Management,* Yates continues with this perspective, offering a fascinating example of how a series of Western Railroad train collisions in the 1890s became the impetus behind that corporation's transition from an oral tradition to its extensive reliance on a disciplined management approach, earmarked by the use of memos and other forms of written communication.

Responding to a series of collisions, the company's first response was to establish clear lines of authority and communication. Having established this foundation, the Directors of Western Railroad (which ran between Worcester and West Stockbridge, Massachusetts) mandated that a single, official timetable would be maintained for all train traffic. This timetable would be maintained and published by the Engineer. Changes to the timetable could only be introduced by the Office of the Superintendent and would be implemented only after they had "been received and are understood by all concerned." Having established clear pathways for downward and lateral communication, the company next established policies for record keeping and put in place procedures to ensure timely upward reporting.

Managers, the Road Master, and the master mechanic were required to keep records about operations and to report to their superiors once a month. The scope of these reports was clearly articulated, as illustrated in the directions to the Road Master: "The Road Master shall keep a journal of his operations stating the several points at which labor has been performed—the nature and extent of the same and results produced in order that the experience thus acquired may be rendered serviceable in subsequent operations . . . . He will at the end of each month make a report to the Engineer of his proceedings—with such suggestions as he may deem necessary." The purpose for transmitting these reports upward through the management chain was also clearly stated: "Each agent, under the chief engineer, in all grades of service, is to report once a month, to the Engineer, his operations, for the preceding month, so that the whole management of the road shall, at short, stated intervals, come under review of the Engineer's department."

Summarizing the overall implication of this change in culture and philosophy, Yates concludes:

> The published rules, the journal of operations, and the monthly reports all reflected a desire to rise above the individual memory and to establish an organizational memory tied to job positions and functions, rather than to

specific individuals. Downward communication via written rules and orders provided a mechanism for embodying the required wisdom at any given moment. The regular, though still slight, flow of upward communication provided a mechanism for updating that wisdom in light of experience.[7]

With the expanding need for control and documentation, memos established a firm footing in American industry. By the early part of the twentieth century, writing texts were taking notice. As an example, in J. B. Griffith's 1909 text on correspondence and filing, we find the following comment: "Of considerable importance in every large organization is the inter-department correspondence—the notes from one department head to another. Every department head finds it necessary at times to request information from other departments. Even with an inter-communicating telephone system with which every large office and plant should be equipped, many of these requests are of a nature that, to guard against misunderstandings, demand written communications."[8]

A MARRIAGE OF FORM AND FUNCTION

In our discussion of e-mail, we illustrated that its format and style had been influenced by the medium. In memos, we find another interesting relationship: the style and voice of memos are driven by the document's application.

As we just established, the memo grew out of a need to establish control and to provide documentation. Originally, the memo was merely the internally-based equivalent of the business letter, relying essentially on the same formatting and stylistic conventions. However, as the document's application became better pronounced and defined, the memo began to develop its own identity. The change was so significant that, although the telegraph and the e-mail system made deep impressions on writing style, in the case of memos, the reverse is true: The memo made its impression on the machines of the times, most notably the typewriter. Beyond the effects on secretarial desks and vertical filing systems, the memo—or more precisely the stylistic changes reflected in the evolution of the memo—influenced the design and evolution of the typewriter.

As documentation needs and office pressures increased, the design of the typewriter changed to keep pace. Originally introduced in the 1870s, the typewriter advanced along with the sculpting of the memo's role in nineteenth- and twentieth-century enterprise. By the mid-1880s, the typewriter's changing design reflected the pronounced differences between the memo and its external counterpart, the business letter. Underlining and uppercase letters were introduced to the typewriter, allowing for such structural features as subheads. In addition, lists, a common feature of memos but not as common an attribute of business letters, were made easier to create when tabs were added to the typewriter around the turn of the century.

Moreover, typists, an occupation that grew up in direct correlation with the increased acceptance of the typewriter, became an influential force: efficiency was achieved by promoting format standardization, further delineating the memo from the business letter. Accordingly, as the memo became more established and more distinct from the business letter, the genre secured a more permanent position among the various forms of written communication.[9]

The particular function of the memo as established in the early days of the twentieth century continues largely unchanged today. The substance of memos has not changed much in the century and a half since its introduction into business. Not much different from the directions given to the railroad management and engineers in the 1840s is the advice still given today regarding when to use memos. Sample advice from the 1970s and 1980s demonstrates that the memo's role and vitality have not been substantively changed by the advent of e-mail (Figure 11.1). More than a century after the Western Railroad demanded a more disciplined set of interoffice communications, we see that the same themes remain constant in the professional literature pertaining to the preparation of memos.

Providing a clearer insight into the use of the memo as a means to sound the voice of management, one article correctly declares a twofold purpose for the genre: to serve as a reminder of social norms or company rules and to announce information of corporate consequence. As with the case of Western Railroad, memos represent the means to reacquaint employees with rules, policies, etiquette, and expected modes of behavior. Memos, as the Western Railroad example illustrated, are often the management's response to a problem. Depending on the seriousness of the problem, memos may also be used to explain potential follow-up activities and sanctions. For example, employees reminded that e-mail should be used exclusively for business purposes may also be informed in the same memo that repeated violations can result in termination.

In comparison, sometimes rather than reacquainting employees with policies and practices, memos may serve to introduce new corporate practices or expectations, especially those that—because of their anticipated reception—warrant the authority of management's voice, e.g., cutbacks in staff or benefits. When used to announce decisions, the analyses have already been completed, the course of action fixed. Therefore, memos are not issued with the expectation that much debate or discussion will follow; rather, the message is generally irreversible, open only to minor modifications or clarifications aimed at better understanding the management's expectations. Acceptance of the changes and commitment to the proposed new rules are simply assumed.[10]

Recognizing that the use and application of memos have remained relatively static for the past century and a half, we might easily understand the formatting logic of the memo. It is a streamlined letter, designed to carry managerial authority

---

FIGURE 11.1

A Look Back at the Advice on Memos

"Since the memorandum is an internal communication, it is more management-oriented than a business letter and is a more objective type of communication. As a memo writer, a manager may need to disseminate information concerning new policies and business decisions, relay asked-for information, present facts for decision making by others, report progress on what is happening within the organization, suggest ideas, justify or set responsibility for certain courses of action, or take a stand on an issue. Managers frequently use memos to communicate useful facts and data within their organization. Memos are especially useful if there is the possibility that information communicated verbally may be forgotten or misunderstood." (1978)[11]

"The memo remains the best single device for communicating substantial chunks of detailed information to a co-worker. Particularly if what you are communicating consists largely of numbers, and particularly if you are going to need a record of the information . . . . The memo is the managerial tool of choice when you want to put out word to lots of people, more than you can conveniently assemble for an oral exhortation." (1986)[12]

with minimal length, accomplished by the careful alignment of form and function. A first step in marrying form and substance came with the addition of a subject line, a convention added to support the efficient filing and retrieval of information. More stylistic adjustments were quick to follow. As Yates notes in her article "The Emergence of the Memo As a Managerial Genre," purpose drove forward the streamlining of the memo: "The traditional salutation and closing with their formal and polite style were eliminated to save time in writing and typing. Letterhead stationery was replaced by a cheaper and more efficient form heading that included spaces for all the information the sender and receiver might need to file and retrieve the communication, including a subject line."[13]

The drive for a less expensive, streamlined communication form is made evident in a 1904 article on "inter-house correspondence" (i.e., correspondence between different locations of a single company) in which the author advocates various stylistic means to save time, words, and paper:

> In the first place, all unnecessary courtesy, such as "Fred Brown & Co." "Gentlemen," "yours very truly," and other phrases are omitted entirely. In a business where hundreds and sometimes thousands of interhouse letters are written daily the saving of time is considerable. Next, an expensive letterhead is done away with, and this also is a factor in reducing expense. The blank [standard form] is made with simply the words, "From Chicago," "From Atlanta," or whatever may be the name of the town where the letter is written, printed in the upper left-hand corner, and underneath the word, "Subject." In the upper right-hand corner is the serial number of the letters and the words, "In reply refer to No." and "Replying to No." It will thus be seen that the only typewriting necessary in addressing a letter consists of the location of the house to which the letter is to be sent, a short summary of the matter contained in the letter for indexing purposes, the number of the letter, and date, with the initials of the writer, and the number and date of the letter which is under reply (in case there has been previous correspondence), with the initials of the former correspondent.[14]

This march toward brevity and efficiency went forward for at least the first two decades of the twentieth century, tearing away elements of traditional business correspondence seen as too cumbersome for everyday office communications. A high point came in 1912 when President Taft established a Commission on Economy and Efficiency. This commission, among other subjects, examined "the principles that should govern in the matter of handling and filing correspondence and preparing and mailing communications in connection with the work of several departments of the government."

In a report entitled "Memorandum of Conclusions Concerning the Principles That Should Govern in the Matter of Handling and Filing Correspondence and Preparing and Mailing Communications in Connection with the Work of Several Departments of the Government, Together with Suggestions for the Use of Labor-Saving Devices in Preparing and Mailing Letters, etc.," the Commission advocated dozens of changes. These changes included many recommendations that are still used in business, such as the use of envelopes with clear cellophane windows that allow the address on the letter to serve as the external mailing address as well.

The Commission also took clear aim at the contents of the letters being prepared in government offices. In a tone much more assertive than any business communication text, the Commission declared that "The essential elements of a letter are the date, the person from whom or office from which the letter emanates, the person to whom the letter is sent, the body of the communication, and the signature. The salutation and the complimentary close add nothing to the letter from the standpoint of conducting the business of the Government. These elements, serving no practical purpose, could be eliminated without detriment to the public business at a considerable saving of time and expense."

The recommendations advocated by the Commission for use throughout the government were already beginning to be deployed in business and elsewhere. Although still perceived of as an experiment, the changes in formatting were catching on fast. As the Commission took note:

> That this proposition is not merely theoretical is seen by the fact that several foreign Governments in some of their large departments have actually eliminated from their correspondence the salutation and complimentary close as well as abbreviated the titles of their public officers. In the United States some large corporations are doing the same thing. One of the greatest railroad companies in America is simplifying its correspondence to the extent of eliminating the salutation and complimentary close as well as using the initials of the individual from whom the letter emanates and to whom it is addressed in correspondence within certain divisions of its service. This is being done as an experiment and is meeting with such success that its use now bids fair to be extended all over the system. [15]

In a fervor that previewed the "efficiency experts" of the 1970s and 1980s, many companies sought to go further than the Commission. To do this, they chartered "Efficiency Departments" that took aim, with equal zeal, at technical processes and administrative chores alike. As an example, a report issued by the Efficiency Division of Du Pont's High Explosives Operating Division saw it as fair game when "emphasizing efficiency over authority." Like the Presidential Commission, Du Pont saw an opportunity to eliminate the salutation and complimentary close, to simplify the recipient's title and address, to strike unnecessary words, and to standardize format.

Changing the opening, close, and title was expected to save a few dozen words per memo. Standardizing format was expected to yield multiple benefits. First, the action would aid in handling and filing correspondence. Placing the addressee's name and department, relevant file numbers, a subject designation, references to previous letters, and a list of enclosures at the top of the page would make the filing location easier to define and more consistent. Second, the new format was intended to reduce unnecessary words. Standard opening sentences could be eliminated. There was no need for statements such as "We have letters dated October 4 and October 17 from _____ as per attached . . . ." (Figure 11.2 provides a sample Du Pont memo illustrating the before and after versions.[16])

LOSING SIGHT OF FORM AND FUNCTION

As we can now recognize, memos succeed when a tight relationship is maintained between form and function. We must be careful therefore not to let the balance slip. We must also be cautious not to assume that the ideas of form and function may be reduced to or understood as the equivalents of "brief" and "easy." Effectively encapsulating much of the current thinking about preparing memos, a 1999 article in *InfoWorld* noted: "The first element of a good memo is brevity."[17] Brief in the service of the memo's role is good; brief in defiance of the memo's message is not good.

FIGURE 11.2

The Search for a
Cost-Effective Style

A. ORIGINAL
August 16, 1913
Copy to Chemical Department
Mr. C. A. Patterson, Supt.
Gibbstown, N.J.

Dear Sir:

OUR FILE OH-1129. Referring to your letter of June 11, in regard to the deposit of so-called "Triton Whiskers" in your weak nitric acid glass tube lines, we are sending you herewith copy of the letter of August 15th from the Chemical Department on this subject which is self-explanatory.

You will note that Mr. Chickering expects to be at Repauno on Monday or Tuesday of next week to discuss this matter with you. From the estimate given in the Chemical Department's letter, the apparatus which it is proposed to install can be put in under a Minor Construction Notice.

Yours very truly,

(Sgd.) W. C. Spruance, Jr.

(118 words)

B. REVISED
August 16, 1913
Copy to Chemical Dept.
SUPT. REPAUNO.

OUR FILE OH-1129. TRITON DEPOSITED IN
WEAK NITRIC ACID GLASS LINES.
Your letter 6/11/13.
Enclosure Chemical Department letter 8/15/13.

Mr. Chickering will discuss this with you Monday or Tuesday.

The apparatus proposed can be put in under a Minor Construction Notice.

(Sgd.) J. Thompson Brown

(49 words)

Source: Joanne Yates, "The Emergence of the Memo as a Managerial Genre," *Management Communication Quarterly,* vol. 2, no. 4, pp. 485-510, copyright ©1989 By Sage Publications, Inc. Reprinted by permission of Sage Publications, Inc.

Ironically, despite the protestations of Ross Perot and others who have disparaged the memo, the underscoring objective of being terse has been the prime force in allowing the basic format of the memo to remain essentially unchanged for more than a century (Figure 11.3).[18] However, as we are beginning to understand, being brief is not sufficient understanding of the memo and its corporate responsibilities.

You do not want brevity for brevity's sake; neither do you want to replace managerial authority with informality and simplicity. Memos are not the hardcopy equivalent of e-mail—a mistake commonly communicated in typical descriptions of the memo:

The organizational title, department heading, salutation, complimentary close, and writer's complete handwritten signature are omitted in a memo. The memorandum, one of the most widely used pieces of correspondence within a business organization, is an informal, concise method

FIGURE 11.3

Memorandum Head	MEMORANDUM
To Line	TO:
From Line	FROM:
Date Line	DATE:
Subject Line	SUBJECT:
Body	
Reference Initials	jh
Enclosure Notation	Enclosure

The Basic Memo Structure

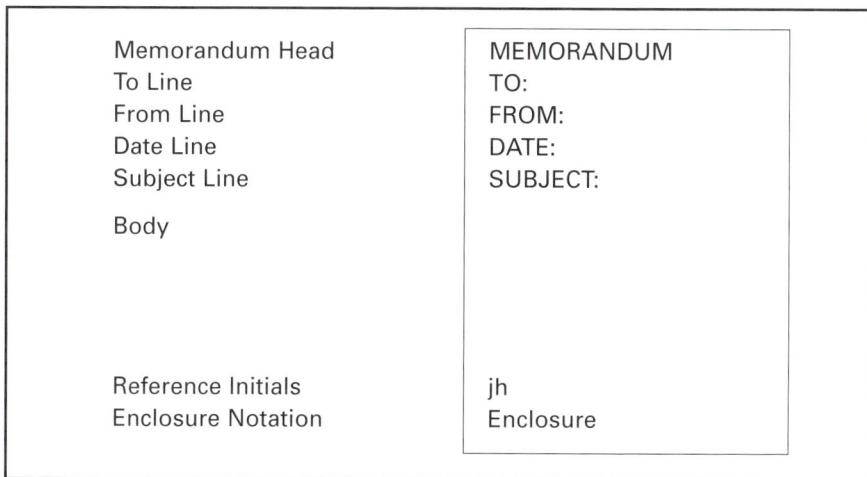

of communication. It is an effective management tool used to simplify correspondence procedures and to improve communication as it carries written information rapidly and conveniently between members of an organization. The use of memorandums with headings illustrates simplicity in organization of internal correspondence, contributes to easy reading, makes quick messages between colleagues more businesslike, and provides a key to strong managerial communication. Communication by memorandum represents one of today's most important opportunities to save valuable managerial time. The effective manager knows when and how to use the following simplified memorandum format as a tool to improve written communication within an organization.[19]

Brevity is here emphasized to the detriment of function and message. Informality is promoted without regard to the memo's essential function as the voice of management. We need, as the quotation above should remind us, to look to our earlier lessons to maintain proper perspective. Was the documentation achieved subsequent to the railroad collisions intentionally "informal"? Were the stern admonitions of the Taft Commission given over to advocating a certain casual tone that should be embraced by government agencies? Was the goal of Du Pont's Efficiency Department to be precise and concise at the expense of the message, or, conversely, was the focus on making the critical message all the more visible? The voice, the purpose, the structure, and the substance of memos are very much formal. They are brief precisely to reinforce the tone and make the message more overt. Memos cannot conceivably "save valuable managerial time" if they are employed as just another means of creating the informality and brevity better suited to face-to-face discussions or e-mail. When reduced to this level, memos are fair and appropriate targets for Ross Perot, Thomas Peters, and every busy professional and manager.

WHEN GOOD MARRIAGES GO BAD

Brevity may distract us momentarily from maintaining attention on function. Dismissing the memo's function as something easy to master is a more deceptive concept. As one article tries to claim: "Don't be intimidated by having ended up in a job where, seemingly, writing memos is going to take up a good part of your day. It really isn't difficult to become a fluid, effective writer of business correspondence and satisfy your boss's needs."[20]

Both the form and the substance of memos grew out of particular business needs and circumstances. Inappropriately manipulating the memo's form or substance can lead to a series of problems:

1. Incompatibility—mistaking memos for e-mail
2. Not acting one's age—giving in to the basic faults of professional communication
3. Generally misbehaving—making memos try to do the work of other forms of communication
4. Staying out late—confusing retrievability with permanence

INCOMPATIBILITY

The general dissatisfaction voiced about memos from Ross Perot and other critics results from the imprecise way in which the terms and the genre are used. As we saw at the beginning of this chapter, a memo is understood by seasoned communicators to be a unique piece of interoffice correspondence; however, often the term is used more loosely as if synonymous with e-mail, general notes, and any form of printed report. Try, for instance, to define the particular elements of the memo using the following guidance for writing the effective memo:

• Know the likes and dislikes of the person to whom you're writing.
• Have all the facts at your disposal before starting.
• Outline the memo to make sure it flows logically.
• Assume nothing—and leave nothing to chance. Make sure every detail is fully spelled out to avoid misinterpretation.
• Get to the point quickly. Answer the important five W's: who, what, where, when, and why. Get rid of extraneous verbiage.
• Use simple words. Write in short, declarative sentences.
• Stop at the appropriate time. If action is required, state what it is.[21]

While we might want to excuse this problem as merely a matter of diction, the misuse of the memo's substance and form is a more substantive problem. Too often, writers dash off memos that share little in common with the genre's intended form and substance. As if rubber-stamping the word *memo* on any piece of paper, this strategy dilutes the memo's authority. When Ross Perot advocates a "memo-less" office, it is not necessarily the equivalent of a "paperless" office. The direction, the records, and the institutionalization of knowledge are every bit as important to General Motors and IBM in the twenty-first century as they were to the railroad industry in the middle of the nineteenth century, in fact, more so. So, too, remains the importance of having a means of effectively communicating both a managerial message and managerial authority. In this regard, even companies that aspire to a paperless office or an office with only the simplest of administrative controls, are aspiring to a clearer vision and statement of management direction.

This lesson becomes apparent when we consider the example of Nordstrom department stores, a company whose one-line policy manual ("Use your own best judgment") is often touted as validation that memos and other forms of written managerial direction are unnecessary in effectively conducting business. Nordstrom's reliance on a one-line policy manual is not a denunciation of the memo. It is a forceful demonstration of the corporation's interest in freeing management expectations from a clutter of ill-defined office communications. It is, therefore, a vigorous endorsement of the principles underlying the intent of the memo, and at the same time, a warning to those who (unintentionally though it may be) dilute the effectiveness of the memo. The goal achieved by Nordstrom's one-line policy manual is precisely aligned with the communication responsibilities historically assigned to the memo.

In the case of Nordstrom, the managerial emphasis, as stated by one of the Vice Presidents, is on realigning employee energies by establishing an environment in which the "absence of childish rules" helps shift the "employees' focus of innovation from how to evade toilet break rules to precisely where the firm wishes it to be: in pursuit of serving the customer better."[22] The critical feature, as expressed, is not on brevity, informality, or simplicity; rather, the underlying motivation is to place employee attention precisely "where the firm wishes it to be." In the case of the communicator, the first challenge is to ensure the correct placement of the emphasis, to use the memo purposely in support of management direction, and to make a conscious and deliberate effort to resist allowing the memo to be submersed in a sea of trivialized communications. Memos should be employed exclusively to focus corporate and staff attention on critical information.

Second, the communicator has to maintain the proper voice to reinforce the one-directional nature of memos. The tone and language should make evident that the memo is not soliciting comments or opening debate. Memos should put the issue or problem at hand to bed, not, as some have advocated, create "a forum for opinion," or offer an interactive mode "of dealing with people."[23] If it's conversation you want, then call a meeting; if it's resolution you seek, issue a memo. Using memos correctly (to reinforce formal management decisions, to reinforce critical behaviors and expectations) allows focus and attention where it needs to be. Focused application of memos can provide, as the Nordstrom example has proven, a liberating achievement. Establishing management's position while speaking with management's voice is the foremost demand on the memo writer.

Third, the memo must be understood as setting a final stamp on a question or problem, not offering an additional avenue for debate or discussion. Diluted by trivia or overuse, the memo is transformed from effective communication to corporate noise that echoes only faintly in the distance. Diluting the memo changes it from a force that has weight to one that holds no weight. This factor was also a critical theme underlying development of the one-line policy at Nordstrom: "Sad to say, rule books are referred to only to slow action, defend turf, and assign blame. Have you ever heard of anyone going to a rule book to figure out how to speed things up?" The memo should be absolute in both its authority and its position. Communicators need to avoid allowing memos to descend into a world of turf wars, to be the substance of finger pointing, or to be the reflection of communications that are anything but "truly managerial."

NOT ACTING ONE'S AGE

Our discussion of e-mail addressed a variety of inappropriate and unprofessional behaviors that commonly find their way into on-line communications. Although not as frequent, many of the same problems find their way into memos: making ourselves the focus of the topic, being too informal, employing an inappropriate tone, and assigning blame. We need not go into any elaboration on these behaviors beyond that already provided in Chapter 10. However, we need to qualify one point about memo style.

In our discussion of e-mail, we noted how the language and tone could slip into inappropriate communications (flaming). Memos, when viewed superficially, may appear to border on the harsh and impersonal. Describing the style of memos, we hear comments such as the following: "In departmental letters . . . there is also no need of establishing a personal relationship, so that courtesy should receive less consideration than directness and completeness."[24] Memos are to be complimented for their "explicitness, literalness, and cool impersonality of statement," and praised for their "strictly business-like tone."[25]

One must recognize that a "business-like tone" in a memo is not a cousin of flaming. Memos, as a tool of management, should be expected to get to the point quickly, to speak in an authoritative tone, and to handle only those subjects that are "truly managerial." Putting critical news in proper perspective or inviting compliance with corporate policies or positions demands a style recognized as serious and in charge.

However, it is not hard for memos to earn a reputation for being harsh or overly critical. Typically, this reputation occurs, as with other charges often leveled at the memo, when the memo itself is being misused. Writing in *Fortune* magazine, Walter Kiechel III observes: "Why do managers persist in sending so many memos? The reasons range from the truly managerial, through the psychological, to the political."[26] The "truly managerial" applications include the restatement of policy, formal expectations for performance, and establishing proper context for sharing vitally important information. In contrast, among the psychological reasons cited is discomfort with communicating face-to-face or over the phone.

Under the heading of political reasons for sending memos, the *Fortune* magazine article cites reasons highly reminiscent of the problem behaviors we considered in our discussion of e-mail:

> Managers also send memos for political reasons, good and bad: to get credit for their ideas ("I would like to propose a new way to handle . . ."), cover their you-know-what ("While I am not opposed to the project, I do have certain reservations . . ."), or even to set a trap for others ("Would you please send me your comments on the following proposal . . ."). By and large, a useless memo is rarely held against you, while a good one can advance your cause with the powers above. The chief danger here is that a self-serving ulterior motive—to catapult the writer into the attention of higher-ups, for example—may be all too transparent.[27]

Expressed in its most basic form, we might capture the essence of "not acting one's age" in a single statement: If you're going to use a management communication tool, behave like a manager; keep your attention and your memos focused on dispatching only the "truly managerial."

GENERALLY MISBEHAVING

Just as memos can fail when managers hide behind them, so memos can be less than successful when sent out to do the work better served by another document type. For instance, it is not uncommon to see memos used to try to establish and detail rather than reinforce policies and procedures. One problem with this alternative use is the lack of permanence. The other problem is the general lack of suitability. In particular, using memos to establish procedures tends to dilute both the message and the means of accomplishing the ends. Competing for prominence, the manager's message about an existing urgent condition usually gets through to the staff; however, the sequence of steps that need to be taken (the procedure) is generally less successful. Because the procedure either gets embedded in the text or abbreviated for the sake of brevity, the actions are less visible, are perceived—as a consequence of their positioning—as less critical, and, therefore, are less likely to be heeded. The memo, instead of setting the procedure, should call attention to the need to comply with the procedure, define the consequences of not doing so, and provide references that will allow employees to locate the procedure being discussed.

Another problem category is associated with misuse of managerial authority. Memos generally have a less rigorous review and approval process than do many other document types that set corporate direction. Consequently, memos tend to be issued more unilaterally by a single manager. A manager establishing policy or procedure via memo is less likely to be assisted or tempered by the comments of colleagues or by a formal review process. The result can be memos that establish positions unintentionally contrary to the best interests of the company.

As an example, at one production facility, a middle manager issued a memo establishing a process for discarding oily rags used in cleaning and maintaining equipment. The manager felt fully empowered to issue the memo, rationalizing that as the senior facility manager he had both responsibility and authority to maintain the integrity of the operation. The process as he set forth in the memo was followed faithfully until an environmental audit pointed out that the process, while efficient, was in violation of federal environmental statutes. The facility manager, while clearly an expert on operations, was not nearly as thoroughly versed on the nuances of environmental law.

STAYING OUT LATE

To the disappointment of many senior personnel, managerial pertinence does not secure a permanent home in the corporate literature, at least not when it comes to issuing memos. A common mistake stems from confusion between what constitutes an active document and one with permanence. Here we face a problem almost the opposite of that cited in our discussion of e-mail.

While many e-mail authors have been surprised at the retrievability of supposedly deleted e-mails, authors of memos often mistakenly believe that the political weight of a memo will cause it to have both a lasting effect on its readers and a lasting place in everyone's active files. While it's true that memos, like e-mail and all documents of corporate significance, can be retrieved, staying power, not retrieval, is at stake when a memo is issued (Figure 11.4).[28] The reality is that memos, whether issued in paper or electronically, have a limited lifetime on the corporate shelves.

FIGURE 11.4

The Retrieved Memo

> **Tobacco industry memo reveals passive smoking strategy.**
>
> A leaked industry memo promises to blow apart the façade that the tobacco industry carries out neutral research into passive smoking. The memo plainly sets out the details of the Philip Morris Company's worldwide strategy to coordinate and pay so many scientists on an international basis to keep the environmental tobacco smoke controversy alive.

Unlike documents such as company policies or procedures that are maintained through a formal revision control program, memos have permanence, but not a continuously active status. In comparison, documents that set the foundations for corporate performance, quality standards, and federal compliance are maintained current to ensure that only the most recently approved copy is in use by personnel.

Accordingly, one typical feature distinguishing a permanent (retrievable) document from one that is part of the active, working structure is a revision number, a specific notation denoting the document's version (e.g., Rev. A, Rev. 1). In contrast, other document types may have a number by which they can be referenced or retrieved (such as a letter number or report number), but no revision number is assigned; either it is unlikely that revisions will be issued, or it is understood that even if revisions are issued, they will have limited immediate consequence relative to the integrity of business activities.

Those document types that are in the "active" collection (often referred to as "controlled documents") are the ones that own the prime corporate shelf space; the other document types, such as memos, have a limited presence, thereafter slipping into the corporate archives where they can be retrieved if needed at some future date. Failing to acknowledge this distinction, the manager who issues a memo with expectations that the staff will use and reference a particular memo far into the future may be surprised at just how ephemeral the written corporate word can be.

A COUPLE REUNITED

We now have a clear set of factors to consider when preparing to draft a memo:

- Is the memo doing the work of a memo (i.e., reinforcing policy) or is it involved in informal exchange better served by e-mail or personal interaction?
- Is the memo stating or reinforcing policy, practices, or behaviors?
- Is the memo maintaining the correct tone and structure, thereby retaining the management voice and weight?
- Is the memo doing the right job, or is it attempting the work more appropriately assigned to a procedure or other genre?
- Is the memo stating a fixed position, or is it soliciting feedback, discussion, or alternatives?
- Is the memo providing a short-term remedy (reinforcement of a policy or corporate announcement) to a problem, or is it trying to establish a position requiring greater permanence and protracted visibility?

We now see that memos have a clear and distinct role in contemporary business. They have a clear identity in terms of purpose, direction of communication, tone, and style (Table 11.2). Recognizing that the foremost use of memos is as a tangible reflection of management's voice, we can construct a straightforward means of developing effective memos. Maintaining the proper tone and style derives from our growing appreciation of corporate audiences. Achieving the precise purpose of memos is accomplished by our recognition that memos, at their most fundamental heart, are a narrative translation of a policy statement. Therefore, if we understand the nature of policy statements, we can translate and transform this knowledge into a skill in preparing effective memos.

FROM CORPORATE POLICY TO MEMO: A SHORT WALK

As Figure 11.5 shows, policy is made up of four elements—the same four elements that provide the structure for writing effective memos. To show the clear relationship between policy and memo, Figure 11.6 is a policy statement issued by the U.S. Department of State in the aftermath of the bombing of the World Trade Center on September 11, 2001. Figure 11.7 is the resulting memo that was issued to all personnel working for the Department of Energy. The correspondence between the intent, voice, style, and structure of the policy statement and its implementing and reinforcing memo is readily apparent.

In turn, the same structure, direct tone, and style are the fundamentals of all effective memos, whether they are targeted at large corporate departments, the entire population of a university, or even to a single class of students. To illustrate this point, we have included three additional memos: 1) Figure 11.8 is a restatement of corporate policy intended to reinforce compliance with company rules regarding the practice of making up for missed time. 2) Figure 11.9 is a

TABLE

11.2 THE ESSENCE OF MEMO STYLE	
Primary Purpose	Reinforce corporate expectations Provide reminders of rules and protocols Ensure managerial context to the sharing of critical information
Directions	Primarily downward (i.e., from management to staff and employees)
Tone	Managerial, authoritative
Style	Terse, businesslike, etiquette consistent with conducting business operations

FIGURE 11.5

An Overview of Policy Statements

Statement of intent (usually fewer than three pages) that defines the scope and establishes a commitment pertaining to a specific aspect of the company's primary scope of work. Policies are typically approved by the Executive Committee or the Office of the President to ensure a consistent method of doing business across all elements of the company.

Policy Format Elements

Policy
State the overall intent and/or commitment in a manner defining the basic principles and methods of doing business across the business unit or company.

Requirements
Define the scope of the policy and describe the basic activities, guidelines, or programs, which are necessary to implement the policy in a consistent and effective manner.

Responsibilities
Identify the assigned organizations and their major responsibilities for accomplishing the requirements of the policy.

References
List the legal, corporate, and other references on which the policy is based.

FIGURE 11.6

Travel Policy
Issued by State
Department

U.S. DEPARTMENT OF STATE
Office of the Spokesman
Worldwide Caution
September 12, 2001

The events of September 11 at the World Trade Center, the Pentagon and Somerset, Pennsylvania, serve as a cruel reminder of the continuing threat from terrorists and extremist groups to Americans and American interests worldwide. This situation remains fluid and American citizens should be aware of the potential risks and to take these into consideration when making travel plans. The Department will continue to develop information about potential threats to Americans overseas and to share credible threat information through its Consular Information Program . . . .

U.S. citizens are urged to maintain a high level of vigilance and to increase their security awareness. Americans should maintain a low profile, vary routes and times for all required travel, and treat mail and packages from unfamiliar sources with suspicion. American citizens are also urged to avoid contact with any suspicious, unfamiliar objects, and to report the presence of the objects to local authorities. Vehicles should not be left unattended and should be kept locked at all times. U.S. Government personnel overseas have been advised to take the same precautions.

FIGURE 11.7   Travel Memo Issued by the Department of Energy

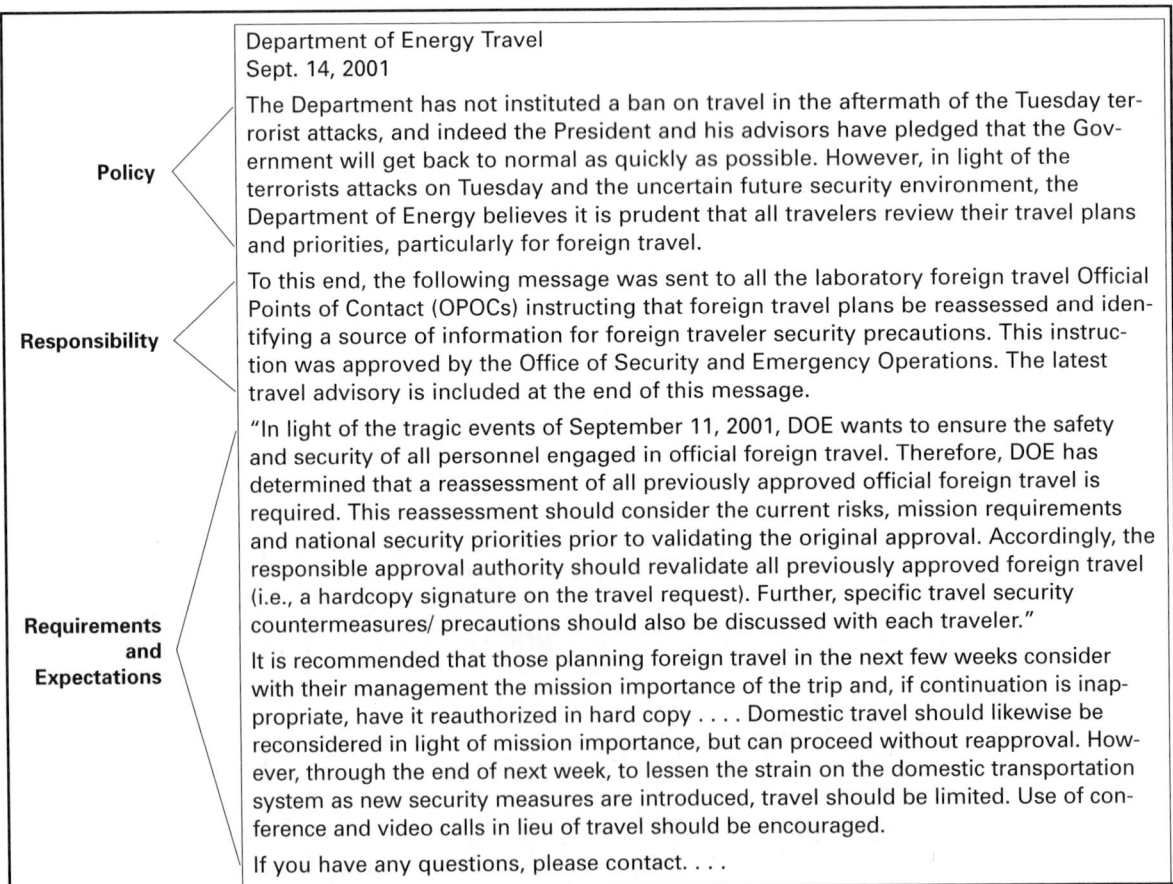

Department of Energy Travel
Sept. 14, 2001

Policy

The Department has not instituted a ban on travel in the aftermath of the Tuesday terrorist attacks, and indeed the President and his advisors have pledged that the Government will get back to normal as quickly as possible. However, in light of the terrorists attacks on Tuesday and the uncertain future security environment, the Department of Energy believes it is prudent that all travelers review their travel plans and priorities, particularly for foreign travel.

Responsibility

To this end, the following message was sent to all the laboratory foreign travel Official Points of Contact (OPOCs) instructing that foreign travel plans be reassessed and identifying a source of information for foreign traveler security precautions. This instruction was approved by the Office of Security and Emergency Operations. The latest travel advisory is included at the end of this message.

**Requirements
and
Expectations**

"In light of the tragic events of September 11, 2001, DOE wants to ensure the safety and security of all personnel engaged in official foreign travel. Therefore, DOE has determined that a reassessment of all previously approved official foreign travel is required. This reassessment should consider the current risks, mission requirements and national security priorities prior to validating the original approval. Accordingly, the responsible approval authority should revalidate all previously approved foreign travel (i.e., a hardcopy signature on the travel request). Further, specific travel security countermeasures/ precautions should also be discussed with each traveler."

It is recommended that those planning foreign travel in the next few weeks consider with their management the mission importance of the trip and, if continuation is inappropriate, have it reauthorized in hard copy . . . . Domestic travel should likewise be reconsidered in light of mission importance, but can proceed without reapproval. However, through the end of next week, to lessen the strain on the domestic transportation system as new security measures are introduced, travel should be limited. Use of conference and video calls in lieu of travel should be encouraged.

If you have any questions, please contact. . . .

statement from a university Chancellor reminding personnel about the appropriate use of the Internet. 3) Figure 11.10, a very familiar form of the memo, is an explanation of expectations for students in a business communication course. Given its common heritage with the other memos, the notice to students likewise expresses policy and behavior in the form of expectations.

MEMOS—THE LESSONS

Memos have a relatively short history, but an extremely important role in American enterprise. Derived as an outgrowth of specific needs and honed through a disciplined approach to communication, the memo has an exclusive role in helping management do its job. The memo provides a recognized genre for promoting management's voice in helping remind personnel of rules and expectations and in sharing information of critical importance that warrants

---

FIGURE 11.8   An Example of a Memo Used as a Reminder of Company Rules

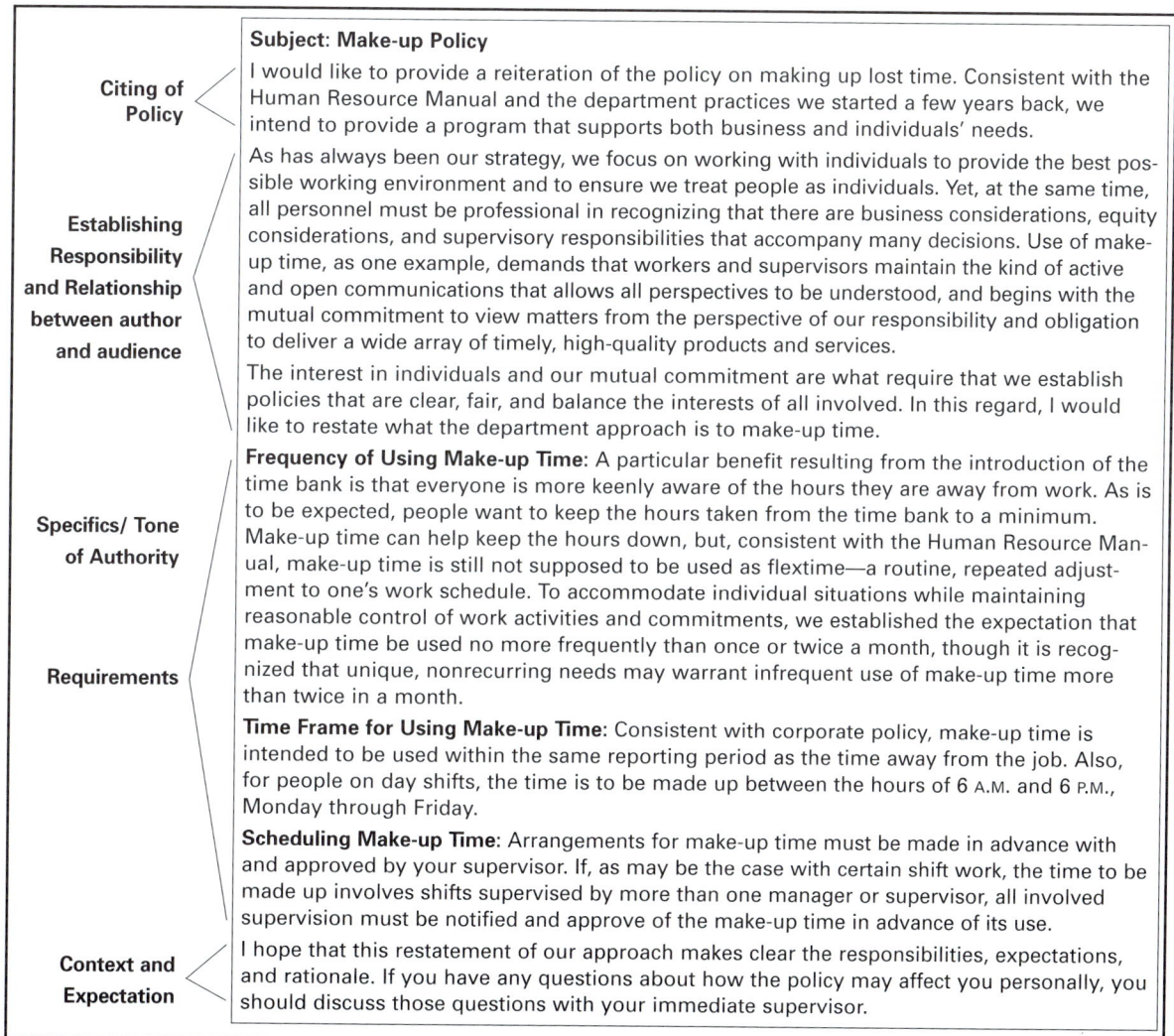

Citing of Policy

Subject: Make-up Policy

I would like to provide a reiteration of the policy on making up lost time. Consistent with the Human Resource Manual and the department practices we started a few years back, we intend to provide a program that supports both business and individuals' needs.

Establishing Responsibility and Relationship between author and audience

As has always been our strategy, we focus on working with individuals to provide the best possible working environment and to ensure we treat people as individuals. Yet, at the same time, all personnel must be professional in recognizing that there are business considerations, equity considerations, and supervisory responsibilities that accompany many decisions. Use of make-up time, as one example, demands that workers and supervisors maintain the kind of active and open communications that allows all perspectives to be understood, and begins with the mutual commitment to view matters from the perspective of our responsibility and obligation to deliver a wide array of timely, high-quality products and services.

The interest in individuals and our mutual commitment are what require that we establish policies that are clear, fair, and balance the interests of all involved. In this regard, I would like to restate what the department approach is to make-up time.

Specifics/ Tone of Authority

Requirements

Frequency of Using Make-up Time: A particular benefit resulting from the introduction of the time bank is that everyone is more keenly aware of the hours they are away from work. As is to be expected, people want to keep the hours taken from the time bank to a minimum. Make-up time can help keep the hours down, but, consistent with the Human Resource Manual, make-up time is still not supposed to be used as flextime—a routine, repeated adjustment to one's work schedule. To accommodate individual situations while maintaining reasonable control of work activities and commitments, we established the expectation that make-up time be used no more frequently than once or twice a month, though it is recognized that unique, nonrecurring needs may warrant infrequent use of make-up time more than twice in a month.

Time Frame for Using Make-up Time: Consistent with corporate policy, make-up time is intended to be used within the same reporting period as the time away from the job. Also, for people on day shifts, the time is to be made up between the hours of 6 A.M. and 6 P.M., Monday through Friday.

Scheduling Make-up Time: Arrangements for make-up time must be made in advance with and approved by your supervisor. If, as may be the case with certain shift work, the time to be made up involves shifts supervised by more than one manager or supervisor, all involved supervision must be notified and approve of the make-up time in advance of its use.

Context and Expectation

I hope that this restatement of our approach makes clear the responsibilities, expectations, and rationale. If you have any questions about how the policy may affect you personally, you should discuss those questions with your immediate supervisor.

FIGURE 11.9

An Example of
a Memo as a
Reminder of
Social Norms

From:	Chancellor
To:	Faculty; Students
CC:	
Subject:	Appropriate Use of Computers
Attachments:	

In light of the recent local news coverage about access to pornography through campus computers at . . . I feel it is appropriate at this time to remind everyone of the proper use of campus computers. The computer systems provided for use by the faculty, staff, and students are an integral and important resource in fulfillment of our research, academic, and administrative responsibilities. As is noted in the Student Handbook and in the Computer Services Division's Statement of Ethical and Responsible Use of Computer Facilities, "(i)t must be understood that this . . . resource must be used in strictly legal and ethical ways, not only to maximize the effectiveness and efficiency of these systems, but also to respect canons of honesty and integrity upon which all academic institutions rely."

To that end, downloading or viewing pornographic material on computers without legitimate research objectives is inappropriate for members of the faculty and staff, students, and visitors. Of particular note, in addition, are the severe legal implications under federal law attendant to downloading and possessing child pornography. As an example, possessing material that contains a visual representation of a minor engaged in sexual activity is a felony punishable by up to 5 years in prison. The applicable federal law is found at 18 2252A. State laws regulating obscenity and materials harmful to minors are found at Sections 16-15-305 through 16-15-445 of the State Code of Laws.

I ask that each of you help me ensure that our computer systems are used for legitimate and appropriate purposes. Persons found to be using them for other purposes are subject to institutional disciplinary action and/or civil or criminal proceedings according to appropriate state and/or federal law.

Chancellor

TABLE 11.3 THE BASIC ATTRIBUTES OF THE MEMO

Primary Uses	Request compliance with company rules and protocols; remind personnel of expectations and social norms; provide critical information that shows a management perspective
Expectations	Adherence to the request; follow-up inquiry by audience if there is issue or further clarification needed
Audience	Internal; generally directed downward to staff (although in instances, horizontally directed memos can be employed)
Style	Terse, businesslike. Tone should reinforce managerial authority
Length	Generally no more than one to two pages. (If longer, the memo may be involved in doing the work best left to other document types.)
Breadth	Single topic; identified in the subject line
Accountability	Author is assumed to have both the authority to propose the action and enforce the compliance; manager is also directly accountable for the document and resulting actions
Format	Standard internal correspondence format; abbreviated structure; may be issued in either paper or electronic form
Retrievability	Represents an official corporate document; generally will have an assigned reference number that will serve as the basis for future retrieval
Potential Problems	—incompatibility of purpose —stylistic problems (e.g., inappropriate informality; loss of managerial tone) —use of memos to do the work of other document types (e.g., e-mail, procedures) —hiding behind memo when more direct interaction is warranted —issuing a memo when a document of greater permanence is needed

FIGURE 11.10

An Example of a
Memo Used to
Share Information

Some Class Expectations/Information

Assignments: Assignments will include a variety of exercises—some done in class, some to be completed out-of-class. There will also be one major project. Assignments done out-of-class are to be typed, double spaced, using a size 11 or 12 font size. Turn exercises in when due. Late papers are accepted, but will have grades decreased.

Attendance: Being here in body is expected; being here in spirit would be preferred (and may potentially be rewarded). Because missing a single class is missing an entire week's work, more than one absence will result in a reduced grade.

My Approach: My goal is to focus on principles rather than on templates and to make these principles meaningful through practical exercises and examples. Accordingly, class time will generally be occupied with some lecturing (sometimes it can't be avoided) but mainly by a discovery process assisting you in coming to grips with the tools you will need to communicate effectively in today's business world.

Your Role: Discovery rather than lecture demands a mature contribution by the students. I expect you to think, to challenge, to participate; in other words, to make an honest, mature effort to learn.

Textbook: The handouts in class represent the major source of information for this course. The textbook can be helpful. Read sections in the book as they correspond to the areas on the syllabus. Don't bring the textbook to class; there is no goal or grade associated with weight training.

Grading: The final grade represents several components:

Element	app. % of grade
5–7 writing/oral assignments	50
Major project	20
Final	20
Participation	10

Access to Instructor: I will try to be in my office for the half hour immediately before class. However, since I am generally only on campus the one evening I teach, the best ways to get a message or assignments to me outside of class are:

1) e-mail (assignments can be attached)

2) contact the department secretary/leave material in my box

3) call me

4) arrange to meet at a time mutually convenient for the two of us

management perspective. Memos are a vital means for transmitting a management message, for providing management context, and for signaling importance—a measure largely achieved by invoking the natural authority the memo has as a tool of management.

Writing effective memos is achieved not by envisioning the memo as a hard-copy equivalent to e-mail or as the alter ego of the business letter, but as a unique document type that takes its cue from corporate policy. The successful memo is not the one that adheres to the template or uses the fewest words, but the one that remains true to its historically defined purpose, expectations, tone, and style (Table 11.3).

You manage a regional office of e-con.com, a company that designs professional training packages and consulting services for corporations interested in on-line commerce. In total, the company has five offices. Your office has approximately 75 employees, all very highly educated, broadly experienced, and—because of their particular talents—very mobile. Compensation and benefits packages are, in your estimation, quite attractive, a feature designed to attract and maintain top-notch talent.

There are stringent performance expectations. For instance, corporate policy, set at the national headquarters, states that "casual overtime" is considered part of the routine work and therefore not compensated (see inset). Recently, you have noticed that a growing number of employees are attempting various means to "recover" these uncompensated hours. They are coming in late, leaving early for lunch, taking extended breaks, and leaving without notice.

> **Employee Manual: Section 5. Overtime Pay**
>
> **Overtime Pay:** "Professional staff are expected to put in the hours needed to get assignments done. Overtime in excess of 8 hours in a single week will be compensated at a rate of 1½ the base pay; hours in excess of 12 hours in a single week will be compensated at a rate of 2 times the base pay. Casual overtime—fewer than 8 hours in a single week—will not be compensated."

You have been watching this development for a while, but now your boss, Ms. Vasquez, has scheduled an audit of your operation (a routine activity). Ms. Vasquez is known to be a stickler for discipline. The lax employee attitude may be bad for your image.

To fix the problem, you have developed an on-line time clock. Employees will "punch in" on their computers when they arrive at work, every time they leave their workstations for more than 20 minutes, and when they leave at the end of the day. Use of the time clock will be mandatory, and every absence of greater than 20 minutes will result in a deduction from the employee's salary.

☐ Group

Divide into groups.

1. Select at least three memos written by classmates (Individual exercise 1) about the time-clock policy and analyze how effective they are and why.

2. As a group, develop an improved version of at least one of the memos and present it to the class for discussion.

☐ Individual

1 Write a memo announcing the new time-clock policy.

2. Review at least three memos issued by your company or university. Prepare an evaluation explaining how well they represent the voice of management and what improvements in arrangement, tone, or information you would suggest.

3. Select a policy issued by your company or university. Draft a memo reinforcing its use by the entire organization.

[1] Table 11.1 is adapted from: Joanne Yates and Wanda J. Orlikowski, "Genres of Organizational Communication: A Structurational Approach to Studying Communication and Media," *Academy of Management Review,* Vol. 17, No. 2 (1992), pp. 299–326.

[2] Thomas J. Peters, "To: Corporate Managers, Re: Bureaucracy; Don't Send Memos!" *Washington Monthly,* Vol. 19, No. 10 (Nov. 1987), pp. 12–15.

[3] *Ibid.*

[4] Joanne Yates, "The Emergence of the Memo As a Managerial Genre," *Management Communication Quarterly,* Vol. 2, No. 4 (May 1989), pp. 485–510.

[5] H. William Rice, "Teaching the Art of the Memo: Politics and Precision." *Business Communication Quarterly,* Vol. 58, No. 1 (March 1995), pp. 31–34.

[6] Yates and Orlikowski, "Genres of Organizational Communication."

[7] Joanne Yates, *Control Through Communication: The Rise of System in American Management.* Baltimore: The Johns Hopkins University Press, 1989, pp. 5–6.

[8] Yates, "The Emergence of the Memo As a Managerial Genre."

[9] Yates and Orlikowski, "Genres of Organizational Communication."

[10] Carol David and Margaret Ann Baker, "Rereading Bad News: Compliance-Gaining Features in Management Memos," *Journal of Business Communication,* Vol. 31, No. 4 (Oct. 1994), pp. 267–290.

[11] Jo Ann Hennington, "Memorandums—An Effective Communication Tool for Management," *The ABCA Bulletin,* Sept. 1978, pp. 10–14.

[12] Walter Kiechel, III, "Memo Punctilio," *Fortune,* Sept. 15, 1986, pp. 185–186.

[13] Yates, "The Emergence of the Memo As a Managerial Genre."

[14] *Ibid.*

[15] *Economy and Efficiency in Government Service, Message of the President of the United States.* Doc. #670. 62nd Congress, 2nd Session, Washington, DC, 1912.

[16] Yates, "The Emergence of the Memo."

[17] Paula Jacobs, "Rules Still Apply for Memos' New Medium," *InfoWorld,* Vol. 21, No. 19 (May 10, 1999), p. 112.

[18] Figure 11.3 is adapted from Jo Ann Hennington, "Memorandums."

[19] Jo Ann Hennington, "Memorandums."

[20] Robert Half, "How Can I Write an Effective Memo?" *Management Accounting,* Vol. 73, No. 6 (Dec. 1991), p. 11.

[21] Robert Half, "How Can I Write an Effective Memo?"

[22] Thomas J. Peters, "To: Corporate Managers."

[23] H. William Rice, "Teaching the Art of the Memo."

[24] Quoted in Yates, "The Emergence of the Memo As a Managerial Genre."

[25] Quoted in Yates, *Control Through Communication,* p. 97.

[26] Kiechel, "Memo Punctilio."

[27] Kiechel, "Memo Punctilio."

[28] Simon Chapman, "Tobacco Industry Memo Reveals Passive Smoking Strategy," *British Medical Journal,* Vol. 314, No. 7094 (May 31, 1997), p. 1569.

Business Letters
Reasserting Our Innate Linguistic and Decision-Making Abilities

Although e-mail and memos may have surpassed business letters in terms of sheer volume, business letters are the clear winner when considered from the standpoint of longevity. The standard structure of a business letter has been around for several hundred years (Figure 12.1). However, what we are most familiar with are the formatting conventions, the basic use and positioning of such features as the date, salutation, and signature. The format is merely the shell of the communication. In addition, we need to concentrate on the substance of the letter—the relationship among form, audience, purpose, style, and reasoning. These elements, though equally (if not more) important as the format, are far less simple to master. Writing effective business letters has a long tradition but also has a number of relatively young challenges. We need to make certain that we know not only what the letter should look like, but also what we need to do to make our point straightforwardly and effectively.

A MODEL HISTORY

Beginning at least 800 years ago, standard formats and expectations existed for the preparation of business letters. As explained by Malcolm Richardson in "Business Writing and the Spread of Literacy in Late Medieval England," medieval students interested in writing business letters studied various

A model history

A bit of distortion

A bit of fancy modeling

- Mum's the word

- Gaining compliance

- Being polite

- . . . and getting off course

Where the model goes wrong

- Misunderstanding the business audience

- Mischaracterizing the business circumstance

- Misrepresenting the business purpose

The model recast

- Doing what comes naturally

- Revisiting the early guidance

- Employing the motivated sequence

- Ensuring the right balance

A closing note on politeness

Business letters—the lessons

models intended to address the spectrum of potential business and personal topics. The rhetorical style these students learned for use both in letters and legal documents was known as the *Ars dictaminis,* or more often as the *dictamin.* The stylistic elements of the *dictamin* were the basis of virtually all writing performed by scribes. As early as the beginning of the twelfth century, study of the *dictamin* was incorporated into the curricula of many European universities.

Further reinforcing the standard components of letters, students used formularies, books comprised mainly of model letters that were both imitated and adapted in the course of study. These models addressed a broad range of writing forms, including purely legal and diplomatic documents, personal letters, and business communications. With this heritage, by the time business began to grow in the fifteenth and sixteenth centuries, a standard set of formatting conventions had evolved from the *dictamin* (Table 12.1).[1]

Encouraging the spread of the *dictamin*'s teachings, formularies began to appear in popularized form, known as "letter-writers." Rather than functioning

FIGURE 12.1 • A Typical Business Letter Format

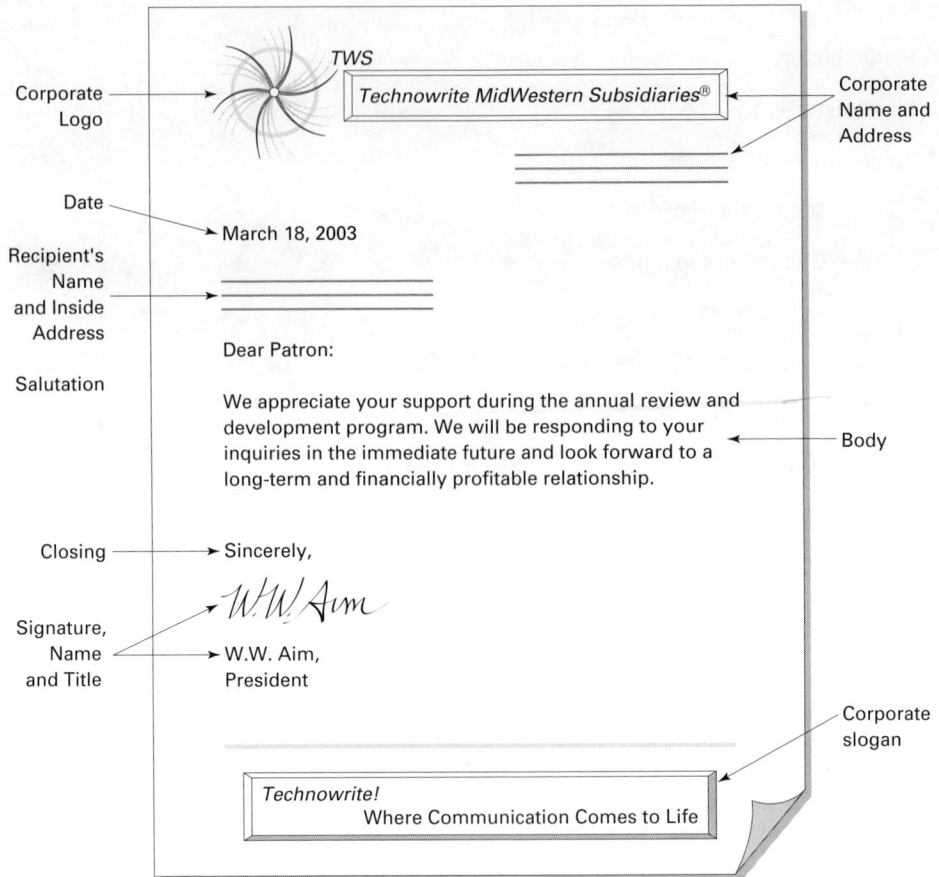

Corporate Logo

TWS
Technowrite MidWestern Subsidiaries®

Corporate Name and Address

Date

March 18, 2003

Recipient's Name and Inside Address

Salutation

Dear Patron:

We appreciate your support during the annual review and development program. We will be responding to your inquiries in the immediate future and look forward to a long-term and financially profitable relationship.

Body

Closing

Sincerely,

Signature, Name and Title

W.W. Aim,
President

Corporate slogan

Technowrite!
Where Communication Comes to Life

TABLE 12.1 THE BASIC SECTIONS OF THE *DICTAMIN*

Section	Expression
Address	"right trusty and well beloved". . . .
Salutation	"we greet you well"; "I recommend me to you,"
Notification	"and we let you wit [know] that . . ."
Exposition	"whereas . . ." "for as much as . . .,"
Disposition or Injunction	"wherefore we wol [will]"; in private correspondence usually beginning "wherefore," "therefore,"
Valediction	"and God have you in his keeping,"
Attestation and Date	" Written at . . . ," and the date, sometimes noted by the year of the king's reign (i.e., "the sixth year of King Harry the Sixth")

FIGURE 12.2

The Secretary's Guide, or Young Man's Companion
The Young Secretary's Guide: or, A Speedy Help to Learning
The Complete Letter-Writer: or, Young Secretary's Instructor
The Complete Letter-Writer: or, Polite English Secretary
The Complete Letter-Writer, Containing Familiar Letters
The New Complete American Letter-Writer: or, The Art of Correspondence
Juvenile Correspondence
The American Letter-Writer
Models of Letters in French and English
A New Academy of Compliments: or, The Lover's Secretary
The American Academy of Compliments
The New Universal Letter-Writer: or, Complete Art of Polite Correspondence

The Most Popular, Most Reprinted Letter-writers of the Eighteenth Century

primarily as university texts, letter-writers provided average citizens with models for use in all forms of "familiar" correspondence as might occur in business and family life. When *The Enimie of Idlenesse,* the first letter-writer written in English, was published in London in 1568, the popularity of these books soared.[2]

As one bibliographer of letter-writers notes, for hundreds of years beginning with *The Enimie of Idlenesse,* "letter-writers have been published in a steady flow and have circulated among those who wanted to write eloquent, polite, and effective letters of all sorts of subjects, but who lacked the skill to express themselves adequately. Confronted by the situation, such persons could, and still can, turn to a letter-writer or handbook containing model letters for all occasions."[3]

As evidence of the popularity of letter-writers, one bibliography of English letter-writers lists 239 titles published between 1560 and 1800; another bibliography, which addresses the period between 1698 and 1943, lists 416 titles. The letter-writers reached similar popularity in America, with some titles going through dozens of editions. In fact, as one leading bibliographer of letter-writers concludes "for about 100 years, or from 1698–1800, American needs were apparently served by a dozen titles" (Figure 12.2).[4]

Proceeding to the nineteenth century and the growth of American enterprise, we see these popular letter-writers shifting emphasis from a predominant focus on personal letters to an expanded set of guidance on writing business letters. This emphasis first becomes evident in the 1840s and steadily increased through the Civil War. By the 1870s, many manuals included entire chapters on business correspondence. With the prosperity of the 1880s and 1890s, manuals offered a variety of business models: application letters, collection letters, letters of inquiry, and letters conveying good news, bad news, and congratulations.[5]

Typical among the types of letter-writers and guidance of the late nineteenth century was *Hill's Manual of Social and Business Forms.* In addition to providing typical models (Figure 12.3), Thomas Hill also distilled the essence of writing effective business letters into nine pragmatic rules:

1. In letters of business, use as few words as possible.

2. Business letters should be promptly answered.

3. Use a clear, distinct writing, avoiding all flourish of penmanship or language.

4. Come at once to your subject, and state it so clearly that it will not be necessary to guess your meaning.

FIGURE 12.3

Hill's Business
Letter Guidance

60   LETTERS APPLYING FOR EMPLOYMENT.

Applications for Situations.

Letters Answering Advertisements.

THE following advertisements, taken from metropolitan papers, are but samples of hundreds of such to be seen every day in the advertising columns of the leading daily newspapers in the great cities; showing that abundant opportunities constantly offer for obtaining employment, the positions to be secured, however, by letters making application for them.

As a hundred different persons will sometimes make application for one position, which will be given to the individual writing the best letter, everything else being equal, this illustrates in a striking manner the importance of being able to write a letter elegantly and correctly.

Answer to an Advertisement for an Assistant Editor.

WANTED.

Miscellaneous.

WANTED—AN EDITORIAL ASSISTANT ON A literary paper. A thoroughly competent lady preferred. Address D 71, Herald office, New York.

WANTED—IN A GRAIN COMMISSION HOUSE, a smart lad for office work; must be a good penman. Address, in own handwriting, stating age and salary expected, W 32, Ledger office.

WANTED—A YOUNG LADY CLERK IN A DRY goods store. Must be accustomed to the business. Address, with reference, B 80, Picayune office.

WANTED—AN ASSISTANT BOOKKEEPER, one who writes neatly and rapidly; willing to work for a moderate salary, and who can bring A No. 1 recommendations. Address, stating experience and particulars, X. Y. Z., Bulletin office.

WANTED—AN EXPERIENCED BOOKKEEPER in a bank. Address, with reference, Z 61, Journal office.

WANTED—LADY COPYIST, ABLE TO WRITE A bold, distinct hand. Salary good. Address, in applicant's own handwriting, COPY, Republican office.

WANTED—A COMPETENT SALESMAN TO sell pianos—one who has experience and good references. Address, stating salary expected, PIANOS, Tribune office.

WANTED—AN ACCOMPLISHED, EDUCATED young lady as a companion, to travel for six months in Europe, with a gentleman, wife, and daughter. Must be a ready writer, a good conversationalist, and possess vivacity and pleasing manners. Wardrobe furnished, and money to pay all expenses. Address Z. B. M., Commercial office, stating where an interview can be had.

Maplewood, Mass., April 1, 18—.

Dear Sir:

Observing the enclosed advertisement in this morning's "Herald," I improve the opportunity by writing you an application for the place, as I am at present disengaged.

I graduated four years ago at Mrs. Willard's Seminary, Troy, N. Y., since which time I conducted the literary department of Frank Leslie's "Magazine of Fashion" up to October last, when failing health, resulting from too much close confinement, compelled me to travel abroad, from which journey, principally through England and France, I have just returned, with health completely restored.

I beg to refer you to Mrs. Leslie for testimonials. Being exceedingly fond of literary pursuits, I shall be happy to occupy the position you offer, if mutually agreeable.

Yours, Most Respectfully,

Harriet Sibley (May Myrtle.)

5. Give town, county, state, and date explicitly. It is frequently of great importance to know *when* a letter was written.

6. Read your letter carefully when finished, to see that you have made no omissions and mistakes. Also carefully examine your envelope to see that it is rightly directed, with postage-stamp affixed.

7. Copy all business letters, of your own, by hand, or with the copying press made for the purpose.

8. Send money by Draft, P. O. Money-Order, or Express, taking a receipt therefore; thus you have something to show for money guaranteeing you against loss. Always state in your letter the amount of money you send, and by what means sent.

9. Write date, and by whom sent, across the end of each letter received, and file for future reference, fastening the letters together with rubber bands, or

binding in a letter-file adapted to the purpose. The possession of a letter sometimes prevents litigation and serious misunderstanding.[6]

By the early part of the twentieth century, business communication (or Business English, as it was generally termed) became a subject in itself, as did business correspondence. At this point, correspondence models were explained in the context of writing principles, diction, reasoning, the nature of business, and, even, the psychology of human interaction. For example, let's look at the admonitions of George Burton Hotchkiss whose book entitled *Business English* was one of the earliest and most popular texts on business writing. In his 1916 text, Hotchkiss, who was head of the Department of Business English at the New York University School of Commerce, Accounts, and Finance, set three main requirements for "a complete mastery of Business English." The first requirement was, perhaps, the earliest call for an appreciation of the psychology of audience: "You must know people and the way their minds act—yes, psychology, if you choose to call it by a scientific name. You must know what qualities produce favorable impressions upon people and make them respond. And you must know how to secure these qualities." The second requirement was to gain a facility with the "technique of language": grammar, sentence-structure, word use, and punctuation. Third was an appreciation of basic patterns and models: "how to make a sale; how to adjust a complaint; how to collect money; how to handle each of the other typical situations that confront the correspondent."[7]

Tempered by the psychology of communication, models—as Hotchkiss's guidance makes apparent—were no longer sufficient. Models had to be understood in terms of personal interaction and the business context. As such, the three dimensions Hotchkiss advocated were integrated into a single course of study. Lessons about understanding the reader's point of view were coupled with discussions of appropriateness of phrasing and with examination of various types of business correspondence. Explanations about internal coherence accompanied study of sentence structure and preparation of credit and financial letters. (The Appendix provides an overview of the structure of study in Hotchkiss's text.)

Today, given the sophistication of communication study and the ever-expanding diversity, breadth, and complexity of American enterprise, we should find it even less tenable than did Hotchkiss and his contemporaries to rely on models. Clearly, it would be difficult, if not impossible, to provide a definitive set of models that represent the broad spectrum of business activities. We should recognize that models, such as the one offered at the beginning of this chapter, reflect only the structure, not the substance. The simplicity of business as conducted in the years from 1568 to the early twentieth century offered a much narrower expanse, one that conceivably could be addressed in a series of business letter models. The contemporary business landscape, in contrast, is much more diverse and specialized, representing not just industry-specific but also company- and department-specific communication needs.

Yet the struggle with complex purposes often leads to an attempt to greatly simplify and categorize the types of activities in which business engages on a daily basis. This same exercise in simplification can also color the study of business letters. Reminiscent of the formularies and letter-writers, the study of business correspondence is often distilled into examination of three categories of letters: the informative letter, the bad news letter, and the good news letter (Figure 12.4).[8] Circumventing Hotchkiss's mandate that "business English covers the substance of ideas, as well as the ways of thinking and the form of expression"

FIGURE 12.4

The Typical
Business Letter
Threesome

Letter-Writing Assignments

Approximately four weeks are spent on letter writing. During the first week, the students learn the dynamics of the writing process: planning, composing and revising. They then write the first of three letter assignments, a direct request (for information about career opportunities within an organization, a company's position on a certain issue or a government official's position on an issue, or anything that fits the description of "direct request"). The second letter assignment is a message of goodwill praising an organization about a product or service or an individual for something praiseworthy . . . . The third letter assignment is a letter of complaint, which is also mailed to someone responsible for dealing with such complaints.

and diminishing the significance of the rhetorical attributes of correspondence, the contemporary models, like their predecessors, provide far too narrow a perspective on the expectations or challenges of contemporary business letters.

A BIT OF DISTORTION

We should be careful not to let simple organization schemes and basic replication of models lead us away from the realities of day-to-day business life. First, we must not lose the opportunity to establish our personal stamp on the written products we produce. Even Thomas Hill, the author of the very popular letter-writer we quoted earlier, recognized this expectation, explaining to his readers that even though models might be of some assistance, "Letter writing affords a fine opportunity for the display of originality."

Second, we must not treat real demands, audiences, and purposes as if they are simply the members of a predictable equation, a concern that dates from at least the early days of the twentieth century. In his 1910 essay, "How Shall I Word It?," Max Beerbohm, an essayist and social critic, challenged both the letter-writers and those who relied on them. With tongue in cheek, Beerbohm took aim at those who were pursuing being "'original, fresh, and interesting' by dint of more or less strict adherence to sample":

> Indeed, if you were in any other one of the crises which this book is designed to alleviate, you might copy out and post the specially-provided letter without making yourself ridiculous in the eyes of its receiver— unless, of course, he or she also possessed a copy of the book. But—well, can you conceive any one copying out and posting one of these letters, or even taking it as the basis for composition? You cannot. That shows how little you know of your fellow-creatures. Not you nor I can plumb the abyss at the bottom of which such humility is possible. Nevertheless, as we know by that great and constant "demand," there the abyss is, and there multitudes are at the bottom of it. Let's peer down . . . . No, all is darkness. But faintly, if we listen hard, is borne up to us a sound of the scratching of innumerable pens—pens whose wielders are all trying, as the author of this handbook urges them, to "be original, fresh, and interesting" by dint of more or less strict adherence to sample.[9]

Third, we must recognize that the models themselves have faults. One characteristic problem is that reliance on models creates a strong possibility that the exchange will be robbed of its very being. Like the need for the "human moment" we spoke of in Chapter 8, models are generally devoid of and in opposition to dealing openly with the conflict, drama, and true dynamics of business interaction. The challenge, as Beerbohm extended it, would be for model authors to "sprinkle . . . a few less righteous examples" among the sample letters, "thereby purging [their] book of its monotony." (The Appendix provides one of these "less righteous" examples, a letter Beerbohm proposes as a model for anyone contemplating blackmail.)

Fourth, models (the early formularies, the popular letter-writers, or the contemporary threesome of good news, bad news, and information request) share a common problem—a mistaken belief that all purposes demanding written correspondence can be both identified and categorized. Identification of all circumstances (business or otherwise) is implausible. Although the specific purposes of a particular company might be reflected in a series of models, that set of models cannot be applied elsewhere in the industry, sometimes not even elsewhere in the same corporation.

These simplified categorization schemes were referenced at length in Chapter 1 when we examined various attempts to dismiss the complexity of business purpose: denials of knowable purposes, attempts to sidestep the multiplicity of purposes, and incomplete assessments of purpose. As we noted then, these dismissals of complexity inevitably lead to poor and incomplete responses. The same conclusion holds true when considering business correspondence. As Table 12.2 begins to make evident, business correspondence must address and accommodate a range of activities far beyond that reflected in a good news/bad news categorization scheme.[10]

Examining Table 12.2 brings numerous questions to mind. We might wonder, for instance, whether all "inquiries" are the same. Do they arise from the same circumstances? Do they share influencing and informing characteristics? Are the audience expectations the same, or even similar? The same questions might be asked of each of the other categories of letters listed. The answer to these questions is that the letters do not represent a single, predictable set of circumstances. Each category, in fact each letter, is potentially different. Adherence to models not only diminishes the sophistication of American enterprise, it also diminishes the integrity of the business message, the soundness of business reasoning, the appropriateness of business style, and the appreciation of the business audience. Yet, before we can dismiss these contemporary models, we need to understand not only how but why we have progressed from the diverse scope of the formularies to a more restricted set of business models in the letter-writers, and from there to the contemporary interest in good news letters, bad news letters, and information requests.

A BIT OF FANCY MODELING

A common thread that underlies formularies, letter-writers, and the contemporary models is an intense interest in maintaining social or business etiquette, in being polite. This interest becomes most evident in discussions of the bad news letter: "writing negative messages is one of the most difficult tasks facing business communicators. Because we usually find saying 'no' harder than saying 'yes,' and because refusing a request often is misinterpreted by a reader as personal rejection, most writers know enough to approach the task of writing negative

12.2 USE OF BUSINESS LETTERS

Letter Type	Managerial/Organizational Level*		
	Low (%)	Middle (%)	Upper (%)
Inquiries	41.7	19.1	20.6
Requests for products or services	36.4	21.1	25.0
Favorable replies	25.0	11.8	5.6
Orders	12.5	20.0	27.3
Claims	20.0	11.1	10.0
Refused requests	20.0	12.5	0
Refused adjustments	20.0	0	0
Collection	16.7	0	16.7
Credit reports	20.0	0	0
Back and incomplete orders	11.1	0	0
Applications	14.3	0	7.7

* Low-level managers directly manage operations and activities.
  Middle-level managers have supervisors and managers who report to them.
  Upper-level managers report directly to vice-presidential levels or higher.

Source: Reprinted with permission of the Association for Business Communication.

messages with some degree of caution."[11] Accordingly, we will focus on this one letter type, which is not only portrayed as the most difficult of the three, but also receives the greatest attention in the literature. We'll begin our analysis by looking at the two prevailing philosophies about transmitting bad news; then we'll take a look at the techniques these strategies promote.

MUM'S THE WORD

People are naturally reluctant to relay bad news. In a rare show of directness, two psychology professors at the University of Georgia named "this alleged tendency to keep mum about unpleasant messages the 'mum' effect." Explaining the effect, these psychologists pointed out in one of their studies that "The mum effect has been shown to be a pervasive, systematic bias in interpersonal communication. Over diverse settings, communicators, recipients, and messages, good news tends to be communicated more frequently, more quickly, more fully, and more spontaneously than bad news."[12]

Since the identification—or at least the labeling—of the mum effect in 1975, numerous studies have looked at the common reluctance to transmit bad news.

Yet, as we all know, bad news happens. To understand how we choose to transmit bad news (i.e., the bad news letter), we need to begin by understanding the options and decisions involved in transmitting bad news.

The first decision when we possess bad news is whether or not to transmit the information. A decision not to transmit the bad news leads to three options: 1) say nothing, 2) delegate, or 3) simply pass the buck. Saying nothing ends the issue (of course, until the matter surfaces in some other context). Delegation involves an appropriate assignment of the communication to someone lower in the hierarchy. An example of appropriate delegation might be transmitting results of disciplinary decisions, an action usually assigned to an employee's immediate manager, even if more senior managers contributed to the decision. In contrast, ducking responsibility, "discriminatory buck-passing," involves making someone else do your job, delegating the hatchet work to an assistant or staff member. Although they are clearly distinct actions, discriminating between delegation and passing the buck is not always easy.

As an example, consider the four options available to a personnel manager who must inform job applicants of the company's hiring decisions. The personnel manager has four possible options: 1) speak to all candidates directly, 2) delegate all communications to an assistant, 3) speak to candidates directly when the decision is to hire the individual, but have the assistant inform those candidates who will not be receiving a job offer, or 4) speak directly to those candidates who are not being hired, but have the assistant pass along good news to candidates about to receive a job offer. Options 2 and 3 may be either delegation or buck-passing depending on the motivation. If the personnel manager assigns the responsibility to an assistant as part of that individual's professional development, the act represents acceptable delegation. In contrast, if the manager is seeking to avoid confrontation, then the act is conscious buck-passing.[13]

Knowing how someone has come to the assignment of transmitting bad news clearly influences the next decision. Whoever ends up with the assignment to transmit the bad news now has three additional options: 1) communicate the bad news in a matter-of-fact manner, 2) downplay the negative components or consequences (e.g., suggest a reduced importance or relevance of the bad news), or 3) amplify and intensify the negative elements (e.g., be pessimistic or assign an overly dramatic significance to the news).[14]

The means by which the assignment was made and the following decisions about how to relay the information are eventually translated into attention to three variables that govern the relationship between the sender and the receiver of the bad news, variables that also underlie and influence the two primary schools of thought regarding how best to prepare bad news letters:

1. Distance—the relationship that exists between the communicator and audience
2. Power—who has the controlling role in the relationship
3. Imposition—the loss of prestige (or face) that may result as a consequence of the exchange

Theorists who concentrate on the implications associated with changes in the "power" variable tend to advocate that effectively transmitting bad news is best achieved by means of "compliance-gaining strategies." Theorists who prefer to ameliorate the consequences of the bad news or to maintain a cordial relationship, in contrast, advocate "politeness theory." In addition, each camp depends on an idealized concept of communication. As the principal founders of politeness theory acknowledge: "We attempt to account for some systematic aspects of language usage by constructing, tongue-in-cheek, a model person."[15] The model for writing bad news letters thus, as we are about to examine, becomes the second-generation derivative of an idealized, questionable conception of who business people are, how business people interact, and how business is thought to be conducted.

GAINING COMPLIANCE

Compliance-gaining, as its name implies, represents attempts by the communicator to elicit a particular, "preconceived response" from the audience by concentrating on and taking advantage of the power variable. Compliance-gaining strategies may, at first, sound in total alignment with other reasonable attempts to persuade an audience. However, the critical differentiating factor between compliance-gaining and other methods is the objective of controlling power. The intent is not merely to persuade. The preconceived response, as one extensive analysis reports, is achieved only when "the actor manipulates the

TABLE 12.3

SAMPLE POSITIVE AND NEUTRAL COMPLIANCE-GAINING TECHNIQUES

Techniques	Phrasing examples
Reward-Oriented	
1. Immediate Reward From Behavior	You will find it interesting.
2. Deferred Reward From Behavior	It will help you with upcoming work-related assignments.
3. Reward From Supervisor	I will make it beneficial.
4. Reward From Others	Other employees will respect you for it.
5. Self-Esteem	You always do such a good job.
6. Positive Superior-Subordinate Relationship	I will think more highly of you.
7. Altruism	Other employees will benefit if you do this.
Neutral Techniques	
8. Normative Rules	It's the way we do things around here.
9. Expertise	From my experience, it is a good idea.
10. Supervisor Feedback	It will help me know your problem areas.
11. Peer Modeling	Your coworker friends are doing it.
12. Supervisor Modeling	This is the way I always do it.

target's behavior, altering it from what would have been without the actor's involvement."[16]

Compliance-gaining as an organizing strategy represents more manipulation than cooperation, more outcome-oriented than audience-oriented action. Sometimes the compliance-gaining techniques can be neutral or even positive (Table 12.3).[17] More commonly, the strategies, based as they are on establishing sanctions and engaging audience needs, represent a broad spectrum of questionable appeals, many of which (even when positive) represent the types of logical fallacies we have been coached against in English and speech courses because they intentionally seek to manipulate our emotions rather than appeal to our reason (Table 12.4).[18]

Given its reliance on power, the only truly appropriate opportunities to employ compliance-gaining techniques in a manner where there is not a manipulative quality are when maintaining the significant power imbalance is an overt theme of the correspondence, or when the goal is to shift the balance of power in favor of the recipient.

TABLE

12.4   A SUMMARY OF COMPLIANCE-GAINING APPEALS

Strategy	How Invoked
Allurement	Compliance will indirectly benefit the audience by creating a circumstance in which others will benefit; those recipients, in turn, will be beholding to the audience
Altruism	An intense appeal for help or assistance from the recipient, creating an argument that in so responding the audience will be perceived as kind, heroic, generous, or self-sacrificing
Aversive Stimulation	Compliance is portrayed as the only perceived means of ending some form of punishment, pain, or ridicule.
Deceit	Compliance is gained by misrepresenting the situation, the context, or the consequences. For example, a big reward for action might be offered, but the offerer knows they do not have the authority to deliver on the promise
Esteem	Promises are made; in exchange for compliance, the audience will gain increased power, status, competency, or moral/ethical standing
Guilt	A failure to comply will result in diminished self-worth, political station or clout, integrity, or respect of the community
Hinting	Compliance is gained by indirect suggestion, pointing the audience in the desired direction. (As an example, the statement might be something like: "If someone were to report this to the Board, they'd probably be in for a promotion.")
Ingratiation	A range of tangible and intangible reinforcement is offered, extending from subtle acknowledgements to unctuous displays of "brown-nosing"
Promise	A trade or compromise (some future action) is offered in exchange for compliance
Threat	A failure to comply will result in significant adverse conditions, e.g., loss of job

Promoting and sustaining the power differential may occur in correspondence where you have the force of law or some equivalent power on your side. Probably no better example of compliance-gaining invoked in the name of law exists than in letters authored by the Internal Revenue Service (IRS). Granted significant authority by government regulation, the IRS has designed some of its correspondence purposely to intimidate the audience by emphasizing the power differential between itself and the taxpayer. For example, consider the power relationship implied in the letter the IRS issues to people assumed to owe back taxes (Figure 12.5).

In contrast, sales letters demonstrate precisely the opposite realignment of power—transferring the balance of power to the recipient. These letters, as one might expect, rely heavily on positive compliance-gaining techniques (e.g., reward, self-esteem, promise, and allurement) to foster a sustained relationship. We are regularly enticed by solicitations that promise to make us better people in some way. Done well, these letters create a bond, promoting trust, confidence, and well-being through use of a fairly recognizable vocabulary and phrasing:

world-renowned	veteran	promise
time-tested	protects	secure
seasonal	pledge	stable
performs	rigorous standards	warmly
pioneer	testimonial	sound
gets results	strong	you may cancel at any time[19]

FIGURE 12.5

Speaking With the Authority of Law

> THIS NOTICE REQUIRES A RESPONSE
> WE ARE PROPOSING CHANGES TO YOUR TAX RETURN
>
> We are proposing changes to your . . . tax return because information you reported does not match what was reported to us by your employers, banks, and/or other payers. Our proposed amount you owe is $ . . . . See our proposed changes on page 2 and the detailed information beginning on page 3.
>
> Please compare your records with the payer information that begins on page 3. To assist you in reviewing your return, the taxpayer information may show both reported and unreported amounts. However, the proposed changes shown on page 2 are based on the unreported amounts only.
>
> If you AGREE with our proposed changes:
> * Check Box A on the response page
> * Sign and date the total agreement statement. Both spouses must sign if you filed a joint return.
> *If possible, enclose your payment in full.
> If you can not pay the entire amount, you can request an installment agreement by completing the last page of this notice.
>
> If you DISAGREE with our proposed changes:
> * Check Box B on the response page
> * Enclose a signed statement explaining each change you disagree with and why you disagree
> *Send us the response page with your statement and supporting documents in the enclosed . envelope
>
> It is important that we receive your response by . . . . If we don't receive your response, we will conclude that our proposed changes are correct. Then we will send you a Notice of Deficiency followed by a bill for the proposed amount you owe including tax and any penalties plus additional interest.

BEING POLITE

Essentially concurrent with the organizational psychologists who concentrated on the power variable of the author-audience relationship, linguists turned their attention to the variables of distance and imposition to assess how best to transmit bad news. They developed "politeness theory," an attempt to maintain the relationship and lessen the severity of "face-threatening acts." According to this theory, "politeness is used to redress face-threatening acts, or actions that threaten another's needs to be publicly appreciated and be free of impositions." Not surprisingly, politeness theory is thereby assumed to be of significant value when "communicating bad news because bad news is a face-threatening act that directly threatens the recipient's needs to be appreciated and acknowledged."[20]

Explained by Penelope Brown and Stephen Levinson, the principal authors of politeness theory, the relationship between sender and receiver is controlled by 1) positive politeness—attempts to build bridges by claiming common ground, focusing on cooperation, and seeking to fulfill the receiver's wants or interests, and 2) negative politeness—attempts to minimize friction by allowing more freedom of action, minimizing the degree of severity of the imposition, and disassociating either the sender or receiver from the activity. These strategies, like their compliance-gaining counterparts, can be evidenced in telltale linguistic traits (Figures 12.6 and 12.7).[21]

Between politeness theory and compliance-gaining techniques, all three variables affecting the sender-receiver relationship are subject to management and manipulation. Compliance-gaining is advocated where power is predominant, when communicating "boldly without redress." Politeness theory, in contrast, is advocated in those interactions where "(1) the authors do not have vastly superior power over their clients; (2) the danger to their client's face is not minimal . . . ; (3) and face demands cannot be left unattended because of overwhelming urgency or efficiency."[22]

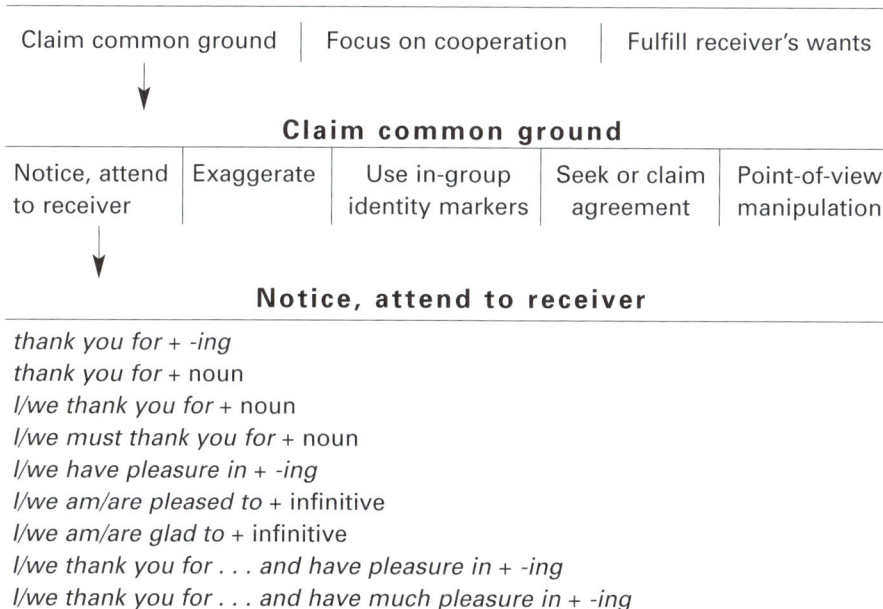

Claim common ground	Focus on cooperation	Fulfill receiver's wants

Claim common ground

Notice, attend to receiver	Exaggerate	Use in-group identity markers	Seek or claim agreement	Point-of-view manipulation

Notice, attend to receiver

thank you for + -ing
thank you for + noun
I/we thank you for + noun
I/we must thank you for + noun
I/we have pleasure in + -ing
I/we am/are pleased to + infinitive
I/we am/are glad to + infinitive
I/we thank you for . . . and have pleasure in + -ing
I/we thank you for . . . and have much pleasure in + -ing

FIGURE 12.6

Positive Politeness Strategies

Source: Reprinted from *Journal of Pragmatics,* Vol. 28, Morten Pilegaard, "Politeness in Written Discourse; A Textlinguistic Perspective on Requests," pp. 223–244, Copyright 1997, with permission of Elsevier Science.

FIGURE 12.7

Negative Politeness Strategies

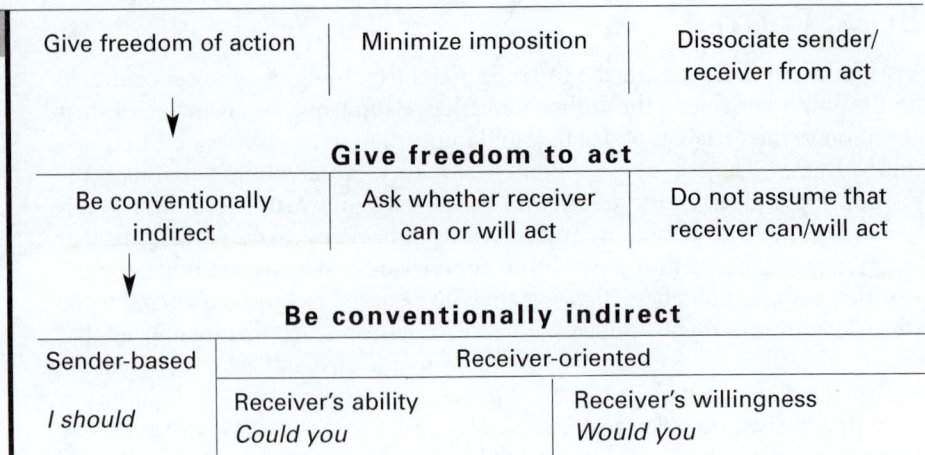

Give freedom of action	Minimize imposition	Dissociate sender/ receiver from act

↓

Give freedom to act

Be conventionally indirect	Ask whether receiver can or will act	Do not assume that receiver can/will act

↓

Be conventionally indirect

Sender-based	Receiver-oriented	
	Receiver's ability	Receiver's willingness
I should	*Could you*	*Would you*

Source: Reprinted from *Journal of Pragmatics,* Vol. 28, Morten Pilegaard, "Politeness in Written Discourse; A Textlinguistic Perspective on Requests," pp. 223–244, Copyright 1997, with permission of Elsevier Science.

GETTING OFF COURSE

Politeness and compliance-gaining are natural attributes of human interaction and business communication. Despite this fact, the most serious problem arises when either technique is used to manipulate the audience. A less ominous, but equally serious, communication problem surfaces when these techniques are used to manipulate the message through indirectness or evasion.

INDIRECTNESS. Whether predicated on politeness theory or compliance-gaining techniques, almost every business communication textbook suggests that some form of indirectness be used when transmitting bad news. In contrast to Hill's nineteenth-century rule to "come at once to your subject," the contemporary thinking is to come eventually to your subject. The popular advice is to use some form of a "buffer"—in opening sentences or the opening paragraph—to avoid coming directly to the message. As one study of 10 business communication textbooks summarized, "all ten recommend using an 'indirect strategy' consisting of a 'buffer' opening, a neutral statement of the reasons for the bad news, a diplomatic or implied statement of the negative decision itself, and a helpful, friendly, positive close . . ."[23] The buffer is "intended to ensure the writer appears interested in and appreciative of the reader's point of view, and generally to establish a positive attitude." Eventually, albeit indirectly, we arrive at the message. However, the "appearance" of interest may have already created a perception that we are not at all interested, and, moreover, that we are not being candid, forthright, or sincere.

EVASION. More troubling than indirectness is advocating misdirection and evasion. It is only a brief distance from the "diplomatic or implied statement of the negative decision" noted above to a more evasive strategy. Like the manager who chooses not to communicate bad news, written evasion is the equivalent of willfully manipulating important information. Table 12.5 illustrates how certain techniques contribute to evasion.[24]

Yet, simple evasion creates a slippery slope and can easily spin out of control. In such cases, evasion techniques are much more explicit, going so far as to substitute excuses for truth. Beginning from the fundamental axiom that "most negatives are responses to requests," one article suggests five principal strategies are employed "when addressees of a request want not to comply, but also to lessen

TABLE 12.5   EMPLOYED POLITENESS STRATEGIES

Politeness strategy	How expressed	Face-saving goal
1. Discredit the source directly	"How would they know?"	Minimize threat
2. Decrease importance	"This is only interim"	Minimize threat
3. Disagree explicitly	"They are wrong"	Minimize threat
4. Providing acts for improvement	"Let's work on . . ."	Hedging

the social threat of refusing":

1. Deny that an item referred to in the request exists.
2. Deny having the authority or responsibility for the action.
3. Deny that the circumstances allow the action to be completed.
4. Claim inability to perform the requested act.
5. Cite reasons why something other than the requested action is what's needed. [25]

Accompanying these evasive techniques, buried in the article's footnotes, is a sixth potential strategy: "Cite reasons for your unwillingness to perform the requested act." The reason why telling the truth is relegated to the footnotes is, as the author explains: "Obviously, it is more polite to claim inability than unwillingness since inability presupposes that the writer's reasons for refusing are not within his or her control." Arguing that it is better to be polite than to tell the truth, the same footnote invites us as communicators to turn our communication assignments into exercises in situational ethics: "It is important to remember that the use of a particular strategy for refusing a request need not necessarily reflect the actual reason for the refusal; the purpose of the strategies is to maintain social relations (i.e., to be polite). Therefore, even though many decisions to refuse the reader's request in the business world may be the actual result of the writer's unwillingness, if the writer wants to maintain the goodwill of the reader by being polite as possible, he will be better off implying that he is unable to fulfill the reader's request." We might conclude from this reasoning that "goodwill rather than good communication" is our paramount responsibility. Certainly, that can't be the basis of our actions.

Acceptance of indirectness as a communication strategy has given rise to evasion; evasion has, in turn, become distortion. Distortion has become denial and, ultimately, denial has become deceit. Compliance-gaining and politeness theory have fused together in the act of defeating effective communication. While we were unlikely to have great respect for the manager who ducked responsibility when expected to transmit bad news, are we likely to have respect for the letter-writer who uses fabrication to escape discomfort? Would we want to sign correspondence that is misleading? (Not to mention that these ethical lapses are also likely to invoke strong corporate responses, including the possibility of termination.)

WHERE THE MODEL GOES WRONG

Although our business correspondence should always be polite, we should now feel uncomfortable about compliance-gaining and politeness techniques as overt communication strategies. Further, even in those limited applications where politeness theory or compliance-gaining techniques might be warranted, using these approaches as organizing strategies leaves us to face a maze of inexact and confusing guidance. Summarizing the dilemma associated with practicing these techniques, one article notes the following difficulties:

> How exactly are business communicators, especially students, to know *when* to "subordinate an unpleasant thought"? What counts as "unpleasant"? When is an agent "unimportant" . . . . The textbooks remain silent on these and similar points . . . . In addition, textbook advice on handling negative messages appears contradictory. Students are told, as leading principle, to follow the "C's" of Clarity, Conciseness, and Confidence—to go baldly, on record, as it were; but they are also told to be diplomatic, to imply negative news—to use redressive on-record strategies or even apparently, to go off-record. But students *aren't* told *how* one uses language to be diplomatic or to imply. [However,] . . . in many contexts, business communicators *cannot* imply, or go off-record. Students, then, rarely, if ever receive principled, research-based explanations of how Clarity, Conciseness, and Confidence . . . often conflict with another important "C" often invoked in the textbooks—Courtesy.[26]

Balancing the four C's (clarity, conciseness, confidence, and courtesy) appears to represent a trade-off between concise statements that are less polite and longer statements that, while more polite, introduce their own communication challenges. However, the real trade-off is between the choices of attending to the message or adopting a manipulative, indirect, or evasive strategy. Exercising these strategies—manipulation, indirectness, and evasion—does business a serious disservice, one that can best be understood in terms of the rhetorical principles we examined in Part 1 of this text: The strategies badly misunderstand the business audience, mischaracterize the business circumstance, and misrepresent the business purpose.

MISUNDERSTANDING THE BUSINESS AUDIENCE

Advocates of politeness theory and compliance-gaining tend to implicitly misstate the nature of the business audience, making questionable assumptions about what the audience expects and how it will react. Business is a world of give-and-take, of negotiated actions and agreements. Businesspeople can accept negatives, bad news, and rejected requests. Contrary to the theory, bad news is not always a "face-threatening act that directly threatens the recipient's needs to be appreciated and acknowledged." Nor is it true that a recipient necessarily takes no as a personal affront. To the contrary, many business exchanges have greater probability of producing a negative rather than a positive response. For example, a search for a job or a request for reassignment is often more likely to result in rejection than in approval. The suggestion that "readers never want to hear 'no' in a letter, for they desire and expect a 'yes' answer to a request" is simply wrong.[27]

The issues can be seen plainly in advice about buffers (text added with the single purpose of allowing the audience to save face or to lessen the intensity of the bad news). The most grievous problem occurs when the buffer is proposed and sanctioned as a manipulative device, as demonstrated in the following illustration: "The fact is that you start bad news messages by 'beating around the bush,' but you do it skillfully. Beating around the bush has a bad reputation because most people do it so clumsily that it's quite obvious. It works only when the reader doesn't notice what you're up to. By the end of this chapter, you'll be an expert at it."[28]

Additionally, placement of the buffer also suggests a certain misunderstanding of the audience. Placing a buffer in the first paragraph as is typically the process may actually have little benefit for or effect on the business reader who, through experience, knows where the key information is likely to appear in a particular type of correspondence. Just as students receiving responses to college applications can be expected to scan to find the critical phrases indicating their acceptance or rejection, so too, business professionals can be expected to skim by a letter's contents on the way to the critical part of the correspondence.

Use of the buffer suggests several other misunderstandings about the business audience. Buffers suggest that a writer can, as one critic notes, "use sequence to manipulate a reader's response." The expectation stems from an assumption that readers not only read, but also react in a particular sequence: "The implicit assumption is that readers . . . will read sentence 1 and have reaction A. Then they will read sentence 2, and have reaction B—or rather, A', since the original reaction will not be replaced but only modified by the next sentence. Thus, when they read sentence 5, the zinger, they will not have reaction E, the reaction that they would have had if they had read the sentence by itself, but rather reaction A'''', a reaction mediated by all previous ones."[29]

Although readers might be assumed to suspend reaction until they can infer where the message is heading, they may—in response to the buffer—make intuitive leaps. The business professional who senses misdirection or an intentional effort to procure agreement rather than unfold or advance an argument is likely to become suspicious. That suspicion will trigger one of two responses: that the reader will skip ahead to identify the real message, or that the reader, alerted by the buffer, will become more guarded and will avoid walking into a trap by consciously reacting in a fashion designed to counter the buffer. In either case, the value of the buffer is negated, a fact substantiated in several studies looking at both the positioning and impact of buffers.

One such study looked at more than 200 rejection letters sent to people seeking publication in academic journals. Contrary to the suggested formula for transmitting bad news, 53.8% of the letters stated the rejection in the first paragraph, and 17.9% started the letter with the rejection. Another 38.5% included the rejection in the second sentence. As the authors of the survey noted, the placement of the bad news did not adversely affect the recipients' sense of self, or their attitudes toward the letter or its author: "Placement was not correlated with either recipients' self-perceptions or their perceptions of the negative letter and the sender." These two facts (unbuffered placement of bad news and the recipients' acceptance of getting the news immediately) led to two important conclusions in the study: 1) "The placement of the rejection is not significant: Real-life letters may deviate significantly from textbook standard." 2) Buffers, in practical, professional environments, add little value to presenting bad news: "Instructors may stop insisting that their students provide buffers."[30]

To allow us personally to test these conclusions about buffer placement and impact, consider your reaction to the following buffer paragraph included in a letter from a bank Vice President:

> Congratulations on the beautiful landscaping job you've done on your property. Last summer I drove by your home on my way to work and was very impressed with your garden—particularly the roses. I know you must have worked almost every weekend to get such quick results.[31]

Few of us would react without some skepticism. Is the Vice President really interested in complimenting our garden? Somewhere, shortly, we expect to see the sales pitch or the bad news. Are we about to be offered a new credit card, a new mortgage rate, or—more concerning—are we delinquent on some payment? Our natural alarm mechanism will not allow us to keep reading in a linear fashion. We want to know the real agenda. The delaying tactic is not perceived as a positive reflection on the letter or its author. Our response, similar to that experienced by the recipients of the rejection letters, negates the value of the buffer; it confirms the actual nature of reactions people have when encountering manipulation, indirection, and evasion.

FIGURE 12.8

Good News From the Government

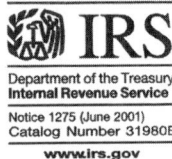

IRS

Department of the Treasury
Internal Revenue Service

Notice 1275 (June 2001)
Catalog Number 31980B

www.irs.gov

Notice of Status and Amount of Immediate Tax Relief

Dear Taxpayer:

We are pleased to inform you that the United States Congress passed and President George W. Bush signed into law the Economic Growth and Tax Relief Reconciliation Act of 2001, which provides long-term tax relief for all Americans who pay income taxes.

The new tax law provides immediate tax relief in 2001 and long-term tax relief for the years to come.

As part of the immediate tax relief, you will be receiving a check in the amount of

   $600.00   during the week of   08/27/2001.

Your amount is based on information you submitted on your 2000 federal tax return and is just the first installment of the long-term tax relief provided by the new law. The amount of the check could be reduced by any outstanding federal debt you owe, such as past due child support or federal or state income taxes. You need to take no additional steps. Your check will be mailed to you. You will not be required to report the amount as taxable income on your federal tax return.

On the reverse side of this letter is information on how your check amount was calculated. If you need additional information, please visit the IRS web site at **www.irs.gov** or call 1-800-829-4477. Please keep a copy of this notice with your tax records.

One last example, one encountered by millions of Americans, should seal this point. As part of an economic stimulus plan enacted during President George W. Bush's first year in office, the IRS sent letters to every taxpayer in America announcing a program of tax rebates. Letters were designed to let taxpayers know precisely how much they were going to receive and when. Looking at Figure 12.8, just how long did it take for you to isolate this key information? Probably not long. Like most Americans, you probably skipped right past the introductory information. Even when the news is good, as in Figure 12.8, we disprove the theory that we can be expected to read and react in sequence.

Yet, what happens when the IRS's letter is designed to communicate bad news? Will a buffer make the information more palatable? Figure 12.9 is the letter received by taxpayers who were not eligible for a rebate. The bad news—no money is on its way—doesn't surface until the last sentence of paragraph 2. Do you believe recipients felt better because of the buffer? Do you expect recipients of this letter came away with a sense of goodwill or with a sense of dissatisfaction? The buffer, more than softening the blow, amplifies the aggravation. The reader, as this final example illustrates, is generally better served, and probably less put out, by a straightforward answer rather than by indirectness, evasion, or manipulation.

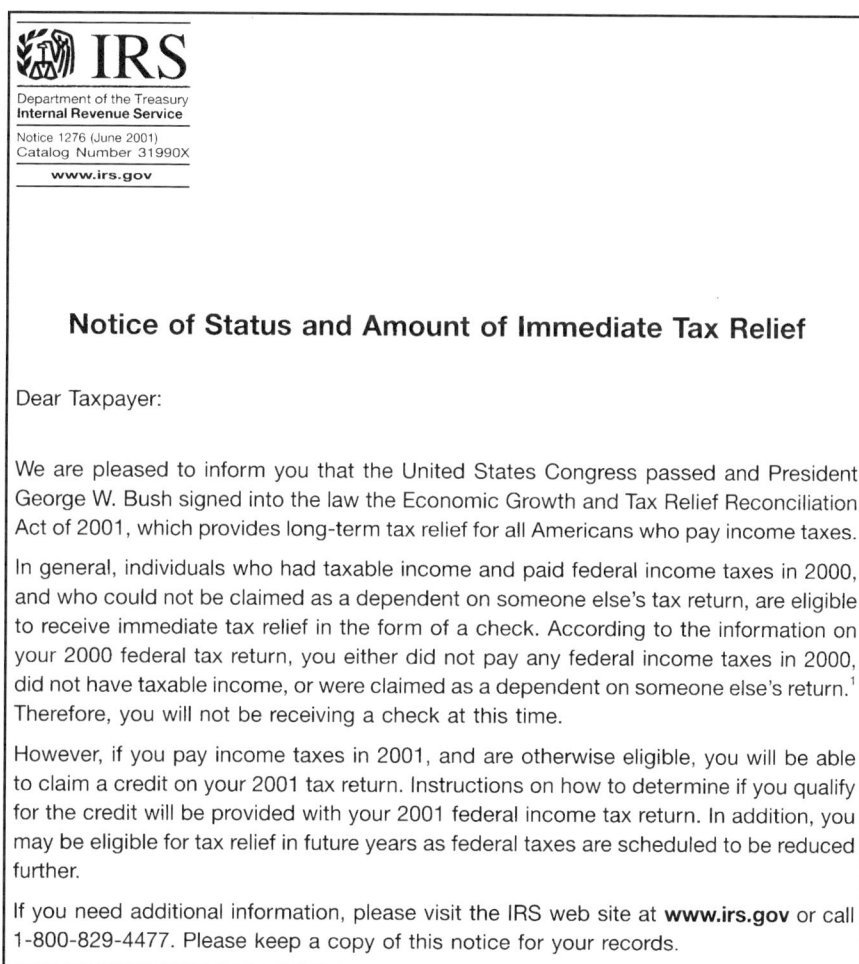

FIGURE 12.9

Or So You Thought

IRS
Department of the Treasury
Internal Revenue Service
Notice 1276 (June 2001)
Catalog Number 31990X
www.irs.gov

Notice of Status and Amount of Immediate Tax Relief

Dear Taxpayer:

We are pleased to inform you that the United States Congress passed and President George W. Bush signed into the law the Economic Growth and Tax Relief Reconciliation Act of 2001, which provides long-term tax relief for all Americans who pay income taxes.

In general, individuals who had taxable income and paid federal income taxes in 2000, and who could not be claimed as a dependent on someone else's tax return, are eligible to receive immediate tax relief in the form of a check. According to the information on your 2000 federal tax return, you either did not pay any federal income taxes in 2000, did not have taxable income, or were claimed as a dependent on someone else's return.[1] Therefore, you will not be receiving a check at this time.

However, if you pay income taxes in 2001, and are otherwise eligible, you will be able to claim a credit on your 2001 tax return. Instructions on how to determine if you qualify for the credit will be provided with your 2001 federal income tax return. In addition, you may be eligible for tax relief in future years as federal taxes are scheduled to be reduced further.

If you need additional information, please visit the IRS web site at **www.irs.gov** or call 1-800-829-4477. Please keep a copy of this notice for your records.

MISCHARACTERIZING THE BUSINESS CIRCUMSTANCE

A problem also exists regarding what these strategies say about how business is conducted. Two inferences might be drawn from the popular advice: 1) There is an adversarial relationship between author and recipient. 2) Business is not conducted using a series of exchanges, but, rather, through isolated, one-directional communications. However, neither inference is correct.

The mistaken adversarial notion is implied by the proposed need to mislead or misdirect the audience (whether done skillfully or not). Instead of reflecting an adversarial relationship, business correspondence is an active reflection of the three phases of the business process: making contact, negotiating, and resolving conflict. Each of these phases of the business relationship demands directness, honesty, and integrity. In addition, each phase has unique expectations and employs unique types of business correspondence.

The working relationship may begin, for instance, with a seller issuing sales letters announcing savings opportunities. In this contact stage, there may be a series of inquiries and associated follow-up responses. Negotiating is next conducted using various quotations, definitions of terms and agreements, and—if the relationship extends to its successful conclusion—correspondence pertaining to placement of orders. Beyond the negotiation stage, there may be a final series of exchanges: reminders (about delivery or payment), complaints about lapses in fulfilling agreed-to obligations, and a variety of legal and contractual correspondence depending on the degree and severity of the conflict.

Unlike the static business universe implicit in promotion of compliance-gaining techniques and politeness theory, each of these phases is characterized by changes in the relationship between participants—a continuous shifting in the dynamics of distance, power, and imposition. Distance generally diminishes as the sender-receiver relationship matures. While there is a large distance between parties initially, this distance closes rapidly as the relationship moves from the contact to the negotiation stage; thereafter the distance remains relatively fixed. The power variable also tends to shift. Initially the primary power resides with the recipient, who has the option of whether or not to continue the relationship.

The power is then equalized in the negotiation stage, where both parties deal from equally strong vantage points. If the relationship enters the conflict stage, the power may be with either party. A refusal to respond would give the advantage to the sender; proceeding with some formal action (e.g., a lawsuit) would place the power advantage with the recipient. Last, imposition, in most cases, is a function of how well the interactions remain within accepted business rules and norms. Like those authors who received rejection notices, imposition (bad news) is understood consistent with accepted practice and generally anticipated outcomes.[32]

The dynamics of the relationship, therefore, also diminish the suitability of relying on formulaic models and manipulative strategies. The reliance on these tactics does not acknowledge the uniqueness of the business audience; neither does it show a keen appreciation for business circumstance. The strategies mistake business purposes.

MISREPRESENTING THE BUSINESS PURPOSE

Business purpose, intentionally or not, is often placed in a secondary role when the communicator's emphasis is redirected to compliance-gaining or politeness.

"Couching with politeness strategies," as one author explains, presents the "highest potential for information distortion, because the communicator is actually trying to decrease the threat of an inherently face-threatening act."[33] The road stretches directly from politeness to distraction, distraction to indirectness, indirectness to evasion, and finally from evasion to information distortion—the loss of the message.

Try to determine the message intended in the following letter received by an applicant for a university position:

> Thank you for your inquiry about the advertised position at Superior. We have been making headway identifying candidates whose credentials and experience seem to meet our needs, and we have made plans to invite two or three for an interview. Our needs, of course, could change, so we will keep your letter and supporting information on file through the summer. Thank you for your interest in the position and for being patient while we have reviewed the applications.

Is the applicant going to get the job? Is the candidate at least on a short list that is undergoing further evaluation? Not certain? In fact, the original purpose of the letter was to inform the candidate that this application had not been selected for further consideration. As the author of this example notes: "The reader of this letter could be forgiven for assuming that those interview plans might still include him or her, since the letter fails clearly to state otherwise. Even a change as simple as saying 'we have invited' rather than 'we have made plans to invite' would help make it clear that the recipient of this letter is not on the guest list."

Clearly, in this example, being polite and saving face are achieved at the expense of purpose. Purpose has taken on a secondary role. The letter's recipient—or for that matter the recipient of any business letter—deserves better: "The motive behind these rejection letters that fail to reject is no doubt a humane one, an effort to cushion the applicant from an unpleasant truth. The effect of such circumlocution is often, however, anything but comforting . . . . The least the hopeful applicant deserves is a clear statement of where he or she stands, even if it comes in just a two- or three-sentence missive."[34]

Although losing complete sight of our purpose may be a relatively infrequent consequence of an undue emphasis on minimizing face-threatening acts, a distortion of purpose is relatively common. This problem stems from exaggerated attention to manipulating power, distance, or imposition rather than an intent focus on achieving the purpose at hand.

The irony is, however, that all these missteps might be remedied by reacquainting ourselves with what has been called our natural "pragmatic competence," our innate ability to transfer our facility with human interactions to our business correspondence. Such a step would not demand any deep psychological study; rather, we need merely to reinvoke the originally-intended meaning of that fourth "C"—courtesy. We need to reacquaint ourselves with the nineteenth- and early twentieth-century concept of "business courtesy," which was understood as a natural capability of all communicators. Acknowledging our innate capabilities, in turn, will free us to move away from a study of manipulative techniques and instead devote ourselves more fully to the task of effectively communicating business information.

THE MODEL RECAST

DOING WHAT COMES NATURALLY

The solution to the manipulation, indirectness, and evasion is simple. Rather than focusing our energies on crafting politeness strategies and compliance-gaining techniques, we should entrust these linguistic responsibilities to business convention and to our innate abilities: tact, diplomacy, civility, and courtesy. Even in business correspondence and business communication, our innate abilities at maintaining effective, sustained interpersonal relationships is well documented—at all levels of the organization.

For example, an extensive study of writing done at an auditing firm showed that the writing was well adapted to the audience, the business circumstance, and the purpose. In particular, the researchers recognized that compliance-gaining factors, buffers, and politeness techniques—where applicable—were an inherent component of the professional discourse. "Real-world business communicators like the firm's auditors rarely must convey context only; usually they also must [take] great pains to adjust their language to the delicate demands of interpersonal diplomacy."

Although we might be inclined to criticize the apparent stilted style reflected in the auditors' writing (Figure 12.10), the researchers concluded that the writing style accurately incorporated needed compliance-gaining and politeness techniques. Further, as they reported, each device was "employed with good reason." Given the significance of this insight, the researchers' conclusion is worth quoting at length:

> The impersonal, hedging style The Firm prefers protects it from overstepping its boundaries by making explicit its limited role in drawing conclusions from necessarily incomplete data. Furthermore, impersonal, mitigated constructions minimize potential impositions on clients by playing down The Firm's recommendations. The characteristic style of The Firm's letters is *the language of diplomacy,* which enables interactions in any potentially threatening social setting to stay within their preordained preserves, insulating them from direct confrontations . . . .
>
> The linguistic politeness strategies in The Firm's writing and the intentions motivating them do not reflect the esoteric practices of auditors or diplomats alone. Rather, they are readily explicable instances of the universal politeness patterns all language users employ in daily interaction.[35]

This natural capacity to apply reasonable compliance-gaining and politeness strategies where needed is equally evident at the top of the business chain, in the

FIGURE 12.10

When Compliance and Politeness Come Naturally

Based on our *limited* view, *it appears* that internal audit *could* contribute significantly to the Corporation through increased *involvement* in user testing and *reviews* of specific applications before *implementation* and on a *post-implementation* basis. At a minimum, internal audit *should be notified* of all program changes and major scheduling/processing changes. Additionally, internal audit *should* participate in the *development and testing* of new systems and major changes *whenever possible*. Internal audit *may* also *be of assistance* in *preparation and planning* for the new facility.

writing done by CEOs. In Chapter 11, we reviewed an entire genre that illustrated the kinds of compliance-gaining techniques employed by senior management. Analyses have also identified numerous politeness techniques employed in the writing by this same group. Among the devices commonly employed were such techniques as relational markers (e.g., second-person pronouns, first-person pronouns, questions, and asides) used to involve the reader and emphasize a relationship.[36] These politeness and compliance-gaining techniques were in evidence in all forms of business correspondence, internal and external, and in all business phases (making contact, negotiation, and resolution). In sales letters, inquiries, quotations, reminders, and other letter types, management writing displayed such positive and negative politeness techniques as claiming common ground, focusing on cooperation, responding to the requestor's interests, and minimizing imposition.[37] (The Appendix contains a table detailing the results of the analysis of politeness techniques in CEO correspondence.)

The need to gain compliance, to be polite, and to set proper context for bad news were, as these studies support, never at issue. These communication activities are important in creating and maintaining all business relationships. However, precisely because "handling the delicate demands of interpersonal diplomacy" is a natural consequence of our intrinsic "pragmatic competence," it doesn't necessarily warrant the extensive attention currently given it in the professional literature. Further, the communication techniques should be understood as helpful insights, not templates.

REVISITING THE EARLY GUIDANCE

As we have identified, the underlying premises of compliance-gaining and politeness theory trace their heritage to issues of courteously dealing with problematic communications. However, to better appreciate the heritage, they might have traced the lineage back a little further. As professional communicators, we have always had a responsibility to impart the message while being civil, courteous and considerate. We have also had an obligation to position purpose in the primary role, to maintain a keen awareness of audience, and to ensure a complete responsiveness to purpose.

Recognizing the proper relationship of purpose and politeness, Hotchkiss, in his 1916 text, speaks of the "spirit behind the expression," a need to weave together a clarity of purpose with a genuine concern for the reader's interest:

Politeness is really an element of force, because it makes the reader feel that you are treating him as an equal, and consequently makes him more responsive.

Courtesy, however, means a great deal more than mere politeness. It is possible for a letter to be polite, and still be extremely irritating. At best, politeness is only the surface of courtesy—the outward dress, so to speak. Often it is mere formality that is no more a proof of courtesy than a full-dress suit is a proof that the wearer is a gentleman. Courtesy goes deeper than mere expression; it refers to the spirit behind the expression. In the case of a letter, it means that the writer is genuinely concerned with the reader's interest, and is attempting to work in his behalf. It is, in fact, the essence of the "you" attitude.[38]

To illustrate this distinction, Hotchkiss offers samples of a curt letter, a polite letter, and what he calls "a truly courteous letter" (Figure 12.11).

FIGURE 12.11

Delineating
Courtesy From
Politeness

CURT

Gentlemen:

We have your letter of September 16, inclosing check for $196 to cover our invoice No. 1011 for $200. You have deducted a discount to which you are not entitled. Remit balance immediately.

Very truly ours,

POLITE

Gentlemen:

We thank you for your letter of September 16, inclosing check for $196 in payment of our invoice No. 1011 for $200. It appears that a mistake has been made in deducting a discount of 2 per cent, to which you are not entitled. We are crediting your account with the amount of your check, and request that you kindly remit balance at your earliest convenience.

Very truly yours,

COURTEOUS

Gentlemen:

We thank you for your letter of September 16, and the inclosed check for $196 which you sent to cover our invoice No. 1011 for $200. We notice a slight discrepancy in the amount, which was no doubt caused by your bookkeeper's deducting a discount of 2 per cent for cash. As the period during which you were entitled to a cash discount expired on September 1, we are unable to allow this deduction.

Our terms, as you know, are printed on the invoice, and are the same for all customers. It would be inconsistent with our policy of square-dealing to allow you a discount which we cannot grant to others. We are therefore returning your remittance, and ask that you send us a check for the correct amount, $200.

Very truly yours,

Yet, we might continue to step back even farther than the work of Hotchkiss. Let's return to the starting point for our discussion of business letters—the *dictamin*. Politeness was clearly evident in the earliest business letters. Politeness was exercised in support of the message and the logical representation of the argument. Speaking of business letters prepared using the guidance of the *dictamin*, one scholar notes, "the logical progression of thought is unusually clear, much more so than in many modern business letters."[39] While history has remained true to the formatting conventions expounded in the *dictamin*, ironically, we have lost sight of the clarity of argument that brought about those very conventions. Specifically the *dictamin* provided for "notification," in which the problem was identified; "exposition," in which the context and circumstances were explained; and "disposition," in which a suitable resolution was proposed. Simplifying the structure and the underlying argument even further, the body of most letters was divided into two parts: The first section chiefly gave background, describing or recalling the reasons for the letter; the second part told the reader what the writer wanted done in response to the situation.

As the *dictamin* laid out several hundred years ago, business letters need both to reinvoke our innate linguistic abilities and reenlist our natural decision-making faculties. Business letters need to establish the assertion, set the context, and lead to a conclusion that derives naturally from the substance and sequence of the information. This structure can readily be achieved in business correspondence by presenting information in a pattern known as the "motivated sequence."

Employing the Motivated Sequence

Indirectly descended from the *dictamin,* the motivated sequence derives more immediately from 1933 and the work of John Dewey. In his book, *How We Think,* Dewey provided insights into the basic reasoning structure people use when solving day-to-day problems.[40] As he laid out the process, we go through five stages:

1. we locate and define the problem
2. we analyze the problem
3. we establish the goals or criteria
4. we select the best solution
5. we implement the selected solution

In business correspondence, the equivalent steps are attention, need, satisfaction, visualization, and action. Table 12.6 shows Dewey's basic reasoning structure and the corresponding elements of the communication structure. Figure 12.12 provides greater detail on the substance of each of the five steps in the motivated sequence.

TABLE 12.6 BASIC REASONING OF THE MOTIVATED SEQUENCE

Dewey's Insights	Example	Communication Step
1. We locate and define the problem.	"Which movie should I see tonight?"	1. Attention Step
2. We analyze the problem.	"Which movies are even playing?"	2. Need Step
3. We establish the goals or criteria for a preferred solution.	"I really don't want to drive far, and I think I'd rather see a comedy than anything else."	3. Satisfaction Step
4. We select the best solution.	". . . is playing at the . . ."	4. Visualization Step
5. We implement.	"Come on. Let's go."	5. Action Step

FIGURE 12.12

Basic Elements of the Motivated Sequence

1. Attention Step
   principal topic of discussion
2. Need Step
   what is the problem specifically
   what is the scope of the problem
   demonstrate problem is real and immediate
3. Satisfaction Step
   what needs to be done
   show how what you propose is a correct fix
   practical experience with the solution
   meet objections and alternatives (why your answer is "it")
4. Visualization Step
   what happens if your plan isn't used
   what benefits will occur if your plan is used
5. Action Step
   precisely what the vendor has to do

To explain how the motivated sequence fits in a business letter, let's assume you have a challenge. You're an inventor who has completed extensive research on games and the psychology of games. You feel you have developed a surefire successor to Monopoly. Your game, Giants of the World, has all the proven qualities of a winner. Further, you know the associated production costs and profit projections. You're even well-versed on a company, Novel Toy Co., where you feel the game can best be marketed. Novel Toy Co., though historically interested primarily in stuffed animals, is in financial difficulty and needs a strong contender to regain market share. Figure 12.13 shows how the motivated sequence assists with presenting your case in a concise, straightforward, and effective business letter.

In addition to reinforcing assertions, the motivated sequence works equally well transmitting good or bad news. By tailoring the emphasis of each of the

---

FIGURE 12.13 The Effective Business Letter: Using the Motivated Sequence

I appreciate the opportunity to meet with you. I am confident I have a product that will make a positive difference in Novelty Toy Co.'s bottom line.

Attention Step
Topic introduced

As you are well aware, we need to be looking for a new product that will give Novelty Toy a strong hold on the market. Sales on toys have been slipping, and sales on stuffed animals are off by more than 40% over just the past 2 years. Only your office has the opportunity and authority to turn this trend around and to fulfill the vision your father had for this company.

Need Step
Problem developed, made real and immediate

For the past year, I've been researching what attributes are needed to make games successful and I now know the formula. Using this information, which I will explain to you in detail if you're interested, I have developed a game that is certain to become another Monopoly if not bigger. Giants of the World is a thrill-ride through a fictional world. It has all the success factors determined by my research: luck and strategy, unpredictability, excitement. Moreover, its subject will capture the imaginations of all age groups.

Satisfaction Step
Explanation of what needs to be done, how and why it fits, and a response to objections

Giants of the World is well aligned with the directions you have established for the company. Best of all, production time and cost are low. The game can be available for the upcoming holiday season, and altogether (production, marketing, and distribution) will cost only $250,000. This is less than that of the last three product lines we launched, and can be provided using the available product development reserves. My projections show full cost recovery in only 18 months, followed by annual net profiles on the order of $300,000.

Visualization Step
What happens if your plan is used: consequences and benefits

This is the time for Novelty Toy to move forward and to take that bold new step. Without a dynamic new product of this caliber, Novelty Toy can anticipate continued revenue losses and loss of market share. With Giants of the World, Novelty Toy will have a path back to the top of our industry and will provide the revenue for introducing that new animal line you spoke of at the last management meeting.

Action Step
What precisely you want your reader to do

I appreciate you agreeing to see me this afternoon. I look forward to sharing the details of Giants of the World, getting your endorsement for the game, and your appointing me to lead the project development team that will make Novelty Toy the household name your father envisioned.

steps, by expanding or contracting steps consistent with the business phase and the variables of distance, power, and imposition, you can provide the appropriate degrees of politeness, compliance-gaining, directness, and clarity. Thus, the message always remains the item of principal focus of your—and your reader's—attention.

To demonstrate this point, we have included three letters. First we offer a disciplinary letter (Figure 12.14). It would be hard to find a business letter, either internal or external, bearing greater bad news than a formal reprimand with an explicit threat of termination. The second letter is a template for a typical cover letter accompanying a resume (Figure 12.15). The third sample is a form letter developed by the Office of Consumer Affairs for use when negotiating a

---

FIGURE 12.14 · A Disciplinary Letter

Implementation of Disciplinary Action:

Sequence Number

Attention Step

In the nearly 2 years that you have reported to the Administrative Services Department, you have demonstrated a lack of professional responsibility: remaining openly resistant to operational changes, repeatedly displaying disregard for the directions provided by management, and promoting an inappropriate attitude toward your work and your coworkers.

1

Need Step

In the past 2 months:
1. Multiple requests had to be made of you to update the equipment report.
2. The budget report due to the manager's office was ignored until the last moment and then done incorrectly, jeopardizing critical funding.
3. Repeated requests had to be made to obtain a response to the out-processing of subcontracted employees, and then had to be done by the manager.
4. Outbursts in staff meetings, as occurred in the recent discussion of assignments, are both unprofessional and discourteous to management and coworkers.

2

Satisfaction Step

These recent examples are part of a lengthy pattern in which you have demonstrated your unwillingness to support management direction. Despite numerous opportunities and invitations to participate in setting the strategies and directions for the department, you continue to disregard and disparage the efforts of management and coworkers. Despite efforts by management to draw upon your extensive experience, you choose to demonstrate a lack of initiative and professional commitment. Despite attempts to establish a better working environment among the staff, you have continued to demonstrate an open hostility that has contributed to a heightened tension and anxiety among the staff. None of these attributes is acceptable, and certainly not from a senior professional.

3–7

Visualization Step

Therefore, it has become necessary to establish a clear set of expectations and performance measures:
1. Effective immediately, you are being relocated to the operations department. You are responsible for a smooth transition.
2. Every 4 months, or more frequently if warranted, you will be provided with a detailed schedule of tasks to be completed during the next period.
3. Monthly, you will provide a written report on the status of all open tasks.
4. A follow-up meeting will be held monthly among you, me, and your immediate manager to review and document your performance.

8

Action Step

If your performance and attitude do not improve, further disciplinary action—up to and including termination—will be taken. A formal response to this letter should be filed with Human Resources within 5 working days.

9

10

FIGURE 12.15

General Outline
for a Cover Letter

**Attention
Step**

Need Step

**Satisfaction/
Visualization
Steps**

Action Step

Your Street Address
City, State, ZIP Code
Phone Number

Current Date

Name of Person & Title
Company/Organization
Street Address
City, State, Zip Code

Dear Mr./Ms. _____:

INTRODUCTION PARAGRAPH 1: Introduce yourself, and state the reason for writing. (Example: As a graduating senior, majoring in English, I am writing to inquire about the possibility of a position as editorial assistant with your company.)

BODY PARAGRAPH 2: Explain why you are interested in working for that employer or in that field of work, and what your qualifications are. Point out achievements related to the field, and why you enjoy that work. (Example: Based upon my rigorous academic preparation, my work experiences, and my strong interest in the field of publishing, I believe I could be an asset to your firm. During high school, I was editor of our newspaper. Also, my internship with a local newspaper helped to sharpen my editing skills, and heightened my interest in the field of publishing.)

CLOSING PARAGRAPH 3: Refer the reader to the enclosed resume and state your desire for an interview. Indicate you will call on a specific day to see if an interview is possible. (Example: As I will be in town the week of March 3–7, I would very much appreciate an opportunity to talk with you. I look forward to speaking with you.)

Sincerely,

(Sign here)
Your Name

enclosure

problem regarding a defective product or service (Figure 12.16).[41] Together, including the toy company letter, these four samples cover all three of the commonly addressed categories of business letter: good news, bad news, informative letter. Further, the letters are representative of communications that may occur in each of the three phases of business: 1) the transmittal letter is part of making contact; 2) the letter to the toy company and the form letter from Consumer Affairs constitute elements of negotiation; and 3) the disciplinary letter represents activities encountered in the conflict phase.

ENSURING THE RIGHT BALANCE

As the samples show, the motivated sequence provides an ideal strategy for preparing effective business correspondence (Table 12.7). This remains true whatever the categorization scheme might be. However, we still actively need to guard against the mum effect, our innate inclination to shy away from transmitting bad news. Therefore, as a follow-up to drafting a business letter, we recommend that you use a Business Letter Analysis form to reassess your product (Figure 12.17).

FIGURE 12.16

Sample Consumer
Affairs Complaint
Letter

```
                                        (Your Address)
                                        (Your City, State, ZIP Code)
                                        (Date)
(Name of Contact Person, if available)
(Title, if available)
(Company Name)
(Consumer Complaint Division, if you have no contact person)
(Street Address)
(City, State, ZIP Code)

Dear (Contact Person)

Re: (account number, if applicable)

On (date), I (bought, leased, rented, or had repaired) a (name of product with serial or model
number or service performed) at (location, date, and other important details of the transaction).

Unfortunately, your product (or service) has not performed well (or the service was inadequate)
because (state the problem). I am disappointed because (explain the problem; for example, the
product does not work properly, the service was not performed correctly, I was billed the wrong
amount, something was not disclosed clearly, or was misrepresented, etc.).

To resolve this problem, I would appreciate your (state the specific action you want—money
back, charge card credit, repair, exchange, etc.). Enclosed are copies (do not send originals) of
my records (include receipts, guarantees, warranties, canceled checks, contracts, model and
serial numbers, and any other documents).

I look forward to your reply and a resolution to my problem, and will wait until (set a time
limit) before seeking help from a consumer protection agency or the Better Business Bureau.
Please contact me at the address above or by phone at (home and/or office numbers with area
codes).

        Sincerely,

        (Your Name)

Enclosure(s)
Cc: (reference to whom you are sending a copy of this letter, if anyone)
KEEP COPIES OF YOUR LETTER AND ALL RELATED DOCUMENTS
```

Source: Reprinted with permission of the Association for Business Communication.

TABLE 12.7 — MOTIVATED SEQUENCE APPLICATIONS

Step	Informative Letter	Good News Letter	Persuasive Letter	Bad News Letter
Attention Step	Respond to reader's inquiry or concern	Establish subject of good news	Catch reader's attention; establish the mutual goals	Establish the subject of the bad news; don't distract with buffer
Need Step	Define the topic of discussion, problem being solved	Provide details	Define the problem you both share	Explain how the decision was reached
Satisfaction Step	Examine the negative elements (e.g., special requirements or limitations)	Explain any limitations (e.g., time limits)	Describe the solution; explain how the negatives are addressed in your solution	Explain why the decision directly applies to the circumstances at hand
Visualization Step	Describe the benefits and consequences	Describe the benefits and consequences	Describe the benefits and consequences	Describe the benefits and consequences
Action Step	Explain any actions that need to be taken	Explain any actions that need to be taken	Explain any actions that need to be taken	Explain any actions that need to be taken

Completing the form presents a graphical illustration of the balance among the five steps of the motivated sequence, and helps ensure whatever the bad news that needed to be transmitted has not been distorted or evaded. Also, while the goal is not necessarily to create an even distribution among the steps, the balance should be consistent with all the factors we have been discussing throughout this chapter: 1) distance, 2) power, 3) imposition, 4) business phase, and 5) purpose. For short letters, the Organizing Rationale section is used to represent individual sentences. For longer letters, the section may be used for blocks of sentences or for entire paragraphs. As an illustration, Figure 12.18 provides a Business Letter Analysis form completed for the disciplinary letter (Figure 12.14).

The completed form indicates the letter has maintained a tight focus on its objective. The notations relative to Business Phase, Audience, and Audience Factors are consistent with the letter's Specific Purpose. The explanations of the Assertions and Supporting Evidence indicate the key points are pertinent and supported by sufficient detail. The graph in the Organizing Rationale section depicts three important points in assessing the effectiveness of our letter. 1) The line shows the letter emphasizes discussion of performance problems (context), a focus critical to demonstrating that serious personnel actions are warranted. 2)

FIGURE 12.17

Business Letter Analysis Form

Business Letter Analysis

Business Phase	Audience		Audience Factors		
Making Contact ❏ Negotiating ❏ Resolving Issues ❏	Primary	Secondary	Power	Distance	Potential Loss of Face
Specific Letter Type:	Executive ❏ Counterpart ❏ Staff ❏ Public ❏ Other ❏	Executive ❏ Counterpart ❏ Staff ❏ Public ❏ Other ❏	Sender ❏ Recipient ❏ Neutral ❏	Close ❏ Neutral ❏ Not yet estab- lished ❏	Significant ❏ Minimal ❏ None ❏

Specific Purpose:

Main Assertions	Supporting Information
1. 2. 3. 4.	

Organizing Rationale

	Define Problem/Issue	Provide Context	Offer Resolution	Detail Benefits/ Consequences	Request Action/ Response	Balanced?
1.						
2.						
3.						Yes ❏
4.						
5.						
6.						No ❏
7.						
8.						
9.						
10.						

Balance Justification:

The graph depicts the other elements of the Motivated Sequence have received equal attention, appropriate for a letter attuned to analyzing the seriousness of the problem. 3) The line suggests the argument unfolds in a progression consistent with the series advocated in the Motivated Sequence. Overall, the completed form attests to the fact that the letter is on target, balanced and straightforward in explaining the bad news and detailing a specific path forward.

A CLOSING NOTE ON POLITENESS

In addition to the expectation that all business communication is carried out politely and courteously, there are a few specific demonstrations of politeness associated with business letters. Some of these considerations are similar to those we discussed when considering e-mail:

- Maintain an appropriate level of formality, especially in addressing the recipient.

- Limit the distribution (CCs) to essential recipients; don't invite everyone into your business or your correspondence.

Business Letter Analysis

Business Phase	Audience		Audience Factors		
Making Contact ❑ Negotiating ❑ Resolving Issues ☑	**Primary**	**Secondary**	**Power**	**Distance**	**Potential Loss of Face**
Specific Letter Type:	Executive ❑ Counterpart ❑ Staff ☑ Public ❑ Other ❑	Executive ❑ Counterpart ❑ Staff ❑ Public ❑ Other ☑	Sender ☑ Recipient ❑ Neutral ❑	Close ☑ Neutral ❑ Not yet estab- lished ❑	Significant ☑ Minimal ❑ None ❑
Disciplinary Letter					

Specific Purpose: Establish a sound basis, consistent with Human Resources policy, for placing the employee on probation. Also to establish performance expectations

Main Assertions	Supporting Information
1. Unacceptable performance in past	Lack of response to requests/assignments
2. Pattern of unacceptable behavior	Unwillingness to take/follow through on direction
3. Formal performance measures needed	Periods and specific expectations
4. Explanation of consequences	Practical disciplinary actions that may follow

Organizing Rationale

	Define Problem/Issue	Provide Context	Offer Resolution	Detail Benefits/ Consequences	Request Action/ Response	Balanced?
1.						
2.						
3.						Yes ☑
4.						
5.						
6.						
7.						No ❑
8.						
9.						
10.						

Balance Justification: Emphasis on context necessary to establish a legally supportable action consistent with the stated requirements of the corporate Human Resources Manual

FIGURE 12.18

A Sample Completed Business Letter Analysis Form

- Respond quickly to incoming correspondence; prompt responses tend to show interest (and respect), even when bad news is involved.

Last, look for means to give a personalized touch to your correspondence. Even though you are acting as an agent of the company, the recipient will react more positively if there is a sense of "somebody" behind the correspondence. The less anonymous the interaction, the more likely it is that contacts will be made, negotiations will go smoothly, and conflicts can be resolved.

One simple suggestion for personalizing your correspondence is a brief hand-written note at the bottom of the letter, or even a distinctive signature that makes evident that the recipient is not in possession of a machine-generated letter. Whether sending out a single letter or letters to dozens of potential clients, you need to sign each one. Make your mark—and your presence—clear. It's not a surprise that in an age of automation and signature machines that there is a resurgence in the use of fountain pens. "Back in the 1950s, it sent an important message if your business correspondence was perfectly typed . . . . It meant you were powerful enough to have a secretary who could type a whole page without a mistake. But now that everyone has a word processor, error-free correspondence isn't a power symbol anymore. Instead . . . it's the note, handwritten with a fountain pen and appended to the bottom of a letter, that indicates power."[42] Call it power or call it politeness, you want to be sure that even the driest of subjects, even the worst news, carries with it a sense that the matter is receiving your personal attention. Make certain your letters reflect the "you attitude," what Hotchkiss referred to as the genuine concern for audience.

BUSINESS LETTERS—THE LESSONS

Business letters demand a good deal of attention, not so much to formatting (which derives from centuries of guidance), and not so much to the basics of interpersonal etiquette (which derive from our innate "pragmatic competencies"), but to be sure that a tight focus is maintained on purpose. You don't need to work on the template, which more than likely will be provided by your company. You also don't want to work on how to keep the message hidden from your audience or how to manipulate your audience. In these matters, you need to trust in your internal, ethical compass.

You do need to make certain that you have a clear purpose in mind and that you communicate your purpose clearly and forthrightly. The best means for accomplishing this goal is to use the motivated sequence, which allows customized presentation of information in an arrangement consistent with the natural process of reaching decisions. Focusing on the type of information to be conveyed (good news, bad news, indifferent news) offers little in terms of an organizing principle. The only measure of success is that you have treated your audience as they deserve to be treated, both in terms of providing a clear and reasoned message and in terms of treating them as partners in a business exchange.

As summarized in Table 12.8, writing an effective business letter demands a masterful application of the art and discipline we have studied throughout Part 1 of this text: appreciating the audience, having a complete measure of the purposes involved, introducing the necessary information, using a reasoned organization, and employing language appropriate to the interaction.

12.8 BUSINESS LETTERS: A SUMMARY OVERVIEW

Primary Uses	Used in all phases of business to establish/maintain contractual relationship; may also be used for internal communication where a significant corporate liability demands formal documentation
Style	Standard format, generally using company letterhead. Tone and language are formal and businesslike.
Distribution	Limited to specific recipients (addressees); copies identified on the distribution list should be limited to essential personnel
Permanence	Copies retained in corporate archives; may become public record
Accountability	Accountability assigned directly to the person who signed the letter; when issued on company letterhead, the corporation also becomes obligated and accountable for fulfilling agreements/expectations
Response Expected	Responses are expected consistent with the type of letter and the status of the business process (making contact, negotiation, conflict resolution)
Breadth	Like a memo, letter usually addresses a specific subject, which may, based on company policy, be reflected in a subject line
Review/Approval	Generally external business letters will undergo some form of formal review by management to ensure position is consistent with company practices, policy, and philosophy
Authorship	Authority generally assigned as a function of one's corporate role and level of management; authority runs generally in parallel with authority for setting or changing corporate policy
Associated Risks	Making inappropriate commitments Appearing to manipulate the reader Appearing to evade the reader Failure to communicate a sense of interest in the reader

EXERCISES

☐ Group

Divide into groups.

1. Identify how you might improve the IRS's letter proposing an adjustment in taxes (Figure 12.5). Then rewrite the letter using the motivated sequence. Discuss the problems you addressed in the letter and the reasons for your proposed resolutions.

2. Prepare a letter to convince a previous client of e-con.com to do business with your firm despite a previous missed deadline on a major project. Share the letter with the class, highlighting any examples of politeness or compliance-gaining techniques.

3. Draft a letter to one of your firm's clients. Explain that you have implemented a new productivity device (the on-line time clock discussed in Exercise 1 of

Chapter 11). You want to assure her that this device will eliminate the kinds of late deliveries she has experienced with her last two contracts.

    a) In the left-hand margin, indicate where each of the steps in the motivated sequence begins.

    b) Identify any phrases (compliance-gaining or politeness) that you have used to promote a relationship with the audience.

    c) Complete a Business Analysis form for your letter.

    d) Discuss parts a–c above with the class.

☐ Individual

1. Revise the letters from the IRS (Figures 12.8 and 12.9) to provide a clearer, more direct message. Explain what changes were needed and why.

2. Collect a week's worth of unsolicited mail. Identify the compliance-gaining and politeness techniques that are used. Prepare an analysis explaining which techniques work, which don't, and why.

3. Redo the letter to the Novelty Toy Co. (Figure 12.13) and prepare a Business Analysis form showing how you would adjust the five elements of the motivated sequence if the two following conditions existed:

    a) you knew the company owners were strongly against investing in a new game, and

    b) the company had shown a significant profit in the previous year.

END NOTES

[1] Malcolm Richardson, "Business Writing and the Spread of Literacy in Late Medieval England," in *Studies in the History of Business Writing*, ed. George W. Douglas and Herbert W. Hildebrandt. Urbana, IL: The Association of Business Communication, 1985, pp. 1–11.

[2] Henry B. Weiss, *American Letter-Writers 1698–1943*. New York: The New York Public Library, 1945, p. 4.

[3] *Ibid.*, p. 3.

[4] *Ibid.*, p. 10.

[5] L.W. Denton, "The Etiquette of American Business Correspondence," in *Studies in the History of Business Writing*, pp. 87–96.

[6] Thomas E. Hill, *Hill's Manual of Social and Business Forms: A Guide to Correct Writing*. Chicago: Hill Standard Book Co., Publishers, 1886.

[7] George Burton Hotchkiss, *Business English: Being the First Text in a Course in Business English*. New York: Business Training Corporation, 1916.

[8] Lorraine Krajewski and Gwendolyn Smith, "From Letter Writing to Report Writing: Bridging the Gap," *Business Communication Quarterly*, Vol. 60, No. 4 (Dec. 1997), pp. 88–90.

[9] Max Beerbohm, "How Shall I Word It?" in *And Even Now*. London: William Heinemann, 1921.

[10] Table 12.2 is adapted from: Marie E. Flatley, "A Comparative Analysis of the Written Communication of Managers at Various Organizational Levels in the Private Business Sector," *Journal of Business Communication*, Vol. 19, No. 3 (Summer 1982), pp. 35–50.

[11] Douglas Solerno, "An Interpersonal Approach to Writing Negative Messages," *The Journal of Business Communication*, Vol. 25, No. 1 (Winter 1988), pp. 41–51.

[12] Abraham Tesser and Sidney Rosen, "The Reluctance to Transmit Bad News," *Advances in Experimental Social Psychology*, Vol. 8 (1975), ed. Leonard Berkowitz, pp. 193–232.

[13] Sidney Rosen, Richard Grandison, and John Stewart II, "Discriminatory Buckpassing: Delegating Transmission of Bad News," *Organizational Behavior and Human Performance,* Vol. 12 (1974), pp. 249–263.

[14] Fiona Lee, "Being Polite and Keeping MUM: How Bad News Is Communicated in Organizational Hierarchies," *Journal of Applied Social Psychology,* Vol. 23, No. 14 (1993), pp. 1124–1149.

[15] Penelope Brown and Stephen Levinson, *Politeness: Some Universals in Language Usage.* New York: Cambridge University Press, 1987.

[16] Morten Pilegaard, "Politeness in Written Discourse: A Textlinguistic Perspective on Requests," *Journal of Pragmatics,* Vol. 28 (1997), pp. 223–244.

[17] Kevin Lamude and Joseph Scudder, "Compliance-Gaining Techniques of Type-A Managers," *Journal of Business Communication,* Vol. 31, No. 1 (1993), pp. 63–79.

[18] Shenck-Hamlin, Richard Wiseman, and G. Georgacarakos, "A Model of Compliance-Gaining Strategies," *Communication Quarterly,* Vol. 30, No. 7 (Spring 1982), pp. 92–100.

[19] Linda Westphal, "How to Create Believability When You Write." *Direct Marketing,* Vol. 67, No. 7 (Nov. 1998), pp. 24–25.

[20] Lee, "Being Polite and Keeping MUM."

[21] Figures 12.6 and 12.7 are adapted from: Pilegaard, "Politeness in Written Discourse."

[22] John Hagge and Charles Kostelnick, "Linguistic Politeness in Professional Prose," *Written Communication,* Vol. 6, No. 3 (July 1989), pp. 312–339.

[23] *Ibid.*

[24] Lee, "Being Polite and Keeping MUM."

[25] Kim Sydow Campbell, "Explanations in Negative Messages: More Insights from Speech Act Theory," *The Journal of Business Communication,* Vol. 27, No. 4 (Fall 1990), pp. 357–375.

[26] John Hagge and Charles Kostelnick, "Linguistic Politeness in Professional Prose."

[27] Quoted in: Solerno, "An Interpersonal Approach to Writing Negative Messages."

[28] *Ibid.*

[29] Douglas Brent, "Indirect Structure and Reader Response," *The Journal of Business Communication,* Vol. 22, No. 2 (1985), pp. 5–8.

[30] Mohan Limaye, "Buffers in Bad News Messages and Recipients' Perceptions," *Management Communication Quarterly,* Vol. 2, No. 1 (Aug. 1988), pp. 90–101.

[31] Brent, "Indirect Structure and Reader Response."

[32] Pilegaard, "Politeness in Written Discourse."

[33] Lee, "Being Polite and Keeping MUM."

[34] Ted Brown, "Unkind Cuts: Rethinking the Rhetoric of Academic Job Rejection Letters," *College English,* Vol. 55, No. 7 (Nov. 1993), pp. 770–778.

[35] John Hagge and Charles Kostelnick, "Linguistic Politeness in Professional Prose."

[36] Ken Hyland, "Exploring Corporate Rhetoric: Metadiscourse in the CEO's Letter," *The Journal of Business Communication,* Vol. 35, No. 2 (April 1998), pp. 224–245.

[37] Pilegaard, "Politeness in Written Discourse."

[38] George Burton Hotchkiss, *Business English.*

[39] Malcolm Richardson, "Business Writing and the Spread of Literacy in Late Medieval England."

[40] John Dewey, *How We Think: A Restatement of the Relation of Reflective Thinking to the Education Process.* Boston: D.C. Heath Co., 1933.

[41] Cited in P.K. Shula, "The Complaint Letter and Response," *Business Communication Quarterly,* Vol. 61, No. 4 (Dec 1998), pp. 107–108.

[42] Laura Bird, "Marketers Sell Pen As Signature of Style," *The Wall Street Journal,* Nov. 3, 1993, p. B-1.

13

The Long Report
Negotiating a Complexity of Purpose, Audience, and Design

In business, many situations give rise to the development of lengthy reports that are used to develop a more complete treatment of a subject than reflected in memos or business letters. Each of the elements on Figure 13.1, for instance, can involve extensive evaluations, analyses, and decisions—each supported by one or more long, detailed reports. Moving beyond the focus of creating new product lines, we can generalize a number of reasons for developing a lengthy report:

1. The need to refine or redefine business

2. The need to respond to a specific business problem or opportunity

3. The need to submit special or periodic reports to auditors, oversight agencies, shareholders, or investors

4. The need to go after new business or business markets

Numerous report types are involved in responding to these needs. The challenge, however, lies not in sustaining the argument over a number of pages, but the challenge has a keenly rhetorical basis. Simply stopping to assign templates or define formats will create nothing more than a shell. Completing the long report correctly demands not so much an appreciation of the length of the writing chore, but the sustained clarity of purpose. To this end, we will begin by looking at several types of long reports and will then narrow our focus to two types that can effectively stand as representative of the major challenges of writing long reports.

The four primary types of long reports
- Business plans
- Business/Technical reports
- Annual reports
- Proposals

Defining the challenge—what it's not
- Reasoning
- Stylistic considerations
- Structure/Formatting
- Audience identification

The real challenge: a complexity of purpose and audience

The business report: matching structure and audience
- The Title and Cover Page
- Executive Summary
- Table of Contents
- Introduction
- The body, the recommendations, and the conclusions
- Appendixes
- Mythical beasts and structural unity

The Annual Report: aligning voice, design, and purpose
- From fraud to CPA to design house
- . . . and finally to the province of the communicator
- Sending the right message
- The final partnership

The long report—the lessons

FIGURE 13.1   Essential Components of New Product Development

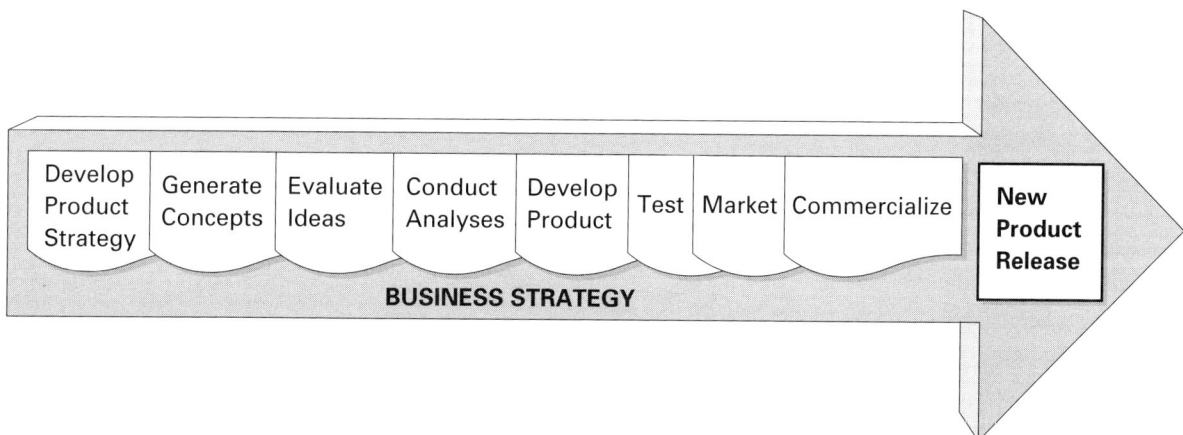

Develop Product Strategy | Generate Concepts | Evaluate Ideas | Conduct Analyses | Develop Product | Test | Market | Commercialize | **New Product Release**

BUSINESS STRATEGY

THE FOUR PRIMARY TYPES OF LONG REPORTS

Corresponding to the four categories of events that trigger development of lengthy business documents are four document types:

1. Business Plans
2. Business/Technical Reports
3. Annual Reports
4. Proposals

Before further discussion, we need to get a basic sense of each of these document types.

BUSINESS PLANS

According to the U.S. Census Bureau, 695,657 new businesses were started in 1995. Of these, 567,337 had failed by the end of 1998. A primary cause is poor planning: "While many factors can contribute to a business failure, inadequate planning is probably the single greatest cause of new business failure."[1] Planning is an integral component of all business ventures—whether done formally or not, and whether it involves formal documented plans or simply reasonable forethought. The American Management Association uses an example of a local gas station versus an oil company to explain this range of planning:

> For the neighborhood gas station, the planning issues include appropriate inventory levels of a limited range of products, product/service pricing, and cash-flow management; the time horizon of the plan is no more than one year and is frequently on a month-to-month basis; all of the required information and decision-making authority resides with the station owner. In contrast, the planning process for the international petroleum company must address a much broader range of issues—for example, the acquisition of raw materials; appropriate inventory levels at several stages in a complex manufacturing process; cost control; pricing for a wide range of products; investments in capital equipment, facilities, and new product development; management and motivation of thousands of employees; and distribution of hundreds of products to thousands of consumers. The information required for planning decisions exists in formal data systems and in the brains of hundreds of management personnel. The time horizon may extend more than twenty years into the future.[2]

The formal means by which planning strategies are developed and articulated is the business plan, a kind of basic road map. As depicted in Figure 13.2, the business plan integrates five strategies:

1. The market strategy—the customer base and the products of interest to them
2. The production strategy—the process, technology, and infrastructure needed to produce the products
3. The research and development strategy—the areas where the company may have a competitive edge because of expertise or intellectual property rights
4. Organization and management strategy—the alignment of personnel to meet the demands of the company and its objectives and commitments
5. Financial strategy—the management of finances, in terms of operation, the company, investments, and use of profits

FIGURE 13.2

The Integrated Components of the Business Plan

BUSINESS/TECHNICAL REPORTS

Business reports provide distilled statements of the support work done to aid business decisions. The breadth of circumstance that can introduce the need to draft a business report is almost beyond definition. Any situation where a large body of information may need to be communicated may create a need for a business or technical report (generally differentiated from each other by the principal topic or focus). As an example, almost every circle in Figure 13.3, a depiction of the complex sequence involved in bringing a product to market,

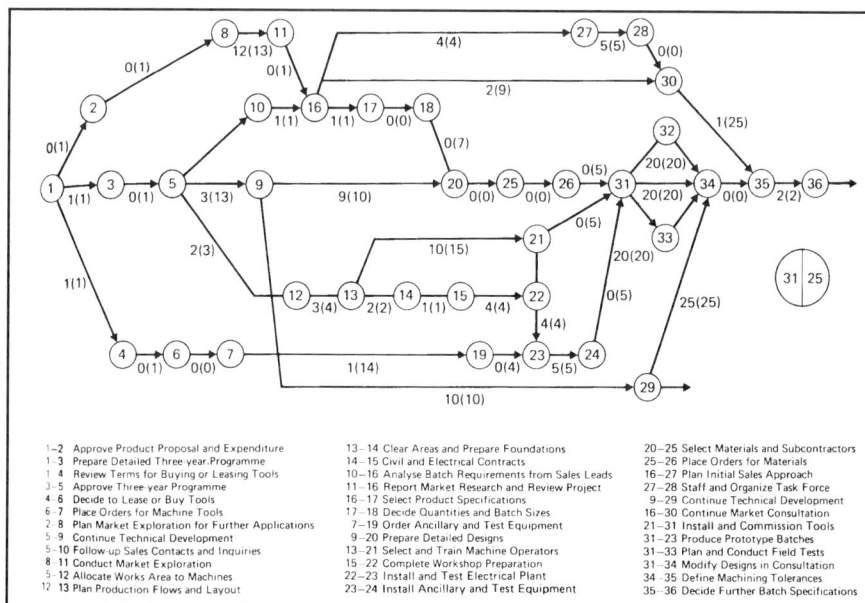

FIGURE 13.3

A Detailed Sequencing of New Product Development

1–2 Approve Product Proposal and Expenditure	13–14 Clear Areas and Prepare Foundations	20–25 Select Materials and Subcontractors
1–3 Prepare Detailed Three-year Programme	14–15 Civil and Electrical Contracts	25–26 Place Orders for Materials
1–4 Review Terms for Buying or Leasing Tools	10–16 Analyse Batch Requirements from Sales Leads	16–27 Plan Initial Sales Approach
3–5 Approve Three-year Programme	11–16 Report Market Research and Review Project	27–28 Staff and Organize Task Force
4–6 Decide to Lease or Buy Tools	16–17 Select Product Specifications	9–29 Continue Market Consultation
6–7 Place Orders for Machine Tools	17–18 Decide Quantities and Batch Sizes	16–30 Continue Technical Development
2–8 Plan Market Exploration for Further Applications	7–19 Order Ancillary and Test Equipment	21–31 Install and Commission Tools
5–9 Continue Technical Development	9–20 Prepare Detailed Designs	31–23 Produce Prototype Batches
5–10 Follow-up Sales Contacts and Inquiries	13–21 Select and Train Machine Operators	31–33 Plan and Conduct Field Tests
8–11 Conduct Market Exploration	15–22 Complete Workshop Preparation	31–34 Modify Designs in Consultation
5–12 Allocate Works Area to Machines	22–23 Install and Test Electrical Plant	34–35 Define Machining Tolerances
12–13 Plan Production Flows and Layout	23–24 Install Ancillary and Test Equipment	35–36 Decide Further Batch Specifications

Source: Reprinted from *Long Range Planning,* vol. 14, E. Peter Ward, "Planning for Technological Innovation: Developing the Necessary Nerve," pp. 59–71, copyright ©1981, with permission of Elsevier Science.

may warrant one or more reports before proceeding to the next step. Another condition that may require report writing occurs when the reports themselves are the product—as is the case in contracted research agreements.[3]

Illustrating this expectation, the following quotation comes from a 1954 report E.I. Du Pont de Nemours & Co. (Du Pont) issued to its technical staff at a major development project.

> We are behind an eightball. We owe a large number of Research and Development (DP) reports to the AEC [Atomic Energy Commission], with whom we have contracted to perform certain work and report on it. We owe these reports to our bosses, who pay us to write them. We also owe them to ourselves, to get our work on record so that it is not lost; and to our scientific colleagues, in this and other AEC laboratories, to help them in their work and to avoid needless duplication of effort. To date, the Laboratory has published a very few formal DP reports. This is all we have to show for more than a year's labor by more than two hundred technical men. It isn't much.[4]

ANNUAL REPORTS

The annual report is a stylized answer to a requirement that is approximately 70 years old. In the mid-nineteenth century, the New York Stock Exchange (NYSE) urged corporations to publish annual assessments of their financial performance. This request became codified in the 1930s following a series of financial frauds that bilked shareholders and moneylenders out of some $500 million—not an insignificant amount in the 1920s and 1930s. In response to the unfolding scandals, the government passed the Security Act of 1933, known as the "truth in securities" law. This act required that corporations provide investors with financial and other significant information concerning securities being offered for public trade. The law also addressed deceit, misrepresentation, and fraud in the sale of securities. The following year, the government enacted the Securities Exchange Act of 1934, which, in addition to establishing the Securities and Exchange Commission (SEC), mandated that companies with more than $10 million in publicly traded assets must issue independently audited annual reports.

Today, the business of producing annual reports is estimated as a $5 billion per year industry worldwide, about $2 billion of which is spent in the United States where about 12,000 annual reports are published. As established in the 1933 and 1934 laws, these annual reports have been expected to include approximately 40 different categories of financial information. Categories include:

1) a review of business development activities
2) details of dividends paid
3) details of directors and their shareholdings
4) significant changes in fixed assets
5) significant differences between book and market values of assets, and
6) various financial reports
   i. a profit and loss account for the period;
   ii. group accounts;
   iii. source and application of funds statements;

iv. a balance sheet as of the last day of the period; and

v. a statement of the accounting policies.

PROPOSALS

No matter what type of business you engage in or where that business lies in terms of its position within its market, the financial health of the business is dependent on continually bringing in new and expanding sources of revenue. In some cases, this might be done by marketing campaigns or the business may employ a body of salespeople whose job it is to go out and drum up new business. Another approach is developing business proposals in response to Requests for Proposals (RFPs). Requests for Proposals are generated by private enterprise, government agencies, universities, and privately funded organizations. These RFPs solicit firms from around the globe to provide quotations (competitive statements) and to explain their capability to perform the needed work. (Figure 13.4 is a sample RFP posted on the Internet version of the government publication *Commerce Business Daily*.)

Generally, RFPs are comprised of four sections: ground rules, requirements, evaluation criteria, and formatting requirements.

Ground Rules—Identify the purpose of the RFP and explain basic expectations such as the timetable of dates relevant to the project.

Requirements—Define the users' needs or problems (the work to be done).

Evaluation Criteria—Identify how the award decision is to be made, how the best or most appropriate supplier and product will be selected (e.g., cost, fit).

Format Requirements—Establish standards for preparing the proposal, for example, how cost information or credentials of principal personnel are to be displayed. Generally, this section is only included for complex proposals where the soliciting agency wants to be sure that it can readily make accurate comparisons among bids.

The proposal takes its cues from the RFP. Some proposals may be relatively short and straightforward; others may demand extensive development. (The Appendix includes a typical flowchart for developing a modest-sized proposal.)

Part: U.S. GOVERNMENT PROCUREMENTS
 SUBPART: SERVICES
CLSSCODE: R—Professional, Administrative, and Management services
Subject : R—Student Intern Support
DESC: The contractor shall furnish three part-time student interns, transportation, supervision, and materials necessary to provide . . . staff and management with administrative and computer support in managing and implementing the environmental program. On site part time student interns from accredited colleges and universities within a 50-mile radius of . . . will be considered. The anticipated period of performance is 1 January 2002 through 31 December 2003. Fax request for solicitations will be accepted at Fax no. . . . All responsible sources may submit an offer which will be considered.

FIGURE 13.4

A Sample of a Simple RFP

DEFINING THE CHALLENGE—
WHAT IT'S NOT

Although at first glance the major challenge to these reports may be their imposing length, the most significant challenge is not length. The business world is not challenged in terms of finding sufficient information to create thousands of lengthy reports. Knowledge management and sophisticated corporate intranets negate issues of availability of sufficient information.

The problem is also not one of how to present the information. Chapter 4 provided the necessary tools for presenting large volumes of complex data. Knowing the basics of organizational strategies and the effective use of graphical devices provides the foundations for portraying information in the lengthiest of documents. Therefore, we need to look elsewhere to gain an appreciation of the challenges these documents represent. Areas often suggested are: reasoning, stylistic considerations, formatting, and audience.

REASONING

One avenue that may concern communicators is the ability to establish and sustain a convincing line of reasoning throughout a lengthy document. While the matter may appear daunting, it may have already become evident that these four document types bear considerable similarity to the four lines of argument we discussed at length in Chapter 5. This resemblance is not accidental. In fact, the four document types correspond directly with the four strategies of argument:

- Business plan = proposition
- Business/Technical report = analysis
- Annual report = evaluation
- Response to RFP = proposal

The business plan responds to questions about what the business is or should be. It is largely an exercise in definition and classification. The goal is to better position the company or venture—the tangible demonstration of a proposition. The business/technical report is an expanded demonstration of analysis. What is the problem? How does it affect the business? What needs to be done to resolve the issue or to take advantage of the opportunity? Responding to these numerous elements of business activity and product development require the communicator to perform a protracted analysis.

When we turn to the annual report, we see an example of evaluation. After all, the entire document seeks to answer one overriding question: How has the corporation performed? As we noted, the origin of the Securities Acts of 1933 and 1934 was a perceived need to require corporations to provide forthright and independently validated evaluations of the previous year's financial performance. Last, the response to an RFP is, as appropriately entitled, a proposal. The document seeks to convince the audience that the corporation is best suited—in terms of expertise, experience, and cost—to do the job. The document is a persuasive argument—why the company represented by the proposal should get the award.

While the dimensions of the reasoning may have expanded in the long report, the overall structure of the argument remains consistent with strategies presented in Chapter 5. The length of the document does not, in and of itself, introduce any novel dimensions to the subject of reasoning or to the basic structure of argument. The effectiveness of the argument remains contingent on maintaining a structured approach to presenting information in support of the contentions and assertions.

STYLISTIC CONSIDERATIONS

If not a unique challenge in reasoning, perhaps the documents have some unique stylistic demands. In a recent article in the *Business Communication Quarterly,* one instructor published survey statistics attempting to define what business communication instructors expect students to learn and what skills they will improve as a consequence of completing the business report assignment. The survey results were reported in terms of organization, clarity, and completeness.[5] (The Appendix includes the detailed results of this survey.)

While the students and instructors reported the assignment was most beneficial in teaching organization and management of substantive content, stylistic benefits associated with headings, charts, graphs, tables, and references were also noted. These considerations, though clearly valid, suggest little new in the long report when it comes to stylistic concerns. Therefore, style does not appear to be a unique challenge when preparing these documents.

STRUCTURE/FORMATTING

Perhaps, then, the challenge lies in the formatting demands of each of the document types. Certainly, the documents have distinctive, recognizable structures. But is there really a difficulty in learning these structures? Format for a business plan, for example, can be defined simply by following templates that come as standard fare in many office management software packages. Proposals, as we noted, are governed by the requestor.

Structure and format for annual reports and technical reports are also very well-known commodities. Much of the annual report format has been fixed through 70 years of government direction. The business or technical report has a standard set of sections: executive summary, conclusions, appendixes, etc. Therefore, we can conclude that structure and formatting are either relatively fixed or at least readily discerned (Figure 13.5). As such, we might conclude formatting is also not the most significant challenge when dealing with this genre.

AUDIENCE IDENTIFICATION

A full quarter of the students in the survey just cited saw little improvement in audience analysis as a consequence of preparing a long report, suggesting only

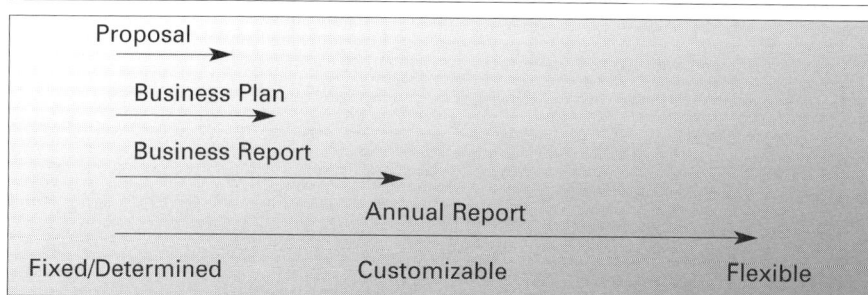

FIGURE 13.5

The Dynamics of Structure

Proposal

Business Plan

Business Report

Annual Report

Fixed/Determined   Customizable   Flexible

limited analysis of audience is required. After all, even for the document type with the largest distribution, the annual report, audience is predefined; 40 percent of the copies go to shareholders; the other 60 percent are distributed to employees, suppliers, customers (current and prospective), government officials, acquisition candidates, and the media. As reflected in Table 13.1 and Figure 13.6, the basic audience configuration for these documents is generally well understood.

THE REAL CHALLENGE: A COMPLEXITY OF PURPOSE AND AUDIENCE

If the challenge is not the length, gathering information, the reasoning, stylistic considerations, or identification of audience, where does the challenge lie? The challenges lie with recognizing and responding to the relationship among the unique sets of audience expectations, the document purposes, and the report structures. The challenge is appreciating and taking advantage of structures that, like the memo, have evolved as an outgrowth of a precise delineation of the many purposes and multiple audiences associated with the development and design of these document types.

Communicators must precisely understand who the principal audiences are and then must strive to identify, isolate, and prioritize the purposes. Responses must then be tailored to audiences that have distinct and differing interests, not only in the document types, but, more particularly, in different sections of the

TABLE

13.1 | A MORE DETAILED PERSPECTIVE OF TARGETED READERS

	Management	Counterparts	Staff	Known External	Unknown External
Business Plan	✓	✓	✓	✓	
Business Report	✓	✓	✓		
Annual Report	✓	✓	✓	✓	✓
Proposal	✓	✓	✓	✓	

FIGURE 13.6

Primary Audience

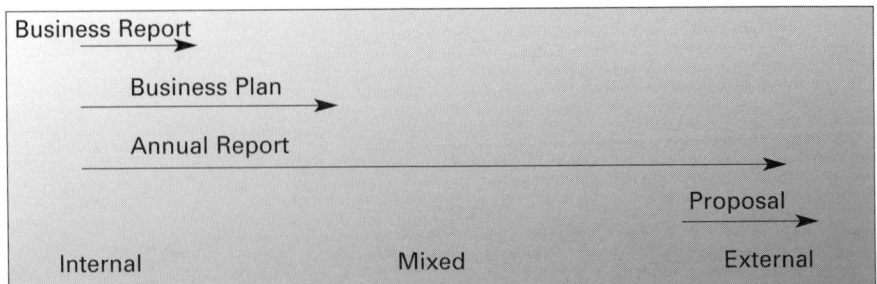

Business Report →

Business Plan →

Annual Report →

Proposal →

Internal   Mixed   External

documents. These insights and determinations, in turn, drive the logic and design of the documents.

Unlike the document types we have examined thus far in this text, long reports must be designed with an eye to accommodating a variety of audiences and purposes. In contrast, memos, for example, have a singular purpose and a relatively homogeneous audience—the employees of the corporation. Business letters and e-mail may involve a large distribution, but still have a primary target audience that is clearly differentiated from the other recipients. In contrast, the long report has multiple primary readerships; no equivalent delineation between primary and secondary audiences is evident or intended. Accordingly, these document types demand that we balance the expectations of audiences with widely divergent interests (Table 13.2).

Although any document has the possibility of being widely read and disseminated, that doesn't necessarily establish the expectation that the particular interests of each reader community will or must be accommodated. In contrast, for these four document types, not accounting for or responding to the diverse interests is a prescription for reader dissatisfaction and failed purposes. Yet, at the same time, an unfocused or ill-constructed attempt to respond to these diverse readerships may represent a formula for chaos, loss of credibility, and reduced readability. Using annual reports as an example, the communicator, in responding to the need to balance diverse interests, may, if not careful, create a certain "uneasy compromise": "The annual report has run into trouble trying to reconcile the different needs of its audience . . . . Corporate communications specialists have long known that annual reports should do more than divulge the information required by regulators—they should 'sell' the company not only to investors but also other audiences, including opinion formers, employees and customers. But this quest to add marketing and PR value to financial reports has recently been running into sand . . . . The two halves don't add up. The first lacks credibility. The second lacks readability." This unhappy merger, "the strain of shoe-horning ever more messages into traditional accounts," eventually results in a communication that lacks consistency and credibility.[6]

To understand the relationship among audience, form, and function, let's begin by examining the two categories of audience expectations shared by all four document types: those of management and those of a known external audience. First, each type must be responsive to and take its lead from management. The business plan has to reflect the aspirations of the management and its vision

TABLE

13.2 **UNIQUE READER EXPECTATIONS**

	Management	Staff	Known External	Unknown External
Business Plan	✓		✓	
Business Report	✓	✓	✓	
Annual Report	✓	✓	✓	✓
Proposal	✓		✓	

of what constitutes success. The business report needs to offer solutions within parameters that reflect the corporate approach to business. In the annual report, management needs to breathe vitality and character into the spreadsheets produced by financial analysts. And, last, the proposal needs to be built around a corporate vision that establishes the themes that highlight the company's unique offerings to the requestor.

Without management vision, the reports lose focus. After losing a succession of proposals to its competitors, a Fortune 500 corporation pulled together a senior-level team to look at methods to overhaul the corporation's proposal development process. The analysis revealed the need for three strategic changes. The first two dealt with a need for organizational realignment of the function and a more streamlined means of retrieving vital corporate information. The third recommendation, and the one most immediately linked to our course of study, was that production activities should not be initiated on any proposal until the senior managers had defined the particular "success strategies," the specific themes and orientation needed to shape and direct the storyline. As the team reported, the lack of a defined management vision adversely contributed to the company's poor performance in winning proposals as well as to the rising cost of the products. Lack of developed forethought contributed both to unconvincing proposals and to excessive rewrites.

The second audience category shared by all the document types is a known external readership. The proposal and the business plan begin in response to and are precisely defined by the primary external audience. The proposal, as we have identified, has a single-minded purpose—to prove itself the superior candidate to accomplish a well-defined scope of work. The business plan, while potentially of educational value to the corporate staff, is also defined by and targeted at a single external audience—financial investors. Addressing this audience, the business plan seeks to examine its unique set of integrated business characteristics: people, opportunity, context, risk, and reward. Building upon a solid base of qualified and experienced personnel, the business plan argues that there is an attractive, sustainable business model—a definable competitive edge. This advantage is complemented by beneficial regulatory and macroeconomic environments (context) and by a clear understanding of the risks and the strategies by which difficult events can be mitigated.

This precise definition of the external audiences for business plans and proposals results in a straightforward relationship between the form and purposes of these documents. The proposal structure is tailored to meet the requirements stipulated by the requestor. The business plan, which seeks to establish a relationship with a particular external audience—investors—also has a generally fixed structure. That structure has evolved to allow the reader to make clear, substantive, and prudent assessments of the company's financial health and investment potential.

The external audiences for the annual report and the business report, although evident, are significantly less well-defined. On the surface, the annual report must be responsive to the SEC, as well as to current and potential investors. The business report, depending on the specific topic, is likely to have an audience of external colleagues, particularly for those reports authored with the intent of public release (either in the professional literature or on the company's web page). Yet, speaking of these readers as if a one-dimensional external audience is somewhat misleading. The designation as a known external audience is only meaningful in the sense that the group members are reached via a common mode of distribution. In reality, from the perspective of the communicator, this audience grouping comprises multiple reader communities, each with its own expectations, and each of which—over time—has contributed to the development of the documents' designs.

As such, we have a new insight into these two particular long reports. They have an array of purposes, each of which governs the structure and the communication logic of the report. These complexities of purpose and audience, in turn, intensify the challenge. More deliberate attention must be paid to the relationship between form and function and to the relationship among structure, format, and design features. Recognizing and taking advantage of these relationships is what allows an author to use these documents as effective communication genres.

Given the greater communication challenge of these two document types and the need to provide full insight into the means by which the communication challenges are met, we will concentrate the remainder of this chapter on the study of business reports and annual reports.

THE BUSINESS REPORT: MATCHING STRUCTURE AND AUDIENCE

In a study we quoted earlier, an attempt was made to determine what students and instructors learn from preparing a business report. Buried among the concern for the more mechanical attributes was a very important acknowledgement that students need to understand how reports contribute to the process of corporate decision-making: "There are specific concepts that the students should learn and skills that they should improve by completing the business report assignment. These include organizing, writing, editing, revising, formatting, data gathering and evaluation, audience analysis, understanding how the report will be used for decision-making, and the need to pay careful attention to detail when writing so that their report is mechanically correct."

Explaining this relationship between reports and decision-making, the 1954 Du Pont report we quoted earlier (and to which we will return several times in the course of our discussion of reports) cites report writing as a fundamental obligation of the professional staff: "You are employed by Uncle Du Pont, who watches over your doings with interest and sometimes with concern. Every month he sends a messenger to you with a little piece of green paper in token of his affection and esteem. It may not occur to you at the time, but a significant fraction of that check is to pay you for writing reports that are clear, factual, and to the point. Management can't make good decisions if you write poor reports."

To assist with this challenge, the business report is expected to answer four basic questions:

1. Where are we now?

2. Where are we headed?

3. How do we propose to get there?

4. How will we know when we've arrived?

Answering these four questions creates a natural problem-solving structure parallel to standard scientific, technical, and business processes employed for examining and solving problems (Table 13.3). Fundamentally, therefore,

13.3 TELLING THE STORY: BUSINESS AND TECHNICAL

Scientific Method	Technical Development	Business Development	Product Development
Postulate a hypothesis	Set objective	Define problem	Define potential product
Define the experiment	Select apparatus and methods	Define scope	Conduct corporate and market research
Conduct the experiment	Conduct methods and process	Determine solution	Begin development
Capture observations	Record observations	Record results	Complete market testing
Formulate conclusions	Reach conclusions	Enact recommendation	Market introduction and communication

understanding the report begins with recognizing that its structure has evolved over time as an efficient means of translating research done in the lab, the library, or in the field into an appropriately detailed package that effectively contributes to and supports front-office decision-making (Figure 13.7).[7]

The overall goal is achieved by creating an integrated package, by weaving together several relatively independent components of the report. While the package must hang together, each component is designed for a particular primary readership, each serves a unique purpose, and each is constructed precisely to meet the expectations of that audience and purpose. To examine this independence and interdependence, we need to look briefly at the report's principal parts:

1. Title and cover page
2. Executive summary
3. Table of contents
4. Introduction
5. Body
6. Recommendations/conclusions
7. Appendixes

THE TITLE AND COVER PAGE

Titles and cover pages generally receive little attention and yet are important features of the report. In the years before the Internet and intranets when monumental volumes of information did not compete for our attention, titles were intended to do little more than announce the general subject: "The title is the subject of the report. It contains a noun or two, plus an assortment of adjectives, articles, and prepositions. No verb. It merely announces a subject; it doesn't make the subject do anything. It should be brief and reasonably definitive. In a

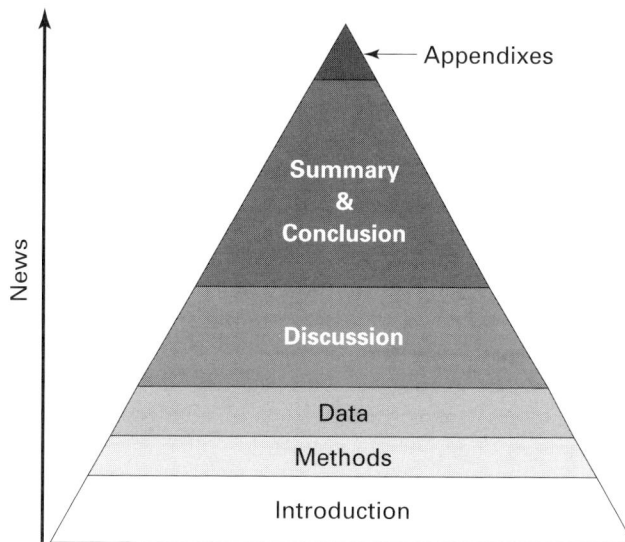

FIGURE 13.7

Reporting the News

showdown, you have the right to sacrifice completeness on the altar of brevity. Few titles need be more than four words long."[8]

Today, information must fight to be heard. In 1932, the first edition of *Ulrich's International Periodicals Directory,* a major index of professional literature, listed 6,000 titles. In contrast, current editions list more than 110,000 titles. In just the sciences, more than 2,000,000 papers are published each year. Book production is equally prolific. The Library of Congress collection increases by more than 1,000,000 titles a year.

In this explosion of information and research, four-word titles may sentence reports to a premature oblivion. Title lengths have been growing in response to the information competition. Titles in scientific and medical journals, for instance, have 36–70% more words than were used prior to the inception of the Internet. Compared to merely announcing the general subject, today's report titles, as recommended by one technical society to prospective authors, need to accomplish three goals: "a good title (i) identifies the subject, (ii) indicates the purpose of the study, and (iii) gives important high-impact words early."

The increased number of words is also needed to help report titles accomplish the two functional goals of the report: to increase the probability of a first reading and to increase the probability of subsequent retrieval. As researchers point out: "A person usually decides to read an article [or report] based on the title's content . . . . Many readers peruse the titles . . . to decide whether or not to turn to a specific abstract. The title must interest these readers. Overly specific, narrow titles with words understandable only to specialists will be passed over. Further, literature searchers will ignore titles that are incomprehensible to all but a few individuals."[9]

The second goal, retrieval, is met by aligning titles with the logic employed by indexing systems, an action that can "make the difference between wide dissemination and lost research."[10] Wide dissemination is achieved by purposely selecting recognizable keywords and terminology that increase accessibility and retrieval. Hierarchical indexes, like the Library of Congress, use the wording of the title to position your work in relation to terminology established in extensive thesauruses. Post-coordination, or keyword, indexes typically scan terms in titles and abstracts. Keyword in Context (KWIC) listings create thesauruses using permutations of keywords, listing the work under each of the main words in the title. (For instance, a report entitled *Attributes of Effective Implementation* would appear in the index under "Attributes" as well as under "Implementation.")

A distinctive cover design may also improve both the initial read and the report's subsequent retrieval. Often a report gets attention because it is recognized as having an association with a particular company, organization, or agency. When this happens, the report may receive greater attention. Once shelved somewhere in the audience's office or library, the number one factor affecting the success of retrieval, as we would readily expect, is whether the audience had previously made use of the report. The second most significant factor affecting retrieval is the distinctive character (the design, logo, and title) we spoke of. Like the identifying corporate icons we advised be used in formal presentations, a distinctive design, logo, or title will positively influence report recall, retrievability, and, ultimately, credibility.[11]

Together, the title and cover page are what make the first and, potentially, the last impression. Make certain you devote sufficient time and energy to put your best face (and message) forward.

EXECUTIVE SUMMARY

The important news in a business report tends to unfold as the reader progresses through the report, with much of the key information withheld until the Conclusion and Recommendations sections. Most busy executives want a clear synopsis of what was done, what the conclusions are, and what follow-through is needed. Even the busy executive who skips ahead to the Conclusion section will, no doubt, be somewhat frustrated: without the context, the conclusions will probably be no more clear or satisfying than if we jump to the final pages of a mystery to learn who did the crime. The pieces have to be understood in context to be fully appreciated.

The resolution of this dilemma (too much information and not enough time) is the Executive Summary—(originally referred to as merely "Summary"). The Executive Summary is a report in miniature, which is generated after all the remaining sections of the report have been written. Generally not more than a page or so, the Executive Summary pulls the critical information from throughout the report, providing quick insight into and context for the results, conclusions, recommendations, and actions. Figure 13.8 is an Executive Summary illustrating the intent and sources of the information presented.

As correctly explained in the supportive guidance of the 1950s, the Executive Summary has "to do with answers, not with plots":

> The [Executive] Summary is addressed, above all, to the reader who must skim a hundred reports a day. He cares not a whit how you wound up to toss the egg, but is intensely interested in what useful results were obtained when it hit the fan. Tell him that, and no more. He isn't going to throw any eggs himself, and he isn't going to advise anybody how to throw eggs. To him, the result and its implications are the important things . . . . The Summary is also addressed to the reader who is so captivated by the subject matter that he is going to read every word you say. The Summary gives this reader some idea of the relative importance and significance of the details that he is going to read later . . . .

FIGURE 13.8 Sample Executive Summary

	Information	Source
In May 1996, the Department Standards Committee (DSC) chartered a team to develop a tool that would help guide the implementation of standards derived and approved using the Necessary & Sufficient (N&S) Closure Process.	Background/ issue being addressed	I. Introduction
The team first defined implementation within the context of DOE work activities, establishing clear boundaries for the team's efforts. Once the scope had been precisely defined, the team then visited a number of DOE sites to learn about implementation practices.	Methodology applied	II. Report Body
Using the field observations as a foundation, the team identified common themes evidenced at the sites, and from these derived a set of 25 attributes correlated with effective implementation.	Results achieved	III. Conclusion
This attribute set is intended for use by all participants involved in implementing standards. The set is intended to accomplish three key goals: 1) Promote more effective and informed decision-making about how implementation is accomplished. 2) Encourage each of the communities involved to make more valuable contributions toward ensuring work is done safely and efficiently. 3) Promote and foster a logic of implementation predicated on the N&S Closure Process.	General application	IV. Recommendations
The set of attributes is a starting point. Derived exclusively from limited observation of DOE programs, the list is not intended to be definitive. Rather, the team expects that experience with the set will encourage expanding and refining the attribute list, and will serve to increase its usefulness in helping meet the DOE's objectives of establishing itself as a world class, standards-based operation.	Specific steps to take	

No matter how much it hurts, minimize the discussion of the motions that you went through in arriving at your conclusions, and keep your order of presentation logical rather than historical. The summary of a report is not an abridged narrative: it has to do with answers, not with plots. You can plot all you want to on your own time.

TABLE OF CONTENTS

The Table of Contents offers a ready road map, allowing the reader to navigate the logic you inherently employed in creating the report: "The Table of Contents is nothing more than the outline from which you prepared your report. It is the skeletal structure on which you hang the muscles and organs of your report .... The Table of Contents answers the questions: 'How is this report hung together, anyway, and where do I look to find the particular topic that I'm interested in?'"[12]

The substance of this "skeleton" was not always apparent from the Table of Contents. It was common practice late into the nineteenth century to indicate items on the Table of Contents in alphabetical order. (Figure 13.9 is the Table of Contents from a report published in 1897.) As reports assumed an increased role in corporate decision-making, the alphabetical arrangement was abandoned in favor of a structure that represented and reflected the actual organization.

FIGURE 13.9

A Nineteenth
Century Table
of Contents—
Alphabetical Order

Therefore, an effective Table of Contents is assumed to satisfy four criteria:

1. It is logically structured, leading the reader on a clear, straightforward path through the evolution of the information and the associated conclusions and decisions.

2. It must be complete enough to illuminate the road without leaving the reader to guess where poorly-lit side streets might lead.

3. It must use language and vocabulary meaningful to the principal audiences.

4. It must help fulfill the report's responsibilities to inform and educate the readership (a goal achieved by balancing the conventional, empathetic, and pedagogical dimensions of the report—Figure 13.10).[13]

FIGURE 13.10 — A Closer Look at Designing a Table of Contents

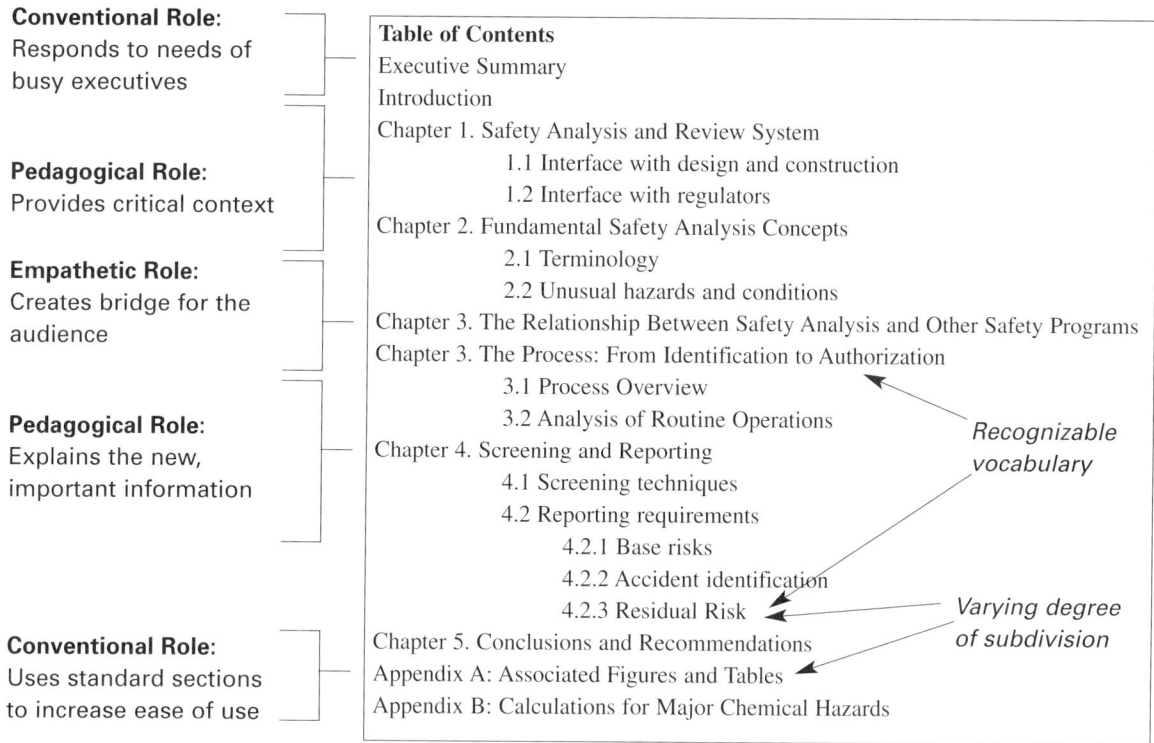

Conventional Role:
Responds to needs of busy executives

Pedagogical Role:
Provides critical context

Empathetic Role:
Creates bridge for the audience

Pedagogical Role:
Explains the new, important information

Conventional Role:
Uses standard sections to increase ease of use

Table of Contents
Executive Summary
Introduction
Chapter 1. Safety Analysis and Review System
    1.1 Interface with design and construction
    1.2 Interface with regulators
Chapter 2. Fundamental Safety Analysis Concepts
    2.1 Terminology
    2.2 Unusual hazards and conditions
Chapter 3. The Relationship Between Safety Analysis and Other Safety Programs
Chapter 3. The Process: From Identification to Authorization
    3.1 Process Overview
    3.2 Analysis of Routine Operations
Chapter 4. Screening and Reporting
    4.1 Screening techniques
    4.2 Reporting requirements
      4.2.1 Base risks
      4.2.2 Accident identification
      4.2.3 Residual Risk
Chapter 5. Conclusions and Recommendations
Appendix A: Associated Figures and Tables
Appendix B: Calculations for Major Chemical Hazards

Recognizable vocabulary

Varying degree of subdivision

Source: Reprinted by permission of Palmer Wright, "The Logic and Rhetoric of a Table of Contents," *Journal of Technical Writing and Communication,* Vol. 2(3), pp. 211–223 (1972). Copyright Baywood Publishing Co., Inc.

INTRODUCTION

As the Du Pont guidance cleverly points out, "The Introduction must distract the reader from whatever he's thinking about and zero him in on your job." To accomplish this "distraction," the introduction seeks to establish a context for the report and establish a reasonable motivation for bothering the reader with any further reading. Setting context, the Introduction is obliged to answer a series of questions:

- What is the problem?
- Why is it important enough for you and me to spend time on it?
- What were the objectives of the work: primary, secondary, and so on?
- How does this work fit in with what has gone before? Did you pick up the idea from someone else or did you think it up yourself?
- What is the scope of the job that you did?
- Where did it start and where did it stop?

In addition to setting the external context—the information predating and setting the report in motion—the Introduction has one additional job: summarizing the internal logic. Generally, the concluding paragraphs of the Introduction explain the report's organization. Although the Table of Contents provides the skeleton, a brief narrative statement in the Introduction helps establish the nature of the journey (Figure 13.11).

THE BODY, THE RECOMMENDATIONS, AND THE CONCLUSIONS

The body of the report is intended to be a reasoned, integrated discussion. In developing the body, you need to keep in mind the general line of reasoning, the appropriate organizational principles, and the appropriate pacing (use of white space, figures, tables, and headings). All of these features give the reader a chance to digest materials efficiently. The recommendations and conclusions

---

FIGURE 13.11 ◆ Defining the Sources of Information for the Introduction

1. INTRODUCTION

When the Department of Energy (DOE) issued the Criteria for the Department's Standards Program (DOE/EH/-0416) in August 1994, it established a new direction and vision for the complex: Standards-Based Management. Beyond the mechanical changes needed to achieve the vision, the Criteria, also identified a new set of management principles and values that had to be reflected universally throughout DOE, its contractors, and all their diverse operations.

> **The History:** the general background leading up to the project/research

The first tangible demonstration of how these "Work Smart" principles contribute to achieving the goals established in the Criteria was provided in the Department Standards Committee's (DSC's) development of a Necessary and Sufficient (N&S) Closure Process for the identification and approval of Work Smart Standards. Using the expectations set forth in the Criteria, the DSC engineered a process that calls for establishing knowledgeable teams to conduct a rigorous examination of the work and to determine the associated hazards—followed by a disciplined, cooperative determination of the standards necessary to allow the work to be performed both safely and efficiently.

> **Previous Work:** A look at the primary foundations upon which the present effort intends to build

Successes achieved in pilot applications validated both the N&S Closure Process and the inherent value and benefits resulting from the underlying Work Smart principles. However, owners of potential applications recognized that selecting and approving an appropriate set of standards is only the first step. Once the standards are approved, they still must be translated into the performance of work.

> **The Need:** A statement of the basic rationale why the effort has merit and value

As with development of the N&S Closure Process, the issue with implementation was not that no previous method or system existed. For as long as DOE has been doing work, standards and program requirements have generally been captured in and translated into work through the use of policies, plans, and procedures.

The missing ingredient is not availability of a method, but, rather, availability of a strategy that embeds the Work Smart principles within the implementation function. Specifically what was determined to be needed was 1) an appreciation of precisely what is meant by "effective implementation," and 2) availability of a tool to promote and provide a measure of enhanced effective implementation.

> **Intended Results:** A statement of what specifically constitutes resolution of the need

Therefore, the DSC chartered a team to accomplish precisely these ends:

- develop a definition and understanding of effective implementation
- establish a framework to guide implementation
- establish a framework to promote improved implementation for those activities already underway.

> **The Initiation:** How the work got authorized and underway; the transition to the detail in the Body

This report provides the results of the team's efforts. The sections of the report correspond with the objectives established for the team by the DSC:

Chapter I. Introduction—provides the context and background of this project

Chapter II. Implementation—provides an explanation of implementation—its scope and focus

Chapter III. Attributes as a Tool—provides an explanation of why attributes were selected as the tool most appropriate and the process used to derive them.

Chapter IV. Attribute Descriptions—provides descriptions of each of the attributes, including descriptions of conditions found when the attribute is in evidence, benefits of the attribute, and field examples as observed during team visits.

> **Organization:** The logic of how the materials collected and developed will be presented to the reader

should be reviewed to be certain that they are derived naturally from the information presented in the body of the report. The conclusions and recommendations should be recognizable as reasonable outcomes and inferences drawn from the materials presented. Equivalent to the concluding slide in a formal presentation, they should also summarize the thoughts you want the reader to take away from the report.

You can use a variety of methods for the order of the recommendations and conclusions: 1) in order from most to least significant; 2) in order from most to least immediate, either in terms of urgency or likelihood of implementation; or 3) chronological, in order from near-term to long-term actions. Whichever order you choose, it should be consistent and evident to the reader.

APPENDIXES

The Appendix is the most specialized of the report's contents. The Appendix should contain material necessary to round out the picture, but that would disrupt the flow, continuity, and persuasiveness of the report if it were included in the main body of the report. The Appendix is intended almost exclusively for colleagues and other researchers who need additional specifics to allow them to pursue related lines of inquiry: detailed spreadsheets, lengthy process diagrams, extensive discussions of theoretical bases, historical foundations, or precise methodologies.

Appendixes are very valuable, but their value is to a limited audience. While almost everyone will read the executive summary, and a good percentage of those same readers will scan the recommendations and conclusions, a relatively small subset of your readers will have a keen interest in reading through the Appendixes (Figure 13.12).[14]

MYTHICAL BEASTS AND STRUCTURAL UNITY

The business report is a persuasive document designed to respond to a number of different audiences and constituencies. The report is an integrated package

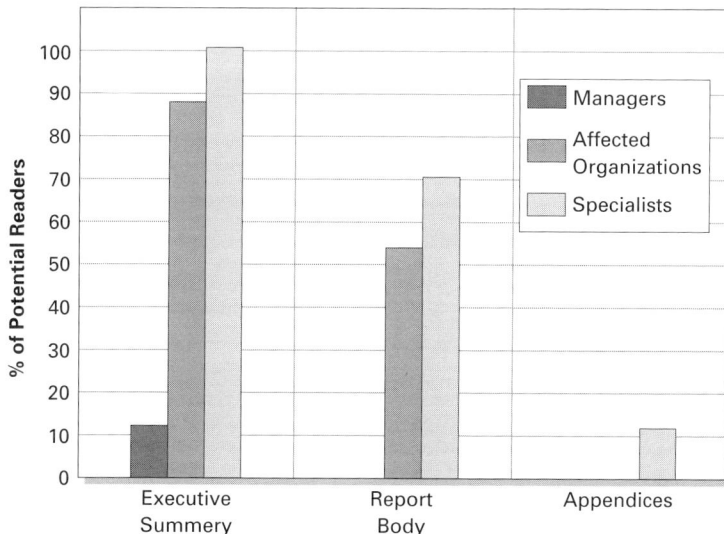

FIGURE 13.12

A Readership Perspective

woven out of several carefully designed components. Crafted effectively, these components satisfy the various sets of audience expectations in a manner that avoids the possible chaos, loss of credibility, and issues with readability that can result when a poorly orchestrated attempt is made to satisfy multiple audiences and purposes (Figure 13.13). The challenge is to remain mindful of the work of each of the elements—its purpose, as well as its primary and secondary readerships (Table 13.4).

At the same time, the obligation is to maintain "structural unity," to avoid the appearance of an inartfully pieced-together answer to the initiating condition. The unique voice of the 1950s Du Pont guidance makes this point extremely well:

> Your report must have structural unity. The whole report deals with a single subject. Each section deals with one aspect of that subject. Each paragraph treats one phase of that aspect. Keep out the extraneous stuff, and you'll cut your work in half. Don't pad your report with adventitious rubbish. A good report is direct and complete. Length doesn't matter. A short report that goes to the point is far better than a long report that rambles.
>
> If you graft together a man's upper body, a goat's hindquarters, and a heifer's horns, you, the creator, may think the result looks good. But people will look at you askance because your product violates their ideas of structural unity. Besides, everybody knows that satyrs are mythical beasts and therefore implausible. Let your animal be a man, a goat, or a heifer, but don't mix them up.
>
> Aside from the blood, sweat, and tears of which you are so acutely conscious, your report is composed of sections, paragraphs, sentences, and words . . . . Your job is to make each of these components carry its share of the load, so that the resulting structure will hang together and won't fall apart the first time one of your critics sniggers at it.

Understanding how attention to audience needs and precise purposes can produce a document uniquely suited to assisting the decision-making processes of the corporation or organization, we next turn to a document that is geared toward advancing the corporate image and financial stature. Just as we learned by analyzing the structure of the business report, we will also see that the annual report has evolved—in a relatively short period of time—from a document written by analysts for analysts into a document that is a truly challenging communication assignment.

FIGURE 13.13

The Long Report—
A Perspective

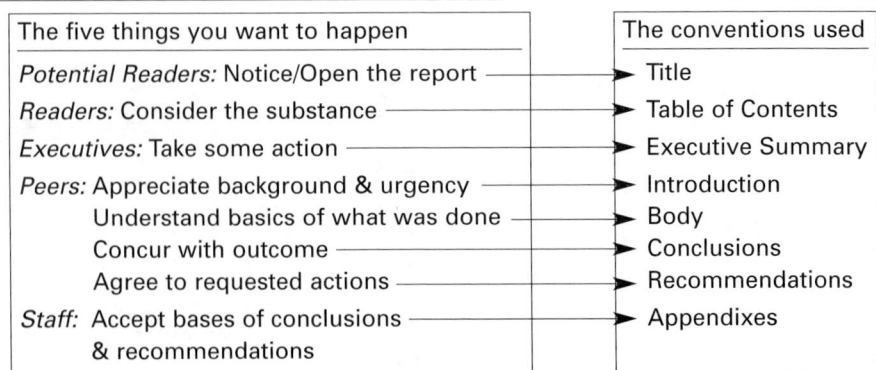

The five things you want to happen	The conventions used
Potential Readers: Notice/Open the report	Title
Readers: Consider the substance	Table of Contents
Executives: Take some action	Executive Summary
Peers: Appreciate background & urgency	Introduction
Understand basics of what was done	Body
Concur with outcome	Conclusions
Agree to requested actions	Recommendations
Staff: Accept bases of conclusions & recommendations	Appendixes

13.4 THE BUSINESS REPORT STRUCTURE—AN OVERVIEW

Component	Description	Purpose	Audiences
Title	The title has three components: 1) a descriptive phrase that summarizes and captures the report's scope and intent; 2) the audience for whom the report was prepared; and 3) the date (at minimum, month and year) of publication. In addition, there may be other corporate/organizational identifiers, e.g, report numbers, logos.	Allow full breadth of potential readers to determine if the report warrants their attention. This includes both direct recipients of the report and those who learn of it through on-line searches.	Primary: All potential readers

Secondary: Indexers |
| Executive Summary | A compact synopsis of the primary high points of the report; generally includes summary of methods, issues, and emphasizes the principal recommendations and conclusions | Allow busy executives to gain quick insights into and abbreviated knowledge of the report's critical substance | Primary: Executives

Secondary: All other readers |
| Table of Contents | Using section titles that are variants of the report title, sets forth the overall organization. The amount of detail (headings and subheadings) is a reflection of the need to define the logic and assist the reader with accessing information of key interest. | Allow easy navigation of information, clarify the relationship among sections and subsections | Primary: Colleagues

Secondary: Executives |
| Introduction | An explanation of the background and context: what set the work in motion, what the limitations were, related efforts, and methods used. Why was the work important, and why now? Generally concludes with an overview of the structure and organization of the report | Establish the framework from which to understand the conclusions and recommendations | Primary: Colleagues

Secondary: Executives |
| Body | Provides the relevant details explaining the processes used, the outcomes, the limitations, and other information vital to allowing the reader to appreciate the appropriateness of the conclusions and recommendations | Detail, at an appropriate level of specificity, the activities and processes involved | Primary: Colleagues

Secondary: Staff |
| Conclusions | Summary of the principal results of the work and the key inferences drawn from the research and analyses | Highlight the precise points that result from the research, presented in an order consistent with either the order in which they arise from the work reported, or a classification strategy promoted by the report's purposes (e.g., sequential, primacy) | Primary: Executives and Colleagues

Secondary: Staff and Specialists |
| Recommendations | A list of the specific actions or follow-up items that need to be initiated. These recommendations may be accompanied by schedules and specific assignment of responsibility. | Translate the conclusions into a specific course of action | Primary: Executives and Staff

Secondary: Peers |
| Appendixes | Specific, highly-detailed information necessary to support the report's assertions and conclusions, but which, because of its specificity, would impede the flow of the argument and story. | Allow other researchers and specialists to better understand the presentation and to build upon the foundation established | Primary: Specialists

Secondary: Colleagues |
| Distribution List | The specific individuals and programs who either need or are affected by the report, particularly the recommendations and conclusions. Includes those who may have assignment for any follow-up actions | Ensure the receipt by all who need to be apprised of the report: sponsors, affected organizations, and those who should receive the report as part of corporate policy and protocol (e.g., the records and information management program) | N/A |

THE ANNUAL REPORT: ALIGNING VOICE, DESIGN, AND PURPOSE

FROM FRAUD TO CPA TO DESIGN HOUSE

Without doubt, the documents most people associate with the stock market and with investments is the corporate financial report, more popularly referred to as the annual report. This document type, though not as old as the NYSE, is about 175 years old, dating from approximately 1827. However, its role has not always been as clear as it is today. In fact, the legal requirement for annual reporting is, as we noted earlier in this chapter, less than 75 years old.

Stocks began trading on the NYSE in 1792. Some 70 years later in 1860, when the NYSE first asked companies for regular reports, the idea was less than wildly accepted. The Delaware, Lackawanna and Western Railroad, as example, said in reply: "This company makes no reports and provides no statements."[15] This lack of enthusiasm didn't keep the NYSE from pushing the idea.

For those companies who, unlike the Delaware, Lackawanna and Western Railroad, willingly complied with the NYSE request, reports were fairly simple, often not much more than a few columns of financial data printed in *The New York Times* or *The Wall Street Journal.* (The Appendix includes a sample annual report as appeared in *The Wall Street Journal,* January 24, 1895.) Other companies approached the request more thoroughly, reporting financial performance in great detail. For example, the first annual report of the Northern Pacific Railway Company in 1897 included 54 pages of narrative and spreadsheets examining every element of the operation from maintenance of equipment, tunnels, and fencing to the costs of "oil, tallow, and waste for locomotives" (which totaled $23,424.50).[16] All these financial conclusions were duly attested to on the General Balance Sheet by "Price, Waterhouse & Co., Auditors."

Further, the report was accompanied by a bound volume of "Official Reports Used in the Preparation of the First Annual Report," a volume that included nearly 100 pages of minutely detailed supporting reports authored by the General Manager, the General Traffic Manager, the General Passenger and Ticket Agent, and the Chief Engineer. Whereas the annual report, for instance, makes a single notation of all "general expenses" ($529,827.34), the supporting detail identifies 23 contributing elements, including notations by the General Traffic Manager regarding his deep concern that the corporate advertising budget ($46,784.22) had been exceeded by $1,889.22 (neither of which amount would warrant inclusion—no less concern—in any contemporary annual report or corporate balance sheet).

A growing public desire for full disclosure, attested to by the signature of a certified auditor, gave great impetus to advancing the stature and standardization of the accounting profession. In the early 1880s, the first society of public accountants was formed, followed shortly in 1886 by introduction of a national certification program—the CPA (Certified Public Account) exam.[17] Like the NYSE, which had politely solicited reports from corporations, the accounting professions were nonetheless also initially limited to working with those corporations willing to open their books to the public. Acknowledging this lack of corporate openness, in 1903, the Bureau of Corporations (an agency chartered by Congress) published a scathing report citing the "principal evil" of stock and security activity: "secrecy and dishonesty in promotion" complemented by "secrecy of corporation and administration" and abetted by "misleading or dishonest financial statements."[18]

Throughout the early decades of the twentieth century, the number of participating corporations continued to grow, most of which, as studies have shown, made honest disclosures. However, honesty did not always translate into clarity. Reports, in general, remained difficult for investors to interpret accurately. For example, let's consider the 1931 annual report from the Coca-Cola Company. Issued as a 6" × 8" document, the brief 16 pages begins with a short statement from the President to the stockholders announcing the year's "favorable profit." The President's statement is then supported by a balance sheet, a handful of graphs, and a half dozen pictures highlighting Coca-Cola's expanding international presence (Figure 13.14).

Despite demonstrating an evident interest in honest disclosure, the information presented in the report is hard to interpret. Figure 13.15, for instance, shows units of production that are unclear. Figure 13.16 argues for the company's current and projected financial health, but provides no values or units by which to ascertain just how rosy the picture really is.[19]

Juxtaposed with the disclosures that simply created a grain of suspicion, other companies were involved in outright fraud. As one Harvard law professor asserts, the first 30 years of the twentieth century represented "three decades of intermittent securities fraud waves. Securities fraud was considered to be so severe a problem that every state but Nevada enacted a securities regulation statute between 1911 and 1933."[20] The public outcry against deception,

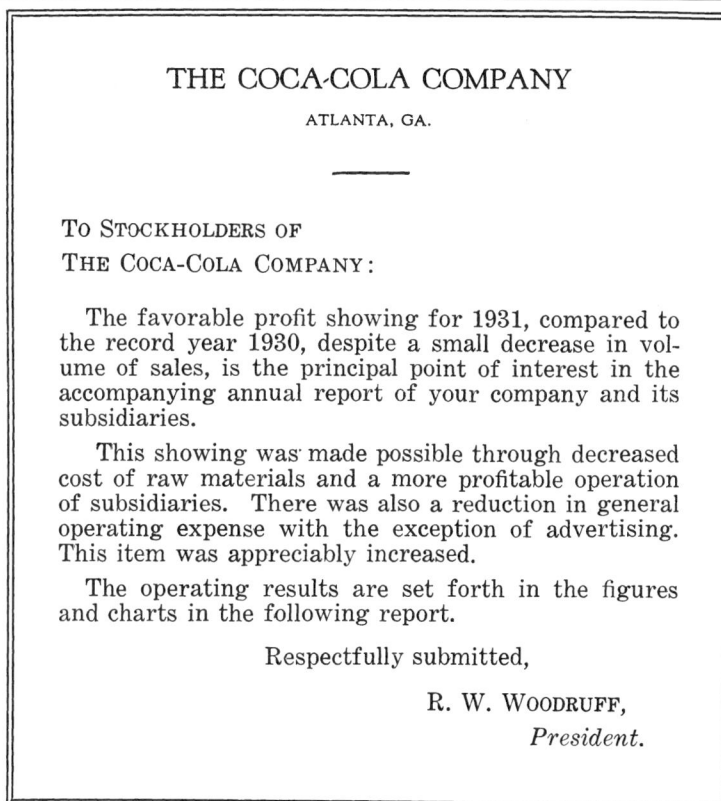

FIGURE 13.14

A Short Word of Introduction to Stockholders

THE COCA-COLA COMPANY

ATLANTA, GA.

TO STOCKHOLDERS OF

THE COCA-COLA COMPANY:

The favorable profit showing for 1931, compared to the record year 1930, despite a small decrease in volume of sales, is the principal point of interest in the accompanying annual report of your company and its subsidiaries.

This showing was made possible through decreased cost of raw materials and a more profitable operation of subsidiaries. There was also a reduction in general operating expense with the exception of advertising. This item was appreciably increased.

The operating results are set forth in the figures and charts in the following report.

Respectfully submitted,

R. W. WOODRUFF,

President.

FIGURE 13.15

A Hard-to-Interpret Annual Report Chart

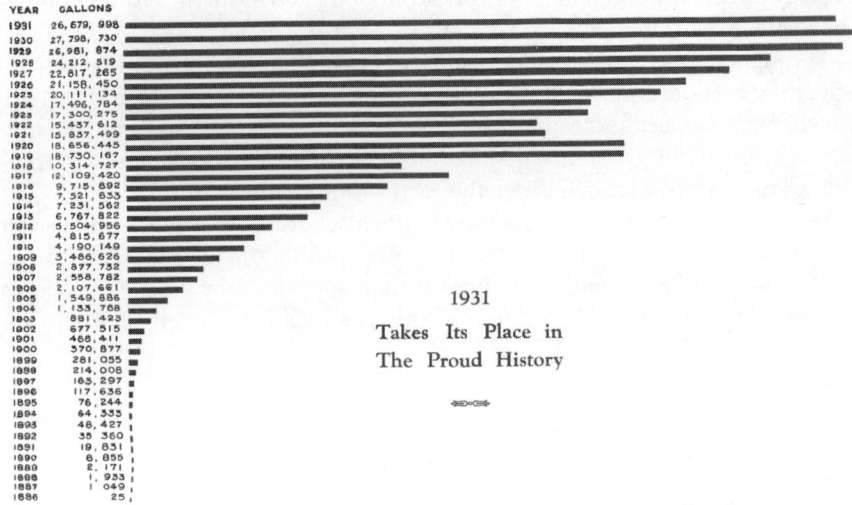

YEAR	GALLONS
1931	26,679,998
1930	27,798,730
1929	26,981,874
1928	24,212,519
1927	22,817,265
1926	21,158,450
1925	20,111,134
1924	17,496,784
1923	17,300,275
1922	15,437,612
1921	15,837,499
1920	18,656,445
1919	18,730,167
1918	10,314,727
1917	12,109,420
1916	9,715,692
1915	7,521,833
1914	7,231,562
1913	6,767,822
1912	5,504,956
1911	4,815,677
1910	4,190,149
1909	3,486,626
1908	2,877,732
1907	2,558,782
1906	2,107,661
1905	1,549,886
1904	1,133,788
1903	881,423
1902	677,515
1901	468,411
1900	370,877
1899	281,055
1898	214,008
1897	163,297
1896	117,636
1895	76,244
1894	64,333
1893	48,427
1892	35,360
1891	19,851
1890	6,855
1889	2,171
1888	1,933
1887	1,049
1886	25

1931
Takes Its Place in
The Proud History

FIGURE 13.16

Presenting Pictures Without Values

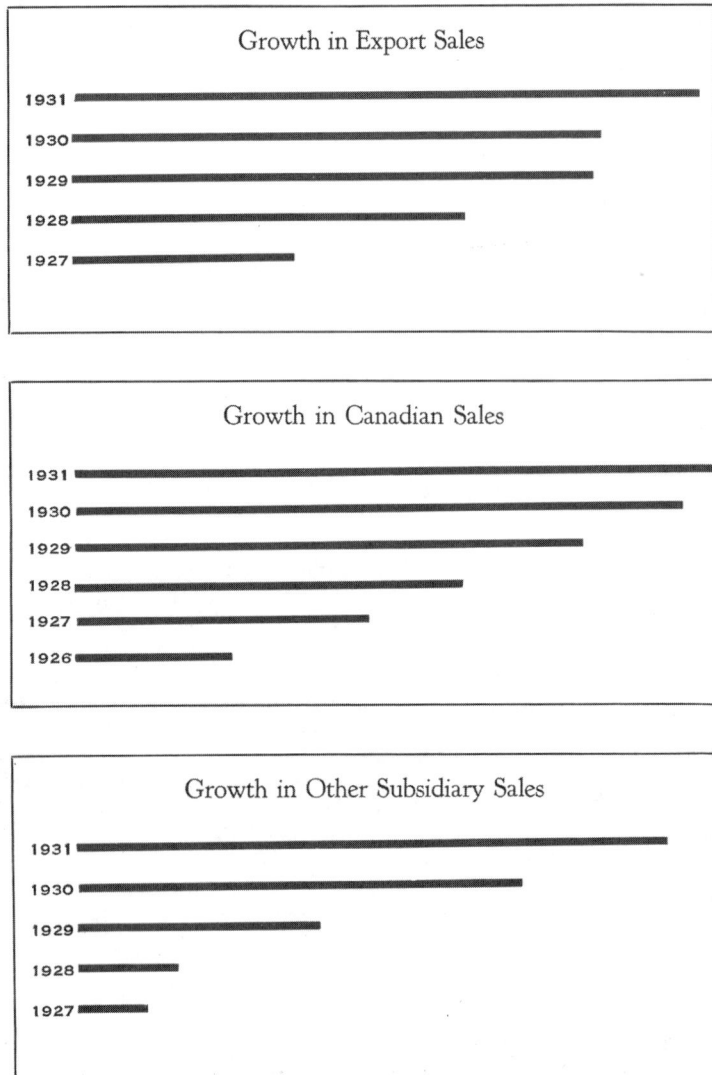

Growth in Export Sales

1931
1930
1929
1928
1927

Growth in Canadian Sales

1931
1930
1929
1928
1927
1926

Growth in Other Subsidiary Sales

1931
1930
1929
1928
1927

dishonesty, and lack of clarity reached its crescendo with the "Matchbook" scandals of the late 1920s. The "Matchbook King," Ivan Kreuger, controlled three-quarters of the world's match production via his company, International Match Corp. A darling of the social set, Kreuger, once known as the "Puritan of Finance," bilked shareholders and moneylenders out of some $500 million by transferring funds around the United States and abroad among 400 subsidiary corporations. The fraud, the "largest financial statement scam in history," was made possible because Kreuger absolutely refused to allow his books or those of his partners to be independently audited.

Responding to the outcry, Congress enacted what some people have entitled the "ultimate sunshine laws": the Securities Exchange Acts of 1933 and 1934. As President Franklin Roosevelt proclaimed when recommending passage of the 1933 Securities bill, the act "should give impetus to honest dealing in securities and thereby bring back public confidence."[21] As established in the two laws, all publicly traded corporations were thereafter required annually to produce four consolidated reports: 1) a statement of earnings, 2) a balance sheet, 3) a statement of cash flow, and 4) a statement of stockholders' equity. The reports also had to provide relevant footnotes detailing quantitative and qualitative information (i.e., accounting policies) needed to allow readers to better understand the data.

While boosting the participation of accounting firms, who now had legislatively mandated responsibility for attesting to the accuracy of the financial data, the law, seemingly, also turned the remaining text of the reports over to the analysts as well. As stipulated in Section 15(d) of the 1934 Securities Exchange Act, the section requiring independent audits of financial information, corporate officers are forbidden from making "any untrue statement of a material fact or to omit to state a material fact necessary in order to make the statements made, in the light of the circumstances under which they were made, not misleading."[22]

As generally interpreted, this requirement was understood to mean that narrative should be limited to those observations needed to clarify and expand information contained on the financial statements. Accordingly, not only the Management Discussion and Analysis (MDA) section of the annual report, but the other two pieces where narrative generally appears—the letter to shareholders and the company report—by extension, also were given over to the province of the analyst. (Figure 13.17, the President's statement from the 1957 Delta Air Lines annual report, typifies the concept of narrative as written with the sole intent of highlighting and interpreting the report's financial data.)

Using this interpretation, annual reports continued fairly unchanged for 30 or so years following the passage of the Security Exchange Acts. Then a new idea emerged. Maybe in addition to answering the financial obligations, the annual report could serve as the corporation's principal public relations document. The advent of the reconstituted annual report had begun. "In the 1960s, some companies went to glossy paper, color photographs, stylized graphics, and fancy layouts in attempts to set themselves apart from other companies chasing the favor of the same investors."[23] The design houses were soon engaged in the marketing of American enterprise. The $5 billion dollar annual report business took off, forcing every company into a competition for the attentions and investments of the American public. For example, when celebrating its 100-year anniversary in 1969, Ringling Bros. and Barnum & Bailey issued an annual report rivaling its stylized circus programs. Among other notable features, the report pictured the CEO, President, and Treasurer sharing the spotlight with two other "stellar

FIGURE 13.17

The CEO
Statement as
Amplification
of Financial
Information

1957 | Annual Report

DELTA AIR LINES, INC.

TO THE STOCKHOLDERS

The 1957 fiscal year was a period of further growth and development for Delta Air Lines. We improved and expanded our services over both domestic and international route systems, and we became firmly established and identified in our new markets. Twelve airplanes were added to our operating fleet, seat miles produced increased 28% over the preceding year (to 2,206 million) and the additional personnel required by this higher volume of operations were employed and trained. Preparation was made for the ten DC-7B airplanes to be placed in service during the 1958 fiscal year, along with further planning for jet operations that becomes progressively more detailed.

The higher prices encountered in almost every phase of our operations were vigorously combatted. Through those efforts, revenue ton mile costs increased only 3% over the preceding year and the break-even passenger load factor (the load factor that produces passenger revenue, which, combined with all other operating revenues, equals operating expenses) remained relatively unchanged.

The substantial increase in seat miles produced, and the augmentation of service over the newly-certificated routes to the Northeast, are reflected

Source: 1957 annual report, Delta Air Lines, reprinted with permission.

performers" from the company—an elephant and an animal trainer.[24] Yet, even that effort represented a modest degree of extravagance. Among the more noteworthy contenders for king of extravagance is the 1984 annual report of H.J. Heinz, Inc., the food processing giant. At a cost of $8 a copy, the company issued an annual report featuring a 40-page salute to the tomato.[25]

As costs for producing annual reports continued to rise and the perceived value to the investors and shareholders continued to decline, more and more corporations began to question the wisdom and value of the annual report. As senior management at Pfizer company summarized, and we as communicators can appreciate, annual reports "are getting out of hand . . . . Sometimes design overwhelms message."[26] By 1986, the criticism was raised to the SEC. Just as the era of the CPA had been replaced by the era of the design house, the annual report was preparing for one more major transition.

THE PROVINCE OF THE COMMUNICATOR

For the majority of the twentieth century, the narrative portions of the annual report focused on explaining and amplifying the financial information. During the era of the design house, the goal, as most annual reports implicitly argued, was to make companies look as good as possible without overstepping the bounds dictated by the 1934 Securities Exchange Act. Rethought as a public relations tool, annual reports were described as "undisguised advertisement," "mindless marketing blather," and as a management platform for "practicing their philosophies and touting themselves and their companies."[27]

In 1986, a shift in thinking occurred: "the first real innovation to annual reports since the days when they were handwritten."[28] The innovation was an agreement with the SEC that companies could tuck their detailed financial information into a separate document (the Proxy Statement, commonly referred to as a 10-K) and create a Summary Annual Report (SAR). This SAR, a product of a 3-year study, would be more compact, concise, and more readable. As its proponents argued to the SEC, the SAR would reflect "significant content changes, such as moving footnote material into the narrative, using graphs more generously, and rewriting the financial report in laymans' terms."[29]

Reconfirming many of the principles we examined in Part 1 of this text, authors of the proposed restructuring argued that the SAR would not only reduce production costs, it would also assist investors who, as surveys showed, wanted shorter reports that gave clearer perspective on earning potential: "Investors would like to see additional information in the annual report such as company outlook, potential valuables, and industry projections. They would like to know the company's plans for the future."[30]

In arguing for an SAR, General Motors learned an important lesson that we have been stressing in this text: Make certain you understand not only the explicit, but also the implicit and embedded purposes of your communication. Although industry had been quick to attribute the rising costs and reduced value of the annual report to the legal requirements established by the Securities Exchange Act, the problems had been largely manufactured by the industries themselves. As the SEC pointed out to General Motors, the law required annual reporting; neither the law nor the SEC had ever stipulated or mandated that the annual report was the exclusive means of satisfying the requirement. In the first 50 years following passage of the law, corporations, rather than accurately deciphering precisely what was being requested of them, had handcuffed themselves.

Armed with the new interpretation, companies such as General Motors, which at that time issued 2 million copies of its annual report a year, had a renewed control of their own fates—at least regarding the design, intent, and use of their Annual Reports. The SAR effectively recast the report into the province of the communicator, who would now be assisted by, rather than dictated to by, the analysts and design houses. Rather than a purely financial orientation or a public relations spin of a financial orientation, an SAR focuses on six primary objectives, many of which echo the lessons we have been discussing:

1. Encourage readership by making the report easier to read and understand.

2. Provide readers with relevant and concise financial and nonfinancial information without creating information overload.

3. Improve the quality and effectiveness of financial communications.

4. Enhance shareholder relations and management credibility through more effective communications.

5. Bring production costs in line with the message.

6. Design the document with its multiple purposes (public relations, financial disclosure, recruiting) in mind.

Having been the instrumental force in securing agreement for a Summary Annual Report from the SEC, General Motors did not take the leadership role in producing such a document. Maintaining it did not have sufficient time to react to the SEC's decision, General Motors proceeded with release of a colorful, 44-page magazine. Instead, McKesson Corporation, having learned of the SAR idea through *The Wall Street Journal* story about the negotiations between General Motors and the SEC, took advantage of the development.[31] In the final weeks of June 1987, the shareholders of McKesson Corporation became the first ever to receive a Summary Annual Report. McKesson claimed the action was an immediate success. The company saved approximately $60,000 in production costs (roughly 20% of the total spent annually on its annual report). More important to us as communicators, according to the corporate Vice President, the revised approach was living up to its expectations; it had "greatly improved the readability of the report and its use as a communication device."[32]

The opportunity we have today as communicators, evident from the SAR's objectives, was announced in the same article from *The Wall Street Journal* that first revealed the ongoing discussions between the SEC and General Motors: "Once the word spreads that the myth has been shattered, we believe many corporations will unleash a lot of pent-up creativity and invent a better glossy report. Inevitably, the reports will become the province of communicators and not accountants and lawyers. And that should be good for companies and investors alike."[33] As the annual report continues to gain recognition as a communication tool, the enhanced cooperative nature of the task increases the need for personnel with a keen appreciation of the rhetorical principles underlying all effective communication. (Figure 13.18 depicts the evolution of the annual report.)

SENDING THE RIGHT MESSAGE

The annual report has always been about credibility, about giving investors complete and truthful information. The movement away from a narrative that is

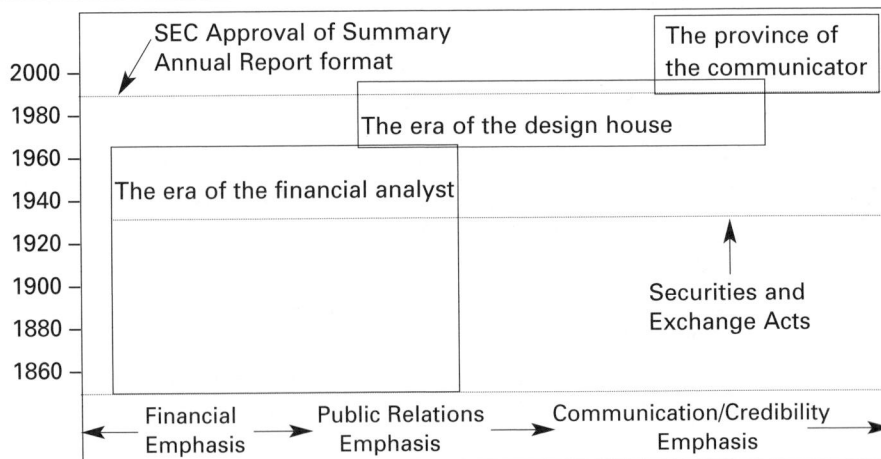

FIGURE 13.18

The Primary Historical Phases of the Annual Report

exclusively an amplification of financial data to an "undisguised advertisement," and finally to a communication tool is both liberating and challenging: "U.S. corporations are now free to reinvent and, one hopes, to improve the annual report . . . . From now on, companies can use the report to convey any truthful message that suits them. If they choose, they can even eliminate the annual report altogether."[34] The creation of a truthful message where for decades readers only believed they were witnessing corporate deceit and misrepresentation is a massive undertaking. It means that we must concentrate on a few critical dimensions—credibility and consistency—factors that demand careful and purposeful alignment of the stated message and the message conveyed by the design.

CONFIDENCE AND CREDIBILITY. Beginning with President Roosevelt's call to bring back "integrity" and "public confidence" in the securities industry, the watchword for the annual report has been "credibility." The financial data, subject as it is to intensive scrutiny, is not generally where the issue of credibility lies (or if it does, it lies outside our capabilities and immediate interests). Rather, credibility must be established foremost in the President's or CEO's message to the stockholders, the most widely read segment of the report. (An SEC survey found that 77% of those who read annual reports reported they read the President's letter at least "somewhat thoroughly.")[35] As one article on "making the most" of the annual report describes, "Just because an annual report is a SEC-filed document doesn't mean it has to wear a lawyer's pinstripe suit and horn-rimmed glasses."[36] The message has to bear not only the personal imprint of the CEO, but an imprint that engenders trust and credibility.

Credibility is a function of character, of a truthful personality. The story needs to be told the way it actually is, not the way the company might like it to be. Communicators, as the agents of the CEO and the corporation, can do only so much to balance the public relations and financial reporting requirements of the annual report. When corporate credibility is lacking or lost, it is almost impossible to recover. Read in the aftermath of the corporation's financial implosion, the CEO's statements in the annual reports of Enron Corporation appear eerily suspicious. In retrospect, we read statements about "innovative culture" and a workforce "empowered to do what they do best" as early indicators of a company interested in bending the boundaries of fiscal integrity. We look cynically at the company's core values of communication, respect, integrity, and excellence—values that Enron proudly touted on the inside back covers of its annual reports beginning in 1997 (Figure 13.19). In the light of the scandal, we hear not the voice of Enron's leadership, but the language of the congressional accusations when we read Enron's proclamation that "ruthlessness, callousness, and arrogance don't belong here." No communicator can rescue a program that practices a total disregard for client—and reader.

In comparison, communicators—as agents of the CEO and the corporation—can play an important role in creating and sustaining an image of straight talk, candor, and honesty. The first step is assisting with creating a voice or an identity for the CEO and the corporation. Instead of a bland repetition of trivialized phrases of accomplishment, communicators can help create an image of a corporate leadership engaged in an open and frank exchange with shareholders.

As untraditional as the model might be, we can make this point most forcefully by turning to the 1931 annual report of Alphonse (Al) Capone Enterprises, a parody manufactured by the Simpson Paper Company. As the report makes

FIGURE 13.19

The Core Values
Cited in the Enron
Annual Report

OUR VALUES

COMMUNICATION
We have an obligation to communicate. Here we take the time to talk with one another . . . and to listen. We believe that information is meant to move and that information moves people.

INTEGRITY
We work with customers and prospects openly, honestly, and sincerely. When we say we will do something, we will do it; when we say we cannot or will not do something, then we won't do it.

RESPECT
We treat others as we would like to be treated ourselves. We do not tolerate abusive or disrespectful treatment. Ruthlessness, callousness, and arrogance don't belong here.

EXCELLENCE
We are satisfied with nothing less than the very best in everything we do. We will continue to raise the bar for everyone. The great fun here will be for all of us to discover just how good we can really be.

evident, unfortunately for the mob, the Great Depression has resulted in a dramatic reversal in fortunes. While the corporation had a $5 million profit in 1930, 1931 ended with a $5 million loss. Even with such decisive fiscal maneuvering as reducing "Federal and Foreign Income Taxes" from $7 in 1930 to $2 in 1931, management has not rescued the enterprise. Given this lackluster performance, Al Capone begins his letter to the shareholders with a truly memorable phrase: "1931 stunk." The letter goes on to discuss a number of interesting reasons and remedies—including "the involuntary retirement or disappearance of several executives" (Figure 13.20). The candor is refreshing, even though it certainly would have been unsettling to the Board of Directors, which includes such unsavory characters as Frank "the Enforcer" Nitti, "Machine Gun" Jack McGurn, and Jake "Greasy Thumb" Guzik.[37]

The second contribution to credibility we can make as communicators is to increase the forthrightness. Even when telling a truthful story, annual reports, reminiscent of the evasive tactics we saw when we discussed business correspondence, can reflect a certain reluctance to being fully candid. One attribute of this reluctance is evidenced when management accepts credit, but denies blame. As one set of researchers succinctly explains this phenomenon: "Management attributes good performance to itself and poor performance to external factors."[38] Sometimes, as we would all expect, it's not just external factors such as the Great Depression that can adversely influence performance; sometimes the management team simply wasn't able to fulfill every lofty performance goal.

We also need to carefully assess the implications of inappropriately downplaying the less attractive dimensions of the year's activity. As a case in point, we might return momentarily to the 1986 General Motors annual report, the one that was supposed to be the first Summary Annual Report. That year, General Motors experienced a titanic struggle between H. Ross Perot and other corporate personnel. The annual report, however, saw fit to report as if nothing had happened, a lack of forthrightness that, once exposed, diminished the credibility of the entire report. As reported in *The Wall Street Journal*, "If you had spent the last year in a monastery, you might not be aware that the world's biggest company and one of its richest men locked horns in a messy corporate

FIGURE 13.20

Capone's Letter to His Stockholders

1

LETTER TO SHAREHOLDERS

1931 stunk.

Following years of unimpeded growth and diversification, with annual sales increasing from 12 million dollars in 1922 to a record 105 million in 1930, your company has started to come apart.

The depression isn't helping anybody trying to run a business, but the worst problem in our industry is increasing government interference. The federal bureaucracy, particularly as regards the Federal Bureau of Investigation, is sticking in their nose too much where it don't belong. Likewise, our initiative is being handcuffed by excessive government regulations, a particular example being the Internal Revenue Service.

Your company is working every day, and night, to handle these situations, including hiring the smartest lawyers. However, even the honest ones send up our operating overhead much more than graft and bribery used to.

As to political relations, we see another serious threat. If that crazy Roosevelt in New York ever gets to be President, that will be the end of Prohibition. When booze becomes legal, we can't be expected to continue as a legitimate business. We'll be back to broads and gambling.

I am pleased to report, however, that there are some encouraging signs of business improvement. Our publicity continues to make us look like glamorous characters, and there are some hit movies and plays which show what an exciting business this is to invest in, providing you don't get hurt. An additional benefit is the contacts we have made with Hollywood and Broadway, meaning we can start muscling into those areas so long as we maintain good public relations with various talent agents and labor goons.

To improve our profit picture, we are now concentrating on reducing our payroll. This program has had considerable success what with the involuntary retirement or disappearance of several

executives. Our hiring is now confined to the abundant cheap help found standing in breadlines or selling apples on street corners.

Looking ahead to new fields of operation to replace obsolescent markets, we can see a nice future in armaments, assasination, kidnapping, terrorism, and subversion. In new product development, we are conducting extensive market research into drugs and dirty movies although we don't want to get into disgusting things like that unless we can project a healthy return on our investment.

I remain confident in the future of your company. Consumer demand for our products and services is as frantic as ever. You may depend on maximum performance from management, which I will personally attend to, and full cooperation from your Board of Directors, what's left of them.

Al Capone
Chief Executive Officer

Source: Reprinted with permission of the Simpson Paper Company.

donnybrook. And you certainly wouldn't know it from reading the annual report."[39] Paragraph 43 of the CEO's 45 paragraph letter to the stockholders offers the only evidence of the feud: "Ross Perot resigned as Chief Executive of Electronic Data Systems Corporation on Dec 1." The financial implications of the struggle are even less evident, residing in a footnote six pages from the end of the report. On page 38, footnote 15 informs investors that 11,791,790 Class E shares were "reacquired from certain employees and former stockholders of

EDS."[40] Without forthrightness, credibility is sacrificed. Like a strong leadership voice, forthrightness is an essential component of credibility.

However, we need not rely on the likes of Al Capone to find examples of clear identity, candor, and forthrightness. Many annual reports effectively employ a distinctive voice and a forthright demeanor. Perhaps most often cited among these positive illustrations is the Berkshire Hathaway annual report. Warren Buffett, the corporation's CEO, makes a purposeful effort to use the report as a vehicle for an enlightened exchange with shareholders: "I assume I've got a very intelligent partner who has been away for a year and needs to be filled in on all that happened . . . . Rather than repeat the same things each year . . . I take up topics that further their education."[41]

As illustrated in the short excerpts from some of the more recent Berkshire Hathaway reports (Figure 13.21), Buffet has an honest and engaging style that promotes a perception of a real, interested, and candid leader of and spokesper-

---

FIGURE 13.21

Telling It Like It Is

1995
There's no reason to do handsprings over 1995's gains. This was a year in which any fool could make a bundle in the stock market. And we did. To paraphrase President Kennedy, a rising tide lifts all yachts.

1996
Though our primary goal is to maximize the amount that our shareholders, in total, reap from their ownership of Berkshire, we wish also to minimize the benefits going to some shareholders at the expense of others. These are goals we would have were we managing a family partnership, and we believe they make equal sense for the manager of a public company. In a partnership, fairness requires that partnership interests be valued equitably when partners enter or exit; in a public company, fairness prevails when market price and intrinsic value are in sync. Obviously, they won't always meet that ideal, but a manager—by his policies and communication—can do much to foster equity.

1997
Given our gain of 34.1%, it is tempting to declare victory and move on. But last year's performance was no great triumph: Any investor can chalk up large returns when stocks soar, as they did in 1997. In a bull market, one must avoid the error of the preening duck that quacks boastfully after a torrential rainstorm, thinking that its paddling skills have caused it to rise in the world. A right-thinking duck would instead compare its position after the downpour to that of the other ducks on the pond.

1998
Normally, a gain of 48.3% would call for handsprings—but not this year. Remember Wagner, whose music has been described as better than it sounds? Well, Berkshires's progress in 1998—though more than satisfactory—was not as good as it looks. That's because most of that 48.3% gain came from our issuing shares in acquisitions.

1999
The numbers on the facing page show just how poor our 1999 record was. We had the worst absolute performance of my tenure and, compared to the S&P, the worst relative performance as well. Relative results are what concern us: Over time, bad relative numbers will produce unsatisfactory absolute results.
Even Inspector Clouseau could find last year's guilty party: your Chairman. My performance reminds me of the quarterback whose report card showed four "Fs and a D but who nonetheless had an understanding coach. "Son," he drawled, "I think you're spending too much time on that one subject." My "one subject" is capital allocation, and my grade for 1999 most assuredly is a D.

2000
I can't resist pointing out that Berkshire—whose top management has long been mired in the nineteenth century—is now one of the very few authentic "clicks-and-bricks" businesses around . . . . You can bet this move by Berkshire is making them sweat in Silicon Valley.

son for the corporation. He thereby elicits the kind of response that any communicator would be pleased to earn: "Not only is the writing clear and informative, but Buffett's folksy, disarming style makes it a downright entertaining read."[42] In the language of Part 1 of this text, the lesson offered is that the communication strategy needs to concentrate on ensuring that statements are not only honest, but complete and targeted at the intended audience. The next step is to create a "structural unity," a consistency of tone and message communicated by the text and the design.

CONSISTENCY. Like a resume, which needs to establish the individual's identity and set that individual apart from others competing for the same job, the annual report must foster an identity and a distinct character. The report must creatively align the financial message, the chairman's message, and the design's message to create this distinct corporate identity. It's not the most costly or elaborate package that promotes the investors' trust and confidence. It is the package constructed with keen appreciation and awareness that annual reports rely on three components to send the message: 1) the financial data, 2) the narrative, and 3) the design. Issuing an annual report in a canvas bag with a carrying strap as Domino's Pizza did one year may get you noticed, but may not send the intended message. A CEO statement that has personality and character but is unsupported by a well-aligned design may lay flat—and unopened—on the recipient's desk. Or, design may overwhelm message.

Imagine the impact of juxtaposing an elaborate, multicolor, glossy report with Warren Buffett's "folksy" style. Because of their contradictory nature, the two pieces might cancel each other out, or the straight talk could get lost in the glare. The design, overtaken by the CEO's engaging style, might simply add up to a sizeable, unnecessary expenditure.

However, a more damaging calculation can be that the CEO message minus design consistency will equal loss of credibility. Understanding this relationship between the components of the message, Berkshire Hathaway shareholders "get no photographs, no colored inks in foil embossing, no bar charts or graphs—not even a logo. It looks like the kind of annual you see from a company whose bubble has finally burst, only Berkshire Hathaway . . . shows no signs of bursting."[43] What the annual report achieves is a comfortable consistency of tone and message.

Any number of approaches can be taken to fuse message and design while at the same time releasing the "pent-up creativity." Cover and internal images might be artfully associated with the brand and product line in a manner that enhances the readability and the communicative value of the information. For example, the Marvel Comics annual report is designed to look like a comic book—same size, same colors, and with the recognized army of superheroes assisting with and integrated into the text to help tell the story (Figure 13.22).[44] Another method, similar to the kind involved in developing proposals, is to build the platform around a primary message that may be critical to fostering an improved relationship with investors.

One example of this strategy at work was evidenced in the first annual report issued by eBay, the popular on-line auction house. The cover of the report featured a white 8"-diameter, revolving disk; when spun, the disk revealed—through three cut-out circles—images of on-line trading activities and merchandise. Inside the report, an array of quarter- and half-panel pages were designed to attract potential investors by demonstrating the relative ease with which buyers and sellers navigate the eBay web site—thereby attracting users and raising prof-

FIGURE 13.22

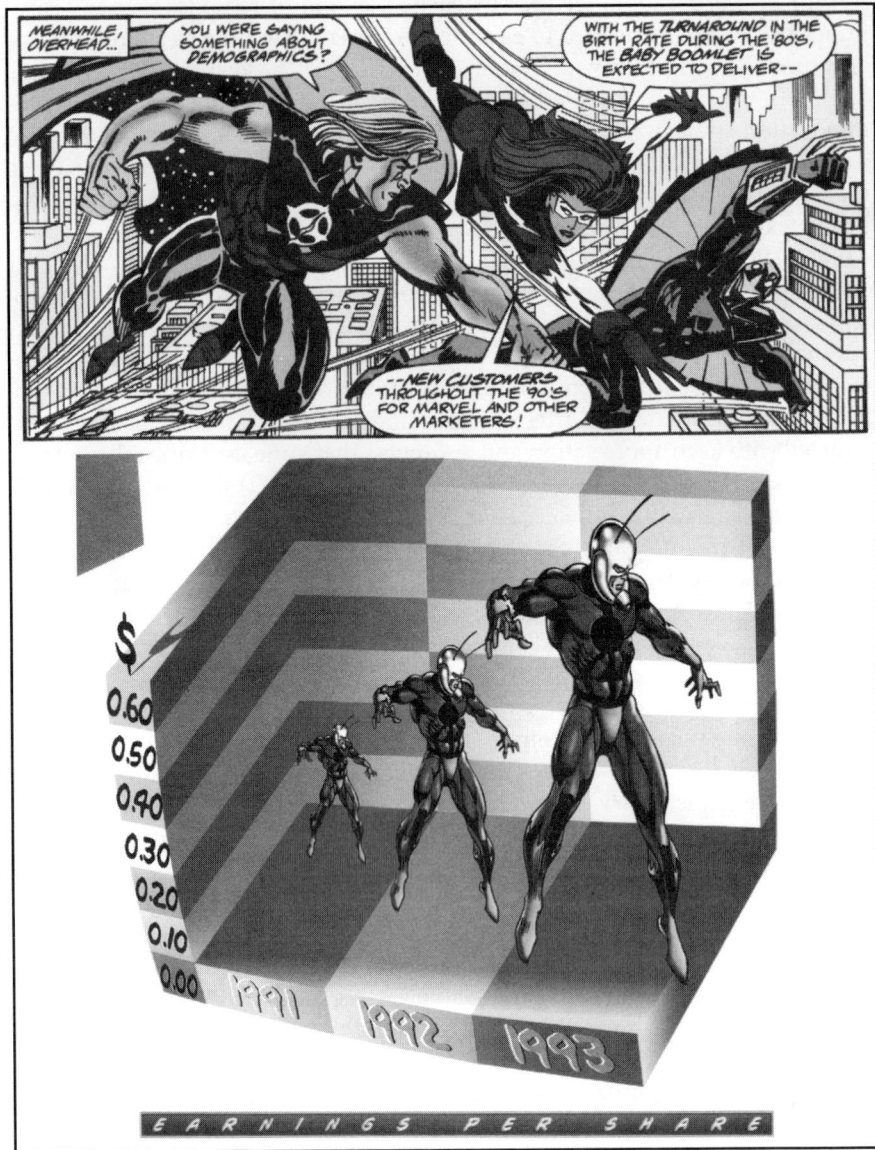

Source: Copyright ©2002 Marvel Characters, Inc., used with permission.

its (Figure 13.23).[45] Explaining how the design reinforces the report's overt messages, the company's senior marketing communications director notes: "We didn't want to show how successful eBay is, but rather what it is . . . . We knew some of the stockholders were not Internet users. We wanted the annual report to mimic our Website on paper."[46] The unique voice, the forthrightness, and the consistent message of the text and design—as eBay and Berkshire Hathaway illustrate—add up to a successful and well-received annual report.

THE FINAL PARTNERSHIP

Getting the annual report to reflect the province of the communicator demands strict attention to audience, purpose, and presentation. The package has to be characterized by credibility and consistency. Paraphrasing the recommendations

FIGURE 13.23

How It All Works

The Nuts and Bolts About eBay:

So admit it: you're intrigued by the whole thing, and you'd like to know a little bit more about how the process of buying and selling works on the eBay site. Here are a few easy steps:

4. The Hunt

Here's where it gets interesting. Just like any competitive situation, anyone can outbid you at any time for an item—and raise the bar for all potential buyers. Even if you're in the lead for days, it's who's on top at the end that ultimately matters. Things can get pretty competitive when it gets down to the wire and time is running out. But if you're lucky, vigilant and just plain want an item more than anyone else, you just might win.

5. The Transaction

Once it's all over, eBay automatically notifies the buyer and seller via email. At that point, the two consummate the transaction independently of eBay, arranging for shipment of and payment for the item. While we're not directly involved in the transaction, we have a number of programs designed to protect the interests of both buyers and sellers, including escrow services, insurance available from Lloyd's of London, and the eBay Feedback Forum.

6. Do It All Over Again

Whether you were successful in buying that object of your desire, or narrowly missed out on it this time around, you'll probably be back. Same thing for sellers. There's something

Source: These materials have been reproduced with the permission of eBay Inc. Copyright ©eBay Inc. All rights reserved.

cited in an article in *Management Review,* these are eight major guidelines to consider:

1. Define the message and the themes. Concentrate on the message and themes at every stage of the development and review process. Think outward from them, not around them or despite them.

2. Speak to your audience: Take Warren Buffett's approach of treating the audience as "partners."

3. Face up to disappointing results. Take responsibility for problems and present solutions.

4. Admit there are competitors and tell what is being done to maintain or build upon market position.

5. Make your projections real, substantive, and meaningful.

6. Use clear language, graphs, and charts to make information and financial data understandable and meaningful.

7. Use a design that reinforces the message and the corporate identity. Make graphics work as hard as your text in sending the right message.

8. Invite your "partners" into the discussion. Make certain you know precisely what they want, what they need, and what they're not getting. As with all communications, in the province of the communicator, the audience is king.

THE LONG REPORT—THE LESSONS

The long report is not a challenge due to its length. It is a challenge because it requires careful understanding of and attention to the integration between form and function, and between message and design. The long report is also a challenge because it represents a complicated terrain—multiple audiences, diverse purposes—and very large consequences if the terrain is not negotiated correctly. Knowing what's expected, how the report structures evolved, and how the pieces work (both individually and in concert with one another) is the only way to be sure that these documents achieve the fullest measure of benefits from residing in the province of the communicator.

EXERCISES

☐ Group

1. Divide into three groups. Choose an RFP from the *Commerce Business Daily* or another source.

   a) Develop outlines for both a proposal to go after the award and for a business plan that will allow you to secure the necessary financial backing to do the work.

   b) Exchange your outlines with another group for their evaluation. (When evaluating the proposal, the evaluating group assumes itself to be the author of the RFP. When evaluating the business plan, the evaluating team represents potential investors.)

2. Your team represents a major American plastics firm. In the past year, your company lost nearly $25 million in net revenue (against an operating base of $100 million). Based on preliminary forecasts, next year will not be much better. If your management team cannot turn things around in the next 2 years, the company may be facing bankruptcy.

   a) Draft the letter from the CEO for inclusion in the company's annual report.

   b) Exchange letters between groups and evaluate what strategies have been used and how effective those letters are in promoting shareholder trust and confidence.

3. You have been selected by a local charity to help prepare a new strategy for improving its fund-raising performance. Develop ideas for how this might be accomplished and then prepare the Executive Summary and Introduction for the report you intend to submit to the charity's management team.

☐ Individual

1. Select 3 annual reports from companies in the same industry (e.g., tourism, airlines, manufacturing). Compare the success of the following reports:

   a) the effectiveness of the CEO's letter to shareholders

   b) the consistency of messages sent by the design and text

   c) the appearance of candor and forthrightness

2. Choose an article in the literature on the subject of professional communication. Prepare an Executive Summary for the article.

[1] Cited in Thomas W. Schneider, "Building a Business Plan," *Journal of Property Management,* Vol. 63, No. 6 (Nov.–Dec. 1998), pp. 30–32.

[2] Edwin T. Crego, Brian Wheaton, and Peter Schiffren, *How to Write a Business Plan,* Boston: American Management Association Extension Institute, 1986. Figure 13.2 is also derived from this source.

[3] E. Peter Ward, "Planning for Technological Innovation: Developing the Necessary Nerve," *Long-Range Planning,* Vol. 14 (April 1981), pp. 59–71.

[4] *The D(ratted) P(rogress) Report.* Report No. DP-00. E.I. Du Pont & Nemours, Inc. Savannah River Laboratory: Aiken, SC, July 12, 1954.

[5] Kathleen M. Hiemstra, "Instructor and Student Perceptions of What Is Learned by Writing the Business Report," *Business Communication Quarterly,* Vol. 64, No. 2 (June 2001), pp. 44–54.

[6] Alan Mitchell, "Annual Brand Report," *Management Today* (Jan. 1998), p. 110.

[7] Figure 13.7 is adapted from: Melba W. Murray, *Engineered Report Writing.* Tulsa, OK: The Petroleum Publishing Co., 1969, pp. 51–57.

[8] *The D(ratted) P(rogress) Report.*

[9] Donnelyn Curtis and Stephen Bernhardt, "Keywords, Titles, Abstracts, and On-Line Searches: Implications for Technical Writing," *The Technical Writing Teacher,* Vol. 18, No. 2 (Spring 1991), pp. 142–161.

[10] *Ibid.*

[11] M. W. Lansdale, "Remembering about Documents: Memory for Appearance, Format, and Location," *Ergonomics* (1991), pp. 1161–1178.

[12] *The D(ratted) P(rogress) Report.*

[13] Figure 13.10 is adapted from: Palmer Wright, "The Logic and Rhetoric of a Table of Contents," *Journal of Technical Writing and Communication,* Vol. 2, No. 3 (July 1972), pp. 211–223.

[14] Quoted in: John W. Hazard, "How to Read Those Annual Reports," *U.S. News and World Report* (Feb. 18, 1985), p. 74.

[15] Adapted from: Melba W. Murray, *Engineered Report Writing.*

[16] *First Annual Report of the Northern Pacific Railway Company for the fiscal year (ten months) ending June 30, 1897.*

[17] Dale L. Flesher, Paul J. Miranti, and Gary John Previts, "The First Century of the CPA," *Journal of Accountancy,* Vol. 182, No. 4 (Oct. 1996), p. 51 (7).

[18] Joel Seligman, "The Historical Need for a Mandatory Corporate Disclosure System," *The Journal of Corporation Law,* Vol. 9, No. 1 (Fall 1983), pp. 1–61.

[19] *Annual Report to Stockholders for the Year 1931,* Coca-Cola Company, Atlanta, Georgia, March 4, 1932.

[20] Seligman, "The Historical Need for a Mandatory Corporate Disclosure System."

[21] *Ibid.*

[22] Eric Abrahamson and Choelsoon Park, "Concealment of Negative Organizational Outcomes: An Agency Theory Perspective," *Academy of Management Journal,* Vol. 37, No. 5 (Oct. 1994), pp. 1302–1334.

[23] "How Valuable is Your Annual Report?" *Management Review,* Vol. 77, No. 10 (Oct. 1988), pp. 51–53.

[24] *Ringling Bros. Barnum & Bailey Combined Shows, Inc., 1969 Annual Report.*

[25] Bryan Burrough, "Here Is Our Report on a Report About Corporate Annual Reports," *The Wall Street Journal,* Oct. 23, 1986, p. 35.

[26] *Ibid.*

[27] Robert W. Ingram and Katherine Beal Frazier, "Narrative Disclosures in Annual Reports," *Journal of Business Research,* Vol. 11 (1983), pp. 49–60. "Some Annual Reports Are Worth Reading," *Inc.* (July 1999), p. 85.

[28] Sid Cato, "When Preparing Annual Reports, Less Is Definitely More," *The Wall Street Journal,* April 22, 1988, p. 12.

[29] Edmund Kulkosky, "Brave New World of Annual Reports," *The Wall Street Journal,* Feb. 10, 1987, p. 38.

[30] Zebollah Razaee and Grover W. Porter, "Can the Annual Report Be Improved?" *Review of Business,* Vol. 15, No. 1 (Summer–Fall 1993), pp. 38–41.

[31] Thomas B. Simone, "Behind the Scenes: How McKesson Produced the First Summary Annual Report," *Financial Executive,* Vol. 4, No. 1 (Jan./Feb. 1988), pp. 49–52.

[32] Zebollah Razaee and Grover W. Porter, "Summary Annual Reports: Is Shorter Better?" *Journal of Accountancy,* May 1988, pp. 52–54.

[33] Kulkosky, "Brave New World of Annual Reports."

[34] *Ibid.*

[35] Quoted in Gary J. Kobut and Albert H. Segars, "The President's Letter to Stockholders: An Examination of Corporate Communication Strategy," *Journal of Business Communication,* Vol. 29, No. 1 (Winter 1992), pp. 7–21.

[36] Ronald B. Millman, "Making the Most of Your Annual Report," *Management Review,* Vol. 79, No. 10 (Oct. 1990), pp. 52–55.

[37] *The Alphonse Capone Enterprises Annual Report of 1931.* San Francisco: Simpson Paper Company, 1981.

[38] Robert W. Ingram and Katherine Beal Frazier, "Narrative Disclosures in Annual Reports."

[39] Devon P. Levin, "OK, Who Out There Remembers Details of Every Ex-Employee?" *The Wall Street Journal,* March 18, 1987, p. 33.

[40] *Ibid.*

[41] Andrew Tobias, "Letters from Chairman Buffett," *Fortune,* Vol. 108 (Aug. 22, 1983), pp. 137–140.

[42] "Some Annual Reports Are Worth Reading," *Inc.* (July 1999), p. 85. The quoted material in Figure 13.21 is taken from the Berkshire-Hathaway web site (http://www.berkshirehathaway.com).

[43] Tobias, "Letters from Chairman Buffett."

[44] *Marvell Annual Report (1992 & 1993).*

[45] *eBay Annual Report 1998,* eBay, Inc., San Jose, California.

[46] Jack Rosenberger, "Not Your Typical Annual Report," *Graphic Arts Monthly,* Vol. 72, No. 5 (May 2000), p. 149.

14

Procedures
Doing the Work of Business

We live in a world of instructions, directions, and procedures. Instructions accompany everything we buy—how to assemble, operate, or maintain the item. We are given directions on how to complete forms and how to navigate streets and highways. Procedures are fundamental in completing everyday chores from preparing meals to taking the correct dosage of medicine.

PROCEDURES: A FUNCTIONAL DEFINITION

- comprise a set of sequential operations or steps that, in total, complete a single process
- solve a specific problem that always presents itself in the same way
- need (for safety or financial reasons) to be done in only one way
- produce the same result each time
- limit introduction of theoretical or explanatory information
- focus on use

At one level, procedures prescribe the precise sequences of steps involved in conducting business in the most hazardous environments; at another level, they are the endless stream of self-help books that claim to help us to change careers, improve our health and fitness, live happier and healthier lives, and find our ideal mates. Stated simply, procedures explain to us how to do things, clarify what is expected in our daily performances, and permit us to go along with the flow of life—whether we are speaking literally of crossing streets or speaking metaphorically of contributing to our families, our professions, or our communities.

However, being inundated by procedures is not necessarily assurance that the procedures we must rely on always provide the clarity of direction needed to allow us to proceed with efficiency and confidence.

Most often, people first focus on the procedure's topic and its level of detail. Is the subject highly technical, or is there a demanding degree of specificity? Yet, these are only two dimensions we must consider. Procedures, to be written effectively, have very demanding rhetorical expectations. The accuracy of the technical content does not necessarily correspond to procedure adequacy. To prepare procedures correctly in business and to allow organizations to interact efficiently while ensuring the absolute integrity of business processes demands that we take full advantage of the lessons we have been learning regarding audience, purpose, organization, reasoning, precision of language, and pace. Writing procedures is a very demanding activity and one that can spotlight our abilities as communicators.

Just consider the last time you were given driving directions. If you arrived without difficulty or incident, you thought highly of the person who assisted you with directions; if you had trouble getting where you were going, you didn't blame the fact that the route was complex, but you most likely fumed at the individual who gave you the directions. The technical and communication skills, as this simple illustration makes clear, must be complementary.

We need to measure performance from two vantage points when assessing the effectiveness of procedures: Did we faithfully relate the technical information (our technical responsibility)? Did we relate that information in a manner that allowed the user successfully and efficiently to negotiate the terrain of the task at hand (our communication responsibility)? All too often, authors are prepared to handle their first obligation, but not the second. Fulfilling the first obligation leaves the user well informed, but lost. Only when we have fulfilled both obligations have we efficiently led the reader to the intended destination.

A BASIC SENSE OF PROCEDURES

As a starting point to understand the role and quality of procedures in business, let's begin by getting a perspective on the breadth and depth of procedures in general. To do this, let's use four simple examples. At one end of the spectrum are overly simplistic directions that are so generalized as to limit their meaningful application. There is, for example, little likelihood that we could make substantive application of the direction Dale Carnegie provided to a jittery post-World War II generation on how to relax and stop worrying (Figure 14.1).[1]

Somewhat better, but still lacking in substance, are the seemingly precise directions. This subset of procedures offers the illusion of substance and specificity, but in the most general of terms. Typically, these directions sound good, but offer little more than what would already be well understood by any reasonable user. Consider, as example, a process cited on the local evening news. How much does the following eight-step procedure on preventing "summer tragedies" add to the average listener's body of knowledge and insight (Figure 14.2)?

Rule 1:	Get the facts.
Rule 2:	After carefully weighing all the facts, come to a decision.
Rule 3:	Once a decision is carefully reached, act! Get busy carrying out your decision—and dismiss all anxiety about the outcome.
Rule 4:	When you, or any of your associates, are tempted to worry about a problem, write out and answer the following questions: a. What is the problem? b. What is the cause of the problem? c. What are the possible solutions? d. What is the best solution?

FIGURE 14.1

How to Stop Worrying

Tonight we're going to give you recommendations on how to prevent tragedies this summer.

- Maintain constant supervision. Watch children around any water environment, no matter what skills your child has acquired and no matter how shallow the water.

- Don't rely on substitutes. The use of flotation devices can't replace parental supervision.

- Enroll children in a water safety course or Learn to Swim program.

- Parents should take a CPR course. Knowing these skills can be important around the water.

- Be sure your pool is completely enclosed with a self-locking, self-closing fence.

- Always keep lifesaving equipment near the pool and know how to use it.

- Keep toys away from the pool when it is not in use. Toys can attract young children into the pool.

- Pool covers should be completely removed prior to using the pool.

FIGURE 14.2

Preventing Summer Tragedies

Peering at us from the far end of the spectrum are the detailed, very specific procedural directions, the kind we associate with operating nuclear power plants and highly sophisticated manufacturing processes. An early version of this type of technical procedure is illustrated in Benjamin Franklin's explanation about how to make a lighting rod (Figure 14.3).

Somewhere between the precision of Franklin and the less substantive self-help procedures lie the vast majority of procedures, many of which we daily accept on face value. We expect that, when needed, these procedures will allow us to do our jobs better, make our lives simpler, and protect us in times of stress and confusion. A good example of one of these "invisible" procedures is the direction we are given for responding in the event of a fire. Posted in hallways and stairwells and often addressed as part of routine employee training, like white noise, these procedures lay just outside our conscious attention. Not atypical of this type of procedure is the following direction provided by a university to its personnel (Figure 14.4).

Each of these four procedures shares a common goal—to allow the audience to accomplish a particular task or activity. Yet, among the four samples, we can already begin to sense some of the attributes of a meaningful procedure. We may also begin to see elements that contribute to an effective procedure. To get a better appreciation of what these elements might be, let's return to the commonly shared experience of using travel directions in order to help us assess the rhetorical subtext of procedures. Let's assume we are visiting a distant relative in an unfamiliar town. We would probably employ one of three means to get to our destination: 1) use a map, 2) ask directions as we progress along the route, or 3) use directions already provided to us.

FIGURE 14.3

How to Make Lightning Rods

Prepare a steel rod about five or six feet long, about half an inch thick at its largest end, and tapering to a sharp point. This point should be gilded to prevent its rusting. Secure to the big end of the rod a strong eye or a ring half an inch in diameter. Fix the rod upright to the chimney or the highest part of a house. It should be fixed with some sort of staples or special nails to keep it steady. The pointed end should extend upward, and should rise three or four feet above the chimney or building to which the rod is fixed. Drive into the ground an iron rod about one inch in diameter, and ten or twelve feet long. This rod should also have an eye or ring fixed to its upper end. It is best to place the iron rod some distance from the foundation of the house. Ten feet away is a good distance, if the size of the property permits. Then take as much length of iron rod of a smaller diameter as will be necessary to reach from the eye on the rod above to the eye of the rod below. Fasten this securely to the fixed rods by passing it through the eyes and bending the ends to form rings too. Then close all the joints with lead. This is easily done by making a small bag of strong paper around the joints, tying it tight below, and then pouring in the molten lead. It is useful to have these joints treated in this way so that there will be a considerable area of contact between each piece. To prevent the wind from shaking this long rod, it may be fastened to the building by several staples. If the building is especially large or long, extending more than one hundred feet for example, it is wise to erect a rod at each end. If there is a well sufficiently near to the building to permit placing the iron rod in the water, this is even better than the use of the iron rod in the ground. It may also be wise to paint the iron to prevent it from rusting. A building so protected will not be damaged by lightning.

Each of these options has particular strengths and weaknesses. The map may either be too detailed or insufficiently detailed. A map provided at an airport rental counter, for instance, often generalizes the area. In comparison, a map purchased at a gas station might list every street, no matter how large or how long. Were we dealing with the map shown in Figure 14.5, for instance, we might drive for miles trying to locate our destination if we knew it only as a small street that intersects somewhere with one of the major thoroughfares.

Directions we receive through a service (AAA, destination locators on the Internet, or GPS [Global Positioning Systems], for example) may introduce a different selection of problems for us. Some of these directions overwhelm us

FIGURE 14.5

Getting Directions

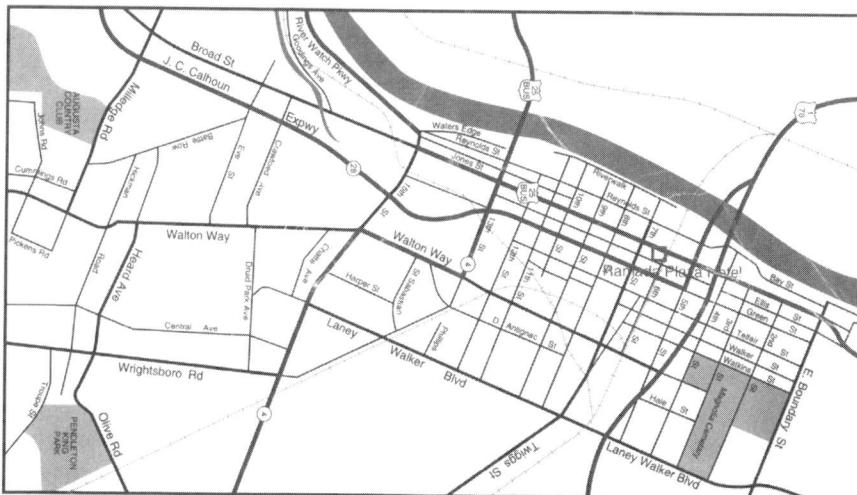

with detail, informing us of required driving maneuvers on a seemingly continuous basis. The amount of information and the form in which it is presented to us may not aid our driving, but may distract us from it. Not only do we divide our attention between the directional information and our driving, but we also may find ourselves focusing more intently on road signs—in hopes of spotting the name of a street—than on the traffic surrounding us. While these two methods offer some variability, a greater degree of uncertainty enters the equation when we operate by the third strategy—asking directions on a periodic basis.

While the first two strategies were founded on well-established, credible documentation, the third method (inquiring of people whom we stop along our way) has questionable reliability. Did the individual we asked really have knowledge of how to get from Point A to Point B? In fact, what certainty do we have that this person even really knows where Point B is at all? (Having received directions from a stranger you've encountered, have you ever proceeded while harboring that gnawing suspicion that your guide is already laughing about the grand joke just played on you?)

Regardless of which strategy we use, certain factors remain constant: the location we're seeking never changes, its relationship to surrounding markers is relatively static, and the traffic patterns on the approaching streets rarely change. Yet, in each case, there is doubt about whether we are making reasonable time, whether we are proceeding in an efficient manner. The problem may not result from the form of the communication, but from the underlying assumptions that are at work.

In each case, the provider of the directions is making certain assumptions about us that may or may not be valid: do we prefer the more direct or scenic route; would we prefer the fastest route or the one with the least traffic congestion; are we at all familiar with the region; are we capable of assimilating numerous specific actions or would we respond better to more generalized directions? Or, to add one more variable, are we comfortable with being told directions in terms of left and right, or would we prefer north and south? Just think back on how many times you have been lost, or felt like you were lost, and the truth about these assumptions and their significance will be evident to you. The technical content (the actual steps) may be part of a fixed universe of facts; however, the variables are related to principles of purpose and audience—how well we have deciphered the code of embedded, overlapping purposes and how well we have accommodated the interests of the audiences.

The success of our trip (on the highways of America or in the procedures of business) is dependent on two factors. Success is dependent both on the technical accuracy of the directions and the appropriateness of the implicit, underlying assumptions. Both elements equally shape the final form of the communication. This dual basis for success explains why—despite living in a world of directions, instructions, and procedures; despite a lengthy history of business failures and calamitous accidents whose root cause was procedure inadequacy; and despite extensive literature on the subject—we still face a reasonable probability that the procedures we rely on will prove inadequate.

MOVING PROCEDURES TO CENTER STAGE

Perhaps this lesson was learned most acutely by the nuclear industry. The catastrophic events at the Three Mile Island (TMI) nuclear plant in 1979 crippled an entire industry for a quarter of a century. On March 28, 1979, the reactor support system designed to keep the reactor cool failed, resulting in 75% of the core melting. The building was in ruins and totally inaccessible due to significant releases of radiation. Within a day, limited evacuations began in the town nearest the facility. For the next 15 years, Metropolitan Edison, the reactor's owner, was immersed in responding to more than 2,500 lawsuits alleging radiation-induced illnesses and in coordinating a massive cleanup project at a cost to the company (and ultimately the taxpayers) of more than $2 billion. The fallout was more than just radioactive gas. While there were approximately 100 reactors in service in the United States and plans for as many as 500 more at the time of the accident, not a single new plant has been built since the TMI failure. Public concern, reflected in volumes of federal regulations and oversight, changed the cheapest source of electricity into, perhaps, the most expensive. Estimates suggest that to build a new power plant today would cost in excess of $5 billion (more than seven times what it cost to build the plant at TMI).

Although not cited as the exclusive contributing agent, among the specific lessons resulting from the TMI event was an "emphasized . . . need for improved . . . procedures to guide the operator under accident conditions."[2] Subsequent reports issued by the Nuclear Regulations Commission (NRC), which provides federal oversight of the nuclear industry, continued to amplify and highlight the role played by procedures in the management and operation of these facilities, a role not unlike the role played by directions in our driving scenario or the role played by procedures in business.

Despite this intense attention, including extensive governmental reviews and hearings, years after the TMI accident, serious procedural problems—many of which have broad-reaching implications for all businesses—are still being cited in this industry:

- Procedures do not provide effective guidance for conducting work.
- Procedures are often incomplete, unusable, or missing critical information.
- Procedures are not properly and effectively used.
- Procedures do not effectively assist in responding to emergency conditions.[3]

Of importance to us, as the items above indicate, is that the majority of issues are not matters regarding technical accuracy of the content, but are matters of the quality of the communication. Even in the nuclear business, where there is an intense focus on responding to the technical complexity of the work, analyses and investigations have concluded that a large percentage of procedure problems go back to audience, purpose, fact, language, and pace—failures in fulfilling basic communication responsibilities (Table 14.1):

> Major characteristics of procedures, in particular accuracy, completeness and understandability, are directly related to the quality of the procedure development process. If a procedure is inaccurate, it is most commonly the result of a faulty analysis by the procedure writer . . . . If a procedure is incomplete with regard to the amount and kind of information needed by the user, it is most commonly attributable to the fact that the writer does not have an adequate definition of the users' skills and knowledge . . . . If a procedure is not understandable to the intended user, it is most commonly the result of inadequate . . . guidelines relating to choice of vocabulary, sentence structure, language control, and other factors involved in the comprehension and retention of information.[4]

14.1   TYPES OF PROBLEMS EXPERIENCED WHEN USING PROCEDURES

Category of Problem	Specific Difficulties Experienced
Organization	• Could not locate information • Excessive levels of subordination or numbers of subheads
Presentation	• Turned to wrong page • Confused by lack of indentation
Terminology	• Could not understand terms • Ambiguous direction led to use of wrong step • Unfamiliar acronyms
Internal Consistency	• Could not follow text • Confused by complex statements • Logical conflicts caused by incompleteness
Numeric Information	• Missed calculations • Unable to calculate values • Could not remember essential formula
Salience	• Overlooked warnings
Comprehensibility	• Confused by large blocks of text • Confused by unclear sentences
Technical Demands	• Could not perform sub-tasks • Was uncertain about where warnings applied
Level of Detail	• Made mistakes when steps were not delineated
Graphs and Tables	• Could not find important information • Could not record required data in space provided
Navigation	• Could not find necessary information due to excessive internal referencing from one part of the procedure to another

Whether the procedure was being used in routine or in emergency conditions, a poorly written document, the analyses demonstrate, has an increased probability of contributing to a variety of errors, any of which could result in financial liabilities, risk to the worker, or failure of a major system or process:

1. The procedure user reacts incorrectly, not providing the appropriate response to the conditions at hand.

2. The user omits steps in the process, inadvertently bypassing important actions.

3. The user completes steps in incorrect order, usually as a consequence of misreading complex statements.

4. Because of difficulties with the procedure, the user decides to rely on expertise and judgment to compensate for the inadequacies of the procedure.

5. The user makes incorrect decisions, resulting from the procedure user's uncertainty about how best to proceed. (The Appendix contains details of the types of activities workers were involved in when procedure errors occurred.)

All five types of errors are avoidable if authors remain attentive to the rhetorical principles we have been studying. Declaring the meaningful contributions that communicators can make in supporting the corporation's goals of doing work efficiently, safely, and effectively, one government report concludes: "Procedures can fill the void where lack of information leads to omission of steps, performing steps in the wrong order, executing steps incorrectly, and dealing with poorly designed controls and indicators. Such gains are accomplished by providing direction at the step level of detail, designing the procedures for maximum usability, and employing notes and cautions to alert the operator to controls and indicators that do not look or function as he might expect."[5]

In making these assertions, the nuclear industry only highlighted what business has known since the beginning of Scientific Management. When procedures are done poorly, business problems mount, error rates rise, and vulnerabilities increase. These vulnerabilities are not simply technical failures, but are also potentially severe business liabilities and losses. Even in the nuclear industry, poor procedures have given rise to business losses (not only to technical challenges). One highly visible implication of the consequences was evident when, in 1997, the Secretary of Energy terminated a long and lucrative contract with one of America's leading research laboratories. A critical phrase used by the Secretary in publicly announcing the action was that "the level of informality was inappropriate . . . ."[6] Unable to demonstrate it had the ability to operate by an effective set of procedures, the contractor had created political, legal, and environmental issues that eclipsed the technical issues. The government, in response, translated the resolution into a financial loss for the contractor.

However, the business consequences were becoming evident in numerous other industries long before the Secretary of Energy took action. With the clear image of the technical and business consequences of poorly written procedures indelibly stamped by the TMI accident, the Federal government began actively encouraging all American industry to pay closer attention both to process control and to the role played by procedures in ensuring that work was accomplished safely and efficiently. Procedures, a centerpiece of the transformation, in turn, were dramatically transformed from a simple task description document into a mirror reflecting industry's formality of operations.

PROCEDURES AND THE BUSINESS OF QUALITY

Procedures had their origins in Scientific Management, assisting business's newfound interest in disciplined operations. Procedures matured with the coming of the "total quality" movement, which created a universal enthusiasm for discipline, monitoring, and control.

The threads of the total quality movement date back at least to the 1920s when Bell Laboratories developed a system for measuring variance in production systems, known as statistical process control. Complementing this engineering tool, Bell Laboratories created the "Plan-Do-Check-Act" cycle of business, which applies a simple yet systematic approach to improving work processes. "Systematic," in its early business usage, implied procedural controls, an orientation that became the cornerstone of business practice beginning around the time of World War II.

The War Department hired W. Edwards Deming, a physicist and Census Bureau researcher, to teach statistical process control to the defense industry. Expected to contribute substantially to America's war efforts, quality control and statistical methods were initially classified as military secrets. However, these tools were not as revered once the war ended. With America's industrial superiority reinforced by the dismantling of both Asian and European industry, these tools, for the most part, were consigned to unimaginative applications in quality control and inspection departments.

Overseas, the devastated nations were struggling for a means to recapture industrial momentum, an environment in great need of a disciplined and orchestrated reformation. As one action to get the momentum going, the U.S. occupation forces in Japan enlisted Deming to assist with Japan's post-war census and to lecture business leaders on statistical process control and quality. In Japan, Deming's work, along with that of two other Americans, Joseph Juran and Armand Feigenbaum, forged the foundations of the modern quality movement. Feigenbaum stressed involving employees in pursuit of what soon became known as "Total Quality Control." Juran introduced Deming's methods into all functions in the organization, not just the production department. The most radical step was yet to come—refocusing corporate attention on the customer. Corporate emphasis, for the first time, was attentively fixed on responding to the urgency of meeting customer expectations.

Employee involvement and customer orientation fueled the Japanese quality movement, which also took advantage of the work of American behavioral scientists such as Abraham Maslow (the hierarchy of needs) and Douglas McGregor (Theory X/Theory Y). One of the principal outcomes was the creation of quality circles—small teams of managers, supervisors, and workers trained in statistical process control and group problem-solving. From 1945 to the early part of the 1970s, Japan continued to expand the application of quality circles, even going so far as to create an external equivalent, "vendor partnerships," in which companies and their suppliers fused their interests and expertise. This enthusiasm, assisted by procedures, which produced and maintained the necessary consistency, reliability, and standardization, transformed the negative connotations of the "Land of the Rising Sun" into a globally recognized trademark signifying quality, excellence, and cost effectiveness—"Made in Japan."

Beaten essentially by our own tools and expertise, America was introduced to a new war, the war for industrial superiority. Suddenly, the quality tools and theories of Deming, Juran, and Feigenbaum were in vogue.

Acknowledging that America's "product and process quality has been challenged strongly," and that these challenges "may require fundamental changes in the way companies and agencies do business," on August 20, 1987, President Reagan signed Public Law 100-107, the Malcolm Baldridge National Quality Improvement Act. An outgrowth of the statistical control momentum of the post World War II days and accelerated by the TMI accident, this law converted a casual interest in efficient and disciplined operations into a celebrated national cause.

In addition to a variety of new initiatives, the act established the Malcolm Baldridge Award, which was intended to recognize leadership in quality and quality management. Named for President Reagan's original Secretary of Commerce, the award, at first, was limited to manufacturing and service industries. Under President Clinton, in 1998, the award was broadened to include not-for-profit health care corporations and educational institutions (from elementary schools to universities and technical schools).

Process quality (originally referred to in the award criteria as "processes and procedures") became one of seven focal points for gauging a business's quality (Table 14.2). [7] As the awards were to prove, consistent with the expectations of Congress, the Commerce Department, and President Reagan, procedures are "directly applicable to small companies as well as large, to service industries as well as manufacturing, and to the public sector as well as private enterprise." The 41 winners since 1988 come from all business segments. For example, the four companies that received the honor in 2000 were 1) a manufacturer of drive shafts for light, medium, heavy-duty and off-highway vehicles; 2) a contract manufacturer of precision sheet metal machined components for the telecommunications, semiconductor, and medical equipment industries; 3) a company that maintains and operates more than 160 public and private sector wastewater and waste treatment facilities in 29 states and in a half-dozen foreign countries; and 4) an independent community bank that provides a full range of financial services to the consumer, commercial, and government markets.

Moreover, as was envisioned in the formulation of the legislation, companies that demonstrated excellence in the seven assessed categories tend to perform above average in the market. Attesting to this fact, since 1995, the Commerce Department's National Institute of Standards and Technology has been monitoring the "Baldridge Index," a measure of the financial performance of Baldridge Award winners. Based on hypothetical investments of $1000, the Baldridge winners consistently produce a return of 4 to 6 times that accomplished by the Standard & Poor's (S & P) 500. In one year, they amassed a "685 percent return on investments compared to a 163 percent return for the S & P 500."

The common denominator among these winners of the award is not size (the 2000 winners range from 167 to 3400 employees), not product, and not

---

TABLE 14.2   **THE SEVEN CATEGORIES ASSESSED IN THE MALCOLM BALDRIDGE COMPETITION**

Business	Education	Health Care
1. Leadership	Leadership	Leadership
2. Strategic Planning	Strategic Planning	Strategic Planning
3. Customer and Market Focus	Customer and Market Focus	Customer and Market Focus
4. Information and Analysis	Information and Analysis	Information and Analysis
5. Human Resource Focus	Faculty and Staff Focus	Staff Focus
6. Process Management	Education and Support Process Management	Process Management
7. Business Results	Organizational Performance Results	Organizational Performance Results

customer base. What they share is a successful management philosophy, codified and solidified in well-constructed procedures. As the award criteria stipulate, companies must explain in their applications how the elements of customer (audience), purpose, information selection, and information presentation are reflected in and accounted for by the processes and procedures that support production, business processes (e.g., strategic planning), and administration (e.g., accounting) (Table 14.3).

Recognizing that procedures are at work in all forms of business, that they represent a blending of technical and communication expertise, and that they reinforce the quality and integrity of business activities, positions us to better understand the merits and values of procedures. Adding the insights gained from the Malcolm Baldridge Award competition criteria improve the clarity about how to gauge the effectiveness of business operations and the procedures that document those processes. As the seven assessment criteria make evident, the success of a business process—and the success of the associated business procedures—is dependent on examining and integrating several key factors: management philosophy, business circumstance, corporate strategy, judgment, negotiation, and usability. However, before we can isolate how these particular factors affect procedures, we need to take a moment to delineate more completely the differences among the major types of procedures.

TABLE

14.3 CRITERIA FOR ASSESSING PROCESSES AND PROCEDURES

1. What are your key processes for supporting your daily operations and your employees in delivering products and services?

2. How do you determine key support process requirements, incorporating input from internal customers, as appropriate? What are the key operational requirements (such as productivity and cycle time) for these processes?

3. How do you design these processes to meet all the key requirements?

4. How does your day-to-day operation of key support processes ensure meeting key performance requirements?

5. What are your key performance measures/indicators used for the control and improvement of these processes? Include how in-process measures and internal customer feedback are used in managing your support processes, as appropriate.

6. How do you minimize overall costs associated with inspections, tests, and process/performance audits?

7. How do you improve your support processes to achieve better performance and to keep them current with business needs and directions? How are improvements shared with other organizational units and processes, as appropriate?

PROCEDURE TYPES: A BASIC PRIMER

Three primary types of procedures are employed in business: technical, response, and management control. Technical procedures focus primarily on the physical operation and maintenance of equipment and engineered systems. These procedures derive from formal technical, statistical, and engineering analyses. Technical procedures are what come to mind when we are shown images of nuclear power control rooms where engineers are confronted by a vast array of switches and flashing lights.

Response procedures explain how to react when systems go bad. They detail steps to take when operations approach established safety thresholds. The response procedure is aimed at accomplishing two things: "recovering" systems (bringing them back into normal operation) and minimizing the probability that a minor irregularity will grow into a major failure. This type of procedure relies on extensive analyses of safety factors, hazards, and vulnerability studies to determine the appropriate set of response steps to take when an abnormal situation occurs.

In contrast to these first two types, the most commonly used procedure type and the one of greatest interest to us here is the management control procedure. Management control procedures are not directly used to operate or maintain facilities or equipment; nor are they employed only when an alert condition exists. Sometimes referred to as administrative procedures, management control procedures provide for the coordination, interactions, and communications that bind business operations together. One way of thinking about management control procedures is that they translate policy into action. They are based less on quantitative analyses and design standards than on the management's philosophy of how they want the company to function. In this regard, they represent the culture of the organization, the personality of the corporation.

To illustrate the concept of management philosophy and corporate culture, let's use a simple example of how companies internally share information. One company might require meetings to share critical new information; another might conduct classroom training to communicate new information. A third company might issue circulars that all employees are required to read, and a fourth company might restrict the transmission of new information to memos issued exclusively to management. Among these options, there is no right way or wrong way; there is no good way or bad way. There are only variations that reflect what management believes are information transfer mechanisms in keeping with the way management believes the system should work—the management philosophy. As similar practices develop that suggest the prevailing management sentiment, personnel (both inside and outside the company) gain a sense of how things work—the corporate culture. (Figure 14.6 is a typical hierarchy of documents suggesting how requirements, expectations, and corporate philosophy flow downward into procedures.)

All three types of procedures share a common purpose. They direct how a job is to be done. But each of the three kinds is distinct from the others. While technical procedures are largely the tools of engineers and technicians, and response procedures are the voice of the safety department, administrative procedures are an embodiment of the management: what they think, what they consider important, how they want organizational units to work together, and what information they think is vital to be collected, shared, and retained. There are also

FIGURE 14.6

The Direction of
Work Direction

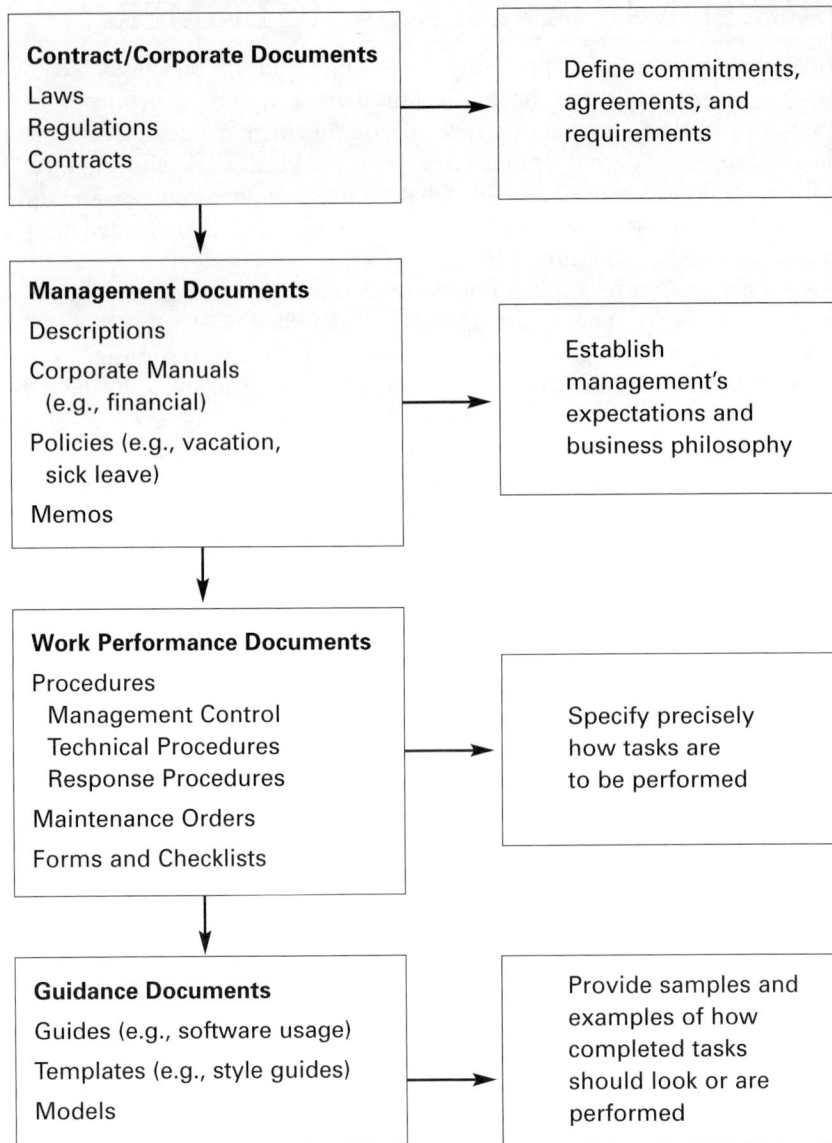

Contract/Corporate Documents Laws Regulations Contracts	Define commitments, agreements, and requirements

Management Documents
Descriptions
Corporate Manuals
  (e.g., financial)
Policies (e.g., vacation,
  sick leave)
Memos
	Establish
	management's
	expectations and
	business philosophy

Work Performance Documents
Procedures
  Management Control
  Technical Procedures
  Response Procedures
Maintenance Orders
Forms and Checklists
	Specify precisely
	how tasks are
	to be performed

Guidance Documents Guides (e.g., software usage) Templates (e.g., style guides) Models	Provide samples and examples of how completed tasks should look or are performed

differing modes of expression: a narrative structure for management control, a command format for technical procedures, and a terse, abbreviated speech for response procedures. These differences in the use, tone, and audience contribute to differences in the look and feel of the three procedure types.

Of the three types, management control procedures are of keenest interest to us as professional communicators. They are the only procedures found in every type of business, technical or otherwise. They are the procedures that place the greatest emphasis on our communication skills. They are the most challenging in terms of understanding and achieving the overt and embedded purposes. For the most part, it takes a technically trained individual to write a technical or response procedure. As we are about to explore, it requires a technically astute communicator to craft an effective management control procedure.

GETTING A HANDLE ON MANAGEMENT CONTROL PROCEDURES

Management control procedures represent a challenging communication task—translating a series of complex, intertwined purposes into an effective communication. Management control procedures require a strong analytical base to analyze the nuances of purpose and the complexity of audience. These skills must be complemented by sound judgment to develop creative, though pragmatic, procedures. At the same time, these procedures must establish a practice that is in agreement not only with the technical and political requirements, but also with the strategy and philosophy of the company.

UNDERSTANDING THE TERRAIN

The first components you need to put together are the three pieces that give you a complete picture of the territory your procedure fits in: 1) management philosophy, 2) business circumstance, and 3) corporate strategy.

MANAGEMENT PHILOSOPHY. Have you ever walked into a government office, driver's license bureau, or city agency and wondered why all the paperwork appeared to demand that you visit an excessive number of windows in order to obtain an excessive number of signatures? You probably found yourself wondering, "Why do we have all those signatures? Why can't one person give us the answers we need? Why can't the various offices share a single copy of the form?" Although we might want to blame the person at the counter, that person is not the process designer. Someone, somewhere "upstairs" of that individual, decided five signatures were better than four, four organizations should be involved upfront instead of three, and three copies of the paperwork were better than two.

Somewhere buried in the bowels of the organization outside our field of vision is the management philosophy that, in the example above, established a process that invoked a reliance on shared accountability and a dependence on redundant filing systems. Unlike President Truman's pronouncement that "the buck stops here," these agencies have established and codified a seemingly troublesome procedure. The one-stop approach Truman advocated and the grossly adulterated accountability embodied in the bureaucracy are, as we now understand, examples of differing management philosophies.

Does that make one philosophy preferable to or better than the other? Although we might be inclined to say yes when we consider the bureaucratic example, when exclusively focused on the question of philosophy, the answer is no. Every company establishes what fits their idealized sense of how best to conduct business. Sometimes a single individual may call the shots (as with the Truman illustration). More frequently, there may be a host of informing clients and influencing conditions. In the case of the government agency, for instance, there may be any number of federal regulations that have paved the road for what we perceive to be an endless highway of unnecessary signatures and redundant paperwork.

Referencing these extreme examples, we can see more clearly why the Malcolm Baldridge Award criteria focus on the fundamental link among process management, business efficiency, and customer satisfaction. We also see more clearly how one measure of a procedure's success is its ability to translate management philosophy into daily practice. But are there still other inputs to the procedure process?

Let's try using a less provocative example than that of a government agency to get our answer. Let's assume you have just been hired by a company that makes computer chips for high-end computer devices. You are asked to review the procedures controlling final fabrication. Your perception is that the procedures appear to require more steps than necessary for final verification of product quality. You're certain with a minimum of work you can reduce the time required to complete this process by at least 20%. Further, knowing as you do that the company has an incentive program that could net you a $10,000 bonus for a productivity savings like this, you vigorously start work on rewriting the procedure.

A few days later you submit your revised procedure. Expecting congratulations, you are quite surprised when you receive a terse note that says the procedure will not be changed per your suggestion. What went wrong? After rechecking your version, you still can't see any problem because the product will be available to ship in less time. Frustrated, you decide to visit your boss. What you learn is that the management team has staked its reputation—and the fiscal health of the company—on producing parts that have $1/_{10}$th the failure rate of any competitor. The means by which this is achieved is a strong quality control program. Your boss and every management level all the way up to the president of the company are not unaware that the increased quality takes time, but that's how the company has achieved and maintained its share of the market. Where the industry commonly does checks at only four points in the process, your company checks twice as frequently, as well as conducts redundant checks anywhere local and industry statistics suggest a failure mode might exist. Your idea was good, but it did not fit correctly with the management philosophy.

Luckily, your idea was derailed before anyone implemented it; otherwise your concept of a cost savings could have come at great cost to your company. You've learned a valuable lesson. Efficiency for efficiency's sake is not the goal of procedure writing. The goal of the final fabrication procedures was not simply to get the product out quickly, but to maintain and reinforce management's quality goals. The procedure may take longer to perform as it currently exists, but it is more correct and more appropriate in terms of mirroring the management philosophy than is your proposed revision. With your revision, you were on the verge of making the same blind leap of faith that earlier entrusted your judgment to Joe in Transportation (Chapter 2).

BUSINESS CIRCUMSTANCE. Preparing a management control procedure entails more than just sitting down and starting to write. It requires a complete understanding of the conditions, constraints, circumstances, and expectations. The design of the process is largely under the control of the author; the boundaries are not. The philosophy accounts for the culture; yet often laws, regulations, and external agencies dictate the boundaries.

As an example, procurement procedures may be governed by federal regulations. Safety programs will find themselves accountable to such agencies as the Office of Safety and Health Administration (OSHA). Anything to do with chemicals will find a host of environmental regulations dictating everything from storage to marking to disposal. Procedures governing personnel actions and benefits will need to maintain compliance with a range of regulations, public laws, and state requirements. As one of the technical dimensions of the task, you, as procedure author, must become knowledgeable of the full range of applicable influences and requirements.

Further, as was shown in Figure 14.6, organizations may rely on extensive document hierarchies. Not only do regulations and requirements flow down in the form of source documents from external agencies, but various management documents may prescribe internally defined requirements and constraints. Your procedure may be influenced by any number of company policies and program manuals, such as commitments to diversity, total quality, and unique accounting regulations. A management control process and its associated procedures cannot be appropriately developed without appreciation of the full territory of controls, expectations, and demands. Developing a procedure without due consideration of all these factors may yield a procedure that is efficient and yet totally unacceptable. It may produce a procedure that is inadequate to achieve the company's goals. Or, it may produce a procedure in direct conflict or competition with another company obligation or expectation.

CORPORATE STRATEGY. As Figure 14.7 suggests, management control procedures operate within a complicated universe of organizational structures and business processes that collectively comprise a corporation's infrastructure. Once you have assembled the complete scope of requirements, expectations, and influences (sometimes referred to as a "management control basis"), the next step is to anticipate how your procedure will interact with other procedures and practices. For example, a simple change in the accounting system may have repercussions through procurement, operations, and training. If we return momentarily to your earlier efforts to streamline the final fabrication process, we see that there are a number of questions that should be answered: Are there other procedures your changes will affect? Are there other organizations that might be directly or indirectly affected by the revised process? Are there any changes in practices underway that could be impacted? The answers to these questions are critical prerequisites to developing a prudent and workable process.

As an easy starting point to isolate some of the unanticipated consequences of your proposed revisions, let's return to our example and assess some of the implications associated with changing existing fabrication procedures. In the current practice, signatures are used to confirm the fact that the required quality control steps have been completed. If your procedure is implemented, then suddenly auditors are no longer signing off the forms as the product moves through the process. When the process is complete, the forms may, therefore,

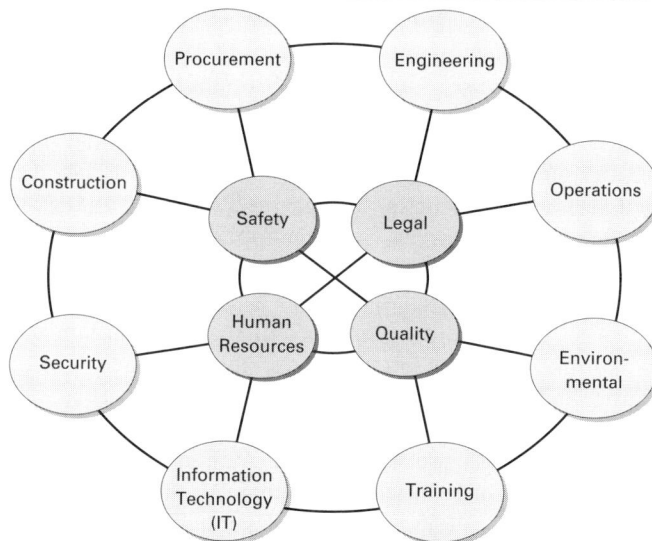

FIGURE 14.7

The Infrastructure Universe of Management Control Procedures appear incomplete. The missing signatures will likely set off alarms with the Quality Control inspectors who are trained to look for and respond to process irregularities. The Purchasing Department, in turn, may not have heard that the process now requires stocking 20% more raw material, an action that may necessitate renegotiating supplier contracts, reallocating warehouse space, and reassigning expeditors. Meanwhile, production management has been approached by the Union Steward, who is filing grievances because schedules are being changed in violation of the union agreement. Last, Human Resources hasn't had an opportunity to evaluate the impact of idled production inspectors.

While this organizational turmoil grows more intense, we may have caused additional problems closer to home. Is the revised procedure consistent with other final fabrication procedures? Will the procedure work with the other procedures? Will the existing procedures work at all once yours is implemented? For example, will the procedures that control the equipment maintenance need to be modified? Will forecasting procedures that relied on final fabrication data still be functional? By the time everything is sorted out, an imprudent action, reflected in a poorly developed procedure, may cause every infrastructure element in the tightly knit network depicted in Figure 14.7 to feel the rippling of your revision.

Stated succinctly, step one is to understand whether your procedure is appropriately aligned with the management philosophy. Step two is to make certain it fits in properly with the external requirements, agreements, and constraints. Step three is to ensure the procedure fits in comfortably with the existing business logic. Only when all three preliminary steps have been completed are you prepared to move on to the chore of constructing the process.

ADDING THE PERSPECTIVE

With the terrain duly surveyed, you can now make some inferences about why the procedure is needed as well as who will use it and how it will be used. This dimension of your task involves a bit of judgment, a lot of negotiation, and a sound attention to usability.

A BIT OF JUDGMENT. Even if it is a good fit with management philosophy and consistent with the game plan, your procedure may still not be perfect. Management control procedures rely on judgment calls—whether the procedure is needed at all and whether the process as you have defined it is in the company's best interests.

Determining whether a procedure is needed is a difficult matter. Often the decision is clear; when there are business risks that need to be mitigated, a procedure is clearly warranted. For example, you have learned that several departments have decided it's faster for them to order materials directly from the vendor than to route requests through the Procurement Department. The departments, however, are not aware of the implications. Distributing procurement activities may jeopardize ongoing pricing negotiations, introduce contract liabilities, and add restocking charges. Left on their own, the departments will put the company at risk, both in terms of financial obligations and potential legal issues. Putting a procedure in place prescribing precisely how departments are to procure materials is clearly warranted, even if some departments find the process inconvenient.

But what if developing a procedure is not a matter of business urgency? Too often procedures are written for the wrong reasons—territoriality or capitulation. The first offense is one that many professionals make. They assume that drafting procedures will secure or sustain territory. There is a mistaken belief that we can make our jobs secure by creating a process that makes us seemingly unexpendable. This is the same thinking that sets bureaucracies in motion, not the thinking that produces efficient operations. The goal in business is, to the contrary, to look for added value, not added steps or added effort. Accordingly, although you may succeed initially in writing procedures others must follow, you may find the long-term outlook less pleasant when the counterfeit processes are exposed. Those who have been artificially burdened by your process will eventually challenge the inconveniences, leaving you to defend not only the suspect processes, but your suspect thinking as well.

Sometimes the issue of territoriality is reflected not in the form of unneeded procedures, but instead in the form of unnecessarily troublesome process steps. For instance, at the driver's license bureau, there clearly is a need to validate that an applicant meets legal requirements. However, most likely the law does not stipulate how the requirement is met. The decision to have the credential validated by one official or by two officials is made by the process designer. This is where efficiency becomes a measure of success.

If, for instance, we can mail a form in versus having to go to a particular location to have it signed in person, we feel better served. If we can get two steps completed in one place instead of two, we feel the process designer has our interests in mind. Each of these process decisions is under the discretion of the process designer. The procedure only serves to document the decisions reached; it does not make any of the decisions.

The second problem regarding procedural need is capitulation, the willing collusion in creating an unnecessarily complicated process. In most cases, this offense occurs when an organization uses the procedures as a means to appease audiences who voice concerns peripheral to the procedures. For example, many regulated industries have amazingly complex procedures; however, careful analysis shows that although a process began as a straightforward sequence of steps, over time the procedures were adulterated. Steps were added as a simple means to answer an audit finding. More steps were added to accommodate a particular pet project of one of the managers. Superfluous information was added in response to a training or safety requirement. Each of these dilutions can occur without raising much attention. An auditor notes an interest in having the process completed in a slightly different way, and the procedure gets changed to incorporate the additional steps. A manager asks a question about reliability of equipment and suddenly a series of new steps are incorporated requiring the users to record information, make calculations, and process extra paperwork to guard against a problem that may not even exist. Training departments or vendors supply new catalogs and, in response, explanations, information notes and appendixes compete with the actual process. The only one who has suffered as a consequence of these actions is the procedure user—the document's primary audience.

Generating a procedure offers a rare opportunity in business for you to have a broad ownership, not only of the communication vehicle, but also of the thinking that went into the process. Accepting this responsibility demands that you exercise due diligence, both in preparing a process and procedure that is appropriate for the business needs and in defending the integrity of that process. The significance should be obvious. If you personally are thought of in terms of how well you think through a process, you want to make sure that your procedure is well thought of. It speaks well of your judgment, your integrity, and your management ability. Otherwise, it can tell the entire corporation that you have fulfilled neither your technical nor your communication responsibilities.

NEGOTIATION. Because procedures represent the means of coordinating and communicating activities, they often bring a large number of organizations into a single discussion. You need to work with each affected organization using your best abilities to demonstrate how the practices you propose are in the company's best interests. You need to be ready to articulate the reasons behind your choices, to explain how the method you propose is both responsive to requirements and respectful of your counterparts' needs and expectations. If you have done a defensible job, have built the proposed process upon a substantive foundation, the interactions should go smoothly, as long as you also have analyzed each of the respective audiences, their orientations, and their concerns about the new process.

Procedure preparation also gives opportunity for evasion by hiding behind the administrative protocols. You can avoid conversation and confrontation by relying on the administrative personnel and the corporate review process to handle your communication responsibilities. Far too often procedures are transmitted to the organization that coordinates the review process and then abandoned. The infrastructure will move the paper around, but will not make your case for you. The procedure, which is stripped of explanation, rationale, and assumptions by design, will be thrust upon the other departments. Several cycles of comments and proposed resolutions will ensue. At some point, most likely because your counterparts will be weary of the continuing exchange, the procedure will be signed off and approved, but the victory will have been won by the weight of the system, not the strength of your argument. You will have gained approval signatures and lost the opportunity to demonstrate your abilities, your strength of conviction, and your clarity of thinking.

USABILITY. For this last component, we need to return to issues cited by the NRC: accuracy, completeness, and comprehensibility. These requirements, along with several related factors (such as currency of information) add up to usability. When discussed in terms of a procedure, usability is the equivalent of efficiency.

The most immediate concern here is one of accuracy and completeness. Although these seem as if they can be dispensed with as obvious prerequisites, their very persistence as a problem reveals a continuing difficulty. Problems with procedures are not typically a function of the author's technical competence, but a problem of losing sight of the intended audience. Too often procedures are written by experts, but are intended for use by those significantly less expert in the subject. The result is a number of problems: 1) The author leaves information out under the mistaken assumption that the omitted material is understood and therefore not needed. 2) The author introduces inexact or overly exact language. 3) Information pace is inappropriate for the reader and circumstance. 4) Superfluous text interferes with the clarity and comprehension of the essential information.

These problems come in the form both of too little and too much information. When too little is provided, the user can make mistakes by trying to intuit actions or by making assumptions. When there is too much information (typically, too many steps), users can feel that the level of prescription impinges on their ability to get work done. Essentially, every one of the five error types we discussed earlier is a consequence (in part or in whole) of not paying close attention to the audience's interests, needs, and expectations.

The procedure author must remain sensitive to those who will be using the procedure. Maintaining a focus on audience will generally resolve the usability issues, but may demand some clever accommodations. For instance, a dual format (text and graphics) may be needed if the user community is highly diverse, particularly if there is a significant division between those who are novices and those who are accomplished at the task under consideration.

THE PROCEDURE FOR PROCEDURES

We can now better understand the true rhetorical complexity of procedures. Explained superficially, procedures are merely a matter of issuing a set of sequential steps. Understood more correctly, they represent a significant communication challenge: balancing numerous contributing purposes, attending to numerous potential audiences, and responding to demands that the product must be a logical, comprehensible, and usable piece of communication. We must be aware of being able to demonstrate, with confidence, that all these dimensions have been addressed purposely and effectively. Given this complexity, we can successfully construct a workable and efficient procedure by progressing through a four-step process (Figure 14.8):

1. Define the territory.
2. Design the process.
3. Determine the usability.
4. Document the thinking.

DEFINE THE TERRITORY

As in all communication tasks, you need to begin with the end in mind. When considering procedures, that end is not the procedure, but the successful completion of the task delineated in the procedure. The end point is not the single issuance of the paper, but the dozens or hundreds of times the process is completed. Your goal, your commitment to the company, is to prepare a document that, when followed, provides for the necessary consistency, mitigates some financial risks, or improves the business performance.

As shown in Figure 14.9, you need to start by envisioning your task in the broadest terms: gathering, analyzing and assessing materials that constitute the input to the procedure process and designing a process that leads efficiently to achieving precisely defined corporate outcomes—the procedure outputs. Recognizing the three large blocks (inputs, process, and outputs) involved helps illuminate why, before actually writing a procedure, you need to have a keen appreciation of requirements, management philosophy, business circumstance, and corporate

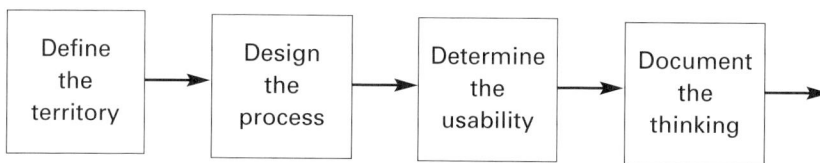

FIGURE 14.8

The Basic Procedure Development Process

FIGURE 14.9

The Procedure Framework: A Basic View

strategy. You need to make certain you have developed comprehensive answers to 10 basic questions that help define these elements (Table 14.4).[8]

As a first step in getting ready to write the procedure, you must assemble and review any sources that contain applicable requirements or commitments: regulations, relevant policies and manuals, applicable correspondence, and information from people experienced in similar processes. As a next step, to the degree applicable, you should review the circumstances in which the procedure will be used: where the procedure will be used, when it will be needed, and who will constitute the user community. If the procedure won't always be performed in an office, environmental or location factors may influence procedure performance or increase the difficulty. For example, a procedure on conducting a physical inventory of company assets may appear straightforward in an office environment, yet may become increasingly difficult to follow when performed at construction sites.

Therefore, you should research potential problems associated with performing the activities. These problems might best be understood by interviewing

---

TABLE 14.4 TEN DEFINING QUESTIONS FOR PROCEDURES

1. What requirements are to be met?	How does the procedure fulfill requirements and commitments?
2. What expectations are to be met?	What does management feel will be a satisfactory approach and output?
3. What materials, equipment, and facilities are to be used?	What is necessary for the activities to be performed?
4. What tasks are to be accomplished?	What precisely must be done?
5. Why must the tasks be accomplished?	What is the relationship of this procedure or task to other related procedures or tasks?
6. Who, other than the user, must be involved?	Are there other individuals or organizations that contribute to completing the tasks?
7. When are the tasks to be accomplished?	Are there specific times or circumstances that dictate when to use the procedure?
8. Where are the tasks to be accomplished?	Is there more than one location in which activities will occur; are the locations evident, easily accessed, and distinctively marked?
9. How are the tasks to be performed?	Are there different methods or techniques available to complete the tasks?
10. How is completion to be confirmed?	What kinds of indicators may be used to monitor that the process is doing the best job at producing the desired results?

---

prospective procedure users and examining problems experienced when performing related procedures. Coordination with other affected organizations should be initiated early in the process. Working with representatives of affected organizations, you must ensure that interactions among all affected organizations are defined and agreed upon, and that any conflicts with existing processes or procedures in the affected organizations are resolved in advance of putting your process into practice. A similar issue that must be addressed is the relationship of the new procedure to other initiatives. Identify any other initiatives that are in effect or under development and coordinate the development of the new management control procedure with those initiatives. For example, a maintenance manager developing a procedure for handling work orders might need to assess how the work order procedure will work in conjunction with production schedules and audit plans.

Equally important, though most often overlooked, is the need to identify performance measures, the means by which you intend to evaluate the effectiveness and efficiency of the process (Question 10 in Table 14.4). Specifically, these measures aid in monitoring whether the process is producing the desired results and in identifying areas of the process requiring further attention. The measures you develop should generally be one of two types: measures focused on the intended output or measures that monitor those factors or performance that should be affected if your process is running correctly. In developing these measures, you should focus on objective, quantifiable factors such as cycle time, error rates, and cost as opposed to qualitative measures such as customer satisfaction. For example, if you were preparing procedures on how the corporate library is operated, you might want to consider such indicators as the costs of conducting computerized literature searches or how long it takes to locate and check out materials.

Last, there is a note of caution when surveying the territory. Although you should solicit and use information gained from experience with similar processes and procedures to guide your efforts, never simply replicate a borrowed procedure from another corporation or business unit, or rely exclusively on it as the sole source of information. The problem with this shortcut is that even if the same regulations apply, it will not likely share the same underlying conditions: the management philosophy, business circumstance, and corporate strategy. Accepting an existing model on face value has a larger potential for introducing problems than for achieving efficiency. Only by conducting your own research, discovering the purposes, and analyzing your audience can you proceed with confidence that you are creating a procedure that will serve your company's interests.

DESIGN THE PROCESS

Having completed the research, you are now ready to begin devising the best process for achieving the intended results. This procedure development process is best achieved in a series of five steps:

1. Getting a measure of the whole
2. Partitioning the activity to the task level
3. Developing the step level
4. Assessing the qualifying conditions
5. Synthesizing the elements of the process

GETTING THE MEASURE OF THE WHOLE. Just as we discussed in developing coherent paragraphs, the best strategy is to begin with an overview of the entire picture to be communicated. For example, if the procedure addresses how to assemble a product, we would want to know in advance what parts are needed and how the product is supposed to appear when completed. If the focus is on installation, the "whole" includes a clear picture of the location where installation is to occur, the conditions, and a comprehensive sense of the various contributing activities (e.g., carpentry, millwork, electrical). In comparison, if the focus is on use, we would expect to have all the inputs and all the possible outputs identified (including both the intended outputs and those that are probable but not intended). (Returning to our discussion of following directions, an unintended output is the equivalent of the direction that lets us know that "if we get to the post office, we have gone too far.") Last, if we are preparing a procedure detailing a process, we would want to understand what action or condition initiates the process, the major components, and the outputs. To illustrate, Figure 14.10 shows the inputs and outputs associated with adding a new copier in the office.[9] (The process portion is not detailed because, in this example, the process is internal to the copier.)

As a second example, let's return to the procedure for evacuating university buildings. Figure 14.11 suggests how the prewriting stage might look in the process of envisioning the whole of that activity.

PARTITIONING TO THE TASK LEVEL. A natural consequence of seeing the whole is beginning to isolate the specific tasks. In most cases, this step offers a hierarchical framework for the work, proceeding first from the whole to the main sections, and then from these major elements to the discrete steps involved in doing the work (Figure 14.12). This format is not unlike envisioning the organizational structure of a large firm, with the tasks flowing down from the President to the Vice Presidents, and then down through successive levels of the organization until each of the elements of the work has been appropriately assigned.

To develop the task level, the easiest method is by drafting a flowchart. A flowchart can be collapsed or expanded as needed, allowing a telescoping of the major sections. In addition, a flowchart is a substantial means of providing an

---

FIGURE 14.10

Seeing the Whole Picture

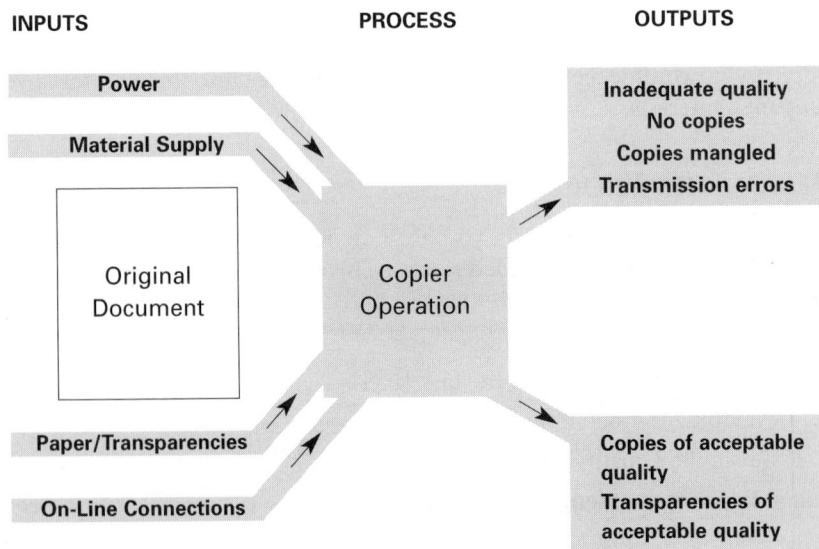

INPUTS | PROCESS | OUTPUTS

Power
Material Supply
Original Document
Paper/Transparencies
On-Line Connections

Copier Operation

Inadequate quality
No copies
Copies mangled
Transmission errors

Copies of acceptable quality
Transparencies of acceptable quality

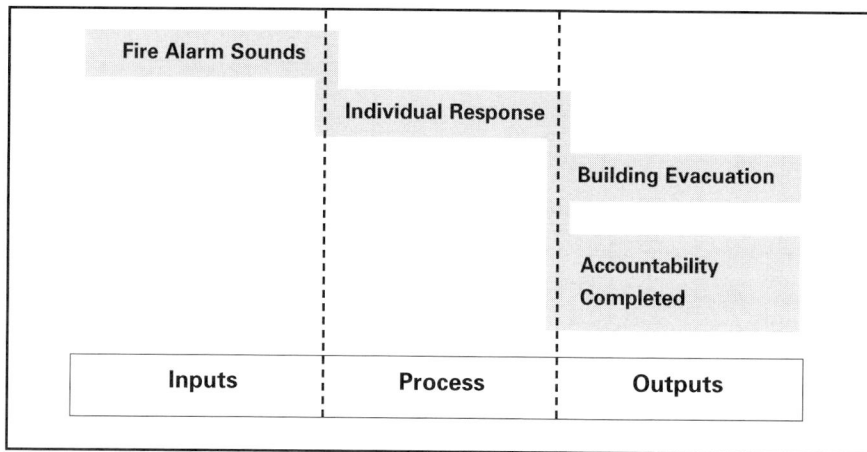

FIGURE 14.11

An Overview
of the Evacuation
Procedure

Fire Alarm Sounds		
	Individual Response	
		Building Evacuation
		Accountability Completed
Inputs	**Process**	**Outputs**

early check that you are on course to developing a procedure. If you can't create a flowchart from the pieces, then you are probably writing something other than a procedure (such as a plan). Sometimes people write policies and philosophy disguised as procedure. This difficulty occurs either as a result of confusion among the designated purposes for the various segments of the document hierarchy or because the author never developed a process to begin with. For example, if you try to convert the directions on "Preventing Summer Tragedies" (Figure 14.2) into a procedure, you will discover that the directions do not represent a process, but a list of policies and recommendations.

To illustrate how the flowchart readily delineates the tasks involved in a process, let's consider the curriculum development process used at Coyote Community College, a fictitious college whose application is used to train assessors for the Malcolm Baldridge Award (Figure 14.13).

DEVELOPING THE STEP LEVEL. Below the task level are the specific steps involved in completing each of the major sections, and ultimately the procedure as a whole. Defining the steps can be done efficiently by expanding upon the level of specificity in the flowchart. Or, if the process is not particularly complicated, the steps can simply be written out.

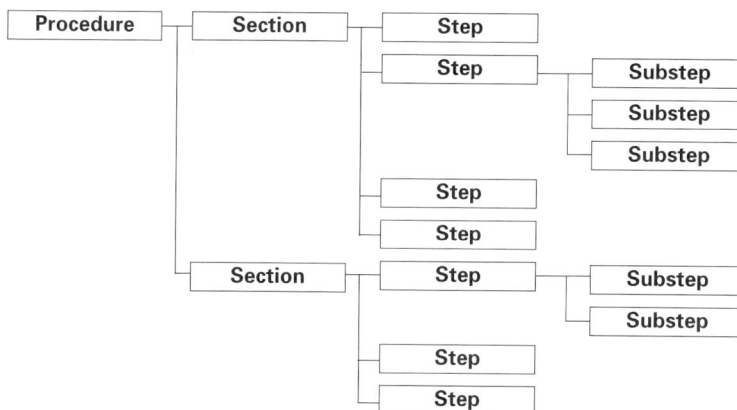

FIGURE 14.12

The Basic
Hierarchical
Structure of
Procedures

FIGURE 14.13

The Curriculum Development Process at Coyote Community College

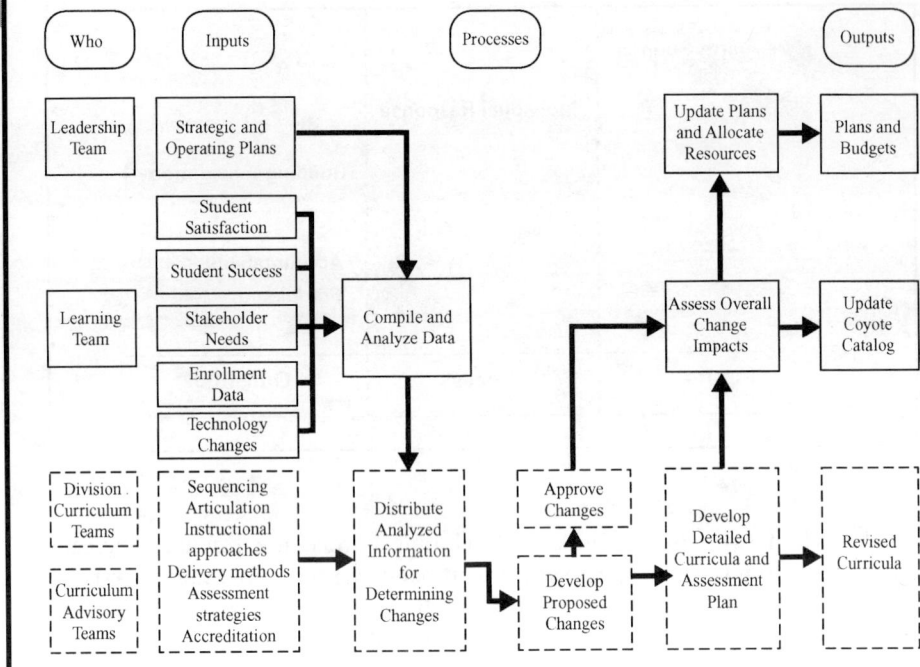

Who	Inputs	Processes		Outputs

Who: Leadership Team — **Inputs:** Strategic and Operating Plans

Student Satisfaction

Student Success

Who: Learning Team — **Inputs:** Stakeholder Needs — **Processes:** Compile and Analyze Data

Enrollment Data

Technology Changes

Who: Division Curriculum Teams; Curriculum Advisory Teams — **Inputs:** Sequencing Articulation Instructional approaches Delivery methods Assessment strategies Accreditation — **Processes:** Distribute Analyzed Information for Determining Changes; Approve Changes; Develop Proposed Changes; Develop Detailed Curricula and Assessment Plan — **Outputs:** Revised Curricula

Processes: Update Plans and Allocate Resources; Assess Overall Change Impacts — **Outputs:** Plans and Budgets; Update Coyote Catalog

At this stage, you need to start thinking about how to help your audience understand and follow the process. One highly successful means of accomplishing these ends is to use graphical aids to help explain the process. This relationship between process definition and graphical illustration is a lengthy one, as reflected in the age-old marriage of text and graphics used to explain complex process descriptions accompanying most patent applications. Since President Washington signed the first American patent in 1790 (for making potash for use in fertilizer), most of the 6.5 million patents issued have used exploded views and other graphical devices to delineate the required "utility" or "design" novelties of their inventions. Doing so without advantage of these devices would have made patent applications considerably longer, and, more importantly, considerably less clear. (Figure 14.14 is a sample patent illustration, a depiction accompanying Eli Whitney's request for a patent for the cotton gin.)

One commonly employed means to promote and encourage graphical thinking is to use a Procedure Development Form, the first two columns of which are for recording the steps (Figure 14.15). In this form, the planning strategy is not far different from that used when developing your materials for a presentation. On the left side, write the step to be completed; on the right side, consider if there are any graphical materials that might aid comprehension.

For instance, let's consider a simple task of changing a broken outlet in the kitchen. Let's assume you work for the company that manufactures outlets and are charged with drafting basic directions to accompany your product, which is sold in greatest volume in hardware and home improvement stores as opposed to electrical warehouses. Also assume you have already developed the flowchart that creates both the vision of the whole as well as the principal main tasks (Figure 14.16).

The structure looks straightforward enough. Yet, remembering an audience of do-it-yourselfers, the audience probably requires more help than provided by

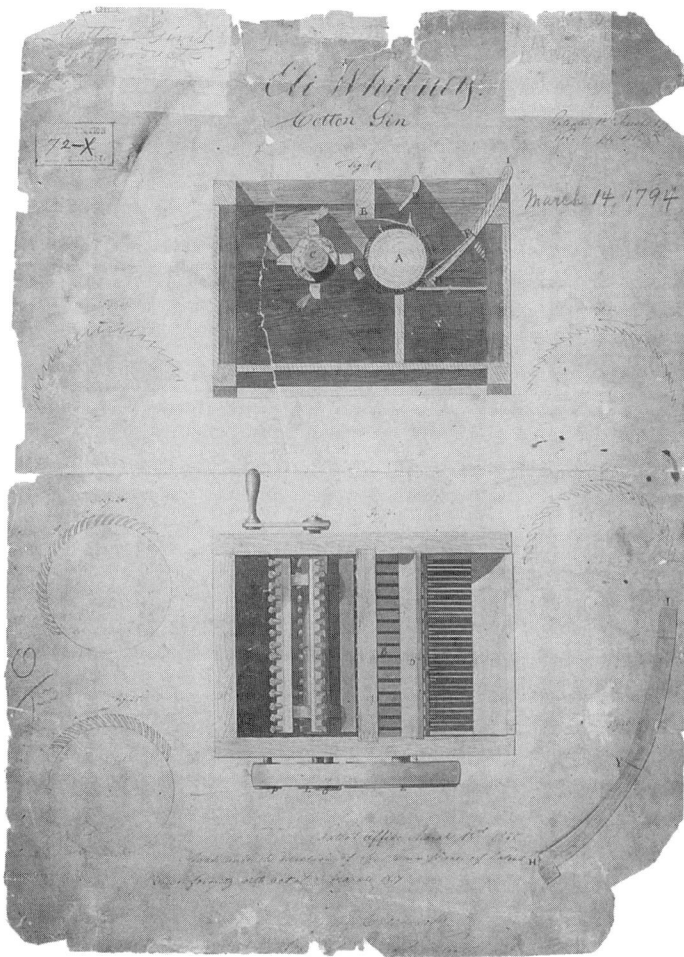

FIGURE 14.14

An Illustration From Eli Whitney's Patent Application for the Cotton Gin (March 14, 1794)

Step (narrative)	Graphical Aid

FIGURE 14.15

Procedure Development Form—Initial Columns

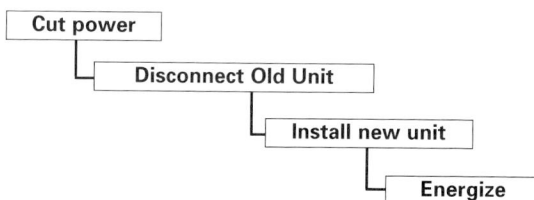

Cut power

Disconnect Old Unit

Install new unit

Energize

FIGURE 14.16

The "Whole" of Replacing an Outlet

these four steps. This audience will need assistance with differentiating lead from ground wires and help in de-energizing the outlet. Simply acquainting users with wires likely encountered when the faceplate is removed may be insufficient. Explaining that standard electrical codes designate the red insulated wire is the lead, black the negative, and green the ground might be sufficient if we could proceed with certainty that all buildings and apartments using your outlets had been similarly wired—a fairly low probability given the frequent changes to building codes.

Instead, using our form to record steps, we can articulate the sequence of actions associated with disconnecting and removing the old unit (Figure 14.17). This notation leads to a graphically aided depiction that is well attuned to your purpose and audience; the depiction is now clear, complete, and comprehensible (Figure 14.18).[10]

ASSESSING QUALIFYING CONDITIONS. Not all steps are equal. Any process may have some steps that, if done incorrectly, introduce particular risks or higher probability of confusion or error than do the other steps. For example, when replacing an outlet, we should pay particular attention to de-energizing the circuit and when handling and connecting wires. Business processes may likewise contain risks that are most likely to occur at certain steps in the process. Failing to complete a step satisfactorily may create financial liability, leave decisions unrecorded, create opportunities for misinterpretation, or jeopardize a client or

FIGURE 14.17

Completing the Step Information

Step (narrative)	Graphical Aid
Remove outer screw.	Show position.
Remove faceplate.	Show position.
Pull outlet.	Show exploded view.
Identify wires.	Show position on outlet.

FIGURE 14.18

A Basic Illustrated Process

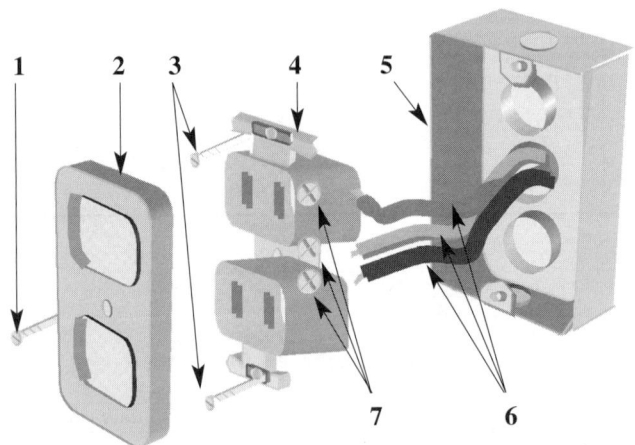

Remove Wall Outlet

-----WARNING-------

Be certain to turn off circuit breaker or remove fuse that controls power to wall outlet being removed.

1) Remove outer screw (1). Remove faceplate (2).

2) Remove two mounting screws (3)

3) Pull outlet (4) from box (5).

To help you remember where each wire connects, label and note position of each of three wires (6) before removing each.

4) Loosen screw (7) for each wire. Remove wires (6) from screws. Remove outlet (4).

vendor relationship. For example, failure to submit an invoice through the proper departments may delay payments to a vendor; that delay, in turn, may create legal liabilities or make that vendor less inclined to make services or products available to your firm in the future.

Here again we must rely on research. If you have done an adequate job of researching the requirements, history, and expectations, you should have already discovered any unique qualifications, potential issues, high-risk factors, and probable miscues. Knowing this information, you next need—as was shown in the outlet example—to position that critical information appropriately in the procedure to be sure that it merits the proper response and attention. Alerting drivers that there is a "Dangerous Curve Ahead" is only of value if the driver is provided sufficient time to react. The same principle applies in the design of procedures.

To be sure that qualifying conditions are cited where needed, we can introduce a third column to our Procedure Development Form—Qualifying Conditions. Together, the three columns now prompt us to consider what needs to be done, how those actions can best be made clear to the procedure user, and what additional clarifying information is vital to accomplishing the step efficiently (Figure 14.19).

SYNTHESIZING THE PROCESS ELEMENTS. Having looked closely at the individual elements, our last job in this portion of the procedure development process is to make certain the pieces fit together properly. Can we reconstruct the whole out of the pieces? To appreciate this problem, you might envision a jigsaw puzzle. You construct the puzzle by assembling the principal images within the picture from the individual pieces. The puzzle is not complete until these images are pulled together in a cohesive, integrated unit.

This synthesizing step is generally referred to as "verification," walking through the entire process to see if you end up where you intended. If you can complete the entire process without hesitating or filling in gaps as you go, you probably have a reasonably designed process. If you're uncertain about the completeness or clarity of a segment or step, go back and rethink the process. Better yet, find individuals who will be expected to use the procedure and ask them to take this hypothetical walk. Any place they stumble or require further clarification represents an area in the process that needs revision or refinement. While this verification process accomplishes some of the goals generally understood as usability testing, a few additional factors still need to be addressed.

DETERMINE THE USABILITY

As might be assumed from the method we advocated for defining graphical aids and qualifying conditions, information pace is a critical dimension of procedures. For instructions to be understood, they must be delivered at a pace commensurate with the capability (expertise and experience) of the intended user

FIGURE 14.19

Step (narrative)	Graphical Aid	Qualifying Conditions
Remove faceplate.	Show position.	Before proceeding to the next step, verify the circuit is de-energized.

Expanded Procedure Development Form

community. This objective is often complicated when multiple user communities exist. Users may range from persons with lengthy service with the company to new employees, from employees with extensive familiarity with a certain process to those who have only the most infrequent exposure to the activity. For example, someone who travels infrequently on business may be expected to be less familiar with the company travel procedure than someone who travels regularly. Your job is to accommodate this range, a challenge met by maintaining attention to those factors that determine pace: narrative versus graphical representation, level of detail, and visual highlighting of important information.

NARRATIVE VERSUS GRAPHICAL REPRESENTATION. Adjusting pace by means of graphical equivalents was briefly illustrated by our example of repairing an electrical outlet. Although many graphical devices aid comprehension, by far the most commonly employed graphical device for communicating process is a flowchart, which provides a representation of the sequence using symbols to delineate various types of actions (Figure 14.20). Flowcharts not only do well at depicting process, they are also adaptable for use with the range of audiences expected for management control procedures. As detailed in Table 14.5, flowcharts can be used alone or in conjunction with a more detailed narrative. When narrative and flowchart are used together in a procedure, the narrative provides the details needed by those less experienced with the process; the flowchart, in contrast, is responsive to the more experienced user who can be expected to move more quickly through the process. A further adaptation can also be made in the degree of correspondence between the narrative and flowchart. Symbols can correspond to each of the narrative steps or can be tailored, highlighting only decisions and qualifying conditions previously identified.

Figure 14.21, for example, shows how a portion of a corporate travel procedure might be presented in a format combining narrative and flowchart. As the flowchart makes evident, the text within the symbols is streamlined for easier use by experienced personnel. Additionally, two other benefits of the flowchart are illustrated in this example. First, the actual steps, decisions, and qualifying conditions are aligned in a straight vertical column, making them readily distinguishable from supporting information that is not part of the actual process. Second, the flowchart makes certain features more visible. The first step, for instance, in the narrative form might be thought of as an action. In fact, the step is asking the user to make a decision.

LEVEL OF DETAIL. For procedures to be useful and credible, they must provide a level of detail commensurate with the knowledge, skill, and experience of the user. Someone who has never replaced a kitchen faucet expects directions accompanying a new faucet to be complete. A sheet that begins "remove old faucet," will invite problems and customer dissatisfaction. Conversely, the accomplished mechanic doesn't expect to be told to take the following actions in preparation to set the tension on a spring:

1. Go to tool box.
2. Locate wrench.
3. Adjust wrench opening to approximate dimension of locknut.
4. Position wrench on locknut.
5. Adjust wrench to size of locknut.
6. Test that wrench fits snugly on locknut by turning $\frac{1}{4}$ inch to left.
7. Turn wrench continuously in counterclockwise direction to loosen nut.
8. When locknut is free of shaft, remove locknut.

FIGURE 14.20

A Typical Set of
Procedure
Flowchart Symbols

Rectangle—Action

Editor writes narrative

A Begins with responsible party

Diamond—Decision

(Branch chief)
Work needed?

A Begins with responsible party
B Summarizes question
C Accounts for multiple potential
outcomes

Oval—Adjunct Information

Flowchart has
been submitted

A Summarizes adjunct information
B Comes off side of activity box
indicating it represents a clarification not an action

Triangle—Reference

See Att. 1

A Should stipulate "go to" or "see"
relationship
B Comes off side of activity box
indicating it is not a required
action

Circle—Warning

Warning!
Wear
Goggles

A Precedes activity where warning
is warranted
B Begins with appropriate warning
word such as *Warning* or *Caution!*

TABLE

14.5 NARRATIVE FLOWCHART EXPLANATION

Narrative	Flowchart
Useful for initial encounter with a given procedure	Useful for those experienced in a given procedure • Identifying decision points • Locating specific steps quickly • Reviewing procedure
Provides detailed description in complete sentences	Provides abbreviated descriptions of each step
Lists complete names, form numbers, responsible parties, all adjunct information	Provides a cross-reference to forms and designates titles and departments by acronyms
Useful for reviewers/auditors to check details	Useful for general review for assessing logic of process

FIGURE 14.21

A Sample
Flowcharted
Procedure

1. Confirm the travel is on the approved Travel List. (See Procedure TL 101).
2. Complete Travel Form (TF101).

3. Obtain immediate supervisor's approval signature on the form.

4. Does the trip involve foreign travel?
5. If it does, obtain approval signatures from the Division Program Manager's Office. (The PMO will submit the form to the Office of Travel and Budget.) Note: Failure to obtain this signature in advance may result in denial of reimbursement.

6. If not, transmit the form to the Office of Travel and Budget.
7. Attach the form to completed Expense form (EF101), when travel is completed. The form must be submitted within 10 working days of completing travel.

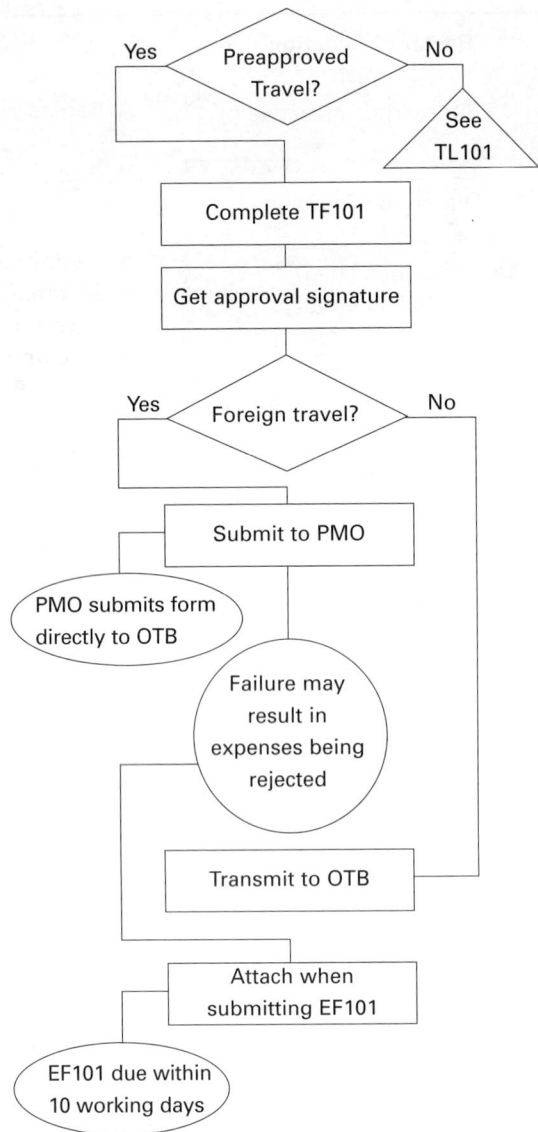

Yes — **Preapproved Travel?** — No → See TL101

Complete TF101

Get approval signature

Yes — **Foreign travel?** — No

Submit to PMO

PMO submits form directly to OTB

Failure may result in expenses being rejected

Transmit to OTB

Attach when submitting EF101

EF101 due within 10 working days

While the instruction to "remove faucet" is too rapid a pace, the locknut direction is painfully slow. Here again a flowcharted procedure can help bridge the divide. The narrative can accommodate the novice's needs; the flowchart can accommodate the expert.

HIGHLIGHTING IMPORTANT INFORMATION. To make the procedure successful, you need to be sure that necessary information is clear and apparent. The first step is to make certain each step is identifiable. For example, consider the following "single" validation step included as part of a routine post-production process (Figure 14.22).

Hidden in this "one step" are nine separate tasks and a decision. Equally problematic for the user, there is no explanation of what to do at the decision point. What is the user supposed to do if the two weights differ by more than 3 grams? In comparison, Figure 14.23 shows how a flowcharted version might have

FIGURE 14.22

A Sample
Congested Step

A Validating Weight

16. Record weight of check weight being used and gross weight of scale readout on DATA SHEET. Compare the gross weight to known check weight by printing the data using the n+1 key. Obtain printout by pressing the Enter key. Clear the check weight by pressing the "C" key and the n+1 key. Clear tare weight by pressing "c" and "T." Attach the printout to the DATA SHEET. If the gross weight and the check weight differ by more than 3 g, notify supervision before proceeding. Attach hoist to check weight and return weight to STORAGE position.

FIGURE 14.23

Illuminating the
Embedded Actions

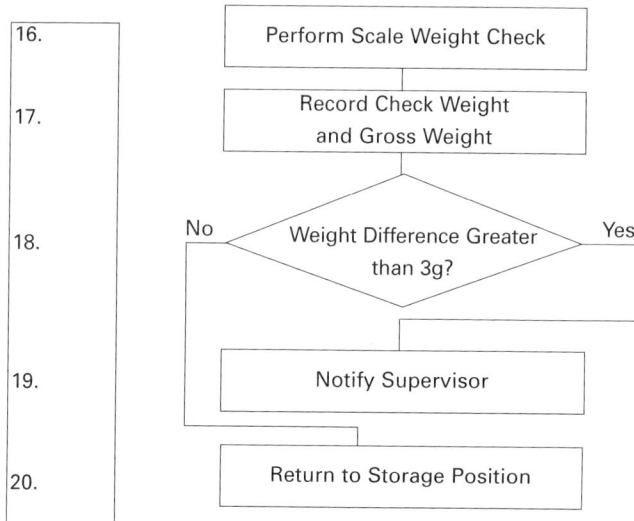

addressed the problem, while at the same time adjusting the level of detail and clearly highlighting critical information. The flowchart uses white space to improve reading ease, the decision is clearly called out, the implications of the decision are now identified, and the pace has been improved by consolidating a few of the steps.

The next step is to use a standardized format that lets the user readily distinguish among the major sections of the procedure and to distinguish between actions to be taken and other forms of information. Generally, the easiest way to do this is to set up a series of highlighting conventions (Table 14.6). Placing what we have learned about procedures in perspective, Table 14.7 summarizes the elements of procedure usability.

PUTTING THE PIECES TOGETHER

At this point, let's revisit the procedure for evacuating university buildings to test our expanded knowledge about procedure construction, design, and usability. Reexamining that procedure, we should see several potential improvements we need to make: 1) increase visibility of specific steps, 2) reorganize information

14.6 **SAMPLE HIGHLIGHTING TECHNIQUES**

Information Type	Emphasis Technique
First-order heading	Bold, all capital letters
Second-order heading	Bold, initial capital letters
Warning	Boxed and centered
References	Italics
Lists	Bulleted/indented

14.7 **THE USABILITY FACTORS: A SUMMARY**

Factors	Expectations
Terminology	Is the language clear and precise?
Technical Demand	Does the user possess the knowledge necessary to complete the procedure?
Comprehensibility	Is the grammar, syntax, wording, and phrasing clearly understood?
Graphs and Tables	Is the important information easily identified and extracted?
Internal Consistency	Does the procedure contain consistent information and directions?
Level of Detail	Is the level of specificity appropriate for the user community?
Navigation	Can the user follow the flow of work?
Salience	Is important information appropriately identified?
Presentation Style	Does the format and legibility facilitate use and comprehension?
Organization	Is material logically sequenced?

so as to combine related information, and 3) highlight the embedded warning against breaking windows. (Figure 14.24 illustrates the revised procedure in text form; Figure 14.25 is in flowchart format.)

Recasting the procedure also exposes another consideration possibly overlooked by the procedure's author. Had the authors begun with a vision of the whole, they might have noticed that the picture they present is perhaps incomplete. Is evacuating offices the only concern in the event of a fire? Evacuating an office may be different from evacuating classrooms, laboratories, or other special-purpose facilities. When evacuating a classroom, for instance, a professor

FIGURE 14.24

Evacuation and Fire Alarms

1. Initial response
   a. Close all office windows
2. Determine if it's appropriate to evacuate
   a. **When not to evacuate**
      (Note: If your door is closed, feel the door to determine if heat is present.)

      > **WARNING: Do not break windows; this may increase smoke.**

      1. Open window if breathing is difficult.
      2. Make your condition known.
      3. Hang a towel from the window.
   b. **When to evacuate**
      If heat is not present, proceed to the nearest exit and then to your reporting station.
3. Personnel accounting
   a. Department Chairs will conduct accountability and notify the Fire Department of personnel not accounted for.
   b. Personnel should remain at the reporting station until dismissed.

The Evacuation Procedure in Text Form

may have certain responsibilities to account for the students' safety. A lab instructor may need to secure chemicals or shut down experiments in advance of evacuating the facility.

DOCUMENTING THE THINKING

This potential omission leads to the final responsibility you have as a procedure author. There is no way to find out if the author of the evacuation procedure intentionally omitted discussion about evacuating classrooms and laboratories. The only means by which this decision would be known is if the author developed a set of documentation that detailed what decisions had been reached relative to the procedure, what sources had been used, and what assumptions had been made. Precisely because procedures do not include an explanation of the research conducted, the thinking behind the design, or the decisions reached regarding particular steps, you should create a file of this type of information. Future discussions about the procedure, for instance, liabilities associated with the process or need for subsequent revisions, are assisted by the availability of such a file.

To assist with this final objective, we recommend that a fourth column be added to the Procedure Development Form—Explanations and Notes. Generally, you will not have notes or explanations associated with every step. You should, however, at minimum, have notes explaining each decision point and qualifying condition (Table 14.8). Filling in relevant details on the sheets you've been using will create a valuable history. Equally important, it will ensure that critical steps are not inadvertently deleted in subsequent revisions. For example,

FIGURE 14.25

The Evacuation
Procedure in
Flowchart Format

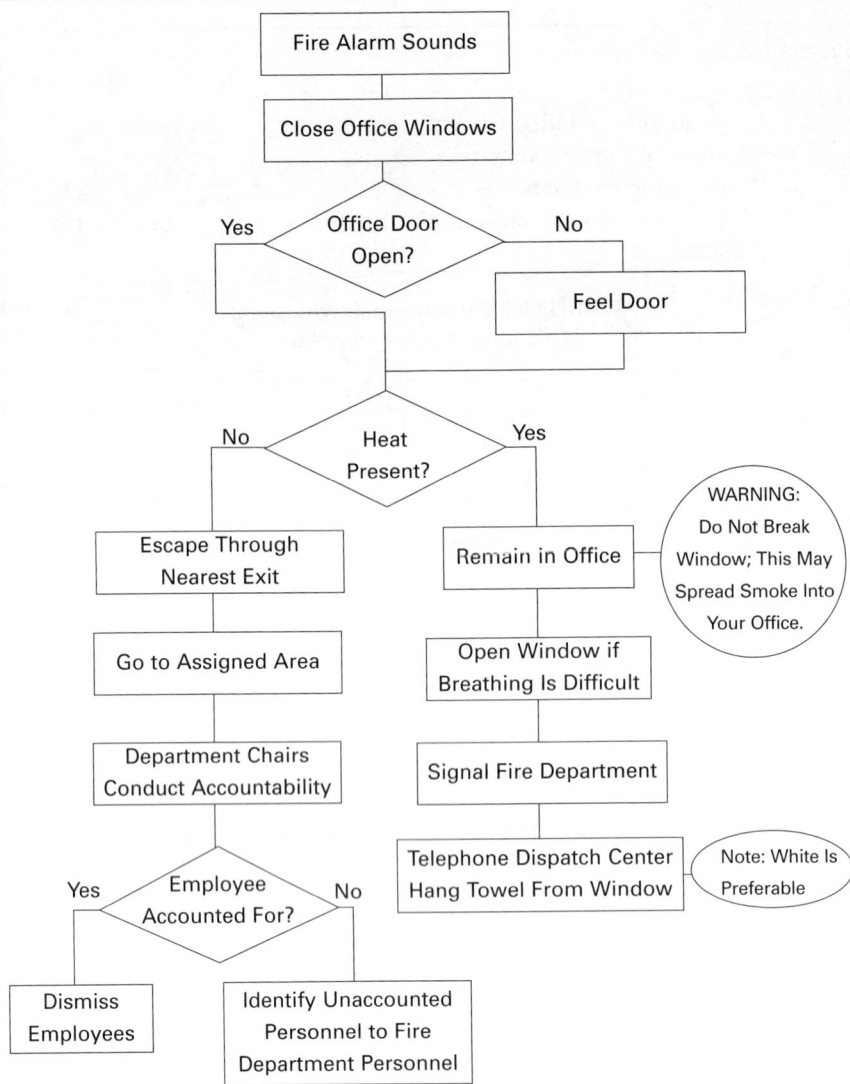

```
                    ┌─────────────────────┐
                    │  Fire Alarm Sounds  │
                    └─────────────────────┘
                               │
                    ┌─────────────────────┐
                    │ Close Office Windows│
                    └─────────────────────┘
                               │
                    ╱─────────────────────╲
          Yes      ╱     Office Door       ╲      No
        ◄─────────┤        Open?            ├─────────►
                   ╲                       ╱
                    ╲─────────────────────╱
                                              ┌──────────────┐
                                              │  Feel Door   │
                                              └──────────────┘

                    ╱─────────────────────╲
          No       ╱        Heat            ╲      Yes
        ◄─────────┤       Present?          ├─────────►
                   ╲                       ╱
                    ╲─────────────────────╱
```

┌─────────────────────┐   ┌─────────────────────┐   WARNING:
│ Escape Through   │   │ Remain in Office   │   Do Not Break
│ Nearest Exit   │   └─────────────────────┘   Window; This May
└─────────────────────┘   Spread Smoke Into
                                                                            Your Office.
┌─────────────────────┐   ┌─────────────────────┐
│ Go to Assigned Area│   │ Open Window if   │
└─────────────────────┘   │ Breathing Is Difficult│
                                           └─────────────────────┘
┌─────────────────────┐   ┌─────────────────────┐
│ Department Chairs   │   │ Signal Fire Department│
│ Conduct Accountability│   └─────────────────────┘
└─────────────────────┘
                                           ┌─────────────────────┐   Note: White Is
          ╱─────────────╲   │ Telephone Dispatch Center│   Preferable
  Yes   ╱   Employee   ╲   No   │ Hang Towel From Window│
◄───────┤ Accounted For? ├───────►   └─────────────────────┘
         ╲   ╱
          ╲─────────────╱

┌──────────┐   ┌─────────────────────┐
│ Dismiss │   │ Identify Unaccounted │
│ Employees│   │ Personnel to Fire   │
└──────────┘   │ Department Personnel │
                      └─────────────────────┘

TABLE   14.8   THE COMPLETE STEP DOCUMENTATION

Step (narrative)	Graphical Aid	Qualifying Condition	Explanation and Notes
Remove faceplate	Show position	Before proceeding, verify the circuit is de-energized.	OSHA rule requires redundant testing; Legal suggested such precaution will mitigate liability. (Letter: LD-01-03)

think how you might have proceeded differently in redesigning the fabrication procedures had you known in advance that the existing procedures reflected business decisions about quality control requirements. Figure 14.26 shows a completed Procedure Development Form documenting the key information for the evacuation procedure.

FIGURE 14.26

A Completed
Procedure
Development
Form

Procedure Number	EM 1-1
Rev. Number	01
Procedure Title	Evacuations and Fire Alarms

Step	Step (narrative)	Graphical Aid	Qualifying Condition	Explanation and Notes
1	Determine if it is safe to leave the office.		Heat outside office may make leaving unsafe.	Fire Safety Guide (Rev 1)—Section 10
2	Leaving office Going to assembly area	Table showing designated staging areas		Fire Safety Guide—Section 12
3	Conducting accountability	Provide copy of Accountability Checklist (Form 2-107).	Individuals unaccounted for must be reported to Fire Department personnel.	Emergency Plan (Rev 3)—section 7
4	Remaining in office		Need to warn against breaking windows— risk of smoke accumulation	Fire Safety Guide—Section 5
5	Making presence in office known –telephone –visual signals	Depict appropriate signaling.	Preferred use of white (or light) materials to signal	Fire Safety Guide—Section 2; confirmed with Safety (Letter DG: 1-03)
6	Evacuating other types of facilities			Per Dean Reimann, other evacuation procedures to be developed by Campus Safety (Memo: DR-1-03a)

PROCEDURES—THE LESSONS

Business procedures represent the means by which work is conducted. Written correctly, procedures produce a smooth, efficiently operated enterprise. Written poorly, they can introduce a host of problems. To prepare procedures effectively, you must recognize that there are numerous factors that influence the substance and design: management philosophy, business circumstances, corporate strategies, and a range of potential user communities. These complexities demand attention to audience, purpose, pace, organization, and reasoning. Doing justice to this communication task requires you to demonstrate your capabilities both as a technical expert and as an expert communicator.

EXERCISES

☐ Group

1. On the next page is another section from a university Employee Safety Handbook. As a team, consider what issues might exist with the procedure and then revise the procedure accordingly.

2. The flowchart on the following page is intended to explain how the Board of Examiners for the Malcolm Baldridge Award conducts the evaluation process. As

> **Radiation Safety**
>
> The University has a radiation safety program that supports the needs of researchers who use radiation as an essential tool in their work. The types of radiation that are used in the laboratories include radioactive materials, x-ray machines, lasers, ultraviolet light, and microwave sources.
>
> The radiation safety program has three main functions:
> - Regulatory compliance and enforcement
> - Essential services for researchers, and
> - Training programs for all employees.
>
> All employees who work with radiation must be active participants in the radiation safety program. They must follow the policies and procedures for the type of radiation that they are using and participate in the various training programs offered by the program. The policies and procedures can be found in the Radiation Safety Manual, which has been issued to laboratories. Before employees can use radiation, they must read the manual and become familiar with the various provisions related to his/her specific uses.
>
> If you plan to use radiation, your principal investigator will provide you with specific information about becoming qualified to work with the materials or devices. The training programs offered by the radiation safety office are designed to provide you with general information that will help you work safely in the laboratory. However, to complete the training process, your principal investigator will provide you with specific safety measures related to the work you are going to perform.

the Senior Examiner, you have been asked to explain in greater detail what you expect of this year's team. Explain how you might expand the flowchart.

3. As a team, develop a process for reducing the amount of time it takes to get a driver's license. Once you have a process defined, do the following

a) Prepare a procedure for training the personnel at the driver's license bureau.

b) Prepare a presentation to the Directors of the Department of Transportation (your class), using your flowchart to explain why your proposal is prudent and practical.

☐ **Individual**

1. Select a personnel procedure at your university or company (e.g., hiring, termination, leaves of absence). Assume you have been asked to revise and update the procedure. Then complete the following:

a) Identify the underlying management philosophy, business circumstances, and corporate strategies at work.

b) Identify areas of the process you think can be improved.

c) Identify the primary audiences/users of the procedure. Create a flowchart version of the procedure.

2. Select a set of instructions accompanying a product you have purchased recently. Review the directions to determine how successful they are in assisting you to use, install, or make the product. Explain the strengths of the directions and the weaknesses, and rewrite a section to demonstrate how your suggestions would change the quality of the procedure.

3. Convert Ben Franklin's process for building a lightning rod (Figure 14.3) into a flowchart. Explain what insights the flowchart gives you about the completeness and quality of the process description.

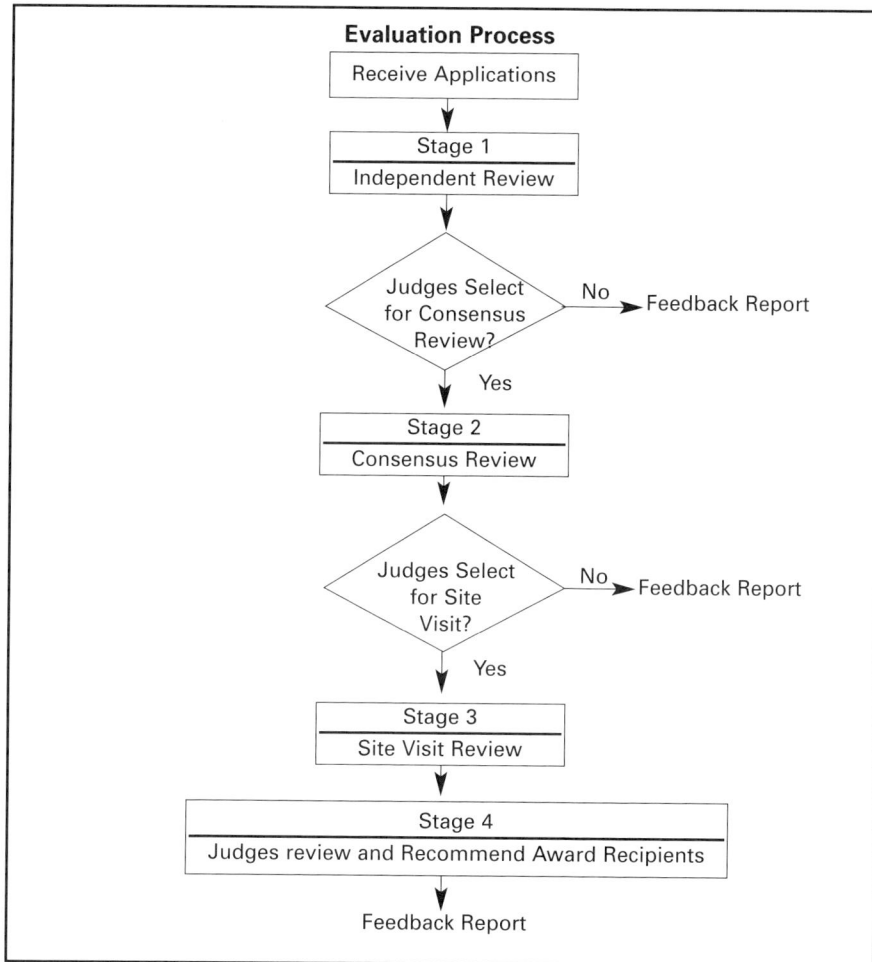

Evaluation Process

```
           Receive Applications
                   │
                   ▼
        ┌─────────────────────┐
        │      Stage 1         │
        │  Independent Review  │
        └─────────────────────┘
                   │
                   ▼
            ◇ Judges Select ◇        No
            ◇ for Consensus ◇ ───────────► Feedback Report
            ◇    Review?    ◇
                   │ Yes
                   ▼
        ┌─────────────────────┐
        │      Stage 2         │
        │  Consensus Review    │
        └─────────────────────┘
                   │
                   ▼
            ◇ Judges Select ◇        No
            ◇   for Site    ◇ ───────────► Feedback Report
            ◇    Visit?     ◇
                   │ Yes
                   ▼
        ┌─────────────────────┐
        │      Stage 3         │
        │  Site Visit Review   │
        └─────────────────────┘
                   │
                   ▼
   ┌─────────────────────────────────────────┐
   │                Stage 4                   │
   │ Judges review and Recommend Award Recipients │
   └─────────────────────────────────────────┘
                   │
                   ▼
            Feedback Report
```

END NOTES

[1] The examples from Dale Carnegie and Ben Franklin are quoted in: Jacqueline Berke, *Twenty Questions for the Writer: A Rhetoric with Readings,* 2nd ed. New York: Harcourt, Brace, Jovanovitch, Inc., 1976.

[2] "Methods for Review and Evaluations of Emergency Procedure Guidelines Volume 1: Methodologies" NUREG/CR-3177, March 1983.

[3] "Analysis of Findings from the First Sixteen Tiger Team Assessments," Department of Energy Report (DOE/EH-0191), May 1991.

[4] "Development of a Checklist for Evaluating Maintenance, Test and Calibration Procedures Used in Nuclear Power Plants," NUREG/CR-1368, May 1980.

[5] "Human Engineering Guidelines for Use in Preparing Emergency Operating Procedures for Nuclear Power Plants," NUREG/CR-1999, April 1981.

[6] "Secretary Pena Terminates Brookhaven Contract," Department of Energy Press Release, May 1, 1997.

[7] The materials in this chapter pertaining to the Malcom Baldridge Law and the Award are taken from the Department of Commerce web site (http://www.quality.nist.gov).

[8] DOE Standard, *Writers Guide for Technical Procedures,* DOE-STD-1029-92, Dec. 1992.

[9] This figure is adapted from Kay Inaba, "Guidelines for Instructions and Procedures to Support Commercial Products," draft standard of the Human Factors Society, April 15, 1997.

[10] *Ibid.*

15

Resumes
Realizing the Rhetoric of Personal Advocacy

We have saved discussion of resumes for the last chapter for three reasons: 1) Developing resumes correctly and effectively may represent the ultimate demonstration of the principles we have been examining throughout this text. The ability to write an effective resume is a tangible and very personalized display of analyzing audience, defining primary and secondary purposes, tailoring information selection and design, creating and maintaining a purposeful argument, and communicating with style. 2) Learning to create resumes reinforces a message reiterated numerous times in this text: Templates are no substitute for thoughtful analysis. Communication students can appreciate how the lessons of effective business communication contribute to assisting them in differentiating themselves from other candidates. 3) Resumes put a decidedly personal face on business communication—yours!

Envisioning future application of writing principles may be difficult for some students, but almost no one has difficulty in envisioning what job or which job title they intend to pursue (in the near or not-too-distant future). Equally clear—to everyone currently in business or seeking to join the corporate world—is the relevance the resume has in the pursuit of job and job title. Therefore, an examination of resume writing, including looking at some inappropriate shortcuts, provides both an appropriate ending to the text and a practical beginning in mastering the art, the discipline, and the methods of effective business communication.

The career-long importance of resumes

The limitations of empirically based strategies

The limitations of stylistic prescriptions

- Length
- Organization
- Design
- Language

Creating the effective resume

- Developing the comparative inventory
- Responding to the opportunity
- Completing the picture
- Refining the messages
- Defining the design
- Double-checking the product
- Drafting the cover letter

Resumes—the lessons

THE CAREER-LONG IMPORTANCE OF RESUMES

Many a personnel administrator, recruiter, college placement officer, and manager have maintained that the resume is the most important document you may ever write. Few people doubt the resume has a particular significance in the life of every professional. However, while we would not contest the idea that the resume is certainly an important document, we strongly disagree with the perspective that writing resumes is a single, intense exercise.

More correctly, your resume**s** are among the most important document**s** you will ever write. The distinction here is important. If, as many have suggested, the resume is largely a one-time or infrequently completed action, then perhaps it is a unique specialty item with little in common with other genres we have examined. As such, it might be reduced to a simple formulaic construction, which, in turn, might best be subcontracted to a "resume writer"—mechanical or human.[1]

In business, the resume is really a document type that demands regular preparation (revision or creation). And, like business letters and proposals, resumes demand reasoned, disciplined, and customized consideration of the fundamental principles we have been learning: audience, purpose, information selection, organization, argument, and style. Attempting to minimize the demands that resumes make on business professionals is a sure means of producing documents that don't work for you, and, as a consequence, don't get the job for you. To appreciate this communication challenge, let's begin by understanding why every professional—student through senior executive—must remain prepared to write an effective resume.

Most business professionals will write a number of resumes. At the onset of our careers, we write resumes to try to land that critical first position or, more precisely, to land the interview. Once beyond this hurdle and employed, we will find additional opportunities to rely on resumes to assist in climbing the corporate ladder and when participating in corporate proposals and marketing.

Professionals today can be expected to go through a succession of jobs, moving among corporations to gain experience and opportunity. Traveling this highway relies on the same diligent effort needed to secure our first professional position. Each move is a kind of corporate dance, with the hopeful candidate trying—by means of a resume—to entice a prospective new partner.

Even if we find the one corporation in which to invest a large portion of our working career, we will still likely need periodically to update and reissue our resumes. At least three circumstances necessitate this activity. The first is when pursuing promotions. Corporations—especially diverse corporations with complex, distributed operations—are no longer able to maintain a full, daily appreciation of the credentials of every member of the staff. As we mature in our jobs, we experience changes in our credentials, in training and education, in corporate perspective, and in leadership and managerial ability. Each of these dimensions may be a vital ingredient in our preparation for a new job or a new job title. No single database or artificial intelligence system has the ability—beyond the superficial level—to align all these constantly changing personal attributes with current and projected corporate vacancies. Instead, to identify suitable candidates, corporations employ a variety of internal reassignment programs to identify candidates. These systems generally expect and rely on evaluation of resumes.

The second corporate use of resumes is to support efforts to market the company or land new work. As was discussed when we examined preparation of business proposals, a key differentiating factor among proposals is the experience and expertise of the proposal team members. If you rise within the company to a point where your skills are vital for securing new work, your resume becomes part of the corporate arsenal, a tool that will be brought out and will require updating as often as the enterprise and business needs dictate. The third use for resumes within the corporation is for routine response to Human Resource information requests. Periodically, every corporation updates its personnel files. Typically, this activity is done by requesting employees to submit resumes.

Regardless of which of these circumstances we are in—recent graduate, potential transfer, upwardly oriented, or, simply, respondent to an information request—the competition to get the break, to get the interview, to get the promotion, to get noticed is perhaps the greatest single competition we enter. In many cases, the competition is open to everyone—the qualified, the semi-qualified, and the poorly qualified. The competition is open to those who live in the immediate vicinity of the job and those who live on the other side of the globe. The competition is open to those who learn of the vacancy through friends, through published advertisements, via Internet announcements, and from headhunters.

Major American corporations such as AT&T or IBM may receive over 1 million resumes a year. During the peak recruiting periods from November to April, even modestly sized corporations may receive an average of 1000 resumes a week.[2] To assume that a single document prepared only once in our career is a suitable representation of our credentials—especially when potentially prepared by a software package or resume service—is patently unreasonable. A simple acknowledgment of the lessons learned about audience, purpose, and application of facts should discourage us from this conclusion. Further, these principles also suggest why formulaic approaches to resume writing—even those based on empirical research—have only limited value to us. To fully appreciate how resume writing benefits from the lessons we have been studying, let's begin with an overview of the formulaic strategies that are often advocated.

THE LIMITATIONS OF EMPIRICALLY BASED STRATEGIES

Studies on almost every aspect of resume production have been conducted, including examining such features as whether personnel managers prefer receiving resumes by mail or by hand.[3] By far the most studied feature is content. Since the late 1960s, various studies have sought to analyze what should and shouldn't be in a resume. Analyses have been conducted to assess the perspectives of Human Resource Managers, corporate executives, personnel administrators, and college guidance counselors. One of the earliest analyses, which summarized guidance provided in the 14 years from 1969 to 1983, concluded the answer was contained in the lists of *do's* and *don't's* summarized in Table 15.1. [4]

TABLE

15.1 BASIC SUMMARY OF EARLY GUIDANCE ON RESUME CONTENT

Resume Content for Inclusion (1969–1983)	Resume Content for Exclusion (1969–1983)
1. Name, Address, Phone	1. Educational Qualifications
2. Professional Objective	2. High School Performance, Ranking
3. Educational Qualifications	—high school activities
—institution	—high school transcripts
—dates of degree	3. College Transcripts
—degree received	4. Employment History
4. Employment History	—supervisors' names
—prior work experience	—company addresses
—previous employers	5. General Information
—job title and description	—professional society activity
—dates of employment	6. Personal Information
—military experience	—personality/background statements, height/weight/race, religion, gender spouse's occupation/willingness to relocate/picture
5. General Information	7. Draft Status
—awards	8. References (to be made available on request)
—professional memberships	
6. Personal Information	
—personal requirements	
—hobbies/outside interests	
—any physical limitations	

At first glance, Table 15.1 appears to provide a sufficient foundation upon which to begin work on our resume. Based on this table, we know to include basic information about ourselves, what we hope to accomplish or gain in the assignment, our essential work experience, and a few insights about ourselves. Yet, before we entrust our future to these lists, several questions need to be answered: Is there consensus on the conclusions of this study? How do I make use of the empirical research? Should I place my trust in these suggestions, and, if I do, how do I go forward?

To get a sense of whether consensus exists, let's compare a number of surveys. Table 15.2 compares the recommendations regarding the single issue of what to include about our education. To add balance and perspective, the table includes recommendations from a variety of sources and from surveys conducted in five different years.[5]

Even a cursory comparison of the survey data points up the fact that there are few areas about which there is consensus. Although we could conduct a statistical analysis of alignment among the scores, a more immediate interpretation is evident. Almost every decision about what to include on the resume is left up to us. Should we put in information about our college activities and scholarships? Should we put in information about our school ranking or grade point average? The answer appears to be—maybe.

TABLE 15.2 PERCENTAGES OF RESPONDENTS FAVORING INCLUSION OF INFORMATION

Educational Information	Years*				
	1984	1989**	1991***	1994	1997
School Name	98	100		99	90
Years Attended		83		84	
Rank/GPA	97	91	85	77	68
Major	95	99	100		92
Minor	65	81		76	72
Specific Courses or Grades	56				55
Transcripts	21				45
Activities and Scholarships	78	91	93	82	80
Year of Graduation	84			89	90
High School Attended	30				38
High School Performance	11			29	43
High School Activities	15			23	39

* Data has been normalized; blanks indicate no data available.
** Survey only included items cited as important by at least 62% of the respondents.
*** Survey only listed items cited as important by at least 68% of the respondents.

Moreover, a similar issue is evident regarding what to omit. For example, the surveys tend to agree that information about our high school is of minimal importance. Even the most fundamental information, the name of our high school, draws the support of only 30–38% of the respondents. The conclusion, therefore, appears to be to leave out all reference to high school. Class President, class valedictorian—leave it out! We think most class valedictorians would think otherwise. While we might concede that most people don't achieve this level of accomplishment in high school and therefore may not see this particular dilemma as relevant, there are still other reasons why an average student might want, just as seriously, to reconsider the survey guidance.

Would it be beneficial, for instance, to include the name of your high school if it had the reputation for producing the highest number of National Merit Scholarship winners several years in a row, if it had a reputation for producing great talent (let's say in music, sports, or science), or even if it afforded the kind of name recognition that might catch the eye of a potential recruiter or corporate personnel manager? In much of the northeast, for example, New York City schools such as Stuyvesant High School and Brooklyn Tech raise the same kinds of positive associations in the minds of recruiters as do the names of many prestigious colleges. We need to use some other measure to decide whether particular information should be included.

The issue at hand is not the integrity of the research, but the simple truth that while empirical research may have statistical relevance, it cannot provide personal pertinence. If your purpose is to distinguish yourself from the crowd, why would you defer your judgment to a statistical sampling of the crowd? It's your resume; you need a sounder basis than statistical relevancy to reach the decision on how to communicate who you are. To make this point more emphatically, let's isolate just those categories of information that one survey clearly delineates as appropriate or inappropriate for inclusion on our resume (Table 15.3). [6]

We now get a very clear—if not very helpful—picture of what information needs to be omitted. Omit all our high school information as well as the information already disallowed according to federal discrimination law (e.g., discussion of age, race, religion, or health). Looking at the other side of the coin is equally unsatisfying. Can we construct a meaningful vision of our professional credentials from the elements suggested for inclusion? Will a brief overview of

---

TABLE

15.3 WHAT'S KEPT AND WHAT'S DISCARDED: ONE PERSPECTIVE

Kept Items	Discarded Items
Degree	High school grades
Academic majors	Courses in minor
Educational institution	List of all courses
Description of jobs related to position sought	High school courses
Dates of employment	High schools attended
Phone number	Class rank
Address	Physical/health status
	Date of birth
	Personal information
	(e.g., marital status/dependents/height/race)

who we are and what we've been doing be sufficient to land that next job or interview? Following this advice, our potential new employer would know where we live, how to get in touch with us, and some limited information about our work background. That potential employer wouldn't know much else, probably couldn't discern what about us merits an interview, and, almost certainly, wouldn't invest the time and money to find out.

Imagining the thousands of competitors with whom we entered the race for this job or promotion, are we really sure this strategy of relying on the empirical analyses will keep us in the running, let alone put us in first place? Equally critical, if we decide to entrust our careers to this research, which specific set of recommendations do we follow? As Table 15.2 has already made evident, there are lots of conflicting proposals. Furthermore, assessing how well these typical recommendations met the expectations of personnel administrators, one extensive survey concluded that the majority of published guidance has extremely limited applicability: "Instructions and advice given in resume writing books may not be appropriate . . . . Several of the items . . . recommended for inclusion on resumes were considered relatively unimportant by the personnel administrators." Moreover, "personnel professionals did not prefer the resume formats in the ways discussed by the resume writing sources." [7]

It's not that these surveys are not asking the right questions or asking them of the wrong people, but the surveys are simply confirming that there is no single, homogeneous group in the corporate world that has reached consensus on how best to assess resumes. Personnel professionals may have titles in common and share similar responsibilities, but that doesn't mean they will react similarly. Each job, each business, and each personnel professional is different. Business circumstances, as well as the professional's preferences, affect hiring decisions. Equally important, every candidate is a distinct individual representing a unique history that may not best be captured using predefined categories.

Contrary to the impressions that may be raised by the commonly repeated assertions about what should and shouldn't be done in resumes, there are no national consensus standards governing the style or design of resumes. Although we can quantitatively and qualitatively analyze empirical data, a survey of preferred contents is just a survey, not a prescription for writing or a predictor of success. This is why, ultimately, it is our ability to apply the principles we have been examining that will make the difference between getting the interview, landing the job, or receiving the polite "we'll keep your information on file" response.

THE LIMITATIONS OF STYLISTIC PRESCRIPTIONS

Where content formulas won't serve as an alternative to disciplined application of the art of professional communication, often we are invited to rely on simple stylistic prescriptions and on resume templates. While many rules and preparation strategies have been advocated, we'll profile a few of the more popular themes: prescriptions about length, organization, design, and language.

LENGTH

There appears to be almost unanimity on the issue of just how long a resume should be. Based on some rather questionable estimates of how long, on average, reviewers spend with each resume, resumes are expected to be one, or, at most, two pages. At one end of the time-allotment spectrum are suggestions that the candidate has as little as 10 seconds to make an impression on the reviewer.[8] In contrast to this 10-second dash, other studies allow the resume anywhere from 30 seconds to 3 minutes to make your case.[9]

Three minutes (180 seconds) is actually a lot of time. Pick up an average city newspaper and begin reading the first page. In the first 30 seconds, you will have sufficient time to take in the banner headlines, scan a number of images, and probably read at least the introductory paragraph of one of the main stories. By the end of the first 2 minutes, you will have had time to read a complete story. By the end of 3 minutes, you've probably already left the cover page and headed for the stories inside. Still intimidated by the time constraints? Well, you shouldn't be. This conclusion is especially true since the time your resume receives—whether 10 seconds or 3 minutes—is not premeasured or preordained as we might be led to believe by the various studies.

The time you get is a function of how well your resume engages the reader. The reason why most resumes get a cursory glance is that they have failed to do their jobs. That job entails communicating an intrinsic value to the reader, a sense that the reader will benefit by reading a few moments longer or a little bit closer. Having been personally involved in hundreds of hiring actions, we can tell you that the poor resume—the one that doesn't make its case—is discarded almost instantaneously, perhaps in fewer than 10 seconds. The resume that makes its case is examined closely, a perusal that may easily exceed the supposed upper limit of 180 seconds.

Any attempt to frighten writers by suggesting mere seconds will be devoted to their resumes has greatly mischaracterized the situation. To explain why time limitations, as reported, are not accurate, let's put the situation into context.

You are a middle manager for XYZ corporation. It's a pleasant Monday morning. The sun is shining. A stack of unreturned phone messages sits in front of you, your secretary has scheduled two more meetings on top of the three already on the calendar, and you have a presentation to make to the executive board at 4 P.M. Yet, you turn your attention to the five dozen or so resumes just delivered to you via the company mail service. With everything else swirling around you, you're reading resumes. Why? Precisely because everything is swirling!

It's not because you like to pass your time daydreaming about other people's credentials, but you need *help*. You already defined, argued about, and secured the funding to staff your organization with new talent. To the harried manager, getting necessary help is a major priority. Therefore, when you stop to view this corporate drama from the hiring manager's perspective or from Human Resource's perspective, you understand that evaluators want your resume to give them reason to screen you **in,** not screen you out![10] They treat evaluation of resumes every bit as (and often more) seriously than most resume writers. They know precisely the importance of getting someone into the company as well as the consequences if they choose unwisely. They are eager to find someone to help with the work and the commitments. The corporate evaluator is not likely to dismiss resumes that effectively represent potential candidates, even the marginally prepared candidate, on a 10-second assessment.

So, what is the right length for the resume? As one nationwide sampling of middle management, hiring officials, and college recruiters reported, one-third of the respondents indicated the resume's length should be determined by substance (Table 15.4).[11] Substance, not statistics, must govern the writing process.

TABLE

| 15.4 | **PREFERRED LENGTH OF RESUMES** |

Preference	Percentage of National Respondents
No longer than one page	24
No longer than two pages	42
Determined by information	33

Yet, we do not want to leave the impression that resumes, therefore, can be any length. While many executive or CEO resumes often run to four pages, the best length is, in fact, one to three pages, but not as an accommodation to reading speed. The length should be one to three pages for two reasons: convention and restraint.

Convention plays heavily in business. Evaluators have a set idea what a resume is supposed to be. Accordingly, they may be generally unprepared (or unwilling) to accept a document that clearly lies outside the boundaries of what they have been conditioned to expect. The difference between a resume that may be a bit outside the norm but is still acceptable and one where lack of convention jeopardizes the resume's reception can be illustrated if we return momentarily to our discussion about what items should be included on the resume.

Although Tables 15.1 and 15.3 made evident that there is no consensus regarding inclusion of references, that does not mean there are not strong opinions on the subject. Yet, even among those evaluators who prefer to have the references included, only 1% believed that not having references constituted grounds for rejecting the resume.[12] Violating the evaluator's particular preference did not cast the resume in a sufficiently negative light to warrant its dismissal.

In comparison, the multipage resume (four or more pages) is readily discernable within a stack of resumes that tend to be primarily one- to two-pages long. Here, forced to make time-dependent decisions, the evaluator may feel imposed upon by the author. The elicited response will probably not favorably dispose the evaluator to the resume or its author. In part, the evaluator may interpret inappropriate length as a demonstration that the author lacks critical communication (and editing) skills.

This perception is tied to the second reason why a resume should be in the range of one to three pages. Used effectively, three pages should provide sufficient space to prove—precisely and substantively—that you're the one for the job. If you cannot make the case, it is not a matter of insufficient space, but poor analysis, poor information selection, and poor design (all of which we will take up shortly in this chapter). Your resume needs to reflect the proper restraint—the ability to create a cogent, compelling, and concise case for you.

For each resume and each time you redo your resume, length should be a response to audience, purpose, and circumstance, not the reflection of artificial determinations about what's a good length and what's a bad length. The same principles need to apply to decisions about organization of the document.

ORGANIZATION

Two types of resumes are commonly described: the chronological and the functional. As one would infer, the chronological organization presents information in sequential history, generally beginning with the most recent education or experience and then proceeding in sequence through all the elements in that section of the resume. This organization structure tends to emphasize the where and when of your history. In contrast, the functional organization arranges materials according to areas of competence, emphasizing accomplishments over specific experience.

The basic rationale advocated for choosing one organizational structure over the other involves what we might refer to as the 3 C's: convention, completeness, and continuity:

1. Convention—The studies point to a preference for the chronological.

2. Completeness— Functional organization may be an easier means of masking gaps (periods of your history when the activities are entirely irrelevant or potentially embarrassing).

3. Continuity—Organizational decisions may be based on whether your goal is to remain within your current discipline or to move to an entirely new career path. Changing jobs within the same field of expertise is best promoted by the chronological format; making the shift from one profession to another is best served, so the argument goes, by a functional organization.[13]

As typically presented, this advice presents the resume author with an "either/or" decision—to proceed with a chronological resume or with a functional resume. The problem is, like page-length guidelines, the dilemma is artificial.

The writer need not—and should not—start off with a question of which organizational strategy to select. That conclusion resolves itself in the course of developing the resume. If there is a choice, it is not between chronological and functional; the choice is between an "open resume" and a "targeted resume." With an open resume, you do not so much have a specific job in mind as you do a profession or an industry. You point in a general direction rather than at a particular target. For example, if you are completing a degree in accounting but have not pinpointed a particular job of interest to you, you will draft a resume profiling those qualities you feel you have in common with accountants as a class; once drafted, the same resume will be sent to all prospective employers.

If, in contrast, you have been attracted to a specific vacancy, you should prepare a targeted resume. Your strategy will factor in the specific position demands, using the attributes common to the profession or industry to establish the context. This multilevel approach allows you to achieve a more precise alignment with the articulated expectations of the particular vacancy. The more targeted the effort, the more precise the response.

To illustrate targeted and open resumes, let's create a hypothetical situation that we will return to periodically throughout the remainder of this chapter. Assume yourself to be the manager of planning and production at Wilbur Company. Your business has an established reputation as a leader in products used in transporting horses: vans, trailers, chutes, portable pens. Your primary customer base is made up of moderately sized quarter-horse farms, as opposed to the casual horse owner or the thoroughbred community. You operate by putting together project teams to develop, market, and commercialize each of your product lines, and have recently advertised a position in the trade publications for a product developer (Figure 15.1). You are receptive to bringing in someone at either a senior or an associate's level, based on their credentials. After sorting through the resumes you received, you have narrowed the field to three applicants.

The first resume is from John who is nearing completion of his undergraduate education in marketing. John has little experience, but his course work in a very intensive program at a highly reputable university has convinced him that he'd enjoy the challenge of product development and commercialization. He wants to join a company actively engaged in producing new products. He is not particularly finicky about which company and was advised by the Career Counseling Office to send a resume to the Wilbur Company as one of three dozen places he is contacting. He had not even seen the Wilbur Company advertisement when he placed his resume in the mail.

The second resume is Jennifer's. She has a mature work history and has learned through extensive experience that she really has a talent for market development and commercialization. Since graduating from college, she has worked exclusively in the furniture industry. During her career, she has worked in most of the activities involved in product development. She knows almost nothing about the transportation or equestrian industries, but saw your ad and decided to apply.

Gary is the third applicant you have selected for further consideration. Gary has a science degree and has worked most of his life in some capacity around animals. His family owns and races quarter horses, and he has firsthand knowledge of the complete line of Wilbur products. Unbeknownst to you, the job was mentioned to him by one of your salespeople who thought Gary would be a natural fit in the new position you created. Although he never really thought about product development before and has never studied marketing, economics, or business administration, Gary figured that this might be a chance to put all his interests and experience to work.

In this instance, the preparation of a targeted or an open resume will be a matter of how each of the candidates sees the opportunities. Without concerning ourselves for now with precisely what the three applicants will say or how they might present it, we can anticipate how each candidate envisions the opportunity and what approach to winning each will take. John sees Wilbur Company, in general, as illustrative of all product development enterprises; he will attempt to show how his recent studies are more significant than expertise or experience with a certain product line or industry. Jennifer sees product development and commercialization as subsets of a business strategy; her approach will be to show how general commercialization experience is the key to success at Wilbur Company.

FIGURE 15.1

The Wilbur
Company
Advertisement

> **Product Planner Needed**
>
> The Wilbur Company, the most respected name in quarter-horse transportation and transportation accessories (chutes, lifts, portable pens), is looking for someone with experience in developing and bringing new product lines to market and repositioning existing product lines. Must be creative, willing to meet the clients head on, able to respond to a quickly growing market. B.A in Marketing or Management. Certification by the American Marketing Association preferred. Knowledge of equestrian industry a plus.
>
> Salary commensurate with experience. Send resume to HR Department, Wilbur Company.

Gary, on the other hand, sees the opportunity as a chance to reorient the sequencing of product development, to let it unfold from the customer's perspective. He will be inclined to assert that his unique appreciation of the product line and its uses will allow him to reinvigorate the product development and "repositioning" logic (though he is uncertain what that means) and thereby to increase the marketability of Wilbur Company products.

To use the terms we have introduced, John has elected to use an open structure; Jennifer and Gary have each selected the targeted approach. As this example illustrates, the fundamental organizational question is not whether the structure should be chronological or functional, but how the information can best be organized to support and communicate precisely the messages you intend. While there should be organizational consistency within each of the resume sections (e.g., experience, education), the document's overall structure, like that of all effective documents, is responsive to convention, but determined by purpose and audience.

We will return to John, Jennifer, and Gary shortly when we address the matter of how to prepare resumes correctly. For now, let's look at two last stylistic prescriptions: design and language.

DESIGN

In much the same way that the empirical strategists argue for specific inclusions or exclusions and for severe limitations on length, so most recommendations steer vehemently away from almost all design considerations beyond the conventional block structure. Almost all deviations from tradition are likely to be dismissed as gimmicks.

To put this advice against the nonstandard format into proper context, let's consider three levels of what are generally categorized as gimmickry: 1) the "notice me at all costs" approaches, 2) the "I want to have something more than text" camp, and 3) the nontraditional resume. The first two levels are clearly questionable (but still have application within certain limits); the third level, the nontraditional design, in contrast, is often worthy of encouragement.

The "notice me at all costs" is a risky venture for even the most talented and creative writers and artisans. Many absurd approaches have been used in the name of getting noticed. One anecdote related in *Forbes* magazine should be sufficient to suggest the extremes used. An executive recruiter was in the process of filling the position of sales and promotion director at a major department store. One day a messenger delivered to him a mannequin's arm and leg; accompanying the limbs was an anonymous note: "I'd give an arm and a leg to have the position of sales and promotion director." Two more deliveries followed. The next day, the mannequin's head arrived. The accompanying note read: "I'm losing my head over this job." And, on the third day, the mannequin's torso was delivered. This note, which also revealed the identity of the mysterious candidate, implored: "I'd put my body and soul into this work." The mannequin got the individual noticed, but it didn't get him an interview.[14] The moral might be that even a dummy can be noticed, but it's the effective resume that lands the interview.

That doesn't necessarily mean that being creative is bad. Reiterating a principle we have stressed throughout this text, the author of the *Forbes* article concludes: "The key to pulling off an offbeat resume is knowing your audience."[15] In addition to knowing the audience, the key to an offbeat resume is very simple: Use it only if you intend your primary message to be that you are a creative spirit not encumbered by convention. The man who sent the mannequin, while certainly creative, not only badly misread his audience, but he also starkly announced that he did not understand the scope of responsibility of a sales and promotion director. The job description did not ask for unpredictability, a trait that—if exercised at an inappropriate moment—might jeopardize not only his own career but also that of the manager who hired him. As the mannequin sender found out too late, the unfettered creative impulse is not a particularly strong selling point.

At the second level of gimmickry are the more modest attempts to get noticed. Here again, the probability of success is a function of alignment between strategy and message. A common error in this category is mistaking cute for effective. Resumes transformed into baseball cards, wanted posters, portraits with the family, and strained images of dynamic professionals at work may—the first time the approach is used—communicate a sense of novelty and playfulness. Yet, even when not dismissed as hackneyed, the approach may still be sending a message in conflict with your intended plan.

Sending the embellished resume just to distinguish it from the crowd may do more damage than good. The lack of attention to convention—a lack of "rhetorical alignment" as one author calls it—may earn your resume an early dismissal.[16] Further, this lack of alignment may cause the resume to exclude itself on the basis of technical grounds. If you're applying, for instance, for a production job, a multimedia format may be putting your resume at risk because the evaluator doesn't have a VCR or the necessary software immediately available. If forced to expend inordinate attention or energy on your resume, the evaluator will, more than likely, simply move on to the next candidate in the stack.

A subset of multimedia resumes may, however, have limited application when used effectively. They work well when the message 1) is about your technical facility with electronic publishing technology; 2) is used to demonstrate a specific multimedia interest of value to the employer, or 3) is necessary to represent the dynamic elements of research and experience that cannot be translated well into a few sentences displayed in simple block form.

Recognizing that there is some applicability among gimmicky resumes leads to the third category, the nontraditional design. Nontraditional, when deferential to convention and attentive to audience and purpose, can create a proper balance of creativity, humility, and individuality. This is particularly true when nontraditional is synonymous with adapting organization, language, and design to support the message.

Examined closely, the argument against the nontraditional resume stems from an overly enthusiastic defense of the unadorned, unembellished block structure sustained by most resume templates. Stated in its purest form, the argument maintains that "employers are buying abilities and skills, not artwork."[17] This reasoning, however, sets up another false dilemma—that design is anathema to clarity of message. In this absolute stance, even the most elemental of design deviations raises suspicion: "Unconventional, gimmicky resumes can win attention, but they rarely win an interview or land the job. Some applicants go to the expense of printing their resumes on expensive paper, in two colors, have the text typeset, and adding their picture in the corner."[18] Can quality paper and effective presentation really be detrimental to your resume? Should we really not vigorously pursue quality of design or presentation? While sending a mannequin through the mail may signal a rash unpredictability, sending a design-dead resume may send an equally damaging message: that you don't have the interest or enthusiasm to do more than the minimum to express your unique qualifications for the position.

Fundamental design features that purposely reflect a mature style, effectively control the pace, and also promote and communicate the intended message are worthwhile and necessary investments whether publishing business proposals, making presentations to the Board of Directors, or creating a resume to represent yourself to prospective new employers. Use of such basic design elements as white space, headings, changes in type size and font, shading, and positioning are all essential ingredients in transforming the executive's initial cursory glance into active interest and, ultimately, into an invitation to an interview. Yet, before we get to assembling a resume, let's look at one final set of stylistic prescriptions.

LANGUAGE

While adhering to the conservative advice on design, resumes are often coaxed into bending into linguistic contortions in order to balance individuality and convention. Epitomizing the unnatural balancing act, one author offers the cryptic mandate to "keep the resume detailed but general."[19] In less cryptic terms, the guidance is generally framed in the form of two injunctions: avoid jargon and use active and precise wording. Let's consider the implications these two mandates have on writing an effective resume.

JARGON. Jargon is in the eye, or rather the ear, of the beholder. The resume writer needs to recognize and differentiate between jargon and language that is used for precision or to control pace. If, for example, we return to our three prospective product planners for the Wilbur Company, we might arrive at three different perspectives on jargon.

John, our graduate-to-be, has been extensively steeped in the newest methods, technologies, and theories of product development, marketing, and commercialization. He is quite conversant in the language. What elements of his new vocabulary are likely to speak effectively to the majority of those marketing personnel who will receive his resume—the language of academia or the language of industry? How much of an academic terminology, for instance, may someone at Wilbur Company be comfortable with? At the same time, can John, who is essentially substituting his academic knowledge for experience, risk not relying heavily on the vernacular of the university to ensure his expertise is evident? The challenge John faces is that, although references to "transformational leadership," "econometric modeling," and "psychographic segmentation" may be the music of the new age corporations on his list, these same terms may be exactly the kind of jargon that will earn John's resume a quick trip to the trash at Wilbur Company.

When we turn to Jennifer, we see a different language challenge. Since Jennifer is venturing outside the domain of the furniture industry, she may need to "recalibrate" herself, gain a sense of how product development language may have distinctly different and specialized meanings and connotations in one industry versus another. While not exactly an exercise in industrial anthropology, Jennifer must recognize that vocabulary common to the furniture industry may not be the language of horses and transportation. Just try to imagine the similarities and differences in interpretation that may arise when someone in the furniture industry and someone in the business of transporting horses engage in a discussion of ergonomics.

Gary's intention to position himself simultaneously as an insider (someone who knows horses and Wilbur Company products) and yet an outsider (someone not married to any standard methodology or theory of marketing and product development) may experience entirely different language challenges than those faced by either John or Jennifer. Gary clearly needs to introduce language on his resume that draws associations to his practical knowledge while maintaining that he has the necessary credentials to handle the technical dimensions of the job. Gary may assert his working knowledge of gooseneck trailers, slant loads, and transport licensing, but he also must incorporate the language of commercialization. In this case, jargon may not be that single, atonal sound that registers negatively in our brain, but the prolonged note that by its very persistence elicits a negative response from us.

Here are three different candidates with three different challenges regarding jargon. Simply calling for each candidate to "eschew jargon" (the common rallying cry) would not, most likely, be beneficial. Various factors, including purpose, structure, as well as audience, influence the determination of what is and is not jargon. If anything, we might conclude that following stylistic prescription has a strong probability of leading to trouble. The more formulaic the orientation, the more probable authors will wander unwittingly into the world of jargon.

ACTIVE AND PRECISE WORDING. The same imprecision in the guidance on jargon is evident in the enthusiastic advice on active and precise wording. However, this imprecision about precision has potentially more serious consequences for us than does a momentary slide into jargon. Sometimes the message to us is to sell hard; at other times, "precision" and "accuracy" are used as euphemistic warnings about misrepresenting ourselves. As part of the advice on how to be "general but specific," that same author advises clients to "Be accurate. Describe your skills, qualifications, and experience as positively as possible without exaggerations or misstatements."[20] Distilling our life work into a page or two is difficult enough; coupling that responsibility with the idea of an anonymous reader and with a deafening drumbeat insisting you jump out from among the pile within 10 seconds can add up to a formula for ethical misjudgments.

This possibility of misrepresentation has not escaped the notice of reviewers, who must now proceed with a degree of suspicion about what each candidate claims and how accurate those claims might be. As one author explained in *Inc.*, a highly respected business publication, executives need to master the "art of reading between the lines of a resume." Balancing an eagerness to fill a vacancy with the need to fill it with a suitable candidate forces employers to be wary: "The pressure to hire right the first time is greater than ever, but so is the pressure for employees to sell themselves to an employer. At the center of the stormy process is the resume, a highly variable, enigmatic, and often fallacious document."[21]

Crossing the boundary between accurate resume and "fallacious document" is unintentionally encouraged by popular recommendations that we express accomplishments by leaning "heavily on power words": "Don't just list where you worked and what you did . . . . Tell how well you did each one. In doing so, lean heavily on 'power words': 'designed,' 'directed,' 'created,' 'caused,' 'saved,' etc. And rather than using the tired '. . . am seeking a challenging position,' say '. . . am seeking a challenging opportunity that will permit me to apply my computer expertise in areas where computing and information resources are not realizing their full potential.'"[13] Responding to this challenge, the average computer programmer being addressed in the quoted material—or any resume writer for that matter—may begin metamorphosing proven, documentable capabilities into exaggerated claims, inflating fundamental skills into overstated abilities to tame errant business processes. It is, as this example suggests, a short walk from emphasis to exaggeration, and from there to misrepresentation.

The web of power words can be equally entrapping regardless of our facility with language. One talented editor, for example, felt that referencing her editorial responsibilities was not eliciting the type of enthusiastic response she was desiring from prospective employers. Their short-term disinterest, she reasoned, could be reversed if she promoted herself more powerfully. Accurate statements about having "edited critical business reports for senior executives" overnight became statements like "led the development of plans critical to the strategic reengineering of the company." The change worked; prospective employers became interested. This interest culminated in embarrassing moments when—having been flown at the company's expense to some distant corporate headquarters—she was forced to explain the real nature of her accomplishments and contributions.

This drive for accuracy and precision might take a lesson from the sciences. In science, there is a very distinct and very well-understood difference between accuracy and precision. If we shoot a series of arrows and every one misses the target, we have 100% precision. Every arrow did precisely the same thing. At the same time, we have 0% accuracy; we didn't get a single bullseye. In resume writing, as in shooting arrows, we should avoid being precise at the expense of being accurate. Our language and explanations must be both 100% precise and 100% accurate—a valid and truthful representation of who we are, what we've accomplished, and how that experience is relevant.

Whether using statistical studies to define the content, the length, the structure, the design, or the language, we are relying on averages to tell us what to do in particular. Turning our futures over to averages or trudging along in deeply worn pathways may not be in our best interest. We need to refine and customize the insights gained through the research and surveys on resume writing. We must apply an integrated process that allows us to balance conventions and individuality in the preparation of an honest and effective resume.

CREATING THE EFFECTIVE RESUME

Defining a truly effective process for constructing quality resumes, as shown in Figure 15.2, entails six primary components:

1. Developing a comparative analysis
2. Responding to the opportunity
3. Refining the message
4. Defining the design
5. Double-checking the product
6. Drafting the cover letter

In this section, we will look at the first five process steps that contribute to the development and production of the resume. In the next section, we will look at the final component, the cover letter. Throughout this section, we will refer to a Resume Development Form, a single form that can be used to record and integrate the four components of the development process (Figure 15.3).

FIGURE 15.2

The Resume
Development
Process

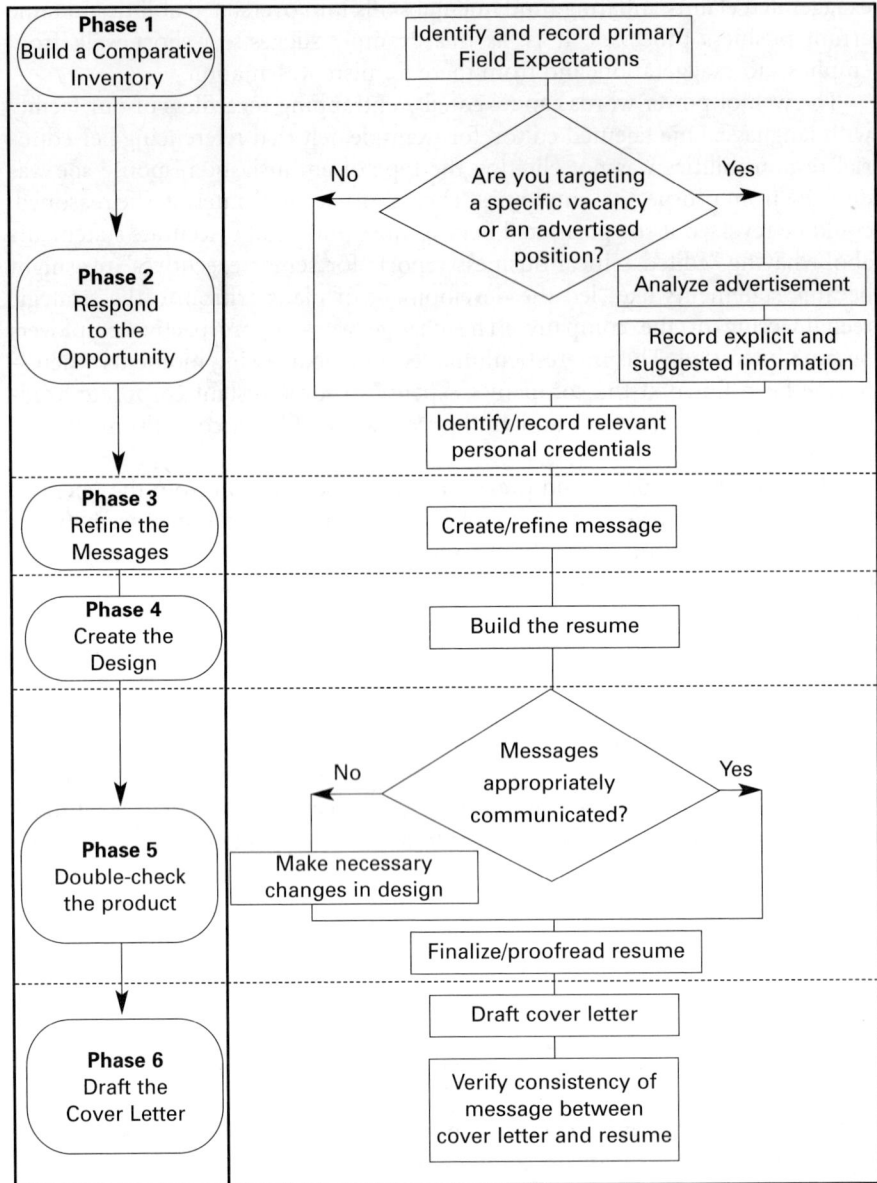

Phase 1
Build a Comparative
Inventory

Identify and record primary
Field Expectations

No / Yes — Are you targeting a specific vacancy or an advertised position?

Phase 2
Respond
to the
Opportunity

Analyze advertisement

Record explicit and
suggested information

Identify/record relevant
personal credentials

Phase 3
Refine the
Messages

Create/refine message

Phase 4
Create the
Design

Build the resume

No / Yes — Messages appropriately communicated?

Phase 5
Double-check
the product

Make necessary
changes in design

Finalize/proofread resume

Draft cover letter

Phase 6
Draft the
Cover Letter

Verify consistency of
message between
cover letter and resume

DEVELOPING THE COMPARATIVE INVENTORY

Almost all advice on resume writing suggests that your work should begin with an inventory of your talents and experience. This autobiographical writing is to be accomplished by closeting yourself away, recollecting, and recording every facet of your education and career: "Take time to research what you've done . . . . Go through your notes and files, because you won't remember everything when you sit down to write your resume . . . . You'll be surprised . . . . Some little project that you spent five minutes on and forgot may be worth a line or two on your resume, and that's the thing that gets you the interview."[23] Unfortunately, this direction encapsulates the two major problems with the autobiographical inventory:

FIGURE 15.3

Resume Development Form			
	Field Expectations	Job-Specific Expectations	Personal Credentials
Education			
Experience			
Attributes			
Intended Messages			

1) Considering our preceding discussion on the ethics of precision and accuracy, we should be troubled by the suggestion that 5 minutes of work (that you need to be prompted to remember, no less) is deserving of "a line or two" on your resume. 2) Writing about yourself, for yourself, is not why a resume is written.

We don't need to amplify our discussion on ethics, but the question of audience is central to the resume process. Perhaps we can best isolate the principal difficulty by considering an article devoted to this inventory process. In "Organizing the Writing of Your Resume," the author establishes a 12-step process, seven steps of which relate to the production of the autobiographical inventory (Figure 15.4). As a lead-in to organization, we are encouraged in this article to create a comprehensive personal inventory: school, education, activities, honors, references.[24]

While this process of deep introspection is certain to produce a large volume of information, it is not certain whether the information will be valuable or relevant. Is the purpose clear, focused, or even established? Unless you are intending to frame and mount the resume in your office so you can admire your accomplishments, you need instead to start, not end, with the goal or job in mind.

THE RATIONALE FOR THE COMPARATIVE INVENTORY. Rather than looking inward, the resume process should begin with a comparative analysis, one that assesses your qualifications against those needed to do the job. Even before you examine a particular announcement or vacancy, you need to have a clear appreciation of the field, discipline, or profession you are considering. This comparative inventory, a kind of personalized benchmarking exercise, begins by completing the "Field Expectations" column of the Resume Preparation Form, a reflection of the typical educational requirements, experience, and attributes of the job or profession.

FIGURE 15.4

Typical Depiction of the Resume Writing Process

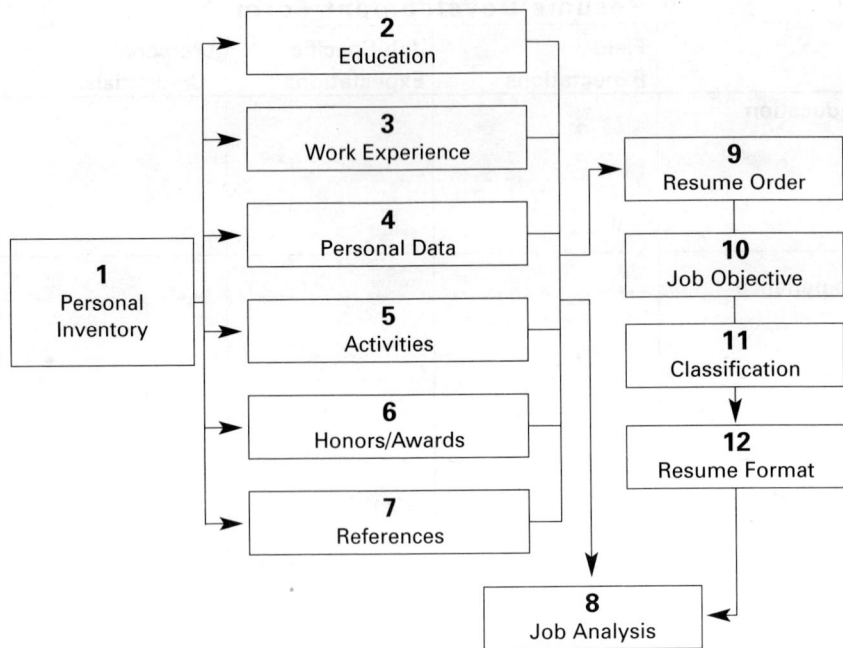

1 Personal Inventory	**2** Education	**9** Resume Order
	3 Work Experience	**10** Job Objective
	4 Personal Data	**11** Classification
	5 Activities	**12** Resume Format
	6 Honors/Awards	
	7 References	
	8 Job Analysis	

Source: Reprinted with permission of the Association for Business Communication.

The reasons for beginning the assessment with identification of the field expectations are threefold. First, whether you are taking an open or targeted approach, you need to select and orchestrate the information on your resume. Identifying what needs to be on the resume and how best to represent it begins by putting a face on your reader. As if foreshadowing the interview, you need to start thinking about what that person is going to expect of you and what standards (education, experience, attributes) will be used as the measuring stick.

Second, the most important thing for you to learn before writing your resume is what you don't know. While the typical autobiographical inventory process results in an unsorted laundry list of your life's work, you need to concern yourself with precisely what it will take to get you in the door. If you have trouble characterizing the fundamental expectations for the job, you need to do more research before beginning your writing. This research can also provide a secondary benefit—allowing you to gain a fuller perspective on whether the career or job you are seeking is right for your personality and temperament. As people learn, often too late, a paycheck is important, but may not prove to be the most important consideration when it comes to a career choice. It is equally important to align your personality with the organization and work environment as it is to align your skills and interests with the work.[25]

The third reason for beginning with an assessment of field expectations is to avoid a common mistake—overlooking a critical dimension of the position. When the focus is wrong, resumes may not respond to the major, most obvious, expectations of the job. Consider, for instance, the following situation.

You are completing your doctoral studies and plan to pursue a position on the faculty of a prestigious university. In the quiet moments between course work and the constant drafting and redrafting of your dissertation, you start putting your resume together. What are the major areas you need to address on your resume? You develop your inventory of research projects, publications, and grants you have received. Armed with this detail and assisted by the guidance from recent surveys explaining what subjects to include, you draft your resume. Just before placing the package in the mail, you ask yourself if any areas might have been overlooked.

In fact, like the majority of resumes assessed in one survey, you have made a critical omission. The two major elements of a university job include research and teaching; the resume mentioned above has only addressed the first of these two aspects of the job. It is hard to imagine, using this illustration, that anyone who plans to make a career at the university would have the least difficulty recognizing that both categories must be addressed in the resume. Yet, in one very revealing study of the cover letters and resumes of approximately 150 doctoral candidates and Ph.D.s applying for a position of Assistant Professor of Cognitive Psychology, 78% of the respondents did not include a teaching statement; nine of the respondents did not even mention teaching despite being coaxed in the advertisement that "the successful candidate will demonstrate excellent teaching potential." [26]

If a majority of people with advanced degrees, even when explicitly solicited to respond to a particular and well-known expectation, can overlook a category as obvious and significant as teaching, is it unreasonable to speculate that this type of categorical omission is extremely common? Add in the fact that many job announcements do not make expectations as explicit as in our illustration and the probability of omitting some critical dimension goes up dramatically.

Equally important, returning to our focus on audience and purpose, we could infer from this study that a good share of respondents did not address teaching responsibilities because they preferred to concentrate on their scholarly strengths and interests. But this problem is precisely the point we are emphasizing. Seventy-eight percent of these candidates may have written what they wanted to write, but not what the school wanted to read. The resolution, or rather the avoidance, of this problem is to do a comparative inventory, to begin your process by completing the "Field Expectations" in order to ensure your focus is correctly assigned to your audience and your purpose.

DEFINING THE FIELD EXPECTATIONS. The Field Expectations represent a basic threshold of requirements, the minimum credentials needed to obtain and do that job. The amount of detail should reflect what you believe is sufficient to capture the primary expectations of the job.

The top row of the Resume Development Form begins with education expected. What is the expected educational preparation? What degrees are expected? Is there a specific course of instruction or training? Are there certifications or licenses required? Can experience be substituted for education? For example, in some engineering disciplines, an engineering degree may be necessary; in other engineering jobs, some combination of training and experience may be sufficient.

In the middle row, identify the minimal experience needed to be considered a serious candidate. The responses in this row can vary greatly depending on the complexity and the seniority of the position. Entry-level positions rarely demand much experience; the hiring managers may be receptive to a demonstration of any work experience, related to the position or not. In contrast, senior positions will generally expect significant experience—often looking for both length and breadth of experience. For example, a senior Human Resources position may not only expect 10 or more years of experience, but may specify experience in compensation, policy, labor relations, recruiting, pension administration, and benefits.

The bottom row focuses on attributes, the "personality" of the corporation or profession. To understand this concept, consider the commonly portrayed perceptions of the used-car salesman. Almost immediately, an image comes to mind. That image is most likely not the face of a specific person, but rather the personality of the profession. While we might immediately entertain the negative attributes of this profession, the owner of a car lot has distinctly different attributes in mind when hiring. To the owner, an accomplished salesperson must be outgoing, a good closer, and a good reader of people. Each of these qualities is an attribute; collectively, they represent the personality of the profession.

The work that is done sets the tangible, functional skill requirements. The way in which the work is done reflects the personality of the profession, what one consulting firm calls the "will do" criteria, "intangible attitudes and attributes, such as ability to work under pressure or being detail oriented." [27]

When considering attributes, try not to get mired in such undifferentiating aspects as "good with people." Instead, try to identify attributes of potential interest to a hiring manager. One method of identifying attributes is to examine what constitutes success in a particular field, how individual performance is measured. Using Table 15.5, for instance, you might gauge which values are most relevant to achieving solid performance in your selected industry or job.

A second strategy may be to identify what commonalities exist among the leaders in the field. An interesting example of this second approach is demonstrated in a list compiled by Peter Drucker, a well-known management theorist. Explaining the attributes of effective corporate leadership, Drucker cited the common attributes of the people whose accomplishments routinely warrant

TABLE

15.5   ATTRIBUTES OF PROFESSIONAL PERFORMANCE

	Discipline	Achievement	Potential
Proficiency	**Knowledge, Skills:** How much an individual knows with respect to his or her area of expertise	**Productivity:** How much an individual accomplishes	**Innovation:** How much improvement an individual is likely to make in the area of proficiency
Functionality	**Pertinence:** How relevant an individual's expertise is to the goals of the company	**Closure:** How successful an individual is in completing work	**Adaptability:** How readily an individual responds to change
Credibility	**Customer Orientation:** How customers perceive the individual	**Contribution:** How much the individual adds to the capabilities and skills base	**Independence:** How customers and co-workers regard the individual's reliability in handling work with minimal direction or oversight

PART 2   THE METHODS OF PROFESSIONAL COMMUNICATION

their inclusion in high school history textbooks (Table 15.6).[28] Similar strategies can be used to characterize the attributes common to any profession—even the transportation specialists employed by Wilbur Company, our fictitious manufacturer of equestrian transportation equipment (Figure 15.5).

RESPONDING TO THE OPPORTUNITY

With the "Field Expectations" column completed, it is time to complete the remaining columns. If you are developing an open resume, you will not have Job-Specific Expectations. Therefore, the next step will be completing the "Personal Credentials" column. To do so, you proceed, row by row, as you did when filling in the Field Expectations, detailing what in your background corresponds to the specifics you recorded in the "Field Expectations" column. In some instances, your qualifications may be in the form of one-to-one correspondences with the expectations. In other instances, you may have multiple items that in total represent the qualification. Two important factors need to be considered when filling

15.6 ATTRIBUTES OF FAMOUS PEOPLE IN HISTORY BOOKS

• Committed	• Creative/Quirky/Peculiar
• Determined to make a difference	• Rebels
• Focused	• Irreverent/Disrespectful
• Passionate	• Masters of improvisation
• Risk seekers	• Asked forgiveness after the fact
• Ahead of their time	• Bone honest
• Impatient	• Flawed
• "Tuned into" followers' needs and aspirations	• Damned good at what they do

Field Expectations	
Education	B.A., Marketing/Management
Experience	Project Management Developing Product Strategies Generating Concepts Evaluating Ideas Conducting Analyses Developing Products Defining and Conducting Testing Marketing Plans and Ideas Commercialization
Attributes	Outgoing Excellent Communications Project Leadership Self-starter Good Initiative

FIGURE 15.5

Completed "Field Expectations" Column

out this column: What do you have in your background that is immediately pertinent and responsive to the field expectation? How well, how completely, do the items you list demonstrate your preparations to do the job? Both these factors will be vitally important when you begin the design phase. Using John, our hypothetical job candidate who is relying on an open resume, Figure 15.6 illustrates how the completed comparative inventory might look.

If, however, you are preparing a targeted resume, then the "Job-Specific Expectations" column is completed before completing the "Personal Credentials" column. (The goal is to have the most complete picture of the job before you in order to allow you to identify your most relevant credentials.)

To complete the "Job-Specific Expectations" column, you need to assess the particulars provided in the job description or announcement. Job-specific information includes both explicit information and suggested information. Explicit information includes details you can transcribe directly from the notice onto the Resume Development Form. Suggested information includes the additional expectations implied by the notice. To better understand these categories of expectations, let's examine two ads, one from a local newspaper for an entry- to mid-level professional, and one from a nationally placed ad soliciting an experienced senior manager.

The local ad (Figure 15.7) describes a moderately defined position. If we were completing the Resume Development Form, we would capture such specific information as job location, specific job, degree, and years of experience needed. Beyond these specifics, the ad suggests several additional expectations valuable to record:

FIGURE 15.6

Resume
Development
Form: John's
Personal
Credentials

		Resume Development Form		
		Field Expectations	Job-Specific Expectations	Personal Credentials
Education		B.A., Marketing/ Management		B.A., Marketing
Experience		Project Management Developing Product Strategies Generating Concepts Evaluating Ideas Conducting Analyses Developing Products Defining and Conducting Testing Marketing Plans and Ideas Commercialization		College Internship College Courses
Attributes		Outgoing Excellent Communications Project Leadership Self-starter Good Initiative		Creative Outgoing

1. Education: The jack-of-all-trades implications of the job description, coupled with open-ended terms such as *computer literacy* suggest you will be running a small office (perhaps a one-person office). Educational elements suggested include any on-the-job training you might have had and any nondegree training you may have received in such areas as office management and business administration.

2. Experience: The call for a "business expert" gives great latitude regarding what types of experience may be acceptable. This business expertise, read in conjunction with the specific responsibilities, suggests a strong inclination to hire someone who has owned or managed a small business. Yet, even if you haven't owned your own business, you can highlight projects that might suggest an equivalent breadth of responsibility and accountability.

3. Attributes: Looking at the job's consulting and coordinating demands suggests that the hiring managers are partial to applicants who stress a collegial spirit, a results-oriented approach, strong personal commitment, and initiative.

The second ad (Figure 15.8), a nationally advertised position for an electronics engineer, reflects a similar balance of specific and suggested information. In this case, the prospective candidate knows many facets that should be highlighted on the resume: degree (Ph.D. or equivalent); specific educational emphases (mathematics and electrical engineering); specific relevant experience; familiarity with military contexts and protocols; a clean security and police record (the need to obtain a secret clearance); and no professional conflicts with the assignment (the need to satisfy the Ethics in Government Act).

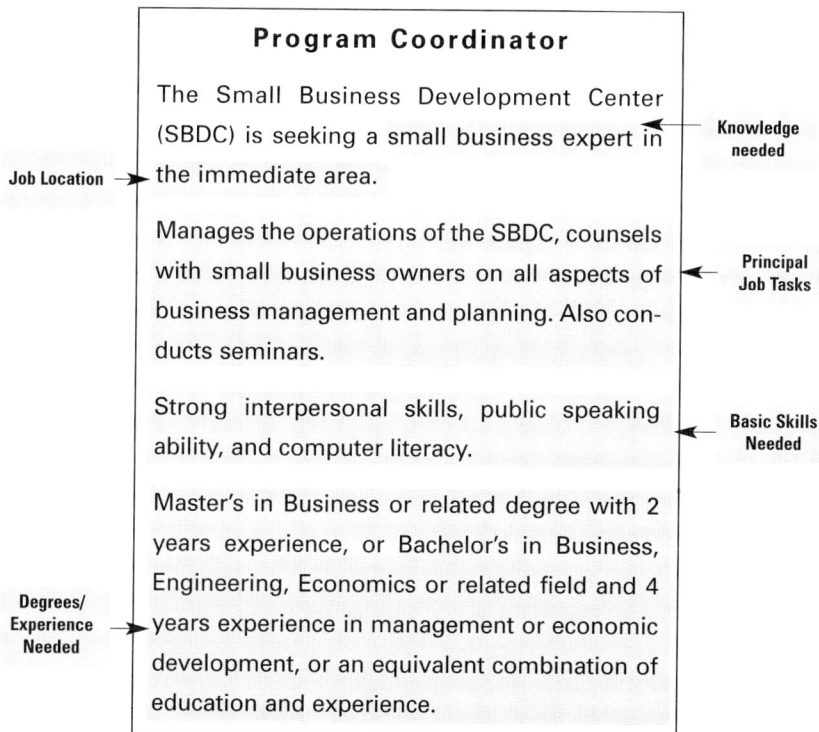

FIGURE 15.7

A Local Job Advertisement

Program Coordinator

Job Location → The Small Business Development Center (SBDC) is seeking a small business expert in the immediate area. ← Knowledge needed

Manages the operations of the SBDC, counsels with small business owners on all aspects of business management and planning. Also conducts seminars. ← Principal Job Tasks

Strong interpersonal skills, public speaking ability, and computer literacy. ← Basic Skills Needed

Degrees/ Experience Needed → Master's in Business or related degree with 2 years experience, or Bachelor's in Business, Engineering, Economics or related field and 4 years experience in management or economic development, or an equivalent combination of education and experience.

FIGURE 15.8

A Nationally
Advertised Position

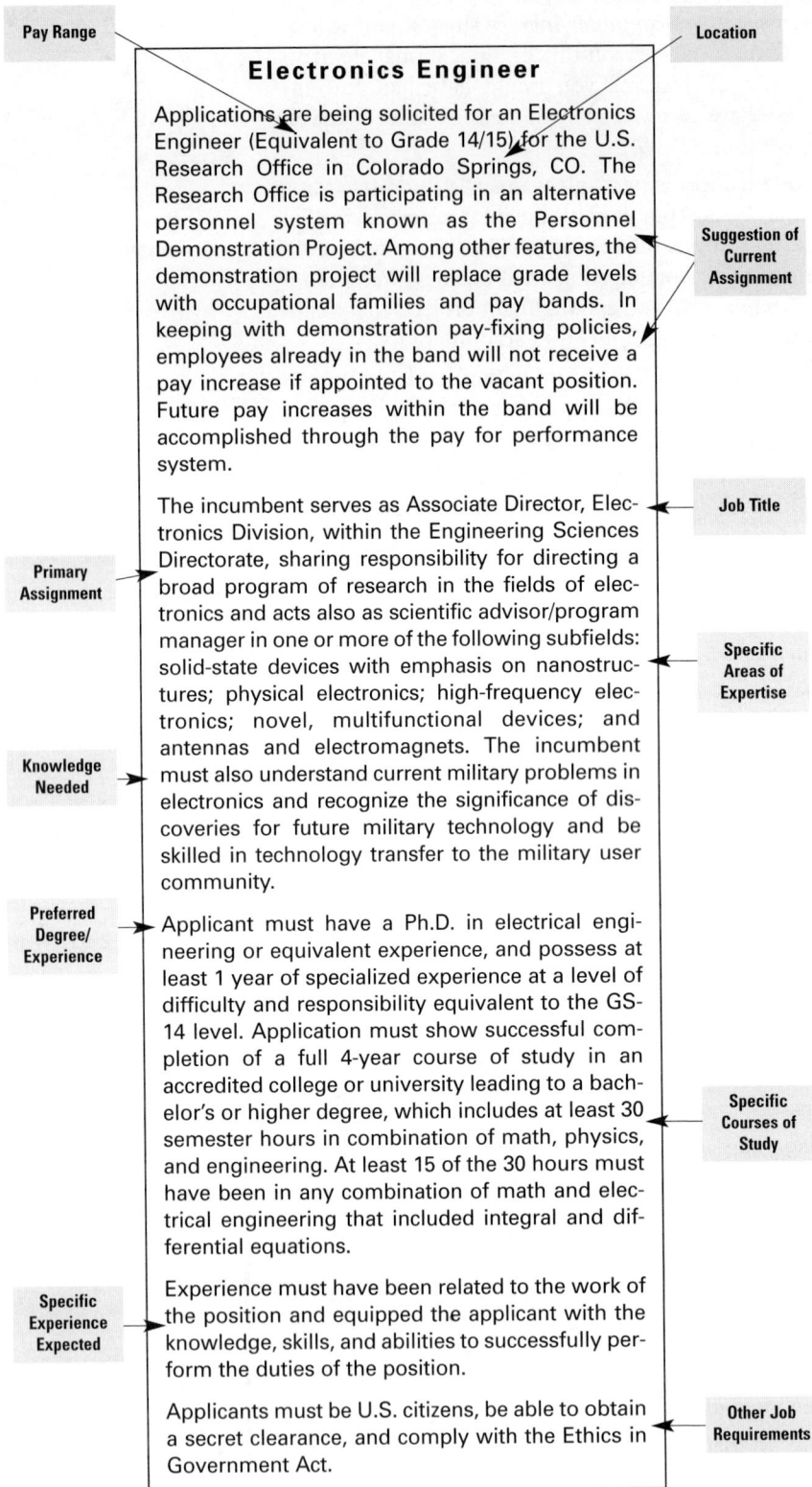

Pay Range

Location

Electronics Engineer

Applications are being solicited for an Electronics Engineer (Equivalent to Grade 14/15) for the U.S. Research Office in Colorado Springs, CO. The Research Office is participating in an alternative personnel system known as the Personnel Demonstration Project. Among other features, the demonstration project will replace grade levels with occupational families and pay bands. In keeping with demonstration pay-fixing policies, employees already in the band will not receive a pay increase if appointed to the vacant position. Future pay increases within the band will be accomplished through the pay for performance system.

Suggestion of Current Assignment

The incumbent serves as Associate Director, Electronics Division, within the Engineering Sciences Directorate, sharing responsibility for directing a broad program of research in the fields of electronics and acts also as scientific advisor/program manager in one or more of the following subfields: solid-state devices with emphasis on nanostructures; physical electronics; high-frequency electronics; novel, multifunctional devices; and antennas and electromagnets. The incumbent must also understand current military problems in electronics and recognize the significance of discoveries for future military technology and be skilled in technology transfer to the military user community.

Job Title

Primary Assignment

Specific Areas of Expertise

Knowledge Needed

Preferred Degree/ Experience

Applicant must have a Ph.D. in electrical engineering or equivalent experience, and possess at least 1 year of specialized experience at a level of difficulty and responsibility equivalent to the GS-14 level. Application must show successful completion of a full 4-year course of study in an accredited college or university leading to a bachelor's or higher degree, which includes at least 30 semester hours in combination of math, physics, and engineering. At least 15 of the 30 hours must have been in any combination of math and electrical engineering that included integral and differential equations.

Specific Courses of Study

Specific Experience Expected

Experience must have been related to the work of the position and equipped the applicant with the knowledge, skills, and abilities to successfully perform the duties of the position.

Applicants must be U.S. citizens, be able to obtain a secret clearance, and comply with the Ethics in Government Act.

Other Job Requirements

As was true with our local advertisement, suggested credentials can also be readily assigned to each of the three job inventory rows on the Resume Development Form:

1. Education: The detailed list of research concentrations suggests skills needed represent not only doctoral studies but also postdoctoral work and on-the-job training. References to specific types of additional training received (for instance, workshops attended in conjunction with professional conferences), and with whom—assuming the provider's name is recognizable as an authority—should be included on the resume.

2. Experience: The lengthy discussion of pay and promotion structures, along with references to federal government salary grades, makes clear that a current or recent affiliation with the military (as a member of the armed forces, a consultant, or a contractor) is expected.

3. Attributes: In addition to the good character signaled by attention to ethical standards and security clearances, the position also demands flexibility and project management expertise. Flexibility is expected, as signaled by the need to relocate and the willingness to accept compensation through an "alternative personnel system." "Sharing responsibility for directing a broad program of research" further signals expectations of superior planning skills, organizational and fiscal management, communication, and coordination.

COMPLETING THE PICTURE

Using the insights we have gained, we can now return to the example we have been employing. Based on the information contained in the job announcement (Figure 15.1), we can complete the "Job-Specific Expectations" column in advance of applying to the Wilbur Company:

1. Education: In addition to a degree, the company is looking for certification.

2. Experience: Familiarity with both the horse business and the transportation industry is needed.

3. Attributes: The company wants an individual who is flexible, creative, and has initiative.

We can also fill in the " Personal Credentials" column for each of the candidates. Gaining the perspective provided by their completed forms, we get a clearer picture of where each candidate stands and how the candidates will need to concentrate their attentions. John's qualifications suggest a significant gap between credentials he possesses and what the company needs, a situation made worse because John's open approach did not even consider the specific needs of the Wilbur Company (Figure 15.9). In comparison, both Jennifer's and Gary's analyses have allowed them to put together responses that show strong qualifications for and alignment with the Wilbur Company expectations (Figures 15.10 and 15.11). With a clearer, more tangible knowledge of what the job entails and how the candidates stack up, we are now ready for a critical stage on the way to designing the resume—refining the messages.

FIGURE 15.9

John's
Development
Form for the
Wilbur Company
Position

Resume Development Form			
	Field Expectations	Job-Specific Expectations	Personal Credentials
Education	B.A., Marketing/ Management	B.A., M.A., Marketing or Management Certification by American Marketing Association preferred	B.A., Marketing
Experience	Project Management Developing Product Strategies Generating Concepts Evaluating Ideas Conducting Analyses Developing Products Defining and Conducting Testing Marketing Plans and Ideas Commercialization	Firsthand experience with all facets of product development from conception through marketing Specific experience with integrating product lines Familiarity with transportation or equestrian industry a plus	College Internship College Courses
Attributes	Outgoing Excellent Communications Project Leadership Self-starter Good Initiative	Want an individual with ideas and talent. Must be willing to go where the clients are. Must be flexible and willing to respond to a changing and exciting market	Creative Outgoing

FIGURE 15.10

Jennifer's
Development
Form for the
Wilbur Company
Position

Resume Development Form			
	Field Expectations	Job-Specific Expectations	Personal Credentials
Education	B.A., Marketing/ Management	B.A., M.A., Marketing or Management Certification by American Marketing Association preferred	B.A., Marketing Training at Merrill Marketing Academy Advanced project management class at Ahill Institute
Experience	Project Management Developing Product Strategies Generating Concepts Evaluating Ideas Conducting Analyses Developing Products Defining and Conducting Testing Marketing Plans and Ideas Commercialization	Firsthand experience with all facets of product development from conception through marketing Specific experience with integrating product lines Familiarity with transportation or equestrian industry a plus	5 years experience at Newcastle Furniture —developed individual bedroom items and suites Received a National Designer's Award 7 years as an assistant project developer at Gershwin's Furniture
Attributes	Outgoing Excellent Communications Project Leadership Self-starter Good Initiative	Want an individual with ideas and talent Must be willing to go where the clients are Must be flexible and willing to respond to a changing and exciting market	Won awards for design Started in-house training for design associates Set up showrooms in Newton, Ontario, and London, England

Resume Development Form			
	Field Expectations	**Job-Specific Expectations**	**Personal Credentials**
Education	B.A., Marketing/ Management	B.A., M.A., Marketing or Management Certification by American Marketing Association preferred	B.A., Animal Husbandry Veterinary Assistant's Program, Ucon Tech
Experience	Project Management Developing Product Strategies Generating Concepts Evaluating Ideas Conducting Analyses Developing Products Defining and Conducting Testing Marketing Plans and Ideas Commercialization	Firsthand experience with all facets of product development from conception through marketing Specific experience with integrating product lines Familiarity with transportation or equestrian industry a plus	Worked numerous assignments at Lancaster Farms Won steer-roping contests at Seattle Invitational National 4H winner/ quarterhorse category
Attributes	Outgoing Excellent Communications Project Leadership Self-starter Good Initiative	Want an individual with ideas and talent Must be willing to go where the clients are Must be flexible and willing to respond to a changing and exciting market	Know Wilbur products well Am a natural around horse people Am outgoing and eager Know what the horse people really need

FIGURE 15.11

Gary's Development Form for the Wilbur Company Position

REFINING THE MESSAGES

As we discussed in Chapter 1, business communications often have primary purposes supported by secondary purposes. The primary purpose of all resumes is the same—to make the assertion that you are the right person for the work, the job, or the position. The secondary purposes are to establish the themes and messages you want to list as the proof of your primary assertion.

John's secondary message is that the quality and recency of his academic training represents a potent tool for advancing Wilbur Company business. Jennifer is intending to persuade the Wilbur Company that practical knowledge of product development is more important than expertise within a particular market. Gary is attempting to demonstrate the value of his practitioner's perspective in promoting and expanding the Wilbur Company line of products.

Although the personal inventory establishes the platform, the specific architecture is a function of a designed message. As is often the case and as was demonstrated by our three candidates, the initial personal inventory is generally in great need of further definition and amplification. In some regards, the inventory does as much to identify weaknesses as it does to establish strengths. Your goal is to amplify strengths and offset, downplay, or compensate for shortcomings. In the case of our three candidates, John's lack of practical experience, Jennifer's lack of familiarity with the transportation industry, and Gary's lack of insight into the specific job duties of a product developer represent hurdles our candidates will need to address. If the candidates were to proceed without further assessment of the themes to employ, they might inadvertently highlight or call more attention to these shortcomings than to their strengths. That is why the final information added to the Resume Development Form is a statement of precisely what messages you intend to communicate.

For each of our candidates, the form has identified important secondary messages. Of the three forms, John's is the least helpful in this regard because he used an open approach. Yet, even in this circumstance, there is at least one message that will warrant consideration when we come to designing the resume: His coursework has provided preparation in all elements of product development and commercialization. He should use his resume to make these correspondences as transparent as possible.

Jennifer's form, in contrast, suggests four messages to be worked into the resume design: 1) Her credentials exceed the expectations implied by the Wilbur Company interest in preferred Certification by the American Marketing Association. Certification is generally called for to provide a kind of external validation of your credentials. In Jennifer's case, courses she has taken at a variety of management institutes and marketing seminars add up to an equivalent validation. 2) Her attributes are immediately compatible with the expressed corporate personality. She has specific examples that demonstrate her creativity, flexibility, initiative, and readiness to go where the customers are (her opening of national and international showrooms). 3) She has firsthand familiarity with all facets of product development. Though it is distributed among her three professional assignments, Jennifer has done all the jobs from conceptual design to commercialization. She needs to make sure these individual chapters of her work life add up to the clear story of her qualifications. 4) She has experience integrating product lines. The integrator's perspective should be highlighted, especially since her primary assertion is that it is in the company's interest to hire a generalist rather than a specialist in a particular product.

Gary's completed form suggests two principal messages: 1) He has the ability to sell. Gary not only knows the Wilbur Company line of products, but he also knows the typical Wilbur Company customer. He needs to use his resume to communicate his ability to move the products he develops. 2) Gary has peripheral training that may not have been considered previously when the Wilbur Company hired product developers—animal physiology. It's one thing to have been raised around horses; it is a different matter to say that you have formal training in animal husbandry and veterinary medicine. Both these messages should be used in the resume design to expand the theme of the original assertion that Gary knows the Wilbur Company product line. Gary has a unique message to share: While some candidates may know the products and some the customers, few are likely to know, as Gary does, the products and *all* the customers—both those who buy and those who use the Wilbur Company products. The opportunity suddenly has expanded appreciably for our candidates as a result of their efforts in completing the Resume Development Form. (Figure 15.12 shows the "Intended Message" row of the Resume Development Form as it would be completed by each of our candidates.)

As this step highlights, the resume needs to be seen not as a chronological representation of your life, but as an integrated line of argument. The resume preparation began with an implicit assertion that you are the best one for the job; the Resume Development Form helps ensure that you identify the avenues to make that argument clear, consistent, and unambiguous to your reader.

You have now completed the first three phases of the resume preparation process: building a comparative inventory, responding to the opportunity, and refining the messages. You are now ready to design and produce a resume that will specifically profile the points you need to make the sale.

FIGURE 15.12

Resume Development Form			
	Field Expectations	Job-Specific Expectations	Personal Credentials
Education	_____ _____	_____ _____	_____ _____
Experience	_____ _____	_____ _____	_____ _____
Attributes	_____ _____	_____ _____	_____ _____

Intended Messages:

John's Principal Messages

1. Course work prepares me for all elements of product development work.

Jennifer's Principal Messages

1. Credentials exceed American Marketing Association certification requirements.
2. Attributes perfectly aligned with Wilbur Company
3. Have experience with all elements of product development
4. Experience with product mixing and integration

Gary's Principal Messages

1. Have the right stuff to sell (products and customers)
2. Veterinary training could be beneficial

Intended Messages of the Three Candidates

DEFINING THE DESIGN

The design of the resume is already implicitly defined for you by the details on the Resume Development Form. You have all the information readily available about what is expected of you and what you have to offer. You have also refined the messages that you intend to communicate. Placing this information alongside what we now know about language, page length, organization, and style defines the primary design options. Production therefore becomes simply a matter of following through on the path you've already implicitly laid out for yourself.

As with earlier discussions of presentation of information (particularly in Chapter 4), we now align design, information, and message. Instead of a simple, fixed template, any number of devices (or combinations of devices) is available to create the fine balance of convention and individuality. To give you a small sampling (of options, not templates), Figures 15.13, 15.14, and 15.15 represent possible resume designs for each of our candidates. Each design is different; each is a customized reflection of targeting the individual's credentials and messages to the specific expectations of the job. Further illustrating our point that the designs can be appropriately customized, Jennifer's resume is two pages long, Gary's and John's are one page each.

Your choices, like those of our candidates, are defined, but not limited, by your responses and messages. The opportunity to have a first-class design—to speak your message effectively—is just a matter of taking that same energy used in completing the analyses and applying it to creating effective graphical representations, much as you did when developing formal presentations.

FIGURE 15.13 ◆ John's Completed Resume

Language implies John's interest in rapid advancement opportunity, but phrased to project a positive image on the corporation

Main sections separated by line

Education lists high school because of the school's suggestive name

Type faces used as symbolic reflections of the two distinct components of John's preparations

Providing the url invites employers to preview John's work & ability

Although the work itself is not relevant to the job John is after, this experience tells the employer at least two important things: 1) John will be a reliable worker, and 2) the full time employment which coincides with John's university studies shows he is extremely motivated

Personal information includes permanent & temporary addresses

Textbox with drop shadowing used to highlight the objective. Terms allow prospective employers broad latitude in determining how John's qualifications may fit their needs

John Malthus

Home Address
2221 Astoria Blvd.
Queens, New York
(212) 555-0488

School Address
169 Hendricks Ave.
Albany, New York
(518) 555-1895

CAREER OBJECTIVE: Looking for opportunity to use my training in design, marketing, and product development to assist a dynamic corporation in bringing new products to market.

EDUCATION: 1996 - 2000, B.A., Marketing, University of New York at Albany

1992-1996, High Scool of Art & Design, New York City

ACADEMIC PREPARATION:

Design
Product Design
Marketing Graphics
Elements of Design
Design Techniques

Development & Marketing
Marketing in Electronic Media
Marketing Research
Entrepeneurship
Marketing & Commercialization
Small Business Management

Designed & implemented e-commerce web site for local business as part of senior class project
(http://www.harbinger's books.com)

EXPERIENCE: Material Handler
University Parcel Service & Couriers, Albany, New York
Part Time April 1998 - July 1999; Full time August 1999 - Present

ACTIVITIES: Member, Student chapter, American Marketing Association
Volunteer, local youth hostel
Varsity footbal team junior and senior year

Career objective used because response is not to a specific job (open structure)

Headings done in bold face with small caps

Boxed off section highlights credentials

Detail articulates message of depth and balance of qualifications

Class internship used to draw practical linkage between design and marketing qualifications

Including these activities shows John is involved, well rounded, and energetic

---

FIGURE 15.14a ◆ Page 1 of Jennifer's Completed Resume

Jennifer's personal information is highlighted by using a larger, bold-faced type

Education listed in reverse chronological order to balance education & training

Bold type used to emphasize job title

Bulleted list emphases &, delineates items while adding white space for ease of reading

Items address intended messages

Language & specifics suggest transferability of expertise

Training coupled with education to allow Jennifer to respond to call for certification

Jennifer Williams
4 Moncrosse Lane
Winocca, Kentucky
(606) 555-1771

EDUCATION/TRAINING:

1979 - 1983, B.A., Marketing, Missouri State University
1987, Executive Training, Product Development, Merrill Academy
1990, Executive Training, Product Pricing Strategies, Merrill Academy
1992, Advanced Project Management, Ahill Institute of Management
1995 Marketing Design Techniques, American Marketing Association Seminar Series
1998, Advanced Project Management II, Ahill Institute of Management

Excellent academic & postgraduate credentials in product planning

EXPERIENCE: Senior Product Developer
Newcastle Home Furnishings Inc.
Lexington, Kentucky
June 1995 - Present

• Led teams that introduced four new lines of furniture in two years, the fastest development and production cycle in corporate history
• Introduced just-in-time manufacturing for new products
• Identified just-in-time locations for prime new distribution centers
• Set up new showrooms central to major American, Canadian, and British markets
• Established in-house design training, reducing corporate costs by an average of 15% for each new product line
• Co-authored the first ever Production Performance Improvement Plan with the company's Senior Vice President, defining strategic directions:
  —shorter machine runs   —more efficient setups
  —enhanced product flexibility —fewer setup parts
  —just-in-time manufacturing   —cellular manufacturing

Cost Reductions Achieved & Projected

Reductions in Production Time

Textbox with reversed image calls attention to and highlights Jennifer's educational message

Sans serif type (helvetica) offers stark contrast to typeface used in text (palatino)

Shaded lines used to separate major segments of the resume

Items begin with a precise and accurate verb explaining what Jennifer contributed to each activity

Graphs depict the explicit contributions Jennifer has made to this company

FIGURE 15.14b   Page 2 of Jennifer's Completed Resume

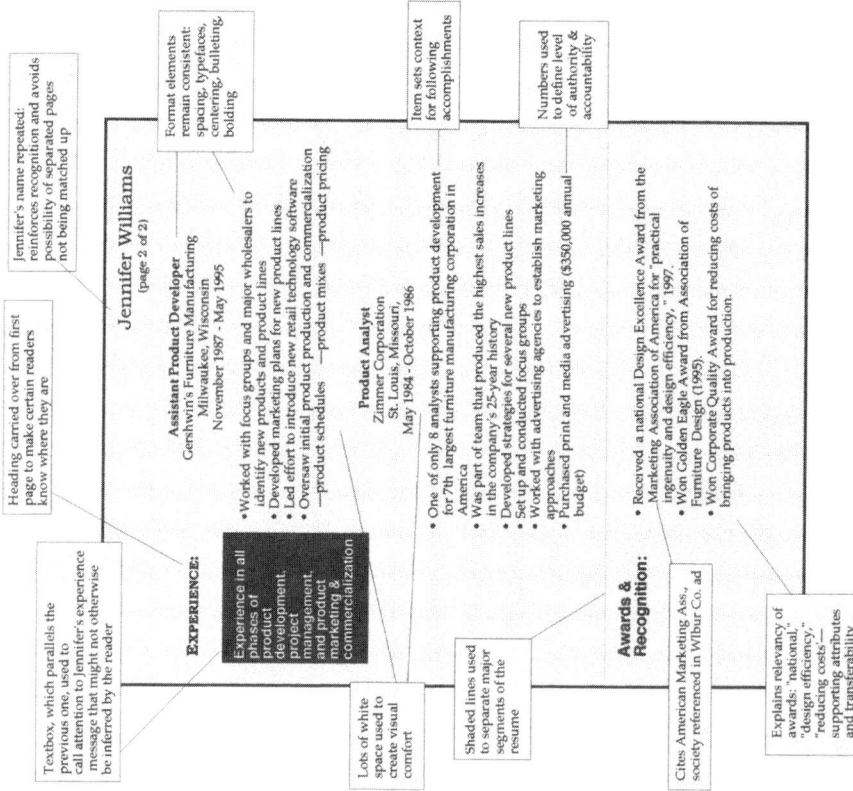

FIGURE 15.14b — Page 2 of Jennifer's Completed Resume

Annotations:

- Jennifer's name repeated: reinforces recognition and avoids possibility of separated pages not being matched up
- Format elements remain consistent: spacing, typefaces, centering, bulleting, bolding
- Heading carried over from first page to make certain readers know where they are
- Item sets context for following accomplishments
- Numbers used to define level of authority & accountability
- Textbox, which parallels the previous one, used to call attention to Jennifer's experience message that might not otherwise be inferred by the reader
- Lots of white space used to create visual comfort
- Shaded lines used to separate major segments of the resume
- Cites American Marketing Ass., society referenced in Wilbur Co. ad
- Explains relevancy of awards: "national," "design efficiency," "reducing costs"—supporting attributes and transferability

Resume content:

Jennifer Williams
(page 2 of 2)

EXPERIENCE:

Experience in all phases of product development, project management and product marketing & commercialization

Assistant Product Developer
Gershwin's Furniture Manufacturing
Milwaukee, Wisconsin
November 1987 - May 1995

- Worked with focus groups and major wholesalers to identify new products and product lines
- Developed marketing plans for new product lines
- Led effort to introduce new retail technology software
- Oversaw initial product production and commercialization —product schedules —product mixes —product pricing

Product Analyst
Zimmer Corporation
St. Louis, Missouri
May 1984 - October 1986

- One of only 8 analysts supporting product development for 7th largest furniture manufacturing corporation in America
- Was part of team that produced the highest sales increases in the company's 25-year history
- Developed strategies for several new product lines
- Set up and conducted focus groups
- Worked with advertising agencies to establish marketing approaches
- Purchased print and media advertising ($350,000 annual budget)

Awards & Recognition:

- Received a national Design Excellence Award from the Marketing Association of America for "practical ingenuity and design efficiency," 1997.
- Won Golden Eagle Award from Association of Furniture Design (1995).
- Won Corporate Quality Award for reducing costs of bringing products into production.

FIGURE 15.15   Gary's Completed Resume

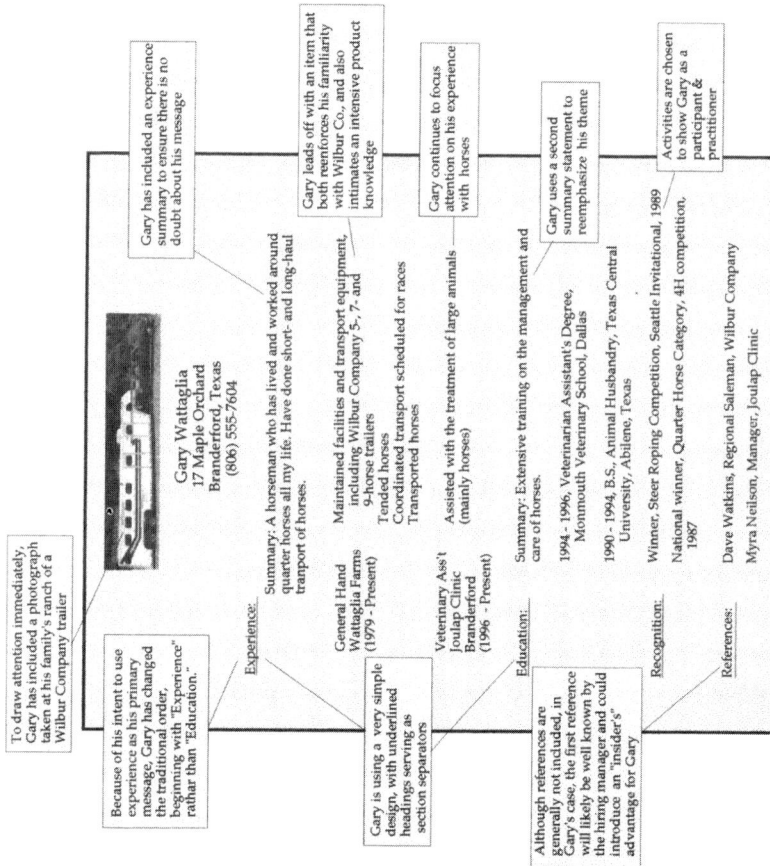

Annotations:

- To draw attention immediately, Gary has included a photograph taken at his family's ranch of a Wilbur Company trailer
- Gary has included an experience summary to ensure there is no doubt about his message
- Gary leads off with an item that both reinforces his familiarity with Wilbur Co., and also intimates an intensive product knowledge
- Gary continues to focus attention on his experience with horses
- Gary uses a second summary statement to reemphasize his theme
- Activities are chosen to show Gary as a participant & practitioner
- Because of his intent to use experience as his primary message, Gary has changed the traditional order, beginning with "Experience" rather than "Education."
- Gary is using a very simple design, with underlined headings serving as section separators
- Although references are generally not included, in Gary's case, the first reference will likely be well known by the hiring manager and could introduce an "insider's" advantage for Gary

Resume content:

Gary Wattaglia
17 Maple Orchard
Branderford, Texas
(806) 555-7604

Experience:

Summary: A horseman who has lived and worked around quarter horses all my life. Have done short- and long-haul tranport of horses.

General Hand
Wattaglia Farms
(1979 - Present)
Maintained facilities and transport equipment, including Wilbur Company 5-, 7- and 9-horse trailers
Tended horses
Coordinated transport scheduled for races
Transported horses

Veterinary Ass't
Joulap Clinic
Branderford
(1996 - Present)
Assisted with the treatment of large animals (mainly horses)

Education:

Summary: Extensive training on the management and care of horses.

1994 - 1996, Veterinarian Assistant's Degree, Monmouth Veterinary School, Dallas

1990 - 1994, B.S., Animal Husbandry, Texas Central University, Abilene, Texas

Recognition:

Winner, Steer Roping Competition, Seattle Invitational, 1989
National Winner, Quarter Horse Category, 4H competition, 1987

References:

Dave Watkins, Regional Saleman, Wilbur Company
Myra Neilson, Manager, Joulap Clinic

DOUBLE-CHECKING THE PRODUCT

The resume is now complete, and you're almost ready to put it in the mail. The last thing that needs to be done other than writing the cover letter is to double-check your product. There are no second chances when it comes to resumes. There's no boss who will send it back with comments or teams that will request you to submit it again with clarifications. Once the resume leaves your hands, it is all or nothing. That all-or-nothing condition demands that your resume be absolutely right the first time. To make certain it is right, we suggest use of a 10-step Resume Quality Control Checklist (Figure 15.16).

FIGURE 15.16

Resume Quality
Control Checklist

☐ 1. Is the resume complete?	Review the Resume Development Form to ensure no important information was accidentally omitted.
☐ 2. Is the content accurate?	Make certain that your word choices reflect precisely and accurately what you did and what your contributions were.
☐ 3. Does the resume establish an identity?	Determine if the resume makes clear not only what your experience is but also who you are as a person.
☐ 4. Does the resume "send" the right messages?	Review the messages you recorded; make certain each message is clearly made evident by the content, organization, and/or design.
☐ 5. Are the messages consistent?	Examine the resume as a whole; be sure to correct any suggestions of competing or ambiguous messages.
☐ 6. Is the resume attractive?	Stand back and look at your resume. Is the design appealing? If it doesn't catch your eye, consider other design ideas or formats.
☐ 7. Is the resume consistent with conventions?	Make certain you have maintained "rhetorical alignment" with the primary conventions.
☐ 8. Does it make you feel good about yourself?	The resume should give you a sense of pride. If you don't feel that pride, then something has either been left out or a message was not developed properly.
☐ 9. Have you checked the facts?	Make certain you have double-checked things like dates, addresses, and company names.
☐ 10. Have you done a quality check?	In addition to checking spelling and grammar, look at such items as alignment of lists, centering, etc.

DRAFTING THE COVER LETTER

For the most part, cover letters follow the same expectations as all business letters: same format, same organization, and same need to create a clear and consistent argument. The only additional requirement associated with cover letters is the need to compare the themes and arguments presented in the letter with those of the resume. This doesn't mean that your two documents mirror each other in detail, but they need to stay anchored to the same sets of themes and messages.

For example, think about the case we discussed earlier about graduate students who forgot to include discussion of teaching in their resumes. If one of those candidates had stressed teaching in the resume, the accompanying cover letter should echo that same theme. Conversely, if the resume concentrated on research to the exclusion of teaching, a cover letter that claimed a serious interest in teaching would create for the reviewer a certain suspicion about the author's veracity or sincerity.

If your cover letter introduces new or different messages from those of your resume, one of two actions is needed: either redesign the resume to align the themes or omit the new themes from the cover letter. Inconsistency between the cover letter and the resume is a signal that either something important has been omitted, or, worse, that the resume is somehow shading the truth. The opportunity to fix this problem—and perhaps rescue your credibility—exists up to the point when the resume has been mailed. At that point, like the editor we discussed, you may find more embarrassment than satisfaction.

RESUMES—THE LESSONS

Writing effective resumes is a chance to put all the art, all the skills, and all the discipline examined in the first half of this text into action for you. Mastering the communication challenges involves analyzing audiences, defining primary and secondary purposes, tailoring information selection and design, communicating with style, and developing an argument. Resume development also brings into play the artful integration of text and graphics, attention to pace, and a keen appreciation of the sounds that words make on paper. Equally important, writing effective resumes brings us full circle to a point we made in the Introduction: When it comes to professional communication, success comes not from following templates and checklists, but from the skill, confidence, and expertise that result from a thorough appreciation of the art, the method, and the discipline of professional communication.

EXERCISES

☐ Group

1. Four new candidates have come forward for the position of Product Developer at Wilbur Company. They all work for the company:

   a) Miguel—a bookkeeper with a degree in finance who has been studying marketing at night

   b) Linda—the Assistant Director of Human Resources

   c) Ryoko—the head of production line maintenance who has no degree but has 15 years of experience in manufacturing

   d) Jack—the salesperson who told Gary about the job

Divide into teams. Prepare a Resume Development Form for one of the four new candidates. (You can make up credentials you feel support your case.) Then discuss the completed forms with the class.

2. Divide into three teams. Using the Personal Credentials and Intended Messages already established, design a second resume for one of our three original candidates for the Wilbur Company position. Review the revised resumes with the class.

3. A friend of yours heard that you were studying how to write effective resumes. He is getting ready to graduate and asked you to comment on his resume (shown below). Divide into teams. Then complete the following:

a) Prepare a set of improvement recommendations.

b) Using the recommendations, prepare a revised resume and review it with the class.

Nathan David Thomas
1404 Wild Marsh Drive
Aiken, South Carolina
(208) 555-7575

Career Objective: To earn a professional position in the marketing field of a major corporation

Education: University of South Carolina-Aiken
Bachelor of Science in Business Administration/Marketing

Work Experience:

Woodhills Plantation, Augusta, Georgia
May 1997 - Present (part- time)
- Gained knowledge of public relations with members
- Cart attendant

Little Cove Country Club, Hilton Head, SC
Summer of 1996 (Part- time)
- It is recognized as one of the most prestigious golf courses in the state of SC
- Advanced my knowledge of public relations with members
- Cart attendant

Sweetwinds Country Club, Cloverville, SC
1994 - 1996 (Part- time)
- Pro-shop assistant and cart attendant
- Gained knowledge of sales
- Gained knowledge in use of cash register operations
- Advanced my knowledge of public relations with customers
- Worked for Master Professional, Mr. Dietrich Ossining

Activities: Volunteer four hours a week at the Peterson Rehabilitation Center (pediatrics)

References: Available upon request

☐ Individual

1. Prepare your own resume. At each of the stages below, review your progress with the class:

a) Completion of a comparative inventory (Field Expectations)

b) Inclusion of information from a specific job announcement (Job-Specific Expectations)

c) Completion of the "Personal Credentials" column

d) Refinement of Messages

e) Design and preparation of the actual resume

END NOTES

[1] See Kay Larocca, "Writing Resumes for Profit," *Home Office Computing,* Vol. 10, No. 4 (Apr. 1992), pp 32–33.

[2] Beverly Culwell-Block and Jean Anna Sellers, "Resume Content and Format—Do the Authorities Agree?" *The Bulletin of the Association for Business Communication,* Vol. 57, No. 4 (Dec. 1994), pp. 27–30.

[3] R.L Lorentz,. J.W. Carland, and J.C. Carland, "The Resume: What Value Is There in References?" *Journal of Technical Writing and Communication,* Vol. 23, No. 4 (1993), pp. 371–377.

[4] Kevin L Hutchinson, "Personnel Administrators' Preferences for Resume Content: A Survey and Review of Empirically Based Conclusions," *The Journal of Business Communication,* Vol. 21, No. 4 (1984), pp. 5–14.

[5] The 1984 survey is from Kevin L. Hutchinson, "Personnel Administrators' Preferences for Resume Content: A Survey and Review of Empirically Based Conclusions," *The Journal of Business Communication,* Vol. 21, No. 4 (1984), pp. 5–14. The 1997 data are from K. L Hutchinson, and D.S. Brefka, "Personnel Administrators' Preferences for Resume Content: Ten Years Later," *Business Communication Quarterly,* Vol. 60, No. 2 (June 1997), pp. 67–75. The three other surveys, respectively, are adapted from: Jules Harcourt and A.C. Krizan, "A Comparison of Resume Content Preferences of Fortune 500 Personnel Administrators and Business Communication Instructors," *The Journal of Business Communication,* Vol. 26, No. 2 (Spring 1989), pp. 177–190. Robert M. Schramm and R. N. Dortch, "An Analysis of Effective Resume Content, Format, and Appearance Based on College Recruiter Perceptions," *The Bulletin,* Vol. 54, No. 3 (Sept. 1991), pp. 18–23. M.A. Griffin and P.L. Anderson, "Resume Content," *Business Education Forum,* Vol. 48, No. 3 (Feb. 1994), pp. 11–14.

[6] Hutchinson and Brefka, "Personnel Administrators' Preferences for Resume Content: Ten Years Later."

[7] B.E. Weeg, "An Evaluation of the Resume Content Recommendations of Resume Writing Books," *The Reference Librarian,* No. 36 (1992) pp. 153–172.

[8] R. Greenly, "How to Write a Resume," *Technical Communication,* First Quarter (1993), pp. 42–48.

[9] See Culwell-Block and Sellers, "Resume Content and Format—Do the Authorities Agree?" J.C. Roderick and H.M. Jelley, "An Innovative Method for Teaching Resume Design," *The Bulletin of the Association for Business Communication,* Vol. 55, No. 2 (June 1992), pp. 1–4. J.S. Hornsby and B.N. Smith, "Resume Content: What Should Be Included and Excluded," *SAM Advanced Management Journal,* Vol. 60, No. 1 (Winter 1995), pp. 4–9.

[10] B. Smith, "How to Screen Resumes," *HR Focus,* Vol. 72, No. 1 (Jan. 1995), p. 24.

[11] Griffin and Anderson, "Resume Content."

[12] Lorentz, Carland, and Carland, "The Resume: What Value Is There in References?"

[13] See S. Hagevik, "What Kind of Resume Should I Choose?" *Journal of Environmental Health,* Vol. 60, No. 5 (Dec. 1997), pp. 35–36.

[14] L. R. Walbert, "A Foot in the Door," *Forbes,* Vol. 136 (Nov. 18, 1985), pp. 240–241.

[15] *Ibid.*

[16] Michael J. Hassett, "Teaching the Rhetoric of Document Design," *Business Communication Quarterly,* Vol. 59, No. 3 (Sept. 1996), pp. 65–67.

[17] R. Ryan, "21 Ways to Improve Your Resume," *Journal of Accountancy,* Vol. 180, No. 6 (Dec. 1995), pp. 83–86.

[18] Greenly, "How to Write a Resume."

[19] A. Bernar, "Use Your Resume to Rebuild Your Career," *EDN,* Vol. 37, No. 3A (Feb. 6, 1992) pp. S29–S30.

[20] Ryan, "21 Ways to Improve Your Resume."

[21] T. Lammers, "How to Read Between the Lines: Tactics for Evaluating a Resume," *Inc.,* Vol. 15, No. 3 (Mar. 1993) , pp. 105–107.

[22] Greenly, "How to Write a Resume."

[23] Bermar, "Use Your Resume to Build Your Career."

[24] P. Stanley Wiegand, "Organizing the Writing of Your Resume," *Bulletin of the Association for Business Communication,* Vol. 54, No. 3 (Sept. 1991), pp. 11–12.

[25] See D.L Plung, "Comprehending and Aligning Professionals and Publication Organizations," in *A Publications Management Source Book,* ed. O.J. Allen and L. Deming. Amityville, NY: Baywood Press, 1994, pp. 41–54.

[26] B. Perlman, J.C. Marxen, S. McFadden, and L. McCann, "Applicants for a Teaching Position Do Not Emphasize Teaching," *Teaching Psychology,* Vol. 23, No. 2 (Apr. 1996), pp. 103–104.

[27] B. Smith, "How to Screen Resumes."

[28] Peter Drucker, "Attributes of Those Who 'Made' the 10th Grade History Textbook," Fourth Annual Worldwide Lessons in Leadership Series, Nov. 17, 1999.

SUPPORTING INFORMATION, ILLUSTRATIONS, AND EXAMPLES

INTRODUCTION

MEDIA ADDRESSED IN BUSINESS AND TECHNICAL COMMUNICATION TEXTBOOKS

Communication Media	Business Communication Textbooks	Technical Communication Textbooks
Memos	9 of 9	5 of 5
Letters	9 of 9	5 of 5
Short Reports	9 of 9	5 of 5
Instructions	3 of 9	5 of 5
Procedures	7 of 9	5 of 5
Proposals	7 of 9	5 of 5
Progress Reports	7 of 9	5 of 5
Evaluations	1 of 9	1 of 5
Technical Reports	2 of 9	5 of 5
Long Reports	9 of 9	5 of 5
Job Descriptions	2 of 9	1 of 5

Table adapted from: P. G. Campbell, "Business Communication or Technical Writing?" *The Bulletin,* Vol. 54, No. 2 (June 1991), pp. 6–10.

Source: Reprinted with permission of the Association for Business Communication

CHAPTER 2.1 AUDIENCE

Audience Analysis: An Oversimplified Example

The last time Barbara Cottrell picked up her 10-year-old television set from your repair shop, you warned her that the set was on its last cathodes. You tried to make a joke, which Ms. Cottrell apparently missed: "In human terms, this set is now 108-years-old." At the time you put in a special order for some long out-of-stock components and tightened the horizontal hold so Ms. Cottrell would no longer have the impression of watching a passing freight train. Now she tells you that in the process you damaged the sound control, leaving her unable to turn the sound off and just "watch the pictures." She expects you to fix the set for nothing, given your 90-day guarantee on repairs.

Your 90-day guarantee applies only to the components that you worked with, so you must refuse her claim. But you appreciate Ms. Cottrell as a customer, however difficult she may be at times. If you could sell her one of the fine new televisions you have in stock, you wouldn't have to spend any more time hunting up long outmoded parts for her ancient television set.

Your task: Write Ms. Cottrell and explain that you are unwilling to fix her set for free.

Quoted in J. Suchen and R. Dulek, "Toward a Better Understanding of Reader Analysis," *Journal of Business Communication,* Vol. 25, No. 2 (Spring 1988), pp. 25–45.

Source: Reprinted with permission of the Association for Business Communication

CHAPTER 3.1 FACTS

```
    PRIMARY CONCERNS -

o   FIELD JOINT - HIGHEST CONCERN

    o   EROSION PENETRATION OF PRIMARY SEAL REQUIRES RELIABLE SECONDARY SEAL
        FOR PRESSURE INTEGRITY
        o   IGNITION TRANSIENT - (0-600 MS)
            o   (0-170 MS)HIGH PROBABILITY OF RELIABLE SECONDARY SEAL
            o   (170-330 MS) REDUCED PROBABILITY OF RELIABLE SECONDARY SEAL
            o   (330-600 MS) HIGH PROBABILITY OF NO SECONDARY SEAL CAPABILITY

        o   STEADY STATE - (600 MS - 2 MINUTES)
        o   IF EROSION PENETRATES PRIMARY O-RING SEAL - HIGH PROBABILITY OF
            NO SECONDARY SEAL CAPABILITY
            o   BENCH TESTING SHOWED O-RING NOT CAPABLE OF MAINTAINING CONTACT
                WITH METAL PARTS GAP OPENING RATE TO MEOP
            o   BENCH TESTING SHOWED CAPABILITY TO MAINTAIN O-RING CONTACT DURING
                INITIAL PHASE (0-170 MS) OF TRANSIENT

                                                            [Ref. 2/14-3 3 of 13]
```

3.2

```
E(I) JOINT    PRIMARY Q _CERNS    SRM 25

  o  A TEMPERATURE LOWER THAN CURRENT DATA BASE RESULTS
     IN CHANGING PRIMARY O-RING SEALING TIMING FUNCTION
                      ARC
  o  SRM 15A — 80° BLACK GREASE BETWEEN O-RINGS
     SRM 15B — 110° ARC BLACK GREASE BETWEEN O-RINGS

  o  LOWER O-RING SQUEEZE DUE TO LOWER TEMP

  o  HIGHER O-RING SHORE HARDNESS

  o  THICKER GREASE VISCOSITY

  o  HIGHER O-RING PRESSURE ACTUATION TIME

  o  IF ACTUATION TIME INCREASES, THRESHOLD OF SECONDARY
     SEAL PRESSURIZATION CAPABILITY IS APPROACHED

  o  IF THRESHOLD IS REACHED THEN SECONDARY SEAL MAY
     NOT BE CAPABLE OF BEING PRESSURIZED
                                            [Ref. 2/14-3 4 of 13]
```

3.3

Monday, May 21, 2001; 4:16 P.M.
Dear Mr. Nasser:

Today, I am informing you that Bridgestone/Firestone Inc. is ending its tire supply relationship with the Ford Motor Company. While we will honor our existing contractual obligations to you, we will not enter into any new tire sales agreements in the Americas with Ford beginning today.

Business relationships, like personal ones, are built upon trust and mutual respect. We have come to the conclusion that we can no longer supply tires to Ford since the basic foundation of our relationship has been seriously eroded. This is not a decision we make lightly after almost 100 years of history. But we must look to the future and the best interests of our company, our employees and our other customers.

Our analysis suggests that there are significant safety issues with a substantial segment of Ford Explorers. We have made your staff aware of our concerns. They have steadfastly refused to acknowledge those issues.

We have always said that in order to insure the safety of the driving public, it is crucial that there be a true sharing of information concerning the vehicle as well as the tires. You simply are not willing to do that. We believe you are attempting to divert scrutiny of your vehicle by casting doubt on the quality of Firestone tires. These tires are safe, and as we have said before, when we have a problem, we will acknowledge that problem and fix it. We expect you to do the same.

I wish you and the Ford Motor Company continued success and regret that we cannot continue our relationship going forward.

Sincerely,
John T. Lampe

Firestone's Letter to Ford

CHAPTER 5.1 REASONING

The planet Jupiter disgorged a large comet, which made a grazing collision with the Earth around 1500 B.C. The various plagues and Pharaonic tribulations of the Book of Exodus all derive directly or indirectly from this cometery encounter: material which made the river Nile turn to blood drops from the comet; the vermin described in Exodus are produced by the comet; flies and perhaps scarabs drop out of the comet, while indigenous terrestrial frogs are induced by the heat of the comet to multiply; and earthquakes produced by the comet level Egyptian but not Hebrew dwellings. (The only thing that does not seem to drop from the comet is cholesterol to harden Pharaoh's heart.)

All this evidently falls from the coma of the comet, because at the moment that Moses strikes his staff upon the rock, the Red Sea parts—due either to the gravitational tidal field of the comet, or to some unspecified electrical or magnetic interaction between the comet and the Red Sea. Then, when the Hebrews have successfully crossed, the comet has evidently passed sufficiently further on for the parted waters to flow back and drown the host of Pharaoh. The Children of Israel during their subsequent forty years of wandering in the Wilderness of Sinai are nourished by manna from heaven, which turns out to be hydrocarbons (or carbohydrates) from the tail of the comet.

Another reading of *Worlds in Collision* makes it appear that the plagues and the Red Sea events represent two different passages of the comet, separated by a month or two. Then after the death of Moses and the passing of the mantle of leadership to Joshua, the same comet comes screeching back for another grazing collision with the Earth. At the moment that Joshua says, "Sun, stand thou still upon Gibeon; and thou, Moon, in the valley of Agalon," the Earth—perhaps because of tidal interaction, again, or perhaps because of an unspecified magnetic induction in the crust of the Earth—obligingly ceased its rotation to permit Joshua victory in battle. The comet then makes a near collision with Mars, so violent as to eject it out of its orbit so that it makes two near collisions with the Earth which destroy the army of Sennacherib, the Assyrian king, as he was making life miserable for some subsequent generation of Israelites. The net result was to eject Mars into its present orbit and the comet into a circular orbit around the sun, where it became the planet Venus. The Earth meantime had somehow begun rotating again at almost exactly the same rate as before these encounters. No subsequent aberrant planetary behavior has occurred since about the sixth century B.C., although it might have been common in the second millennium.

Carl Sagan, "An Analysis of *Worlds in Collision*," in *Scientists Confront Velikovsky*, ed. Donald Goldsmith, Ithaca: Cornell University Press, 1977.

Appendix

AN ATTEMPT TO DIFFERENTIATE REAL AND CRACKPOT SCIENCE

Test	Maximum Points	Physicist	ESP-er	Dowser
1. **Public verifiability** (the science works when tested)	12	12	5	0
2. **Predictability** (the science is based on reasonable expectations)	12	11	2	2
3. **Controlled experimentation** (the research can be replicated)	13	13	5	0
4. **Occam's razor** (when competing theories or explanations exist, the simplest answer should be accepted)	5	4	0	4
5. **Fruitfulness** (the research adds value to the field of science)	10	10	7	5
6. **Authority** (the researcher has recognized credentials)	10	10	3	0
7. **Ability to communicate** (the researcher makes sense to colleagues)	8	8	4	4
8. **Humility** (the researcher acknowledges the foundations being built upon)	5	5	1	0
9. **Open-mindedness** (the researcher is willing to entertain challenges)	5	4	0	0
10. **Fulton non sequitur** (the researcher's assertion that he is just too far ahead of his time to be understood)	5	5	5	5
11. **Paranoia** (the researcher's belief that the world is stacked against him)	5	5	4	4
12. **Dollar complex** (projections of extraordinary value of the findings)	5	5	2	2
13. **Statistics compulsion** (a reliance on questionable calculations and statistics)	5	5	0	2
Total	100	97	38	28

Adapted from Fred J. Gruenberger, "A Measure for Crackpots," *Science,* 145 (Sept. 25, 1964), pp. 1413–1415.

31885

Federal Register

Vol. 63, No. 111

Wednesday, June 10, 1998

Presidential Documents

Title 3—

The President

Memorandum of June 1, 1998

Plain Language in Government Writing

Memorandum for the Heads of Executive Departments and Agencies

The Vice President and I have made reinventing the Federal Government a top priority of my Administration. We are determined to make the Government more responsive, accessible, and understandable in its communications with the public.

The Federal Government's writing must be in plain language. By using plain language, we send a clear message about what the Government is doing, what it requires, and what services it offers. Plain language saves the Government and the private sector time, effort, and money.

Plain language requirements vary from one document to another, depending on the intended audience. Plain language documents have logical organization, easy-to-read design features, and use:

- common, everyday words, except for necessary technical terms;
- "you" and other pronouns;
- the active voice; and
- short sentences.

To ensure the use of plain language, I direct you to do the following:

- By October 1, 1998, use plain language in all new documents, other than regulations, that explain how to obtain a benefit or service or how to comply with a requirement you administer or enforce. For example, these documents may include letters, forms, notices, and instructions. By January 1, 2002, all such documents created prior to October 1, 1998, must also be in plain language.
- By January 1, 1999, use plain language in all proposed and final rule-making documents published in the **Federal Register**, unless you proposed the rule before that date. You should consider rewriting existing regulations in plain language when you have the opportunity and resources to do so.

The National Partnership for Reinventing Government will issue guidance to help you comply with these directives and to explain more fully the elements of plain language. You should also use customer feedback and common sense to guide your plain language efforts.

I ask the independent agencies to comply with these directives.

This memorandum does not confer any right or benefit enforceable by law against the United States or its representatives. The Director of the Office of Management and Budget will publish this memorandum in the Federal Register.

THE WHITE HOUSE,

Washington, June 1, 1998.

FR Doc. 98–15700

'iled 6–9–98; 10:56 am]

illing code 3110–01–M

6.2

A Confusion of Terms

1. Anxious/eager
2. People/persons
3. Avert/avoid
4. Fortuitous/fortunate
5. All right/alright
6. Bring/take
7. Disburse/disperse
8. Amoral/immoral
9. Quotation/quote
10. Aggravated/irritating
11. Eminent/immanent/imminent
12. Quoted/referred to
13. Adverse/averse
14. Practicable/practical
15. Can/may
16. Real/reel/really
17. Hew/hue
18. Principal/principle
19. Pseudo/quasi
20. Affect/effect
21. Continual/continuous
22. Composed/comprised
23. Carat/caret/carrot/karat
24. Alumna/alumnus
25. Diagnosis/prognosis
26. Allusion/delusion/illusion
27. Corespondents/ correspondence/correspondents
28. Emigrate/immigrate
29. Laid/lain/lay
30. Hypercritical/hypocritical
31. Moot/mute
32. Amount/number
33. Healthful/healthy
34. Unique/unusual
35. Consul/council/counsel
36. Hoard/horde
37. Stationary/stationery
38. Credible/creditable/credulous
39. Bimonthly/semimonthly
40. Facetious/factious
41. Vains/vanes/veins
42. Provided/providing
43. Arbitrate/mediate/meditate
44. Loath/loathe
45. Censor/censured
46. Indigenous/indigent/indignant
47. Poor/pore/pour
48. Vice/vise
49. Shear/sheer
50. Perpetrate/perpetuate
51. Ordinance/ordnance
52. Feat/fete
53. Flaunt/flout
54. Track/tract
55. In/in to/into
56. Democrat/democrat/ Democratic/democratic
57. Statue/stature/statute
58. Can not/cannot
59. Populace/populous
60. Die/dye
61. Fazed/phased/phrased
62. Biannual/biennial
63. Decent/dissent/descent
64. Deceased/desisted
65. Invaluable/valuable
66. Extant/extent
67. Lay/lie
68. Elicit/illicit
69. Bad/badly
70. Assure/ensure/insure/inure
71. Anecdote/antidote
72. Farther/further
73. Persecute/prosecute
74. Flair/flare
75. Covert/overt

P. Williams, J.D. Scriven, S. Wayne, "A Ranking of the Top 75 Misused Similar Words that Business Students Confuse Most Often," *The Bulletin,* vol. 34, no. 4 (Dec. 1991), pp 19–25.

Source: Reprinted with permission of the Association for Business Communication.

COMPARISON OF COMMUNICATION ACTIVITIES BY E-MAIL USE

Communication Activities	Percent using E-mail for Specific Task			
	Secretary	Analyst	Director	Total
Document Delivery	89.8	84.4	84.6	86.3
Request Information	78.0	62.2	80.8	73.7
Answer Questions	69.5	77.8	69.2	72.2
Receive Tasks	69.5	53.3	61.5	61.5
Coordinate Office	57.6	55.6	57.7	57.0
Circulate Memos	55.9	60.0	53.8	56.6
Express Opinions	49.2	40.0	65.4	51.5
Maintain Office	47.5	42.2	53.8	47.8
Personal Messages	39.0	40.0	26.9	35.3
Draft Documents	32.2	44.4	26.9	34.5
Assign Tasks	25.4	15.6	50.0	30.3
Make Decisions	13.6	4.4	23.1	13.7

Christopher B. Sullivan, "Preferences for Electronic Mail in Organizational Communication," *The Journal of Business Communication,* Vol. 32, No. 1 (January 1995), p. 49 (16)

Source: Reprinted with permission of the Association for Business Communication

E-MAIL VERSUS FACE-TO-FACE COMMUNICATION ACTIVITIES

Communication Activities	Preferences for Communication Channel		
	Prefer E-mail n (%)	Either n (%)	Prefer Telephone n (%)
Making Decisions	12 (13)	22 (23)	60 (64)
Personal Messages	12 (13)	22 (24)	58 (63)
Expressing Opinions	19 (17)	22 (19)	72 (64)
Answering Questions	21 (18)	36 (31)	59 (51)
Maintaining Office	23 (21)	31 (28)	56 (51)
Assigning Tasks	26 (26)	31 (31)	42 (42)
Requesting Information	29 (26)	36 (32)	48 (42)
Receiving Assignments	30 (28)	37 (34)	41 (38)
Drafting Documents	31 (32)	25 (26)	41 (42)
Coordinating Activities	35 (30)	29 (25)	53 (45)
Document Delivery	58 (50)	28 (24)	29 (25)
Circulating Memorandums	69 (67)	22 (21)	12 (12)

Christopher B. Sullivan, "Preferences for Electronic Mail in Organizational Communication," *The Journal of Business Communication,* Vol. 32, No. 1 (January 1995), p. 49 (16)

Source: Reprinted with permission of the Association for Business Communication

10.3

> **Legal Advice on E-mail Policy: Fulfilling the Notification Requirements ***
>
> 1) Clearly communicate to employees that the security of E-mail is not guaranteed. The company may override individual passwords and codes, and require employees to disclose all passwords and codes.
> 2) Explain monitoring procedures and their use by management.
> 3) Define the limited, authorized access to E-mail, e.g., for business purposes only.
> 4) Explain that electronic communications and the contents of an employee's computer are the sole property of the employer.
> 5) Identify the reasons for surveillance, e.g., preventing excessive personal use of the company's systems, assuring compliance with company policies, and investigating conduct or behavior that may be illegal or adversely affect employees.
> 6) Establish (preferably in writing) that by using company E-mail, the employee knowingly and voluntarily consents to be monitored, and acknowledges the employer's right to conduct such monitoring.
> 7) Prohibit the following uses of E-mail for:
>   a. Personal messages, solicitation of employees, or distribution of information that is not related to the employer's business
>   b. Communications that may constitute verbal abuse, slander, defamation, harassment, or trade disparagement of employees, customers, clients, vendors, or competitors.
>   c. Communications that are vulgar, obscene, or that disparage any characteristics (e.g. race) protected under federal, state, or local law.
>   d. Communications that create, distribute, or solicit sexually-oriented messages or images, unwelcome sexual advances, requests for sexual favors, or other unwelcome conduct of a sexual nature.
>   e. Disseminating copyrighted materials, including articles and software, in violation of copyright laws.
>   f. Exchanging trade secrets, proprietary information, or any other confidential information
>   g. Distributing privileged information, e.g., communications to in-house counsel that may be subject to the attorney-client privilege.
>   h. Accessing or transmitting messages from the E-mail system of another user.
> 8) Explain the significance of the "Delete" and "Wastebasket" functions, and describe procedures for ensuring the permanent destruction of E-mail.
> 9) Inform employees regarding the potential discovery of stored E-mail and the potential use of such messages for litigation against the company.
>
> *Adapted from Donald H. Selfman and Craig W. Trapanier, "Evolution of the Paperless Office: Legal Issues Arising out of Technology in the Workplace," *Employee Relations Law Journal*, Vol. 21, No. 3, (Winter 1995/1996), pp. 5–36.

10.4

A Retrieved E-mail Message
Introduced in the Tower Commission Hearings

MSG FROM:NSOLN --CPUA
09/06/86   15:31:36   To: **NSJMP --CPUA**

*** Reply to note of 09/02/86 16:03

                                                     ■ **SECRET --**
NOTE FROM: **OLIVER NORTH Subject: Iran**

Last night at 2330 our Project Democracy rep. in Costa Rica called to advise that Arias Govt [One line deleted, (b) (1) (s) exemption] "was going to hold press conference today (Saturday) announcing that an illegal support operation for the Contras had been taking place from an airfield in Costa Rica for over a year. The names of two Americans Secord and **[Deleted, (b) (1) (s) exemption]*** were going to be predominantly mentioned. I called **[Deleted, (b) (1) (s) exemption]** to confirm the info and he returned call at 0030 verifying the info. I then had a conference call w/ Tambs, Abrams, and Fiers and we agreed on the following sequence: --North to call Pres. Arias and tell him that if the press conference were held, Arias **[One line deleted, (b) (1) (s) exemption]** wd never see a nickel of the $80M that McPhearson had promised him earlier on Friday. --Tambs then called Arias from his location in W. Va. And confirmed what I had said and suggested that Arias talk to Elliott for further confirmation. --Arias then got the same word from Elliott. **--[One line deleted, (b) (1) (s) exemption]** At 0300 Arias called back to advise that there wd be no press conference and no team of reporters sent to the airfield. As a precaution, the Project a/c were flown to Ilopango last night and no project personnel remain in site at the field other than local guards (8). Fiers advises today that this operation was timed to coincide w/ the Conference on our $100M and was directed by the Cubans. **[Two lines deleted, (b) (1) (s) exemption]** - but that I wd reconsider if things looked better next wk. I recognize that I was well beyond my charter in dealing w/ a head of state this way and in making threats/offers that may be impossible to deliver, but under the circumstances and w/Elliotts concurrence - it seemed like the only thing we could do. Best of all, it seems to have worked. I believe that it is important that you or Al or both make a trip down there again as soon as the $100M is approved so that someone w/ more horsepower than I can look Arias - **[One line deleted, (b) (1) (s) exemption]** very aware of our resolve in making this project work. If Al were to go it wd be a good opportunity for him to become familiar w/ some of the facts which will be critical to this effort if it is to succeed. V/R North

GLOSSARY

Abrams—Elliott Abrams, US assistant secretary of state
Project Democracy—covert Contra support operation
Arias—Oscar Arias, Costa Rican president
Fiers—Alan Fiers, CIA official
Tambs—Lewis Tambs, US Ambassador to Costa Rica

*References to "Deleted, (b) (1) (s) exceptions," are portions removed for national security reasons.

HOTCHKISS'S UNITS OF STUDY

PRINCIPLES	TECHNIQUE	METHODS
UNIT I		
THE READER'S POINT OF VIEW	**GENERAL**	**IMPORTANT TYPES OF LETTERS**
Every letter a sales-letter. Adjustment to the reader. Clearness, and how to secure it. Correctness, its meaning and value. Force, and how to secure it.	Avoidance of stereotyped phrases. Use of simple conversational language. Right and wrong ways to begin a letter. Right and wrong ways to end a letter.	Sales-letters. Applications for positions. Handling inquiries and orders. Adjusting complaints. Making collections.
UNIT IV		
COHERENCE AS AN AID TO CLEARNESS	**SENTENCES**	**CREDIT AND FINANCIAL LETTERS**
Logical progress in the message. The narrative order. The descriptive order. Inductive and deductive order. Transitions.	Order in the sentence. Misrelated modifiers. The "and" habit. Use of connectives. Parallelism. Participial constructions. Punctuation as an aid to coherence.	Making credit inquiries. Answering credit inquiries. Asking credit. Granting credit. Refusing credit. Legal questions.
UNIT VIII		
THE PERSONAL TOUCH	**WORDS**	**SALES-LETTERS**
Analysis of the reader. Adapting style to the reader's character and interest. Taking advantage of the reader's mood. Clinching the sale. Building a list.	Language adapted to the reader. Colloquial diction. The use of "lingo." Idioms. Localisms and slang.	Letters to dealers. Letters to farmers. Letters to business men. Letters to professional men. Letters to technical men. Letters to women. Letters to foreigners.
UNIT XI		
ORGANIZATION OF MATERIAL	**PREPARING FOR PUBLICATION**	**BOOKLETS AND CATALOGS**
Gathering data. Filing and indexing material. Making outlines. Dictating from outlines. Correspondence manuals.	Revision of manuscript. Proof correction. Typographical marks. Copyright. Postal information.	Descriptive booklets. Educational booklets. Inspirational booklets. Evidential booklets. Mail order catalogs. Technical catalogs. Salesmen's catalogs. Dealer's catalogs.
UNIT XII		
LOGICAL PRESENTATION	**OTHER FACTORS—STYLE**	**REPORTS**
Analysis of facts and statistics. Clearness and conciseness in presentation. Tabulation. Graphic charts and diagrams. Exhibits. Conclusions and recommendations.	Idioms. Synonyms. Errors in sentence structure. Errors in words. Oral English. Pronunciation.	General business reports. Accountant's reports. Financial reports. Sales reports. Reports of investigations.

George Burton Hotchkiss, *Business English: Being the First Text in a Course in Business English.* New York: Business Training Corporation, 1916.

12.2

POSITION OF BUFFERS IN ACTUAL REJECTION LETTERS

Letter Attribute/Category	Percentage of Letters
Number of Paragraphs	
1–2	23.1
3–4	33.3
5–6	28.2
more than 6	15.5
Paragraph where rejection sentence occurs	
1	53.8
2	20.5
3	17.9
more than 3	7.8
Sentence in which rejection occurs	
1	17.9
2	38.5
3	12.8
4	7.7
5	12.8
later	10.3

Ted Brown, "Unkind Cuts: Rethinking the Rhetoric of Academic Job Rejection Letters," *College English,* Vol. 55, No. 7 (Nov. 1993), pp. 770–778.

Source: Ted Brown, "Unkind Cuts: Rethinking the Rhetoric of Academic Job Rejection Letters," *College English.* Copyright 1993 by the National Council of Teachers of English.

12.3

POSITIVE AND NEGATIVE POLITENESS IN THE WRITING OF SENIOR MANAGEMENT

Business Phase	Letter type*	Claim common ground		Focus on cooperation		Fulfill receiver's wants		Give freedom of action		Minimize imposition		Dissociate sender/receiver from act	
		Ext	Int	Ext	Int	Ext	Int	Ext	Int	Ext	Int	Ext	Int
Making contact	SAL	41.9	8.7	50.0	86.9	8.1	4.4	57.1	34.1	20.0	25.3	22.8	40.6
	INQ	33.9	11.1	58.9	88.9	8.2	0.0	42.0	47.2	22.5	16.5	35.5	36.3
	OTL	47.6	25.0	50.5	50.0	1.9	25.0	29.2	44.7	23.2	21.0	47.6	34.3
Negotiating	QUO	44.6	47.0	52.5	49.3	2.9	3.7	32.1	28.6	22.4	27.8	45.5	43.6
	ORD	33.3	20.0	66.7	80.0	0.0	0.0	100	23.3	0.0	100	0.0	6.7
	OTL	50.8	30.2	12.8	67.9	6.4	1.9	26.5	38.9	32.3	27.9	41.2	33.2
In conflict	REM	60.0	15.4	40.0	89.6	0.0	0.0	50.0	30.7	0.0	14.5	50.0	54.8
	COM	25.0	50.0	75.0	50.0	0.0	0.0	7.0	25.0	42.9	27.3	50.1	47.7
	OTL	57.1	51.7	42.9	48.8	0.0	3.5	34.4	29.6	21.9	19.8	43.7	51.5

Figures are given in percentage. Abbreviation: "SAL": sales letter, "INQ": inquiry, "OTL": other letters, "QUO": quotation, "ORD": order, "REM": reminder, "COM": complaint, "Ext": external position (beginning or ending of the letter), "Int": internal position (the body of the letter).

Morten Pilegaard, "Politeness in Written Discourse: A Textlinguistic Perspective on Requests," *Journal of Pragmatics,* Vol. 28 (1997), pp. 223–244.

Source: Reprinted from *Journal of Pragmatics,* vol. 28, Morten Pilegaard, "Politeness in Written Discourse: A Textlinguistic Perspective on Requests," pp. 223–244, Copyright 1997, with permission from Elsevier Science.

CHAPTER 13.1 THE LONG REPORT

A Basic Plan for a Moderate to Large-Size Proposal

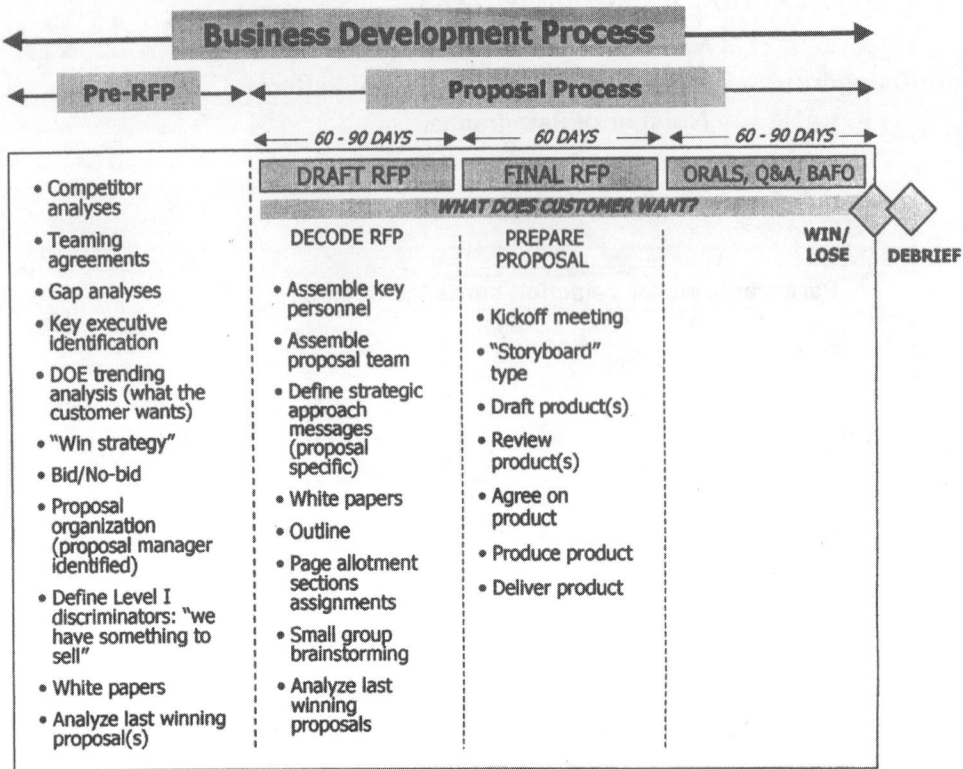

13.2

PERCEPTIONS OF IMPROVEMENT RESULTING FROM WRITING A BUSINESS REPORT (IN PERCENT)

Competency	Strongly Agree		Agree		No Opinion		Disagree		Strongly Disagree	
Organization	29	70	62	29	6	1	3	0	0	0
Clarity	21	47	54	49	20	3	5	1	0	0
Completeness	27	46	50	47	18	5	6	1	0	1
Correctness	25	42	49	51	20	4	5	3	0	0
Conciseness	28	40	51	50	17	7	3	3	1	0
Content	26	53	49	42	17	4	7	2	0	0
Grammar & Mechanics	21	36	40	51	29	7	9	5	1	1
Tone	20	35	50	46	26	13	4	5	0	1
Audience Analysis	31	44	44	38	21	14	4	4	0	0
Confidence in Writing	20	44	45	46	25	7	8	3	1	0

Kathleeen M. Hiemstra, "Instructor and Student Perceptions of What Is Learned by Writing the Business Report," *Business Communication Quarterly,* Vol. 64, No. 2 (June 2001), pp. 44–54.

Source: Reprinted with permission of the Association for Business Communication

13.3

Fourteenth Annual Report
OF THE
MUTUAL RESERVE FUND LIFE ASSOCIATION.

EDWARD B. HARPER,
PRESIDENT.

The Association Has Now in Force a Total Business of Over $293,366,106, a Gain of $30,759,041 Over 1893.

Death Claims Paid in 1894, $3,070,514.01

Assets Are $5,536,115.99 and Liabilities $2,259,936.10—Net Surplus Over All Liabilities, $3,276,179.89.

The fourteenth annual meeting of the [...and] Friends. Gr[ee]tings to you one and all, members of the Mutual Reserve Fund Life [...] and congratulations upon the continued suc-

---

information regarding this association which will for all time to came silence the anonymous slanderer, and give renewed faith in our system and renewed zeal upon the part of our representatives in pushing on the good work of the Association.

We can only repeat to our members what we have said to these Commissioners, that we shall press forward in the future as in the past with all the energy at our command, and with the simple purpose of conducting the affairs of this Association, to the minutest detail, with the most rigid economy and the strictest integrity, and with an eye only in the direction of furthering the very best interest of each member and beneficiary. We have now reached a period in our history where the Mutual Reserve Fund Life Association is so solidly founded, so well established, and so favorably known, that we can point to our eminent success in the past and to our brilliant hope of the future without extended comment.

We shall miss at this Annual Meeting the brilliant, able, and exhaustive report of President Harper, but we hope and believe that in the immediate future he will return to the Home Office entirely restored to health, when we may confidently expect that he will supplement the proceedings of to-day by a statement which will be forwarded to every member and gladden their hearts, as well as those of every friend of the Association.

For the time being, therefore, we shall make but a brief statement of the Fourteenth Annual Report of the Mutual Reserve Fund Life Association, and in presenting the few figures that follow, we simply state that our assets are larger, our surplus greater, our new business of more magnitude, and our payments to beneficiaries more than in any preceding year in our history.

ASSETS.

Our gross assets have increased during the year 1894 from $5,138,510.36 to $5,536,115.99, making a net gain for the year of $397,605.63.

RESERVE FUND.

We have increased our Reserve or Surplus Emergency Fund during the past twelve months from $3,589,326.13 to $3,827,635.12, making a net gain for the year of $238,308.99.

INCOME.

Our income from all sources during the year 1894 amounted to $4,943,739.59, as against $4,498,815 for 1893, making a net increase of $444,924.59.

DEATH CLAIMS.

At the end of the year 1893 we had disbursed to the widows and orphans and representatives of our deceased members the sum of $17,684,833.86. For the same purpose during the year 1894 we have paid out the largest sum in the history of our institution, viz.: $3,070,514.01, making in all, in the fourteen years of our existence, the magnificent total of $20,754,847.87.

CASH AND INVESTED ASSETS.

At the beginning of the year 1894 our cash and invested assets were $3,938,941.15. During the year we have added the sum of $307,202.75, so that at the close of the year these assets amounted to $4,246,143.90. This increase was made notwithstanding the fact, as already stated, that we paid out for death claims a larger sum than during any previous year of our history. We present herewith a detailed schedule of the investments of the Association, with a certificate from the Central Trust Company of New-York, duly signed by the Hon. F. P. Olcott, President, which will enable each member to examine and ascertain for himself the character and absolute security of the investments made by the association.

BUSINESS IN FORCE.

Our books show that on December 31st, 1894, we had in force 66,067 policies, covering insurance amounting to $293,366,106, being a net increase for the year of 13,251 policies, amounting to $30,759,041, while the applications for

NEW BUSINESS.

received during the year amounted to $81,365,145, which does not include one dollar's worth of business received since December 31st, 1894.

The eloquence of these results can perhaps be best illustrated by the following statement, showing

THE PROGRESS OF THE ASSOCIATION.

Year.	Insurance in Force.	Cash and Invested Assets.
1881	$7,633,000	$6,024.33
1882	33,190,750	50,441.53
1883	63,525,500	169,946.24
1884	85,452,000	350,775.05
1885	124,883,500	639,873.41
1886	150,175,250	966,240.16
1887	156,554,100	1,472,200.61
1888	165,902,850	1,955,752.81
1889	181,334,200	2,512,554.56
1890	197,003,435	2,830,178.96
1891	215,307,910	3,234,457.06
1892	236,421,700	3,620,592.78
1893	262,607,065	3,938,941.15
1894	293,366,106	4,246,143.90

Year.	Reserve or Emergency Fund.	Death Claims Paid.
1881	...	...
1882	$11,906.00	$14,250.00
1883	115,762.00	335,675.00
1884	271,440.00	815,575.00

A Typical Nineteenth Century Financial (Annual) Report

Chapter 14.1 Procedures

ACTIVITIES IN WHICH PROCEDURAL ERRORS WERE CITED

Activity Type	% of Errors
Normal Operations	60%
Maintenance	11%
Inspections/Monitoring	8%
Facility/System/Equipment Testing	7%
Construction	5%
Shutdown	5%
Transportation	2%
Startup	1%
Facility Decontamination/Decommission	1%

"Human Engineering Guidelines for Use in Preparing Emergency Operating Procedures for Nuclear Power Plants," NUREG/CR-1999, April 1981.